THE INDEPENDENT SCHOOLS GUIDE

THE INDEPENDENT SCHOOLS GUIDE

2006–2007

12TH EDITION

A FULLY COMPREHENSIVE DIRECTORY

GABBITAS
Educational Consultants

London and Philadelphia

KH

Publisher's note

The information supplied in this *Guide* has been published in good faith on the basis of information submitted by the schools listed. Neither Kogan Page nor Gabbitas Educational Consultants can guarantee the accuracy of the information in this *Guide* and accept no responsibility for any error or misrepresentation. All liability for loss, disappointment, negligence or other damage caused by the reliance on the information contained in this *Guide*, or in the event of bankruptcy or liquidation or cessation of trade of any company, individual or firm mentioned, is hereby excluded.

Photographs on front cover reproduced with kind permission of Hydesville Tower School, Walsall, West Midlands (left), Farleigh School, Andover, Hampshire (centre) and Farnborough Hill School, Farnborough, Hampshire (right).

First published in 1995
This edition published in 2006

Kogan Page Ltd
120 Pentonville Road
London N1 9JN
UK

Kogan Page US
525 South 4th Street, #241
Philadelphia PA 19147
USA

British Library Cataloguing in Publication Data

A CIP record for this book is available from the British Library

ISBN 0 7494 4567 X

ISSN 1478-6893

Typeset by AJS Solutions, Dundee & Huddersfield
Printed and bound in Great Britain by Bell & Bain, Glasgow

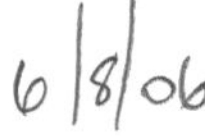

Contents

PART 4: REFERENCE SECTION

Acknowledgements

This Guide is the product of many hours of data collection and meticulous proof-reading by staff at Gabbitas and Kogan Page, together with cooperation and contributions from a wide-ranging team of experts. Gabbitas would like to thank all those who have helped in the preparation of this Guide, in particular Towry Law Financial Services Ltd; Hydesville Tower School, West Midlands, Farleigh School, Hampshire, and Farnborough Hill School, Hampshire, for kind permission to reproduce photographs; and the educational associations, Heads and schools that have so promptly provided the information required for publication.

Gabbitas Educational Consultants Ltd
January 2006

Foreword

Gabbitas Educational Consultants

Welcome to the 12th edition of *The Independent Schools Guide*, the most comprehensive directory of independent schools in the UK. Compiled from our unique database and fully updated every year, the Guide includes nearly 2,000 schools as well as practical advice from the Gabbitas team for parents about to start their search for the right school.

The Guide's accompanying website pages offer an online school search to help you identify schools suited to your requirements as well as direct links to school websites. You can also use 'Ask an Expert' to put questions directly to our team, who will be happy to help you in your search.

Established for over 130 years, Gabbitas is uniquely placed to offer parents expert advice. Each year we help thousands of parents and students in the UK and abroad who seek personal guidance at all stages of education:

- choosing the right independent school or college;
- educational assessment;
- Sixth Form options – A levels, International Baccalaureate and vocational courses;
- university and degree choices and UCAS applications;
- careers assessment and guidance, job searching and interview techniques.

Gabbitas also advises on transfer into the British educational system and provides guardianship services for children from overseas attending boarding schools in the UK. To find out more about Gabbitas, visit our website at www.gabbitas.co.uk or contact us at:

Gabbitas Educational Consultants
Carrington House, 126–130 Regent Street, London W1B 5EE
Tel: +44 (0)20 7734 0161 Fax: +44 (0)20 7437 1764
E-mail: admin@gabbitas.co.uk

How to Use the Guide

About independent schools

The first part of this Guide offers extensive information about independent schools, examinations, fee-planning, scholarships and bursaries as well as guidance on choosing a school.

Researching individual schools

The main index at the back gives all page references for each school.

Selecting schools in a particular location

If you are looking for a school in a specific area, turn to the directory section (Part Two), which is arranged geographically by town and county. Schools in London are listed under their postal areas. Each entry gives the name, postal address, telephone and fax numbers and e-mail address of the school, together with the name of the Head, details of the type and age range of pupils accepted, the number of pupils, number of boarders (where applicable) and the annual fees.

Schools which have an asterisk also appear in the School Profiles section (Part Three), where advertisers provide more detailed information. These schools also have a map reference to show their exact location.

To find any other references to the school, for example to find out whether it offers scholarships, turn to the appropriate index at the back.

Scholarships, bursaries and reserved entrance awards

Many schools offer scholarships for children with a particular talent, bursaries where there is financial hardship or reserved entrance awards for children with a parent in a specific profession such as the Clergy or HM Forces. Part Four contains a complete list of schools, by county, which offer such awards.

This section is necessarily only a brief guide to awards available. More specific information can be obtained from individual schools.

Religious affiliation

The index in Part Four provides a full list of schools under appropriate headings.

Single-sex schools

For a complete list of single-sex schools, turn to Part Four.

Boarding schools

Schools with boarding provision generally offer full, weekly or flexi-boarding options. Some Sixth Form colleges, with no residential facilities, may offer accommodation with host families. The number of boarders is shown in the entries in Part Two. For an index of boarding provision by county, see Part Four.

Dyslexia

Most schools offer help, in varying degrees, for pupils with dyslexia. A list of schools registered with CReSTeD (Council for the Registration of Schools Teaching Dyslexic Pupils) appears in Part Four.

English as a foreign language

Most independent schools offer assistance to overseas pupils who require special English language tuition. A list of schools, arranged by county, appears in Part Four.

Schools accredited by the Independent Schools Council

Part Four contains an index of schools in membership of the associations listed below, which together form the Independent Schools Council (ISC). A satisfactory inspection report by the Independent Schools Inspectorate is a requirement for any school wishing to join one of these associations and for its continued accreditation as a member. For more information on the inspection of independent schools, see Part 1.1.

- Headmasters' and Headmistresses' Conference (HMC)
- Girls' Schools Association (GSA) (including the Girls' Day School Trust GDST)

- Society of Headmasters and Headmistresses of Independent Schools (SHMIS)
- Incorporated Association of Preparatory Schools (IAPS)
- Independent Schools Association (ISA).

Other associations which are constituent members of ISC but are not covered by the index are the Association of Governing Bodies of Independent Schools (AGBIS) and the Independent Schools Bursars' Association (ISBA).

School search online

Remember that you can search for schools, according to your criteria, at www.gabbitas.co.uk.

Part 1

The Independent Sector

1.1
What is an Independent School?

Independent schools educate about 8 per cent of the whole school population. Under the Education Act 1996 all independent schools must be registered with the Department for Education and Skills (DfES) and must meet certain regulations set by the DfES (in Wales the Welsh Office Education Department – WOED). However, independent schools are largely self-governing and are not required to comply with all legislation covering schools maintained by the State.

There is sometimes confusion over the terms used to describe independent schools. 'Public schools' generally refers to old-established schools in membership of the Headmasters' and Headmistresses' Conference (HMC). Because many of these schools date back to the days when education was a luxury, received chiefly through private tutors, the term 'public school' indicated a school which the public could attend. Most schools are now described as independent. A 'private school' simply means a school which charges fees.

How are independent schools funded?

Independent schools are usually funded by fees charged to parents. Some have generous endowments that enable them to keep fees at a lower level than might otherwise be possible. Most independent schools are run as charitable trusts under a Board of Governors. Schools with charitable status are effectively non-profit-making concerns; surplus funds are allocated at the discretion of the Governors. Often they are invested in new facilities or in scholarships or bursaries. A few schools are still privately owned.

Who is responsible for the management of an independent school?

The Board of Governors is the policy-making body for the school. It is responsible for the appointment of the Head, allocation of finances and major decisions affecting the school and its development. Governors give their time voluntarily. Often they can contribute professional expertise in education, business, finance, marketing or other areas relevant to the management of the school. The Board often includes a number of parent-governors who have children at the school.

Day-to-day responsibility for the running of the school is delegated to the Head, who is accountable to the Board of Governors and who is supported by one or more Deputy Heads. Other key figures include the Bursar, who is responsible for the school's financial management, the Director of Studies, who manages the curriculum, timetable, examinations and other academic matters, and the Registrar, who is responsible for admissions and arrangements for parents to visit the school. Many schools also have a Development Director, who is responsible for marketing and presentation.

Academic staff in independent schools are not legally required to hold teaching qualifications, but schools almost always insist on a first degree in a subject which normally forms a part of the secondary school curriculum and a Postgraduate Certificate in Education (PGCE). All schools look for enthusiastic and committed staff with flair and ability. Salary scales at independent schools tend to reflect the wide range of commitment expected of staff and are often more generous than those in the maintained sector, enabling schools to attract higher-calibre teachers. Further information on teaching in the independent sector can be found on the Gabbitas website at www.gabbitas.co.uk.

Do independent schools have to follow the National Curriculum?

Although not bound to follow the National Curriculum, most independent schools choose to do so. Almost all prepare pupils for GCSE and A level examinations (or in Scotland, for Scottish National Qualifications). There is no requirement for independent schools to set pupils the National Tests used in the maintained sector. In practice, most schools have regular assessments throughout the year and set formal, internal exams two or three times a year, the results of which are included in the end-of-term report.

Who inspects independent schools?

While the performance of maintained schools is monitored by the Office for Standards in Education (OFSTED), most independent schools in England and Wales are inspected by the Independent Schools Inspectorate (ISI), which was established in April 2000 and works closely with OFSTED and the DfES.

The ISI is responsible for the inspection of independent schools which are members of the school associations that form the Independent Schools Council (ISC). These are: the Headmasters' and Headmistresses' Conference (HMC); the Girls' Schools Association (GSA), including the Girls' Day School Trust (GDST); the Society of Headmasters and Headmistresses of Independent Schools (SHMIS); the Incorporated Association of Preparatory Schools (IAPS); and the Independent Schools Association (ISA).

A satisfactory ISI report is a requirement for any school wishing to join one of the above associations and for its continued accreditation as a member, and from September 2003 the ISI became a body approved for the purpose of inspection.

Inspection of ISC schools in Scotland and Northern Ireland is the responsibility of the appropriate national bodies.

How often are schools inspected, and what does an inspection cover?

ISC schools are normally inspected by the ISI every six years. The aims, as published by the ISI, are to improve the quality of education provided, to raise levels of achievement by pupils and to confirm whether or not schools comply with the registration standards set by the DfES.

ISI inspections provide a comprehensive assessment of the quality of education offered by the school, educational standards achieved, pastoral care, school management, premises, accommodation and facilities. Inspections normally last three or four days.

The views of parents are also assessed using a confidential questionnaire. The school receives only a statistical summary. Inspectors investigate concerns which are significant and, if they feel it appropriate to do so, make recommendations in their final report. However, they do not enter into individual correspondence with parents.

Who are the inspectors?

Inspection teams are led by a Reporting Inspector, who must be an OFSTED Registered Inspector, a recently retired Her Majesty's Inspector (HMI), a recently retired independent school Head or a highly experienced serving independent school Head. Other members of the team must also fulfil one of the above criteria or be a senior independent school teacher. All ISI inspectors must have satisfactorily completed training courses based on OFSTED principles.

What is done about the findings of the inspection? Can parents get a copy?

All inspection reports are sent to OFSTED and the DfES. As stated above, a satisfactory report is required in order for a school to take up membership of one of the associations that form the ISC or to be re-accredited for continued membership, and the ISI therefore also advises the relevant association accordingly. All parents of children at the school receive a free summary of the inspection findings and may obtain the full report free of charge on request. Reports can also be found on the ISI website at www.isinspect.org.uk.

Schools must submit a plan to their Association to remedy any deficiencies highlighted by the inspectors. This must also be sent to all parents. The association reviews the inspection findings and the proposed action plan and may wish to arrange a further visit to the school to assess progress or offer guidance. The association may also require a follow-up inspection before membership can be confirmed or renewed.

In cases where inspectors report that a school is failing to provide an acceptable standard of education or where the safety and welfare of pupils is in question, the DfES may ask HMI to visit the school and to monitor the situation until the concerns are resolved.

Whom do I contact if I have a complaint about my child's school?

In the first instance complaints should be referred to the Head. Parents who feel thereafter that their concerns have still not been adequately addressed can refer the matter to the Board of Governors. The ISI inspection system also allows parents to express concerns in confidence to the inspection team. If an inspection is due within the next two terms, complaints about the quality of education or safety and welfare of pupils can be addressed in writing to the ISI (see below). All such correspondence is treated in the strictest confidence. Otherwise, concerns may be sent to Margaret Pattinson, Deputy Registrar of Schools, DfES, Mowden Hall, Staindrop Road, Darlington DL3 9BG (tel: 01325 392172; e-mail: margaret.pattinson@dfes.gov.uk).

Who inspects independent schools which are not members of one of the ISC constituent associations?

These schools are inspected by OFSTED at least every six years. Findings are published in a report which is available to the school, parents and wider community. Schools are given copies for distribution. Reports are also available via the OFSTED website at www.ofsted.gov.uk. The DfES may ask OFSTED to revisit a school within the six year period to review progress on any action points drawn up following the first inspection in areas where regulatory requirements had not been met. Parents' views, which are treated in confidence, also form part of the inspection. Reports refer only to the view of parents generally.

New schools must comply with the regulations before they are allowed to open. Information on the registration of new schools is available on the DfES website at www.dfes.gov.uk.

Boarding schools

National Boarding Standards, drawn up by the National Boarding Standards Committee, came into effect in April 2002 for use by the National Care Standards Commission. The Standards are the agreed minimum requirements for good practice in independent and maintained boarding schools and cover all welfare, health and policy issues.

The National Boarding Standards can be downloaded from the Boarding Schools' Association website at www.boarding.org.uk. Alternatively, hard copy can be ordered from The Stationery Office at www.the-stationery-office.co.uk.

Accreditation and inspection of independent colleges

A number of independent colleges are accredited by the British Accreditation Council (BAC) (see below). Some independent Sixth Form and tutorial colleges are also in membership of the Council for Independent Further Education (CIFE) (see below). All colleges taking five or more students below the age of 16 are inspected by OFSTED on behalf of the DfES.

The British Accreditation Council (BAC)

The BAC is the main inspection and accreditation body for independent colleges accepting pupils over the age of 16. Inspections cover: premises and health and safety; administration and staffing, quality management; student welfare; and teaching and learning: delivery and resources. Accredited colleges are re-inspected every five years, with an interim visit during the intervening period. Accreditation may be refused or withdrawn if any aspect of the college does not meet the required standards for accreditation. For further information visit the website at www.the-bac.org.

Council for Independent Further Education (CIFE)

There are 27 independent Sixth Form and tutorial colleges in membership of CIFE. Member colleges offer one- and two-year A level and GCSE courses, retake courses, revision courses and also one-year foundation courses for students who wish to enter a UK university but have been educated outside the British system. At present, one college offers the International Baccalaureate programme. CIFE members are required to hold accreditation from either the BAC or ISC.

Council of International Schools (CIS)

Some international schools in the UK are accredited by CIS, a membership organization comprising international schools in all parts of the world. As part of a range of services offered to its member schools, CIS offers regular and associate schools a programme of evaluation and accreditation specially developed for international schools. Those schools that meet the standards for accreditation are given accredited status and in addition to regular monitoring must undergo a full re-evaluation every ten years.

Useful addresses

Independent Schools Inspectorate (ISI)
CAP House
9–12 Long Lane
London EC1A 9HA
Tel: 020 7600 0100
Fax: 020 7776 8849
E-mail: info@isinspect.org.uk
Website: www.isinspect.org.uk

The British Accreditation Council
42 Manchester Street
London W1U 7LW
Tel: 020 7224 5474
Fax: 020 7224 5475
E-mail: info@the-bac.org
Website: www.the-bac.org

Council for Independent Further Education
75 Foxbourne Road
London SW17 8EN
Tel: 020 8767 8666
Fax: 020 8767 9444
E-mail: enquiries@cife.org.uk
Website: www.cife.org.uk

Council of International Schools (UK office)
21A Lavant Street
Petersfield
Hampshire GU32 3EL
Tel: (01730) 263131
Fax: (01730) 268913
E-mail: cois@cois.org
Website: www.cois.org

Office for Standards in Education (OFSTED)
Alexandra House
33 Kingsway
London WC2B 6SE
Tel: 020 7421 6800
Website: www.ofsted.gov.uk

1.2
The Independent Sector

Why choose independent education?

Variety and choice

The independent sector includes schools of many different styles and philosophies, including both the traditional and the more liberal. Each school has its own ethos and atmosphere. Schools also vary widely in size. Some are based in towns and cities. Most boarding schools have more rural locations. Some are co-educational, others are single-sex, although many boys' schools now have co-educational Sixth Forms.

A school to suit your child

Your child's academic needs are the top priority. Not all independent schools educate highly academic children, but there is always some form of selection. While some schools will only accept pupils able to keep pace with a fast-moving curriculum, there are many others which cater for a wider spectrum of ability and some which specialize in helping those in need of more individual attention in a less academic environment.

Academic success

Good independent schools enable pupils, whatever their academic ability, to achieve their best. Their success in helping children to fulfil their potential is reflected in the exam results both of highly selective schools and of schools with less competitive entry requirements where children may need more individual support and encouragement.

An all-round education

Independent schools encourage pupils to develop their strengths outside as well as inside the classroom, ensuring that special talents, in music, drama, art or sport, are nurtured and providing a range of extra-curricular activities which inspire enthusiasm for a great many wider interests.

Small classes and individual attention

Class size at the lower end of the age range normally averages 15 to 20, GCSE groups about 12 to 18 and A level between 4 and 12, although this varies from one school to another and according to subject. Most independent schools have a staff:pupil ratio which ensures that pupils receive plenty of individual attention in accordance with their needs.

St Teresa's School, Surrey p. 381

Pastoral care

Independent schools generally place great emphasis on the traditional values of tolerance and consideration for others and on personal development within a secure but disciplined environment. Pupils normally have a personal tutor who, as part of an experienced team, monitors progress and emotional welfare throughout their school career.

Excellent facilities

Many schools offer first-class facilities for teaching, accommodation, sports and all aspects of school life.

Maintaining high standards

Independent schools must meet rigorous inspection criteria. Schools in membership of any of the associations which form the Independent Schools Council must conform to strict accreditation requirements and are inspected every six years by the Independent Schools Inspectorate, which works closely with OFSTED and the Department for Education and Skills. Other independent schools in England and Wales are inspected by Her Majesty's Inspectorate for OFSTED (see Section 1.1).

The boarding option

About 15 per cent of all independent school pupils are boarders. Research has shown that boarders enjoy school life and welcome the special opportunities which boarding offers, including long-lasting friendships, self-reliance and immediate access to help with studies and to a full range of facilities and activities.

While traditional full boarding has declined in popularity, interest is growing in more flexible boarding arrangements. Flexi- and weekly boarding are now much more widely available, enabling pupils to spend more time with their families, while still enjoying all the benefits of boarding life. Flexi-boarding generally means an arrangement that enables pupils to board for half the week and attend as day pupils for the remainder. Most schools can also offer a bed on an occasional basis, for example before a school trip or in the event of an emergency at home.

Full boarders normally enjoy busy weekends which offer access to a range of activities. A few schools timetable lessons on Saturday mornings, although this is becoming much less common as weekly boarding becomes more popular. Schools often arrange weekend trips away, for example to centres of cultural or historical interest or for activities such as walking or sailing. Otherwise pupils may be occupied with sports fixtures, musical or theatre performances or favourite hobbies. Most attend chapel on Sundays and have free time in which to study or relax.

Accommodation in boarding schools is often of an exceptionally high standard. Pupils share well-decorated bedrooms for small groups and are encouraged to bring comforts from home such as their own duvet covers, toys and posters. Sixth Form students often have single-study bedrooms in their own accommodation block and are allowed a greater degree of freedom. Houseparents provide constant care and supervision and are there to help with any problems arising. The Housemaster or Housemistress is normally assisted by a qualified Matron and one or two assistants, depending on the number of children in the House.

About 700 schools, including single-sex and co-educational schools, offer boarding places. Very few schools are for boarders only. Most also admit a significant number of day pupils. Whether you are looking for a boarding or a day place, it is wise to check the proportions of boarding and day pupils, since these will influence the overall ethos and character of a school. Numbers of boarders at each school are shown in Part Two. An index of boarding provision by county appears in Part Four.

Prior's Field School, Surrey p. 377

State-maintained and grant-maintained boarding schools

There are some 35 state-maintained schools which accept boarding pupils, although day pupils are usually in the majority. UK and EU nationals and children from outside the EU who have the right of residence in the UK can be accepted as boarders. They pay only for the cost of boarding at these schools and are not charged for tuition. This means that fees, which are generally around £2,000 a term, are much lower than those charged by independent boarding schools. For further information see the school profiles beginning on page 255 or contact the Boarding Schools' Association (see page 513).

Types of independent schools

Independent schools in the UK cover all age ranges; some offer education from nursery level through to 18, others are junior or senior only. Most are day schools, but a large number offer both boarding and day places. There is a variety of co-educational and single-sex schools; many of the latter, particularly boys' schools, offer co-education at Sixth Form level.

Age range	*Type of establishment*
2–7/8	**Nursery or Pre-Preparatory School**
7/8–13	**Preparatory School**
11/13–16/18	**Senior School**
16–18	**Sixth Form**

Nursery and pre-preparatory schools

Nursery education refers to schools for pupils under the age of 5, pre-preparatory education for pupils aged 5–7/8. Many preparatory schools have their own nursery and pre-prep departments.

Pupils under the age of 5 are rarely required to meet more than the very basic practical requirements for entry, although the Head will wish to meet the child in advance. Some schools also set relatively simple tests. Most schools offer entry at the beginning of each term.

The youngest children attend either mornings or afternoons only, before progressing to a full day. Emphasis is given to the development of academic, social, language and aesthetic skills through play, music, drama and handicrafts. Children may cover basic letter and number work, handwriting and spelling. Approaches vary, from traditional teaching styles to more modern methods. Montessori schools teach according to a series of principles which centre on observation of the individual needs of each child and provision of appropriate stimuli and tasks accordingly.

Hendon Preparatory School, London p. 340

Preparatory schools

Many prep schools accept pupils from the age of 3 upwards. Entry is usually dependent upon an interview with the Head and a satisfactory report from the previous school. Some schools also set verbal or written entrance tests in English and Mathematics, although pupils entering the preparatory department of a pre-preparatory school which they already attend may be exempted from such tests. It may be difficult to join a school for the final one or two years of preparatory education when pupils are approaching Common Entrance and other entrance examinations. Schools which prepare pupils primarily for Common Entrance may test older entrants more rigorously to ensure that they have the capacity to pass at 11, 12 or 13.

When single-sex education was more common, it was usual for girls to remain at their prep school until the age of 11 and for boys to remain until 13. However, with the growth of co-education the options are now more flexible.

Dean Close Preparatory School, Gloucestershire p. 282

Most preparatory schools are preparing pupils for the Common Entrance examination, taken at 11+, 12+ or 13+ for entry to senior boarding or day schools, although some schools, particularly city day schools, set their own entrance examinations. Some parts of the country retain the old examinations for entry to local grammar schools, which require no formal preparation. The destination of school leavers and the main academic thrust of the school may well be influenced by available provision at senior level. The Head of your child's school will want to know which senior school you have chosen when he or she reaches the last two years of prep school. Further information about Common Entrance is given on page 42.

Pupils are normally taught by class teachers until the age of about 8. After this they may be grouped according to ability. By the age of 9 or 10 there is increasing emphasis on subject teaching by specialists and close attention to the requirements of the National Curriculum, which may be complemented by other elements such as current affairs and topical studies, group projects and field trips.

Formal assessments of academic progress and achievements as well as performance in sports and other activities are made regularly. Examinations are normally held twice a year or at the end of each term. Grades are entered in the termly report for parents.

Senior schools

Senior schools generally admit pupils from 11 to 18, although some boys' schools still maintain the traditional age of entry at 13. Schools with their own preparatory department may offer a straightforward transfer into the senior school, but most demand successful completion of entrance tests. Some schools set their own entrance tests in English, Mathematics and a general paper. Many use the Common Entrance examination.

Bromsgrove School, Worcestershire p. 292

Many senior schools also offer a range of scholarships for pupils demonstrating exceptional talent and potential in academic studies, music or art. Examinations are normally held in February and March for entry in September.

St Margaret's School, London p. 350

Changing schools at 15 or 17 is not generally recommended because of the likely disruption to GCSE or A level studies, particularly if the move means a change to a different examination syllabus. If a move has to be made after age 13, it may be best to wait until after GCSEs or their equivalent have been completed.

Changing schools at 16 is quite common. Entry to the Sixth Form of most schools is dependent upon interview, together with specified results at GCSE, which will vary from one school to another. Some schools also offer scholarships at this level. Entry requirements for independent Sixth Form colleges tend to be more flexible than in schools.

Independent schools in England and Wales are not required to teach the National Curriculum or to use the National Tests, which are compulsory for state-maintained schools. However, since most are preparing students for public examinations, they generally follow the National Curriculum, complementing it with additional options or areas of study as desired. Independent schools in Scotland are free to form their own curriculum policy, but, like maintained schools in Scotland, they are normally preparing pupils for Standard and Higher examinations.

Almost all senior schools in England and Wales are preparing pupils for the General Certificate of Secondary Education (GCSEs), taken at 16, the Advanced Subsidiary (AS) and Advanced GCE (A2). In Scotland pupils are prepared for the Scottish National Qualifications.

Kingswood School, Bath p. 409

Pupils at the lower end of the age range are often taught in sets, a method which groups children for each subject according to their ability in that subject. Streaming, which groups children according to ability on a cross-curricular basis, is used in a smaller number of schools.

The two-year GCSE course begins at 14. Most pupils take eight or nine subjects. In some cases very able children may take certain GCSE examinations after one year rather than two. In Scotland pupils normally take seven to eight Standard Grade subjects.

Assessments or examinations in each subject may take place each term. Many schools operate a tutorial system under which a House tutor is assigned to each pupil to monitor social and personal development as well as academic progress. Parents receive a full report at the end of each term. In some schools, mock examinations (in preparation for GCSE, AS/A2 or Scottish equivalents) are held in the spring preceding the real examinations. These are marked internally by the school and give an indication of likely performance in the summer.

Most Sixth Form students study a combination of up to four AS levels in the first year, which are normally reduced to three subjects in the final year (A2). Some schools also offer Vocational A levels. For further details see page 45.

A few schools offer the International Baccalaureate (IB), a demanding two-year course which includes six subject groups that comprise both arts and sciences. The IB is accepted as an alternative to A levels by all British universities and as a means of entry to many universities overseas.

Some schools also run one-year courses for students who do not wish to take a full Sixth Form examination course but may wish to take a general course which includes the opportunity to take additional GCSEs, supplemented by vocational options.

Boarding schools in Scotland usually follow the English examination system, though many also offer Scottish qualifications. Higher examinations form the basis for entry to Higher Education and are offered in a wide range of subjects. Some schools also offer vocational programmes. See page 44 for details.

Pupils at Sixth Form level are encouraged to develop a more independent approach to their studies, to learn how to determine priorities and manage their time wisely. As well as timetabled lessons they normally have periods set aside for private study.

All-round education

Aside from academic studies, independent schools place great emphasis on wider activities. Many excel in areas such as sport, where pupils can develop their talents through fixtures against other schools as well as county or national school championships. Most schools recognize, however, that not all pupils enjoy team games. Many offer more individual sports, including, for example, squash, horse-riding, sailing and golf. Music, art and drama are also important aspects of the curriculum and extra-curricular activities. Many schools offer individual music lessons on a range of instruments and encourage students to play in the school orchestra or other music groups or to sing in the choir. Drama is often taught to a very high standard, with performances staged for public festivals as well as in school. Many schools offer preparation for examinations set by the Associated Board of the Royal Schools of Music and the London Academy of Music and Dramatic Art (LAMDA) and there may be regular trips to galleries, concerts, the theatre or the ballet.

Merchiston Castle School, Edinburgh p. 419

Independent Sixth Form colleges

Many students remain in the same school for A level studies, which offers the benefits of continuity and familiarity at a crucial stage of education. Others choose to move to a different school or college, for example if their preferred combination of subjects is not available or if a different type of environment is sought. Independent Sixth Form (tutorial) colleges offer an alternative option for students who are seeking a different style of education, for whom entry to a school Sixth Form is not appropriate or in situations where a mid-course transfer to an alternative mainstream school is not possible. Most colleges offer resit and short revision courses as well as full-time one-year and two-year GCSE and AS/A2 courses. Tuition is in small groups, with special emphasis given to exam technique and study skills. Attendance at lessons and coverage of academic work are strictly monitored, although the overall atmosphere within a college is usually less formal than that in schools.

Cambridge Centre for Sixth Form Studies, Cambridgeshire **p. 272**

Most independent colleges are located in major cities, including London, Oxford, Cambridge, Birmingham and Manchester. Most are day colleges but some offer accommodation in their own halls of residence or with local families. Some colleges provide a range of sports and extra-curricular activities, but few can offer the campus-style environment and full range of on-site facilities and activities offered by some schools.

For students who wish to pursue a more vocational route there is a variety of independent further education colleges. These tend to be much smaller than state-maintained further education colleges and specialize in specific areas such as Business, Secretarial Training, Computing or Beauty Therapy.

Pastoral care and discipline

Many independent schools, whether boarding or day, operate a House system, which divides pupils into smaller communities to ensure a good staff:pupil ratio for pastoral care. Boarders are often accommodated in small groups with resident House staff. The Housemaster or Housemistress is in charge of pastoral care and will also go through the school report with each child at the end of term. House staff monitor overall progress, keep the Head informed about each child and, in boarding schools, may be the first point of contact for parents. Many schools also allocate each pupil a personal tutor, who assists with educational guidance, keeps progress and welfare under constant review and can deal with issues arising on a day-to-day basis. The Children Act also places a legal obligation on schools to provide a statement of the policy and system of care in place for pupils. All schools are required to have a published policy on bullying.

Most schools keep rules simple, encouraging self-discipline and common sense in their pupils and giving praise for good behaviour. Sometimes children may contribute to a

House points system, being awarded points for good work, thoughtful behaviour and for showing initiative or making a particular effort. Points might be deducted for bad behaviour. Other sanctions imposed might include limitations on leaving school premises or detention. A breach of school rules with regard to smoking or alcohol may mean suspension. Breaches involving illegal drugs may mean immediate permanent exclusion. Corporal punishment is illegal in all schools.

Religion

Spiritual growth is an important aspect of life in most independent schools, whatever their affiliation. The range includes Church of England, Roman Catholic, Quaker, Methodist, Jewish and others. Most adopt an inter-denominational approach and are happy to accept children of other faiths, but parents should check with individual schools the extent to which their child, if of a faith other than the majority of pupils, would be expected to participate in school worship. An index of schools by religious affiliation starts on page 478.

Contact with parents

Every child receives a termly report which is sent home to parents. Schools also hold parents' evenings at regular intervals to allow parents to discuss with teaching and pastoral staff any issues of concern and to be fully briefed on their child's progress. The school report will also contain results of any internal exams held during the term. Parents are often invited to attend school sporting, musical or theatrical events, whether or not their child is taking part, and sometimes to help with school projects such as fundraising activities.

Educational guidance and careers assessment

The value of good educational guidance cannot be overestimated, particularly in view of the complexity and variety of options now available to school leavers and the importance of making the right choice. Some schools have a well-stocked, permanently staffed careers department and a full programme of careers guidance which includes formal assessment, talks from visiting speakers and work experience opportunities. Others may have more limited resources. For parents seeking specialist guidance from an independent source, Gabbitas offers extensive one-to-one careers assessment and advice for students aged 15+.

Special educational needs

Parents of children in need of extensive individual attention, usually those with specific learning difficulties such as dyslexia, will find that there is a large number of mainstream independent schools which offer facilities and tuition in varying degrees. Some schools may bring in a specialist teacher to assist pupils at set times during the week. Some may have specialist teachers permanently on the staff. Others may run a specially staffed department or unit. Parents interested in schools which offer provision in some form will find a number of these profiled in Part Three. More detailed information is available from the Dyslexia Institute, the British Dyslexia Association and CReSTeD (see Part Four). Many schools also offer English as a Foreign Language (EFL) support to students coming from overseas, although in most cases pupils will be expected to have a certain level of English on arrival. A list of schools offering EFL support appears in Part Four. More detailed information on special needs provision and special schools may be found in a separate Gabbitas publication, *Schools for Special Needs – A Complete Guide*, available in bookshops or direct from Gabbitas. To search for special schools online, visit www.gabbitas.co.uk.

Extra-curricular activities

Many schools offer an impressive range of options, from art appreciation to abseiling, from fencing to fishing, often at very high standards. Most schools have a range of musical activities – orchestras, choir, madrigal groups, wind ensembles, to name but a few – and offer wide-ranging opportunities for individual music tuition. Most sports form part of extra-curricular activities as well as timetabled lessons. Other activities might include chess, badminton, canoeing, Duke of Edinburgh's Award, horse-riding, Brownies and Scout groups, ballet, cookery, gardening, trampolining, rowing, golf, billiards, furniture restoration, stamps, sailing, carpentry, model-making, DT, pottery, drama, French clubs, community service and outward bound activities. Individual schools should be happy to supply parents with a list of their activities.

Michael Hall, East Sussex p. 386

School staff – who's who?

The Board of Governors

The Board of Governors is the planning and policy-making body which controls the administration and finance of the school. Some may also be parents of children at the school. The Governors are responsible for the appointment of the Head and for all major decisions affecting the school. Governors give their time voluntarily. Many are individuals with expertise in their professional lives, for example in law or accountancy, who can contribute their knowledge for the benefit of the school.

Head

Accountable to the Governors for the safety and welfare of pupils and the competence of staff, the Head is responsible for all aspects of the day-to-day management of the school, including appointment of staff, pupil admission policy and pupil recruitment, staffing and administrative structure, curriculum content and management. As figureheads for their schools, many Heads also regard the marketing of their school as a key part of their role, although some schools now employ a Development Director specifically for the purpose. Most Heads also include several hours' teaching in the week, which helps them to keep in touch and get to know pupils individually.

Bursar

The Bursar, in conjunction with the Governors, is responsible for financial matters within the school. The Bursar also takes charge of maintenance of the grounds, premises and buildings as well as catering arrangements.

Director of Studies

Many schools have a Director of Studies, who is responsible for day-to-day curriculum matters and timetabling and for ensuring that staff are kept informed of new developments.

Registrar/Admissions Secretary

The Registrar is responsible for the admission of pupils and making arrangements for parents to visit the school and meet the Head. He or she also takes care of the practical aspects of registration and joining.

Housemaster/Housemistress

The Housemaster or Housemistress takes care of the welfare and overall progress of children in the House and is normally the first point of contact for parents. He or she will keep the Head informed of each child's progress and may often be the first to hear of any problems. Serious issues are always referred to the Head.

Subject teachers

Subject teachers are responsible for the academic progress of pupils and will produce a termly report for those taking their subject. Open evenings offer parents the opportunity to discuss any matters of concern with subject teachers.

Chaplain

The Chaplain has a special role within school. Independent of academic or disciplinary considerations, the Chaplain is responsible for the spiritual development of pupils and can often provide a sympathetic ear to children who seek guidance on issues of concern.

Matron

The Matron looks after the practical aspects of boarding life, supervising and arranging laundry. Separate Houses normally have their own Matron. She often knows children individually and can provide sympathy and support for those who feel homesick or upset.

Sister

The Sister is a qualified nurse responsible for medical arrangements. She looks after pupils who may be admitted into the sanatorium with minor ailments and may require a few days in bed. Within a boarding school, serious medical matters are always referred to the school doctor and where necessary children will be taken to hospital.

Students

Independent schools encourage their pupils to take on positions of responsibility as part of school life. Senior pupils who show good sense and have contributed to the school by their achievements in academic work, musical or sporting activities for example, may be granted suitable senior positions in recognition of their efforts. Hence an excellent sportsman may be made Games Captain or an outstanding chorister Head of Choir. Pupils with an excellent academic record or who deserve merit for other contributions may be given the post of Head Boy or Girl. Prefects have responsibility for some of the daily routines in school and are encouraged to set a good example to younger pupils.

What will it cost?

Fees vary widely, but as a general guide, in 2005/2006 parents can expect to pay annual fees of between £2,500 and £10,000 at a day preparatory school or £10,000 to £15,000 for boarding. At senior level fees range from about £6,500 to £15,000 at day schools, or £15,000 to £20,000+ for a boarding place. Fees at girls' schools tend to be marginally lower than those at boys' and co-educational schools.

Fees in independent Sixth Form colleges are usually charged per subject, with accommodation charged separately. The overall costs of tuition and accommodation for a student studying three subjects at A level are broadly in line with those charged at a senior boarding school.

Parents are normally asked to pay fees in three termly instalments, one at the start of each term, although some schools may offer a choice of payment methods. If you wish to move your child to another school, the present school will normally require a full term's notice in writing. Otherwise you may find that you are charged an additional term's fees in lieu.

Many schools also encourage parents to take out insurance against the risk of their child not being able to attend school, for example in the event of illness.

Parents may be asked to meet additional costs during the school year for school lunches, school trips, sports kit, music lessons and similar items, so it is important to check what is and what is not included in the basic termly fee and to take account of other essentials when estimating the overall costs. Boarders will also require additional items such as bedlinen and weekend wear.

If you live overseas, bear in mind that there will be other costs associated with a boarding education in the UK. These include the costs of guardianship, discussed in Part 1.4, travel and any specialist dental treatment, eye tests or spectacles which your child may need while he or she is in the UK. Your child will also need a regular supply of pocket money. Schools discourage pupils from carrying large amounts of cash, but your child will probably want to buy music or clothes as well as small treats.

Scholarships and bursaries

If your child is exceptionally talented in a specific area, there may well be scholarship opportunities which could reduce the fees by as much as 50 per cent or possibly more. If financial hardship is an issue, bursaries may be available to help top up the shortfall. The decision to grant a bursary will be taken according to individual circumstances.

Further information about planning for school fees begins on page 34. Information on scholarship and bursary opportunities begins on page 38 and a full list of schools offering scholarships and bursaries appears in Part Four (pp. 435–60).

1.3
Choosing your School

'Which is the best school?'

There is no one school which can provide the best possible education for every child. Begin by working out your child's needs, then look for schools which meet these requirements. You will undoubtedly hear differing views about individual schools but remember that you are the best judge of your own child's needs. The question to ask is 'Which school will suit my child best?'

Avoid drawing up your shortlist on the basis of published league tables. These are an unreliable guide to the suitability of schools for your child and can be misleading. Finding the right school requires a much wider approach.

When to start

For entry to preparatory school at 7 or 8, you should be thinking about your choice once your child reaches the age of about 4. This allows you to be clearer about his or her academic potential, while allowing plenty of time for your research. For entry to senior schools, most parents start to look at the options two to three years ahead.

If you are thinking about a change of school at 16, remember that your child will be expected to sit an entrance exam. These often take place in October or November for entry the following September, with the offer of a place normally conditional upon GCSE results. It is therefore important to begin your search during Year 10, ie, the first year of your child's GCSE course.

Similarly, for entry to schools in Year 10 there is normally some form of entrance exam during the preceding year, so it is wise to allow plenty of time beforehand to consider the options.

What type of school will be appropriate?

- **Single sex or co-educational:** This is really a matter of personal preference; some argue that single-sex education enables pupils to achieve at a higher level without the distraction of the opposite sex. Others believe that co-education offers a more natural environment. An index of single-sex schools appears in Part Four.

- **Day or boarding:** Boarding does not suit all children, but for those who enjoy it there are many benefits. For some children it may be a necessity. Ensure that your knowledge is up to date: most boarding schools today offer flexi-boarding or weekly boarding options which enable pupils to spend more time with their families. Some schools offer 'taster' days and weekends which enable prospective pupils to sample boarding life in advance.
- **Location:** Remember to consider the likely travelling time, particularly by car, during the morning and evening rush hours. Travel to and from school will also be required for parents' evenings, sports days and other school events. If public transport is to be used, how easy is the journey? Schools in more rural areas often offer a minibus service. Many parents of boarders, who today generally have many opportunities to go home during the term, choose schools within about two hours' drive.
- **Religious affiliation:** Would you prefer a school of a particular denomination or are you willing to include others in your choice?

Your child's needs

Academic needs are the first priority. Be realistic about your child's potential and avoid trying to gain a place at a very academic school unless you are confident of your child's ability to cope. Consider also any other interests your child may have, for example in music or sport, as well as your child's overall personality. Some children thrive in a highly active environment offering a multitude of stimuli and the company of other lively and confident youngsters. Others may benefit from being a part of a smaller school community.

Finding out

The Head of your child's present school can probably recommend suitable options, but you may also find it helpful to obtain an independent viewpoint from an educational consultant. Ask those schools which interest you to send you a prospectus. Most schools also have a website, which often has more recent news of activities and developments. Website addresses appear in Part Three of this Guide, or you can access sites for all these schools at www.gabbitas.co.uk. If you would like independent recommendations in line with your needs, contact Gabbitas.

Visiting schools

A personal visit is the only way to find out whether or not you like a particular school and will allow you to meet staff and pupils and experience the overall atmosphere. If possible, try to visit more than one school, so that you have a means of comparison. You may be invited to an Open Day, but the best time to visit is on a normal day during term time. That way you can see the day-to-day routine in place and the children at their usual activities. In most cases you will meet the Head, who will want to interview your child, following which a member of staff or senior pupil may give you a tour of the school.

In a boarding school you should also be able to meet the Housemaster or Housemistress. It is important that you feel comfortable with the Head and other staff who will be responsible for your child. Do they show a genuine interest in your child? Do they make you feel welcome?

There are a number of areas you may wish to ask about during your visit.

Academic policy and destination of leavers

- At prep level, is the school's policy appropriate for your longer-term plans? Some schools may be preparing pupils primarily for entry to senior independent schools; others may have significant numbers whose parents are interested in good local state schools. Scholarship examinations also vary in syllabus from one school to another. Since some prep schools prepare pupils for a limited range of senior schools, you may wish to find out which ones are covered.
- At secondary level, what is the school's academic pace and focus?
- Ask about subjects in which your child has a particular interest or strength. How are these taught? Are pupils encouraged to develop their knowledge and interest through special projects, trips or events?
- How many children take GCSEs and AS/A2 levels, or their equivalents?
- How many GCSE and AS/A2 level subjects are offered?
- How big is the Sixth Form?
- How many pupils stay on into the Sixth Form? If a large proportion of pupils leave after GCSE, why is this and where do they go?
- Is there any evident bias in the numbers taking certain subjects?
- What other courses are offered in the Sixth Form?
- Ask about the destinations of Sixth Form leavers. What proportion go on to university or other forms of higher education or training? In which subject areas?

Exam results

- Exam results, if you can compare them with results in previous years, are a useful measure of the school's academic performance and any trends, but take care when interpreting the figures. A 100 per cent pass rate seems impressive, but how many pupils took the exam? Some schools pre-select candidates, which inevitably improves the pass rate statistics.

Testing and assessment

- What systems are in place to monitor performance?
- How much communication is there between staff and parents?

Educational and careers guidance

- What guidance is offered to pupils choosing subjects for examination study, higher education and career options? At what stage does this begin? How is it developed as pupils progress through school?
- What experience do advisers have?
- What facilities are available? Is there a dedicated careers unit with specialist staff?
- Are there any work experience programmes in place?

Special needs

- If your child has special educational needs, exactly how will the school provide for these? What experience do staff have of meeting these needs? The same applies if your child has any special medical or dietary requirements.

Pastoral care and boarders

- How is the welfare of students monitored? How will you be kept in touch?
- If your child is to be a day pupil in a boarding school, you may wish to know whether day pupils can join in with evening and weekend activities at school.
- Many working parents may find before- and after-school care facilities attractive. Some schools, particularly city day schools, offer this service.
- Parents of boarders must have complete confidence in those who will be responsible for their child's welfare. Ask about the school's policy for the care and supervision of boarders.
- What is the routine at weekends? May pupils leave the premises?
- Who is on duty in the evenings, at night and at weekends? Are they suitably qualified and experienced?
- What happens in the event of an emergency? What is the school's responsibility?
- Do boarders receive regular medical and dental checks?
- Make sure that you are shown the boarding accommodation. Is it clean, warm and welcoming? Is there plenty of space for your child's clothes and personal effects? Is there a secure area for valuables?
- What are boarders permitted to bring to school? Some schools allow small pets.

Teaching staff

- Are staff appropriately qualified? Are they specialists in the subjects they teach?
- How many are full-time?
- Is there a high staff turnover? If so, why?
- How is teaching organized?

Extra-curricular activities

- If your child has a particular interest or strength, will the school encourage and develop it?

Discipline

- Be sure that you agree with the school's policies. How do they deal with incidents involving smoking, alcohol or drugs?
- Will you be informed of any disciplinary matter which involves your child?

Seeing the school

- What do your first impressions tell you? Are staff and pupils polite and welcoming? Is the Reception area easy to find? Are the buildings and grounds neat and well kept?
- Is there a sense of order and purpose? What are the noise levels like?
- Do the noticeboards suggest an active, enthusiastic school?
- How do pupils respond to you? Are they articulate and confident? How do they respond to teachers in class?
- How do staff respond to the Head?

Registration and confirmation

Registering your child commits neither you nor the school. Schools normally charge a non-refundable registration fee, which may be anything up to £100 for a senior school. It is wise to have your child registered at more than one school in case no place is offered or available at your first choice. You will need to make up your mind about a year before your child is due to start. Once you have formally accepted a place there is a contract between you and the school. Should you change your mind, your deposit may or may not be refundable, depending upon the terms set by the school. As with any contractual arrangement, ensure that you understand and accept the school's published terms and conditions before going ahead.

The final choice

After your visits, check the schools' performance against your original criteria. Each school will have its own strengths. Which are most important to you? Your child must also be happy with the final choice, but the decision must be yours. If you have difficulty deciding between two schools, the answer is to trust your instincts. The right school is the one which will allow your child to develop his or her full potential in the company of liked and trusted staff and pupils in an environment where he or she feels happy and at home.

1.4
Coming from Overseas

If you live overseas, the best advice is to plan ahead as far as possible and at least a year in advance. This will give you a wider choice of school and allow you time to research all the options properly and make an informed choice. Parents may find it helpful to bear in mind the following aspects.

Level of English

Most independent schools will expect your child to speak some English on arrival, although additional tuition is often available in school to improve fluency and accuracy and to ensure that your child can cope with a normal curriculum.

If your child is to board in the UK but speaks only a little or no English, he or she may benefit from a short period in one of the specialist boarding schools (often called international study centres) which prepare overseas pupils for entry into mainstream boarding schools at secondary level. A list of international study centres is given at the end of this section.

Alternatively, you may wish to arrange for your child to spend the summer at one of the UK's many language schools before joining a boarding school in September. Details of suitable courses can be obtained from reputable consultants such as Gabbitas.

Academic background

If your child has been educated within the British system, it should not be difficult to join a school in the UK, although care should be taken to avoid changing schools while a student is in the middle of GCSE or A level studies. However, if your child has not been following a British curriculum, entry to a mainstream independent school may be less straightforward. The younger your child, the easier it is likely to be for him or her to adapt to a new school environment. Prep schools may accept overseas pupils at any stage up to the final two years, when pupils are prepared for Common Entrance exams and entry may be more difficult. Senior schools, in particular, will normally look for evidence of ability and achievement comparable with pupils educated in the British system and will probably wish to test your child in English, Maths and Science before deciding whether to offer a place. Students wishing to enter the Sixth Form will probably be tested in the subjects they wish to study. Recent reports and transcripts, in translation, should also be made available to schools.

If your child has been following the International Baccalaureate (IB) programme overseas, you will find a number of schools and colleges in the UK, both state and independent, which offer the IB. Details of the IB and the schools and colleges offering it are given on pages 46–58.

Length of stay

If you are planning to live in the UK for a relatively short period, perhaps no more than a year, you may find it more appropriate for your child to attend an international school. These schools specialize in educating children whose stay is limited and who regularly move around the world with their parents. Most are day schools, though some also offer boarding provision. These schools tend to have a broad mix of nationalities and offer a curriculum, normally based either on the British or the American system, sufficiently flexible to allow a smooth transition afterwards into international schools elsewhere in the world. Many also offer the IB, as described above.

If your stay is relatively short and you plan to return home afterwards, you may be able to enter your child in one of the schools in the UK specifically for nationals of other countries who are based in the UK. France, Germany, Sweden, Norway, Greece and Japan are all represented. Your own embassy in London should be able to provide further details.

Location

If you are looking for a boarding school, try not to restrict your search too narrowly. Most schools, including those in the most beautiful and rural parts of the UK, are within easy reach of major transport links and the UK is well served by air, rail and road routes. In addition, most schools will make arrangements to have your child escorted between school and the airport and vice versa.

Visiting schools

Once you have decided on the most suitable type of school, you can obtain information on specific schools. Gabbitas can identify schools likely to meet your requirements, and arrange for you to receive prospectuses. It is essential that you visit schools before making a choice. Try to plan your visits to schools during term time. The school year in the UK begins in September and comprises three terms: early September to mid-December, early January to mid-March and early April to early July. There are also three half-term breaks, normally from two days to a week, at the end of October, in mid- to late February and at the end of May. Gabbitas can arrange a schedule of visits for you to ensure that you make the best use of your time in the UK.

Questions to ask

English language support

What level of English does the school expect? Is additional support available at school? How is this organized? Is there a qualified teacher?

Pupil mix

International schools naturally have pupils of many different nationalities at any one time. However, if you are looking to enter your child into a mainstream independent school, you may wish to find out how many other pupils of your nationality attend the school and what arrangements are made to encourage them to mix with English pupils.

Pastoral care

If your child has special dietary needs or is required to observe specific religious principles, is the school willing and able to cope? Would your child also be expected to take part in the school's normal worship?

If your child speaks little English, it can be very comforting during the early days when homesickness and minor worries arise, or in the event of an emergency, to have a member of staff on hand to whom the child can speak in his or her own language. Bear in mind, however, that fewer schools are likely to have staff who speak non-European languages.

Ask about arrangements for escorting your child to and from school at the beginning and end of term. Some schools have a minibus service to take children to railway stations and airports or will arrange a taxi where appropriate.

Guardianship

Most schools insist that boarding pupils whose parents live overseas have an appointed guardian living near the school who can offer a home for 'exeats' (weekends out of school), half-term breaks and at the beginning and end of term in case flights do not coincide exactly with school dates. A guardian may be a relative or friend appointed by parents, but it should be remembered that the arrangement may need to continue for some years and that guardianship is a substantial commitment.

For parents with no suitable contacts in the UK, schools may be able to assist in making arrangements. Alternatively there are independent organizations, including

Gabbitas, which specialize in the provision of guardianship services. Good guardian families should offer a 'home from home', looking after the interests and welfare of your child as they would their own, providing a separate room and space for study, attending school events and parents' evenings, involving your child in all aspects of family life and encouraging him or her to feel comfortable and relaxed while away from school. Some guardianship organizations are very experienced in selecting suitable families who will offer a safe and happy home to students a long way from their own parents. The range of services offered and fees charged by different providers will vary, but you should certainly look for a service which:

- personally ensures that families are visited in their homes by an experienced member of staff and that all appropriate checks are made;
- takes a genuine interest in your child's educational and social welfare and progress;
- keeps in touch with you, your child, the school and the guardian family to ensure that all is running smoothly;
- provides, as required, administrative support and assistance with visa and travel requirements, medical and dental checks and insurance, and any other matters such as the purchase of school uniform, sports kit and casual clothes.

Parents seeking a guardianship provider may like to contact AEGIS (the Association for the Education and Guardianship of International Students), of which Gabbitas is a founder member. The purpose of AEGIS is to promote best and legal practice in all areas of guardianship and to safeguard the welfare and happiness of overseas children attending educational institutions in the UK. AEGIS aims to provide accreditation for all reputable guardianship organizations. Applicants for membership are required to undergo assessment and inspection to ensure that they are adhering to the AEGIS Code of Practice and fulfilling the Membership Criteria before full membership can be granted. For further details of the Gabbitas Guardianship Service, contact Catherine Stoker on +44 (0)20 7734 0161 or visit www.gabbitas.co.uk. For further information about AEGIS, visit the website at www.aegisuk.net.

Preparing your child to come to the UK

Coming to school in a different country is an enriching and exciting experience. You can help your child to settle in more quickly by encouraging him or her to take a positive approach and to try to absorb the traditions and social customs of school and family life in the UK. After the first year, most children begin to feel more confident and comfortable in their surroundings, both at school and with their guardian family. A good guardianship organization will ensure that you and your child know what to expect from life in the UK, and that you are aware of the kind of behaviour and approach which the school and guardian family will expect from your child. They will also be able to advise on aspects such as appropriate clothes to bring for a UK climate, which may be very different from that at home. Similarly, they should be able to advise on visas, UK entry requirements and related matters.

Where to go for help

You may be able to obtain information about schools from official sources in your own country. For detailed guidance and assistance in the UK you may wish to contact an independent educational consultancy such as Gabbitas which can advise you on all aspects of education in the UK and transferring into the British system.

International study centres

For contact details, please refer to the entries in Part Two.

- The International Centre, Ackworth School, West Yorkshire
- Bedford School Study Centre, Bedfordshire
- Diana, Princess of Wales Study Centre, Riddlesworth Hall, Norfolk
- Dover College, International Study Centre, Kent
- International College, Sherborne School, Dorset
- International Study Centre at Kent College, Canterbury, Kent
- King's International Study Centre, The King's School, Ely, Cambridgeshire
- Millfield English Language School, Millfield School, Somerset
- Newlands International College, East Sussex
- Rossall School International Study Centre, Lancashire
- Sidcot Academic English School, Sidcot School, North Somerset
- Taunton International Study Centre, Somerset

1.5
Finding the Fees

Towry Law Financial Services Limited

How much will it cost?

Your first decision is what fees you are planning to meet. Do you have a specific school or schools in mind and if so what are the fees? Hopefully you have started planning early, which means that you are unlikely to have made a final choice of school. In this case you need to work on the average or typical fees for the type of school. This can range from day preparatory to senior boarding school. If your child was born in the latter part of the year, check that you are planning for the right period, i.e. don't plan to provide funds a year early, leaving a gap year at the end.

Next, you need to allow for inflation. A school's major cost is teacher and other salaries, which tend to increase in line with earnings rather than prices. Historically, earnings rise faster than prices, so even though inflation is now relatively low, it is certainly not something you can ignore.

The distinctive feature of planning for educational costs

The distinctive nature lies in the fact that you are planning for a 'known commitment'. You know that at the beginning of each term or school year you will have a bill to pay and will need to draw on your investments.

This is where the 'reward–risk' spectrum comes in. At one end, asset-backed investments offer a higher potential reward but also a degree of investment risk or potential volatility. In the longer term, such investments have been the way to achieve real growth and outpace inflation (though the past is not necessarily a guide to future performance). On the other hand, you do not want to rely on such investments if it means encashing them at the worst possible time, just after a stock market setback. Remember, because of the nature of educational planning you probably do not have any choice about when you need funds to pay a bill.

At the other end of the reward–risk spectrum are deposit accounts; just about as safe as safe can be (so long as the institution is safe), but will they even keep up with inflation?

You do not need to plump for either extreme. The answer partly depends on the period over which you are investing. If you are starting soon after birth, asset-backed investment can play a larger role, giving greater potential for real growth. Nearer the time, your holdings can be switched on a phased basis into more secure investment vehicles to lock in any gains and from which you can draw during the schooling period.

An alternative approach is 'mix and match'. A mixture of asset-backed investments and more secure ones will allow you to draw from the former in years when their values are high. In other years, you can draw from the more secure investments.

Existing investments

Your strategy should take into account any existing investments or savings that may be suitable. These may not have been taken out with school fees in mind. For example, you may have started a mortgage endowment some years ago and changed to a repayment mortgage. This would free up the endowment which could be used for school fees.

Tax-efficient investments

You can invest regular contributions or a lump sum into Individual Savings Accounts (ISAs). They are generally a good idea, especially for a higher-rate taxpayer, because the tax benefits should enhance returns. You can use ISAs for cash deposits, equities and also 'corporate bonds'. You will need to check whether 'mini' or 'maxi' ISAs are best for you. There is a limit on the contributions that can be made in each year, but both husband and wife can take out an ISA.

Rather than investing in individual shares, investors nowadays more commonly use 'collective' investments like unit trusts (or Open Ended Investment Companies – OEICs) or investment trusts. Collective funds give access to the benefits of equity investments without the investment risk inherent in investing in one or a small number of individual shares. Collective funds are a low-cost way of spreading risk by investing in a portfolio of shares, with the added advantage of professional fund management.

Investment services are now available that enable you to use your annual ISA allowance to invest in more than one fund with more than one manager. This provides additional diversification of the risk by allowing you to invest with a number of leading fund managers. It also makes a 'mix and match' approach easier. An adviser could put together a portfolio for you that mixes equities and bonds in portions to match your 'risk profile' and the length of time before fees are required, combining equities for the prospect of higher growth and bonds to provide an element of stability. With these investment services it is easy and relatively cheap to make adjustments as you go along, so as you get nearer to the fee paying period you could gradually switch from equities to bonds to lock in gains and increase the predictability of returns.

Any existing ISAs and Personal Equity Plans (PEPs) could, of course, be used as part of your planning. Not everyone is aware that you can transfer existing PEPs from one manager to another if appropriate, so that they will better meet your current objectives.

Other investment options

A range of other investment options is available. For instance, if you will be over 50 when fees (or university expenses) are required, you may be eligible to contribute more to a pension and use the benefits towards the bills (although this will of course reduce the amount available to provide retirement income).

Once you have used your ISA entitlement, you can still invest in the same underlying funds and benefit from the manager's expertise, but without the tax advantages of an ISA.

Besides with-profit bonds, insurance companies offer a number of lump-sum investment options with a range of underlying investments and risk ratings.

Expatriate parents

If you are an expatriate or offshore investor, there are offshore versions of most of the investments described above. Important considerations are your tax position whilst you are offshore, and if you will be returning to the UK during the schooling period, your UK tax position.

Late planning

If you have left it late to start planning, say within five years, you could consider the following:

- Check the school's terms for payment in advance (sometimes called composition fees schemes) as these can be attractive. Ask what happens if, for whatever reason, you switch to another school.
- Consider deposit-based schemes. Tax-efficient investments may play a part (cash ISAs).
- For other deposit accounts, consider internet or postal accounts, as they often offer better rates.
- National Savings, gilts and fixed-interest securities could also be considered.
- Loan schemes may be available whereby you arrange a 'drawdown' facility secured on your house. This assumes you have some 'free equity' (the difference between the value of the house and your mortgage) and is usually set up as a second mortgage. You can then 'drawdown' from the facility as and when you need to pay fees. Hence, you do not start paying interest sooner than necessary, keeping down the total cost. (Think carefully before securing other debts against your home. Your home may be repossessed if you do not keep up repayments on your mortgage.)

- Because of the interest payments, loan schemes are costly, so they should be regarded as a last resort and only after you have reviewed your finances to check that there is no alternative.

The need for protection

For most families, the major resource for educational expenses is the parents' earnings. Death or prolonged illness could destroy a well-laid plan and have a terrible effect on a family's standard of living and a child's education. You should therefore review your existing arrangements (whether from a company scheme or private) and make sure you are sufficiently protected.

University expenses

Although many of the same investment considerations apply, planning needs to cover living expenses plus a small proportion of the fees. There is a system of student loans.

Although university expenses are generally not as high as school fees, they have become more onerous in recent years, a trend that is likely to continue.

'Golden' rules of educational planning

- Plan as early in the child's life as possible.
- Set out what funds you need and when you need them, and plan accordingly.
- Mitigate tax on the investments wherever possible.
- Use capital if available, particularly from grandparents.
- Consult an expert, preferably an independent financial adviser.

This article briefly outlines some of the considerations and investment opportunities and does not make specific or individual recommendations. There is no one answer to suit everyone. The solution depends on a number of considerations and for a strategy tailored to your individual circumstances, seek independent financial advice.

Towry Law Financial Services Limited
Towry Law House,
Western Road,
Bracknell RG12 1TL
Tel: 0845 788 9933 (calls may be recorded)
E-mail: info@towrylaw.com

1.6
Scholarships, Bursaries and Other Awards

In addition to the many financial planning schemes available, assistance with the payment of fees may be obtainable from a variety of other sources.

Scholarships

Many senior schools offer scholarship opportunities. These are awarded, at the discretion of the school, to pupils displaying particular ability or promise, either in academic subjects, as an all-rounder or in specific areas such as music or art. Candidates are normally assessed on the basis of their performance in an examination or audition. Scholarship examinations are normally held in the February or March preceding September entry. Pupils awarded scholarships in, for example, music or art, may be required to sit the Common Entrance examination to ensure that they meet the normal academic requirements of the awarding school.

Scholarships are normally offered upon the usual age of entry to the school. Some schools also offer awards for Sixth Form entry, for example for students who have performed particularly well in the GCSE examinations. These awards may be restricted to pupils already attending the school or may also be open to prospective entrants coming from other schools.

Scholarships vary in value, although full-fee scholarships are now rarely available. Scholarships are awarded as a percentage of the full tuition fee to allow for inflation.

Fewer scholarships are available at preparatory school level. Choristers, however, are a special category. Choir schools generally offer much reduced fees for Choristers, well below the normal day fee. Help may also be available at senior schools, although in practice it is common for Choristers to gain music scholarships at their senior schools. A list of schools belonging to the Choir Schools Association appears on page 515. Details of schools specializing in the arts, dance and music appear on page 461.

Information about other music awards at independent schools is available from the Music Masters' and Mistresses' Association (MMA) at www.mma-online.org.uk. The site includes a searchable database of music awards offered by individual schools. The

MMA's annual guide to 'Music Awards at Independent Schools' is also available in printed form in music shops and libraries or by mail order from the MMA.

For a general guide to scholarships offered by individual schools, turn to the Scholarships index in Part Four.

Bursaries

Bursaries are intended primarily to ensure that children obtain provision suited to their needs and ability in cases where parents cannot afford the normal fees. They are awarded on the basis of financial hardship, rather than particular ability. All pupils applying for a bursary, however, will be required to show, normally by passing Common Entrance or the school's own entry tests, that they meet academic requirements. The size of the award is entirely at the discretion of the school.

A list of schools that offer bursaries is given in Part Four.

Reserved entrance awards

Some schools reserve awards for children with parents in a specific profession, for example in HM Forces, the clergy or in teaching. These are similar to bursaries in that the child must meet the normal entry requirements of the school, but eligibility for the award will be dependent upon fulfilment of one of the criteria stated above. Normally schools will reserve only a few places on this basis. Once a place for a specific award has been filled, it will not become available again until the pupil currently in receipt leaves the school. Hence the award may be available only once every five years or so.

A list of schools and brief summary of the reserved entrance awards offered by each is given in Part Four. The awards covered include those offered to children with one or both parents working in any of HM Forces, the Foreign Office, the medical profession, teaching, the clergy or as Christian missionaries.

Other awards

Schools may also offer concessions for brothers and sisters or for the children of former pupils.

If you are interested in the possibility of a scholarship or bursary or in other awards which might be available from schools in which you are interested, it is a good idea to advise schools accordingly when you first contact them.

The GDST Scholarship and Bursary Scheme

The GDST (Girls' Day School Trust), which comprises 25 independent girls' schools educating over 19,000 girls, has traditionally aimed to make its schools accessible to bright, motivated girls from families who could not afford a place at a GDST school without financial assistance. It has a Scholarship and Bursary Scheme specifically designed for low-income families. Grants are only awarded at GDST schools.

Most bursaries under the Scheme are awarded to girls from families with a total income of under £15,000, and it is unlikely that a bursary would be awarded in cases where total gross income exceeds £43,000. Bursaries are means-tested and may cover up to full fees. Scholarships, which are not means-tested, are awarded on merit and may cover up to half the fees. Most awards are available either on entry at 11 or for girls entering the Sixth Form. The Scheme is also designed to assist pupils already attending a GDST school whose parents face unexpected financial difficulties which could mean having to remove their daughter from the school and disrupt her education.

Awards are made at the discretion of individual school Heads rather than the Trust and requests for further information should therefore be directed to the Head of the school at which parents wish to apply for a place. A full list of GDST schools appears on page 518.

Other government grants

Assistance with the payment of fees is also offered to personnel employed by the Foreign and Commonwealth Office and by the Ministry of Defence, where a boarding education may be the only feasible option for parents whose professional lives demand frequent moves or postings overseas.

The FCO termly boarding allowance is available to FCO parents on request and is reviewed annually. Parents in need of further information should contact the FCO Personnel Services Department on 020 7238 4357.

Services personnel may seek guidance from the Service Children's Education Advisory Service, which can advise on choosing a boarding school and on the boarding allowance made. In 2005/2006 the boarding allowance is £3,496 per term for junior pupils and £4,557 per term for senior pupils. An allowance is also available for children with special educational needs. Further information may be obtained from Children's Education Advisory Service, Trenchard Lines, Upavon, Pewsey, Wiltshire SN9 6BE; Tel: 01980 618244. You may also find it helpful to visit www.army.mod.uk and www.sceschools.com.

Parents may also find it helpful to consult the list of schools offering reserved entrance awards. Some schools may be able to supplement allowances offered by employers through a reserved entrance award offered to pupils who meet the relevant criteria, eg with a parent in HM Forces.

Grant-giving Trusts

There are various educational and charitable Trusts which exist to provide help with the payment of independent school fees. Usually the criteria restrict eligibility to particular groups, for example orphans, or in cases of sudden and unforeseen financial hardship. In many cases a grant may be given only to enable a child to complete the present stage of education, eg to finish a GCSE or A Level course. Applications are normally considered on an individual basis by an appointed committee. The criteria for eligibility and for the award of a grant will vary according to individual policy. In some cases several Trusts may each contribute an agreed sum towards one individual case in order to make up the fees required. It should be noted that such Trusts receive many more applications for grants than can possibly be issued and competition is fierce. Applications for financial help purely on the grounds that parents would like an independent education for their child but cannot afford it from their own resources will be rejected. Parents are advised to consider carefully before applying for an independent school place and entering a child for the entrance examination if they cannot meet the fees unaided nor demonstrate a genuine need, as defined by the criteria published by the awarding Trusts, for an independent school education. Parents may find it helpful to consult the *Educational Grants Directory*, published by the Directory of Social Change. For further information about charitable funding contact ISC Educational Grants Advisory Service, Joint Educational Trust, 6 Lovat Lane, London EC3R 8DT; Tel: 020 7626 4583 (weekdays 9 to 11 am).

Local Authority grants

Grants from Local Authorities are sometimes available where a need for a child to board can be demonstrated, for example where the child has special educational needs which cannot be met in a day school environment or where travel on a daily basis is not feasible. Such grants are few in number. Awards for boarding fees at an independent school may not be granted unless it can be shown that there is no boarding place available at one of the state boarding schools, of which there are 36 nationwide.

Awards from Local Authorities are a complex issue. Parents wishing to find out more should contact the Director of Education for the Authority in which they live.

1.7 Examinations and Qualifications in the UK

Common Entrance

The Common Entrance examination forms the basis of entry to most independent senior schools, although some schools set their own entrance exams. Traditionally it is taken by boys at the age of 13 and by girls at the age of 11. However, with the growth of co-education at senior level the divisions have become less sharply defined and the examinations are open to both boys and girls.

The Common Entrance papers are set centrally by the Independent Schools Examinations Board, which comprises members of the Headmasters' and Headmistresses' Conference (HMC), the Girls' Schools Association (GSA) and the Incorporated Association of Preparatory Schools (IAPS). The papers are marked, however, by the individual schools, which have their own marking schemes and set their own entry standards. Common Entrance is not an exam which candidates pass by reaching a national standard.

The content of the Common Entrance papers has undergone regular review and the Independent Schools Examinations Board has adapted syllabuses to bring them into line with National Curriculum requirements.

Candidates are entered for Independent Schools Examinations by their junior or preparatory schools. Parents whose children attend state primary schools should apply to the Independent School Examinations Board direct, ideally four months before the scheduled examination date. Some pupils may need additional coaching for the exam if they are not attending an independent preparatory school. To be eligible, pupils must normally have been offered a place by a senior school subject to their performance in the exam. Pupils applying for scholarships may be required to pass Common Entrance before sitting the scholarship exam. Candidates normally take the exam in their own junior or preparatory school.

At 11+ the Common Entrance exam consists of papers in English, Mathematics and Science, and is designed to be suitable for all pupils, whether they attend an independent or a state school. Most pupils who take the exam at 13+ come from independent preparatory schools. Subjects are English, Mathematics, Science (compulsory); French,

History, Geography, Religious Studies, German, Spanish, Latin and Greek (optional). English as an Additional Language is an option at 11+ and 13+.

The examination for 13+ entry takes place in February and June. For entry at 11+ the exam is held in January. For further information on Common Entrance, or copies of past papers, contact: The General Secretary, Independent Schools Examinations Board, Jordan House, Christchurch Road, New Milton, Hampshire BH25 6QJ; Tel: 01425 621111; fax: 01425 620044; E-mail: ce@iseb.co.uk.

General Certificate of Secondary Education (GCSE)

The GCSE forms the principal means of assessing the National Curriculum at the end of compulsory schooling. GCSE courses are generally taught over the two years of Key Stage 4 of the National Curriculum from age 14.

GCSEs are assessed through a combination of coursework and terminal examination. The coursework enables pupils to gain credit from work produced during the two years of the course rather than exclusively on the basis of examination performance.

GCSE results are graded on a scale from A* to G.

Most GCSE examinations have differentiated or tiered papers that are targeted at different ranges of ability within the A*–G grade range. Nearly all large-entry GCSE subjects are examined through a foundation tier covering grades G–C and a higher tier covering grades D–A*.

Most pupils of average ability take eight or nine GCSE subjects, although some may take 10 or 11. Very able pupils may take some GCSE exams after one year. Pupils are asked to choose their subjects at 13. Schools can offer advice on those they think most suitable. GCSE (Short Course) qualifications are also available, which are designed to take only half the study time of full GCSE and are the equivalent of half a GCSE. They are graded on the same scale as a full GCSE but cover fewer topics. The GCSE (Short Course) can be used in various ways: to offer able students additional choices such as a second modern language or to offer a subject which could not otherwise be studied as a full GCSE because of other subject choices. It may also be attractive to students who need extra time in their studies and would be better suited to a two-year course devoted to a GCSE (Short Course) rather than a full GCSE. GCSEs in vocational subjects are available in the following eight subjects: Applied Art and Design; Applied Business; Applied ICT; Applied Science; Engineering; Health and Social Care; Leisure and Tourism; and Manufacturing. More information can be found on the DfES website at www.dfes.gov.uk/qualifications.

GCE A levels and GCE Advanced Subsidiary

Most A levels comprise six units. For each subject, three units form an Advanced Subsidiary level (AS) course and represent the first half of the Advanced GCE (A level) course. The remaining three units (known as A2) represent the final year's study.

Completion of all six units is required for the award of an A level. An A level grade is reached by combining AS and A2 grades. AS and A levels have UCAS (Universities and Colleges Admissions Service) point scores for the purposes of university entry. An AS level receives half the points of an A level.

Students who do not pursue a subject beyond the first year but who successfully complete the first three units will be awarded an AS. However, completion of the three A2 units on their own does not represent a qualification.

There are a few free-standing AS subjects where no corresponding A level is available. AS is designed to provide extra breadth to Sixth Form studies. Students may take four or five AS subjects in the first year of Sixth Form, but they may narrow down to three A2 units in the second year.

AS units focus on material appropriate for the first year of an A level course, and are assessed accordingly. A2 is more demanding and is assessed at full A level standard. Overall assessment is based on examinations and/or coursework and may be made at the end of the course (linear) or at stages during the course (modular). There is a compulsory 20 per cent synoptic assessment for all unitized A levels to demonstrate understanding of the course as a whole and the connections between its different elements.

The AS and A levels are graded on a scale of A to E for passes. U (unclassified) indicates a fail. Restrictions on re-sitting individual units were dropped from January 2004, and students are therefore able to resit units more than once. When a request is made for certification, the best attempt will count towards an award.

There is also a programme of Key Skills qualifications. The first three, covering Communication, Application of Number and Information Technology, are separate qualifications in their own right and are usually taken alongside other qualifications and groups of qualifications. They are offered at Levels 1 to 4 and the assessment consists of a portfolio of evidence and an external test. Many A level subjects offer opportunities for students to provide evidence for their Key Skills portfolio. Key Skills qualifications also attract UCAS points; for example a Level 3 in all three skills qualifications is worth 60 tariff points, the same value as an A grade AS level.

The Advanced Extension Award was designed to challenge the most able students and was first examined in 2002. It is available in 19 A level subjects with Psychology and Business examined for the first time in 2005. The AEA in Business is accessible to students studying related subjects at both Vocational A level (VCE) and GCE A level.

Vocational education and training

There are 113 awarding bodies. Many of these are sector-based and provide specific qualifications for their particular industry. However, there are also a number of key awarding bodies that provide a wide range of vocational qualifications across sectors and subjects. These include:

- Edexcel (offers BTEC qualifications);
- City & Guilds (includes Pitman qualifications);

- Cambridge International Examinations (CIE qualifications are mainly available outside of the UK and not within the national framework);
- Oxford, Cambridge and RSA Examinations;
- AQA;
- Education Development International (formerly known as LCCIEB).

Many vocational qualifications come within the National Qualifications Framework, falling into one of two broad categories, namely Vocationally-Related Qualifications and National Vocational Qualifications (NVQs). The latter are competence-based occupational qualifications and are generally taken while the candidate is in employment. The body responsible for the overall framework is the Qualifications and Curriculum Authority. In Scotland the equivalent body for the Scottish Vocational Qualifications framework (SVQ) and (GSVQ) is the Scottish Qualifications Authority.

GCSEs in Applied Subjects and GNVQs

These qualifications are designed for students who seek a course that gives a general introduction to a broad vocational area. GCSEs in applied subjects are currently all double award GCSEs and are graded from A*A* to GG.

GNVQs are still available at two levels:

Foundation: broadly equivalent to 4 GCSEs at Grade D to G or an NVQ level 1;
Intermediate: broadly equivalent to 4 GCSEs at Grade A* to C or an NVQ level 2.

Foundation and Intermediate GNVQs are being replaced by other vocational qualifications and some have already been phased out.

GCEs in Applied Subjects

Vocational A levels (VCEs) were designed as level 3 general qualifications set in the context of a broad vocational area. Like other A levels, they are usually taken over two years and students are normally expected to have achieved at least four or five GCSEs at grades A* to C or an Intermediate GNVQ. Like all A levels, the vocational A levels provide a preparation for both higher education and employment. Vocational A levels assess the students' abilities to apply their skills and understanding in a vocational context. Assessment is one-third external and two-thirds internal. From September 2005 the VCEs were redesigned with an AS/A2 structure and the title VCE was changed to GCE. VCE subject titles such as Art and Design, Business, ICT and Science (which were offered as VCE and GCE) are now known as 'GCE in Applied Art and Design' and so on.
In Scotland, General Scottish Vocational Qualifications (GSVQs) have been brought under the new National Qualifications framework. Vocational A levels and GSVQs are recognized by universities as a basis for entry to Higher Education.

As well as qualifications within the vocational framework, the Awarding Bodies offer a range of other qualifications. Further guidance may be obtained from schools, colleges and careers advisers. Alternatively, contact a reputable independent consultancy such as Gabbitas.

Scottish National Qualifications

Most schools in Scotland prepare students for Standard Grade examinations taken at 16. All students who stay on in education after Standard Grade follow a qualifications system which begins at one of five levels, depending on their examination results.

Access, Intermediate 1 and Intermediate 2 are progressive levels which a student might take to gain a better grounding in a subject before going on to take one of two higher levels: Higher and Advanced Higher. The lower three levels are not compulsory for students with aptitude, who may move straight on to study one of the Higher level courses. With the exception of Standard Grade, each National Qualification is built on units, courses and group awards:

- National Units – these are the smallest elements of a qualification and are internally assessed; most require 40 hours of study.
- Courses – National Courses are usually taken in S5 or S6 and at college. They are made up of three units each, and are assessed internally and by examination for which grades A–C are awarded.
- Scottish Group Awards (SGAs) – these are programmes of courses and units that cover 16 broad subject areas. An SGA can be obtained within one year, or worked towards over a longer period.

There are 70 subjects available, including job-orientated subjects such as Travel and Tourism and traditional ones such as Maths and English. All National Qualifications have core skills embedded in them, although it is possible to take stand-alone units, for example Problem Solving, Communication, Numeracy and Information Technology.

General Scottish Vocational Qualifications (GSVQs) have now been brought under the National Qualifications framework.

For further information contact the Scottish Qualifications Authority.

The International Baccalaureate

(Information supplied by the International Baccalaureate Organisation)

The International Baccalaureate Organisation (IBO) is a non-profit, international educational foundation registered in Switzerland that was established in 1968. The Diploma Programme, for which the IBO is best known, was developed by a group of schools seeking to establish a common curriculum and a university-entry credential for geographically mobile students. They believed that an education that emphasized critical thinking and exposure to a variety of points of view would encourage intercultural understanding and acceptance of others by young people. They designed a comprehensive curriculum for the last two years of secondary school that could be administered in any country and that would be recognized by universities worldwide.

Today the IBO offers three programmes to schools. The Diploma Programme is for students aged 16 to 19 in the final two years of secondary school. The Middle Years Programme, adopted in 1994, is for students aged 11 to 16. The Primary Years Programme, adopted in 1997, is for students aged 3 to 12. In July 2005 the IBO had 1,579 authorized schools in 121 countries. This number is almost evenly divided between state schools and private (including international) schools.

The Diploma Programme

The Diploma Programme (DP), for students aged 16 to 19, is a two-year course of study. Recognized internationally as a qualification for university entrance, it also allows students to fulfil the requirements of their national education system. Students share an educational experience that emphasizes critical thinking as well as intercultural understanding and respect for others in the global community.

The DP offers a broad and balanced curriculum in which students are encouraged to apply what they learn in the classroom to real-world issues and problems. Wherever possible, subjects are taught from an international perspective. In economics, for example, students look at economic systems from around the world. Students study six courses (including both the sciences and the humanities) selected from the following six subject groups:

Group 1	language A1
Group 2	(second language) language *ab initio*, language B, language A2, classical languages
Group 3	individuals and societies
Group 4	experimental sciences
Group 5	mathematics and computer science
Group 6	the arts

Students must also submit an extended essay, follow a course in theory of knowledge (TOK) and take part in activities to complete the creativity, action and service (CAS) requirement.

The assessment of student work in the DP is largely external. At the end of the course, students take examinations that are marked by external examiners who work closely with the IBO. The types of questions asked in the examination papers include multiple-choice questions, essay questions, data-analysis questions and case studies. Students are also graded on the extended essay and on an essay and oral presentation for the TOK course.

A smaller part of the assessment of student work is carried out within schools by DP teachers. The work that is assessed includes oral commentaries in the languages, practical experimental work in the sciences, fieldwork and investigations in the humanities, and exhibitions and performances in the arts. Examiners check the assessment of samples of work from each school to ensure that IBO standards are consistently applied. For each examination session, approximately 80 per cent of DP students are awarded the

Diploma. The majority of students register for the Diploma, but students may also register for a limited number of Diploma subjects, for each of which they are awarded a certificate with the final grade.

The Middle Years Programme (MYP)

The Middle Years Programme (MYP), for students aged 11 to 16, recognizes that students in this age group are particularly sensitive to social and cultural influences and are struggling to define themselves and their relationships to others. The programme helps students develop the skills to cope with this period of uncertainty. It encourages them to think critically and independently, to work collaboratively and to take a disciplined approach to studying.

The aim of the MYP is to give students an international perspective to help them become informed about the experiences of people and cultures throughout the world. It also fosters a commitment to help others and to act as a responsible member of the community at the local, national and international levels.

Students in the MYP study all the major disciplines, including languages, humanities, sciences, mathematics, arts, technology and physical education. The framework is flexible enough to allow a school to include subjects that are not part of the MYP curriculum but that might be required by local authorities. While the courses provide students with a strong knowledge base, they emphasize the principles and concepts of the subject and approach topics from a variety of points of view, including the perspectives of other cultures.

MYP teachers use a variety of tools to assess student progress, including oral presentations, tests, essays and projects, and they apply the assessment criteria established by the IBO to students' work. Schools may opt for official IBO certification by asking the IBO to validate their internal assessment. This is often referred to as the 'moderation system'. In this process, the IBO reviews samples of the schools' assessment of student work and checks that schools are correctly applying the MYP assessment criteria. The IBO offers guidance for teachers in the form of published examples of assessment.

The Primary Years Programme

The Primary Years Programme (PYP), for students aged 3 to 12, focuses on the development of the whole child, addressing social, physical, emotional and cultural needs. At the same time, it gives students a strong foundation in all the major areas of knowledge: mathematics, social studies, drama, language, music, visual arts, science, personal and social education, and physical education. The PYP aims to help students develop an international perspective – to become aware of and sensitive to the points of view of people in other parts of the world.

The PYP curriculum is organized around six themes:

- who we are
- where we are in place and time

- how we express ourselves
- how the world works
- how we organize ourselves
- sharing the planet.

These themes are intended to help students make sense of themselves, of other people and of the physical environment, and to give them different ways of looking at the world.

Assessment is used for two purposes: to guide teaching and to give students an opportunity to show, in a variety of ways, what they know and what they can do. In the PYP, assessment takes many forms. It ranges from completing checklists to monitor progress to compiling a portfolio of a student's work. The IBO offers schools substantial guidance for conducting assessment, including a detailed handbook and professional development workshops. Student portfolios and records of PYP exhibitions are reviewed on a regular basis by the IBO as part of programme evaluation.

For further information about the IB programmes, please contact:

International Baccalaureate Programme
Route des Morillons 15
CH-1218 Grand-Saconnex
Geneva
Switzerland
Tel: +41 22 791 7740
Fax: + 41 22 791 0277
E-mail: ibaem@ibo.org
Website: www.ibo.org

Schools authorized to offer the International Baccalaureate Organisation's Diploma Programme in the United Kingdom

ENGLAND

Bedfordshire

Bedford High School
Bromham Road
Bedford MK40 2BS
Tel: 01234 360221
Fax: 01234 353552
E-mail: ph@bedfordhigh.co.uk
IB Co-ordinator: Mr Philip Herrick

Bedford School
De Parys Avenue
Bedford MK40 7TU
Tel: 01234 362200
Fax: 01234 362283
E-mail: ib@bedfordschool.org.uk
IB Co-ordinator: Mr Adrian Johnson

Luton Sixth Form College
Bradgers Hill Road
Luton LU2 7EW
Tel: 01582 877501
E-mail: cn@lutonsfc.ac.uk
IB Co-ordinator: Mr Colin Hall

Berkshire

Slough Grammar School
Lascelles Road
Slough
Berkshire SL3 7PR
Tel: 01753 537068
Fax: 01753 538618
E-mail: ibcoordinator@ sloughgrammar.berks.sch.uk
IB Co-ordinator: Ms Ruth Symons

Waingel's Copse School
Denmark Avenue
Woodley
Reading RG5 4RF
Tel: 0118 969 0336
Fax: 0118 944 2843
E-mail: wilrw@ waingels.wokingham.sch.uk
IB Co-ordinator: Mr Robert Wilkinson

Cambridgeshire

Deacon's School
Queen's Gardens
Peterborough PE1 2UW
Tel: 01733 562451
Fax: 01733 891601
E-mail: jdk@ deaconschool.peterborough.sch.uk
IB Co-ordinator: Mrs Julie Kirby

Impington College
New Road
Impington
Cambridge CB4 9LX
Tel: 01223 200402
Fax: 01223 718961
E-mail: sixthform@ impingtonvc.cambs-schools.net
IB Co-ordinator: Mrs Sandra Morton

Cornwall

The Bolitho School
Polwithen
Penzance TR18 4JR
Tel: 01736 363271
Fax: 01736 330960
E-mail: enquiries@bolitho.cornwall.sch.uk
IB Co-ordinator: Mr Patrick Ian Minm

Truro College
College Road
Truro
Cornwall TR1 3XX
Tel: 01872 267000
Fax: 01872 267100
E-mail: andyw@trurocollege.ac.uk
IB Co-ordinator: Mr Andy Wildin

Devon

Exeter College
Hele Road
Exeter
Devon EX4 4JS
Tel: 01392 205340
Fax: 01392 205324
E-mail: atruscott@exe-coll.ac.uk
IB Co-ordinator: Mr Andy Truscott

Dorset

Bournemouth & Poole College
North Road
Parkstone
Poole BH14 0QB
Tel: 01202 747600
Fax: 01202 465720
E-mail: ssoutherden@bpc.ac.uk
IB Co-ordinator: Ms Sara Southerden

Essex

Anglo-European School
Willow Green
Ingatestone
Essex CM4 0DJ
Tel: 01277 354018
Fax: 01277 355623
E-mail: strachanj@aesessex.co.uk
IB Co-ordinator: Mrs Jane Strachan

The Sixth Form College
North Hill
Colchester
Essex CO1 1SN
Tel: 01206 500700
Fax: 01206 500770
E-mail: bainess@colchsfc.ac.uk
IB Co-ordinator: Mr Stephen Christopher Baines

Gloucestershire

Cirencester College
Stroud Road
Cirencester
Gloucestershire GL7 1XA
Tel: 01285 640994
Fax: 01285 644171
E-mail: kba@cirencester.ac.uk
IB Co-ordinator: Ms Katy Albiston

Hampshire

Alton College
Old Odiham Road
Alton
Hampshire GU34 2LX
Tel: 01420 592200
Fax: 01420 592253
E-mail: martin.savery@altoncollege.ac.uk
IB Co-ordinator: Mr Martin Savery

Brockenhurst College
Lyndhurst Road
Brockenhurst
Hampshire SO42 7ZE
Tel: 01590 625555
Fax: 01590 625256
E-mail: ncousins@brock.ac.uk
IB Co-ordinator: Mr Nick Cousins

Taunton's College
Hill Lane
Southampton SO15 5RL
Tel: 02380 511811
Fax: 02380 511991
E-mail: grantw@tauntons.ac.uk
IB Co-ordinator: Mr Bill Grant

Hertfordshire

Goffs School
Goffs Lane
Cheshunt
Hertfordshire EN7 5QW
Tel: 01992 424200
Fax: 01992 424201
E-mail: gma@goffs.herts.sch.uk
IB Co-ordinator: Mr Gordon Mather

Haileybury
Hertford
Hertfordshire SG13 7NU
Tel: 01992 706205
Fax: 01992 706276
E-mail: jameshk@haileybury.com
IB Co-ordinator: Mr James Kazi

Hockerill Anglo-European School
Dunmow Road
Bishop's Stortford
Hertfordshire CM23 5HX
Tel: 01279 658451
Fax: 01279 755918
E-mail: admin.hockerill@thegrid.org.uk
IB Co-ordinator: Mrs Vicki Worsnop

Isle of Man

King William's College
Castletown
Isle of Man IM9 1TP
Tel: 01624 822551
Fax: 01624 824207
E-mail: rene.filho@kwc.sch.im
IB Co-ordinator: Dr Rene Filho

Kent

Bexley Grammar School
Danson Lane
Welling
Kent DA16 2BL
Tel: 020 8304 8538
Fax: 020 8304 0248
E-mail: CET@bexleygs.co.uk
IB Co-ordinator: Ms Claire Tipping

The Business Academy Bexley
Yarnton Way
Erith
Kent DA18 4DW
Tel: 020 8312 4800
Fax: 020 8320 4810
E-mail: robert.burton@tba.bexley.sch.uk
IB Co-ordinator: Mr Robert Burton

Dartford Grammar School
West Hill
Dartford
Kent DA1 2HW
Tel: 01322 223039
Fax: 01322 291426
E-mail: j.maidment@dartfordgrammar.kent.sch.uk
IB Co-ordinator: Ms Jayne Maidment

Dartford Grammar School for Girls
Shepherds Lane
Dartford
Kent DA1 2NT
Tel: 01322 223123
Fax: 01322 294786
E-mail: ANGELA@dartfordgrammargirls.kent.sch.uk
IB Co-ordinator: Mrs Angela Pearson

Maidstone Grammar School
Barton Road
Maidstone
Kent ME15 7BT
Tel: 01622 752101
Fax: 01622 753680
E-mail: keith.derrett@mgs-kent.org.uk
IB Co-ordinator: Dr Keith Derrett

Sevenoaks School
Sevenoaks
Kent TN13 1HU
Tel: 01732 455133
Fax: 01732 456143
E-mail: sma@sevenoaksschool.org
IB Co-ordinator: Sue Austin

Tonbridge Grammar School
Deakin Leas
Tonbridge
Kent TN9 2JR
Tel: 01732 365125
Fax: 01732 359417
E-mail: ROSEMARYCHEETHAM@tgsg.kent.sch.uk
IB Co-ordinator: Ms Rosemary Cheetham

Lancashire

Rossall School
Broadway
Fleetwood
Lancashire FY7 8JW
Tel: 01253 774201
Fax: 01253 772052
E-mail: ibatrossall@hotmail.com
IB Co-ordinator: Dr Doris Dohmen

London

The Godolphin and Latymer School
Iffley Road
Hammersmith
London W6 0PG
Tel: 020 8741 1936
Fax: 020 8746 3352
E-mail: ctrimming@godolphinandlatymer.com
IB Co-ordinator: Mrs Caroline Trimming

Highlands School
148 Worlds End Lane
London N21 1QQ
Tel: 020 8370 1100
Fax: 020 8370 1110
E-mail: tutonk@highlands.enfield.sch.uk
IB Co-ordinator: Mr Karl Tuton

International School of London
139 Gunnersbury Avenue
London W3 8LG
Tel: 020 8992 5823
Fax: 020 8993 7012
E-mail: huwbach@btopenworld.com
IB Co-ordinator: Mr Huw Davies

King's College School
Southside
Wimbledon Common
London SW19 4TT
Tel: 020 8255 5300
Fax: 020 8255 5309
E-mail: grs@kcs.org.uk
IB Co-ordinator: Mr Graeme Salt

St Dunstan's College
Stanstead Road
London SE6 4TY
Tel: 020 8516 7200
Fax: 020 8516 7300
E-mail: salgeo@sdmail.co.uk
IB Co-ordinator: Sue Algeo

Southbank International School
36–40 Kensington Park Road
London W11 3BU
Tel: 020 7229 8230
Fax: 020 7229 3784
E-mail: GMA@southbank.org
IB Co-ordinator: Ms Gwen Martinez

Woodside Park School
Friern Barnet Road
Friern Barnet
London N11 3DR
Tel: 020 8368 3777
Fax: 020 8368 3220
E-mail: acobbin@wpis.org
IB Co-ordinator: Ms Alison Cobbin

Merseyside

Broadgreen High School
Queen's Drive
Liverpool L13 5UQ
Tel: 0151 228 6800
Fax: 0151 220 9256
E-mail: apatterson@broadgreenhigh.org.uk
IB Co-ordinator: Mr Austin Patterson

Middlesex

The American Community School
108 Vine Lane
Hillingdon
Uxbridge
Middlesex UB10 0BE
Tel: 01895 259771
Fax: 01895 256974
E-mail: dwynne-jones@acs-england.co.uk
IB Co-ordinator: Mr David Wynne-Jones

North London Collegiate School
Canons
Edgware
Middlesex HA8 7RJ
Tel: 020 8952 0912
Fax: 020 8951 1391
E-mail: mburke@nlcs.org.uk
IB Co-ordinator: Mr Michael Burke

Richmond upon Thames College
Egerton Road
Twickenham
Middlesex TW2 7SJ
Tel: 020 8607 8269
Fax: 020 8891 5998
E-mail: kwildman@rutc.ac.uk
IB Co-ordinator: Mr Stephen Winfield

St Helen's School
Eastbury Road
Northwood
Middlesex HA6 3AS
Tel: 01923 843210
Fax: 01923 843211
E-mail: mbowman@sthelensnorthwood.co.uk
IB Co-ordinator: Mrs Mary Bowman

Northamptonshire

Prince William School
Herne Road
Oundle
Northamptonshire PE8 4BS
Tel: 01832 272881
Fax: 01832 274942
E-mail: reception@pwschool.northants.sch.uk
IB Co-ordinator: Ms Barbara Richards

Oxfordshire

Henley College
Deanfield Avenue
Henley-on-Thames
Oxfordshire RG9 1UH
Tel: 01491 579988
Fax: 01491 410099
E-mail: bhug@henleycol.ac.uk
IB Co-ordinator: Mrs Bridie Hughes

St Clare's
139 Banbury Road
Oxford OX2 7AL
Tel: 01865 517332
Fax: 01865 310002
E-mail: nick.lee@stclares.ac.uk
IB Co-ordinator: Mr Nick Lee

Rutland

Oakham School
Chapel Close
Oakham
Rutland LE15 6DT
Tel: 01572 758698
Fax: 01572 758623
E-mail: jr@oakham.rutland.sch.uk
IB Co-ordinator: Dr Jill Rutherford

Surrey

The American Community School
Portsmouth Road
Cobham
Surrey KT11 1BL
Tel: 01932 867251
Fax: 01932 869791
E-mail: cworthington@acs-england.co.uk
IB Co-ordinator: Mr Craig Worthington

The American Community School
London Road
Egham
Surrey TW20 0HS
Tel: 01784 430800
Fax: 01784 430153
E-mail: tstobie@acs-england.co.uk
IB Co-ordinator: Mr Tristian Stobie

King Edward's School
Witley
Godalming
Surrey GU8 5SG
Tel: 01428 686700
Fax: 01428 682850
E-mail: mehargc@kesw.surrey.sch.uk
IB Co-ordinator: Ms Christine Meharg

Kings College for the Arts and Technology
Southway
Guildford
Surrey GU2 8DU
Tel: 01483 458956
Fax: 01483 458957
E-mail: n.clay@kingscollegeguildford.com
IB Co-ordinator: Mr Nick Clay

Kings International College
Watchetts Drive
Camberley
Surrey GU15 2PQ
Tel: 01276 683539
Fax: 01276 709503
E-mail: a.reynolds@kings-international.co.uk
IB Co-ordinator: Ms Anne Reynolds

Marymount International School
George Road
Kingston upon Thames
Surrey KT2 7PE
Tel: 020 8949 0571
Fax: 020 8336 2485
E-mail: acdean@marymount.kingston.sch.uk
IB Co-ordinator: Dr Brian Johnson

TASIS The American School in England
Coldharbour Lane
Thorpe
Egham
Surrey TW20 8TE
Tel: 01932 565252
Fax: 01932 564644
E-mail: cgoldon@tasis.com
IB Co-ordinator: Mrs Chantal Goldon

Whitgift School
Haling Park
South Croydon
Surrey CR2 6YT
Tel: 020 8688 9222
Fax: 020 8760 0682
E-mail: stewartcook@totalise.co.uk
IB Co-ordinator: Mr Stewart Cook

Sussex

Ardingly College
College Road
Ardingly
Haywards Heath
West Sussex RH17 6SQ
Tel: 01444 893000
Fax: 01444 893001
E-mail: widgetcat@hotmail.com
IB Co-ordinator: Mr John Langford

Hastings College
Archery Road
St Leonard's on Sea
East Sussex TN38 0HX
Tel: 01424 442222
Fax: 01424 720376
E-mail: padams@hastings.ac.uk
IB Co-ordinator: Mr Patrick Adams

Park College
Kings Drive
Eastbourne
East Sussex BN21 2UN
Tel: 01323 637111
Fax: 01323 508778
E-mail: WE_Gilbert@park-college.ac.uk
IB Co-ordinator: Mr William Gilbert

Worth School
Paddockhurst Road
Turners Hill
West Sussex RH10 4SD
Tel: 01342 710222
Fax: 01342 710230
E-mail: nconnolly@worth.org.uk
IB Co-ordinator: Mr Nicholas Connolly

Tyne and Wear

Tyne Metropolitan College
Embleton Avenue
Wallsend
Tyne and Wear NE28 9NJ
Tel: 0191 229 5000
Fax: 0191 229 5301
E-mail: anne.briffa@tynemet.ac.uk
IB Co-ordinator: Ms Anne Briffa

Warwickshire

Finham Park School
Green Lane
Coventry CV3 6EA
Tel: 02476 418135
Fax: 02476 840890
E-mail: v.chandley@finhampark.co.uk
IB Co-ordinator: Mrs Victoria Chandley

Warwickshire College
Warwick New Road
Leamington Spa
Warwickshire CV32 5JE
Tel: 01926 318231
Fax: 01926 318048
E-mail: aholland@warkscol.ac.uk
IB Co-ordinator: Mr Andy Holland

West Midlands

The City Technology College
Kingshurst
PO Box 1017
Cooks Lane
Birmingham B37 6NZ
Tel: 0121 329 8300
Fax: 0121 770 0879
E-mail: julie.dent@kingshurst.ac.uk
IB Co-ordinator: Mrs Julie Dent

George Dixon International School
City Road
Edgbaston
Birmingham B17 8LF
Tel: 0121 434 4488
Fax: 0121 434 3721
E-mail: colinmac@gn.ac.org
IB Co-ordinator: Mr Colin McKenzie

Worcestershire

Malvern College
College Road
Malvern
Worcestershire WR14 3DF
Tel: 01684 581500
Fax: 01684 581617
E-mail: jpk@malcol.org
IB Co-ordinator: Mr John Knee

Yorkshire

Harrogate Grammar School
Arthurs Avenue
Harrogate HG2 0DZ
Tel: 01423 531127
Fax: 01423 521325
E-mail: mbailey@hgs-n-yorks.sch.uk
IB Co-ordinator: Mr Michael Bailey

Rhodesway School
Oaks Lane
Allerton
Bradford
West Yorkshire BD15 7RU
Tel: 01274 770230
Fax: 01274 770231
E-mail: school@rhodesway-bradford.sch.uk
IB Co-ordinator: Mrs Marian Pearson

SCOTLAND

Aberdeenshire

The International School of Aberdeen
'Fairgirth'
296 North Deeside Road
Milltimber
Aberdeen AB13 0AB
Tel: 01224 732267
Fax: 01224 734879
E-mail: marybeth.kiley@isa.aberdeen.sch.uk
IB Co-ordinator: Mrs Beth Kiley

WALES

Cardiff

Whitchurch High School
Penlline Road
Whitchurch
Cardiff CF4 2XJ
Tel: 029 2062 9700
Fax: 029 2062 9701
E-mail: nh@whitchurch.cardiff.sch.uk
IB Co-ordinator: Ms Nicola Hansford

Conwy

Llandrillo College
Llandudno Road
Rhos-on-Sea
Colwyn Bay
Conwy LL28 4HZ
Tel: 01492 546666
Fax: 01492 543891
E-mail: m.monteith@llandrillo.ac.uk
IB Co-ordinator: Ms Melanie Monteith

Rydal Penrhos
Pwllycrochan Avenue
Colwyn Bay
Conwy LL29 7BT
Tel: 01492 530155
Fax: 01492 531872
E-mail: wynniewil@hotmail.com
IB Co-ordinator: Mr Wyn Williams

South Glamorgan

United World College of the Atlantic
St Donat's Castle
Llantwit Major
Vale of Glamorgan CF6 1WF
Tel: 01446 799002
Fax: 01446 799013
E-mail: gareth.rees@uwc.net
IB Co-ordinator: Mr Gareth Rees

Examining and awarding bodies: useful addresses

Assessment and Qualifications Alliance (AQA)
Devas Street
Manchester M15 6EX
Tel: 0161 953 1180
Fax: 0161 273 7572
E-mail: mailbox@aqa.org.uk
Website: www.aqa.org.uk

Stag Hill House
Guildford
Surrey GU2 7XJ
Tel: 01483 506506
Fax: 01483 300152
E-mail: postmaster@aqa.org.uk
Website: www.aqa.org.uk

Unit 10
City Business Park
Easton Road
Bristol BS5 0SP
Tel: 0117 927 3434
Fax: 0117 929 0268

31–33 Springfield Avenue
Harrogate
North Yorkshire HG1 2HW
Tel: 01423 840015
Fax: 01423 523678

City & Guilds
1 Giltspur Street
London EC1A 9DD
Tel: 020 7294 2800
Fax: 020 7294 2400
E-mail: enquiry@city-and-guilds.co.uk
Website: www.city-and-guilds.co.uk

Edexcel Foundation
One90 High Holborn
London WC1V 7BH
Tel: 0870 240 9800
Fax: 020 7190 5700
E-mail: enquiries@edexcel.org.uk
Website: www.edexcel.org.uk

OCR (Oxford, Cambridge and RSA Examinations)
9 Hills Road
Cambridge CB2 1PB
Tel: 01223 553311
Fax: 01223 460278
E-mail: helpdesk@ocr.org.uk
Website: www.ocr.org.uk

Qualifications and Curriculum Authority
Customer Relations
83 Piccadilly
London W1J 8QA
Tel: 020 7509 5555
Fax: 020 7509 6666
E-mail: info@qca.org.uk
Website: www.qca.org.uk

Scottish Qualifications Authority
Hanover House
24 Douglas Street
Glasgow G2 7NQ
Tel: 0845 279 1000
Fax: 0141 242 2244
E-mail: customer@sqa.org.uk
Website: www.sqa.org.uk

Welsh Joint Education Committee
245 Western Avenue
Cardiff CF5 2YX
Tel: 029 2026 5000
Fax: 029 2057 5994
E-mail: info@wjec.co.uk
Website: www.wjec.co.uk

1.8
The Sixth Form and Beyond – a Parent's Guide

If you have a son or daughter studying for GCSEs or the equivalent, he or she, like most 15 and 16 year olds, is probably still some way from decisions about higher education and careers. At this stage there is, of course, plenty of room for the development of ideas and interests, and it is important to have an open mind about all the options. Some preliminary planning, however, is essential.

Choosing the right Sixth Form course is becoming increasingly important as the options at 18 become more complex. Students who have given some thought to their future plans, to their own strengths and personal qualities, will find it easier to identify broad potential career areas. This in turn will enable them to choose suitable Sixth Form and higher education options which still allow flexibility for the development of their skills and personality over the next few years. At the same time, extra-curricular activities, relevant work experience and other research will help to build up the essential personal and practical skills sought by today's employers.

Good advice is essential. Some schools have excellent careers guidance programmes and materials and may also arrange talks from visiting speakers and work experience opportunities. Others may have more limited resources. Computerized careers assessments are often used in schools. These are not designed to provide all the answers, and it is vital that they should form part of a much more extensive discussion that includes consideration of academic achievements and aspirations, attitudes, interests and any special needs.

Your son or daughter may also find it helpful to speak to an independent consultant, who can offer an objective view and perhaps a wider perspective of the possibilities.

Choosing Sixth Form options

The main options available after GCSE are: Advanced Subsidiary GCE (AS) and Advanced GCE (A2); in Scotland, National Qualifications (Highers); the International Baccalaureate (IB); and Vocational A levels (formerly Advanced GNVQs). The basic structure of these courses is covered in Part 1.7.

All can be used as a means of entry to British universities. The IB, as its name implies, is an international qualification and is also recognized for admission purposes by universities worldwide. Unlike the other options above, however, the IB Diploma course is not widely available in the UK. A list of UK schools and colleges authorized to run the IB Diploma course is given on pages 49–58.

Before making a choice, students may find it helpful to consider the following.

Subjects or areas of study

Is depth or breadth the most important factor? A levels offer a high degree of specialization. The IB is a demanding academic qualification but covers a wider range of subjects in less depth. A vocational course will probably have a focus on a particular career area such as Business, Leisure & Tourism or Information Technology.

Course load

Most students take four AS choices in the lower sixth and continue three of these subjects as A2s in the upper sixth, thus emerging from school with three full A levels and one AS in a fourth subject. Because of the diversity of the current Sixth Form programme, entry requirements vary significantly between one course and another. In some cases universities may ask for specific grades in specific subjects; in others they may seek an overall number of UCAS points. The equivalent of three A level passes remains the core requirement, with an interest in any additional qualification obtained. In this relatively uncertain climate, sixth formers should appreciate that quality is more important than quantity – in other words additional courses should not be taken if this would jeopardize the grades obtained in core subjects. Secondly, if they are in any doubt about the combination of A/AS levels and grades which will be acceptable to a university, they should not hesitate to contact admissions staff or seek other forms of professional advice.

Availability

Is the required course available at your child's present school or, if not, at another school or college locally? Is living away from home an option? Vocational A level courses are widely available in maintained colleges. Some vocational courses are also offered by a much smaller number of independent schools.

Assessment method and course structure

Some students prefer regular assessment through submission of coursework or projects rather than exam-based assessment. Many A level courses, traditionally assessed through a final exam, now include coursework as part of the assessment. The IB is assessed chiefly by examinations. Vocational A levels are assessed largely on coursework.

Academic ability

A level courses often demand a good deal of reading and the ability to write well-argued essays, but some students may prefer a more practical approach.

Future plans

Students aiming for a specific career should check whether their preferred options are suitable. Those still undecided should choose a programme which allows some flexibility.

Which A levels?

It is natural for students to want to continue with subjects they enjoy. Clearly, a high GCSE result suggests that a similar result may be expected at A level. This is important, of course, but students must also consider whether or not their preferred combination of subjects is suitable for higher education or career plans. It is also possible to take A level courses in subjects not previously studied.

Career choice

Some careers, typically medicine and architecture, demand a specific degree. This may limit, or sometimes dictate, the choice of A level subjects and students must be confident that they can do well in these. If career plans are undecided, it is wise to choose subjects which will leave a number of options open.

Ability

It is advisable to have achieved at least a grade B at GCSE in any subjects being considered for A level (ideally grade A in Maths, Science and Modern Languages). Some A level subjects such as Economics can be taken without any previous knowledge, but students should consider what skills are required, eg numerical, analytical or essay-writing, and whether or not it will suit them.

Different examining bodies may assess the same subject in different ways. If your son or daughter has concerns about a final exam-based assessment, he or she might consider a syllabus which offers a modular structure and a higher degree of assessment through coursework. Remember, however, that if all the subjects chosen are assessed on this basis, the workload and the pressure to meet deadlines during the course could be very heavy.

Interest

Genuine interest is essential if a student is to feel motivated throughout the two-year course and achieve high grades. Students in a dilemma over the choice between a subject they enjoy and a subject which they feel they ought to do might be well advised to opt for the former, but should check that this is suitable for their future plans. Students who are thinking of taking up a new subject, for example Psychology, may find it helpful to read a few books on the subject to test their interest before making any decisions.

Which subject combinations?

If no specific combination is demanded, how can students ensure a suitable choice? At least two subjects should be complementary, ie two arts/social sciences or two sciences. It is quite common for students to combine arts and sciences. It should be remembered that even those career areas which do not demand specific degree courses may still require certain skills, which some A level subjects will develop better than others.

If a particular degree course does not require an A level in the subject, eg Psychology, it may be better to choose a different A level subject or perhaps a complementary vocational option and so demonstrate a wider knowledge/skills base to university admissions tutors. This also avoids the risk of repeating the A level syllabus in the first year at university.

Other matters to consider include the timetabling restraints at school, which may make a certain combination impossible, in which case students may have to compromise or change to a school or college with greater flexibility, and the school's record of success in A level grades in the subjects chosen.

Where shall I study?

Staying on into the Sixth Form of the present school does have advantages, including continuity and familiarity with surroundings, staff and fellow students. It is not unusual, however, for students to change schools at 16. Some may be looking for a course, subjects or combination of subjects not available at their present school; others may simply want a change of atmosphere or a different style of education.

If a change to a different school is sought, consider the school's academic pace and examination results, its university entry record, the criteria for entry to the Sixth Form and the availability of places, the size of the Sixth Form and of the teaching groups and, where appropriate, the opportunities to develop skills or pursue interests aside from A level studies.

Independent Sixth Form or tutorial colleges offer an alternative environment and are described on page 16. There are also specialist independent colleges which focus on specific vocational areas such as business, accountancy or computing.

Maintained Sixth Form colleges offer a wide range of A levels and, increasingly, vocational options such as Vocational A levels. They may have between 500 and 1,000 students and because of their size can normally offer quite extensive facilities. However, teaching groups may be much larger than those in the independent sector.

Maintained further education colleges are located in all parts of the country and offer a vast range of A levels and vocational courses to students of all ages, many on a part-time basis. Colleges can be huge in size and may occupy several sites. Some also offer degree and diploma courses and may therefore be able to offer extensive facilities and resources, particularly for vocational studies. The age range of such colleges is much wider than in the independent sector, so it is also important to check that there is a suitable system of pastoral care for 16–18-year-olds.

There are also Apprenticeship schemes, which incorporate employment with part-time study. The best source of information on these is usually the local careers office. Such programmes have a national NVQ rating equivalent to GCSE or Sixth Form studies, depending on the level and the content.

The university challenge

Access to degree courses in the UK is now wider than ever before. Despite continuing pressures on graduate employment opportunities and the introduction of tuition fees, students entering higher education have reached record numbers.

Higher education offers a unique range of academic, career and social opportunities. However, poor preparation for university can prove disastrous. There are growing concerns about the rising number of students – currently nearly one in five – who do not complete their degree courses. The sense of having made the wrong choice is an often-cited factor.

Why does your son or daughter want to go to university? Is he or she genuinely motivated and keen to study a particular subject in depth, to qualify for a specific career, and to take advantage of all the benefits which university life offers? All these reasons are valid, but some students may apply to university largely because they feel under pressure at home and/or at school to do so. Timing is also important. Students still unsure what to study should not rush into a decision. It may be better to take a year out and to use the additional time constructively before making a choice.

Most schools encourage students to begin thinking seriously about higher education soon after entering the Sixth Form. During the spring and summer terms of the Lower Sixth, students should be doing their research. Information is available from reference guides, from the internet and from university prospectuses. Most universities organize open days, when students can visit and talk to staff and students. This means that students should be well prepared for the autumn when application forms should be sent to UCAS (the Universities and Colleges Admissions Service): by 15 October for applications that include Oxford, Cambridge or Medicine and by 15 January for all other applications (with the exception of some for Art and Design).

Support and guidance from school, from external advisers and from parents is essential throughout this period, but the final choice of course and university lies with the student, and he or she should be taking an active part in the process. So what are the key points to consider?

Which course?

Is a specific degree necessary for a specific career? In some cases, typically Medicine, yes. In many cases, however, including Law, students have more flexibility. If there are no specific requirements, prospective employers will often take account of the quality of degree obtained and the reputation of the university as much as the subject studied, and will look for other skills and qualities which match their requirements. This means that students should take a subject in which they expect to do well rather than something which they may, perhaps wrongly, believe to be 'the right thing'. It is also important to demonstrate a breadth of knowledge and skills, for example interpersonal skills, language skills, commercial awareness or an understanding of science or information technology, in addition to the subject studied. There are differing views over the importance of taking some career-related degree subjects, for example, Business Studies or Media/Communication Studies. Some employers may prefer to employ graduates with a wider education background and train them in-house. Others may prefer applicants to be able to demonstrate practical knowledge and interest. Taking the above examples, this might include work experience with a company or involvement with the university newspaper or radio station.

Sandwich courses, offered mainly in science, engineering and social sciences, include work experience as part of the course. This can help employment prospects, enhance practical skills and allow students to test their interest in a particular career before committing themselves. In some cases placements may turn into permanent positions with the same employer after graduation. Some students, however, may not want to delay graduation (a sandwich course may take an extra year), and may dislike the disruption between work and study. Many universities also offer students (and not only those taking modern language degrees) the opportunity to study abroad as part of their course.

Foundation degrees

Foundation degrees are vocational in content and focus, and offer a qualification just below the level of an Honours degree. Foundation degrees take two years' full-time study, but they can also be studied part time. They combine work experience with the traditional academic structure of a degree course and are intended to equip students with the skills required by today's employers and to enable them to go straight into their chosen career upon successful completion of the course. Each foundation degree is linked with at least one Honours degree in the same subject area, which means that those who wish to further their qualification can go on to a BA (Hons) qualification if they choose to do so. Entry to Foundation degrees is flexible in order to attract not just school leavers but also those who are already in employment and who have the right level of ability.

Specialization

Students have a choice of studying one subject (single honours) or a combination (joint honours or a modular degree). A combined course offers more breadth and the opportunity to follow complementary studies, but almost always means a heavier workload.

For students unsure about taking a subject not studied at school or going directly into a specialized field, for example Civil Engineering, a more general foundation year may be helpful in providing essential core skills before deciding on a specialization.

Checking course content

Courses with the same name may be very different in content, so it is essential to read the prospectus for details. Modern language degrees, for example, vary widely in focus. Some place particular emphasis on practical language skills and an understanding of current affairs; others may have a more traditional emphasis on literature. Course titles like Communication Studies can also mean a wide variety of things.

Entry requirements

What subjects and grades does the course specify? Is the student likely to achieve these grades or should he or she look for a course with less stringent entry requirements? Remember that published grades are given only as a guide and may be adjusted upwards or downwards when offers are made to individual students. With the variety of Sixth Form programmes being taken, Gabbitas strongly recommends students contact universities direct to find out what they may be expected to achieve. For arts A level students who wish to take a degree in a science-based subject such as Medicine or Engineering, one year conversion courses are available, but students will be expected to have good GCSE grades in Maths and Science. Many modern language courses do not require previous knowledge, although evidence of competency in another foreign language is usually essential.

Remember too that as the A level pass rate rises, admissions tutors increasingly use GCSE results as well as A level grades as an indicator of ability and level of interest in a subject.

Which university?

Quality and reputation are as important for the individual course and department as for the institution as a whole. Beware of published league tables, which will not necessarily answer your questions. Find out about the career or employment destinations of recent graduates. This information may be available direct from the university or in one of the many published handbooks. If you have in mind a particular career or employer, it may be useful to contact the recruitment department to find out their views on specific universities or degree courses. You may also want to ask the university about the teaching styles, methods of assessment and the level of supervision available.

There is, of course, much more to finding the right university than simply the course. Aspects such as accommodation (both on and off campus), location or social atmosphere can generate just as much anxiety and dissatisfaction if things go wrong and may just as likely lead to abandonment of the course.

Some students may be attracted to a collegiate style university such as Oxford, Cambridge or London. Others may prefer a self-contained campus where all academic, social and other facilities are available on-site. Some may prefer a big city environment; others a smaller, more rural location. Living costs are a further important but often neglected issue. What is the quality and frequency of local transport? Is a car necessary? How safe is the area after dark? How important is the distance from home? What other facilities are offered to cater for individual hobbies and interests?

Alternatives to university entry

Students who are not attracted by the idea of full-time study at university will find that there are a number of alternatives available. It is possible to study for a degree part time by distance learning through private institutions, or if practical skills are sought there are many short courses available in areas such as business, computer and keyboard skills, marketing and PR, and languages.

There are companies and other organizations which take on young people with A levels or the equivalent and which offer them part-time academic training leading to relevant professional qualifications, some of which are regarded as the equivalent of a first degree. Examples include the Armed Forces and Emergency Services, the Merchant Navy, retail, hotel and catering, IT, accountancy, estate agents, and certain branches of the Law.

Finding out more

There are, of course, many other options and issues which your son or daughter may want to discuss. These might include the pros and cons of taking a year out after school and how to make the best use of it, sponsorship to help finance a degree course, presenting a well-structured and effective UCAS application, interview techniques, CV writing and job applications.

Advice should be available from your child's school. Expert, independent guidance is available from Gabbitas, who can also advise students who are unhappy at university as well as recent graduates and those looking for a career move in later life. If you would like to know more about the Gabbitas Advisory and Careers Assessment Services, please telephone Richard Leathes on 020 7734 0161 or e-mail richard.leathes@gabbitas.co.uk.

Part 2

Geographical Directory

2.1 Notes on Information given in the Directory Section

Type of school

The directory comprises schools listed within the Department for Education and Skills Register of Independent Schools. Maintained schools, Foundation schools, special schools, independent further education colleges and overseas schools are not included, unless they have a profile in Part Three.

Each school is given a brief description, which explains whether the school is single-sex or co-educational. In some cases single-sex schools take small numbers of the opposite sex within a specified age range. These are indicated where appropriate, eg: Boys boarding and day 3–18 (Day girls 16–18).

Schools are described as 'boarding' (which indicates boarding pupils only), 'boarding and day', 'day and boarding' (indicating a predominance of day pupils) or 'day' only.

Number of boarders

Where appropriate these are divided into full boarders (F) and weekly boarders (W). Weekly boarding arrangements vary according to individual school policy.

Fees

All fees are given annually from September 2005 unless otherwise stated. It should be remembered, however, that some schools increase fees during the year and the figures shown may therefore be subject to change after September 2005. Where the date given is other than September 2005, the information provided is the latest available from the school. Figures are shown for full boarding (FB), weekly boarding (WB) and day fees. In some instances the fees for full and weekly boarding are the same (F/WB £). A minimum and a maximum fee are given for each range. These figures are intended as a guide only. For more precise information schools should be contacted direct.

Key

* denotes that the school has a profile in Part Three;

† denotes that the school is registered with the Council for the Registration of Schools Teaching Dyslexic Pupils.

2.2 England

BEDFORDSHIRE

BEDFORD

ACORN SCHOOL
15 St Andrews Road, Bedford, Bedfordshire MK40 2LL
Tel: (01234) 343449
Fax: (01234) 343449
Email: acornschool@btinternet.com
Head: Mrs M Mason
Type: Co-educational Day 2–8
No of pupils: 130
Fees: (September 04)
Day £3900–£4680

BEDFORD HIGH SCHOOL
Bromham Road, Bedford, Bedfordshire MK40 2BS
Tel: (01234) 360221
Fax: (01234) 353552
Email: admissions@bedfordhigh.co.uk
Head: Mrs G Piotrowska
Type: Girls Day and Boarding 7–18 Flexi-boarding available
No of pupils: 900
No of boarders: F130
Fees: (September 03)
FB £13116–£15600
Day £6048–£8532

BEDFORD MODERN SCHOOL
Manton Lane, Bedford, Bedfordshire MK41 7NT
Tel: (01234) 332500
Fax: (01234) 332550
Email: info@bedmod.co.uk
Head: Mr S Smith
Type: Co-educational Day 7–18
No of pupils: B1018 G143
Fees: (September 05)
Day £6225–£8727

BEDFORD PREPARATORY SCHOOL
De Parys Avenue, Bedford, Bedfordshire MK40 2TU
Tel: (01234) 362274
Fax: (01234) 362285
Email: prepinfo@bedfordschool.org.uk
Head: Mr C Godwin
Type: Boys Boarding and Day 7–13 Flexi-boarding available
No of pupils: 458
No of boarders: F18 W7
Fees: (September 05)
FB £13491–£16020
WB £12861–£15390
Day £8151–£10680

BEDFORD SCHOOL
De Parys Avenue, Bedford, Bedfordshire MK40 2TU
Tel: (01234) 362200
Fax: (01234) 362283
Email: registrar@bedfordschool.org.uk
Head: Dr I P Evans
Type: Boys Boarding and Day 7–18 Flexi-boarding available
No of pupils: 1112
No of boarders: F180 W84
Fees: (September 05)
FB £13491–£19812
WB £12861–£19161
Day £8151–£12600

BEDFORD SCHOOL STUDY CENTRE
67 De Parys Avenue, Bedford, Bedfordshire MK40 2TR
Tel: (01234) 362300
Fax: (01234) 362305
Email: bssc@bedfordschool.org.uk
Head: Mrs O Heffill
Type: Co-educational Boarding 10–17
No of pupils: B20 G10
No of boarders: F30
Fees: (September 05) FB £24750

DAME ALICE HARPUR SCHOOL
Cardington Road, Bedford, Bedfordshire MK42 0BX
Tel: (01234) 340871
Fax: (01234) 344125
Email: admissions@dahs.co.uk
Head: Mrs J Berry
Type: Girls Day 7–18
No of pupils: 910
Fees: (September 05) Day £6225–£8694

PILGRIMS PRE-PREPARATORY SCHOOL
Brickhill Drive, Bedford, Bedfordshire MK41 7QZ
Tel: (01234) 369555
Fax: (01234) 359556
Email: pilgrims@harpur-trust.org.uk
Head: Mrs M Shaw
Type: Co-educational Day 0–8
No of pupils: B144 G134
Fees: (September 04) Day £3666–£6351

POLAM SCHOOL*
45 Lansdowne Road, Bedford, Bedfordshire MK40 2BY
Tel: (01234) 261864
Fax: (01234) 261194
Email: polam@supanet.com
Head: Mr A R Brown
Type: Co-educational Day 2–9
No of pupils: B110 G110
Fees: (September 05) Day £2691–£5190

RUSHMOOR SCHOOL
58–60 Shakespeare Road, Bedford, Bedfordshire MK40 2DL
Tel: (01234) 352031
Fax: (01234) 348395
Email: office@rushmoorschool.co.uk
Head: Mr K M Knight
Type: Co-educational Day Boys 11–16 Girls 3–10
No of pupils: B310 G10
Fees: (September 05) Day £3630–£7530

ST ANDREW'S SCHOOL
78 Kimbolton Road, Bedford, Bedfordshire MK40 2PA
Tel: (01234) 267272
Fax: (01234) 355105
Email: standrews@standrewsschoolbedford.com
Head: Mrs J Marsland
Type: Girls Day 3–16 (Boys 3–7)
No of pupils: B38 G295
Fees: (September 05) Day £4905–£8025

DUNSTABLE

ST GEORGE'S
28 Priory Road, Dunstable, Bedfordshire LU5 4HR
Tel: (01582) 661471
Fax: (01582) 663605
Head: Mrs Plater
Type: Co-educational Day 2–11
No of pupils: B65 G65
Fees: (September 02) Day £1560–£4260

FLITWICK

WAVERLY PREPARATORY SCHOOL
20 Steppingly Road, Flitwick, Bedfordshire MK45 1AJ
Tel: (01525) 718866
Head: Ms Karen Clegg

LUTON

BROADMEAD SCHOOL
Tennyson Road, Luton, Bedfordshire LU1 3RR
Tel: (01582) 722570
Fax: (01582) 486675
Email: Broadmead1@aol.com
Head: Mr A F Compton
Type: Co-educational Day 3–11
No of pupils: B65 G65
Fees: (September 05) Day £4374

MOORLANDS SCHOOL
Leagrave Hall, Luton, Bedfordshire LU4 9LE
Tel: (01582) 573376
Fax: (01582) 509008
Email: moorlands@moorlandsschool.demon.co.uk
Head: Mrs D K Attias
Type: Co-educational Day 2–11
No of pupils: B171 G180
Fees: (September 03) Day £4299–£4653

SHEFFORD

EAST LODGE SCHOOL
Ampthill Road, Campton, Shefford, Bedfordshire SG17 5BH
Tel: (01462) 812644
Fax: (01462) 815909
Email: east-lodge-school@supanet.com
Head: Mrs V A Green
Type: Co-educational Day 3–8
No of pupils: B25 G25
Fees: (September 05) Day £1671–£3910

BERKSHIRE

ALDERMASTON

CEDARS SCHOOL
Church Road, Aldermaston, Berkshire RG7 4LR
Tel: (0118) 971 4251
Head: Mrs J O'Halloran
Type: Co-educational Day 4–11
No of pupils: B25 G25
Fees: (September 05) Day £4875

ASCOT

HEATHFIELD SCHOOL*
London Road, Ascot, Berkshire SL5 8BQ
Tel: (01344) 898342
Fax: (01344) 890689
Email: registrar@heathfieldschool.net
Head: Mrs F King
Type: Girls Boarding 11–18
No of boarders: F220
Fees: (September 05) FB £22890

HURST LODGE SCHOOL
Bagshot Road, Ascot, Berkshire SL5 9JU
Tel: (01344) 622154
Fax: (01344) 627049
Email: admissions@hurstlodgesch.co.uk
Head: Miss V S Smit
Type: Girls Day and Boarding 3–18 (Boys 3–7) Flexi-boarding available
No of pupils: B25 G225
No of boarders: W25
Fees: (September 05) WB £17250 Day £5682–£10500

LICENSED VICTUALLERS' SCHOOL
London Road, Ascot, Berkshire SL5 8DR
Tel: (01344) 882770
Fax: (01344) 890648
Email: registrar@lvs.ascot.sch.uk
Head: Mr I A Mullins
Type: Co-educational Boarding and Day 4–18
No of pupils: B534 G359
No of boarders: F69 W120
Fees: (September 05) F/WB £ £15630–£17235 Day £6105–£9810

THE MARIST SENIOR SCHOOL
Kings Road, Sunninghill, Ascot, Berkshire SL5 7PS
Tel: (01344) 624291
Fax: (01344) 874963
Email: pa2head@marist.ascot.org.uk
Head: Mr K McCloskey
Type: Girls Day 11–18
No of pupils: 315
Fees: (September 05) Day £8475

THE MARIST PREPARATORY SCHOOL
Kings Road, Sunninghill, Ascot, Berkshire SL5 7PS
Tel: (01344) 626137
Fax: (01344) 621566
Email: head@marist-prep.windsor-maidenhead.sch.uk
Head: Mrs J A Peachey
Type: Girls Day 3–11
No of pupils: 247
Fees: (September 05) Day £6300–£6405

PAPPLEWICK SCHOOL*
Windsor Road, Ascot, Berkshire SL5 7LH
Tel: (01344) 621488
Fax: (01344) 874639
Email: hm@papplewick.org.uk
Head: Mr T W Bunbury
Type: Boys Boarding and Day 7–13
No of pupils: 203
No of boarders: F130
Fees: (September 05) FB £17775 Day £13650

ST GEORGE'S SCHOOL*
Ascot, Berkshire SL5 7DZ
Tel: (01344) 629900
Fax: (01344) 629901
Email: office@stgeorges-ascot.org.uk
Head: Mrs C Jordan
Type: Girls Boarding and Day 11–18 Flexi-boarding available
No of pupils: 293
No of boarders: F143
Fees: (September 05) FB £21600 Day £13950

ST MARY'S SCHOOL, ASCOT*
St Mary's Road, Ascot, Berkshire SL5 9JF
Tel: (01344) 623721
Fax: (01344) 873281
Email: admissions@st-marys-ascot.co.uk
Head: Mrs M Breen
Type: Girls Boarding and Day 11–18
No of pupils: 356
No of boarders: F340
Fees: (September 05) FB £22047 Day £15384

BRACKNELL

LAMBROOK HAILEYBURY
Winkfield Row, Bracknell, Berkshire RG42 6LU
Tel: (01344) 882717
Fax: (01344) 891114
Email: info@lambrook.berks.sch.uk
Head: Mr J E A Barnes
Type: Co-educational Boarding and Day 4–13 Flexi-boarding available
No of pupils: B300 G130
No of boarders: F3 W30
Fees: (September 04) F/WB £ £14280–£15975 Day £6990–£10950

MEADOWBROOK MONTESSORI SCHOOL
Malt Hill, Warfield, Bracknell, Berkshire RG42 6JQ
Tel: (01344) 890869
Fax: (01344) 890869
Email: mbrookuk@aol.com
Head: Mrs S Gunn
Type: Co-educational Day 3–11
No of pupils: B50 G50
Fees: (September 03) Day £950–£1950

NEWBOLD SCHOOL
Popeswood Road, Binfield, Bracknell, Berkshire RG42 4AH
Tel: (01344) 421088
Fax: (01344) 421088
Head: Mr M Brooks
Type: Co-educational Day 3–11
No of pupils: 95
Fees: (September 02) Day £2100–£2460

CROWTHORNE

OUR LADY'S PREPARATORY SCHOOL
The Avenue, Crowthorne, Berkshire RG45 6PB
Tel: (01344) 773394
Fax: (01344) 773394
Email: office@olps.co.uk
Head: Mrs S Bell
Type: Co-educational Day 3–11
No of pupils: B50 G50
Fees: (September 05)
Day £2328–£5124

WELLINGTON COLLEGE*
Duke's Ride, Crowthorne, Berkshire RG45 7PU
Tel: (01344) 444012
Fax: (01344) 444005
Email: registrar@wellingtoncollege.org.uk
Head: Dr A Seldon
Type: Co-educational Boarding and Day 13–18 (Co-ed VIth Form, fully co-ed from 09/06)
No of pupils: B707 G50
No of boarders: F640
Fees: (September 05) FB £22995
Day £18396

MAIDENHEAD

CLAIRES COURT SCHOOL
Ray Mill Road East, Maidenhead, Berkshire SL6 8TE
Tel: (01628) 411470
Fax: (01628) 411466
Email: Head@clairescourt.co.uk
Head: Mr J T Wilding
Type: Boys Day 11–16 (Co-ed VIth Form)
No of pupils: 300
Fees: (September 05)
Day £7875–£9180

CLAIRES COURT SCHOOLS, RIDGEWAY
Maidenhead Thicket, Maidenhead, Berkshire SL6 3QE
Tel: (01628) 411490
Fax: (01628) 411465
Email: Head@clairescourt.co.uk
Head: Mrs K M Rogg
Type: Boys Day 4–11
No of pupils: 231
Fees: (September 05)
Day £5895–£7875

CLAIRES COURT SCHOOLS, THE COLLEGE
1 College Avenue, Maidenhead, Berkshire SL6 6AW
Tel: (01628) 411480
Fax: (01628) 411467
Email: Head@clairescourt.co.uk
Head: Mrs L Green
Type: Girls Day 3–16 (Boys 3–5, co-ed VIth Form)
No of pupils: B101 G295
Fees: (September 04)
Day £5580–£8280

HERRIES SCHOOL
Dean Lane, Cookham Dean, Maidenhead, Berkshire SL6 9BD
Tel: (01628) 483350
Fax: (01628) 483329
Email: office@herries.ws
Head: Mrs A M Bradberry
Type: Co-educational Day 3–11
No of pupils: B30 G60
Fees: (September 05)
Day £4350–£6090

HIGHFIELD SCHOOL
2 West Road, Maidenhead, Berkshire SL6 1PD
Tel: (01628) 624918
Fax: (01628) 635747
Email: office@highfield.berks.sch.uk
Head: Mrs C M A Lane
Type: Girls Day 3–11
No of pupils: 180
Fees: (September 04)
Day £2655–£6285

REDROOFS THEATRE SCHOOL
Littlewick Green, Maidenhead, Berkshire SL6 3QY
Tel: (01628) 822461
Email: sam@redroofs.co.uk
Head: Ms June Rose
Type: Co-educational Day 9+
Fees: (September 05)
Day £6900–£9800

ST PIRAN'S PREPARATORY SCHOOL*
Gringer Hill, Maidenhead, Berkshire SL6 7LZ
Tel: (01628) 594300
Fax: (01628) 594301
Email: office@stpirans.co.uk
Head: Mr J Carroll
Type: Co-educational Day 3–13
No of pupils: B218 G110
Fees: (September 05)
Day £2598–£8790

SILCHESTER HOUSE SCHOOL
Silchester House, Bath Road, Taplow, Maidenhead, Berkshire SL6 0AP
Tel: (01628) 620549
Fax: (01628) 620549
Head: Mrs S Eaton
Type: Co-educational Day 2–5
No of pupils: B39 G46
Fees: (September 03)
Day £3600–£7500

WINBURY SCHOOL
Hibbert Road, Bray, Maidenhead, Berkshire SL6 1UU
Tel: (01628) 627412
Fax: (01628) 627412
Email: info@winbury.freeserve.co.uk
Head: Mrs P L Prewett
Type: Co-educational Day 2–8
No of pupils: B50 G50
Fees: (September 04)
Day £2550–£4425

NEWBURY

BROCKHURST AND MARLSTON HOUSE SCHOOLS
Hermitage, Newbury, Berkshire RG18 9UL
Tel: (01635) 200293
Fax: (01635) 200190
Email: info@brockmarl.org.uk
Head: Mr D Fleming and Mrs C Riley
Type: Co-educational Boarding and Day 3–13 (Single-sex ed) Flexi-boarding available
No of pupils: B137 G91
No of boarders: F3 W70
Fees: (September 05) FB £14850
Day £7140–£11175

CHEAM SCHOOL*
Headley, Newbury, Berkshire RG19 8LD
Tel: (01635) 268381
Fax: (01635) 269345
Email: registrar@cheamschool.co.uk
Head: Mr M R Johnson
Type: Co-educational Boarding and Day 3–13 Flexi-boarding available
No of pupils: B218 G153
No of boarders: F19 W74
Fees: (September 05) FB £17325
Day £7335–£12825

HORRIS HILL
Newtown, Newbury, Berkshire RG20 9DJ
Tel: (01635) 40594
Fax: (01635) 35241
Email: enquiries@horrishill.com
Head: Mr N J Chapman
Type: Boys Boarding and Day 7–13
No of pupils: 125
No of boarders: F120
Fees: (September 05) FB £16950 Day £13950

ST GABRIEL'S SCHOOL
Sandleford Priory, Newbury, Berkshire RG20 9BD
Tel: (01635) 555680
Fax: (01635) 37351
Email: info@stgabriels.co.uk
Head: Mr A Jones
Type: Girls Day 3–18 (Boys 3–7)
No of pupils: B10 G520
Fees: (September 04) Day £6195–£8850

ST MICHAELS SCHOOL
Harts Lane, Burghclere, Newbury, Berkshire RG20 9JW
Tel: (01635) 278137
Fax: (01635) 278601
Head: Father J Dreher
Type: Co-educational Boarding and Day 7–18 (Single-sex ed 13–18) Flexi-boarding available
No of pupils: B37 G35
No of boarders: F20 W33
Fees: (September 03) FB £3000–£8100 WB £2550–£7500 Day £1800–£4500

THORNGROVE SCHOOL
The Mount, Highclere, Newbury, Berkshire RG20 9PS
Tel: (01635) 253172
Fax: (01635) 254135
Email: admin@thorngroveschool.co.uk
Head: Mr N J Broughton
Type: Co-educational Day 2–13
No of pupils: B125 G99
Fees: (September 05) Day £6795–£8340

PANGBOURNE

PANGBOURNE COLLEGE*
Pangbourne, Berkshire RG8 8LA
Tel: (0118) 984 2101
Fax: (0118) 984 5443
Email: registrar@pangcoll.co.uk
Head: Mr T J C Garnier
Type: Co-educational Boarding and Day 11–18 Flexi-boarding available
No of pupils: B294 G100
No of boarders: F193
Fees: (September 05) FB £14955–£20595 Day £10515–£14445

READING

THE ABBEY SCHOOL
Kendrick Road, Reading, Berkshire RG1 5DZ
Tel: (0118) 987 2256
Fax: (0118) 987 1478
Email: schooloffice@theabbey.co.uk
Head: Mrs B E Stanley
Type: Girls Day 3–18
No of pupils: 1000
Fees: (September 05) Day £5250–£8940

ALDER BRIDGE SCHOOL
Bridge House, Mill Lane, Padworth, Reading, Berkshire RG7 4JU
Tel: (0118) 971 4471
Fax: (07092) 042631
Email: info@alderbridge.w-berks.sch.uk
Type: Co-educational Day 3–11
No of pupils: B27 G16
Fees: (September 04) Day £3255–£4200

THE ARK SCHOOL
School Road, Padworth, Reading, Berkshire RG7 4JA
Tel: (0118) 983 4802
Fax: (0118) 983 6894
Email: office@arkschool.fsnet.co.uk
Head: Mrs P A Oakley
Type: Co-educational Day 0–11
No of pupils: B53 G58
Fees: (September 04) Day £3510–£3705

BRADFIELD COLLEGE*
Bradfield, Reading, Berkshire RG7 6AR
Tel: (0118) 964 4510
Fax: (0118) 964 4511
Email: headmaster@bradfieldcollege.org.uk
Head: Mr P J M Roberts
Type: Co-educational Boarding and Day 13–18
No of pupils: B480 G150
No of boarders: F550
Fees: (September 05) FB £21750 Day £17400

CHILTERN COLLEGE SCHOOL
16 Peppard Road, Caversham, Reading, Berkshire RG4 8JZ
Tel: (0118) 947 1847
Fax: (0118) 946 3218
Email: info@chilterncollege.com
Head: Mrs J Halliday
Type: Co-educational Day 4–11
No of pupils: 80
Fees: (September 03) Day £4260

CROSFIELDS SCHOOL
Shinfield, Reading, Berkshire RG2 9BL
Tel: (0118) 987 1810
Fax: (0118) 931 0806
Email: office@crosfields.com
Head: Mr J P Wansey
Type: Boys Day 4–13
No of pupils: 466
Fees: (September 03) Day £4905–£8205

DOLPHIN SCHOOL
Hurst, Reading, Berkshire RG10 0BP
Tel: (0118) 934 1277
Fax: (0118) 934 4110
Email: omnes@dolphinschool.com
Head: Mrs H Brough and Mr J Wall
Type: Co-educational Day 3–13
No of pupils: B153 G138
Fees: (September 05) Day £4110–£8490

ELSTREE SCHOOL
Woolhampton, Reading, Berkshire RG7 5TD
Tel: (0118) 971 3302
Fax: (0118) 971 4280
Email: secretary@elstreeschool.org.uk
Head: Mr S M Hill
Type: Boys Boarding and Day 3–13 (Girls 3–7) Flexi-boarding available
No of pupils: B240 G20
No of boarders: F80 W10
Fees: (September 05) FB £16380 Day £6996–£12090

THE ELVIAN SCHOOL
61 Bath Road, Reading, Berkshire RG30 2BB
Tel: (0118) 957 2861
Fax: (0118) 957 2220
Email: mansers@elvian.reading.sch.uk
Head: Mrs S Manser
Type: Co-educational Day 3–18
No of pupils: B126 G10
Fees: (September 05) Day £4923–£6825

HEMDEAN HOUSE SCHOOL
Hemdean Road, Caversham, Reading, Berkshire RG4 7SD
Tel: (0118) 947 2590
Fax: (0118) 946 4474
Email: office@hemdeanhouse.co.uk
Head: Mrs J Harris
Type: Co-educational Day Boys 3–11 Girls 3–16
No of pupils: B50 G130
Fees: (September 05) Day £3750–£5550

THE HIGHLANDS SCHOOL
Wardle Avenue, Tilehurst, Reading, Berkshire RG31 6JR
Tel: (0118) 942 7186
Fax: (0118) 945 4953
Head: Mrs C A Bennett
Type: Co-educational Day Boys 2–7 Girls 2–11
No of pupils: B39 G100
Fees: (September 03) Day £1635–£1915

LEIGHTON PARK SCHOOL
Shinfield Road, Reading, Berkshire RG2 7ED
Tel: (0118) 987 9600
Fax: (0118) 987 9589
Email: admissions@leightonpark.reading.sch.uk
Head: Mr J Dunston
Type: Co-educational Boarding and Day 11–18 Flexi-boarding available
No of pupils: B291 G166
No of boarders: F91 W61
Fees: (September 05) FB £17718–£20850 WB £15801–£18588 Day £11778–£13854

THE ORATORY PREPARATORY SCHOOL*
Goring Heath, Reading, Berkshire RG8 7SF
Tel: (0118) 984 4511
Fax: (0118) 984 4806
Email: office@oratoryprep.co.uk
Head: Mr D L Sexon
Type: Co-educational Day and Boarding 3–13 Flexi-boarding available
No of pupils: B282 G122
No of boarders: F23
Fees: (September 04) FB £12555 Day £2700–£9105

THE ORATORY SCHOOL
Woodcote, Reading, Berkshire RG8 0PJ
Tel: (01491) 683500
Fax: (01491) 680020
Email: enquiries@oratory.co.uk
Head: Mr C I Dytor
Type: Boys Day and Boarding 11–18 Flexi-boarding available
No of boarders: F220
Fees: (September 05) FB £16140–£21300 Day £11970–£15375

PADWORTH COLLEGE*
Padworth, Reading, Berkshire RG7 4NR
Tel: (0118) 983 2644
Fax: (0118) 983 4515
Email: info@padworth.com
Head: Mr R Swan
Type: Co-educational Boarding and Day 13–19 Flexi-boarding available
No of pupils: B15 G100
No of boarders: F65 W10
Fees: (September 05) FB £18600 WB £13500 Day £7500

QUEEN ANNE'S SCHOOL*
6 Henley Road, Caversham, Reading, Berkshire RG4 6DX
Tel: (0118) 918 7333
Fax: (0118) 918 7310
Email: admis@queenannes.reading.sch.uk
Head: Mrs D Forbes
Type: Girls Boarding and Day 11–18 Flexi-boarding available
No of pupils: 340
No of boarders: F100 W80
Fees: (September 05) FB £21222 Day £14334

READING BLUE COAT SCHOOL*
Holme Park, Sonning-on-Thames, Reading, Berkshire RG4 6SU
Tel: (0118) 944 1005
Fax: (0118) 944 2690
Email: vmf@blue-coat.reading.sch.uk
Head: Mr S J W McArthur
Type: Boys Day 11–18 (Co-ed VIth Form)
No of pupils: B614 G55
Fees: (September 05) Day £9900

ST ANDREW'S SCHOOL
Buckhold, Pangbourne, Reading, Berkshire RG8 8QA
Tel: (0118) 974 4276
Fax: (0118) 974 5049
Email: registrar@standrewspangbourne.co.uk
Head: Mr J M Snow
Type: Co-educational Day and Boarding 3–13 Flexi-boarding available
No of pupils: B160 G127
Fees: (September 05) WB £12000 Day £2580–£10500

ST EDWARD'S SCHOOL
64 Tilehurst Road, Reading, Berkshire RG30 2JH
Tel: (0118) 957 4342
Fax: (0118) 950 3736
Email: admin@stedwards.org.uk
Head: Mr P Keddie
Type: Boys Day 4–13
No of pupils: 170
Fees: (September 05) Day £5385–£6945

ST JOSEPH'S CONVENT SCHOOL
Upper Redlands Road, Reading, Berkshire RG1 5JT
Tel: (0118) 966 1000
Fax: (0118) 926 9932
Email: mailbox@st-josephs.reading.sch.uk
Head: Mrs M T Sheridan
Type: Girls Day 3–18
No of pupils: B6 G352
Fees: (September 05)
Day £4110–£8730

SANDHURST

EAGLE HOUSE
Crowthorne Road, Sandhurst, Berkshire GU47 8PH
Tel: (01344) 772134
Fax: (01344) 779039
Email: info@eaglehouseschool.com
Head: Mr S J Carder
Type: Co-educational Day and Boarding 3–13 Flexi-boarding available
No of pupils: B216 G66
No of boarders: F10 W19
Fees: (September 05)
F/WB £ £15600 Day £11250

SLOUGH

ETON END PNEU
35 Eton Road, Datchet, Slough, Berkshire SL3 9AX
Tel: (01753) 541075
Fax: (01753) 541123
Email: admin@etonend.org
Head: Mrs V M Pilgerstorfer
Type: Co-educational Day Girls 3–11 (Boys 3–7)
No of pupils: B50 G200
Fees: (September 05)
Day £3330–£6900

LANGLEY MANOR SCHOOL
St Marys Road, Langley, Slough, Berkshire SL3 6BZ
Tel: (01753) 825368
Fax: (01753) 821451
Head: Mrs J Sculpher
Type: Co-educational Day 3–11
No of pupils: B140 G123
Fees: (September 05)
Day £5730–£5988

ST BERNARD'S PREPARATORY SCHOOL
Hawtrey Close, Slough, Berkshire SL1 1TB
Tel: (01753) 521821
Fax: (01753) 552364
Email: schooloffice@stbernardsprep.fsnet.co.uk
Head: Mrs M B Smith
Type: Co-educational Day 3–11
No of pupils: B125 G71
Fees: (September 05)
Day £4620–£5700

SUNNINGDALE

SUNNINGDALE SCHOOL
Sunningdale, Berkshire SL5 9PY
Tel: (01344) 620159
Fax: (01344) 873304
Email: headmaster@sunningdaleschool.co.uk
Head: Mr T A C N Dawson and Mr A J N Dawson
Type: Boys Boarding 8–13
No of pupils: 100
No of boarders: F95
Fees: (September 04) FB £13050

THATCHAM

BROCKHURST & MARLSTON HOUSE PRE-PREPARATORY SCHOOL
Hermitage, Thatcham, Berkshire RG18 9UL
Tel: (01635) 200293
Fax: (01635) 200190
Email: info@brockmarl.org.uk
Head: Mrs C Riley
Type: Co-educational Day 3–6
No of pupils: 56

DOWNE HOUSE*
Cold Ash, Thatcham, Berkshire RG18 9JJ
Tel: (01635) 200286
Fax: (01635) 202026
Email: correspondence@downehouse.net
Head: Mrs E McKendrick
Type: Girls Boarding and Day 11–18
No of pupils: 554
No of boarders: F538
Fees: (September 04) FB £21600
Day £15630

UPTON

LONG CLOSE SCHOOL*
Upton Court Road, Upton, Berkshire SL3 7LU
Tel: (01753) 520095
Fax: (01753) 821463
Email: info@longcloseschool.co.uk
Head: Mrs W Holland
Type: Co-educational Day 2–13
Fees: (September 05)
Day £4860–£8580

WINDSOR

BRIGIDINE SCHOOL WINDSOR
Queensmead, Kings Road, Windsor, Berkshire SL4 2AX
Tel: (01753) 863779
Fax: (01753) 850278
Email: mail@brigidine.org.uk
Head: Mrs J Dunn
Type: Girls Day 3–18 (Boys 3–7)
No of pupils: B4 G248
Fees: (September 05)
Day £7110–£10755

ETON COLLEGE
Windsor, Berkshire SL4 6DW
Tel: (01753) 671249
Fax: (01753) 671248
Email: admissions@etoncollege.org.uk
Head: Mr A R M Little
Type: Boys Boarding 13–18
No of pupils: 1298
No of boarders: F1298
Fees: (September 04) FB £23688

ST GEORGE'S SCHOOL
Windsor Castle, Windsor, Berkshire SL4 1QF
Tel: (01753) 865553
Fax: (01753) 842093
Email: enqs@stgwindsor.co.uk
Head: Mr J R Jones
Type: Co-educational Boarding and Day 3–13 Flexi-boarding available
No of pupils: B362 G120
No of boarders: F23 W9
Fees: (September 04) FB £13830
WB £13467 Day £2448–£10140

ST JOHN'S BEAUMONT*
Priest Hill, Old Windsor, Windsor, Berkshire SL4 2JN
Tel: (01784) 432428
Fax: (01784) 494048
Email: admissions@stjohnsbeaumont.co.uk
Acting Head: Mr G Delaney
Type: Boys Boarding and Day 4–13
No of pupils: 342
No of boarders: F30 W30
Fees: (September 05) FB £17286 WB £14580 Day £5997–£11046

UPTON HOUSE SCHOOL*
115 St Leonard's Road, Windsor, Berkshire SL4 3DF
Tel: (01753) 862610
Fax: (01753) 621950
Email: info@uptonhouse.org.uk
Head: Mrs M Collins
Type: Co-educational Day Girls 2–11 Boys 3–7
No of pupils: B50 G160
Fees: (September 05) Day £1160–£3660

WOKINGHAM

BEARWOOD COLLEGE*
Bearwood Road, Wokingham, Berkshire RG41 5BG
Tel: (0118) 974 8300
Fax: (0118) 977 3186
Email: headmaster@bearwoodcollege.berks.sch.uk
Head: Mr S Aiano
Type: Co-educational Boarding and Day 11–18 Flexi-boarding available
No of pupils: B250 G68
No of boarders: F65 W44
Fees: (September 05) F/WB £ £17910–£20640 Day £11160–£13020

HOLME GRANGE SCHOOL
Heathlands Road, Wokingham, Berkshire RG40 3AL
Tel: (0118) 978 1566
Fax: (0118) 977 0810
Email: school@holmegrange.org
Head: Mr N J Brodrick
Type: Co-educational Day 3–13
No of pupils: B150 G134
Fees: (September 05) Day £3360–£8340

LUCKLEY-OAKFIELD SCHOOL*
Luckley Road, Wokingham, Berkshire RG40 3EU
Tel: (0118) 978 4175
Fax: (0118) 977 0305
Email: registrar@luckley.wokingham.sch.uk
Head: Miss V A Davis
Type: Girls Boarding and Day 11–18 Flexi-boarding available
No of pupils: 304
No of boarders: F24 W8
Fees: (September 05) FB £17604 WB £16236 Day £10314

LUDGROVE
Wokingham, Berkshire RG40 3AB
Tel: (0118) 978 9881
Fax: (0118) 979 2973
Email: office@ludgroveschool.co.uk
Head: Mr G W P Barber and Mr C N J Marston
Type: Boys Boarding 8–13
No of pupils: 199
No of boarders: F199
Fees: (September 03) FB £15150

WAVERLEY SCHOOL
Waverley Way, Finchampstead, Wokingham, Berkshire RG40 4YD
Tel: (0118) 973 1121
Fax: (0118) 973 1131
Email: waverleyschool@waverley.wokingham.sch.uk
Head: Mr S G Melton
Type: Co-educational Day 3–11
No of pupils: B65 G63
Fees: (September 05) Day £2530–£7080

WHITE HOUSE PREPARATORY SCHOOL
Finchampstead Road, Wokingham, Berkshire RG40 3HD
Tel: (0118) 978 5151
Fax: (0118) 979 4716
Email: office@whitehouse.wokingham.sch.uk
Head: Mrs K Allen
Type: Girls Day 2–11 (Boys 2–4)
No of pupils: B4 G116
Fees: (September 05) Day £3640–£7152

BRISTOL

BRISTOL

BADMINTON SCHOOL
Westbury-on-Trym, Bristol
BS9 3BA
Tel: (0117) 905 5200
Fax: (0117) 962 8963
Email: cbarker@
badminton.bristol.sch.uk
Head: Mrs J Scarrow
Type: Girls Boarding and Day
4–18 Flexi-boarding available
No of pupils: 400
No of boarders: F155 W42
Fees: (September 05)
F/WB £ £21660 Day £12180

BRISTOL CATHEDRAL SCHOOL
College Square, Bristol BS1 5TS
Tel: (0117) 929 1872
Fax: (0117) 930 4219
Email: info@
bristolcathedral.org.uk
Head: Mrs Anne Davey
Type: Boys Day 10–18
(Co-ed VIth Form)
No of pupils: B410 G38
Fees: (September 04) Day £7488

BRISTOL GRAMMAR SCHOOL
University Road, Bristol BS8 1SR
Tel: (0117) 973 6006
Fax: (0117) 946 7485
Email: headmaster@
bgs.bristol.sch.uk
Head: Dr D J Mascord
Type: Co-educational Day 7–18
No of pupils: B808 G398
Fees: (September 05)
FB £4788–£8115

BRISTOL STEINER SCHOOL
Redland Hill House, Redland Hill,
Bristol BS6 6UX
Tel: (0117) 933 9990
Fax: (0117) 933 9999
Head: Mr C Nelson
Type: Co-educational Day 3–14
No of pupils: 200
Fees: (September 03)
Day £2040–£3720

CHEW MAGNA

SACRED HEART PREPARATORY SCHOOL
Winford Road, Chew Magna,
Bristol BS40 8QY
Tel: (01275) 332470
Fax: (01275) 332039
Email: info@
sacredheartprepschool.co.uk
Head: Mrs J E Lee
Type: Co-educational Day 3–11
No of pupils: B36 G57
Fees: (September 05)
Day £960–£5130

CLEVE HOUSE SCHOOL
254 Wells Road, Bristol BS4 2PN
Tel: (0117) 977 7218
Fax: (0117) 977 3915
Email: clevehouseschool@
btconnect.com
Head: Mr D Lawson and
Mrs E Lawson
Type: Co-educational Day 3–11
No of pupils: B61 G71
Fees: (September 05) Day £3885

CLIFTON COLLEGE*
32 College Road, Clifton, Bristol
BS8 3JH
Tel: (0117) 315 7000
Fax: (0117) 315 7101
Email: admissions@
clifton-college.avon.sch.uk
Head: Mr Mark Moore
Type: Co-educational Boarding
and Day 13–18 Flexi-boarding
available
No of pupils: B425 G228
No of boarders: F370
Fees: (September 05) FB £21915
Day £14505

CLIFTON COLLEGE PRE-PREP – BUTCOMBE
Guthrie Road, Bristol BS8 3EZ
Tel: (0117) 315 7591
Fax: (0117) 315 7592
Email: wbowring@
clifton-college.avon.sch.uk
Head: Dr W E Bowring
Type: Co-educational Day 3–8
No of pupils: B156 G88
Fees: (September 05)
Day £1920–£7080

CLIFTON COLLEGE PREPARATORY SCHOOL†
The Avenue, Clifton, Bristol
BS8 3HE
Tel: (0117) 315 7501
Fax: (0117) 315 7504
Email: lturley@
clifton-college.avon.sch.uk
Head: Dr R J Acheson
Type: Co-educational Boarding
and Day 3–13 Flexi-boarding
available
No of pupils: B389 G185
No of boarders: F41 W13
Fees: (September 05)
FB £15555–£16260
WB £14910–£15525
Day £5025–£10725

CLIFTON HIGH SCHOOL
College Road, Clifton, Bristol
BS8 3JD
Tel: (0117) 973 0201
Fax: (0117) 923 8962
Email: enquiries@
cliftonhigh.bristol.sch.uk
Head: Mrs M C Culligan
Type: Co-educational Day and
Boarding 3–18 Flexi-boarding
available
No of pupils: B143 G622
No of boarders: F3
Fees: (September 04) FB £13515
WB £11505 Day £2250–£7815

COLSTON'S GIRLS' SCHOOL
Cheltenham Road, Bristol BS6 5RD
Tel: (0117) 942 4328
Fax: (0117) 942 1052
Email: admin@
colstonsgirls.bristol.sch.uk
Head: Mrs L A Jones
Type: Girls Day 10–18
No of pupils: 450
Fees: (September 03)
Day £4410–£6447

COLSTON'S COLLEGIATE SCHOOL
Stapleton, Bristol BS16 1BJ
Tel: (0117) 965 5207
Fax: (0117) 958 5652
Email: enquiries@colstons.bristol.sch.uk
Head: Mr D G Crawford
Type: Co-educational Boarding and Day 3–18 Flexi-boarding available
No of pupils: B611 G257
No of boarders: F20 W40
Fees: (September 03) FB £13680 Day £5166–£6936

COLSTON'S LOWER SCHOOL
Park Road, Bristol BS16 1BA
Tel: (0117) 965 5297
Fax: (0117) 965 6330
Email: schooladmin@colstons.bristol.sch.uk
Head: Mrs C A Aspden
Type: Co-educational Day 3–11
No of pupils: B156 G74
Fees: (September 05) Day £4365–£6405

FAIRFIELD SCHOOL
Fairfield Way, Backwell, Bristol BS48 3PD
Tel: (01275) 462743
Fax: (01275) 464347
Email: secretary@fairfieldschool.org.uk
Head: Mrs L Barton
Type: Co-educational Day 3–11
No of pupils: B65 G73
Fees: (September 05) Day £5160–£5655

GRACEFIELD PREPARATORY SCHOOL
266 Overndale Road, Fishponds, Bristol BS16 2RG
Tel: (0117) 956 7977
Fax: (0117) 956 3397
Email: enquiries@gracefieldschool.co.uk
Head: Mrs E Morgan
Type: Co-educational Day 4–11
No of pupils: B45 G45
Fees: (September 05) Day £2976

OVERNDALE SCHOOL
Chapel Lane, Old Sodbury, Bristol BS37 6NQ
Tel: (01454) 310332
Head: Mrs K Winstanley
Type: Co-educational Day 1–11
No of pupils: B55 G45
Fees: (September 03) Day £2845

QUEEN ELIZABETH'S HOSPITAL
Berkeley Place, Bristol BS8 1JX
Tel: (0117) 930 3040
Fax: (0117) 929 3106
Email: headmaster@gehbristol.co.uk
Head: Mr S W Holliday
Type: Boys Day and Boarding 11–18 Flexi-boarding available
No of pupils: 567
No of boarders: F16 W16
Fees: (September 05) FB £14727 WB £13395 Day £7992

THE RED MAIDS' SCHOOL
Westbury-on-Trym, Bristol BS9 3AW
Tel: (0117) 962 2641
Fax: (0117) 962 1687
Email: admin@redmaids.bristol.sch.uk
Head: Mrs I Tobias
Type: Girls Day 11–18
No of pupils: 420
Fees: (September 05) Day £7575

REDLAND HIGH SCHOOL
Redland Court, Bristol BS6 7EF
Tel: (0117) 924 5796
Fax: (0117) 924 1127
Email: admissions@redland.bristol.sch.uk
Head: Dr R Weeks
Type: Girls Day 3–18
No of pupils: 672
Fees: (September 04) Day £2440–£7410

ST URSULA'S HIGH SCHOOL
Brecon Road, Westbury-on-Trym, Bristol BS9 4DT
Tel: (0117) 962 2616
Fax: (0117) 962 2616
Email: office@st-ursulas.bristol.sch.uk
Head: Mrs L Carter
Type: Co-educational Day 3–16
No of pupils: B185 G138
Fees: (September 05) Day £4320–£6600

TOCKINGTON MANOR SCHOOL
Tockington, Bristol BS32 4NY
Tel: (01454) 613229
Fax: (01454) 613676
Email: admin@tockington.bristol.sch.uk
Head: Mr R G Tovey
Type: Co-educational Day and Boarding 2–14 Flexi-boarding available
No of pupils: B168 G87
No of boarders: F14
Fees: (September 05) FB £12600–£14010 Day £5730–£9585

TORWOOD HOUSE SCHOOL
29 Durdham Park, Redland, Bristol BS6 6XE
Tel: (0117) 973 5620
Fax: (0117) 973 5620
Email: emailus@torwoodhouse.bristol.sch.uk
Head: Mrs D Seagrove
Type: Co-educational Day 0–11
No of pupils: B100 G102
Fees: (September 04) Day £630–£1227

BUCKINGHAMSHIRE

AMERSHAM

THE BEACON SCHOOL

Chesham Bois, Amersham,
Buckinghamshire HP6 5PF
Tel: (01494) 433654
Fax: (01494) 727849
Email: enquiries@beaconschool.co.uk
Head: Mr M W Spinney
Type: Boys Day 3–13
No of pupils: 430
Fees: (September 05)
Day £3630–£9870

HEATHERTON HOUSE SCHOOL

Copperkins Lane, Chesham Bois,
Amersham, Buckinghamshire
HP6 5QB
Tel: (01494) 726433
Fax: (01494) 729628
Email: admissions@heathertonhouse.co.uk
Head: Mr P Rushforth
Type: Girls Day 3–11 (Boys 2–5)
No of pupils: B17 G158
Fees: (September 05)
Day £1245–£7785

AYLESBURY

ASHFOLD SCHOOL

Dorton, Aylesbury,
Buckinghamshire HP18 9NG
Tel: (01844) 238237
Fax: (01844) 238505
Email: hmsecretary@ashfoldschool.co.uk
Head: Mr M O M Chitty
Type: Co-educational Boarding and Day 3–13 Flexi-boarding available
No of pupils: B187 G86
No of boarders: W25
Fees: (September 05) WB £12480
Day £11010

LADYMEDE

Little Kimble, Aylesbury,
Buckinghamshire HP17 0XP
Tel: (01844) 346154
Fax: (01844) 275660
Email: loffice@ladymede.com
Head: Mrs B.A. Peters
Type: Co-educational Day 3–11
No of pupils: B50 G60
Fees: (September 05)
Day £3225–£6516

BEACONSFIELD

DAVENIES SCHOOL

Beaconsfield, Buckinghamshire
HP9 1AA
Tel: (01494) 685400
Fax: (01494) 685408
Email: office@davenies.co.uk
Head: Mr A J P Nott
Type: Boys Day 4–13
No of pupils: 325
Fees: (September 05)
Day £8400–£9600

HIGH MARCH SCHOOL

23 Ledborough Lane,
Beaconsfield, Buckinghamshire
HP9 2PZ
Tel: (01494) 675186
Fax: (01494) 675377
Email: head@highmarch.bucks.sch.uk
Head: Mrs S J Clifford
Type: Girls Day 3–12 (Boys 3–5)
No of pupils: B12 G290
Fees: (September 05)
Day £2700–£8190

BUCKINGHAM

AKELEY WOOD SCHOOL*

Akeley Wood, Buckingham,
Buckinghamshire MK18 5AE
Tel: (01280) 814110
Fax: (01280) 822945
Email: enquiries@akeleywoodschool.co.uk
Head: Dr J Grundy
Type: Co-educational Day 3–18
No of pupils: B521 G367
Fees: (September 05)
Day £2880–£8475

STOWE SCHOOL

Buckingham, Buckinghamshire
MK18 5EH
Tel: (01280) 818323
Fax: (01280) 818181
Email: enquiries@stowe.co.uk
Head: Dr A K Wallersteiner
Type: Co-educational Boarding and Day 13–18
No of pupils: B497 G102
No of boarders: F535
Fees: (September 04) FB £21780
Day £16335

CHESHAM

CHESHAM PREPARATORY SCHOOL

Orchard Leigh, Chesham,
Buckinghamshire HP5 3QF
Tel: (01494) 782619
Fax: (01494) 791645
Email: secretary@chesham-prep.bucks.sch.uk
Head: Mr J Marjoribanks
Type: Co-educational Day 4–13
No of pupils: B212 G148
Fees: (September 03)
Day £5265–£6255

FARNHAM ROYAL

CALDICOTT SCHOOL*

Crown Lane, Farnham Royal,
Buckinghamshire SL2 3SL
Tel: (01753) 649300
Fax: (01753) 649325
Email: office@caldicott.com
Head: Mr S J G Doggart
Type: Boys Boarding and Day 7–13
No of pupils: 240
No of boarders: F116 W126
Fees: (September 05) FB £15966
Day £11970

DAIR HOUSE SCHOOL TRUST LTD
Bishops Blake, Beaconsfield Road, Farnham Royal, Buckinghamshire SL2 3BY
Tel: (01753) 643964
Fax: (01753) 642376
Email: info@dairhouse.co.uk
Head: Mrs L J Hudson
Type: Co-educational Day 3–11
No of pupils: B59 G27
Fees: (September 05)
Day £2295–£6555

GERRARDS CROSS

GAYHURST SCHOOL
Bull Lane, Gerrards Cross, Buckinghamshire SL9 8RJ
Tel: (01753) 882690
Fax: (01753) 887451
Email: gayhurst@gayhurst.bucks.sch.uk
Head: Mr A J Sims
Type: Boys Day 4–13
Fees: (September 05)
Day £6720–£8538

HOLY CROSS CONVENT
The Grange, Chalfont St Peter, Gerrards Cross, Buckinghamshire SL9 9DW
Tel: (01753) 895600
Fax: (01753) 882147
Email: enquiries@holy-cross.fsnet.co.uk
Head: Mrs M C Shinkwin
Type: Girls Day 3–18
No of pupils: 248
Fees: (September 05)
Day £4092–£8232

KINGSCOTE PRE-PREPARATORY SCHOOL
Oval Way, Gerrards Cross, Buckinghamshire SL9 8PZ
Tel: (01753) 885535
Fax: (01753) 891783
Email: office@kingscoteschool.info
Head: Mrs S A Tunstall
Type: Boys Day 3–7
No of pupils: 115
Fees: (September 05)
Day £3243–£6486

MALTMAN'S GREEN SCHOOL
Maltmans Lane, Gerrards Cross, Buckinghamshire SL9 8RR
Tel: (01753) 883022
Fax: (01753) 891237
Email: office@maltmansgreenschool.bucks.sch.uk
Head: Mrs J R Pardon
Type: Girls Day 3–11
No of pupils: 395
Fees: (September 05)
Day £8175–£8655

ST MARY'S SCHOOL
Packhorse Road, Gerrards Cross, Buckinghamshire SL9 8JQ
Tel: (01753) 883370
Fax: (01753) 890966
Email: registrar@stmarys-gx.org
Head: Mrs F A Balcombe
Type: Girls Day 3–18
No of pupils: 300
Fees: (September 05)
Day £4590–£9605

THORPE HOUSE SCHOOL
Oval Way, Gerrards Cross, Buckinghamshire SL9 8PZ
Tel: (01753) 882474
Fax: (01753) 889755
Email: office@thorpehouse.bucks.sch.uk
Head: Mr A F Lock
Type: Boys Day 3–13
No of pupils: 280
Fees: (September 05)
Day £8490–£8684

GREAT MISSENDEN

GATEWAY SCHOOL
1 High Street, Great Missenden, Buckinghamshire HP16 9AA
Tel: (01494) 862407
Fax: (01494) 865787
Email: headteacher@gateway.bucks.sch.uk
Head: Mr S Wade
Type: Co-educational Day 2–12
No of pupils: B174 G126
Fees: (September 04) Day £6324

HIGH WYCOMBE

CROWN HOUSE SCHOOL
19 London Road, High Wycombe, Buckinghamshire HP11 1BJ
Tel: (01494) 529927
Fax: (01494) 525693
Email: crownhouse.school@virgin.net
Head: Mr L Clark
Type: Co-educational Day 4–11
No of pupils: B78 G59
Fees: (September 04) Day £5850

GODSTOWE PREPARATORY SCHOOL
Shrubbery Road, High Wycombe, Buckinghamshire HP13 6PR
Tel: (01494) 529273
Fax: (01494) 429009
Email: headmistress@godstowe.org
Head: Mrs F J Henson
Type: Girls Day and Boarding 3–13 (Boys 3–8)
No of pupils: B14 G435
No of boarders: F96 W35
Fees: (September 05)
F/WB £ £14625–£15720
Day £6180–£10695

PIPERS CORNER SCHOOL*
Pipers Lane, Great Kingshill, High Wycombe, Buckinghamshire HP15 6LP
Tel: (01494) 718255
Fax: (01494) 719806
Email: school@piperscorner.co.uk
Head: Mrs V M Stattersfield
Type: Girls Day and Boarding 4–18 Flexi-boarding available
No of pupils: 470
No of boarders: F25 W25
Fees: (September 04)
FB £13035–£15945
WB £12825–£15735
Day £4350–£9645

WYCOMBE ABBEY SCHOOL
High Wycombe, Buckinghamshire HP11 1PE
Tel: (01494) 520381
Fax: (01494) 473836
Email: schoolsecretary@wycombeabbey.com
Head: Mrs P E Davies
Type: Girls Boarding 11–18 (A few day places)
No of pupils: 553
No of boarders: F526
Fees: (September 05) FB £23100
Day £17325

MILTON KEYNES

BURY LAWN SCHOOL
Soskin Drive, Stantonbury Fields, Milton Keynes, Buckinghamshire MK14 6DP
Tel: (01908) 220345
Fax: (01908) 220363
Email: burylawnoffice@aol.com
Head: Mr F Roche
Type: Co-educational Day 1–18
No of pupils: B277 G214
Fees: (September 04)
Day £5325–£7710

GROVE INDEPENDENT SCHOOL
Redland Drive, Loughton, Milton Keynes, Buckinghamshire MK5 8HD
Tel: (01908) 690590
Fax: (01908) 649043
Email: office@groveindependentschool.co.uk
Head: Mrs D M Berkin
Type: Co-educational Day 2–13
No of pupils: 214
Fees: (September 04)
Day £7776–£8220

GYOSEI INTERNATIONAL SCHOOL UK
Japonica Lane, Willen Park, Milton Keynes, Buckinghamshire MK15 9JX
Tel: (01908) 690100
Fax: (01908) 690150
Head: Mr Y Mikuriya
Type: Co-educational Boarding and Day 13–18
No of pupils: B62 G38
No of boarders: F100

MILTON KEYNES PREPARATORY SCHOOL
Tattenhoe Lane, Milton Keynes, Buckinghamshire MK3 7EG
Tel: (01908) 642111
Fax: (01908) 366365
Email: info@mkps.co.uk
Head: Mrs H A Pauley
Type: Co-educational Day 0–11
No of pupils: B250 G250
Fees: (September 04)
Day £3840–£8520

SWANBOURNE HOUSE SCHOOL*
Swanbourne, Milton Keynes, Buckinghamshire MK17 0HZ
Tel: (01296) 720264
Fax: (01296) 728089
Email: office@swanbourne.org
Head: Mr S D Goodhart and Mrs J S Goodhart
Type: Co-educational Boarding and Day 3–13 Flexi-boarding available
No of pupils: B225 G188
No of boarders: F28 Flexi 60
Fees: (September 05)
F/Flexi £ £14580
Day £3000–£11370

THORNTON COLLEGE CONVENT OF JESUS AND MARY
Thornton, Milton Keynes, Buckinghamshire MK17 0HJ
Tel: (01280) 812610
Fax: (01280) 824042
Email: registrar@thorntoncollege.com
Head: Miss A Williams
Type: Girls Day and Boarding 2–16 (Boys 2–4) Flexi-boarding available
No of pupils: 310
No of boarders: F32 W18
Fees: (September 05)
FB £12000–£14000
WB £10950–£12525
Day £5550–£8325

NEWPORT PAGNELL

FILGRAVE SCHOOL
Filgrave, Newport Pagnell, Buckinghamshire MK16 9ET
Tel: (01234) 711534
Email: enquiries@filgraveschool.org.uk
Head: Mrs S Marriott
Type: Co-educational Day 3–9
No of pupils: B20 G21
Fees: (September 04) Day £4680

PRINCES RISBOROUGH

ST TERESA'S CATHOLIC INDEPENDENT & NURSERY SCHOOL
Aylesbury Road, Princes Risborough, Buckinghamshire HP27 0JW
Tel: (01844) 345005
Fax: (01844) 345131
Email: office@st-teresas.bucks.sch.uk
Head: Mr R P Duigan
Type: Co-educational Day 3–11
No of pupils: B86 G59
Fees: (September 04)
Day £4950–£5300

CAMBRIDGESHIRE

CAMBRIDGE

BELLERBYS COLLEGE
Queens Campus, Bateman Street, Cambridge, Cambridgeshire CB2 1LZ
Tel: (01223) 363159
Fax: (01223) 307425
Email: cambridge@bellerbys.com
Head: Mr E J Squires
Type: Co-educational Boarding 14–25
No of pupils: B180 G160
No of boarders: F340
Fees: (September 05) FB £16077

CAMBRIDGE ARTS & SCIENCES (CATS)*
Round Church Street, Cambridge, Cambridgeshire CB5 8AD
Tel: (01223) 314431
Fax: (01223) 467773
Email: enquiries@catscollege.com
Head: Mrs E Armstrong and Mr P McLaughlin
Type: Co-educational Boarding and Day 14–19
No of pupils: B114 G133
No of boarders: F220 W5
Fees: (September 05)
FB £15610–£19155
Day £12640–£14465

CAMBRIDGE CENTRE FOR SIXTH-FORM STUDIES*
1 Salisbury Villas, Station Road, Cambridge, Cambridgeshire CB1 2JF
Tel: (01223) 716890
Fax: (01223) 517530
Email: enquiries@ccss.co.uk
Head: Mr Neil Roskilly
Type: Co-educational Day and Boarding 15–19 Flexi-boarding available
No of pupils: B90 G70
No of boarders: F106
Fees: (September 05)
F/WB £16791–£21915
Day £8643–£13767

THE LEYS SCHOOL
Trumpington Road, Cambridge, Cambridgeshire CB2 2AD
Tel: (01223) 508900
Fax: (01223) 505303
Email: office@theleys.net
Head: Mr Mark Slater
Type: Co-educational Boarding and Day 11–18
No of pupils: B324 G202
No of boarders: F280
Fees: (September 05)
FB £15105–£20970
Day £9570–£13425

MADINGLEY PRE-PREPARATORY SCHOOL
Cambridge Road, Madingley, Cambridge, Cambridgeshire CB3 8AH
Tel: (01954) 210309
Fax: (01233) 264169
Email: admin@madingleyschool.co.uk
Head: Mrs P Evans
Type: Co-educational Day 3–8
No of pupils: B30 G30
Fees: (September 05) Day £5850

MPW (MANDER PORTMAN WOODWARD)
3/4 Brookside, Cambridge, Cambridgeshire CB2 1JE
Tel: (01223) 350158
Fax: (01223) 366429
Email: enquiries@cambridge.mpw.co.uk
Head: Dr N Marriott
Type: Co-educational Day and Boarding 15–21 Flexi-boarding available
No of pupils: B50 G50
No of boarders: F20 W20

THE PERSE SCHOOL
Hills Road, Cambridge, Cambridgeshire CB2 2QF
Tel: (01223) 403800
Fax: (01223) 403810
Email: office@perse.co.uk
Head: Mr Nigel Richardson
Type: Boys Day 11–18
No of pupils: B595 G49
Fees: (September 05) Day £10395

THE PERSE SCHOOL FOR GIRLS
Union Road, Cambridge, Cambridgeshire CB2 1HF
Tel: (01223) 454700
Fax: (01223) 467420
Email: office@admin.perse.cambs.sch.uk
Head: Miss P M Kelleher
Type: Girls Day 7–18
No of pupils: 690
Fees: (September 05)
Day £8430–£9900

ST ANDREW'S
2A Free School Lane, Cambridge, Cambridgeshire CB2 3QA
Tel: (01223) 360040
Fax: (01223) 467150
Email: registrar@standrewscambridge.co.uk
Head: Mrs C Williams
Type: Co-educational Boarding and Day 14–18 Flexi-boarding available
No of pupils: B67 G53
No of boarders: F120

ST CATHERINES PREPARATORY SCHOOL
1 Brookside, Cambridge, Cambridgeshire CB2 1JE
Tel: (01223) 311666
Fax: (01223) 472168
Email: stcatherinesprep@aol.com
Head: Mrs D O'Sullivan
Type: Girls Day 4–11
No of pupils: 145
Fees: (September 05)
Day £5925–£6750

ST COLETTE'S SCHOOL
Tenison Road, Cambridge, Cambridgeshire CB1 2DP
Tel: (01223) 353696
Fax: (01223) 517784
Email: stcolettes@indschool.org
Head: Mrs A C Wilson
Type: Co-educational Day 2–7
No of pupils: B70 G70
Fees: (September 05)
Day £5043–£5778

ST FAITH'S
Trumpington Road, Cambridge, Cambridgeshire CB2 2AG
Tel: (01223) 352073
Fax: (01223) 314757
Email: admissions@stfaiths.co.uk
Head: Mr C S S Drew
Type: Co-educational Day 4–13
No of pupils: B318 G196
Fees: (September 05)
Day £7305–£9225

ST JOHN'S COLLEGE SCHOOL
The Garden House, 75 Grange Road, Cambridge, Cambridgeshire CB3 9AA
Tel: (01223) 353532
Fax: (01223) 355846
Email: shoffice@sjcs.co.uk
Head: Mr K L Jones
Type: Co-educational Day and Boarding 4–13 Flexi-boarding available
No of pupils: B270 G190
No of boarders: F38
Fees: (September 05)
FB £5023–£15069
Day £5754–£9540

ST MARY'S SCHOOL*
Bateman Street, Cambridge, Cambridgeshire CB2 1LY
Tel: (01223) 353253
Fax: (01223) 357451
Email: enquiries@stmaryscambridge.co.uk
Head: Mrs J Triffitt
Type: Girls Day and Boarding 11–18 Flexi-boarding available
No of boarders: F46 W7
Fees: (September 05) FB £19650
WB £17370 Day £9870

SANCTON WOOD SCHOOL
2 St Paul's Road, Cambridge, Cambridgeshire CB1 2EZ
Tel: (01223) 359488
Fax: (01223) 359488
Email: sturdy@sturdy.demon.co.uk
Head: Mrs J Avis
Type: Co-educational Day 1–16
No of pupils: B105 G69
Fees: (September 03)
Day £5520–£6510

ELY

THE KING'S SCHOOL ELY*
Ely, Cambridgeshire CB7 4DB
Tel: (01353) 660702
Fax: (01353) 667485
Email: admissions@kings-ely.cambs.sch.uk
Head: Mrs S E Freestone
Type: Co-educational Boarding and Day 2–18 Flexi-boarding available
No of pupils: B542 G365
No of boarders: F163 W61
Fees: (September 05)
F/WB £ £14175–£19410
Day £5835–£13410

HUNTINGDON

KIMBOLTON SCHOOL
Kimbolton, Huntingdon, Cambridgeshire PE28 0EA
Tel: (01480) 860505
Fax: (01480) 860386
Email: registrar@kimbolton.cambs.sch.uk
Head: Mr J Belbin
Type: Co-educational Boarding and Day 4–18 (Boarders from 11) Flexi-boarding available
No of pupils: B462 G400
No of boarders: F54
Fees: (September 05) FB £16560
Day £6300–£9960

WHITEHALL SCHOOL
117 High Street, Somersham, Huntingdon, Cambridgeshire PE28 3EH
Tel: (01487) 840966
Fax: (01487) 840966
Email: office@whitehallschool.com
Head: Mr C Hutson
Type: Co-educational Day 3–11
No of pupils: B50 G50
Fees: (September 05)
Day £3906–£5076

PETERBOROUGH

PETERBOROUGH HIGH SCHOOL
Thorpe Road, Peterborough, Cambridgeshire PE3 6JF
Tel: (01733) 343357
Fax: (01733) 355710
Email: phs@peterboroughhigh.co.uk
Head: Mrs S A Dixon
Type: Girls Day and Boarding 3–18 (Boys 3–11) Flexi-boarding available
No of pupils: B81 G295
No of boarders: F18 W14
Fees: (September 05)
FB £15297–£16404
WB £13437–£14544
Day £6480–£8967

WISBECH

WISBECH GRAMMAR SCHOOL
North Brink, Wisbech, Cambridgeshire PE13 1JX
Tel: (01945) 583631
Fax: (01945) 476746
Email: hmsecretary@wisbechgs.demon.co.uk
Head: Mr R S Repper
Type: Co-educational Day 4–18
No of pupils: B375 G356
Fees: (September 05)
Day £5610–£8280

CHANNEL ISLANDS

ALDERNEY

ORMER HOUSE PREPARATORY SCHOOL
La Vallee, Alderney, Channel Islands GY9 3XA
Tel: (01481) 823287
Fax: (01481) 824053
Email: enquiries@ormerhouse.com
Head: Mrs M Burridge
Type: Co-educational Day 2–13
No of pupils: B28 G24
Fees: (September 03)
Day £1500–£3896

GUERNSEY

CONVENT OF MERCY
Cordier Hill, St Peter Port, Guernsey, Channel Islands GY1 1JH
Tel: (01481) 720729
Fax: (01481) 716339
Head: Sister C Blackburn
Type: Co-educational Day 3–7
No of pupils: B57 G46
Fees: (September 03) Day £1700

ELIZABETH COLLEGE
Guernsey, Channel Islands GY1 2PY
Tel: (01481) 726544
Fax: (01481) 714839
Head: Dr N Argent
Type: Boys Day 2–18 (Co-ed VIth Form)
No of pupils: 740
Fees: (September 05) Day £5400

THE LADIES' COLLEGE
Les Gravees, St Peter Port, Guernsey, Channel Islands GY1 1RW
Tel: (01481) 721602
Fax: (01481) 724209
Email: secretary@ladiescollege.education.gg
Head: Miss M E Macdonald
Type: Girls Day 4–18
No of pupils: 557
Fees: (September 05)
Day £4185–£4425

JERSEY

BEAULIEU CONVENT SCHOOL
Wellington Road, Saint Helier, Jersey, Channel Islands JE2 4RJ
Tel: (01534) 731280
Fax: (01534) 888607
Email: secondaryadmin@beaulieu.sch.je
Head: Mrs R A Hill
Type: Girls Day 4–18
No of pupils: 623
Fees: (September 03) Day £3180

FCJ PRIMARY SCHOOL
Deloraine Road, St Saviour, Jersey, Channel Islands JE2 7XB
Tel: (01534) 723063
Fax: (01534) 880353
Email: admin@fcj.sch.je
Head: Ms M Doyle
Type: Co-educational Day 4–11
No of pupils: B110 G180
Fees: (September 04) Day £2220

ST GEORGE'S PREPARATORY SCHOOL
La Hague Manor, Rue de la Hague, St Peter, Jersey, Channel Islands JE3 7DB
Tel: (01534) 481593
Fax: (01534) 484304
Email: admin@stgeorgesprep.co.uk
Head: Mr Colin Moore
Type: Co-educational Day 3–13
No of pupils: B106 G91
Fees: (September 05)
Day £3255–£10440

ST MICHAEL'S PREPARATORY SCHOOL
La Rue de la Houguette, St Saviour, Jersey, Channel Islands JE2 7UG
Tel: (01534) 856904
Fax: (01534) 856620
Email: ew@stmichaels.je
Head: Mr R De Figueiredo
Type: Co-educational Day 3–13
No of pupils: B167 G132
Fees: (September 04)
Day £6660–£10239

VICTORIA COLLEGE
Jersey, Channel Islands JE1 4HT
Tel: (01534) 638200
Fax: (01534) 727448
Email: admin@vcj.sch.je
Head: Mr R Cook
Type: Boys Day 11–19
No of pupils: 650
Fees: (September 03) Day £3252

VICTORIA COLLEGE PREPARATORY SCHOOL
Pleasant Street, St Helier, Jersey, Channel Islands
Tel: (01534) 723468
Fax: (01534) 780596
Email: admin@vcp.sch.je
Head: Mr P Stevenson
Type: Boys Day 7–11
No of pupils: 280
Fees: (September 05) Day £3600

CHESHIRE

ALDERLEY EDGE

ALDERLEY EDGE SCHOOL FOR GIRLS
Wilmslow Road, Alderley Edge, Cheshire SK9 7QE
Tel: (01625) 583028
Fax: (01625) 590271
Email: schoolmail@aesg.co.uk
Head: Mrs K Mills
Type: Girls Day 3–18
No of pupils: 600
Fees: (September 05) Day £4734–£7146

THE RYLEYS
Ryleys Lane, Alderley Edge, Cheshire SK9 7UY
Tel: (01625) 583241
Fax: (01625) 581900
Email: headmaster@ryleys.cheshire.sch.uk
Head: Mr P G Barrett
Type: Boys Day 3–13
No of pupils: 236
Fees: (September 05) Day £6855–£7845

ALTRINCHAM

ALTRINCHAM PREPARATORY SCHOOL
Marlborough Road, Bowdon, Altrincham, Cheshire WA14 2RR
Tel: (0161) 928 3366
Fax: (0161) 929 6747
Email: admin@altprep.co.uk
Head: Mr A Potts
Type: Boys Day 4–11
No of pupils: 310
Fees: (September 05) Day £4602–£5253

BOWDON PREPARATORY SCHOOL FOR GIRLS
48 Stamford Road, Bowdon, Altrincham, Cheshire WA14 2JP
Tel: (0161) 928 0678
Email: bps@bowdonprep.org.uk
Head: Mrs J H Tan
Type: Girls Day 2–12
No of pupils: 220
Fees: (September 03) Day £3690–£3825

CULCHETH HALL
Ashley Road, Altrincham, Cheshire WA14 2LT
Tel: (0161) 928 1862
Fax: (0161) 929 6893
Email: admin@culcheth-hall.org.uk
Head: Miss M A Stockwell
Type: Girls Day 2–16 (Boys 2–4)
No of pupils: B22 G203
Fees: (September 04) Day £1560–£5850

FOREST SCHOOL
Moss Lane, Timperley, Altrincham, Cheshire WA15 6LJ
Tel: (0161) 980 4075
Fax: (0161) 903 9275
Email: headteacher@forestschool.co.uk
Head: Mrs E A Irons
Type: Co-educational Day 2–11
No of pupils: B79 G73
Fees: (September 05) Day £3915–£4455

HALE PREPARATORY SCHOOL
Broomfield Lane, Hale, Altrincham, Cheshire WA15 9AS
Tel: (0161) 928 2386
Fax: (0161) 941 7934
Email: johnconnor@b.t.connect.com
Head: Mr J Connor
Type: Co-educational Day 4–11
No of pupils: B99 G83
Fees: (September 04) Day £4275

LORETO PREPARATORY SCHOOL
Dunham Road, Altrincham, Cheshire WA14 4AH
Tel: (0161) 928 8310
Fax: (0161) 929 5801
Email: info.loretoprep@btconnect.com
Head: Mrs R A Hedger
Type: Girls Day 3–11 (Boys 4–7)
No of pupils: B1 G163
Fees: (September 05) Day £3750

NORTH CESTRIAN GRAMMAR SCHOOL
Dunham Road, Altrincham, Cheshire WA14 4AJ
Tel: (0161) 928 1856
Fax: (0161) 929 8657
Email: office@ncgs.co.uk
Head: Mr D G Vanstone
Type: Boys Day 11–18
No of pupils: B290 G6
Fees: (September 05) Day £6270

ST AMBROSE PREPARATORY SCHOOL
Hale Barns, Altrincham, Cheshire WA15 0HE
Tel: (0161) 903 9193
Fax: (0161) 903 8138
Email: stambroseprep.admin@traffordlearning.org
Head: Mr M J Lochery
Type: Boys Day 4–11
No of pupils: 170
Fees: (September 05) Day £4320–£4500

CHEADLE

CHEADLE HULME SCHOOL
Claremont Road, Cheadle Hulme, Cheadle, Cheshire SK8 6EF
Tel: (0161) 488 3330
Fax: (0161) 488 3344
Email: headmaster@chschool.co.uk
Head: Mr P V Dixon
Type: Co-educational Day 4–18
No of pupils: B681 G716
Fees: (September 05) Day £5904–£7470

GREENBANK
Heathbank Road, Cheadle Hulme, Cheadle, Cheshire SK8 6HU
Tel: (0161) 485 3724
Fax: (0161) 485 5519
Email: kevinphillips@greenbank.stockport.sch.uk
Head: Mr K Phillips
Type: Co-educational Day 3–11
No of pupils: B102 G71
Fees: (September 05) Day £2820–£5100

HULME HALL SCHOOLS
75 Hulme Hall Road, Cheadle Hulme, Cheadle, Cheshire SK8 6LA
Tel: (0161) 485 4638/3524
Fax: (0161) 485 5966
Email: secretary@hulmehallschool.co.uk
Head: Mr P Marland
Type: Co-educational Day 2–16
No of pupils: B255 G130
Fees: (September 05)
Day £3870–£6225

HULME HALL SCHOOLS (JUNIOR DIVISION)
75 Hulme Hall Road, Cheadle Hulme, Cheadle, Cheshire SK8 6LA
Tel: (0161) 486 9970
Fax: (0161) 485 5966
Email: secretary@hulmehallschool.co.uk
Head: Mr P Marland
Type: Co-educational Day 3–11
No of pupils: B58 G32
Fees: (September 04)
Day £3690–£4590

LADY BARN HOUSE SCHOOL
Langlands, Schools Hill, Cheadle Hulme, Cheadle, Cheshire SK8 1JE
Tel: (0161) 428 2912
Fax: (0161) 428 5798
Email: info@ladybarnhouse.stockport.sch.uk
Head: Mrs S Yule
Type: Co-educational Day 3–11
No of pupils: B280 G187
Fees: (September 04)
Day £3915–£4485

RAMILLIES HALL SCHOOL†
Cheadle Hulme, Cheadle, Cheshire SK8 7AJ
Tel: (0161) 485 3804
Fax: (0161) 486 6021
Email: info@ramillieshall.co.uk
Head: Mrs A L Poole and Miss D M Patterson
Type: Co-educational Boarding and Day 0–16
No of pupils: B110 G76
No of boarders: F10 W6
Fees: (September 04)
WB £9666–£9834
Day £4485–£5994

CHESTER

ABBEY GATE COLLEGE
Saighton Grange, Saighton, Chester, Cheshire CH3 6EN
Tel: (01244) 332077
Fax: (01244) 335510
Email: bursar@abbeygatecollege.co.uk
Head: Mr E W Mitchell
Type: Co-educational Day 4–18
No of pupils: B223 G181
Fees: (September 05)
Day £4560–£7788

ABBEY GATE SCHOOL
Victoria Road, Chester, Cheshire CH2 2AY
Tel: (01244) 380552
Email: abbeygateschool@talk21.com
Head: Mrs S Fisher
Type: Co-educational Day 2–11
Flexi-boarding available
No of pupils: B45 G50
Fees: (September 04)
Day £4498–£4798

THE FIRS SCHOOL
45 Newton Lane, Chester, Cheshire CH2 2HJ
Tel: (01244) 322443
Fax: (01244) 400450
Email: firsschool.admin@btopenworld.com
Head: Mrs M Denton
Type: Co-educational Day 4–11
No of pupils: B134 G81
Fees: (September 05) Day £4995

HAMMOND SCHOOL
Hoole Bank House, Mannings Lane, Chester, Cheshire CH2 4ES
Tel: (01244) 305350
Fax: (01244) 305351
Email: enquiries@thehammondschool.co.uk
Head: Mrs M P Dangerfield
Type: Co-educational Day and Boarding 11–18
No of pupils: B50 G170
No of boarders: F59
Fees: (September 05)
FB £14085–£18360
Day £7155–£11430

THE KING'S SCHOOL
Wrexham Road, Chester, Cheshire CH4 7QL
Tel: (01244) 689500
Fax: (01244) 689501
Email: admissions@kingschester.co.uk
Head: Mr T J Turvey
Type: Co-educational Day 7–18
No of pupils: B699 G117
Fees: (September 04)
Day £5685–£7425

MERTON HOUSE (DOWNSWOOD)
Downswood Drive, West Bank, Off Abbots Park, Chester, Cheshire CH1 4BD
Tel: (01244) 377165
Fax: (01244) 374569
Email: mertonhousesch@aol.com
Head: Mrs M Webb
Type: Co-educational Day 3–11
No of pupils: B58 G82
Fees: (September 03)
Day £3600–£3900

THE QUEEN'S SCHOOL
City Walls Road, Chester, Cheshire CH1 2NN
Tel: (01244) 312078
Fax: (01244) 321507
Email: secretary@queens.cheshire.sch.uk
Head: Mrs C M Buckley
Type: Girls Day 4–18
No of pupils: 600
Fees: (September 05)
Day £5265–£7935

HOLMES CHAPEL

TERRA NOVA SCHOOL
Jodrell Bank, Holmes Chapel, Cheshire CW4 8BT
Tel: (01477) 571251
Fax: (01477) 571646
Email: enquiries@tnschool.org
Head: Mr N Johnson
Type: Co-educational Boarding and Day 3–13 Flexi-boarding available
No of pupils: B143 G101
No of boarders: F7 W17
Fees: (September 05)
F/WB £ £12510
Day £2760–£10080

KNUTSFORD

YORSTON LODGE SCHOOL
18 St John's Road, Knutsford, Cheshire WA16 0DP
Tel: (01565) 633177
Fax: (01565) 631245
Email: headmaster@yorstonlodgeschool.co.uk
Head: Mr R Edgar
Type: Co-educational Day 2–11
No of pupils: B63 G61
Fees: (September 03)
Day £2250–£2950

MACCLESFIELD

BEECH HALL SCHOOL
Beech Hall Drive, Tytherington, Macclesfield, Cheshire SK10 2EG
Tel: (01625) 422192
Fax: (01625) 502424
Email: secretary@beechhallschool.freeserve.co.uk
Head: Mr M Atkins
Type: Co-educational Day 4–13 (Kindergarten 1–5)
No of pupils: B130 G62
Fees: (September 03)
Day £3990–£6120

THE KING'S SCHOOL
Macclesfield, Cheshire SK10 1DA
Tel: (01625) 260000
Fax: (01625) 260022
Email: mail@kingsmac.co.uk
Head: Dr S Coyne
Type: Co-educational Day 3–18 (Single-sex ed 11–16)
No of pupils: B800 G600
Fees: (September 04)
Day £4410–£6600

MACCLESFIELD PREPARATORY SCHOOL
142 Chester Road, Macclesfield, Cheshire SK11 8PX
Tel: (01625) 422315
Fax: (01625) 614434
Email: macprep@stormguard.co.uk
Head: Mr G Davies
Type: Co-educational Day 0–11
No of pupils: B35 G40
Fees: (September 03)
Day £3100–£3300

NORTHWICH

CRANSLEY SCHOOL
Belmont Hall, Great Budworth, Northwich, Cheshire CW9 6HN
Tel: (01606) 891747
Fax: (01606) 892122
Email: cransleyschool@btinternet.com
Head: Mrs J E Jones
Type: Girls Day 3–16 (Boys 3–11)
No of pupils: B23 G137
Fees: (September 04)
Day £2835–£6459

THE GRANGE SCHOOL
Bradburns Lane, Hartford, Northwich, Cheshire CW8 1LU
Tel: (01606) 74007
Fax: (01606) 784581
Email: office@grange.org.uk
Head: Mr C P Jeffery
Type: Co-educational Day 4–18
No of pupils: B574 G539
Fees: (September 05)
Day £5175–£6915

SALE

CHRIST THE KING SCHOOL
The King's Centre, Raglan Road, Sale, Cheshire M33 4AQ
Tel: (0161) 969 1906
Fax: (0161) 905 1586
Email: info@ctks.org.uk
Head: Mr D Baynes
Type: Co-educational Day 5–16
No of pupils: B25 G27
Fees: (September 03) Day £3000

FOREST PARK SCHOOL
Lauriston House, 27 Oakfield, Sale, Cheshire M33 6NB
Tel: (0161) 973 4835
Fax: (0161) 282 9021
Email: post@forestparkschool.freeserve.co.uk
Head: Mr L B R Groves
Type: Co-educational Day 3–11
No of pupils: B80 G60
Fees: (September 05)
Day £4086–£4473

SANDBACH

NORFOLK HOUSE PREPARATORY & KIDS CORNER NURSERY
Norfolk House, 120 Congleton Road, Sandbach, Cheshire CW11 1HF
Tel: (01270) 759257
Fax: (01270) 753519
Email: post@norfolkhouse.net
Head: Mrs P M Jones
Type: Co-educational Day 0–11
No of pupils: B42 G43
Fees: (September 04) Day £3600

SOUTH WIRRAL

MOSTYN HOUSE SCHOOL†
Parkgate, Neston, South Wirral, Cheshire CH64 6SG
Tel: (0151) 336 1010
Fax: (0151) 353 1040
Email: enquiries@mostynhouse.co.uk
Head: Miss S M T Grenfell
Type: Co-educational Day 4–18
No of pupils: B139 G76
Fees: (September 05)
Day £5850–£8985

STALYBRIDGE

TRINITY SCHOOL
Birbeck Street, Stalybridge, Cheshire SK15 1SH
Tel: (0161) 303 0674
Head: Mr W R Evans
Type: Co-educational Day 4–18
No of pupils: B67 G64
Fees: (September 03) Day £3840

STOCKPORT

BRABYNS SCHOOL
34–36 Arkwright Road, Marple, Stockport, Cheshire SK6 7DB
Tel: (0161) 427 2395
Fax: (0161) 449 0704
Email: brabyns@indschool.org
Head: Mr L Sanders
Type: Co-educational Day 2–11
No of pupils: B57 G59
Fees: (September 04)
Day £2985–£4197

HILLCREST GRAMMAR SCHOOL
Beech Avenue, Stockport, Cheshire SK3 8HB
Tel: (0161) 480 0329
Fax: (0161) 476 2814
Email: headmaster@hillcrest.stockport.sch.uk
Head: Mr D K Blackburn
Type: Co-educational Day 3–16
No of pupils: B198 G145
Fees: (September 04) Day £3927–£5388

ORIEL BANK
Devonshire Park Road, Davenport, Stockport, Cheshire SK2 6JP
Tel: (0161) 483 2935
Fax: (0161) 456 5990
Email: secretary@orielbank.org
Head: Mr R A Bye
Type: Girls Day 3–16
No of pupils: 180
Fees: (September 04) Day £3690–£6057

ST CATHERINE'S PREPARATORY SCHOOL
Hollins Lane, Marple Bridge, Stockport, Cheshire SK6 5BB
Tel: (0161) 449 8800
Fax: (0161) 449 8181
Email: info@stcatherinesprep.stockport.sch.uk
Head: Mrs R A Brierley
Type: Co-educational Day 3–11
No of pupils: B61 G88
Fees: (September 05) Day £4350

STELLA MARIS JUNIOR SCHOOL
St Johns Road, Heaton Mersey, Stockport, Cheshire SK4 3BR
Tel: (0161) 432 0532
Fax: (0161) 432 9440
Email: office@stellamaris.stockport.sch.uk
Head: Mrs I L Gannon
Type: Co-educational Day 4–11
No of pupils: B32 G40
Fees: (September 04) Day £3300–£3675

STOCKPORT GRAMMAR SCHOOL
Buxton Road, Stockport, Cheshire SK2 7AF
Tel: (0161) 456 9000
Fax: (0161) 419 2407
Email: sgs@stockportgrammar.co.uk
Head: Mr A H Chicken
Type: Co-educational Day 4–18
No of pupils: B768 G664
Fees: (September 05) Day £5355–£6957

WILMSLOW

POWNALL HALL SCHOOL
Carrwood Road, Wilmslow, Cheshire SK9 5DW
Tel: (01625) 523141
Fax: (01625) 525209
Email: genoffice@pownallhall.cheshire.sch.uk
Head: Mr J J Meadmore
Type: Co-educational Day 2–11
No of pupils: B134 G65
Fees: (September 05) Day £5025–£6990

WILMSLOW PREPARATORY SCHOOL
Grove Avenue, Wilmslow, Cheshire SK9 5EG
Tel: (01625) 524246
Fax: (01625) 536660
Email: secretary@wilmslowprep.co.uk
Head: Mrs H J Shaw
Type: Girls Day 2–11
No of pupils: 155
Fees: (September 05) Day £1854–£6540

CORNWALL

BUDE

ST PETROC'S SCHOOL
Ocean View Road, Bude, Cornwall EX23 8NJ
Tel: (01288) 352876
Fax: (01288) 352876
Email: office@stpetrocs.com
Head: Dr I T Whitehurst
Type: Co-educational Day 3–12 (Nursery from 3 mths)
No of pupils: B43 G40
Fees: (September 05) Day £4140–£6435

LAUNCESTON

ST JOSEPH'S SCHOOL
St Stephen's Hill, Launceston, Cornwall PL15 8HN
Tel: (01566) 772580
Fax: (01566) 775902
Email: registrar@stjosephs.eclipse.co.uk
Head: Dr Alan Doe
Type: Girls Day 3–16 (Boys 3–11)
No of pupils: B31 G160
Fees: (September 04) Day £766–£6915

NEWQUAY

WHEELGATE HOUSE SCHOOL
Trevowah Road, Crantock, Newquay, Cornwall TR8 5RU
Tel: (01637) 830680
Fax: (01637) 830680
Head: Mrs G Wilson
Type: Co-educational Day 3–12
No of pupils: B25 G27
Fees: (September 03) Day £2000–£3000

PAR

ROSELYON
St Blazey Road, Par, Cornwall
PL24 2HZ
Tel: (01726) 812110
Fax: (01726) 812110
Email: office@roselyonsch.fsnet.co.uk
Head: Mr S C Bradley
Type: Co-educational Day 2–11
No of pupils: B38 G45
Fees: (September 05)
Day £5096–£5510

PENZANCE

THE BOLITHO SCHOOL
Polwithen, Penzance, Cornwall
TR18 4JR
Tel: (01736) 363271
Fax: (01736) 330960
Email: enquiries@bolitho.cornwall.sch.uk
Head: Mr D Dobson
Type: Co-educational Day and Boarding 4–18 Flexi-boarding available
No of pupils: B167 G137
No of boarders: F41 W45
Fees: (September 05)
FB £13800–£15900
WB £12000–£14400
Day £4500–£9000

REDRUTH

HIGHFIELDS PRIVATE SCHOOL
Cardrew Lane, Redruth, Cornwall
TR15 1SY
Tel: (01209) 210665
Fax: (01209) 210667
Email: highfieldschool@aol.com
Head: Mrs M D Haddy
Type: Co-educational Day 4–16
Fees: (September 05) Day £3600

ST IVES

ST IA SCHOOL
St Ives Road, Carbis Bay, St Ives, Cornwall TR26 2SF
Tel: (01736) 796963
Email: betsan@hill3129.freeserve.co.uk
Head: Miss B R Hill
Type: Co-educational Day 3–11
No of pupils: B10 G8
Fees: (September 04)
Day £1350–£1470

TRURO

POLWHELE HOUSE SCHOOL
Newquay Road, Truro, Cornwall
TR4 9AE
Tel: (01872) 273011
Fax: (01872) 273011
Email: polwhele@talk21.com
Head: Mr J Mason
Type: Co-educational Day and Boarding 3–13 Flexi-boarding available
No of pupils: B96 G84
No of boarders: W15
Fees: (September 03)
WB £11040–£12285

ST PIRAN'S SCHOOL
Trelissick Road, Hayle, Truro, Cornwall TR27 4HY
Tel: (01736) 752612
Fax: (01736) 752612
Email: office@stpirans.fsbusiness.co.uk
Head: Mr D Wilson
Type: Co-educational Day 3–16
No of pupils: B45 G45
Fees: (September 05)
Day £3480–£4500

TRURO HIGH SCHOOL
Falmouth Road, Truro, Cornwall
TR1 2HU
Tel: (01872) 272830
Fax: (01872) 279393
Email: admin@trurohigh.co.uk
Head: Mr M McDowell
Type: Girls Boarding and Day 3–18 (Boys 3–5) Flexi-boarding available
No of pupils: B2 G463
No of boarders: F38 W10
Fees: (September 05)
FB £14901–£15429
WB £14706–£15234
Day £3405–£8184

TRURO SCHOOL PREPARATORY SCHOOL
Highertown, Truro, Cornwall
TR1 3QN
Tel: (01872) 243120
Fax: (01872) 222377
Email: enquiries@truroprep.com
Head: Mr M Lovett
Type: Co-educational Day 3–11
No of pupils: B132 G76
Fees: (September 05)
Day £1745–£2553

TRURO SCHOOL
Trennick Lane, Truro, Cornwall
TR1 1TH
Tel: (01872) 272763
Fax: (01872) 223431
Email: enquiries@truro-school.cornwall.sch.uk
Head: Mr P K Smith
Type: Co-educational Day and Boarding 11–18 Flexi-boarding available
No of pupils: B507 G315
No of boarders: F93
Fees: (September 04) FB £15669
Day £8034

CUMBRIA

BARROW-IN-FURNESS

CHETWYNDE SCHOOL*

Croslands, Rating Lane, Barrow-in-Furness, Cumbria LA13 0NY
Tel: (01229) 824210
Fax: (01229) 871440
Email: info@chetwynde.cumbria.sch.uk
Head: Mrs I Nixon
Type: Co-educational Day 3–18
Fees: (September 04)
Day £4245–£4599

CARLISLE

AUSTIN FRIARS ST MONICA'S SCHOOL

Etterby Scaur, Carlisle, Cumbria CA3 9PB
Tel: (01228) 528042
Fax: (01228) 810327
Email: secretary@austinfriars.cumbria.sch.uk
Head: Mr C J Lumb
Type: Co-educational Day 3–18
No of pupils: B301 G205
Fees: (September 05)
Day £4140–£8607

LIME HOUSE SCHOOL*†

Holm Hill, Dalston, Carlisle, Cumbria CA5 7BX
Tel: (01228) 710225
Fax: (01228) 710508
Email: lhsoffice@aol.com
Head: Mr N A Rice
Type: Co-educational Boarding and Day 4–18
No of pupils: B130 G80
No of boarders: F140 W10
Fees: (September 04) FB £12000
Day £6000

WELLSPRING CHRISTIAN SCHOOL

Cotehill, Carlisle, Cumbria CA4 0EA
Tel: (01228) 562023
Head: Mr A G Field
Type: Co-educational Day 3–18
No of pupils: B12 G8
Fees: (September 02)
Day £1300–£2340

KENDAL

HOLME PARK SCHOOL

Hill Top, New Hutton, Kendal, Cumbria LA8 0AE
Tel: (01539) 721245
Fax: (01539) 721245
Email: holmeparkschool@hotmail.com
Head: Ms V Curry
Type: Co-educational Day and Boarding 2–12 Flexi-boarding available
No of pupils: B50 G15
Fees: (September 04) Day £6300

KIRKBY LONSDALE

CASTERTON SCHOOL*

Kirkby Lonsdale, Cumbria LA6 2SG
Tel: (01524) 279200
Fax: (01524) 279208
Email: admissions@castertonschool.co.uk
Head: Dr P McLaughlin
Type: Girls Boarding and Day 3–18 (Day boys 3–11) Flexi-boarding available
No of pupils: B15 G355
No of boarders: F281
Fees: (September 04)
FB £13257–£16587
WB £12909–£13854
Day £4578–£9924

PENRITH

HUNTER HALL SCHOOL

Frenchfield, Penrith, Cumbria CA11 8UA
Tel: (01768) 891291
Fax: (01768) 899161
Email: office@hunterhall.cumbria.sch.uk
Head: Mr A J Short
Type: Co-educational Day 3–11
No of pupils: B68 G80
Fees: (September 04) Day £4779

SEASCALE

HARECROFT HALL SCHOOL

Gosforth, Seascale, Cumbria CA20 1HS
Tel: (01946) 725220
Fax: (01946) 725885
Email: harecroft.hall@btopenworld.com
Head: Mr P Block
Type: Co-educational Boarding and Day 3–16 Flexi-boarding available
No of pupils: B81 G36
No of boarders: F29 W3
Fees: (September 04)
FB £10371–£11364
WB £9900–£10932
Day £3330–£7224

SEDBERGH

SEDBERGH SCHOOL

Sedbergh, Cumbria LA10 5HG
Tel: (01539) 620535
Fax: (015242) 621301
Email: hm@sedberghschool.org
Head: Mr C H Hirst
Type: Co-educational Boarding and Day 13–18
No of pupils: B333 G113
No of boarders: F426
Fees: (September 05) FB £20700
Day £15420

ST BEES

ST BEES SCHOOL*†

St Bees, Cumbria CA27 0DS
Tel: (01946) 828010
Fax: (01946) 828011
Email: helen.miller@st-bees-school.co.uk
Head: Mr P J Capes
Type: Co-educational Boarding and Day 11–18 Flexi-boarding available
No of pupils: B189 G119
No of boarders: F88 W38
Fees: (September 05)
FB £14568–£20088
WB £11955–£17139
Day £9321–£12039

WIGTON

ST URSULAS CONVENT SCHOOL

Burnfoot, Wigton, Cumbria
CA7 9HL
Tel: (01697) 344359
Fax: (01697) 344420
Email: stursula@supanet.com
Head: Mrs C V Pearson
Type: Co-educational Day 2–11
No of pupils: B35 G33
Fees: (September 05) Day £3909

WINDERMERE

WINDERMERE ST ANNE'S*

Windermere, Cumbria LA23 1NW
Tel: (01539) 446164
Fax: (01539) 488414
Email: office@wsaschool.com
Head: Miss W A Ellis
Type: Co-educational Boarding and Day 11–18
No of pupils: B129 G145
No of boarders: F83 W44
Fees: (September 05)
FB £16005–£18000
WB £15120–£17100
Day £9000–£9966

DERBYSHIRE

ASHBOURNE

ASHBOURNE PNEU SCHOOL

St Monica's House, Windmill Lane, Ashbourne, Derbyshire
DE6 1EY
Tel: (01335) 343294
Fax: (01335) 343294
Head: Mrs M A Broadbent
Type: Co-educational Day 0–13
No of pupils: 60
Fees: (September 02)
Day £1350–£4575

BAKEWELL

ST ANSELM'S

Bakewell, Derbyshire DE45 1DP
Tel: (01629) 812734
Fax: (01629) 812742
Email: headmaster@anselms.co.uk
Head: Mr R J Foster
Type: Co-educational Boarding and Day 7–13 Flexi-boarding available
No of pupils: B120 G80
No of boarders: F96
Fees: (September 05) FB £14790
Day £10020–£12600

CHESTERFIELD

BARLBOROUGH HALL SCHOOL

Barlborough, Chesterfield, Derbyshire S43 4TJ
Tel: (01246) 810511
Fax: (01246) 570605
Email: barlborough.hall@virgin.net
Head: Mrs W E Parkinson
Type: Co-educational Day 3–11
No of pupils: B140 G115
Fees: (September 05)
Day £4590–£6630

ST JOSEPH'S CONVENT

42 Newbold Road, Chesterfield, Derbyshire S41 7PL
Tel: (01246) 232392
Fax: (01246) 201965
Email: info@st-josephs-convent-sch.org.uk
Head: Mrs B Deane
Type: Co-educational Day 2–11
No of pupils: B69 G66
Fees: (September 04)
Day £3690–£4140

ST PETER & ST PAUL SCHOOL

Brambling House, Hady Hill, Chesterfield, Derbyshire S41 0EF
Tel: (01246) 278522
Fax: (01246) 273861
Email: head@stpeterandstpaul.fsnet.co.uk
Head: Mr A Lamb
Type: Co-educational Day 2–11
No of pupils: B102 G107
Fees: (September 04) Day £4515

DERBY

DERBY GRAMMAR SCHOOL FOR BOYS

Rykneld Road, Littleover, Derby, Derbyshire DE23 4BX
Tel: (01332) 523027
Fax: (01332) 518670
Email: headmaster@derbygrammar.co.uk
Head: Mr R D Waller
Type: Boys Day 7–18
No of pupils: 310
Fees: (September 03)
Day £5940–£7425

DERBY HIGH SCHOOL
Hillsway, Littleover, Derby, Derbyshire DE23 3DT
Tel: (01332) 514267
Fax: (01332) 516085
Email: headsecretary@derbyhigh.derby.sch.uk
Head: Mr C T Callaghan
Type: Co-educational Day Boys 3–11 Girls 3–18
No of pupils: B77 G464
Fees: (September 04)
Day £5460–£7185

EMMANUEL SCHOOL
Juniper Lodge, 43 Kedleston Road, Derby, Derbyshire DE22 1FP
Tel: (01332) 340505
Fax: (01332) 299168
Email: emmanuelschool@supanet.com
Head: Mr A Townsend
Type: Co-educational Day 3–11
No of pupils: B28 G23
Fees: (September 05)
Day £1440–£2316

FOREMARKE HALL SCHOOL
Milton, Derby, Derbyshire DE65 6EJ
Tel: (01283) 703269
Fax: (01283) 701185
Email: registrar@foremarke.org.uk
Head: Mr P Brewster
Type: Co-educational Day and Boarding 3–13 Flexi-boarding available
No of pupils: B277 G155
No of boarders: F51 W29
Fees: (September 04)
F/WB £ £12750 Day £5775–£9525

MORLEY HALL PREPARATORY SCHOOL
Hill House, Morley Road, Oakwood, Derby, Derbyshire DE21 4QZ
Tel: (01332) 674501
Email: julie.lee@morleyhall-school.co.uk
Head: Mrs R N Hassell
Type: Co-educational Day 3–11
No of pupils: B35 G37
Fees: (September 02)
Day £2313–£3321

OCKBROOK SCHOOL
The Settlement, Ockbrook, Derby, Derbyshire DE72 3RJ
Tel: (01332) 673532
Fax: (01332) 665184
Head: Miss D P Bolland
Type: Girls Day and Boarding 3–18 Flexi-boarding available
No of pupils: B40 G460
No of boarders: F18
Fees: (September 03)
F/WB £ £11592 Day £4920–£6297

THE OLD VICARAGE SCHOOL
11 Church Lane, Darley Abbey, Derby, Derbyshire DE22 1EW
Tel: (01332) 557130
Fax: (01332) 557130
Head: Mrs S L Mclean
Type: Co-educational Day 3–11
No of pupils: B44 G44
Fees: (September 03)
Day £4185–£4485

HEANOR

MICHAEL HOUSE STEINER SCHOOL
The Field, Shipley, Heanor, Derbyshire DE75 7JH
Tel: (01773) 718050
Fax: (01773) 711784
Email: admin@michaelhouseschool.co.uk
Head: Ms D Eccott
Type: Co-educational Day 4–16
No of pupils: B85 G80
Fees: (September 04)
Day £1485–£3735

ILKESTON

GATEWAY CHRISTIAN SCHOOL
Moor Lane, Dale Abbey, Ilkeston, Derbyshire DE7 4PP
Tel: (0115) 944 0609
Fax: (0115) 944 0609
Email: admin@gatewayschool.org.uk
Head: Mrs C Pearson
Type: Co-educational Day 3–11
No of pupils: B12 G21
Fees: (September 04) Day £2250

REPTON

REPTON SCHOOL
Repton, Derby, Derbyshire DE65 6FH
Tel: (01283) 559222
Fax: (01283) 559223
Email: registrar@repton.org.uk
Head: Mr R Holroyd
Type: Co-educational Boarding and Day 13–18
No of pupils: B343 G252
No of boarders: F460
Fees: (September 05) FB £21180
Day £15720

ST WYSTAN'S SCHOOL
High Street, Repton, Derbyshire DE65 6GE
Tel: (01283) 703258
Fax: (01283) 703258
Email: secretary@stwystans.org.uk
Head: Mr B Allen
Type: Co-educational Day 2–11
No of pupils: B61 G57
Fees: (September 05)
Day £2505–£5280

SPINKHILL

MOUNT ST MARY'S COLLEGE*
Spinkhill, Derbyshire S21 3YL
Tel: (01246) 433388
Fax: (01246) 435511
Email: headmaster@msmcollege.com
Head: Mr P G MacDonald
Type: Co-educational Boarding and Day 11–18 Flexi-boarding available
No of pupils: B248 G142
No of boarders: F65 W11
Fees: (September 05)
FB £11865–£15660
WB £10065–£13545
Day £7470–£8685

DEVON

ASHBURTON

SANDS SCHOOL
Greylands, 48 East Street,
Ashburton, Devon TQ13 7AX
Tel: (01364) 653666
Fax: (01364) 653666
Email: enquiry@sandsschool.demon.co.uk
Head: Mr S Bellamy
Type: Co-educational Day 11–17
No of pupils: B36 G34
Fees: (September 05) Day £6168

BARNSTAPLE

ST MICHAEL'S
Tawstock Court, Barnstaple,
Devon EX31 3HY
Tel: (01271) 343242
Fax: (01271) 346771
Email: mail@st-michaels-school.com
Head: Mr J W Pratt
Type: Co-educational Day 0–13
No of pupils: B114 G86
Fees: (September 04)
Day £2472–£8343

WEST BUCKLAND PREPARATORY SCHOOL
West Buckland, Barnstaple, Devon
EX32 0SX
Tel: (01598) 760629
Fax: (01598) 760546
Email: prephm@westbuckland.devon.sch.uk
Head: Mr A Moore
Type: Co-educational Day and Boarding 3–11 Flexi-boarding available
No of pupils: B120 G110
No of boarders: F8
Fees: (September 04)
FB £8625–£10080
Day £3285–£6030

WEST BUCKLAND SCHOOL
Barnstaple, Devon EX32 0SX
Tel: (01598) 760281
Fax: (01598) 760546
Email: headmaster@westbuckland.devon.sch.uk
Head: Mr J F Vick
Type: Co-educational Boarding and Day 3–18 Flexi-boarding available
No of pupils: B369 G314
No of boarders: F93
Fees: (September 05)
F/WB £ £10980–£15870
Day £4455–£9105

BEAWORTHY

SHEBBEAR COLLEGE
Shebbear, Beaworthy, Devon
EX21 5HJ
Tel: (01409) 281228
Fax: (01409) 281784
Email: info@shebbearcollege.co.uk
Head: Mr R S Barnes
Type: Co-educational Boarding and Day 3–18 Flexi-boarding available
No of pupils: B179 G91
No of boarders: F68 W16
Fees: (September 05)
FB £3660–£4930
WB £3060–£4080
Day £1310–£2640

BIDEFORD

EDGEHILL COLLEGE
Northdown Road, Bideford,
Devon EX39 3LY
Tel: (01237) 471701
Fax: (01237) 425981
Email: edgehill@btconnect.com
Head: Mr L Clark
Type: Co-educational Boarding and Day 2–18 Flexi-boarding available
No of pupils: B100 G100
No of boarders: F50 W3
Fees: (September 05)
FB £14850–£15600
WB £14220–£15060
Day £4005–£8565

GRENVILLE COLLEGE†
Bideford, Devon EX39 3JR
Tel: (01237) 472212
Fax: (01237) 477020
Email: office@grenvillecollege.co.uk
Head: Dr S J Wormleighton
Type: Co-educational Boarding and Day 2–19 Flexi-boarding available
No of pupils: B231 G181
No of boarders: F62 W18
Fees: (September 04)
FB £13272–£17004
WB £9948–£12716
Day £3549–£8463

DARTINGTON

RUDOLF STEINER SCHOOL
Hood Manor, Dartington, Devon
TQ9 6AB
Tel: (01803) 762528
Fax: (01803) 762528
Email: enquiries@steiner-south-devon.org
Head: Mr M Whitlock
Type: Co-educational Day 3–16
No of pupils: B139 G145
Fees: (September 04)
Day £2700–£3450

DAWLISH

LANHERNE NURSERY AND JUNIOR SCHOOL
18 Longlands, Dawlish, Devon
EX7 9NG
Tel: (01626) 863091
Email: lanherneschool@aol.com
Head: Mr R Hazeldene
Type: Co-educational Day 1–5
No of pupils: 58

EXETER

BENDARROCH SCHOOL
Aylesbeare, Exeter, Devon
EX5 2BY
Tel: (01395) 233553
Email: info@bendarroch.co.uk
Head: Mr N R Home
Type: Co-educational Day 5–13
No of pupils: B25 G25
Fees: (September 03)
Day £3315–£3765

BRAMDEAN SCHOOL
Richmond Lodge, Homefield Road, Heavitree, Exeter, Devon EX1 2QR
Tel: (01392) 273387
Fax: (01392) 439330
Email: info@bramdeanschool.com
Head: Mr D A Connett
Type: Co-educational Boarding and Day 3–18 Flexi-boarding available
No of pupils: B110 G90
No of boarders: W10
Fees: (September 04) WB £10152

ELM GROVE SCHOOL
Elm Grove Road, Topsham, Exeter, Devon EX3 0EQ
Tel: (01392) 873031
Email: elmgroveschool@btconnect.com
Head: Mrs K M Parsons and Mr B E Parsons
Type: Co-educational Day 2–8
No of pupils: B30 G30

EMMANUEL SCHOOL
36–38 Blackboy Road, Exeter, Devon EX4 6SZ
Tel: (01392) 258150
Fax: (01392) 258150
Email: emmanuelschool@tiscali.co.uk
Head: Mr D Rust
Type: Co-educational Day 5–16
No of pupils: B24 G27
Fees: (September 05) Day £2784

EXETER CATHEDRAL SCHOOL
The Chantry, Palace Gate, Exeter, Devon EX1 1HX
Tel: (01392) 255298
Fax: (01392) 422718
Email: exetercs@aol.com
Head: Mr B J McDowell
Type: Co-educational Day and Boarding 3–13 Flexi-boarding available
No of pupils: B112 G60
No of boarders: F25 W4
Fees: (September 04)
FB £10920–£11115
WB £10455–£10650
Day £4020–£6870

EXETER JUNIOR SCHOOL
Victoria Park Road, Exeter, Devon EX2 4NS
Tel: (01392) 258712
Fax: (01392) 498144
Email: admissions@exeterschool.org.uk
Head: Mrs A J Turner
Type: Co-educational Day 7–11
No of pupils: B99 G60
Fees: (September 05) Day £7155

EXETER SCHOOL
Victoria Park Road, Exeter, Devon EX2 4NS
Tel: (01392) 258710
Fax: (01392) 498144
Email: admissions@exeterschool.org.uk
Head: Mr R Griffin
Type: Co-educational Day 7–18
No of pupils: B583 G240
Fees: (September 05)
Day £7155–£7980

EXETER TUTORIAL COLLEGE
44/46 Magdalen Road, Exeter, Devon EX2 4TE
Tel: (01392) 278101
Fax: (01392) 494853
Email: info@tutorialcollege.com
Head: Mr K D Jack
Type: Co-educational Day 15+
No of pupils: B20 G20
Fees: (September 04)
Day £2805–£8415

HYLTON KINDERGARTEN & PRE-PREPARATORY SCHOOL
13A Lyndhurst Road, Exeter, Devon EX2 4PA
Tel: (01392) 254755
Fax: (01392) 435725
Email: info@hyltonschool.co.uk
Head: Mrs R C Leveridge
Type: Co-educational Day 2–8
No of pupils: 75
Fees: (September 04)
Day £466–£3300

MAGDALEN COURT SCHOOL
Mulberry House, Victoria Park Road, Exeter, Devon EX2 4NU
Tel: (01392) 494919
Fax: (01392) 494919
Email: admin@mcs-exeter.co.uk
Head: Mr J G Bushrod
Type: Co-educational Day 2–18
No of pupils: B85 G80
Fees: (September 04)
Day £3150–£6000

THE MAYNARD SCHOOL
Denmark Road, Exeter, Devon EX1 1SJ
Tel: (01392) 273417
Fax: (01392) 355999
Email: office@maynard.co.uk
Head: Dr D West
Type: Girls Day 7–18
No of pupils: 504
Fees: (September 05)
Day £6468–£8094

NEW SCHOOL
The Avenue, Exminster, Exeter, Devon EX6 8AT
Tel: (01392) 496122
Fax: (01392) 496122
Head: Mrs G Redman
Type: Co-educational Day 3–8
No of pupils: B32 G31
Fees: (September 04)
Day £2985–£3545

ST MARGARET'S SCHOOL
147 Magdalen Road, Exeter, Devon EX2 4TS
Tel: (01392) 273197
Fax: (01392) 251402
Email: mail@stmargarets-school.co.uk
Head: Miss R Edbrooke
Type: Girls Day 7–18
No of pupils: 380
Fees: (September 04)
Day £5994–£7242

ST WILFRID'S SCHOOL
29 St David's Hill, Exeter, Devon EX4 4DA
Tel: (01392) 276171
Fax: (01392) 438666
Email: office@stwilfrids.devon.sch.uk
Head: Mrs A E M Macdonald-Dent
Type: Co-educational Day 5–16
No of pupils: B75 G70
Fees: (September 04)
Day £3900–£5739

EXMOUTH

CASTLE DOWN SCHOOL
Littleham Road, Exmouth, Devon EX8 2RD
Tel: (01395) 269998
Fax: (01395) 279200
Head: Miss H Lee
Type: Co-educational Day 3–7
No of pupils: B23 G20
Fees: (September 03)
Day £1800–£2850

THE DOLPHIN SCHOOL
Raddenstile Lane, Exmouth, Devon EX8 2JH
Tel: (01395) 272418
Head: Mr Bill Gott
Type: Co-educational Day 3–11
No of pupils: B43 G42

ST PETER'S SCHOOL
Harefield, Lympstone, Exmouth, Devon EX8 5AU
Tel: (01395) 272148
Fax: (01395) 222410
Email: hmsec@stpetersprep.co.uk
Head: Mr R J Williams
Type: Co-educational Day and Boarding 3–13 Flexi-boarding available
No of pupils: B177 G82
No of boarders: W17
Fees: (September 05) WB £12090 Day £4665–£7950

HONITON

MANOR HOUSE SCHOOL
Springfield House, Honiton, Devon EX14 9TL
Tel: (01404) 42026
Fax: (01404) 41153
Email: office@manorhouseschoolhoniton.co.uk
Head: Mr S J Bage
Type: Co-educational Day 3–11
No of pupils: B85 G85
Fees: (September 04) Day £3360–£5100

NEWTON ABBOT

ABBOTSBURY SCHOOL
90 Torquay Road, Newton Abbot, Devon TQ12 2JD
Tel: (01626) 352164
Head: Mr R J Manley
Type: Co-educational Day 2–7
No of pupils: B50 G50
Fees: (September 05) Day £795–£2634

STOVER SCHOOL
Newton Abbot, Devon TQ12 6QG
Tel: (01626) 354505
Fax: (01626) 361475
Email: mail@stover.co.uk
Head: Mrs S Bradley
Type: Co-educational Day and Boarding 3–18 (Boys 2–11) Flexi-boarding available
No of pupils: B130 G380
No of boarders: F40 W38
Fees: (September 05) FB £12585–£16635 WB £11235–£14085 Day £1089–£2715

PAIGNTON

TOWER HOUSE SCHOOL
Fisher Street, Paignton, Devon TQ4 5EW
Tel: (01803) 557077
Fax: (01803) 557077
Email: twrhouse@aol.com
Head: Mr W M Miller
Type: Co-educational Day 2–16
No of pupils: B148 G135
Fees: (September 04) Day £3672–£5544

PLYMOUTH

FLETEWOOD SCHOOL
88 North Road East, Plymouth, Devon PL4 6AN
Tel: (01752) 663782
Fax: (01752) 663782
Email: headteacher@fletewoodschool.co.uk
Head: Mr J Martin
Type: Co-educational Day 3–11
No of pupils: B35 G35
Fees: (September 04) Day £2460

KING'S SCHOOL
Hartley Road, Mannamead, Plymouth, Devon PL3 5LW
Tel: (01752) 771789
Fax: (01752) 770826
Head: Mrs J Lee
Type: Co-educational Day 3–11
No of pupils: B84 G73
Fees: (September 04) Day £3300–£3975

PLYMOUTH COLLEGE
Ford Park, Plymouth, Devon PL4 6RN
Tel: (01752) 203300
Fax: (01752) 203246
Email: admin@plymouthcollege.com
Head: Mr A J Morsley
Type: Co-educational Day and Boarding 11–18
No of pupils: B360 G274
No of boarders: F90 W11
Fees: (September 05) FB £16872–£17349 WB £16782–£17259 Day £8592–£9069

ST DUNSTAN'S ABBEY-PLYMOUTH COLLEGE JUNIOR SCHOOL
The Millfields, Plymouth, Devon PL1 3SL
Tel: (01752) 201352
Fax: (01752) 201351
Email: juniorschool@plymouthcollege.com
Head: Mr R P Jeynes
Type: Co-educational Day 3–11
No of pupils: B142 G127
Fees: (September 05) Day £4000–£6360

SIDMOUTH

ST JOHN'S SCHOOL†
Broadway, Sidmouth, Devon EX10 8RG
Tel: (01395) 513984
Fax: (01395) 514539
Email: nrp@stjohndevon.demon.co.uk
Head: Mrs Tessa Smith
Type: Co-educational Day and Boarding 2–13 Flexi-boarding available
No of pupils: B107 G103
No of boarders: F55 W5
Fees: (September 05) FB £12141–£13779 WB £12141 Day £5130–£7164

TAVISTOCK

KELLY COLLEGE
Parkwood Road, Tavistock, Devon PL19 0HZ
Tel: (01822) 813100
Fax: (01822) 612050
Email: registrar@kellycollege.com
Head: Mr M S Steed
Type: Co-educational Boarding and Day 11–18 Flexi-boarding available
No of pupils: B217 G142
No of boarders: F86 W56
Fees: (September 05)
FB £17100–£20700
WB £15600–£19350
Day £9150–£12150

KELLY COLLEGE PREPARATORY SCHOOL
Hazeldon House, Parkwood Road, Tavistock, Devon PL19 0JS
Tel: (01822) 612919
Fax: (01822) 612919
Email: admin@kellycollegeprep.com
Head: Mr R Stevenson
Type: Co-educational Day and Boarding 2–11 Flexi-boarding available
No of pupils: B94 G85
No of boarders: F2 W6
Fees: (September 04) FB £13635 WB £12285 Day £4875–£5985

MOUNT HOUSE SCHOOL
Tavistock, Devon PL19 9JL
Tel: (01822) 612244
Fax: (01822) 610042
Email: mounthouse@aol.com
Head: Mr J R O Massey
Type: Co-educational Boarding and Day 3–13 Flexi-boarding available
No of pupils: B175 G75
No of boarders: F110
Fees: (September 03) FB £12870 Day £4590–£9660

TEIGNMOUTH

TRINITY SCHOOL
Buckeridge Road, Teignmouth, Devon TQ14 8LY
Tel: (01626) 774138
Fax: (01626) 771541
Email: headmaster@trinityschool.co.uk
Head: Mr C J Ashby
Type: Co-educational Day and Boarding 3–19 Flexi-boarding available
No of pupils: B309 G206
No of boarders: F10 W130
Fees: (September 05)
FB £14550–£16665
WB £14280–£16395
Day £5880–£7980

TIVERTON

BLUNDELL'S SCHOOL*
Tiverton, Devon EX16 4DN
Tel: (01884) 252543
Fax: (01884) 243232
Email: registrars@blundells.org
Head: Mr I R Davenport
Type: Co-educational Boarding and Day 11–18 Flexi-boarding available
No of pupils: B335 G230
No of boarders: F120 W280
Fees: (September 05)
FB £13755–£20475
WB £12435–£17940
Day £8220–£13200

ST AUBYN'S SCHOOL
Milestones House, Blundell's Road, Tiverton, Devon EX16 4NA
Tel: (01884) 252393
Fax: (01884) 232333
Email: staubyns@blundells.org
Head: Mr N A Folland
Type: Co-educational Day 3–11
No of pupils: B184 G164
Fees: (September 05)
Day £1395–£7035

TORBAY

GRAMERCY HALL SCHOOL
Churston Ferrers, Torbay, Devon TQ5 0HR
Tel: (01803) 844338
Fax: (01803) 846125
Email: gramercy@indschools.org
Head: Mr N Woolnough
Type: Co-educational Day 3–16 Flexi-boarding available
No of pupils: B132 G83
Fees: (September 03) Day £3840

TORQUAY

THE ABBEY SCHOOL
Hampton Court, St Marychurch, Torquay, Devon TQ1 4PR
Tel: (01803) 327868
Fax: (01803) 327868
Email: mail@abbeyschool.co.uk
Head: Mrs J Joyce
Type: Co-educational Day 0–11
No of pupils: B84 G67

STOODLEY KNOWLE SCHOOL
Ansteys Cove Road, Torquay, Devon TQ1 2JB
Tel: (01803) 293160
Fax: (01803) 214757
Email: headoffice@stoodleyknowle.fsnet.co.uk
Head: Sister Perpetua
Type: Girls Day 2–18
No of pupils: 280
Fees: (September 05)
Day £3165–£5760

TOTNES

PARK SCHOOL
Park Road, Dartington, Totnes, Devon TQ9 6EQ
Tel: (01803) 864588
Email: park@schooldartington.freeserve.co.uk
Head: Mr J Hawley-Higgs
Type: Co-educational Day 3–11
No of pupils: B29 G25
Fees: (September 03)
Day £798–£3291

ST CHRISTOPHERS SCHOOL
Mount Barton, Staverton, Totnes, Devon TQ9 6PF
Tel: (01803) 762202
Fax: (01803) 762202
Head: Mrs J E Kenyon
Type: Co-educational Day 3–11
No of pupils: B60 G40
Fees: (May 05) Day £2784–£4335

DORSET

BLANDFORD FORUM

BRYANSTON SCHOOL
Blandford Forum, Dorset DT11 0PX
Tel: (01258) 452411
Fax: (01258) 484661
Email: headmaster@bryanston.co.uk
Head: Ms S J Thomas
Type: Co-educational Boarding and Day 13–18
No of pupils: B380 G275
No of boarders: F588
Fees: (September 04) FB £21807 Day £17445

CLAYESMORE PREPARATORY SCHOOL†
Iwerne Minster, Blandford Forum, Dorset DT11 8PH
Tel: (01747) 811707
Fax: (01747) 811692
Email: clayesmore@aol.com
Head: Mr A Roberts-Wray
Type: Co-educational Boarding and Day 2–13 Flexi-boarding available
No of pupils: B206 G120
No of boarders: F40 W35
Fees: (September 05) F/WB £ £14025–£15180 Day £5103–£11415

CLAYESMORE SCHOOL*†
Iwerne Minster, Blandford Forum, Dorset DT11 8LL
Tel: (01747) 812122
Fax: (01747) 811343
Email: hmsec@clayesmore.com
Head: Mr M G Cooke
Type: Co-educational Boarding and Day 13–18
No of pupils: B241 G135
No of boarders: F218
Fees: (September 05) FB £20745 Day £15180

HANFORD SCHOOL
Childe Okeford, Blandford Forum, Dorset DT11 8HL
Tel: (01258) 860219
Fax: (01258) 861255
Email: hanfordsch@aol.com
Head: Mr N S Mackay
Type: Girls Boarding 7–13
No of pupils: 110
No of boarders: F100
Fees: (September 05) FB £14700 Day £11700

KNIGHTON HOUSE
Durweston, Blandford Forum, Dorset DT11 0PY
Tel: (01258) 452065
Fax: (01258) 450744
Email: enquiries@knighton-house.co.uk
Head: Mrs C L Renton
Type: Girls Day and Boarding 3–13 (Day boys 4–7) Flexi-boarding available
No of pupils: B10 G120
No of boarders: F24 W24
Fees: (September 05) F/WB £ £15423 Day £5865–£11589

MILTON ABBEY SCHOOL†
Blandford Forum, Dorset DT11 0BZ
Tel: (01258) 880484
Fax: (01258) 881194
Email: info@miltonabbey.co.uk
Head: Mr J Hughes-D'Aeth
Type: Co-educational Boarding and Day Boys 13–18 Girls 16–18
No of pupils: B205 G10
No of boarders: F184
Fees: (September 05) FB £22470 Day £16860

BOURNEMOUTH

THE PARK SCHOOL
Queen's Park South Drive, Bournemouth, Dorset BH8 9BJ
Tel: (01202) 396640
Fax: (01202) 392705
Email: headmaster.parkschool@virgin.net
Head: Mr C Cole
Type: Co-educational Day 4–11
No of pupils: B162 G116
Fees: (September 05) Day £4500–£6150

ST MARTIN'S SCHOOL
15 Stokewood Road, Bournemouth, Dorset BH3 7NA
Tel: (01202) 760744
Head: Mr T B T Shenton
Type: Co-educational Day 4–12
No of pupils: B50 G50
Fees: (September 04) Day £3000–£4200

ST THOMAS GARNET'S SCHOOL
Parkwood Road, Boscombe, Bournemouth, Dorset BH5 2BH
Tel: (01202) 420172 / Pre-school: 01202 431286
Fax: (01202) 773060
Head: Mr P R Gillings
Type: Co-educational Day 0–11
No of pupils: B75 G80
Fees: (September 04) Day £3750–£4800

TALBOT HEATH
Rothesay Road, Bournemouth, Dorset BH4 9NJ
Tel: (01202) 761881
Fax: (01202) 768155
Email: admissions@talbotheath.org.uk
Head: Mrs C Dipple
Type: Girls Day and Boarding 3–18 (Boys 3–7) Flexi-boarding available
No of pupils: B10 G628
No of boarders: F22 W6
Fees: (September 04) FB £14400 WB £14100 Day £2760–£8700

TALBOT HOUSE PREPARATORY SCHOOL
8 Firs Glen Road, Bournemouth, Dorset BH9 2LR
Tel: (01202) 510348
Fax: (01202) 775904
Email: admin.talbot@ntlworld.com
Head: Mrs C Oosthuizen and Mr M Broadway
Type: Co-educational Day 3–12
No of pupils: B66 G49
Fees: (September 04)
Day £2250–£4287

WENTWORTH COLLEGE*
College Road, Bournemouth, Dorset BH5 2DY
Tel: (01202) 423266
Fax: (01202) 418030
Email: enquiries@wentworthcollege.com
Head: Miss S Coe
Type: Girls Boarding and Day 11–18 Flexi-boarding available
No of pupils: 220
No of boarders: F40 W20
Fees: (September 05)
F/WB £ £15570 Day £9675

DORCHESTER

DORCHESTER PREPARATORY SCHOOL
25/26 Icen Way, Dorchester, Dorset DT1 1EP
Tel: (01305) 264925
Fax: (01305) 264925
Email: info@dorchesterprepschool.co.uk
Head: Dr C J Rattew
Type: Co-educational Day 3–18
No of pupils: B40 G40
Fees: (September 05)
Day £1500–£6960

SUNNINGHILL PREPARATORY SCHOOL
South Court, South Walks, Dorchester, Dorset DT1 1EB
Tel: (01305) 262306
Fax: (01305) 261254
Email: sunninghillschool@lineone.net
Head: Mr Alan Dickey
Type: Co-educational Day 3–13
No of pupils: B97 G94
Fees: (September 03)
Day £2505–£5520

POOLE

BUCKHOLME TOWERS
18 Commercial Road, Parkstone, Poole, Dorset BH14 0JW
Tel: (01202) 742871
Fax: (01202) 740754
Email: office@buckholme.dorset.sch.uk
Head: Mrs S Mercer
Type: Co-educational Day 3–12
No of pupils: B70 G70
Fees: (September 05)
Day £3777–£4521

UPLANDS SCHOOL
40 St Osmund's Road, Parkstone, Poole, Dorset BH14 9JY
Tel: (01202) 742626
Fax: (01202) 731037
Email: headteacher@uplands.poole.sch.uk
Head: Mrs L Shah
Type: Co-educational Day 2–16
No of pupils: B182 G102
Fees: (September 05)
Day £2814–£8700

YARRELLS SCHOOL
Yarrells House, Upton, Poole, Dorset BH16 5EU
Tel: (01202) 622229
Fax: (01202) 620870
Email: enquiries@yarrells.co.uk
Head: Mrs N A Covell
Type: Co-educational Day 2–13
No of pupils: B104 G119
Fees: (September 05)
Day £336–£7740

SHAFTESBURY

PORT REGIS SCHOOL
Motcombe Park, Shaftesbury, Dorset SP7 9QA
Tel: (01747) 852566
Fax: (01747) 854684
Email: office@portregis.com
Head: Mr P A E Dix
Type: Co-educational Boarding and Day 3–13 Flexi-boarding available
No of pupils: B229 G185
No of boarders: F149 W120
Fees: (September 05)
F/WB £ £18465
Day £6150–£14385

ST MARY'S SCHOOL
Shaftesbury, Dorset SP7 9LP
Tel: (01747) 854005
Fax: (01747) 851557
Email: head@st-marys-shaftesbury.co.uk
Head: Mrs M C McSwiggan
Type: Girls Boarding and Day 9–18
No of pupils: 324
No of boarders: F206
Fees: (September 05)
FB £18195–£19170
Day £12420–£13050

SHERBORNE

INTERNATIONAL COLLEGE, SHERBORNE SCHOOL*
Newell Grange, Sherborne, Dorset DT9 4EZ
Tel: (01935) 814743
Fax: (01935) 816863
Email: reception@sherborne-ic.net
Head: Dr C J Greenfield
Type: Co-educational Boarding 11–17
No of pupils: B80 G50
No of boarders: F140
Fees: (September 05)
FB £24810–£27060

ST ANTONY'S LEWESTON SCHOOLS
St Antony's Leweston, Sherborne, Dorset DT9 6EN
Tel: (01963) 210691
Fax: (01963) 210786
Email: admissions@leweston.dorset.sch.uk
Head: Mr H J MacDonald
Type: Girls Boarding and Day 2–18 (Boys 2–11) Flexi-boarding available
No of pupils: B16 G345
No of boarders: F99
Fees: (September 05) FB £18870 Day £12270

SHERBORNE PREPARATORY SCHOOL
Acreman Street, Sherborne, Dorset DT9 3NY
Tel: (01935) 812097
Fax: (01935) 813948
Email: sherborneprep@hotmail.com
Head: Mr P S Tait
Type: Co-educational Day and Boarding 2–13 Flexi-boarding available
No of pupils: B181 G77
No of boarders: F39 W11
Fees: (September 04) F/WB £ £14220–£14850 Day £2835–£10350

SHERBORNE SCHOOL
Abbey Road, Sherborne, Dorset DT9 3AP
Tel: (01935) 812249
Fax: (01935) 810426
Email: enquiries@sherborne.org
Head: Mr S F Eliot
Type: Boys Boarding 13–18
No of boarders: F520
Fees: (September 05) FB £22785 Day £17985

SHERBORNE SCHOOL FOR GIRLS
Bradford Road, Sherborne, Dorset DT9 3QN
Tel: (01935) 812245
Fax: (01935) 389445
Email: office@sherborne.com
Head: Mrs G Kerton-Johnson
Type: Girls Boarding and Day 11–18
No of pupils: 370
No of boarders: F340
Fees: (September 05) FB £22875 Day £16725

SWANAGE

THE OLD MALTHOUSE
Langton Matravers, Swanage, Dorset BH19 3HB
Tel: (01929) 422302
Fax: (01929) 422154
Email: office@oldmalthouseschool.co.uk
Head: Mr R A Keeble
Type: Co-educational Boarding and Day 3–13 Flexi-boarding available
No of pupils: B75 G25
No of boarders: W30
Fees: (September 05) WB £14985 Day £11385

WEYMOUTH

THORNLOW PREPARATORY SCHOOL
Connaught Road, Weymouth, Dorset DT4 0SA
Tel: (01305) 785703
Fax: (01305) 780976
Email: admin@thornlow.co.uk
Head: Mr R A Fowke
Type: Co-educational Day 3–13 Flexi-boarding available
No of pupils: B43 G35
Fees: (September 05) Day £1870

WIMBORNE

CANFORD SCHOOL
Wimborne, Dorset BH21 3AD
Tel: (01202) 847207
Fax: (01202) 881723
Email: admissions@canford.com
Head: Mr J D Lever
Type: Co-educational Boarding and Day 13–18
No of pupils: B373 G232
No of boarders: F401
Fees: (September 05) FB £22080 Day £16575

CASTLE COURT PREPARATORY SCHOOL
The Knoll House, Knoll Lane, Corfe Mullen, Wimborne, Dorset BH21 3RF
Tel: (01202) 694438
Fax: (01202) 659063
Email: office@castlecourt.com
Head: Mr R E T Nicholl
Type: Co-educational Day 3–13
No of pupils: B205 G121
Fees: (September 05) Day £5100–£11340

DUMPTON SCHOOL
Deans Grove House, Wimborne, Dorset BH21 7AF
Tel: (01202) 883818
Fax: (01202) 848760
Email: headmaster@dumpton.com
Head: Mr A W Browning
Type: Co-educational Day 2–13
No of pupils: B180 G102
Fees: (September 05) Day £5985–£10755

COUNTY DURHAM

BARNARD CASTLE

BARNARD CASTLE SCHOOL
Barnard Castle, County Durham DL12 8UN
Tel: (01833) 690222
Fax: (01833) 638985
Email: secretary@barneyschool.org.uk
Head: Mr D H Ewart
Type: Co-educational Boarding and Day 4–18 Flexi-boarding available
No of pupils: B443 G248
No of boarders: F194
Fees: (September 05)
F/WB £ £11577–£15393
Day £3909–£8940

DARLINGTON

HURWORTH HOUSE SCHOOL
The Green, Hurworth-on-Tees, Darlington, County Durham DL2 2AD
Tel: (01325) 720645
Fax: (01325) 720122
Email: info@hurworthhouse.co.uk
Head: Mr C R T Fenwick
Type: Boys Day 3–18
No of pupils: B193 G22
Fees: (September 03)
Day £2985–£6765

POLAM HALL
Grange Road, Darlington, County Durham DL1 5PA
Tel: (01325) 463383
Fax: (01325) 383539
Email: information@polamhall.com
Head: Miss M Green
Type: Girls Boarding and Day 4–18 Flexi-boarding available
No of pupils: 430
No of boarders: F50 W10
Fees: (September 05)
FB £13680–£16875
WB £13230–£16425
Day £4335–£8760

RAVENTHORPE PREPARATORY SCHOOL
96 Carmel Road North, Darlington, County Durham DL3 8JB
Tel: (01325) 463373
Fax: (01325) 353086
Email: admin@raventhorpe.org.uk
Head: Mr K I Parker
Type: Co-educational Day 3–11
No of pupils: B55 G56
Fees: (September 05)
Day £2820–£3690

DURHAM

BOW SCHOOL
South Road, Durham, County Durham DH1 3LS
Tel: (0191) 384 8233
Fax: (0191) 384 1371
Email: office@bowschool.co.uk
Head: Mr R N Baird
Type: Boys Day 3–13
No of pupils: 125
Fees: (September 05)
Day £4332–£7995

THE CHORISTER SCHOOL
Durham, County Durham DH1 3EL
Tel: (0191) 384 2935
Fax: (0191) 383 1275
Email: head@choristers.durham.sch.uk
Head: Mr I Hawksby
Type: Co-educational Day and Boarding 4–13
No of pupils: B143 G46
No of boarders: F25 W5
Fees: (September 04)
F/WB £ £5790–£10950
Day £5232–£7485

DURHAM HIGH SCHOOL FOR GIRLS
Farewell Hall, Durham, County Durham DH1 3TB
Tel: (0191) 384 3226
Fax: (0191) 386 7381
Email: headmistress@dhsfg.org.uk
Head: Mrs A J Templeman
Type: Girls Day 3–18
No of pupils: 592
Fees: (September 04)
Day £4905–£7305

DURHAM SCHOOL
Quarryheads Lane, Durham, County Durham DH1 4SZ
Tel: (0191) 386 4783
Fax: (0191) 383 1025
Email: enquiries@durhamschool.co.uk
Head: Mr N G Kern
Type: Co-educational Day and Boarding 11–18 Flexi-boarding available
No of pupils: B284 G102
No of boarders: F44 W21
Fees: (September 04) FB £17496
WB £14994 Day £7995–£11496

ESSEX

BILLERICAY

ST JOHN'S SCHOOL
Stock Road, Billericay, Essex CM12 0AR
Tel: (01277) 623070
Fax: (01277) 651288
Email: bursarstjohns@aol.com
Head: Mrs F Armour
Type: Co-educational Day 3–16
No of pupils: B260 G185
Fees: (September 04)
Day £3435–£6495

BRENTWOOD

BRENTWOOD SCHOOL
Ingrave Road, Brentwood, Essex CM15 8AS
Tel: (01277) 243243
Fax: (01277) 243299
Email: headmaster@brentwood.essex.sch.uk
Head: Mr D I Davies
Type: Co-educational Day and Boarding 3–18 (Single-sex ed 11–16)
No of pupils: B898 G599
No of boarders: F52 W18
Fees: (September 05)
F/WB £ £18954 Day £10941

HERINGTON HOUSE SCHOOL
Mount Avenue, Hutton, Brentwood, Essex CM13 2NS
Tel: (01277) 211595
Fax: (01277) 200404
Head: Mr R Dudley-Cooke
Type: Co-educational Day 3–11
No of pupils: B43 G92
Fees: (September 03)
Day £3150–£6210

URSULINE PREPARATORY SCHOOL
Old Great Ropers, Great Ropers Lane, Warley, Brentwood, Essex CM13 3HR
Tel: (01277) 227152
Fax: (01277) 202559
Email: rozdownes@ursulineprepwarley.co.uk
Head: Mrs P M Wilson
Type: Co-educational Day 3–11
No of pupils: B74 G81
Fees: (September 05)
Day £1155–£2150

WOODLANDS SCHOOL
Warley Street, Great Warley, Brentwood, Essex CM13 3LA
Tel: (01277) 211699
Fax: (01277) 232715
Email: ukinfo@woodlandsschools.co.uk
Head: Mr R O'Doherty
Type: Co-educational Day 3–11
No of pupils: B147 G134
Fees: (September 04)
Day £5535–£9090

BUCKHURST HILL

BRAESIDE SCHOOL FOR GIRLS
130 High Road, Buckhurst Hill, Essex IG9 5SD
Tel: (020) 8504 1133
Fax: (020) 8505 6675
Email: enquiries@braesideschool.co.uk
Head: Mrs C Naismith
Type: Girls Day 3–16
No of pupils: 212
Fees: (September 05)
Day £4650–£7320

THE DAIGLEN SCHOOL
68 Palmerston Road, Buckhurst Hill, Essex IG9 5LG
Tel: (020) 8504 7108
Fax: (020) 8502 9608
Email: admin@daiglenschool.co.uk
Head: Mrs M Bradfield
Type: Boys Day 4–11
No of pupils: 152
Fees: (September 04) Day £5490

LOYOLA PREPARATORY SCHOOL
103 Palmerston Road, Buckhurst Hill, Essex IG9 5NH
Tel: (020) 8504 7372
Fax: (020) 8504 7372
Email: office@loyola.essex.sch.uk
Head: Mr P G Nicholson
Type: Boys Day 3–11
No of pupils: 184
Fees: (September 03)
Day £3405–£5685

CHELMSFORD

ELM GREEN PREPARATORY SCHOOL
Parsonage Lane, Little Baddow, Chelmsford, Essex CM3 4SU
Tel: (01245) 225230
Fax: (01245) 226008
Email: admin@elmgreen.essex.sch.uk
Head: Ms A Milner
Type: Co-educational Day 4–11
No of pupils: B110 G110
Fees: (September 05) Day £6078

HEATHCOTE SCHOOL
Eves Corner, Danbury, Chelmsford, Essex CM3 4QB
Tel: (01245) 223131
Fax: (01245) 224568
Email: enquiries@heathcote.co.uk
Head: Mr K Gladwin
Type: Co-educational Day 2–11
No of pupils: B96 G88
Fees: (September 04)
Day £1050–£5250

NEW HALL SCHOOL
Boreham, Chelmsford, Essex CM3 3HS
Tel: (01245) 467588
Fax: (01245) 464348
Email: registrar@newhallschool.co.uk
Head: Mrs K Jeffrey
Type: Co-educational Boarding and Day 4–18 (Boys day 4–11)
Flexi-boarding available
No of pupils: B96 G624
No of boarders: F120
Fees: (September 05)
FB £15060–£18970
Day £6120–£12540

ST ANNE'S PREPARATORY SCHOOL
154 New London Road, Chelmsford, Essex CM2 0AW
Tel: (01245) 353488
Fax: (01245) 353488
Email: headmistress@stannesprep.essex.sch.uk
Head: Mrs H Guard
Type: Co-educational Day 3–11
No of pupils: B70 G90
Fees: (September 05)
FB £4650–£4920

ST CEDD'S SCHOOL
Maltese Road, Chelmsford, Essex CM1 2PB
Tel: (01245) 354380
Fax: (01245) 348635
Email: tthorogood@stcedds.org.uk
Head: Mr R J Mathrick
Type: Co-educational Day 4–11
No of pupils: B155 G170
Fees: (September 04)
Day £5070–£5475

WIDFORD LODGE
Widford Road, Chelmsford, Essex CM2 9AN
Tel: (01245) 352581
Fax: (01245) 281329
Email: enquiries@widfordlodge.co.uk
Head: Mr S C Trowell
Type: Co-educational Day 2–11
No of pupils: B77 G45
Fees: (September 04)
Day £4815–£6300

CHIGWELL

CHIGWELL SCHOOL*
High Road, Chigwell, Essex IG7 6QF
Tel: (020) 8501 5700
Fax: (020) 8500 6232
Email: hm@chigwell-school.org
Head: Mr D F Gibbs
Type: Co-educational Day and Boarding 7–18 Flexi-boarding available
No of pupils: B439 G291
No of boarders: F30 W10
Fees: (September 05) FB £16866
WB £15042–£15966
Day £7215–£11097

GURU GOBIND SINGH KHALSA COLLEGE
Roding Lane, Chigwell, Essex IG7 6BQ
Tel: (020) 8559 9160
Head: Mr A S Toor
Type: Co-educational Day 4–18
No of pupils: 200

COLCHESTER

COLCHESTER HIGH SCHOOL*
Wellesley Road, Colchester, Essex CO3 3HD
Tel: (01206) 573389
Fax: (01206) 573114
Email: info@colchesterhighschool.co.uk
Head: Mr D E Wood
Type: Co-educational Day Boys 3–16 Girls 3–11
No of pupils: B424 G62
Fees: (September 05)
Day £5220–£7080

HOLMWOOD HOUSE†
Chitts Hill, Lexden, Colchester, Essex CO3 9ST
Tel: (01206) 574305
Fax: (01206) 768269
Email: hst@holmwood.essex.sch.uk
Head: Mr H S Thackrah
Type: Co-educational Day and Boarding 4–13 Flexi-boarding available
No of pupils: B246 G151
No of boarders: W28
Fees: (September 05)
WB £12873–£14415
Day £6255–£11145

LITTLEGARTH SCHOOL
Horkesley Park, Nayland, Colchester, Essex CO6 4JR
Tel: (01206) 262332
Fax: (01206) 263101
Email: l.garth@virgin.net
Head: Mr P H Jones
Type: Co-educational Day 2–11
No of pupils: B178 G137
Fees: (September 05)
Day £1380–£6420

OXFORD HOUSE SCHOOL
2 Lexden Road, Colchester, Essex CO3 3NE
Tel: (01206) 576686
Fax: (01206) 577670
Email: ohs@supanet.com
Head: Mr R P Spendlove
Type: Co-educational Day 2–11
No of pupils: B65 G65
Fees: (September 05)
Day £2925–£5790

ST MARY'S SCHOOL
91 Lexden Road, Colchester, Essex CO3 3RB
Tel: (01206) 572544
Fax: (01206) 576437
Email: stmaryschoolcol@tinyonline.co.uk
Head: Mrs G M Mouser
Type: Girls Day 4–16
No of pupils: 450
Fees: (September 05)
Day £5175–£7215

DUNMOW

FELSTED PREPARATORY SCHOOL
Felsted, Dunmow, Essex CM6 3JL
Tel: (01371) 820252
Fax: (01371) 821443
Head: Mr E Newton
Type: Co-educational Boarding and Day 4–13
No of pupils: B213 G147
No of boarders: F19
Fees: (September 03) FB £13680
Day £4860–£10635

FELSTED SCHOOL
Felsted, Dunmow, Essex CM6 3LL
Tel: (01371) 822600
Fax: (01371) 822607
Email: hms@felsted.org
Head: Mr S C Roberts
Type: Co-educational Boarding and Day 13–18 Flexi-boarding available
No of pupils: B287 G166
No of boarders: F300
Fees: (September 05) FB £20541
Day £15372

EPPING

COOPERSALE HALL SCHOOL
Flux's Lane, off Steward's Green Road, Epping, Essex CM16 7PE
Tel: (01992) 577133
Fax: (01992) 571544
Email: info@coopersalehallschool.co.uk
Head: Mrs S Bowdler
Type: Co-educational Day 3–11
No of pupils: B150 G110
Fees: (September 05)
Day £2070–£6600

FRINTON-ON-SEA

ST PHILOMENA'S PREPARATORY SCHOOL

Hadleigh Road, Frinton-on-Sea, Essex CO13 9HQ
Tel: (01255) 674492
Fax: (01255) 674459
Email: contactus@stphilomenas.com
Head: Mrs B Buck
Type: Co-educational Day 3–11
No of pupils: 169
Fees: (September 04) Day £3750

HALSTEAD

GOSFIELD SCHOOL

Halstead Road, Gosfield, Halstead, Essex CO9 1PF
Tel: (01787) 474040
Fax: (01787) 478228
Email: principal@gosfieldschool.org.uk
Head: Mrs C Goodchild
Type: Co-educational Day and Boarding 2–18 Flexi-boarding available
No of pupils: B124 G71
No of boarders: F13 W13
Fees: (September 03)
FB £9300–£10500
Day £3870–£7080

ST MARGARET'S SCHOOL

Gosfield Hall Park, Gosfield, Halstead, Essex CO9 1SE
Tel: (01787) 472134
Fax: (01787) 478207
Email: enq@stmargaretsschool.com
Head: Mrs B Y Boyton-Corbett
Type: Co-educational Day 2–11
No of pupils: B117 G120
Fees: (September 04)
Day £4992–£6357

HARLOW

ST NICHOLAS SCHOOL

Hillingdon House, Hobbs Cross Road, Harlow, Essex CM17 0NJ
Tel: (01279) 429910
Fax: (01279) 450224
Head: Mr R Cusworth
Type: Co-educational Day 4–16
No of pupils: B180 G180
Fees: (September 04)
Day £5115–£6750

HORNCHURCH

GOODRINGTON SCHOOL

17 Walden Road, Emerson Park, Hornchurch, Essex RM11 2JT
Tel: (01708) 448349
Email: info@goodrington.org
Head: Mrs R Ellenby
Type: Co-educational Day 3–11
No of pupils: B69 G34
Fees: (September 05) Day £3150

ILFORD

BEEHIVE PREPARATORY SCHOOL

233 Beehive Lane, Redbridge, Ilford, Essex IG4 5ED
Tel: (020) 8550 3224
Head: Mr C J Beasant
Type: Co-educational Day 4–11
No of pupils: B50 G45
Fees: (September 02) Day £2850

CLARKS PREPARATORY SCHOOL

81/85 York Road, Ilford, Essex IG1 3AF
Tel: (020) 8478 6510
Fax: (020) 8553 1202
Head: Ms N C Woodman
Type: Co-educational Day 0–7
No of pupils: B46 G39
Fees: (September 03)
Day £4140–£7748

CRANBROOK COLLEGE

Mansfield Road, Ilford, Essex IG1 3BD
Tel: (020) 8554 1757
Fax: (020) 8518 0317
Email: info@cranbrookcollege.org.uk
Head: Mr C P Lacey
Type: Boys Day 4–16
No of pupils: 210
Fees: (September 04)
Day £4833–£6195

EASTCOURT INDEPENDENT SCHOOL

1 Eastwood Road, Goodmayes, Ilford, Essex IG3 8UW
Tel: (020) 8590 5472
Fax: (020) 8597 8313
Email: eastcourtschool@talk21.com
Head: Mrs C Redgrave
Type: Co-educational Day 4–11
No of pupils: B163 G177
Fees: (September 04) Day £3175

GLENARM COLLEGE

20 Coventry Road, Ilford, Essex IG1 4QR
Tel: (020) 8554 1760
Email: head@glenarmcollege.com
Head: Mr C Perkins
Type: Co-educational Day 3–11
No of pupils: B53 G80
Fees: (September 04) Day £5460

ILFORD PREPARATORY SCHOOL

Carnegie Buildings, 785 High Road, Ilford, Essex IG3 8RW
Tel: (020) 8599 8822
Fax: (020) 8597 2797
Email: head@ilfprep.demon.co.uk
Head: Mrs B P M Wiggs
Type: Co-educational Day 3–11
No of pupils: B100 G92
Fees: (September 04)
Day £3900–£4500

ILFORD URSULINE PREPARATORY SCHOOL

2 Coventry Road, Ilford, Essex IG1 4QR
Tel: (020) 8518 4050
Fax: (020) 8518 2060
Email: iups@ilfordursuline-prep.redbridge.sch.uk
Head: Mrs C Spinner
Type: Girls Day 3–11
Fees: (September 05) Day £5568

PARK SCHOOL FOR GIRLS

20 Park Avenue, Ilford, Essex IG1 4RS
Tel: (020) 8554 2466
Fax: (020) 8554 3003
Email: enquiries@parkschoolforgirls.co.uk
Head: Mrs N O'Brien
Type: Girls Day 7–18
No of pupils: 235
Fees: (September 03)
Day £4422–£5847

LEIGH-ON-SEA

COLLEGE SAINT-PIERRE

16 Leigh Road, Leigh-on-Sea, Essex SS9 1LE
Tel: (01702) 474164
Fax: (01702) 474164
Email: college@saintpierre.fsnet.co.uk
Head: Mr K Davies
Type: Co-educational Day 2–11
No of pupils: B60 G40
Fees: (September 04)
Day £4374–£5325

ST MICHAEL'S SCHOOL
198 Hadleigh Road, Leigh-on-Sea, Essex SS9 2LP
Tel: (01702) 478719
Fax: (01702) 710183
Email: info@stmichaelsschool.com
Head: Mrs L Morshead
Type: Co-educational Day 3–11
No of pupils: B158 G129
Fees: (September 04) Day £4815–£5430

LOUGHTON

OAKLANDS SCHOOL
8 Albion Hill, Loughton, Essex IG10 4RA
Tel: (020) 8508 3517
Fax: (020) 8508 4454
Email: info@oaklandsschool.co.uk
Head: Mrs P Simmonds
Type: Co-educational Day Boys 2–7 Girls 2–11
No of pupils: B62 G185
Fees: (September 05) Day £3570

MALDON

MALDON COURT PREPARATORY SCHOOL
Silver Street, Maldon, Essex CM9 4QE
Tel: (01621) 853529
Fax: (01621) 853529
Email: enquiries@maldoncourtschool.org
Head: Mrs L F Coyle
Type: Co-educational Day 4–11
No of pupils: B66 G57
Fees: (September 05) Day £5670–£5820

ROCHFORD

CROWSTONE PREPARATORY SCHOOL (SUTTON ANNEXE)
Fleethall Lane, Shopland Road, Rochford, Essex SS4 1LL
Tel: (01702) 540629
Head: Mr J P Thayer
Type: Co-educational Day 2–11
No of pupils: 110

ROMFORD

GIDEA PARK COLLEGE
Balgores House, 2 Balgores Lane, Romford, Essex RM2 5JR
Tel: (01708) 740381
Fax: (01708) 740381
Email: office@gideaparkcollege.co.uk
Head: Mrs V S Lee
Type: Co-educational Day 2–11
No of pupils: B99 G113
Fees: (September 04) Day £4881

IMMANUEL SCHOOL
Havering Grange Centre, Havering Road, Romford, Essex RM1 4HR
Tel: (01708) 764449
Head: Miss F Norcross
Type: Co-educational Day 3–16
No of pupils: B71 G54
Fees: (September 03) Day £3300

RAPHAEL INDEPENDENT SCHOOL
Park Lane, Romford, Essex RM11 1XY
Tel: (01708) 744735
Fax: (01708) 722432
Email: raphaelschool@hotmail.com
Head: Mr N W Malicka
Type: Co-educational Day 3–16
No of pupils: B117 G70
Fees: (September 05) Day £1705–£6405

ST MARY'S HARE PARK SCHOOL
South Drive, Gidea Park, Romford, Essex RM2 6HH
Tel: (01708) 761220
Fax: (01708) 380255
Email: harepark@btconnect.com
Head: Mrs K Karwacinski
Type: Co-educational Day 2–11
No of pupils: B70 G84
Fees: (September 05) Day £5190

SAFFRON WALDEN

DAME JOHANE BRADBURY'S SCHOOL
Ashdon Road, Saffron Walden, Essex CB10 2AL
Tel: (01799) 522348
Fax: (01799) 516762
Email: info@djbs.org
Head: Mrs Jane Crouch
Type: Co-educational Day 3–11
No of pupils: B148 G159
Fees: (September 04) Day £4506–£5970

FRIENDS' SCHOOL
Mount Pleasant Road, Saffron Walden, Essex CB11 3EB
Tel: (01799) 525351
Fax: (01799) 523808
Email: admin@friends.org.uk
Head: Mr A Waters
Type: Co-educational Boarding and Day 3–18 Flexi-boarding available
No of pupils: B209 G169
No of boarders: F32 W17
Fees: (September 05) FB £17370 WB £15870 Day £6150–£10770

SOUTHEND-ON-SEA

ALLEYN COURT PREPARATORY SCHOOL
Wakering Road, Great Wakering, Southend-on-Sea, Essex SS3 0PW
Tel: (01702) 582553
Fax: (01702) 584574
Email: acitsuite@tiscali.co.uk
Head: Mr R Chandler
Type: Co-educational Day 2–11
No of pupils: B175 G126
Fees: (September 04) Day £4029–£6996

THORPE HALL SCHOOL
Wakering Road, Southend-on-Sea, Essex SS1 3RD
Tel: (01702) 582340
Fax: (01702) 587070
Email: sec@thorpehall.southend.sch.uk
Head: Mr D W Gibbins
Type: Co-educational Day 2–16
No of pupils: B226 G139
Fees: (September 04) Day £4080–£5703

UPMINSTER

OAKFIELDS MONTESSORI SCHOOLS LTD
Harwood Hall, Harwood Hall Lane, Corbets Tey, Upminster, Essex RM14 2YG
Tel: (01708) 220117
Fax: (01708) 227911
Email: office@oakfieldsmontessorischool.org.uk
Head: Mrs K Malandreniotis
Type: Co-educational Day 2–11
No of pupils: B82 G90
Fees: (September 03) Day £2860–£4755

WESTCLIFF-ON-SEA

CROWSTONE PREPARATORY SCHOOL
121–123 Crowstone Road, Westcliff-on-Sea, Essex SS0 8LH
Tel: (01702) 346758
Fax: (01702) 390632
Email: info@crowstone.southend.sch.uk
Head: Mr J P Thayer
Type: Co-educational Day 2–11
No of pupils: B120 G110

ST HILDA'S SCHOOL
15 Imperial Avenue, Westcliff-on-Sea, Essex SS0 8NE
Tel: (01702) 344542
Fax: (01702)344547
Email: sthilda15@aol.com
Head: Mrs S O'Riordan
Type: Girls Day 2–16 (Boys 2–7)
No of pupils: 180
Fees: (September 03) Day £3687–£5169

WESTCLIFF PREPARATORY SCHOOL
100 Crowstone Road, Westcliff-on-Sea, Essex SSO 8LQ
Tel: (01702) 340664
Fax: (01702) 300057
Head: Mrs A K Moore
Type: Co-educational Day 3–11
No of pupils: 50
Fees: (September 03) Day £2790–£2840

WOODFORD GREEN

AVON HOUSE*†
490 High Road, Woodford Green, Essex IG8 0PN
Tel: (020) 8504 1749
Head: Mrs S Ferrari
Type: Co-educational Day 3–11
No of pupils: B117 G102
Fees: (September 05) Day £5280–£6360

BANCROFT'S SCHOOL
Woodford Green, Essex IG8 0RF
Tel: (020) 8505 4821
Fax: (020) 8559 0032
Email: office@bancrofts.essex.sch.uk
Head: Dr P R Scott
Type: Co-educational Day 7–18
No of pupils: B494 G449
Fees: (September 05) Day £7389–£9756

ST AUBYN'S SCHOOL
Bunces Lane, Woodford Green, Essex IG8 9DU
Tel: (020) 8504 1577
Fax: (020) 8504 2053
Email: registrar@staubyns.com
Head: Mr G James
Type: Co-educational Day 3–13
No of pupils: B286 G204
Fees: (April 04) Day £2475–£7020

WOODFORD GREEN PREPARATORY SCHOOL
Glengall Road, Snakes Lane West, Woodford Green, Essex IG8 0BZ
Tel: (020) 8504 5045
Fax: (020) 8505 0639
Email: head@wgps.co.uk
Head: Mr A J Blackhurst
Type: Co-educational Day 3–11
No of pupils: B190 G191
Fees: (September 05) Day £3240–£5460

GLOUCESTERSHIRE

CHELTENHAM

AIRTHRIE SCHOOL
29 Christ Church Road, Cheltenham, Gloucestershire GL50 2NY
Tel: (01242) 512837
Fax: (01242) 579583
Email: mail@airthrie-school.co.uk
Head: Mrs A E Sullivan
Type: Co-educational Day 3–11
No of pupils: B90 G90
Fees: (September 04) Day £3900–£5337

BERKHAMPSTEAD SCHOOL
Pittville Circus Road, Cheltenham, Gloucestershire GL52 2QA
Tel: (01242) 523263
Fax: (01242) 514114
Email: headberky@aol.com
Head: Mr T Owen
Type: Co-educational Day 3–11
No of pupils: B114 G124
Fees: (September 03) Day £3180–£5490

CHELTENHAM COLLEGE
Bath Road, Cheltenham, Gloucestershire GL53 7LD
Tel: (01242) 265600
Fax: (01242) 265630
Email: admissions@cheltcoll.gloucs.sch.uk
Head: Mr J S Richardson
Type: Co-educational Boarding and Day 13–18
No of pupils: B375 G191
No of boarders: F450
Fees: (September 05) FB £23280 Day £17445

CHELTENHAM COLLEGE JUNIOR SCHOOL
Thirlestaine Road, Cheltenham, Gloucestershire GL53 7AB
Tel: (01242) 522697
Fax: (01242) 265620
Email: ccjs@cheltcoll.gloucs.sch.uk
Head: Mr N I Archdale
Type: Co-educational Boarding and Day 3–13 Flexi-boarding available
No of pupils: B245 G185
No of boarders: F45
Fees: (September 05)
FB £12375–£16200
Day £5115–£12480

THE CHELTENHAM LADIES' COLLEGE
Bayshill Road, Cheltenham, Gloucestershire GL50 3EP
Tel: (01242) 520691
Fax: (01242) 227882
Email: enquiries@cheltladiescollege.org
Head: Mrs V Tuck
Type: Girls Boarding and Day 11–18
No of pupils: 850
No of boarders: F625
Fees: (September 05) FB £21729
Day £14589

DEAN CLOSE PREPARATORY SCHOOL*
Lansdown Road, Cheltenham, Gloucestershire GL51 6QS
Tel: (01242) 512217
Fax: (01242) 258005
Email: dcpsoffice@deanclose.org.uk
Head: Rev L Browne
Type: Co-educational Boarding and Day 2–13 Flexi-boarding available
No of pupils: B267 G205
No of boarders: F60
Fees: (September 05)
FB £12585–£15885
WB £8670–£12225
Day £7545–£11100

DEAN CLOSE SCHOOL*
Shelburne Road, Cheltenham, Gloucestershire GL51 6HE
Tel: (01242) 258044
Fax: (01242) 258003
Email: registrar@deanclose.org.uk
Head: Rev T M Hastie-Smith
Type: Co-educational Boarding and Day 13–18
No of pupils: B274 G208
No of boarders: F271
Fees: (September 05) FB £22485
Day £15885

THE RICHARD PATE SCHOOL
Southern Road, Leckhampton, Cheltenham, Gloucestershire GL53 9RP
Tel: (01242) 522086
Fax: (01242) 584035
Email: hm@richardpate.co.uk
Head: Mr E L Rowland
Type: Co-educational Day 3–11
No of pupils: B154 G128
Fees: (September 05)
Day £2040–£6480

ST EDWARD'S SCHOOL CHELTENHAM
Cirencester Road, Cheltenham, Gloucestershire GL53 8EY
Tel: (01242) 538600
Fax: (01242) 538160
Email: headmaster@stedwards.co.uk
Head: Dr A J Nash
Type: Co-educational Day 11–18
No of pupils: B258 G211
Fees: (September 04)
Day £7755–£9075

CINDERFORD

ST ANTHONYS SCHOOL
93 Bellevue Road, Cinderford, Gloucestershire GL14 2AA
Tel: (01594) 823558
Fax: (01594) 824799
Email: sister@gli42aafsnet.co.uk
Head: Sister M C McKenna
Type: Co-educational Day 3–11
No of pupils: B61 G61
Fees: (September 04) Day £2910

CIRENCESTER

HATHEROP CASTLE SCHOOL
Hatherop, Cirencester, Gloucestershire GL7 3NB
Tel: (01285) 750206
Fax: (01285) 750430
Email: admissions@hatheropcastle.co.uk
Head: Mr P Easterbrook
Type: Co-educational Boarding and Day 2–13 Flexi-boarding available
No of pupils: B134 G103
No of boarders: F19 W9
Fees: (September 05)
F/WB £ £12810–£13530
Day £5250–£8760

INGLESIDE PNEU SCHOOL
Beeches Road, Cirencester, Gloucestershire GL7 1BN
Tel: (01285) 654046
Fax: (01285) 655073
Email: info@ingleside.gloucs.sch.uk
Head: Mr Ma Anderson
Type: Co-educational Day 3–11
No of pupils: B50 G56
Fees: (September 04)
Day £3225–£3597

RENDCOMB COLLEGE*
Rendcomb, Cirencester, Gloucestershire GL7 7HA
Tel: (01285) 831213
Fax: (01285) 831121
Email: info@rendcomb.gloucs.sch.uk
Head: Mr Gerry Holden
Type: Co-educational Boarding and Day 3–18 Flexi-boarding available
No of pupils: B199 G176
No of boarders: F150
Fees: (September 05)
F/WB £ £14190–£18765
Day £4530–£14580

GLOUCESTER

GLOUCESTERSHIRE ISLAMIC SECONDARY SCHOOL FOR GIRLS
Sinope Street, off Widden Street, Gloucester, Gloucestershire GL1 4AW
Tel: (01452) 300465
Email: iacademy@yahoo.co.uk
Head: Mrs C Sandall
Type: Girls Day 11–16
No of pupils: 90
Fees: (September 04)
Day £700–£900

THE KING'S SCHOOL
Pitt Street, Gloucester, Gloucestershire GL1 2BG
Tel: (01452) 337337
Fax: (01452) 337314
Email: office@thekingsschool.co.uk
Head: Mr P R Lacey
Type: Co-educational Boarding and Day 3–18 Flexi-boarding available
No of pupils: B300 G220
No of boarders: W10
Fees: (September 02)
WB £13290–£14535

SCHOOL OF THE LION
The Judges Lodgings, Spa Road, Gloucester, Gloucestershire GL1 1UY
Tel: (01452) 381601
Fax: (01452) 553331
Email: office@schoolofthelion.org.uk
Head: Mr N Steele
Type: Co-educational Day 3–18
No of pupils: B21 G22

WYNSTONES SCHOOL
Church Lane, Whaddon, Gloucester, Gloucestershire GL4 0UF
Tel: (01452) 429220
Fax: (01452) 429221
Email: info@wynstones.com
Head: Mrs G Kaye
Type: Co-educational Day and Boarding 3–19 Flexi-boarding available
No of pupils: B151 G159
No of boarders: F5 W2
Fees: (September 05)
FB £9331–£9605
WB £7770–£8040
Day £2500–£5700

MORETON-IN-MARSH

THE DORMER HOUSE PNEU SCHOOL
High Street, Moreton-in-Marsh, Gloucestershire GL56 0AD
Tel: (01608) 650758
Fax: (01608) 652238
Email: dtrembath@aol.com
Head: Ms D A Trembath
Type: Co-educational Day 2–11
No of pupils: B54 G58
Fees: (September 03) Day £4044

KITEBROOK HOUSE
Moreton-in-Marsh, Gloucestershire GL56 0RP
Tel: (01608) 674350
Head: Mrs A McDermott
Type: Girls Boarding and Day 4–13 (Boys 4–8)
No of pupils: 150
Fees: (September 02) WB £9540

NAILSWORTH

ACORN SCHOOL
Church Street, Nailsworth, Gloucestershire GL6 0BP
Tel: (01453) 836508
Fax: (01453) 836508
Head: Mr G E B Whiting
Type: Co-educational Day 3–19
No of pupils: 115
Fees: (September 03)
Day £2100–£4560

STONEHOUSE

HOPELANDS SCHOOL
38 Regent Street, Stonehouse, Gloucestershire GL10 2AD
Tel: (01453) 822164
Fax: (01453) 827288
Email: enquiries@hopelands.org.uk
Head: Mrs S Bradburn
Type: Co-educational Day 3–11
No of pupils: B20 G42
Fees: (September 05)
Day £1000–£4708

WYCLIFFE COLLEGE*†
Bath Road, Stonehouse, Gloucestershire GL10 2JQ
Tel: (01453) 822432
Fax: (01453) 827634
Email: senior@wycliffe.co.uk
Head: Mrs M E Burnet Ward
Type: Co-educational Boarding and Day 13–18 Flexi-boarding available
No of pupils: B271 G150
No of boarders: F252
Fees: (September 05)
FB £19545–£23775
Day £12225–£13395

WYCLIFFE PREPARATORY SCHOOL†
Ryeford Hall, Stonehouse, Gloucestershire GL10 2LD
Tel: (01453) 820471
Fax: (01453) 825604
Email: Prep@wycliffe.co.uk
Head: Mr A Palmer
Type: Co-educational Boarding and Day 2–13 Flexi-boarding available
No of pupils: B185 G145
No of boarders: F40
Fees: (September 04)
F/WB £ £9675–£12150
Day £4290–£8625

STROUD

BEAUDESERT PARK SCHOOL
Minchinhampton, Stroud, Gloucestershire GL6 9AF
Tel: (01453) 832072
Fax: (01453) 836040
Email: office@beaudesert.gloucs.sch.uk
Head: Mr J P R Womersley
Type: Co-educational Boarding and Day 4–13 Flexi-boarding available
No of pupils: B204 G198
No of boarders: W40
Fees: (September 05)
WB £12825–£14670
Day £5985–£11205

TETBURY

QUERNS WESTONBIRT SCHOOL*
Tetbury, Gloucestershire GL8 8QG
Tel: (01666) 881390
Fax: (01666) 881391
Email: querns@westonbirt.gloucs.sch.uk
Head: Miss V James
Type: Co-educational Day 4–11
No of pupils: B40 G50
Fees: (September 05)
Day £5115–£7050

WESTONBIRT SCHOOL*
Tetbury, Gloucestershire GL8 8QG
Tel: (01666) 880333
Fax: (01666) 880364
Email: office@westonbirt.gloucs.sch.uk
Head: Mrs M Henderson
Type: Girls Boarding and Day 11–18 Flexi-boarding available
No of pupils: 230
No of boarders: 155
Fees: (September 05)
F/WB £ £19905–£20580
Day £13740–£14280

TEWKESBURY

THE ABBEY SCHOOL
Church Street, Tewkesbury, Gloucestershire GL20 5PD
Tel: (01684) 294460
Fax: (01684) 290797
Email: info@theabbeyschool.org.uk
Head: Mr N W Gardner
Type: Co-educational Day and Boarding 2–13
No of pupils: B46 G31
No of boarders: W4
Fees: (September 05)
WB £9111–£12153
Day £4530–£8781

BREDON SCHOOL†
Pull Court, Bushley, Tewkesbury, Gloucestershire GL20 6AH
Tel: (01684) 293156
Fax: (01684) 276392
Email: enquiries@bredonschool.co.uk
Head: Mr D J Keyte
Type: Co-educational Boarding and Day 7–18 Flexi-boarding available
No of pupils: B171 G59
No of boarders: F87 W40
Fees: (September 05)
FB £13665–£19395
WB £13260–£19065
Day £5475–£12645

WOTTON-UNDER-EDGE

ROSE HILL SCHOOL
Alderley, Wotton-under-Edge, Gloucestershire GL12 7QT
Tel: (01453) 843196
Fax: (01453) 846126
Email: office@rosehillschool.com
Head: Mr P Cawley-Wakefield
Type: Co-educational Boarding and Day 3–13 Flexi-boarding available
No of pupils: B100 G80
No of boarders: F25 W30
Fees: (September 05)
F/WB £ £11550–£14250
Day £1790–£3380

SOUTH GLOUCESTERSHIRE

WINTERBOURNE

SILVERHILL SCHOOL
Swan Lane, Winterbourne, South Gloucestershire BS36 1RL
Tel: (01454) 772156
Fax: (01454) 777141
Email: silverhill@btconnect.com
Head: Mrs C M Phillipson-Masters
Type: Co-educational Day 2–11
No of pupils: B114 G117
Fees: (September 05)
Day £3720–£5100

HAMPSHIRE

ALDERSHOT

STOCKTON HOUSE SCHOOL
Stockton Avenue, Fleet, Aldershot, Hampshire GU51 4NS
Tel: (01252) 616323
Fax: (01252) 627011
Head: Mrs C Tweedie-Smith
Type: Co-educational Day 2–6
No of pupils: B30 G30
Fees: (September 04)
Day £300–£3600

ALTON

ALTON CONVENT SCHOOL
Anstey Lane, Alton, Hampshire GU34 2NG
Tel: (01420) 82070
Fax: (01420) 541711
Email: enquiries@alton-convent.com
Head: Mrs S Kirkham
Type: Girls Day 2–18 (Co-ed 2–11)
No of pupils: B75 G380
Fees: (September 05)
Day £4755–£7800

ANDOVER

FARLEIGH SCHOOL*
Red Rice, Andover, Hampshire SP11 7PW
Tel: (01264) 710766
Fax: (01264) 710070
Email: office@farleighschool.co.uk
Head: Mr S Everson
Type: Co-educational Boarding and Day 3–13 Flexi-boarding available
No of pupils: B233 G160
No of boarders: 115
Fees: (September 05) F/WB £16155
Day £3360–£12225

ROOKWOOD SCHOOL*
Weyhill Road, Andover, Hampshire SP10 3AL
Tel: (01264) 325900
Fax: (01264) 325909
Email: office@rookwood.hants.sch.uk
Head: Mrs M P Langley
Type: Co-educational Day and Boarding 3–16 (Day boys only) Flexi-boarding available
No of pupils: B120 G187
No of boarders: F26
Fees: (September 05)
FB £14040–£16479
Day £5625–£9240

BASINGSTOKE

DANESHILL SCHOOL
Stratfield Turgis, Basingstoke, Hampshire RG27 0AR
Tel: (01256) 882707
Fax: (01256) 882007
Email: office@daneshill.hants.sch.uk
Head: Mr S V Spencer
Type: Co-educational Day Boys 2–13 Girls 2–11
No of pupils: B106 G138
Fees: (September 05)
Day £3300–£7800

GREY HOUSE PREPARATORY SCHOOL
Mount Pleasant Road, Hartley Wintney, Basingstoke, Hampshire RG27 8PW
Tel: (01252) 842353
Fax: (01252) 845527
Email: schooloffice@grey-house.co.uk
Head: Mrs C Allen
Type: Co-educational Day 4–11
No of pupils: B86 G66
Fees: (September 04)
Day £4920–£6057

BRAMDEAN

BROCKWOOD PARK SCHOOL
Bramdean, Hampshire SO24 0LQ
Tel: (01962) 771744
Fax: (01962) 771875
Email: enquiry@brockwood.org.uk
Head: Mr B Taylor
Type: Co-educational Boarding 14–19
No of pupils: B29 G33
No of boarders: F62
Fees: (September 05) FB £11800

CHANDLER'S FORD

WOODHILL SCHOOL
61 Brownhill Road, Chandler's Ford, Hampshire SO53 2EH
Tel: (023) 8026 8012
Fax: (023) 8026 8012
Head: Mrs M Dacombe
Type: Co-educational Day 3–11
No of pupils: B60 G60
Fees: (September 04)
Day £1785–£3480

EASTLEIGH

THE KING'S SCHOOL SENIOR
Lakesmere House, Allington Lane, Fair Oak, Eastleigh, Hampshire SO50 7DB
Tel: (023) 8060 0956
Fax: (023) 8060 0956
Email: office@kingssenior.hants.sch.uk
Head: Mrs R Pierson
Type: Co-educational Day 11–16
No of pupils: B62 G43
Fees: (September 04) Day £3960

SHERBORNE HOUSE SCHOOL
Lakewood Road, Chandler's Ford, Eastleigh, Hampshire SO53 1EU
Tel: (023) 8025 2440
Fax: (023) 8025 2553
Email: enquiries@sherbornehouse.co.uk
Head: Mrs A Entwisle
Type: Co-educational Day 2–11
No of pupils: B124 G138
Fees: (September 05)
Day £1701–£6756

FAREHAM

BOUNDARY OAK SCHOOL

Roche Court, Wickham Road, Fareham, Hampshire PO17 5BL
Tel: (01329) 280955
Fax: (01329) 827656
Email: secretary@boundaryoak.co.uk
Head: Mr B L Brown
Type: Co-educational Boarding and Day 3–13 Flexi-boarding available
No of pupils: B166 G49
No of boarders: W25
Fees: (September 04)
F/WB £ £11835–£13200
Day £1590–£8370

MEONCROSS SCHOOL

Burnt House Lane, Stubbington, Fareham, Hampshire PO14 2EF
Tel: (01329) 662182
Fax: (01329) 664680
Email: meoncross@aol.com
Head: Mr C J Ford
Type: Co-educational Day 3–16
No of pupils: B225 G180
Fees: (September 04)
Day £4860–£6870

WYKEHAM HOUSE SCHOOL

17 East Street, Fareham, Hampshire PO16 0BW
Tel: (01329) 280178
Fax: (01329) 823964
Email: office@wykehamhouse.hants.sch.uk
Head: Mrs R M Kamaryc
Type: Girls Day 2–16
No of pupils: 300
Fees: (September 04)
Day £2889–£6993

FARNBOROUGH

FARNBOROUGH HILL*

Farnborough, Hampshire GU14 8AT
Tel: (01252) 545197
Fax: (01252) 513037
Email: devdir@farnborough-hill.org.uk
Head: Miss J Thomas
Type: Girls Day 11–18
No of pupils: 505
Fees: (September 05) Day £8280

SALESIAN COLLEGE

Reading Road, Farnborough, Hampshire GU14 6PA
Tel: (01252) 893000
Fax: (01252) 893032
Email: office@salesian.hants.sch.uk
Head: Mr P A Wilson
Type: Boys Day 11–18
Fees: (September 03) Day £5625

FLEET

ST NICHOLAS' SCHOOL*

Redfields House, Redfields Lane, Church Crookham, Fleet, Hampshire GU52 0RF
Tel: (01252) 850121
Fax: (01252) 850718
Email: registrar@st-nicholas.hants.sch.uk
Head: Mrs A V Whatmough
Type: Girls Day 3–16 (Boys 3–7)
No of pupils: B20 G350
Fees: (September 05)
Day £3150–£8520

FORDINGBRIDGE

FORRES SANDLE MANOR

Fordingbridge, Hampshire SP6 1NS
Tel: (01425) 653181
Fax: (01425) 655676
Email: office@forressandlemanor.hants.sch.uk
Head: Mr R P J Moore
Type: Co-educational Boarding and Day 3–13 Flexi-boarding available
No of pupils: B144 G129
No of boarders: F61 W35
Fees: (September 05)
F/WB £ £15840
Day £2625–£11640

GOSPORT

MARYCOURT SCHOOL

27 Crescent Road, Alverstoke, Gosport, Hampshire PO12 2DJ
Tel: (023) 9258 1766
Fax: (023) 9258 1766
Head: Mrs J Norman
Type: Co-educational Day 3–11
No of pupils: B40 G45
Fees: (September 04)
Day £1752–£3339

HAVANT

GLENHURST SCHOOL

16 Beechworth Road, Havant, Hampshire PO9 1AX
Tel: (023) 9248 4054
Fax: (023) 9248 4054
Email: office@glenhurstschool.co.uk
Head: Mrs E Haines
Type: Co-educational Day 2–9
No of pupils: B40 G40
Fees: (September 05) Day £3300

HOOK

LORD WANDSWORTH COLLEGE

Long Sutton, Hook, Hampshire RG29 1TB
Tel: (01256) 862201
Fax: (01256) 860363
Email: info@lordwandsworth.org
Head: Mr I G Power
Type: Co-educational Boarding and Day 11–18 Flexi-boarding available
No of pupils: B343 G176
No of boarders: F51 W195
Fees: (September 05)
FB £18465–£20460
WB £18465–£19485
Day £13785–£14520

ST NEOT'S SCHOOL

Eversley, Hook, Hampshire RG27 0PN
Tel: (0118) 973 2118
Fax: (0118) 973 9949
Email: office@st-neots-prep.co.uk
Head: Mr R J Thorp
Type: Co-educational Day and Boarding 1–13 Flexi-boarding available
No of pupils: B180 G130
No of boarders: W26
Fees: (September 05) WB £13230
Day £4110–£10710

SHERFIELD SCHOOL

Reading Road, Sherfield-on-Loddon, Hook, Hampshire RG27 0HT
Tel: (01256) 884800
Fax: (01256) 883172
Email: info@sherfieldschool.co.uk
Type: Co-educational Day 2–13 (Age increasing to 18)
No of pupils: 90
Fees: (September 04)
Day £5400–£9879

LEE-ON-THE-SOLENT

ST ANNE'S NURSERY & PRE-PREPARATORY SCHOOL
13 Milvil Road, Lee-on-the-Solent, Hampshire PO13 9LU
Tel: (023) 9255 0820
Email: st_annes_school@yahoo.co.uk
Head: Mrs A M Whitting
Type: Co-educational Day 2–8
No of pupils: B15 G15
Fees: (September 04) Day £2550

LIPHOOK

HIGHFIELD SCHOOL*
Highfield Lane, Liphook, Hampshire GU30 7LQ
Tel: (01428) 728000
Fax: (01428) 728001
Email: office@highfieldschool.org.uk
Head: Mr P G S Evitt
Type: Co-educational Boarding and Day 8–13
No of pupils: B122 G113
No of boarders: F79
Fees: (September 05)
FB £14100–£16050
Day £10800–£14100

LYMINGTON

HORDLE WALHAMPTON SCHOOL[†]
Lymington, Hampshire SO41 5ZG
Tel: (01590) 672013
Fax: (01590) 678498
Email: registrar@hordlewalhampton.co.uk
Head: Mr R H C Phillips
Type: Co-educational Boarding and Day 2–13 Flexi-boarding available
No of pupils: B183 G143
No of boarders: F41
Fees: (September 05)
F/WB £ £14250
Day £5415–£10830

NEW MILTON

BALLARD SCHOOL
Fernhill Lane, New Milton, Hampshire BH25 5SU
Tel: (01425) 611153
Fax: (01425) 622099
Email: admissions@ballardschool.co.uk
Head: Mr S P Duckitt
Type: Co-educational Day 2–16
No of pupils: B318 G206
Fees: (September 05)
Day £1557–£9510

DURLSTON COURT
Becton Lane, Barton-on-Sea, New Milton, Hampshire BH25 7AQ
Tel: (01425) 610010
Fax: (01425) 622731
Email: secretary@durlstoncourt.org.uk
Head: Mr D C Wansey
Type: Co-educational Day 2–13
No of pupils: B166 G114
Fees: (September 05)
Day £2850–£9855

PETERSFIELD

BEDALES SCHOOL
Petersfield, Hampshire GU32 2DG
Tel: (01730) 300100
Fax: (01730) 300500
Email: admissions@bedales.org.uk
Head: Mr K Budge
Type: Co-educational Boarding and Day 13–18
No of pupils: B219 G227
No of boarders: F301
Fees: (September 05) FB £23535
Day £18120

CHURCHERS COLLEGE
Portsmouth Road, Petersfield, Hampshire GU31 4AS
Tel: (01730) 263033
Fax: (01730) 231437
Email: enquiries@churcherscollege.com
Head: Mr S H Williams
Type: Co-educational Day 4–18
No of pupils: B475 G360
Fees: (September 05)
Day £5475–£8895

CHURCHERS COLLEGE JUNIOR SCHOOL
The Spain, Petersfield, Hampshire GU32 3LA
Tel: (01730) 263724
Fax: (01730) 263724
Head: Mrs S Rivett
Type: Co-educational Day 4–11
No of pupils: B98 G81
Fees: (September 03)
Day £5820–£6440

DITCHAM PARK SCHOOL
Ditcham Park, Petersfield, Hampshire GU31 5RN
Tel: (01730) 825659
Fax: (01730) 825070
Email: info@ditchampark.com
Head: Mrs K S Morton
Type: Co-educational Day 4–16
No of pupils: B193 G158
Fees: (September 05)
Day £5448–£9093

DUNHURST (BEDALES JUNIOR SCHOOL)
Petersfield, Hampshire GU32 2DP
Tel: (01730) 300200
Fax: (01730) 300600
Email: dunhurst@bedales.org.uk
Head: Mr C Sanderson
Type: Co-educational Boarding and Day 8–13 Flexi-boarding available
No of pupils: B90 G94
No of boarders: F53
Fees: (September 03) FB £14706
Day £10980

PORTSMOUTH

THE PORTSMOUTH GRAMMAR SCHOOL
High Street, Portsmouth, Hampshire PO1 2LN
Tel: (023) 9281 9125
Fax: (023) 9236 4256
Email: admissions@pgs.org.uk
Head: Dr T R Hands
Type: Co-educational Day 2–18
No of pupils: B950 G500
Fees: (September 05)
Day £5928–£9246

ROOKESBURY PARK SCHOOL
Southwick Road, Wickham, Portsmouth, Hampshire PO17 6HT
Tel: (01329) 833108
Fax: (01329) 835090
Email: rookesburypark@btconnect.com
Head: Mr P G Savage
Type: Co-educational Boarding and Day 3–13 Flexi-boarding available
No of pupils: B41 G59
No of boarders: F8 W5
Fees: (September 05)
F/WB £ £12435–£14670
Day £5010–£9885

RINGWOOD

MOYLES COURT SCHOOL†
Moyles Court, Ringwood, Hampshire BH24 3NF
Tel: (01425) 472856
Fax: (01425) 474715
Email: moylescourt@btinternet.com
Head: Mr R A Dean
Type: Co-educational Day and Boarding 3–16
No of pupils: B105 G74
No of boarders: F48
Fees: (September 03)
FB £11850–£14835
Day £3894–£7956

RINGWOOD WALDORF SCHOOL
Ashley, Ringwood, Hampshire BH24 2NN
Tel: (01425) 472664
Type: Co-educational Day 4–14
No of pupils: B100 G100

ROMSEY

HAMPSHIRE COLLEGIATE SCHOOL, EMBLEY PARK*
Embley Park, Romsey, Hampshire SO51 6ZE
Tel: (01794) 512206
Fax: (01794) 518737
Email: info@hampshirecs.org.uk
Head: Mr D F Chapman
Type: Co-educational Boarding and Day 3–18 Flexi-boarding available
No of pupils: B300 G180
No of boarders: F30 W46
Fees: (September 05)
F/WB £ £8310–£16620
Day £5000–£10005

STANBRIDGE EARLS SCHOOL†
Stanbridge Lane, Romsey, Hampshire SO51 0ZS
Tel: (01794) 529400
Fax: (01794) 511201
Email: admin@stanbridgeearls.co.uk
Head: Mr G P Link
Type: Co-educational Boarding and Day 10–19
No of pupils: B140 G24
No of boarders: F131
Fees: (September 05)
FB £19095–£20895
Day £14232–£15489

THE STROUD SCHOOL
Highwood House, Highwood Lane, Romsey, Hampshire SO51 9ZH
Tel: (01794) 513231
Fax: (01794) 514432
Email: secretary@stroud-romsey-sch.co.uk
Head: Mr A J Dodds
Type: Co-educational Day 3–13
No of pupils: B188 G127
Fees: (September 05)
Day £2835–£10035

SOUTHAMPTON

THE ATHERLEY SCHOOL
Grove Place, Upton Lane, Nursling, Southampton, Hampshire SO16 0AB
Tel: (023) 8074 1629
Fax: (023) 8074 1631
Email: office.atherley@church-schools.com
Head: Mrs M Bradley
Type: Girls Day 3–18 (Boys 3–11)
No of pupils: B75 G375
Fees: (September 03)
Day £5000–£7500

THE GREGG SCHOOL
Townhill Park House, Cutbush Lane, Southampton, Hampshire SO18 2GF
Tel: (023) 8047 2133
Head: Mr R D Hart
Type: Co-educational Day 11–16
No of pupils: B200 G134
Fees: (September 03) Day £6810

KING EDWARD VI SCHOOL
Kellett Road, Southampton, Hampshire SO15 7UQ
Tel: (023) 8070 4561
Fax: (023) 8070 5937
Email: registrar@kes.hants.sch.uk
Head: Mr A J Thould
Type: Co-educational Day 11–18
No of pupils: B624 G345
Fees: (September 05) Day £8886

KINGS PRIMARY SCHOOL
26 Quob Lane, West End, Southampton, Hampshire SO30 3HN
Tel: (023) 8047 2266
Fax: (023) 8047 2282
Email: kingschool@lineone.net
Head: Mr K Ford
Type: Co-educational Day 5–11
No of pupils: 120
Fees: (September 04) Day £2265

ST MARY'S COLLEGE
57 Midanbury Lane, Bitterne Park, Southampton, Hampshire SO18 4DJ
Tel: (023) 8067 1267
Fax: (023) 8067 7575
Email: stmarysoffice@aol.com
Head: Rev J J Davis
Type: Co-educational Day 3–18
Fees: (September 05) Day £5800

ST WINIFRED'S SCHOOL
17–19 Winn Road, Southampton, Hampshire S017 1EJ
Tel: (023) 8055 7352
Fax: (023) 8055 7352
Email: office@stwinifreds.southampton.sch.uk
Head: Mrs J Collins
Type: Co-educational Day 2–11
Fees: (September 05) Day £5040

VINE SCHOOL
Church Lane, Curdridge, Southampton, Hampshire SO32 2DR
Tel: (01489) 789123
Email: the@vineschool.fsnet.co.uk
Head: Mr A J Saunders
Type: Co-educational Day 3–11
No of pupils: B38 G39
Fees: (September 04) Day £3333

WOODHILL PREPARATORY SCHOOL
Brook Lane, Botley, Southampton, Hampshire SO30 2ER
Tel: (01489) 781112
Fax: (01489) 799362
Email: m.dacombe@woodhill.hants.sch.uk
Head: Mrs M Dacombe
Type: Co-educational Day 3–11
No of pupils: B62 G48
Fees: (September 03) Day £1539–£3015

SOUTHSEA

MAYVILLE HIGH SCHOOL†
35 St Simon's Road, Southsea, Hampshire PO5 2PE
Tel: (023) 9273 4847
Fax: (023) 9229 3649
Email: mayvillehighschool@talk21.com
Head: Mrs L Owens
Type: Co-educational Day Boys 6–16 Girls 1–16
No of pupils: B210 G237
Fees: (September 05) Day £4500–£6510

PORTSMOUTH HIGH SCHOOL GDST
Kent Road, Southsea, Hampshire PO5 3EQ
Tel: (023) 9282 6714
Fax: (023) 9281 4814
Email: headsec@por.gdst.net
Head: Miss P Hulse
Type: Girls Day 3–18
No of pupils: 620
Fees: (September 05) Day £4410–£7365

ST JOHN'S COLLEGE
Grove Road South, Southsea, Hampshire PO5 3QW
Tel: (023) 9281 5118
Fax: (023) 9287 3603
Email: info@stjohnscollege.co.uk
Head: Mr N W Thorne
Type: Co-educational Boarding and Day 2–18 Flexi-boarding available
No of pupils: B458 G179
No of boarders: F103
Fees: (September 03) FB £13650–£15300 Day £4500–£6450

WINCHESTER

CHILTERN TUTORIAL SCHOOL
Otterbourne Halls, Cranbourne Drive, Otterbourne, Winchester, Hampshire SO21 2ET
Tel: (01962) 860482
Fax: (01962) 860482
Head: Mrs J Gaudie
Type: Co-educational Day 7–11
No of pupils: B11 G7
Fees: (September 03) Day £5220

THE PILGRIMS' SCHOOL*
3 The Close, Winchester, Hampshire SO23 9LT
Tel: (01962) 854189
Fax: (01962) 843610
Email: info@pilgrims-school.co.uk
Head: Dr B A Rees
Type: Boys Boarding and Day 7–13
No of pupils: 200
No of boarders: F40 W25
Fees: (September 05) FB £14790 Day £11790

PRINCE'S MEAD SCHOOL
Worthy Park House, Kingsworthy, Winchester, Hampshire SO21 1AN
Tel: (01962) 886000
Fax: (01962) 886888
Email: admin@princesmeadschool.org.uk
Head: Miss P Kirk
Type: Co-educational Day 3–11
No of pupils: B93 G158
Fees: (September 05) Day £7500–£8850

ST SWITHUN'S SCHOOL
Alresford Road, Winchester, Hampshire SO21 1HA
Tel: (01962) 835700
Fax: (01962) 835779
Email: office@stswithuns.com
Head: Dr H L Harvey
Type: Girls Boarding and Day 11–18
No of pupils: 480
No of boarders: F46 W175
Fees: (September 05) F/WB £ £19530 Day £11850

TWYFORD SCHOOL
Winchester, Hampshire SO21 1NW
Tel: (01962) 712269
Fax: (01962) 712100
Email: registrar@twyfordschool.com
Head: Dr D Livingstone
Type: Co-educational Day and Boarding 3–13 Flexi-boarding available
No of pupils: B195 G102
No of boarders: W29
Fees: (September 05) WB £15345 Day £3270–£11865

WINCHESTER COLLEGE*
College Street, Winchester, Hampshire SO23 9NA
Tel: (01962) 621247
Fax: (01962) 621106
Email: information@wincoll.ac.uk
Head: Dr R D Townsend
Type: Boys Boarding and Day 13–18
No of pupils: 689
No of boarders: F667
Fees: (September 05) FB £23500 Day £22325

YATELEY

YATELEY MANOR PREPARATORY SCHOOL
51 Reading Road, Yateley, Hampshire GU46 7UQ
Tel: (01252) 405500
Fax: (01252) 405504
Email: registrar@yateleymanor.com
Head: Mr F G Howard
Type: Co-educational Day 3–13
No of pupils: B344 G189
Fees: (September 05) Day £3366–£9321

HEREFORDSHIRE

BROMYARD

ST RICHARD'S
Bredenbury Court, Bromyard, Herefordshire HR7 4TD
Tel: (01885) 482491
Fax: (01885) 488982
Email: st.dix@virgin.net
Head: Mr N Cheesman
Type: Co-educational Boarding and Day 3–13 Flexi-boarding available
No of pupils: B93 G70
No of boarders: F40 W37
Fees: (September 03) FB £12048 WB £11430 Day £3021–£8292

HEREFORD

HABERDASHERS' REDCAP SCHOOL
32 Broomy Hill, Hereford, Herefordshire HR4 0LH
Tel: (01432) 273594
Fax: (01432) 273594
Email: enquiries@haberdashersredcap.org
Head: Mrs A Ellis
Type: Girls Day 2–11
No of pupils: 80
Fees: (September 03) Day £4095–£5430

THE HEREFORD CATHEDRAL JUNIOR SCHOOL
28 Castle Street, Hereford, Herefordshire HR1 2NW
Tel: (01432) 363511
Fax: (01432) 363515
Email: secretary@hcjs.co.uk
Head: Mr T R Lowe
Type: Co-educational Day 3–11
No of pupils: B190 G137
Fees: (September 04) Day £3864–£5655

THE HEREFORD CATHEDRAL SCHOOL
Old Deanery, Cathedral Close, Hereford, Herefordshire HR1 2NG
Tel: (01432) 363522
Fax: (01432) 363525
Email: enquiry@hcsch.org
Head: Mr P A Smith
Type: Co-educational Day 11–18
No of pupils: B322 G272
Fees: (September 02) Day £6894

LEOMINSTER

LUCTON SCHOOL
Leominster, Herefordshire HR6 9PN
Tel: (01568) 782000
Fax: (01568) 782001
Email: enquiries@luctonschool.org
Head: Mrs G Thorne
Type: Co-educational Boarding and Day 0–16 (VIth Form from Sept 2005) Flexi-boarding available
No of pupils: B80 G72
No of boarders: F38 W15
Fees: (September 04) FB £11340–£14145 WB £9540–£11817 Day £3450–£7305

HERTFORDSHIRE

ALDENHAM

EDGE GROVE
Aldenham Village, Aldenham, Hertfordshire WD25 8NL
Tel: (01923) 855724
Fax: (01923) 859920
Email: enquiries@edgegrove.indschools.co.uk
Head: Mr M T Wilson
Type: Co-educational Boarding and Day 3–13 Flexi-boarding available
No of pupils: B234 G100
No of boarders: F50 W40
Fees: (September 04)
FB £11640–£14220
Day £3495–£10440

BARNET

LYONSDOWN SCHOOL TRUST LTD
3 Richmond Road, New Barnet, Barnet, Hertfordshire EN5 1SA
Tel: (020) 8449 0225
Fax: (020) 8441 4690
Email: enquiries@lyonsdownschool.co.uk
Head: Mrs L Maggs-Wellings
Type: Co-educational Day Boys 3–7 Girls 3–11
No of pupils: B54 G158
Fees: (September 05)
Day £4929–£5424

NORFOLK LODGE NURSERY & PREPARATORY SCHOOL
Dancers Hill Road, Barnet, Hertfordshire EN5 4RP
Tel: (020) 8447 1565
Fax: (020) 8447 1888
Head: Mrs K Conroy
Type: Co-educational Day 1–11
No of pupils: B110 G90
Fees: (September 04)
Day £1179–£5709

ST MARTHA'S SENIOR SCHOOL
Camlet Way, Hadley, Barnet, Hertfordshire EN4 0NJ
Tel: (020) 8449 6889
Fax: (020) 8441 5632
Email: office@st-marthas.org.uk
Head: Mr J Sheridan
Type: Girls Day 11–18
No of pupils: 320
Fees: (September 03) Day £5475

SUZI EARNSHAW THEATRE SCHOOL
68 High Street, Barnet, Hertfordshire EN5 5SJ
Tel: (020) 8441 5010
Fax: (020) 8364 9618
Email: school@susiearnshaw.co.uk
Head: Mr D Earnshaw
Type: Co-educational Day 11–19
No of pupils: B22 G39
Fees: (September 05)
Day £5550–£7150

BERKHAMSTED

BERKHAMSTED COLLEGIATE PREPARATORY SCHOOL
Kings Road, Berkhamsted, Hertfordshire HP4 3YP
Tel: (01442) 358201/2
Fax: (01442) 358203
Email: info@bcschool.org
Head: Mr A J Taylor
Type: Co-educational Day 3–11
No of pupils: B229 G234
Fees: (September 03)
Day £5007–£8001

BERKHAMSTED COLLEGIATE SCHOOL
Castle Street, Berkhamsted, Hertfordshire HP4 2BB
Tel: (01442) 358000
Fax: (01442) 358040
Email: info@bcschool.org
Head: Dr P Chadwick
Type: Co-educational Day and Boarding 11–18 (Single-sex ed 11–16) Flexi-boarding available
No of pupils: B600 G400
No of boarders: F60 W10
Fees: (September 05)
F/WB £ £17976–£19854
Day £10647–£12525

EGERTON-ROTHESAY SCHOOL
Durrants Lane, Berkhamsted, Hertfordshire HP4 3UJ
Tel: (01442) 865275
Fax: (01442) 864977
Email: admin@egerton2.u-net.com
Head: Mrs N Boddam-Whetham
Type: Co-educational Day 3–16
No of pupils: B255 G109
Fees: (September 05) Day £9495

HARESFOOT PREPARATORY SCHOOL
Chesham Road, Berkhamsted, Hertfordshire HP4 2SZ
Tel: (01442) 872742
Fax: (01442) 872742
Email: office@haresfoot.herts.sch.uk
Head: Mrs G Waterhouse
Type: Co-educational Day 3–11
Fees: (September 03)
Day £870–£6000

BISHOP'S STORTFORD

BISHOP'S STORTFORD COLLEGE
Maze Green Road, Bishop's Stortford, Hertfordshire CM23 2PJ
Tel: (01279) 838575
Fax: (01279) 836570
Email: admissions@bsc.biblio.net
Head: Mr J G Trotman
Type: Co-educational Boarding and Day 4–18 Flexi-boarding available
No of pupils: B564 G396
No of boarders: F117
Fees: (September 05)
FB £11580–£16608
Day £5580–£11970

HOWE GREEN HOUSE SCHOOL
Great Hallingbury, Bishop's Stortford, Hertfordshire CM22 7UF
Tel: (01279) 657706
Fax: (01279) 501333
Email: info@howegreenhouseschool.co.uk
Head: Mr G R Gorton
Type: Co-educational Day 2–11
No of pupils: B101 G88
Fees: (September 05)
Day £4671–£7425

THE JUNIOR SCHOOL, BISHOP'S STORTFORD COLLEGE

Maze Green Road, Bishop's Stortford, Hertfordshire CM23 2PH
Tel: (01279) 838607
Fax: (01279) 306110
Email: jsadmissions@bsc.biblio.net
Head: Mr J A Greathead
Type: Co-educational Boarding and Day 4–13
No of pupils: B289 G208
No of boarders: F20 W21
Fees: (September 04)
F/WB £ £10626–£11574
Day £5118–£8781

BUSHEY

IMMANUEL COLLEGE

87/91 Elstree Road, Bushey, Hertfordshire WD23 4EB
Tel: (020) 8950 0604
Fax: (020) 8950 8687
Head: Mr P Skelker
Type: Co-educational Day 11–18
No of pupils: B273 G287
Fees: (September 05) Day £10398

LITTLE ACORNS MONTESSORI SCHOOL

Lincolnsfields Centre, Bushey Hall Drive, Bushey, Hertfordshire WD2 2ER
Tel: (01923) 230705
Fax: (01923) 230705
Head: Ms J Nugent and Ms R Lau
Type: Co-educational Day 2–7
No of pupils: 24

LONGWOOD SCHOOL

Bushey Hall Drive, Bushey, Hertfordshire WD23 2QG
Tel: (01923) 253715
Fax: (01923) 222760
Email: longwoodnursery@aol.com
Head: Mr M Livesey
Type: Co-educational Day 3–11
No of pupils: B63 G45
Fees: (September 03)
Day £2520–£3870

THE PURCELL SCHOOL

Aldenham Road, Bushey, Hertfordshire WD23 2TS
Tel: (01923) 331100
Fax: (01923) 331166
Email: info@purcell-school.org
Head: Mr J Tolputt
Type: Co-educational Day and Boarding 8–18
No of pupils: B59 G109
No of boarders: F100
Fees: (September 02)
FB £14013–£16677
Day £7692–£9993

ST HILDA'S SCHOOL*

High Street, Bushey, Hertfordshire WD23 3DA
Tel: (020) 8950 1751
Fax: (020) 8420 4523
Email: registrar@sthildasbushey.co.uk
Head: Mrs L Cavanagh
Type: Girls Day 3–11 (Boys 3–5)
No of pupils: B5 G120
Fees: (September 05)
Day £4080–£7500

ST MARGARET'S SCHOOL*

Merry Hill Road, Bushey, Hertfordshire WD23 1DT
Tel: (020) 8901 0870
Fax: (020) 8950 1677
Email: schooloffice@stmargarets.herts.sch.uk
Head: Mr Mark Ferris
Type: Girls Boarding and Day 4–18 Flexi-boarding available
No of pupils: 400
No of boarders: F60
Fees: (September 05)
F/WB £ £18885
Day £7005–£10545

BUSHEY HEATH

WESTWOOD

6 Hartsbourne Road, Bushey Heath, Hertfordshire WD23 1JH
Tel: (020) 8950 1138
Email: westwood.school@virgin.net
Head: Mrs J Hill
Type: Co-educational Day 4–8
No of pupils: B36 G36
Fees: (September 05) Day £4950

ELSTREE

ALDENHAM SCHOOL*

Elstree, Hertfordshire WD6 3AJ
Tel: (01923) 858122
Fax: (01923) 854410
Email: enquiries@aldenham.com
Head: Mr J C Fowler
Type: Co-educational Boarding and Day 2–18 Flexi-boarding available
No of pupils: B547 G88
No of boarders: F100 W45
Fees: (September 05)
FB £14676–£20664
WB £12294–£16982
Day £9798–£14223

HABERDASHERS' ASKE'S BOYS' SCHOOL

Butterfly Lane, Elstree, Hertfordshire WD6 3AF
Tel: (020) 8266 1700
Fax: (020) 8266 1800
Email: office@habsboys.org.uk
Head: Mr P B Hamilton
Type: Boys Day 5–18
No of pupils: 1300
Fees: (September 05)
Day £10140–£10800

HABERDASHERS' ASKE'S SCHOOL FOR GIRLS

Aldenham Road, Elstree, Hertfordshire WD6 3BT
Tel: (020) 8266 2300
Fax: (020) 8266 2303
Email: theschool@habsgirls.org.uk
Head: Mrs E J Radice
Type: Girls Day 4–18
Fees: (September 05)
Day £7524–£8970

HARPENDEN

ALDWICKBURY SCHOOL

Wheathampstead Road, Harpenden, Hertfordshire AL5 1AD
Tel: (01582) 713022
Fax: (01582) 767696
Email: registrar@aldwickbury.org.uk
Head: Mr V W Hales
Type: Boys Day and Boarding 4–13 Flexi-boarding available
No of boarders: W30
Fees: (September 05)
WB £10530–£11061
Day £6539–£8445

HARPENDEN PREPARATORY SCHOOL
53 Luton Road, Harpenden, Hertfordshire AL5 2UE
Tel: (01582) 712361
Fax: (01582) 763553
Email: harpendenprep@lineone.net
Head: Mrs E R Broughton
Type: Co-educational Day 2–11
No of pupils: B75 G75
Fees: (September 03)
Day £2280–£5388

KINGS SCHOOL
Elmfield, Ambrose Lane, Harpenden, Hertfordshire AL5 4DU
Tel: (01582) 767566
Fax: (01582) 765406
Email: office@thekingsschool.com
Head: Mr C J Case
Type: Co-educational Day 4–16
No of pupils: 196
Fees: (September 03) Day £3096

ST HILDA'S SCHOOL
28 Douglas Road, Harpenden, Hertfordshire AL5 2ES
Tel: (01582) 712307
Fax: (01582) 763892
Email: office@st-hildasschool.herts.sch.uk
Head: Mrs F Schofield
Type: Girls Day 2–11
No of pupils: 180
Fees: (September 05)
Day £1110–£6285

HATFIELD

QUEENSWOOD SCHOOL
Shepherds Way, Brookmans Park, Hatfield, Hertfordshire AL9 6NS
Tel: (01707) 602500
Fax: (01707) 602597
Email: registry@queenswood.herts.sch.uk
Head: Ms C Farr
Type: Girls Boarding and Day 11–18 Flexi-boarding available
No of pupils: 411
No of boarders: F214
Fees: (September 05)
FB £19995–£21795
Day £15060–£16440

HEMEL HEMPSTEAD

ABBOT'S HILL SCHOOL*
Bunkers Lane, Hemel Hempstead, Hertfordshire HP3 8RP
Tel: (01442) 240333
Fax: (01442) 269981
Email: registrar@abbotshill.herts.sch.uk
Head: Mrs K Lewis
Type: Girls Day 3–16 (Boys 3–7)
No of pupils: B5 G438
Fees: (September 05)
Day £6180–£10950

LOCKERS PARK
Lockers Park Lane, Hemel Hempstead, Hertfordshire HP1 1TL
Tel: (01442) 251712
Fax: (01442) 234150
Email: secretary@lockerspark.herts.sch.uk
Head: Mr D R Lees-Jones
Type: Boys Boarding and Day 7–13 Flexi-boarding available
No of pupils: 138
No of boarders: F37 W33
Fees: (September 05) FB £14700
Day £9195–£11895

WESTBROOK HAY PREPARATORY SCHOOL
London Road, Hemel Hempstead, Hertfordshire HP1 2RF
Tel: (01442) 256143
Fax: (01442) 232076
Email: admin@westbrookhay.co.uk
Head: Mr K Young
Type: Co-educational Boarding and Day 2–13 Flexi-boarding available
No of pupils: B167 G83
Fees: (September 05)
Day £5328–£9885

HERTFORD

DUNCOMBE SCHOOL*
4 Warren Park Road, Bengeo, Hertford, Hertfordshire SG14 3JA
Tel: (01992) 414100
Fax: (01992) 414111
Email: admissions@duncombe-school.co.uk
Head: Mr D Baldwin
Type: Co-educational Day 2–11
No of pupils: B156 G149
Fees: (September 05)
Day £1536–£8040

HAILEYBURY*
Hertford, Hertfordshire SG13 7NU
Tel: (01992) 463353
Fax: (01992) 470663
Email: registrar@haileybury.com
Head: Mr S A Westley
Type: Co-educational Boarding and Day 11–18 Flexi-boarding available
No of pupils: B429 G315
No of boarders: F469
Fees: (September 05)
FB £15735–£21990
Day £10980–£16515

HEATH MOUNT SCHOOL
Woodhall Park, Watton-at-Stone, Hertford, Hertfordshire SG14 3NG
Tel: (01920) 830230
Fax: (01920) 830357
Email: office@heathmount.org
Head: Mr H J Matthews
Type: Co-educational Boarding and Day 3–13 Flexi-boarding available
No of pupils: B207 G150
No of boarders: W15
Fees: (September 04)
WB £13251–£13599

ST JOSEPH'S IN THE PARK
St Mary's Lane, Hertingfordbury, Hertford, Hertfordshire SG14 2LX
Tel: (01992) 581378
Fax: (01992) 505202
Email: admin@stjosephsinthepark.co.uk
Head: Mr A Platt
Type: Co-educational Day 3–11
No of pupils: B88 G73
Fees: (September 05) Day £2535

HITCHIN

KINGSHOTT SCHOOL*
St Ippolyts, Hitchin, Hertfordshire SG4 7JX
Tel: (01462) 432009
Fax: (01462) 421652
Email: pi@kingshott.herts.sch.uk
Head: Mr P R Ilott
Type: Co-educational Day 4–13
No of pupils: B236 G120
Fees: (September 05)
Day £6600–£8220

THE PRINCESS HELENA COLLEGE
Preston, Hitchin, Hertfordshire SG4 7RT
Tel: (01462) 432100
Fax: (01462) 443871
Email: head@phc.herts.sch.uk
Head: Mrs A M Hodgkiss
Type: Girls Day and Boarding 11–18 Flexi-boarding available
No of pupils: 200
No of boarders: F27 W53
Fees: (September 05)
F/WB £ £14970–£19110
Day £10470–£13230

KINGS LANGLEY

RUDOLF STEINER SCHOOL
Langley Hill, Kings Langley, Hertfordshire WD4 9HG
Tel: (01923) 262505
Fax: (01923) 270958
Email: info@rsskl.org.uk
Type: Co-educational Day 3–19
No of pupils: B224 G189
Fees: (September 05)
Day £2790–£6300

LETCHWORTH

ST CHRISTOPHER SCHOOL*
Barrington Road, Letchworth, Hertfordshire SG6 3JZ
Tel: (01462) 650850
Fax: (01462) 481578
Email: admissions@stchris.co.uk
Head: Mr D Wilkinson
Type: Co-educational Boarding and Day 2–19 Flexi-boarding available
No of pupils: B314 G234
No of boarders: F67
Fees: (September 05)
FB £16242–£20325
Day £2910–£11565

ST FRANCIS' COLLEGE
The Broadway, Letchworth, Hertfordshire SG6 3PJ
Tel: (01462) 670511
Fax: (01462) 682361
Email: enquiries@st-francis.herts.sch.uk
Head: Miss M Hegarty
Type: Girls Boarding and Day 3–18 Flexi-boarding available
No of pupils: 509
No of boarders: F34 W6
Fees: (September 05)
FB £15420–£17880
WB £12405–£15030
Day £4665–£9090

POTTERS BAR

LOCHINVER HOUSE SCHOOL
Heath Road, Little Heath, Potters Bar, Hertfordshire EN6 1LW
Tel: (01707) 653064
Fax: (01707) 620030
Email: registrar@lochinverhouse.herts.sch.uk
Head: Mr J Gear
Type: Boys Day 4–13
No of pupils: 343
Fees: (September 03)
Day £6405–£8391

ST JOHN'S PREPARATORY SCHOOL
Brownlowes, The Ridgeway, Potters Bar, Hertfordshire EN6 5QT
Tel: (01707) 657294
Fax: (020) 8363 4439
Email: stjohnssc@aol.com
Head: Mrs C Tardios
Type: Co-educational Day 4–11
No of pupils: B106 G142
Fees: (September 05)
Day £6000–£7000

STORMONT
The Causeway, Potters Bar, Hertfordshire EN6 5HA
Tel: (01707) 654037
Fax: (01707) 663295
Email: admin@stormont.herts.sch.uk
Head: Mrs M E Johnston
Type: Girls Day 4–11
No of pupils: 168
Fees: (September 05)
Day £7590–£8070

RADLETT

MANOR LODGE SCHOOL
Rectory Lane, Ridge Hill, Radlett, Hertfordshire WD7 9BG
Tel: (01707) 642424
Fax: (01707) 645206
Email: prospectus@manorlodgeschool.com
Head: Mrs J M Smart
Type: Co-educational Day 4–11
No of pupils: B206 G174
Fees: (September 05)
Day £6330–£7488

RADLETT NURSERY & INFANTS SCHOOL
Cobden Hill, Radlett, Hertfordshire WD7 7JL
Tel: (01923) 856374
Fax: (10923) 858365
Head: Mrs J R Briggs
Type: Co-educational Day 3–7
No of pupils: B60 G50
Fees: (September 02)
Day £1485–£1925

RADLETT PREPARATORY SCHOOL
Kendal Hall, Watling Street, Radlett, Hertfordshire WD7 7LY
Tel: (01923) 856812
Fax: (01923) 855880
Email: admin@radlett-prep.herts.sch.uk
Head: Mr W N Warren
Type: Co-educational Day 4–11
No of pupils: B265 G225
Fees: (September 04) Day £5400

RICKMANSWORTH

NORTHWOOD PREPARATORY SCHOOL
Moor Farm, Sandy Lodge Road, Rickmansworth, Hertfordshire WD3 1LW
Tel: (01923) 825648
Fax: (01923) 835802
Head: Mr T Lee
Type: Boys Day 4–13 (Girls 3–4)
No of pupils: 300
Fees: (September 03)
Day £7413–£7806

RICKMANSWORTH PNEU SCHOOL
88 The Drive, Rickmansworth, Hertfordshire WD3 4DU
Tel: (01923) 772101
Fax: (01923) 776268
Email: office@rickmansworthpneu.co.uk
Head: Mrs C R Callegari
Type: Girls Day 3–11
No of pupils: 150
Fees: (September 05)
Day £2202–£6315

THE ROYAL MASONIC SCHOOL FOR GIRLS*
Rickmansworth Park, Rickmansworth, Hertfordshire WD3 4HF
Tel: (01923) 773168
Fax: (01923) 896729
Email: enquiries@royalmasonic.herts.sch.uk
Head: Mrs D Rose
Type: Girls Boarding and Day 4–18 Flexi-boarding available
No of pupils: 781
No of boarders: F110 W56
Fees: (September 05)
FB £9675–£15720
WB £9600–£15645
Day £5445–£9705

YORK HOUSE SCHOOL*
Redheath, Sarratt Road, Croxley Green, Rickmansworth, Hertfordshire WD3 4LW
Tel: (01923) 772395
Fax: (01923) 779231
Email: yhsoffice@aol.com
Head: Mr P R MacDougall
Type: Boys Day 3–13 (Co-ed 2–5)
No of pupils: B270 G15
Fees: (September 05) Day £8130

ST ALBANS

BEECHWOOD PARK SCHOOL
Markyate, St Albans, Hertfordshire AL3 8AW
Tel: (01582) 840333
Fax: (01582) 842372
Email: admissions@beechwoodpark.herts.sch.uk
Head: Mr P C E Atkinson
Type: Co-educational Day and Boarding 4–13 Flexi-boarding available
No of pupils: B300 G160
No of boarders: W50
Fees: (September 04) WB £13335

HOMEWOOD PRE-PREPARATORY SCHOOL
Hazel Road, Park Street, St Albans, Hertfordshire AL2 2AH
Tel: (01727) 873542
Email: homewood@chalkface.net
Head: Mr B Cooper
Type: Co-educational Day 3–8
No of pupils: B37 G41
Fees: (September 05)
Day £2055–£6300

ST ALBANS HIGH SCHOOL FOR GIRLS*
Townsend Avenue, St Albans, Hertfordshire AL1 3SJ
Tel: (01727) 853800
Fax: (01727) 792516
Email: admissions@stalbans-high.herts.sch.uk
Head: Ms J C Pain
Type: Girls Day 4–18
No of pupils: 950
Fees: (September 05)
Day £6975–£8865

ST ALBANS SCHOOL*
Abbey Gateway, St Albans, Hertfordshire AL3 4HB
Tel: (01727) 855521
Fax: (01727) 843447
Email: hm@st-albans-school.org.uk
Head: Mr A R Grant
Type: Boys Day 11–18 (Co-ed VIth Form)
No of pupils: B740 G38
Fees: (September 05) Day £10542

ST COLUMBA'S COLLEGE
King Harry Lane, St Albans, Hertfordshire AL3 4AW
Tel: (01727) 855185
Fax: (01727) 892024
Email: admissions@st-columbas.herts.sch.uk
Head: Mr N J B O'Sullivan
Type: Boys Day 4–18
No of pupils: 870
Fees: (September 05)
Day £7080–£8310

STEVENAGE

REDEMPTION ACADEMY
Cottswood House, Ridgemond Park, Telford, Stevenage, Hertfordshire SG2 0AU
Tel: (01438) 727370
Email: academy@redemption-church.org.uk
Head: Rev D Neale
Type: Co-educational Day 4–18
No of pupils: B8 G11
Fees: (September 05)
Day £3600–£5400

TRING

THE ARTS EDUCATIONAL SCHOOL*
Tring Park, Tring, Hertfordshire HP23 5LX
Tel: (01442) 824255
Fax: (01442) 891069
Email: info@aes-tring.com
Head: Mr S Anderson
Type: Co-educational Boarding and Day 8–18
No of pupils: B51 G222
No of boarders: F205
Fees: (September 05)
FB £16380–£23130
Day £11895–£18600

FRANCIS HOUSE
Aylesbury Road, Tring, Hertfordshire HP23 4DL
Tel: (01442) 822315
Fax: (01442) 827080
Head: Mrs Jane Billing
Type: Co-educational Day 2–11
No of pupils: B68 G63
Fees: (September 03)
Day £1395–£5190

WARE

ST EDMUND'S COLLEGE*
Old Hall Green, Ware, Hertfordshire SG11 1DS
Tel: (01920) 824247
Fax: (01920) 823011
Email: admissions@stedmundscollege.org
Head: Mr C P Long
Type: Co-educational Day and Boarding 3–18 Flexi-boarding available
No of pupils: B453 G252
No of boarders: F70 W27
Fees: (September 05) FB £16200
WB £14700 Day £7290

WATFORD

ST ANDREW'S MONTESSORI SCHOOL
High Elms Lane, Watford, Hertfordshire WD25 0JX
Tel: (01923) 681103
Fax: (01923) 681103
Email: son@care4free.net
Head: Mrs S O'Neill
Type: Co-educational Day 0–16
No of pupils: B40 G42
Fees: (September 05)
Day £1200–£6000

STANBOROUGH SCHOOL
Stanborough Park, Garston, Watford, Hertfordshire WD25 9JT
Tel: (01923) 673268
Fax: (01923) 893943
Head: Mr S Rivers
Type: Co-educational Day and Boarding 3–16 Flexi-boarding available
No of pupils: B150 G150
No of boarders: F30 W20
Fees: (September 04)
FB £13560–£15792 WB £9285
Day £3660–£6237

WELWYN

SHERRARDSWOOD SCHOOL
Lockleys, Welwyn, Hertfordshire AL6 0BJ
Tel: (01438) 714282
Fax: (01438) 840616
Email: admin@sherrardswood.plus.com
Head: Mrs L E Corry
Type: Co-educational Day 2–18
No of pupils: 310
Fees: (September 04)
Day £4845–£7800

ISLE OF MAN

CASTLETOWN

THE BUCHAN SCHOOL
Arbory Road, West Hill, Castletown, Isle of Man IM9 1RD
Tel: (01624) 820481
Fax: (01624) 820403
Email: principal@kwc.sch.im
Head: Mrs Alison Hope-Hedley
Type: Co-educational Day 4–11
No of pupils: B111 G92
Fees: (September 05)
Day £2070–£2700

KING WILLIAM'S COLLEGE
Castletown, Isle of Man IM9 1TP
Tel: (01624) 820428
Fax: (01624) 820401
Email: principal@kwc.sch.im
Head: Mr P D John
Type: Co-educational Boarding and Day 11–18 Flexi-boarding available
No of pupils: B192 G158
No of boarders: F84
Fees: (September 05)
FB £16005–£20100
Day £9705–£13800

ISLE OF WIGHT

NEWPORT

WESTMONT SCHOOL
82/88 Carisbrooke Road, Newport, Isle of Wight PO30 1BY
Tel: (01983) 523051
Fax: (01953) 523051
Email: head@westmontschool.freeserve.co.uk
Head: Mr D Reading
Type: Co-educational Day 0–19
No of pupils: B53 G49
Fees: (September 02)
Day £324–£4200

RYDE

RYDE SCHOOL
Queen's Road, Ryde, Isle of Wight PO33 3BE
Tel: (01983) 562229
Fax: (01983) 564714
Email: school.office@rydeschool.org.uk
Head: Dr N J England
Type: Co-educational Day and Boarding 3–18 Flexi-boarding available
No of pupils: B391 G367
No of boarders: F27 W12
Fees: (September 05)
FB £15960–£16740
WB £14895–£15675
Day £3900–£8190

SHANKLIN

PRIORY SCHOOL
Alverstone Manor, Luccombe Road, Shanklin, Isle of Wight PO37 7JB
Tel: (01983) 861222
Head: Mrs K D'Costa
Type: Co-educational Day 2–18
No of pupils: B56 G53
Fees: (September 03)
Day £277–£3285

KENT

ASHFORD

ASHFORD SCHOOL*

East Hill, Ashford, Kent TN24 8PB
Tel: (01233) 625171
Fax: (01233) 647185
Email: registrar@ashfordschool.co.uk
Head: Mr M R Buchanan
Type: Co-educational Day and Boarding Boys 3+ Girls 3–18 (Co-ed 3–11) Flexi-boarding available
No of pupils: B143 G522
No of boarders: F80 W10
Fees: (September 05)
FB £16785–£20190
WB £15105–£17553
Day £4764–£11088

SPRING GROVE SCHOOL

Harville Road, Wye, Ashford, Kent TN25 5EZ
Tel: (01233) 812337
Fax: (01233) 813390
Email: gibscan@btinternet.com
Head: Mr C A Gibbs
Type: Co-educational Day 3–11
No of pupils: B85 G90
Fees: (September 04)
Day £2400–£7500

BECKENHAM

ST CHRISTOPHER'S SCHOOL

49 Bromley Road, Beckenham, Kent BR3 5PA
Tel: (020) 8650 2200
Fax: (020) 8650 1031
Email: secretary@stchristophersthehall.co.uk
Head: Mr A Velasco
Type: Co-educational Day 3–11
No of pupils: B142 G126
Fees: (September 04)
Day £5205–£5610

BROADSTAIRS

HADDON DENE SCHOOL

57 Gladstone Road, Broadstairs, Kent CT10 2HY
Tel: (01843) 861176
Head: Mr N Armstrong
Type: Co-educational Day 3–11
No of pupils: 150
Fees: (September 04)
Day £2100–£4470

WELLESLEY HOUSE SCHOOL

Broadstairs, Kent CT10 2DG
Tel: (01843) 862991
Fax: (01843) 602068
Email: Wellesley.office@lineone.net
Head: Mr R R Steel
Type: Co-educational Boarding and Day 7–13
No of pupils: B80 G44
No of boarders: F69 W38
Fees: (September 05)
F/WB £ £15525 Day £13125

BROMLEY

ASHGROVE SCHOOL

116 Widmore Road, Bromley, Kent BR1 3BE
Tel: (020) 8460 4143
Email: enquiries@ashgrove.org.uk
Head: Dr P Ash
Type: Co-educational Day 3–11
No of pupils: 118
Fees: (September 04) Day £6075

BASTON SCHOOL

Baston Road, Hayes, Bromley, Kent BR2 7AB
Tel: (020) 8462 1010
Fax: (020) 8462 0438
Email: admin@bastonschool.org.uk
Head: Miss K A Greenwod
Type: Girls Day 2–16
No of pupils: 160
Fees: (September 05)
Day £6465–£8280

BICKLEY PARK SCHOOL

14/24 Page Heath Lane, Bickley, Bromley, Kent BR1 2DS
Tel: (020) 8467 2195
Fax: (020) 8325 5511
Email: info@bickleyparkschool.co.uk
Head: Mr P Ashley
Type: Boys Day 2–13
No of pupils: B380 G20
Fees: (September 05)
Day £3225–£9720

BISHOP CHALLONER RC SCHOOL

228 Bromley Road, Shortlands, Bromley, Kent BR2 0BS
Tel: (020) 8460 3546
Fax: (020) 8466 8885
Email: office@bishopchallonerschool.com
Head: Mr J A de Waal
Type: Co-educational Day 3–18
No of pupils: B271 G139
Fees: (September 05)
Day £4920–£6990

BREASIDE PREPARATORY SCHOOL*

41 Orchard Road, Bromley, Kent BR1 2PR
Tel: (020) 8460 0916
Fax: (020) 8466 5664
Email: info@breaside.co.uk
Head: Mr N D Kynaston
Type: Co-educational Day 3–11
No of pupils: B142 G107
Fees: (September 05)
Day £3630–£7185

BROMLEY HIGH SCHOOL GDST

Blackbrook Lane, Bickley, Bromley, Kent BR1 2TW
Tel: (020) 8468 7981
Fax: (020) 8295 1062
Email: bhs@bro.gdst.net
Head: Mrs L Duggleby
Type: Girls Day 4–18
No of pupils: 912
Fees: (September 05)
Day £7149–£9189

HOLY TRINITY COLLEGE
81 Plaistow Lane, Bromley, Kent BR1 3LL
Tel: (020) 8313 0399
Fax: (020) 8466 0151
Email: info@htc-bromley.co.uk
Head: Mrs P Lightfoot
Type: Girls Day 2–18 (Boys 3–5)
No of pupils: B10 G570
Fees: (September 04)
Day £6189–£8370

CANTERBURY

JUNIOR KING'S SCHOOL
Milner Court, Sturry, Canterbury, Kent CT2 0AY
Tel: (01227) 714000
Fax: (01227) 713171
Email: head@junior-kings.co.uk
Head: Mr P M Wells
Type: Co-educational Day and Boarding 3–13 Flexi-boarding available
No of pupils: B224 G163
No of boarders: F45 W17
Fees: (September 05)
F/WB £ £15810
Day £6900–£11700

KENT COLLEGE*
Whitstable Road, Canterbury, Kent CT2 9DT
Tel: (01227) 763231
Fax: (01227) 787450
Email: enquiries@kentcollege.co.uk
Head: Mr G G Carminati
Type: Co-educational Boarding and Day 3–18 Flexi-boarding available
No of pupils: B378 G309
No of boarders: F160 W3
Fees: (September 05)
FB £14979–£20535
WB £14979–£19902
Day £6816–£12015

KENT COLLEGE INFANT & JUNIOR SCHOOL
Vernon Holme, Harbledown, Canterbury, Kent CT2 9AQ
Tel: (01227) 762436
Fax: (01227) 763880
Email: gbarry@kentcollege.co.uk
Head: Mr A Carter
Type: Co-educational Day and Boarding 3–11 Flexi-boarding available
No of pupils: B106 G90
No of boarders: F6 W7
Fees: (September 05)
F/WB £ £14979
Day £6816–£10413

THE KING'S SCHOOL
Canterbury, Kent CT1 2ES
Tel: (01227) 595501
Fax: (01227) 595595
Email: headmaster@kings-school.co.uk
Head: Rev Canon K H Wilkinson
Type: Co-educational Boarding and Day 13–18
No of pupils: B434 G364
No of boarders: F639
Fees: (September 04) FB £19335
Day £13590

PERRY COURT RUDOLF STEINER SCHOOL
Garlinge Green, Chartham, Canterbury, Kent CT4 5RU
Tel: (01227) 738285
Fax: (01227) 731158
Head: Mrs M McIntee
Type: Co-educational Day 4–17
No of pupils: 250
Fees: (September 02)
Day £3783–£4404

ST CHRISTOPHER'S SCHOOL
New Dover Road, Canterbury, Kent CT1 3DT
Tel: (01227) 462960
Fax: (01227) 478220
Email: enquiries@stchristopherscanterbury.org.uk
Head: Mr D Evans
Type: Co-educational Day 3–11
No of pupils: B60 G70
Fees: (September 04)
Day £3810–£4425

ST EDMUNDS JUNIOR SCHOOL
St Thomas's Hill, Canterbury, Kent CT2 8HU
Tel: (01227) 475600
Fax: (01227) 471083
Email: info@stedmunds.org.uk
Head: Mr R G Bacon
Type: Co-educational Day and Boarding 3–13 Flexi-boarding available
No of pupils: B160 G80
No of boarders: F30 W10
Fees: (September 05) FB £14634
Day £2244–£10302

ST EDMUND'S SCHOOL
St Thomas Hill, Canterbury, Kent CT2 8HU
Tel: (01227) 475600
Fax: (01227) 471083
Email: headmaster@stedmunds.org.uk
Head: Mr J M Gladwin
Type: Co-educational Day and Boarding 13–18 Flexi-boarding available
No of pupils: B165 G155
No of boarders: F85
Fees: (September 05)
FB £14634–£20931
Day £10302–£13515

ST FAITH'S AT ASH SCHOOL
5 The Street, Ash, Canterbury, Kent CT3 2HH
Tel: (01304) 813409
Fax: (01304) 813235
Email: st-faithsatash@tinyworld.co.uk
Head: Mr S G I Kerruish
Type: Co-educational Day 3–11
No of pupils: B118 G90
Fees: (September 05)
Day £2619–£5187

CHISLEHURST

BABINGTON HOUSE SCHOOL
Grange Drive, Chislehurst, Kent BR7 5ES
Tel: (020) 8467 5537
Fax: (020) 8295 1175
Email: enquiries@babingtonhouse.com
Head: Miss D Odysseas
Type: Girls Day 3–16 (Boys 3–7)
No of pupils: B65 G165
Fees: (September 04)
Day £2268–£7680

DARUL ULOOM LONDON
Foxbury Avenue, Perry Street, Chislehurst, Kent BR7 6SD
Tel: (020) 8295 0637
Fax: (020) 8467 0655
Email: info@darululoomlondon.co.uk
Head: Mr M Musa
Type: Boys Boarding 11+
No of pupils: 160
No of boarders: F160
Fees: (September 03) FB £1800

FARRINGTONS SCHOOL*
Perry Street, Chislehurst, Kent BR7 6LR
Tel: (020) 8467 0256
Fax: (020) 8467 5442
Email: admissions@farringtons.kent.sch.uk
Head: Mrs C James
Type: Co-educational Day and Boarding Boys 4–7 Girls 4–19 Flexi-boarding available
No of pupils: B10 G516
No of boarders: F37 W5
Fees: (September 05)
FB £14850–£17040
WB £14250–£16020
Day £6480–£9270

CRANBROOK

BEDGEBURY SCHOOL*†
Goudhurst, Cranbrook, Kent TN17 2SH
Tel: (01580) 878143
Fax: (01580) 879136
Email: registrar@bedgeburyschool.co.uk
Head: Mrs H Moriarty and Mr J Lambert
Type: Girls Boarding and Day 2–18 (Boys day 2–7) Flexi-boarding available
No of pupils: B4 G293
No of boarders: F96 W49
Fees: (September 05)
F/WB £ £13035–£19725
Day £490–£12345

BENENDEN SCHOOL
Cranbrook, Kent TN17 4AA
Tel: (01580) 240592
Fax: (01580) 240280
Email: registry@benenden.kent.sch.uk
Head: Mrs C M Oulton
Type: Girls Boarding 11–18
No of pupils: 488
No of boarders: F488
Fees: (September 04) FB £21450

BETHANY SCHOOL
Goudhurst, Curtisden Green, Cranbrook, Kent TN17 1LB
Tel: (01580) 211273
Fax: (01580) 211151
Email: registrar@bethanyschool.org.uk
Head: Mr N Dorey
Type: Co-educational Boarding and Day 11–18
No of pupils: B260 G90
No of boarders: F60 W60
Fees: (September 05)
F/WB £ £18135–£19365
Day £11658–£12270

CRANBROOK SCHOOL*
Cranbrook, Kent TN17 3JD
Tel: (01580) 711800
Fax: (01580) 711828
Email: registrar@cranbrook.kent.sch.uk
Head: Mrs A Daly
Type: Co-educational Day and Boarding 13–18
No of pupils: B392 G359
No of boarders: F242
Fees: (September 05)
FB £8025–£8640

DULWICH PREPARATORY SCHOOL, CRANBROOK*
Coursehorn, Cranbrook, Kent TN17 3NP
Tel: (01580) 712179
Fax: (01580) 715322
Email: registrar@dcpskent.org
Head: Mr S L Rigby
Type: Co-educational Day and Boarding 3–13 Flexi-boarding available
No of pupils: B292 G231
No of boarders: F2 W8
Fees: (September 05) WB £15843
Day £3699–£10836

DEAL

NORTHBOURNE PARK SCHOOL
Betteshanger, Deal, Kent CT14 0NW
Tel: (01304) 611215/8
Fax: (01304) 619020
Email: office@northbourne.kent.sch.uk
Head: Mr S Sides
Type: Co-educational Day and Boarding 3–13 Flexi-boarding available
No of pupils: B85 G85
No of boarders: F43
Fees: (September 05)
FB £13860–£17160
Day £6000–£10650

DOVER

DOVER COLLEGE*†
Effingham Crescent, Dover, Kent CT17 9RH
Tel: (01304) 205969
Fax: (01304) 242208
Email: registrar@dovercollege.org.uk
Head: Mr Stephen Jones
Type: Co-educational Boarding and Day 4–18 Flexi-boarding available
No of pupils: B206 G154
No of boarders: F120 W13
Fees: (September 05)
FB £14250–£19065
WB £13260–£14880
Day £4860–£9525

DUKE OF YORK'S ROYAL MILITARY SCHOOL
Dover, Kent CT15 5EQ
Tel: (01304) 245024
Fax: (01304) 245019
Email: headmaster@doyrms.com
Head: Mr J A Cummings
Type: Co-educational Boarding 11–18
No of pupils: B270 G230
No of boarders: F500
Fees: (September 05)
FB £1650–£4500

FAVERSHAM

LORENDEN PREPARATORY SCHOOL
Painter's Forstal, Faversham, Kent ME13 0EN
Tel: (01795) 590030
Fax: (01795) 538002
Email: admin@lorenden.org.uk
Head: Mrs M R Simmonds
Type: Co-educational Day 3–11
No of pupils: B60 G60
Fees: (September 05)
Day £2802–£6648

FOLKESTONE

ST MARY'S WESTBROOK*
Ravenlea Road, Folkestone, Kent CT20 2JU
Tel: (01303) 854006
Fax: (01303) 249901
Email: hm@st-marys-westbrook.co.uk
Head: Mrs L A Watson
Type: Co-educational Boarding and Day 2–17 Flexi-boarding available
No of pupils: B97 G93
No of boarders: F42
Fees: (September 05) FB £14400
Day £4200–£9750

GILLINGHAM

BRYONY SCHOOL
Marshall Road, Rainham, Gillingham, Kent ME8 0AJ
Tel: (01634) 231511
Fax: (01634) 311746
Head: Mr D E Edmunds and Mrs M P Edmunds
Type: Co-educational Day 2–11
No of pupils: B124 G118
Fees: (September 04)
Day £2989–£3465

GRAVESEND

BRONTE SCHOOL
7 Pelham Road, Gravesend, Kent DA11 0HN
Tel: (01474) 533805
Fax: (01474) 352003
Email: bronteschoolenq@aol.com
Head: Mr R A Dyson
Type: Co-educational Day 3–11
No of pupils: B72 G54
Fees: (September 04)
Day £4060–£4785

COBHAM HALL*†
Cobham, Gravesend, Kent DA12 3BL
Tel: (01474) 823371
Fax: (01474) 825906
Email: enquiries@cobhamhall.com
Head: Mrs H Davy
Type: Girls Boarding and Day 11–18 Flexi-boarding available
No of pupils: 220
No of boarders: F114 W16
Fees: (September 05)
F/WB £ £17400–£21300
Day £10400–£14700

CONVENT PREPARATORY SCHOOL
46 Old Road East, Gravesend, Kent DA12 1NR
Tel: (01474) 533012
Fax: (01474) 533012
Email: sisteranne@sjcps.org
Head: Sister A C O'Connell
Type: Co-educational Day 3–11
No of pupils: B110 G105
Fees: (September 05) Day £3900

HAWKHURST

MARLBOROUGH HOUSE SCHOOL
High Street, Hawkhurst, Kent TN18 4PY
Tel: (01580) 753555
Fax: (01580) 754281
Email: head@marlbhouse.demon.co.uk
Head: Mr D N Hopkins
Type: Co-educational Day and Boarding 3–13 Flexi-boarding available
No of pupils: B191 G136
Fees: (September 05)
Day £3180–£11040

ST RONAN'S
Water Lane, Hawkhurst, Kent TN18 5DJ
Tel: (01580) 752271
Fax: (01580) 754882
Email: info@stronans.kent.sch.uk
Head: Mr W Trelawny-Vernon
Type: Co-educational Boarding and Day 3–13 Flexi-boarding available
No of pupils: B150 G90
No of boarders: W4
Fees: (September 04)
Day £1995–£3485

LONGFIELD

STEEPHILL INDEPENDENT SCHOOL*
Castle Hill, Fawkham, Longfield, Kent DA3 7BG
Tel: (01474) 702107
Fax: (01474) 706011
Email: secretary@steephill.co.uk
Head: Mrs C Birtwell
Type: Co-educational Day 3–11
No of pupils: B54 G54
Fees: (September 05) Day £4941

MAIDSTONE

SHERNOLD SCHOOL
Hill Place, Queens Avenue, Maidstone, Kent ME16 0ER
Tel: (01622) 752868
Head: Mrs L Dack
Type: Co-educational Day 3–11
No of pupils: B52 G96
Fees: (September 04)
Day £3600–£4350

SUTTON VALENCE PREPARATORY SCHOOL
Underhill, Chart Sutton, Maidstone, Kent ME17 3RF
Tel: (01622) 842117
Fax: (01622) 844201
Email: enquiries@svprep.svs.org.uk
Head: Mr A M Brooke
Type: Co-educational Day 3–11 Flexi-boarding available
No of pupils: B205 G173
Fees: (September 04)
Day £3210–£8100

SUTTON VALENCE SCHOOL
Sutton Valence, Maidstone, Kent ME17 3HL
Tel: (01622) 845200
Fax: (01622) 844103
Email: enquiries@svs.org.uk
Head: Mr J S Davies
Type: Co-educational Boarding and Day 11–18 Flexi-boarding available
No of pupils: B373 G137
No of boarders: F60 W90
Fees: (September 05)
F/WB £ £16320–£21450
Day £10380–£13560

RAMSGATE

THE JUNIOR SCHOOL, ST LAWRENCE COLLEGE*
College Road, Ramsgate, Kent
CT11 7AF
Tel: (01843) 572931
Fax: (01843) 572917
Email: ah@slcuk.com
Head: Mr R Tunnicliffe
Type: Co-educational Boarding and Day 11–3 Flexi-boarding available
No of pupils: B80 G52
No of boarders: F7
Fees: (September 05)
F/WB £ £16029 Day £4653–£9891

ST LAWRENCE COLLEGE*
College Road, Ramsgate, Kent
CT11 7AE
Tel: (01843) 572931
Fax: (01843) 572917
Email: ah@slcuk.com
Head: Rev C W M Aitken
Type: Co-educational Boarding and Day 3–18 Flexi-boarding available
No of pupils: B261 G172
No of boarders: F169 W2
Fees: (September 05)
F/WB £ £16029–£21780
Day £4653–£12963

ROCHESTER

GAD'S HILL SCHOOL*
Higham, Rochester, Kent ME3 7PA
Tel: (01474) 822366
Fax: (01474) 822977
Email: admissions@gadshillschool.co.uk
Head: Mr D G Craggs
Type: Co-educational Day 3–16
No of pupils: B170 G170
Fees: (September 05)
Day £5300–£6300

KING'S PREPARATORY SCHOOL
King Edward Road, Rochester,
Kent ME1 1UB
Tel: (01634) 888577
Fax: (01634) 888507
Email: walker@kings-school-rochester.co.uk
Head: Mr R Overend
Type: Co-educational Day and Boarding 8–13 Flexi-boarding available
No of pupils: B172 G56
No of boarders: F3 W1
Fees: (September 05)
F/WB £ £16005
Day £9135–£10380

KING'S SCHOOL ROCHESTER†
Satis House, Boley Hill, Rochester,
Kent ME1 1TE
Tel: (01634) 888555
Fax: (01634) 888505
Email: walker@kings-school-rochester.co.uk
Head: Dr I R Walker
Type: Co-educational Day and Boarding 4–18
No of pupils: B468 G198
No of boarders: F40 W8
Fees: (September 05)
F/WB £ £16005–£22560
Day £7125–£13410

ROCHESTER INDEPENDENT COLLEGE*
Star Hill, Rochester, Kent ME1 1XF
Tel: (01634) 828115
Fax: (01634) 405667
Email: admissions@rochester-college.org
Head: Mr A Brownlow and Mr B Pain
Type: Co-educational Day and Boarding 13–21 Flexi-boarding available
No of pupils: B110 G110
No of boarders: F70
Fees: (September 05) FB £19005
Day £12150

ST ANDREW'S SCHOOL
24–28 Watts Avenue, Rochester,
Kent ME1 1SA
Tel: (01634) 843479
Fax: (01634) 840789
Email: nkynaston@cfbt-hq.org.uk
Head: Mr N D Kynaston
Type: Co-educational Day 4–11
No of pupils: B150 G160
Fees: (September 03)
Day £3078–£3273

SEVENOAKS

COMBE BANK SCHOOL*
Sundridge, Sevenoaks, Kent
TN14 6AE
Tel: (01959) 563720
Fax: (01959) 561997
Email: enquiries@combebank.kent.sch.uk
Head: Mrs R Martin
Type: Girls Day 3–18
No of pupils: B10 G339
Fees: (September 05)
Day £6495–£11640

THE GRANVILLE SCHOOL
2 Bradbourne Park Road,
Sevenoaks, Kent TN13 3LJ
Tel: (01732) 453039
Fax: (01732) 743634
Email: evans@granville-school.co.uk
Head: Mrs J D Evans
Type: Girls Day 3–11 (Boys 3–5)
No of pupils: B10 G190
Fees: (September 04)
Day £3060–£7980

THE NEW BEACON
Brittains Lane, Sevenoaks, Kent
TN13 2PB
Tel: (01732) 452131
Fax: (01732) 459509
Email: admin@newbeacon.kent.sch.uk
Head: Mr R Constantine
Type: Boys Day 4–13
Flexi-boarding available
No of pupils: 400
Fees: (September 05)
Day £7200–£9300

RUSSELL HOUSE SCHOOL
Station Road, Otford, Sevenoaks,
Kent TN14 5QU
Tel: (01959) 522352
Fax: (01959) 524913
Email: head@russellhouse.kent.sch.uk
Head: Mrs A Cooke
Type: Co-educational Day 2–11
No of pupils: B100 G100
Fees: (September 05)
Day £1560–£8085

ST MICHAEL'S SCHOOL
Otford Court, Otford, Sevenoaks, Kent TN14 5SA
Tel: (01959) 522137
Fax: (01959) 526044
Email: office@stmichaels.kent.sch.uk
Head: Mr K S Crombie
Type: Co-educational Day 2–13
No of pupils: B233 G180
Fees: (September 04)
Day £651–£8562

SEVENOAKS PREPARATORY SCHOOL
Godden Green, Sevenoaks, Kent TN15 0JU
Tel: (01732) 762336
Fax: (01732) 764279
Email: admin@sevenoaksprep.kent.sch.uk
Head: Mr P J Oldroyd
Type: Co-educational Day 2–13
No of pupils: B230 G136
Fees: (September 05)
Day £5790–£8310

SEVENOAKS SCHOOL*
Sevenoaks, Kent TN13 1HU
Tel: (01732) 455133
Fax: (01732) 456143
Email: regist@sevenoaksschool.org
Head: Mrs C L Ricks
Type: Co-educational Day and Boarding 11–18
No of pupils: B482 G506
No of boarders: F340
Fees: (September 05)
FB £21609–£23430
Day £13413–£15234

SOLEFIELD SCHOOL
Solefields Road, Sevenoaks, Kent TN13 1PH
Tel: (01732) 452142
Fax: (01732) 740388
Email: solefield.school@btinternet.com
Head: Mr P Evans
Type: Boys Day 4–13
No of pupils: 160
Fees: (September 05)
Day £1960–£2575

WALTHAMSTOW HALL*
Hollybush Lane, Sevenoaks, Kent TN13 3UL
Tel: (01732) 451334
Fax: (01732) 740439
Email: registrar@walthamstow-hall.co.uk
Head: Mrs J Milner
Type: Girls Day 3–18
No of pupils: 478
Fees: (September 05)
Day £2520–£3920

SHEERNESS

ELLIOTT PARK SCHOOL
Marina Drive, Minster, Isle of Sheppey, Sheerness, Kent ME12 2DP
Tel: (01795) 873372
Email: elliottparkschool@tiscali.co.uk
Head: Mr R Barson
Type: Co-educational Day 4–11
No of pupils: B42 G36
Fees: (September 05) Day £3300

SIDCUP

BENEDICT HOUSE PREPARATORY SCHOOL
1–5 Victoria Road, Sidcup, Kent DA15 7HD
Tel: (020) 8300 7206
Fax: (020) 8309 6014
Email: Benedict.House@btinternet.com
Head: Mrs A Brown
Type: Co-educational Day 3–11
No of pupils: B70 G70

HARENC SCHOOL TRUST
167 Rectory Lane, Footscray, Sidcup, Kent DA14 5BU
Tel: (020) 8309 0619
Fax: (020) 8309 5051
Email: info@harencschool.co.uk
Head: Miss S Woodward
Type: Boys Day 3–11
No of pupils: 160
Fees: (September 04)
Day £4761–£6231

MERTON COURT PREPARATORY SCHOOL
38 Knoll Road, Sidcup, Kent DA14 4QU
Tel: (020) 8300 2112
Fax: (020) 8300 2112
Email: office.mertoncourt@argonet.co.uk
Head: Mr D Price
Type: Co-educational Day 2–11
No of pupils: B180 G152
Fees: (September 03)
Day £4665–£5850

WEST LODGE PREPARATORY SCHOOL
36 Station Road, Sidcup, Kent DA15 7DU
Tel: (020) 8300 2489
Fax: (020) 8308 1905
Email: info@westlodge.org.uk
Head: Mrs B A Windley
Type: Co-educational Day 3–11
No of pupils: B30 G130
Fees: (September 05)
Day £3240–£5400

TONBRIDGE

DERWENT LODGE SCHOOL FOR GIRLS
Somerhill, Tonbridge, Kent TN11 0NJ
Tel: (01732) 352124
Fax: (01732) 363381
Email: office@schoolsatsomerhill.com
Head: Mrs E Hill and Mr J Coakley
Type: Girls Day 7–11
No of pupils: 127
Fees: (September 05) Day £8790

FOSSE BANK MOUNTAINS SCHOOL
Noble Tree Road, Hildenborough, Tonbridge, Kent TN11 8ND
Tel: (01732) 834212
Fax: (01732) 834884
Email: office@fossebankschool.co.uk
Head: Mrs G Lovatt-Young
Type: Co-educational Day 3–11
No of pupils: B65 G70
Fees: (September 03)
Day £3039–£5601

HILDEN GRANGE SCHOOL
62 Dry Hill Park Road, Tonbridge, Kent TN10 3BX
Tel: (01732) 352706
Fax: (01732) 773360
Email: enquiries@hildengrange.kent.sch.uk
Head: Mr J Withers
Type: Co-educational Day 3–13
No of pupils: B204 G100
Fees: (September 04)
Day £2880–£8400

HILDEN OAKS SCHOOL
38 Dry Hill Park Road, Tonbridge, Kent TN10 3BU
Tel: (01732) 353941
Fax: (01732) 353942
Email: secretary@hildenoaks.co.uk
Head: Mrs S A Sunderland
Type: Co-educational Day Boys 2–7 Girls 2–11
No of pupils: B18 G125
Fees: (September 05)
Day £2580–£7170

SACKVILLE SCHOOL
Tonbridge Road, Hildenborough, Tonbridge, Kent TN11 9HN
Tel: (01732) 838888
Fax: (01732) 834999
Email: office@sackvilleschool.co.uk
Head: Mrs G M L Sinclair
Type: Co-educational Day 11–18
No of pupils: B175 G40
Fees: (September 05)
Day £7875–£9375

SOMERHILL PRE-PREPARATORY SCHOOL
Somerhill, Tonbridge, Kent TN11 0NJ
Tel: (01732) 352124
Fax: (01732) 363381
Email: office@schoolsatsomerhill.com
Head: Mrs J R Sorensen
Type: Co-educational Day 3–7
No of pupils: 278
Fees: (September 04)
Day £5955–£6885

TONBRIDGE SCHOOL*
Tonbridge, Kent TN9 1JP
Tel: (01732) 304297
Fax: (01732) 363424
Email: hmsec@tonbridge-school.org
Head: Mr T H P Haynes
Type: Boys Boarding and Day 13–18
No of pupils: 754
No of boarders: F433
Fees: (September 05) FB £23784
Day £16806

YARDLEY COURT
Somerhill, Tonbridge, Kent TN11 0NJ
Tel: (01732) 352124
Fax: (01732) 363381
Email: office@schoolsatsomerhill.com
Head: Mr J T Coakley
Type: Boys Day 7–13
Fees: (September 05)
Day £9360–£9720

TUNBRIDGE WELLS

BEECHWOOD SACRED HEART SCHOOL*
12 Pembury Road, Tunbridge Wells, Kent TN2 3QD
Tel: (01892) 532747
Fax: (01892) 536164
Email: bsh@beechwood.org.uk
Head: Mr N R Beesley
Type: Girls Boarding and Day 3–18 (Boys 3–11) Flexi-boarding available
No of pupils: B75 G302
No of boarders: F50 W20
Fees: (September 05) FB £18225 WB £16230 Day £11250

HOLMEWOOD HOUSE*
Langton Green, Tunbridge Wells, Kent TN3 0EB
Tel: (01892) 860000
Fax: (01892) 863970
Email: registrar@holmewood.kent.sch.uk
Head: Mr A S R Corbett
Type: Co-educational Boarding and Day 3–13 Flexi-boarding available
No of pupils: B322 G193
No of boarders: W6
Fees: (September 05) WB £16200
Day £4375–£12855

KENT COLLEGE PEMBURY
Tunbridge Wells, Kent TN2 4AX
Tel: (01892) 822006
Fax: (01892) 820221
Email: admissions@kentcollege.kent.sch.uk
Head: Mrs A Upton
Type: Girls Boarding and Day 3–18 Flexi-boarding available
No of pupils: 516
No of boarders: F62 W8
Fees: (September 05)
F/WB £ £15315–£19920
Day £5625–£12345

THE MEAD SCHOOL
16 Frant Road, Tunbridge Wells, Kent TN2 5SN
Tel: (01892) 525837
Fax: (01892) 525837
Email: meadschool@hotmail.com
Head: Mrs A Culley
Type: Co-educational Day 3–11
No of pupils: B85 G85
Fees: (September 04)
Day £2925–£6765

ROSE HILL SCHOOL
Culverden Down, Tunbridge Wells, Kent TN4 9SY
Tel: (01892) 525591
Fax: (01892) 533312
Email: admissions@rosehillschool.co.uk
Head: Mr P D Westcombe
Type: Co-educational Day 3–13
No of pupils: B197 G108
Fees: (September 03)
Day £2940–£8760

WEST WICKHAM

ST DAVID'S COLLEGE
Justin Hall, Beckenham Road, West Wickham, Kent BR4 0QS
Tel: (020) 8777 5852
Fax: (020) 8777 9549
Email: stdavids@dial.pipex.com
Head: Mrs S Adams
Type: Co-educational Day 4–11
No of pupils: B90 G70
Fees: (September 04)
Day £4200–£4350

WICKHAM COURT SCHOOL
Layhams Road, West Wickham,
Kent BR4 9HN
Tel: (020) 8777 2942
Fax: (020) 8777 4276
Email: wickham@schillerintschool.com
Head: Ms B Hunter
Type: Co-educational Day 2–11
No of pupils: B50 G60
Fees: (September 04)
Day £3447–£4608

WESTGATE-ON-SEA

CHARTFIELD SCHOOL
45 Minster Road,
Westgate-on-Sea, Kent CT8 8DA
Tel: (01843) 831716
Fax: (01843)221973
Email: chartfield1@btclick.com
Head: Mrs J L Prebble
Type: Co-educational Day 4–11
No of pupils: B39 G36
Fees: (September 04)
Day £2070–£2280

LANCASHIRE

ACCRINGTON

HEATHLAND COLLEGE
Broadoak, Sandy Lane,
Accrington, Lancashire BB5 2AN
Tel: (01254) 234284
Fax: (01254) 235398
Email: bursar@heathlandcollege.co.uk
Head: Mrs J Harrison
Type: Co-educational Day 0–11
No of pupils: B30 G25
Fees: (September 02)
Day £3291–£3780

ASHTON-UNDER-LYNE

GRAFTON HOUSE PREPARATORY SCHOOL
1 Warrington Street,
Ashton-under-Lyne, Lancashire
OL6 6XB
Tel: (0161) 343 3015
Fax: (0161) 339 1886
Email: grafton.house@btconnect.com
Head: Mrs P A Oakes
Type: Co-educational Day 1–11
No of pupils: 120
Fees: (September 04)
Day £2800–£4500

BLACKBURN

AL-ISLAH SCHOOL
108 Audley Range, Blackburn,
Lancashire BB1 1TF
Tel: (01254) 261573
Fax: (01254) 671604
Head: Mr N I Makda
Type: Co-educational Day 5–16
No of pupils: B32 G213
Fees: (September 03)
Day £425–£750

QUEEN ELIZABETH'S GRAMMAR SCHOOL
West Park Road, Blackburn,
Lancashire BB2 6DF
Tel: (01254) 686300
Fax: (01254) 692314
Email: headmaster@qegs.blackburn.sch.uk
Head: Dr D S Hempsall
Type: Co-educational Day 3–18
No of pupils: B665 G96
Fees: (September 05)
Day £4347–£7701

TAUHEEDUL ISLAM GIRLS HIGH SCHOOL
31 Bicknell Street, Blackburn,
Lancashire BB1 7EY
Tel: (01254) 54021
Fax: (01254) 54021
Email: admin@tighs.com
Head: Mr I Patel
Type: Girls Day 11–16
No of pupils: 265
Fees: (September 02) Day £615

WESTHOLME SCHOOL
Wilmar Lodge, Meins Road,
Blackburn, Lancashire BB2 6QU
Tel: (01254) 506070
Fax: (01254) 506080
Email: principal@westholmeschool.com
Head: Mrs L Croston
Type: Girls Day 3–18 (Boys 3–7)
No of pupils: B102 G987
Fees: (September 05)
Day £4080–£6438

WINDSMOOR HOUSE SCHOOL
Windsmoor House School, Witton
Bank, Spring Lane, Blackburn,
Lancashire BB2 2PW
Tel: (01254) 691195
Fax: (01254) 698221
Email: admin@windsmoorgroup.co.uk
Head: Mr P Strzalko and
Mrs A Lazarevic
Type: Co-educational Day Boys
11–16

BLACKPOOL

ARNOLD SCHOOL
Lytham Road, Blackpool,
Lancashire FY4 1JG
Tel: (01253) 346391
Fax: (01253) 336250
Email: principal@arnoldschool.com
Head: Mr B M Hughes
Type: Co-educational Day 11–18
No of pupils: B352 G387
Fees: (September 05) Day £6996

LANGDALE PREPARATORY SCHOOL
95 Warbreck Drive, Blackpool, Lancashire FY2 9RZ
Tel: (01253) 354812
Fax: (01253) 354812
Email: langdaleschool@btconnect.com
Head: Mr R A Rendell and Mr P G E Clay
Type: Co-educational Day 3–11
No of pupils: B46 G46
Fees: (September 05) Day £2724–£3144

BOLTON

BOLTON MUSLIM GIRLS SCHOOL
Swan Lane, Bolton, Lancashire BL3 6TQ
Tel: (01204) 361103
Fax: (01204) 533220
Head: Mr I A Patel
Type: Girls Day 11–16
No of pupils: 374
Fees: (September 03) Day £800–£950

BOLTON SCHOOL (BOYS' DIVISION)
Chorley New Road, Bolton, Lancashire BL1 4PA
Tel: (01204) 840201
Fax: (01204) 849477
Email: hm@boys.bolton.sch.uk
Head: Mr M E W Brooker
Type: Boys Day 7–18
No of pupils: 1106
Fees: (September 03) Day £5394–£7191

BOLTON SCHOOL (GIRLS' DIVISION)
Chorley New Road, Bolton, Lancashire BL1 4PB
Tel: (01204) 840201
Fax: (01204) 434710
Email: info@girls.bolton.sch.uk
Head: Mrs G Richards
Type: Girls Day 4–18 (Boys 4–7)
No of pupils: B99 G1117
Fees: (September 05) Day £5877–£7833

CLEVELANDS PREPARATORY SCHOOL
Chorley New Road, Bolton, Lancashire BL1 5DH
Tel: (01204) 843898
Fax: (01204) 848007
Email: clevelands@indschool.org
Head: Mrs G T Mitchell
Type: Co-educational Day 2–11
No of pupils: B90 G90
Fees: (September 04) Day £4392

LORD'S COLLEGE
53 Manchester Road, Bolton, Lancashire BL2 1ES
Tel: (01204) 523731
Head: Mrs H Seager
Type: Co-educational Day 10–17
No of pupils: B40 G35
Fees: (September 02) Day £2250

BURNLEY

ST JOSEPH'S CONVENT SCHOOL
Park Hill, Padiham Road, Burnley, Lancashire BB12 6TG
Tel: (01282) 455622
Type: Co-educational Day 3–11
No of pupils: B73 G71
Fees: (September 04) Day £2800

SUNNY BANK PREPARATORY SCHOOL
171–173 Manchester Road, Burnley, Lancashire BB11 4HR
Tel: (01282) 421336
Fax: (01282) 421336
Email: sunnybankkids@aol.com
Head: Mrs B Cross
Type: Co-educational Day 1–11
No of pupils: B45 G30
Fees: (September 03) Day £2520–£4500

BURY

BURY CATHOLIC PREPARATORY SCHOOL
Arden House, 172 Manchester Road, Bury, Lancashire BL9 9BH
Tel: (0161) 764 2346
Fax: (0161) 764 2346
Email: admin@burycatholicprepschool.co.uk
Head: Mrs A C Dean
Type: Co-educational Day 3–11
No of pupils: B80 G70
Fees: (September 05) Day £3540

BURY GRAMMAR SCHOOL
Tenterden Street, Bury, Lancashire BL9 0HN
Tel: (0161) 797 2700
Fax: (0161) 763 4655
Email: info@burygrammarschoolboys.co.uk
Head: Mr K Richards
Type: Boys Day 7–18
No of pupils: 800
Fees: (September 05) Day £4767–£6678

BURY GRAMMAR SCHOOL GIRLS
Bridge Road, Bury, Lancashire BL9 0HH
Tel: (0161) 797 2808
Fax: (0161) 763 4658
Email: info@bgsg.bury.sch.uk
Head: Mrs R S Georghiou
Type: Girls Day 4–18 (Boys 4–7)
No of pupils: B96 G897
Fees: (September 05) Day £4767–£6678

CHORLEY

THE BENNETT HOUSE SCHOOL
332 Eaves Lane, Chorley, Lancashire PR6 0DX
Tel: (01257) 267393
Fax: (01257) 262838
Email: catherine@bennetthouse332.fsnet.co.uk
Head: Mrs C A Mills
Type: Co-educational Day 2–8
No of pupils: B18 G17
Fees: (September 05) Day £4800

CLITHEROE

MOORLAND SCHOOL
Ribblesdale Avenue, Clitheroe, Lancashire BB7 2JA
Tel: (01200) 423833
Fax: (01200) 429339
Email: bursar@moorlandschool.co.uk
Head: Mr P Smith
Type: Co-educational Boarding and Day 4–16 Flexi-boarding available
No of pupils: B44 G47
No of boarders: F10 W8
Fees: (September 03) FB £10500–£11850 WB £9900–£10650 Day £3150–£5190

OAKHILL COLLEGE
Wiswell Lane, Whalley, Clitheroe, Lancashire BB7 9AF
Tel: (01254) 823546
Fax: (01254) 822662
Email: enquiries@oakhillcollege.co.uk
Head: Mr P S Mahon
Type: Co-educational Day 2–16
No of pupils: B143 G137
Fees: (September 04) Day £4431–£6864

STONYHURST COLLEGE*
Stonyhurst, Clitheroe, Lancashire BB7 9PZ
Tel: (01254) 827073
Fax: (01254) 827135
Email: admissions@stonyhurst.ac.uk
Head: Mr A J F Aylward
Type: Co-educational Boarding and Day 13–18 Flexi-boarding available
No of pupils: B306 G134
No of boarders: F252 W30
Fees: (September 05) FB £21303 WB £18225 Day £12456

FLEETWOOD

ROSSALL JUNIOR SCHOOL
Fleetwood, Lancashire FY7 8JW
Tel: (01253) 774222
Fax: (01253) 774222
Email: enquiries@rossallcorporation.co.uk
Head: Mr J Ingham
Type: Co-educational Day and Boarding 2–11 Flexi-boarding available
No of pupils: B71 G67
No of boarders: F3
Fees: (September 03) FB £12285 Day £4155–£4815

ROSSALL SCHOOL
Fleetwood, Lancashire FY7 8JW
Tel: (01253) 774201
Fax: (01253) 772052
Email: enquiries@rossallcorporation.co.uk
Head: Mr T Wilbur
Type: Co-educational Boarding and Day 11–18 Flexi-boarding available
No of pupils: B242 G184
No of boarders: F180
Fees: (September 04) FB £15912–£22710

ROSSALL SCHOOL INTERNATIONAL STUDY CENTRE
Rossall School, Broadway, Fleetwood, Lancashire FY7 8JW
Tel: (01253) 774204
Fax: (01253) 779415
Email: isc@rossallcorporation.co.uk
Head: Mr D Rose
Type: Co-educational Boarding 11–16
No of pupils: B60 G20
No of boarders: F80
Fees: (September 05) FB £15921–£22710

LANCASTER

SEDBERGH JUNIOR SCHOOL
Low Bentham, Lancaster LA2 7DB
Tel: (01524) 261275
Fax: (01524) 262944
Email: hmsjs@sedberghschool.org
Head: Mr P Reynolds
Type: Co-educational Boarding and Day 4–13 Flexi-boarding available
No of pupils: B79 G29
No of boarders: F27 W19
Fees: (September 05) FB £12885–£14610 WB £11970–£13905 Day £4770–£10920

LEYLAND

STONEHOUSE SCHOOL
90 School Lane, Leyland, Lancashire PR25 2TU
Head: Mrs Linda Williams
Type: Co-educational Day 0–11
Fees: (September 05) Day £3315

LYTHAM ST ANNES

KING EDWARD VII AND QUEEN MARY SCHOOL
Clifton Drive South, Lytham St Annes, Lancashire FY8 1DT
Tel: (01253) 784100
Fax: (01253) 784150
Email: admin@keqms.co.uk
Head: Mr R J Karling
Type: Co-educational Day 2–18
No of pupils: B369 G290
Fees: (September 05) Day £4632–£6720

ST ANNE'S COLLEGE GRAMMAR SCHOOL
293 Clifton Drive South, St Annes-on-Sea, Lytham St Annes, Lancashire FY8 1HN
Tel: (01253) 725815
Fax: (01253) 782250
Email: principal@collgram.u-net.com
Head: Mr S R Welsby
Type: Co-educational Day and Boarding 3–18 Flexi-boarding available
No of pupils: B109 G111
No of boarders: F11 W2
Fees: (September 05) FB £7000 WB £5075 Day £3885–£5625

OLDHAM

FARROWDALE HOUSE PREPARATORY SCHOOL
Farrow Street, Shaw, Oldham, Lancashire OL2 7AD
Tel: (01706) 844533
Email: farrowdale@aol.com
Head: Mr F G Wilkinson
Type: Co-educational Day 3–11
No of pupils: B56 G57
Fees: (September 04) Day £3562–£3750

FIRWOOD MANOR PREP SCHOOL
Broadway, Chadderton, Oldham, Lancashire OL9 0AD
Tel: (0161) 620 6570
Fax: (0161) 626 3550
Email: admin@firwoodmanor.org.uk
Head: Mrs P M Wild
Type: Co-educational Day 2–11
No of pupils: B79 G62
Fees: (September 03) Day £3405–£4161

GRASSCROFT INDEPENDENT SCHOOL
Lydgate Parish Hall, Stockport Road, Lydgate, Oldham, Lancashire OL4 4JJ
Tel: (01457) 820485
Head: Mrs J O'Hara
Type: Co-educational Day 2–7
No of pupils: 45
Fees: (September 03) Day £2838–£3000

THE HULME GRAMMAR SCHOOL FOR GIRLS
Chamber Road, Oldham,
Lancashire OL8 4BX
Tel: (0161) 624 2523
Fax: (0161) 620 0234
Email: girlsinfo@hulmegrammarschools.org.uk
Head: Miss M S Smolenski
Type: Girls Day 3–18
No of pupils: 571
Fees: (September 05)
Day £4377–£6735

THE OLDHAM HULME GRAMMAR SCHOOL
Chamber Road, Oldham,
Lancashire OL8 4BX
Tel: (0161) 624 4497
Fax: (0161) 652 4107
Email: boysenq@hulmegrammarschool.org.uk
Head: Mr K E Jones
Type: Boys Day 7–18
No of pupils: 719
Fees: (September 04)
Day £4290–£5997

OLDHAM HULME KINDERGARTEN
Plum Street, Oldham, Lancashire
OL8 1TJ
Tel: (0161) 624 2947
Fax: (0161) 628 9756
Email: kindergarten@hulmegrammar.oldham.sch.uk
Head: Mrs A S Richards
Type: Co-educational Day 3–7
No of pupils: B46 G53
Fees: (September 04) Day £3879

SADDLEWORTH PREPARATORY SCHOOL
Huddersfield Road, Scouthead,
Oldham, Lancashire OL4 4AG
Tel: (01457) 877442
Email: info@saddleworthpreparatoryschool.org.uk
Head: Mrs L W K Hirst
Type: Co-educational Day 4–7
No of pupils: B27 G29
Fees: (September 04) Day £3200

ORMSKIRK

KINGSWOOD COLLEGE AT SCARISBRICK HALL†
Southport Road, Ormskirk,
Lancashire L40 9RQ
Tel: (01704) 880200
Fax: (01704) 880032
Email: admin@kingswoodcollege.co.uk
Head: Mr E J Borowski
Type: Co-educational Day 2–16
No of pupils: B182 G196
Fees: (September 05)
Day £3000–£6225

POULTON-LE-FYLDE

EMMANUEL CHRISTIAN SCHOOL
Singleton Hall, Lodge Lane,
Singleton, Poulton-Le-Fylde,
Lancashire FY6 8LU
Tel: (01253) 876662
Fax: (01253) 882873
Head: Mr M Derry and
Mrs P Derry
Type: Co-educational Day 4–16
No of pupils: B53 G60

PRESTON

HIGHFIELD PRIORY SCHOOL
Fulwood Row, Fulwood, Preston,
Lancashire PR2 6SL
Tel: (01772) 709624
Fax: (01772) 655621
Email: info@highfieldpriory.co.uk
Head: Mr D Williams
Type: Co-educational Day 2–11
No of pupils: B134 G139
Fees: (September 05)
Day £4500–£5172

KIRKHAM GRAMMAR SCHOOL
Ribby Road, Kirkham, Preston,
Lancashire PR4 2BH
Tel: (01772) 671079
Fax: (01772) 672747
Email: info@kirkhamgrammar.co.uk
Head: Mr D R Walker
Type: Co-educational Boarding and Day 3–18 Flexi-boarding available
No of pupils: B504 G476
No of boarders: F65
Fees: (September 05) FB £12408
WB £12699 Day £5196–£6897

ST PIUS X PREPARATORY SCHOOL
200 Garstang Road, Fulwood,
Preston, Lancashire PR2 8RD
Tel: (01772) 719937
Fax: (01772) 787535
Email: st-pius-x@supanet.com
Head: Miss B Banks
Type: Co-educational Day 2–11
No of pupils: B136 G151
Fees: (September 04)
Day £4200–£4635

ROCHDALE

BEECH HOUSE SCHOOL
184 Manchester Road, Rochdale,
Lancashire OL11 4JQ
Tel: (01706) 646309
Fax: (01706) 860685
Email: bschool119@aol.com
Head: Mr K Sartain
Type: Co-educational Day 3–16
No of pupils: B110 G110
Fees: (September 04)
Day £1307–£3636

STONYHURST

ST MARY'S HALL
Stonyhurst, Nr Clitheroe,
Lancashire BB7 9PU
Tel: (01254) 826242
Fax: (01254) 827316
Email: saintmaryshall@stonyhurst.ac.uk
Head: Mr L A Crouch
Type: Co-educational Boarding and Day 4–13 Flexi-boarding available
No of pupils: B136 G110
No of boarders: F34 W13
Fees: (September 05) FB £15012
WB £13206 Day £10416

WIGAN

KINGSWAY SCHOOL
Greenough Street, Wigan,
Lancashire WN1 3SU
Tel: (01942) 244743
Fax: (01942) 244743
Head: Mrs B Jacobs
Type: Co-educational Day 3–16
No of pupils: B30 G30
Fees: (September 03) Day £2535

LEICESTERSHIRE

ASHBY-DE-LA-ZOUCH

MANOR HOUSE SCHOOL
South Street, Ashby-de-la-Zouch, Leicestershire LE65 1BR
Tel: (01530) 412932
Fax: (01530) 417435
Email: enquiries@manorhouseashby.co.uk
Head: Mr I R Clews
Type: Co-educational Day 4–16
No of pupils: B94 G73
Fees: (September 05) Day £4518–£6135

LEICESTER

GRACE DIEU MANOR SCHOOL
Grace Dieu, Thringstone, Leicester, Leicestershire LE67 5UG
Tel: (01530) 222276
Fax: (01530) 223184
Email: registrar@gracedieu.com
Head: Mr C E Foulds
Type: Co-educational Day 3–13
No of pupils: B190 G141
Fees: (September 05) Day £5010–£8110

IRWIN COLLEGE
164 London Road, Leicester, Leicestershire LE2 1ND
Tel: (0116) 255 2648
Fax: (0116) 2854935
Email: registrar@irwincollege.wireless.pipex.net
Head: Mrs L G Tonks
Type: Co-educational Boarding and Day 14–25
No of pupils: B110 G70
No of boarders: F160
Fees: (September 04) FB £11850 Day £700–£6300

LEICESTER GRAMMAR JUNIOR SCHOOL
Evington Hall, Spencefield Lane, Leicester, Leicestershire LE5 6HN
Tel: (0116) 210 1299
Fax: (0116) 210 0432
Email: redfearnm@leicestergrammar.org.uk
Head: Mrs M Redfearn
Type: Co-educational Day 3–11
No of pupils: B131 G117
Fees: (September 04) Day £5880

LEICESTER GRAMMAR SCHOOL
8 Peacock Lane, Leicester, Leicestershire LE1 5PX
Tel: (0116) 222 0400
Fax: (0116) 291 0505
Email: admissions@leicestergrammar.org.uk
Head: Mr C P M King
Type: Co-educational Day 10–18
No of pupils: B383 G305
Fees: (September 04) Day £7530

LEICESTER HIGH SCHOOL FOR GIRLS
454 London Road, Leicester, Leicestershire LE2 2PP
Tel: (0116) 270 5338
Email: enquiries@leicesterhigh.co.uk
Head: Mrs J Burns
Type: Girls Day 3–18
No of pupils: 435
Fees: (September 05) Day £4995–£7560

LEICESTER MONTESSORI GRAMMAR SCHOOL
58 Stoneygate Road, Leicester, Leicestershire LE2 2BN
Tel: (0116) 255 4441
Head: Mrs D Bailey
Type: Co-educational Day 3–18
No of pupils: 300
Fees: (September 03) Day £7020–£7884

LEICESTER MONTESSORI SCHOOL
194 London Road, Leicester, Leicestershire LE1 1ND
Tel: (0116) 270 6667
Fax: (0116) 255 4440
Head: Mrs D Bailey
Type: Co-educational Day 0–18
No of pupils: B90 G100

RATCLIFFE COLLEGE
Fosse Way, Ratcliffe on the Wreake, Leicester, Leicestershire LE7 4SG
Tel: (01509) 817000
Fax: (01509) 817004
Email: registrar@ratcliffe.leics.sch.uk
Head: Mr P Farrar
Type: Co-educational Boarding and Day 3–18 Flexi-boarding available
No of pupils: B401 G236
No of boarders: F96 W5
Fees: (September 05) FB £15993 WB £12723–£15993 Day £5685–£10617

ST CRISPIN'S SCHOOL (LEICESTER) LTD.†
6 St Mary's Road, Leicester, Leicestershire LE2 1XA
Tel: (0116) 270 7648
Email: enquiries@stcrispins.co.uk
Head: Mrs D Lofthouse and Mr J Lofthouse
Type: Co-educational Day 3–16
No of pupils: B75 G25
Fees: (September 04) Day £4293–£6171

STONEYGATE SCHOOL
London Road, Great Glen, Leicestershire LE8 9DJ
Tel: (0116) 259 2282
Email: stoneygate@webleicester.co.uk
Head: Mr J H Morris
Type: Co-educational Day 3–13
No of pupils: B221 G171
Fees: (September 02) Day £4515–£6045

STONEYGATE COLLEGE
2 Albert Road, Stoneygate, Leicester, Leicestershire LE2 2AA
Tel: (0116) 270 7414
Fax: (0116) 270 7414
Email: office@stoneygate.e7even.com
Head: Mr J C Bourlet
Type: Co-educational Day 3–11
No of pupils: B61 G70
Fees: (September 05) Day £4185–£5385

LOUGHBOROUGH

FAIRFIELD PREPARATORY SCHOOL

Leicester Road, Loughborough, Leicestershire LE11 2AE
Tel: (01509) 215172
Fax: (01509) 238648
Head: Mr R Outwin-Flinders
Type: Co-educational Day 4–11
No of pupils: B255 G234
Fees: (September 05) Day £5976

LOUGHBOROUGH GRAMMAR SCHOOL*

Burton Walks, Loughborough, Leicestershire LE11 2DU
Tel: (01509) 233233
Fax: (01509) 218436
Email: registrar@loughgs.leics.sch.uk
Head: Mr P B Fisher
Type: Boys Day and Boarding 10–18 Flexi-boarding available
No of pupils: 1010
No of boarders: F38 W10
Fees: (September 05) FB £14472 WB £12780 Day £8145

LOUGHBOROUGH HIGH SCHOOL

Burton Walks, Loughborough, Leicestershire LE11 2DU
Tel: (01509) 212348
Fax: (01509) 215720
Email: admin@loughhs.leics.sch.uk
Head: Miss B O'Connor
Type: Girls Day 11–18
No of pupils: 580
Fees: (September 05) Day £7479

OUR LADY'S CONVENT SCHOOL

Burton Street, Loughborough, Leicestershire LE11 2DT
Tel: (01509) 263901
Fax: (01509) 236193
Email: office@olcs.leics.sch.uk
Head: Sister S Fynn
Type: Girls Day 3–18 (Boys 3–5)
No of pupils: B7 G500
Fees: (September 05) Day £5376–£7659

PNEU SCHOOL

8 Station Road, East Leake, Loughborough, Leicestershire LE12 6LQ
Tel: (01509) 852229
Fax: (01509) 852229
Email: office@arley.pneu.eastleake.sch.uk
Head: Mrs E A Gibbs
Type: Co-educational Day 3–11
No of pupils: B40 G39
Fees: (September 05) Day £5520–£5550

MARKET BOSWORTH

THE DIXIE GRAMMAR SCHOOL

Station Road, Market Bosworth, Leicestershire CV13 0LE
Tel: (01455) 292244
Fax: (01455) 292151
Email: info@dixie.org.uk
Head: Mr John Wood
Type: Co-educational Day 10–18
No of pupils: B160 G200
Fees: (September 05) Day £7080

MARKET HARBOROUGH

BROOKE HOUSE COLLEGE*

Leicester Road, Market Harborough, Leicestershire LE16 7AU
Tel: (01858) 462452
Fax: (01858) 462487
Email: enquiries@brookehouse.com
Head: Mr G E I Williams
Type: Co-educational Boarding and Day 14–19
No of pupils: B100 G80
No of boarders: F175
Fees: (September 05) FB £16950 Day £9900

England

LINCOLNSHIRE

ALFORD

MAYPOLE HOUSE SCHOOL

Well Vale Hall, Alford, Lincolnshire LN13 0ET
Tel: (01507) 462764
Fax: (01507) 462681
Email: maypolehouseschool@hotmail.com
Head: Mrs A White
Type: Co-educational Day 3–16
No of pupils: B20 G20
Fees: (September 04) Day £2340–£2775

BOSTON

BICKER PREPARATORY SCHOOL

School Lane, Bicker, Boston, Lincolnshire PE20 3DW
Tel: (01775) 821786
Fax: (0177)
Head: Mrs S Page
Type: Co-educational Day 3–11
No of pupils: B40 G40
Fees: (September 05) Day £3200–£3400

CONWAY PREPARATORY SCHOOL

Tunnard Street, Boston, Lincolnshire PE21 6PL
Tel: (01205) 363150/355539
Fax: (01205) 363150
Email: conway@conwayschool.demon.co.uk
Head: Mr D A Wilson
Type: Co-educational Day 2–11
No of pupils: B30 G30
Fees: (September 05) Day £543–£3690

BOURNE

KIRKSTONE HOUSE SCHOOL
Main Street, Baston, Bourne, Lincolnshire PE6 9PA
Tel: (01778) 560350
Fax: (01778) 560547
Email: kirkstone.house@btclick.com
Head: Miss M Pepper
Type: Co-educational Day 3–16
No of pupils: B151 G99
Fees: (September 05)
Day £4110–£7320

WITHAM HALL
Witham-on-the-Hill, Bourne, Lincolnshire PE10 0JJ
Tel: (01778) 590222
Fax: (01778) 590606
Email: heads@withamhall.com
Head: Mr D Telfer & Mrs S Telfer
Type: Co-educational Boarding and Day 3–13 Flexi-boarding available
No of pupils: B116 G123
No of boarders: W50
Fees: (September 05)
F/WB £ £12990 Day £5820–£9480

GAINSBOROUGH

HANDEL HOUSE PREPARATORY SCHOOL
Northolme, Gainsborough, Lincolnshire DN21 2JB
Tel: (01427) 612426
Fax: (01427) 677854
Email: headteacher@handelhouseschool.fsnet.co.uk
Head: Mrs V C Haigh
Type: Co-educational Day 2–11
No of pupils: B34 G33
Fees: (September 05)
Day £2295–£2850

GRANTHAM

DUDLEY HOUSE SCHOOL
1 Dudley Road, Grantham, Lincolnshire NG31 9AA
Tel: (01476) 400184
Fax: (01476) 400184
Email: headteacher@dudleyhouse.lincs.sch.uk
Head: Mrs P Eastwood
Type: Co-educational Day 3–11
No of pupils: B37 G29
Fees: (September 03) Day £2850

THE GRANTHAM PREPARATORY SCHOOL
Gorse Lane, Grantham, Lincolnshire NG31 7UF
Tel: (01476) 593293
Fax: (01476) 593293
Email: admin@granthamprep.co.uk
Head: Mrs K Korcz
Type: Co-educational Day 3–11
No of pupils: B49 G50
Fees: (September 05)
Day £4320–£5400

LINCOLN

LINCOLN MINSTER SCHOOL
Hillside, Lindum Terrace, Lincoln, Lincolnshire LN2 5RW
Tel: (01522) 551300
Fax: (01522) 551310
Email: admin@lincolnminsterschool.co.uk
Head: Mr C Rickart
Type: Co-educational Day and Boarding 2–18 Flexi-boarding available
No of pupils: B355 G397
No of boarders: F42 W40
Fees: (September 03)
FB £12285–£14580
WB £11385–£13515
Day £5160–£7710

ST MARY'S PREPARATORY SCHOOL
5 Pottergate, Lincoln, Lincolnshire LN2 1PH
Tel: (01522) 524622
Fax: (01522) 523637
Email: office@st-marys-prep.lincs.sch.uk
Head: Mr M Upton
Type: Co-educational Day 2–11
No of pupils: B132 G140
Fees: (September 03)
Day £460–£6660

LOUTH

GREENWICH HOUSE INDEPENDENT SCHOOL
106 High Holme Road, Louth, Lincolnshire LN11 0HE
Tel: (01507) 609252
Fax: (01507) 606294
Head: Mrs J M Brindle
Type: Co-educational Day 0–11
No of pupils: 150

SLEAFORD

FEN SCHOOL
Side Bar Lane, Heckington Fen, Sleaford, Lincolnshire NG34 9LY
Tel: (01529) 460966
Head: Mrs J M Dunkley
Type: Co-educational Day 2–16 Flexi-boarding available
No of pupils: B14 G16
Fees: (September 04)
Day £2235–£4650

SPALDING

AYSCOUGHFEE HALL SCHOOL
Welland Hall, London Road, Spalding, Lincolnshire PE11 2TE
Tel: (01775) 724733
Fax: (01775) 724733
Email: admin@ahs.me.uk
Head: Mr B Chittick
Type: Co-educational Day 3–11
No of pupils: B80 G80
Fees: (September 03)
Day £3060–£3705

STAMFORD

COPTHILL SCHOOL
Barnack Road, Uffington, Stamford, Lincolnshire PE9 4TD
Tel: (01780) 757506
Fax: (01780) 482938
Email: copthill@btinternet.com
Head: Mr J A Teesdale
Type: Co-educational Day 2–11
No of pupils: B149 G140
Fees: (September 04)
Day £1020–£5850

STAMFORD HIGH SCHOOL
St Paul's Street, Stamford, Lincolnshire PE9 2BQ
Tel: (01780) 484200
Fax: (01780) 484201
Email: headshs@ses.lincs.sch.uk
Head: Dr P R Mason
Type: Girls Day and Boarding 11–18 Flexi-boarding available
No of pupils: 640
No of boarders: F60 W5
Fees: (September 03) FB £14928 WB £14880 Day £7800

STAMFORD JUNIOR SCHOOL
Stamford, Lincolnshire PE9 2LR
Tel: (01780) 484400
Fax: (01780) 484401
Email: head@shs.lincs.sch.uk
Head: Miss E M Craig
Type: Co-educational Boarding and Day 2–11
No of pupils: 355
Fees: (September 03) FB £12960 WB £12912 Day £6228

STAMFORD SCHOOL
St Paul's Street, Stamford, Lincolnshire PE9 2BQ
Tel: (01780) 750300/1
Fax: (01780) 750336
Email: headss@ses.lincs.sch.uk
Head: Dr P R Mason
Type: Boys Day and Boarding 11–18 Flexi-boarding available
No of boarders: F75 W10
Fees: (September 05) FB £17100 WB £17052 Day £9012

WOODHALL SPA

ST HUGH'S SCHOOL
Cromwell Avenue, Woodhall Spa, Lincolnshire LN10 6TQ
Tel: (01526) 352169
Fax: (01526) 351520
Email: sthughs-schooloffice@btconnect.com
Head: Mr S G Greenish
Type: Co-educational Boarding and Day 2–13 Flexi-boarding available
No of pupils: B95 G80
No of boarders: F20 W40
Fees: (September 05)
F/WB £ £12345–£12585
Day £5055–£9345

NORTH EAST LINCOLNSHIRE

GRIMSBY

ST JAMES' SCHOOL
22 Bargate, Grimsby, North East Lincolnshire DN34 4SY
Tel: (01472) 503260
Fax: (01472) 503275
Email: enquiries@saintjamesschool.co.uk
Head: Mrs S M Isaac
Type: Co-educational Day and Boarding 2–18 Flexi-boarding available
No of pupils: B127 G111
No of boarders: F33 W2
Fees: (September 05)
FB £10662–£14445
WB £9740–£13740
Day £4092–£8834

ST MARTIN'S PREPARATORY SCHOOL
63 Bargate, Grimsby, North East Lincolnshire DN34 5AA
Tel: (01472) 878907
Email: info@smpschool.fsnet.co.uk
Head: Mrs M Preston
Type: Co-educational Day 3–11
No of pupils: 224
Fees: (September 03)
Day £2925–£3300

England

NORTH LINCOLNSHIRE

BRIGG

BRIGG PREPARATORY SCHOOL

Bigby Street, Brigg, North Lincolnshire DN20 8EF
Tel: (01652) 653237
Fax: (01652) 658879
Email: info@briggprepschool.co.uk
Head: Mrs P Newman
Type: Co-educational Day 3–11
No of pupils: B57 G66
Fees: (September 03)
Day £3945–£4035

KEADBY

TRENTVALE PREPARATORY SCHOOL

Trentside, Keadby, North Lincolnshire DN17 3EF
Tel: (01724) 782904
Email: tvps@beeb.net
Head: Mr P Wright
Type: Co-educational Day 3–11
No of pupils: B40 G40
Fees: (September 04)
Day £2250–£2400

SCUNTHORPE

LYNTON PREPARATORY SCHOOL

250 Frodingham Road, Scunthorpe, North Lincolnshire DN15 7NW
Tel: (01724) 850 881
Fax: (01724) 850881
Email: ejbroadbent@btconnect.com
Head: Mrs E J Broadbent
Type: Co-educational Day 3–11
No of pupils: B27 G24
Fees: (September 05)
Day £2580–£2700

LONDON

E1

GREEN GABLES MONTESSORI PRIMARY SCHOOL

The Institute, 302 The Highway, Wapping, London E1W 3DH
Tel: (020) 7488 2374
Fax: (020) 7488 2376
Email: greengablesschool@talk21.com
Head: Mrs J Brierley
Type: Co-educational Day 0–8
No of pupils: B24 G25
Fees: (September 03)
Day £7020–£9960

MADNI GIRLS SCHOOL

Myrdle Street, London E1 1HL
Tel: (020) 377 1992
Fax: (020) 377 1424
Email: madni_school@hotmail.com
Head: Mrs F R Liyawdeen
Type: Girls Day 12–18
No of pupils: 215

E2

GATEHOUSE SCHOOL*

Sewardstone Road, Victoria Park, London E2 9JG
Tel: (020) 8980 2978
Fax: (020) 8983 1642
Email: admin@gatehouse.towerhamlets.sch.uk
Head: Mrs Belinda Canham
Type: Co-educational Day 3–11
No of pupils: B99 G101
Fees: (September 05)
Day £5535–£6765

RIVER HOUSE MONTESSORI SCHOOL

Admin Office, 2 Printingwolde Road, London E2 7PR
Tel: (020) 7680 1288
Fax: (020) 7488 3097
Head: Ms S Greenwood
Type: Co-educational Day 2–12
No of pupils: 25
Fees: (September 03)
Day £4635–£7740

E4

NORMANHURST SCHOOL

68/74 Station Road, Chingford, London E4 7BA
Tel: (020) 8529 4307
Fax: (020) 8524 7737
Email: info@normanhurstschool.co.uk
Head: Mr P J Williams
Type: Co-educational Day 3–16
Fees: (September 05)
Day £5800–£8100

E5

NORTH LONDON RUDOLF STEINER SCHOOL

A Steiner Waldorf Early Years Centre, Office at: 89 Blurton Road, London E5 0NH
Tel: (020) 8986 8968
Fax: (020) 8985 1332
Email: nlrss@talk21.com
Head: Ms G Reemer
Type: Co-educational Day 2–7
No of pupils: B26 G22
Fees: (September 03)
Day £1500–£2760

PARAGON CHRISTIAN ACADEMY
233–241 Glyn Road, London
E5 0JP
Tel: (020) 8985 1119
Head: Mr G Olson
Type: Co-educational Day 3–11
No of pupils: B17 G14
Fees: (September 02) Day £4320

E7

GRANGEWOOD INDEPENDENT SCHOOL
Chester Road, Forest Gate, London
E7 8QT
Tel: (020) 8472 3552
Fax: (020) 8552 8817
Email: admin@grangewoodschool.com
Head: Mrs C A Adams
Type: Co-educational Day 4–11
No of pupils: B45 G35
Fees: (September 04) Day £4107

E8

EAST LONDON CHRISTIAN CHOIR SCHOOL
Hephzibah Christian Centre,
35–43 Beechwood Road, London
E8 3DY
Tel: (0870) 020 1598
Fax: (020) 7254 5760
Email: admissions@elccs.org.uk
Head: Mr F Tobun
Type: Co-educational Day 2–16
No of pupils: B16 G18

E10

NOOR UL ISLAM PRIMARY SCHOOL
135 Dawlish Road, Leyton,
London E10 6QW
Tel: (020) 85588765
Fax: (020) 85585235
Email: primary@noorulislam.co.uk
Head: Mr Aslam Hansa
Type: Co-educational Day 4–11
No of pupils: B80 G79
Fees: (September 05)
Day £1875–£2100

E11

ST JOSEPH'S CONVENT SCHOOL
59 Cambridge Park, London
E11 2PR
Tel: (020) 8989 4700
Fax: (020) 8989 4700
Email: stjosephswanstead@btconnect.com
Head: Mrs C Youle
Type: Girls Day 3–11
No of pupils: 188
Fees: (September 04) Day £3450

E17

FOREST PREPARATORY SCHOOL
College Place, Snaresbrook,
London E17 3PY
Tel: (020) 8520 1744
Fax: (020) 8520 3656
Email: prep@forest.org.uk
Head: Mr I M McIntyre
Type: Co-educational Day 4–11
No of pupils: B108 G104
Fees: (September 05)
Day £6774–£8283

FOREST SCHOOL
College Place, Snaresbrook,
London E17 3PY
Tel: (020) 8520 1744
Fax: (020) 8520 3656
Email: info@forest.org.uk
Head: Mr A G Boggis
Type: Co-educational Day 4–18
(Single-sex ed 7–16)
No of pupils: B600 G600
Fees: (September 05)
Day £6774–£10716

HYLAND HOUSE
896 Forest Road, Walthamstow,
London E17 4AE
Tel: (020) 8520 4186
Fax: (020) 8520 1549
Head: Mrs Abbequaye
Type: Co-educational Day 3–11
No of pupils: B55 G40

E18

SNARESBROOK COLLEGE PREPARATORY SCHOOL
75 Woodford Road, South
Woodford, London E18 2EA
Tel: (020) 8989 2394
Fax: (020) 8989 4379
Email: office@snaresbrookcollege.org.uk
Head: Mrs L J Chiverrell
Type: Co-educational Day 3–11
No of pupils: B76 G84
Fees: (September 03)
Day £4577–£6122

EC1

CHARTERHOUSE SQUARE SCHOOL
40 Charterhouse Square, London
EC1M 6EA
Tel: (020) 7600 3805
Fax: (020) 7600 3805
Email: csschool@msn.com
Head: Mrs J Malden
Type: Co-educational Day 4–11
No of pupils: B90 G70
Fees: (September 03) Day £7650

DALLINGTON SCHOOL
8 Dallington Street, London
EC1V 0BW
Tel: (020) 7251 2284
Fax: (020) 7336 0972
Email: postmaster@dallingtonschool.co.uk
Head: Mrs M C Hercules
Type: Co-educational Day 3–11
No of pupils: B102 G110
Fees: (September 05)
Day £5430–£6555

THE ITALIA CONTI ACADEMY OF THEATRE ARTS
23 Goswell Road, London
EC1M 7AJ
Tel: (020) 8608 0047
Head: Mr C Vote
Type: Co-educational Day 9–21
No of pupils: B45 G200

EC2

CITY OF LONDON SCHOOL FOR GIRLS
St Giles' Terrace, Barbican, London EC2Y 8BB
Tel: (020) 7628 0841
Fax: (020) 7638 3212
Email: info@clsg.org.uk
Head: Dr Y Burne
Type: Girls Day 7–18
No of pupils: 675
Fees: (September 05) Day £10584

THE LYCEUM
6 Paul Street, London EC2A 4JH
Tel: (020) 7247 1588
Fax: (020) 7655 0951
Email: lyceumschool@aol.com
Head: Mr J Rowe and Mrs L Hannay
Type: Co-educational Day 3–11
Fees: (September 05) Day £8550

EC4

ST PAUL'S CATHEDRAL SCHOOL*
2 New Change, London EC4M 9AD
Tel: (020) 7248 5156
Fax: (020) 7329 6568
Email: admissions@spcs.london.sch.uk
Head: Mr A H Dobbin
Type: Co-educational Boarding and Day 4–13
No of pupils: B140 G66
No of boarders: F40
Fees: (September 05) FB £5199 Day £8964

CITY OF LONDON SCHOOL
Queen Victoria Street, London EC4V 3AL
Tel: (020) 7489 0291
Fax: (020) 7329 6887
Email: headmaster@clsb.org.uk
Head: Mr D Levin
Type: Boys Day 10–18
No of pupils: 871
Fees: (September 05) Day £10845

N2

ANNEMOUNT SCHOOL
18 Holne Chase, London N2 0QN
Tel: (020) 8455 2132
Fax: (020) 8381 4010
Email: headteacher@annemount.co.uk
Head: Mrs G Maidment
Type: Co-educational Day 2–7
No of pupils: B50 G50
Fees: (September 05) Day £4710–£7875

THE KEREM SCHOOL
Norrice Lea, London N2 0RE
Tel: (020) 8455 0909
Fax: (020) 8209 0726
Email: admin@kerem.org.uk
Head: Mrs R Goulden
Type: Co-educational Day 4–11
No of pupils: B85 G85
Fees: (September 05) Day £6000–£6300

N3

AKIVA SCHOOL
Levy House, The Sternberg Centre, 80 East End Road, London N3 2SY
Tel: (020) 8349 4980
Fax: (020) 8349 4959
Head: Mrs S de Botton
Type: Co-educational Day 4–11
No of pupils: B81 G73
Fees: (September 03) Day £5280

BEIS SOROH SCHNEIRER
Finchley United Synagogue, Kinloss Gardens, London N3 3DU
Tel: (020) 8343 1190
Head: Mrs R Weiss
Type: Girls Day 3–9
No of pupils: 95

PARDES GRAMMAR BOYS' SCHOOL
Hendon Lane, London N3 1SA
Tel: (020) 8343 3568
Fax: (020) 8343 4804
Head: Rabbi D Dunner
Type: Boys Day 11–17
No of pupils: 250
Fees: (September 03) Day £4500

N4

HOLLY PARK MONTESSORI
The Holly Park, Methodist Church, Crouch Hill, London N4 4BY
Tel: (020) 7263 6563
Fax: (020) 7263 7022
Email: hpms@btinternet.com
Head: Mrs A Lake
Type: Co-educational Day 2–7
No of pupils: B30 G30
Fees: (September 04) Day £1320–£5460

N6

CHANNING JUNIOR SCHOOL
Fairseat, 1 Highgate High Street, London N6 5JR
Tel: (020) 8342 9862
Fax: (020) 8348 3122
Email: fairseat@channing.co.uk
Head: Mrs J Todd
Type: Girls Day 4–11
No of pupils: 167
Fees: (September 05) Day £9585

CHANNING SCHOOL
Highgate, London N6 5HF
Tel: (020) 8340 2328
Fax: (020) 8341 5698
Email: info@channing.co.uk
Head: Mrs B Elliott
Type: Girls Day 4–18
No of pupils: 560
Fees: (September 05) Day £9585–£10440

HIGHGATE SCHOOL
North Road, London N6 4AY
Tel: (020) 8340 1524
Fax: (020) 8340 7674
Email: admissions@highgateschool.org.uk
Head: Mr A S Pettitt
Type: Co-educational Day 3–18
No of pupils: B1009 G179
Fees: (September 05) Day £10695–£12585

N7

THE DEAN SCHOOL (FORMERLY PRIMROSE MONTESSORI SCHOOL)
66 Eden Grove, Holloway, London N7 8EN
Tel: (020) 7700 4955
Fax: (020) 7700 4955
Email: thedeanschool2004@yahoo.co.uk
Head: Mrs L Grandson
Type: Co-educational Day 2–11
No of pupils: B60 G50
Fees: (September 04) Day £5265

N10

MONTESSORI HOUSE AND PRINCES AVENUE SCHOOL
5 Princes Avenue, Muswell Hill, London N10 3LS
Tel: (020) 8444 4399
Email: mail@montessori-house.co.uk
Head: Mrs L Christoforou
Type: Co-educational Day 1–7
No of pupils: B48 G49
Fees: (September 05) Day £1000–£2500

NORFOLK HOUSE SCHOOL
10 Muswell Avenue, Muswell Hill, London N10 2EG
Tel: (020) 8883 4584
Fax: (020) 8883 4584
Email: office@norfolkhouseschool.org
Head: Mr M Malley
Type: Co-educational Day 4–11
No of pupils: B50 G50
Fees: (September 05) Day £7290

N11

WOODSIDE PARK INTERNATIONAL SCHOOL*†
6 Friern Barnet Lane, London N11 3LX
Tel: (020) 8920 0600
Fax: (020) 8368 3220
Email: admissions@wpis.org
Head: Mr D P Rose
Type: Co-educational Day 2–19
No of pupils: B261 G144
Fees: (September 05) Day £1400–£5100

N14

SALCOMBE PREPARATORY SCHOOL*
224–226 Chase Side, Southgate, London N14 4PL
Tel: (020) 8441 5282 / 5356
Fax: (020) 8441 5282
Email: info@salcombeprep.co.uk
Head: Mr F Steadman
Type: Co-educational Day 4–11
No of pupils: B185 G115
Fees: (September 05) Day £6720

VITA ET PAX SCHOOL
Priory Close, Green Road, Southgate, London N14 4AT
Tel: (020) 8449 8336
Fax: (020) 8440 0483
Email: vitaetpax@lineone.net
Head: Mrs M O'Connor
Type: Co-educational Day 3–11
No of pupils: B90 G90
Fees: (September 04) Day £4680

N16

LUBAVITCH HOUSE SENIOR SCHOOL FOR GIRLS
107–115 Stamford Hill, Hackney, London N16 5RP
Tel: (020) 8800 0022
Fax: (020) 8809 7324
Head: Rabbi S Lew
Type: Girls Day 11–18

MECHINAH LIYESHIVAH ZICHRON MOSHE
86 Amhurst Park, London N16 5AR
Tel: (020) 8800 5892
Head: Rabbi M Halpern
Type: Boys Day 11–16
No of pupils: 60

TAYYIBAH GIRLS SCHOOL
88 Filey Avenue, Stamford Hill, London N16 6JJ
Tel: (020) 8880 0085
Fax: (020) 8249 1767
Head: Mrs N B Qureshi
Type: Girls Day 5–18
No of pupils: 247

YESODEY HATORAH JEWISH SCHOOL
2–4 Amhurst Park, London N16 5AE
Tel: (020) 8800 8612
Email: yeshatorah@aol.com
Head: Rabbi Abraham Pinter
Type: Co-educational Day 3–16 (Single-sex ed)
No of pupils: B250 G710

YETEV LEV DAY SCHOOL FOR BOYS
111–115 Cazenove Road, London N16 6AX
Tel: (020) 8806 3834
Head: Mr Delange
Type: Boys Day 3–11
No of pupils: 320

N17

PARKSIDE PREPARATORY SCHOOL
Church Lane, Bruce Grove, Tottenham, London N17 7AA
Tel: (020) 8808 1451
Fax: (020) 8808 1451
Email: parksideprep2002@aol.com
Head: Mrs M Langford
Type: Co-educational Day 3–11
No of pupils: B27 G28
Fees: (September 03) Day £3789

N21

GRANGE PARK PREPARATORY SCHOOL
13 The Chine, Grange Park, London N21 2EA
Tel: (020) 8360 1469
Fax: (020) 8360 4869
Email: office@gpps.org.uk
Head: Mrs S R Gladwin
Type: Girls Day 4–11
No of pupils: 105
Fees: (September 05) Day £6450

KEBLE PREPARATORY SCHOOL
Wades Hill, Winchmore Hill, London N21 1BG
Tel: (020) 8360 3359
Fax: (020) 8360 4000
Email: office@kebleprep.co.uk
Head: Mr V W P Thomas
Type: Boys Day 4–13
No of pupils: 220
Fees: (September 05) Day £7575–£9450

PALMERS GREEN HIGH SCHOOL
104 Hoppers Road, Winchmore Hill, London N21 3LJ
Tel: (020) 8886 1135
Fax: (020) 8882 9473
Email: office@palmersgreen.enfield.sch.uk
Head: Mrs J C Edmundson
Type: Girls Day 3–16
No of pupils: 320
Fees: (September 05)
Day £2835–£8385

NW1

THE CAVENDISH SCHOOL*
31 Inverness Street, London NW1 7HB
Tel: (020) 7485 1958
Fax: (020) 7267 0098
Email: admissions@cavendish-school.co.uk
Head: Mrs L D Hayes
Type: Girls Day 3–11
No of pupils: 160
Fees: (September 05) Day £8598

FRANCIS HOLLAND SCHOOL*
Clarence Gate, Ivor Place, London NW1 6XR
Tel: (020) 7723 0176
Fax: (020) 7706 1522
Email: admin@fhs-nw1.org.uk
Head: Mrs V M Durham
Type: Girls Day 11–18
Fees: (September 04) Day £10875

INTERNATIONAL COMMUNITY SCHOOL*
4 York Terrace East, Regent's Park, London NW1 4PT
Tel: (020) 7935 1206
Fax: (020) 7935 7915
Email: admissions@ics.uk.net
Head: Mr P Hurd
Type: Co-educational Day 3–18
No of pupils: B120 G120
Fees: (September 05)
Day £9696–£12708

NORTH BRIDGE HOUSE LOWER PREP SCHOOL*
1 Gloucester Avenue, London NW1 7AB
Tel: (020) 7485 0661
Fax: (020) 7284 2508
Email: lowerprep@northbridgehouse.com
Head: Ms J Battye
Type: Co-educational Day 8–11
No of pupils: B72 G107
Fees: (September 05) Day £10035

NORTH BRIDGE HOUSE SENIOR SCHOOL*
1 Gloucester Avenue, London NW1 7AB
Tel: (020) 7267 6266
Fax: (020) 7284 2508
Email: seniorschool@northbridgehouse.com
Head: Miss A Ayre
Type: Co-educational Day 11–16
Fees: (September 05) Day £10035

NORTH BRIDGE HOUSE UPPER PREP SCHOOL*
1 Gloucester Avenue, London NW1 7AB
Tel: (020) 7485 9495
Fax: (020) 7284 2508
Email: upperprep@northbridgehouse.com
Head: Mr B Bibby
Type: Boys Day 10–13
No of pupils: 79
Fees: (September 05) Day £10035

SYLVIA YOUNG THEATRE SCHOOL
Rossmore Road, Marylebone, London NW1 6NJ
Tel: (020) 7402 0673
Fax: (020) 7723 1040
Email: info@sylviayoungtheatreschool.co.uk
Head: Ms F E Chave
Type: Co-educational Day and Boarding 10–16
No of pupils: B68 G88
No of boarders: W22
Fees: (September 05)
FB £10737–£13806
WB £8514–£11232
Day £5550–£7800

NW2

THE MULBERRY HOUSE SCHOOL
7 Minster Road, West Hampstead, London NW2 3SD
Tel: (020) 8452 7340
Fax: (020) 8452 7340
Email: info@mulberryhouseschool.com
Head: Ms B Lewis-Powell
Type: Co-educational Day 2–8
No of pupils: 200
Fees: (September 04)
Day £5640–£10387

NW3

DEVONSHIRE HOUSE PREPARATORY SCHOOL*
2 Arkwright Road, Hampstead, London NW3 6AE
Tel: (020) 7435 1916
Fax: (020) 7431 4787
Email: enquiries@devonshirehouseprepschool.co.uk
Head: Mrs S Alexander
Type: Co-educational Day Boys 2–13
No of pupils: B288 G240
Fees: (September 05)
Day £9300–£10200

THE HALL SCHOOL
23 Crossfield Road, Hampstead, London NW3 4NU
Tel: (020) 7722 1700
Fax: (020) 7483 0181
Email: office@hallschool.co.uk
Head: Mr P F Ramage
Type: Boys Day 4–13
No of pupils: 440
Fees: (September 05)
Day £9030–£11010

HAMPSTEAD FINE ARTS INDEPENDENT COLLEGE*
24 Lambolle Place, Hampstead, London NW3 4PG
Tel: (020) 7586 0312
Fax: (020) 7483 0355
Email: mail@hampsteadfinearts.com
Head: Ms C Cave and Mr N Cochrane
Type: Co-educational Day 14–19
No of pupils: B60 G45
Fees: (September 04) Day £12750

HAMPSTEAD HILL PRE-PREPARATORY & NURSERY SCHOOL
St Stephen's Hall, Pond Street, Hampstead, London NW3 2PP
Tel: (020) 7435 6262
Fax: (020) 7435 6262
Email: hampsteadhill@aol.com
Head: Mrs A Taylor
Type: Co-educational Day Boys 2–8 Girls 2–7
No of pupils: B150 G100
Fees: (September 03)
Day £5500–£10250

HEATHSIDE PREPARATORY SCHOOL
16 New End, Hampstead, London NW3 1JA
Tel: (020) 7794 5857
Fax: (020) 7435 6434
Email: heathside@school.freeserve.co.uk
Head: Ms J White and Ms M Remus
Type: Co-educational Day 3–11
No of pupils: B64 G60
Fees: (September 04)
Day £5250–£6900

HEREWARD HOUSE SCHOOL
14 Strathray Gardens, Hampstead, London NW3 4NY
Tel: (020) 7794 4820
Fax: (020) 7794 2024
Head: Mrs L Sampson
Type: Boys Day 4–13
No of pupils: 175
Fees: (September 05)
Day £8475–£10125

LYNDHURST HOUSE PREPARATORY SCHOOL*
24 Lyndhurst Gardens, Hampstead, London NW3 5NW
Tel: (020) 7435 4936
Email: pmg@lyndhursthouse.co.uk
Head: Mr M O Spilberg
Type: Boys Day 4–13
No of pupils: 140
Fees: (September 05)
Day £10050–£11520

MARIA MONTESSORI SCHOOL HAMPSTEAD
26 Lyndhurst Gardens, Hampstead, London NW3 5NW
Tel: (020) 7435 3646
Fax: (020) 7431 8096
Email: info@mariamontessori.org
Head: Mrs L Lawrence
Type: Co-educational Day 2–11
No of pupils: B30 G30
Fees: (September 04)
Day £3690–£6255

NORTH BRIDGE HOUSE JUNIOR SCHOOL*
8 Netherhall Gardens, London NW3 5RR
Tel: (020) 7435 2884
Fax: (020) 7794 1337
Email: junior@northbridgehouse.com
Head: Mrs R Allsopp
Type: Co-educational Day 6–8
No of pupils: B95 G91
Fees: (September 05) Day £10035

NORTH BRIDGE HOUSE NURSERY SCHOOL*
33 Fitzjohn's Avenue, London NW3 5JY
Tel: (020) 7435 9641
Fax: (020) 7431 7930
Email: nursery@northbridgehouse.com
Head: Mrs R Allsopp
Type: Co-educational Day 3–6
Fees: (September 05)
Day £5220–£10035

THE PHOENIX SCHOOL
36 College Crescent, London NW3 5LF
Tel: (020) 7722 4433
Fax: (020) 7722 4601
Email: info@ucsphoenix.org.uk
Head: Ms J Humble
Type: Co-educational Day 3–7
No of pupils: B70 G60
Fees: (September 04)
Day £5000–£9600

THE ROYAL SCHOOL, HAMPSTEAD*
65 Rosslyn Hill, Hampstead, London NW3 5UD
Tel: (020) 7794 7708
Fax: (020) 7431 6741
Email: admissions@royalschoolhampstead.net
Head: Mrs C Hawkins
Type: Girls Boarding and Day 3–18 Flexi-boarding available
No of pupils: 246
No of boarders: F25 W13
Fees: (September 04)
FB £11520–£14295
WB £9510–£11880
Day £5760–£7185

ST ANTHONY'S PREPARATORY SCHOOL
90 Fitzjohns Avenue, Hampstead, London NW3 6NP
Tel: (020) 7435 0316
Fax: (020) 7435 9223
Head: Mr P Anderson
Type: Boys Day 5–13
No of pupils: 288
Fees: (September 04)
Day £9165–£9420

ST MARGARET'S SCHOOL*
18 Kidderpore Gardens, London NW3 7SR
Tel: (020) 7435 2439
Fax: (020) 7431 1308
Email: headmistress@st-margarets.co.uk
Head: Mrs S Meaden
Type: Girls Day 4–16
No of pupils: 135
Fees: (September 05)
Day £7665–£8850

ST MARY'S SCHOOL HAMPSTEAD
47 Fitzjohn's Avenue, London NW3 6PG
Tel: (020) 7435 1868
Fax: (020) 7794 7922
Email: headmistress@stmh.co.uk
Head: Miss A Rawlinson
Type: Girls Day 2–11 (Boys 2–7)
No of pupils: B41 G244
Fees: (September 04)
Day £4092–£7650

SARUM HALL
15 Eton Avenue, London NW3 3EL
Tel: (020) 7794 2261
Fax: (020) 7431 7501
Email: office@sarumhallschool.co.uk
Head: Mrs C J Scott
Type: Girls Day 3–11
No of pupils: 165
Fees: (September 05)
Day £5760–£9585

SOUTH HAMPSTEAD HIGH SCHOOL
3 Maresfield Gardens, London NW3 5SS
Tel: (020) 7435 2899
Fax: (020) 7431 8022
Email: senior@shhs.gdst.net
Head: Mrs J Stephen
Type: Girls Day 4–18
No of pupils: 875
Fees: (September 05)
Day £7149–£9189

SOUTHBANK INTERNATIONAL SCHOOL, HAMPSTEAD*
16 Netherhall Gardens, Hampstead, London NW3 5TH
Tel: (020) 7243 3803
Fax: (020) 7727 3290
Email: admissions@southbank.org
Head: Mr N Hughes
Type: Co-educational Day 3–14
No of pupils: B94 G95
Fees: (September 05)
Day £12600–£17700

TREVOR ROBERTS'
57 Eton Avenue, London NW3 3ET
Tel: (020) 7586 1444
Fax: (020) 7722 0114
Email: trsenior@btconnect.com
Head: Mr S Trevor-Roberts
Type: Co-educational Day 5–13
No of pupils: B98 G80
Fees: (September 05)
Day £8340–£10590

UNIVERSITY COLLEGE SCHOOL
Frognal, Hampstead, London NW3 6XH
Tel: (020) 7435 2215
Fax: (020) 7433 2111
Email: seniorschool@ucs.org.uk
Head: Mr K J Durham
Type: Boys Day 11–18
Fees: (September 05) Day £12495

UNIVERSITY COLLEGE SCHOOL, JUNIOR BRANCH
11 Holly Hill, London NW3 6QN
Tel: (020) 7435 3068
Fax: (020) 7435 7332
Email: info@ucsjb.org.uk
Head: Mr K J Douglas
Type: Boys Day 7–11
Fees: (September 05) Day £11550

THE VILLAGE SCHOOL
2 Parkhill Road, Belsize Park, London NW3 2YN
Tel: (020) 7485 4673
Fax: (020) 7267 8462
Head: Mrs F M Prior
Type: Girls Day 4–11
No of pupils: 140

NW4

ALBANY COLLEGE*
21/24 Queen's Road, Hendon, London NW4 2TL
Tel: (020) 8202 5965
Fax: (020) 8202 8460
Email: info@albany-college.co.uk
Head: Mr R J Arthy
Type: Co-educational Day 14–19
No of pupils: B120 G81
Fees: (September 05)
Day £10500–£12000

BRAMPTON COLLEGE
Lodge House, Lodge Road, London NW4 4DQ
Tel: (020) 8203 5025
Fax: (020) 8203 0052
Email: enqs@bramptoncollege.com
Head: Mr B Canetti
Type: Co-educational Day 15–19
No of pupils: B131 G111
Fees: (September 04)
Day £2735–£12470

HENDON PREPARATORY SCHOOL*
20 Tenterden Grove, Hendon, London NW4 1TD
Tel: (020) 8203 7727
Fax: (020) 8203 3465
Email: info@hendonprep.co.uk
Head: Mr D Weale
Type: Co-educational Day 4–13
No of pupils: B90 G40
Fees: (September 05)
Day £7245–£9435

NW5

L'ILE AUX ENFANTS
22 Vicar's Road, London NW5 4NL
Tel: (020) 7267 7119
Head: Mr A Hadjadj
Type: Co-educational Day 3–11
No of pupils: 200

NW6

AL-SADIQ AND AL-ZAHRA SCHOOLS
134 Salusbury Road, London NW6 6PF
Tel: (020) 7372 6760
Fax: (020) 7372 2752
Email: alsadiq@btconnect.com
Head: Dr M Movahedi
Type: Co-educational Day 4–16 (Single-sex ed)
No of pupils: B181 G201
Fees: (September 03)
Day £1800–£3150

BROADHURST SCHOOL
19 Greencroft Gardens, London NW6 3LP
Tel: (020) 7328 4280
Fax: (020) 7328 9370
Email: office@broadhurstschool.com
Head: Miss D Berkery
Type: Co-educational Day 2–5
No of pupils: B70 G70
Fees: (September 05)
Day £5970–£10050

BRONDESBURY COLLEGE FOR BOYS
8 Brondesbury Park, London NW6 7BT
Tel: (020) 8830 4522
Fax: (020) 8830 4523
Email: brondesburycollege@hotmail.com
Head: Dr N Butt
Type: Boys Day 11–16
No of pupils: 119
Fees: (September 03) Day £5800

ISLAMIA GIRLS' SCHOOL
129 Salisbury Road, London
NW6 6PE
Tel: (020) 7372 3472
Fax: (020) 7604 4061
Email: headteacher@islamiaschools.com
Head: Ms A Ali
Type: Girls Day 11–16
No of pupils: 125
Fees: (September 05) Day £5500

NAIMA JEWISH PREPARATORY SCHOOL
21 Andover Place, London
NW6 5ED
Tel: (020) 7328 2802
Fax: (020) 7624 0161
Head: Mr D Hopkin
Type: Co-educational Day 3–11
No of pupils: B86 G90
Fees: (September 03)
Day £4797–£5970

RAINBOW MONTESSORI JUNIOR SCHOOL
13 Woodchurch Road, West Hampstead, London NW6 3PL
Tel: (020) 7328 8986
Fax: (020) 7624 4046
Email: rms@rainbowmontessori.co.uk
Head: Mrs L Madden
Type: Co-educational Day 5–12
No of pupils: B23 G34
Fees: (September 05)
Day £6960–£7980

NW7

BELMONT (MILL HILL PREPARATORY SCHOOL)
The Ridgeway, Mill Hill, London
NW7 4ED
Tel: (020) 8906 7270
Fax: (020) 8906 3519
Email: registrar@belmontschool.com
Head: Mrs L C Duncan
Type: Co-educational Day 7–13
No of pupils: B237 G148
Fees: (September 04) Day £10770

GOODWYN SCHOOL
Hammers Lane, Mill Hill, London
NW7 4DB
Tel: (020) 8959 3756
Fax: (020) 8906 8961
Head: Mr S W E Robertson
Type: Co-educational Day 3–11
No of pupils: B118 G107
Fees: (September 04)
Day £2805–£5880

MILL HILL SCHOOL*
The Ridgeway, Mill Hill, London
NW7 1QS
Tel: (020) 8959 1221
Fax: (020) 8906 2614
Email: registrations@millhill.org.uk
Head: Mr W R Winfield
Type: Co-educational Boarding and Day 13–18
No of pupils: B441 G160
No of boarders: F170
Fees: (September 05) FB £20715
Day £13206

THE MOUNT SCHOOL
Milespit Hill, Mill Hill, London
NW7 2RX
Tel: (020) 8959 3403
Fax: (020) 8959 1503
Email: admin@mountschool.com
Head: Mrs J K Jackson
Type: Girls Day 4–18
No of pupils: 400
Fees: (September 05)
Day £6885–£8085

ST MARTIN'S
22 Goodwyn Avenue, Mill Hill, London NW7 3RG
Tel: (020) 8959 1965
Fax: (020) 8959 9065
Email: info@stmartinsmillhill.co.uk
Head: Mrs A Wilson
Type: Co-educational Day 3–11
No of pupils: B50 G75
Fees: (September 05) Day £4875

NW8

ABERCORN SCHOOL
28 Abercorn Place, London
NW8 9XP
Tel: (020) 7286 4785
Fax: (020) 7266 0219
Email: a.greystoke@abercornschool.com
Head: Mrs A S Greystoke
Type: Co-educational Day 2–13
No of pupils: B190 G190
Fees: (September 05)
Day £5775–£10785

THE AMERICAN SCHOOL IN LONDON*
1 Waverley Place, London
NW8 0NP
Tel: (020) 7449 1200
Fax: (020) 7449 1350
Email: admissions@asl.org
Head: Dr W C Mules
Type: Co-educational Day 4–18
No of pupils: B676 G636
Fees: (September 05)
Day £15160–£18570

ARNOLD HOUSE SCHOOL
1, Loudoun Road, St John's Wood, London NW8 0LH
Tel: (020) 7266 4840
Fax: (020) 7266 6994
Email: office@arnoldhouse.co.uk
Head: Mr N M Allen
Type: Boys Day 5–13
No of pupils: 250
Fees: (September 05) Day £11250

ST CHRISTINA'S RC PREPARATORY SCHOOL
25 St Edmunds Terrace, Regents Park, London NW8 7PY
Tel: (020) 7722 8784
Fax: (020) 7586 3454
Email: vanda@stchristinasschool.co.uk
Head: Miss N Clyne Wilson
Type: Girls Day 3–11 (Boys 3–7)
No of pupils: B40 G180
Fees: (September 04) Day £6600

ST JOHNS WOOD PRE-PREPARATORY SCHOOL
St Johns Hall, Lords Roundabout, London NW8 7NE
Tel: (020) 7722 7149
Fax: (020) 7586 6093
Email: school@dircon.co.uk
Head: Mrs H Ellis
Type: Co-educational Day 3–7
No of pupils: B30 G30
Fees: (September 05) Day £4875–£9915

NW9

GOWER HOUSE SCHOOL
Blackbird Hill, London NW9 8RR
Tel: (020) 8205 2509
Fax: (020) 8200 6491
Head: Mr M Keane
Type: Co-educational Day 2–11
No of pupils: B120 G110
Fees: (September 02) Day £3765–£4725

ST NICHOLAS SCHOOL
22 Salmon Street, London NW9 8PN
Tel: (020) 8205 7153
Fax: (020) 8205 9744
Email: stnich@happychild.co.uk
Head: Mrs A Gregory
Type: Co-educational Day 2–11
No of pupils: B40 G40
Fees: (September 03) Day £2130–£4260

NW10

THE SWAMINARAYAN SCHOOL
260 Brentfield Road, Neasden, London NW10 8HE
Tel: (020) 8965 8381
Email: admin@swaminarayan.brent.sch.uk
Type: Co-educational Day 2–18

WELSH SCHOOL OF LONDON
Welsh School of London, c/o Stonebridge Primary School, Shakespeare Avenue, London NW10 8NG
Tel: (020) 8965 3585
Email: cymraeg@llundain.freeserve.co.uk
Head: Mr M H Davies
Type: Co-educational Day 3–11
No of pupils: B10 G5
Fees: (September 04) Day £1950

NW11

GOLDERS HILL SCHOOL
666 Finchley Road, London NW11 7NT
Tel: (020) 8455 2589
Fax: (020) 8209 0905
Head: Mrs A Eglash
Type: Co-educational Day 2–7
No of pupils: B110 G80
Fees: (September 03) Day £4080–£6450

THE KING ALFRED SCHOOL
149 North End Road, London NW11 7HY
Tel: (020) 8457 5200
Fax: (020) 8457 5264
Email: KAS@kingalfred.barnet.sch.uk
Head: Mrs D Moore
Type: Co-educational Day 4–18
No of pupils: B300 G300
Fees: (September 05) Day £9000–£11340

WENTWORTH TUTORIAL COLLEGE
6–10 Brentmead Place, London NW11 9LH
Tel: (020) 8458 8524
Head: Mr A Davies
Type: Co-educational Day 14–18
No of pupils: 150

SE3

BLACKHEATH HIGH SCHOOL GDST
Vanbrugh Park, Blackheath, London SE3 7AG
Tel: (020) 8853 2929
Fax: (020) 8853 3663
Email: info@bla.gdst.net
Head: Mrs E Laws
Type: Girls Day 3–18
No of pupils: 600
Fees: (September 05) Day £5514–£9189

BLACKHEATH PREPARATORY SCHOOL
4 St Germans Place, Blackheath, London SE3 0NJ
Tel: (020) 8858 0692
Fax: (020) 8858 7778
Email: info@blackheathprepschool.com
Head: Mrs E Cartwright
Type: Co-educational Day 3–11
No of pupils: B146 G156
Fees: (September 03) Day £2820–£6300

HEATH HOUSE PREPARATORY SCHOOL
37 Wemyss Road, Blackheath, London SE3 0TG
Tel: (020) 8297 1900
Fax: (020) 8297 1550
Email: info@heathhouseprepschool.com
Head: Mr I R Laslett
Type: Co-educational Day 4–11
No of pupils: B44 G38
Fees: (September 04) Day £6900–£7500

THE POINTER SCHOOL
19 Stratheden Road, Blackheath, London SE3 7TH
Tel: (020) 8293 1331
Fax: (020) 8293 1331
Email: secretary@pointers-school.co.uk
Head: Mr R J S Higgins
Type: Co-educational Day 3–11
No of pupils: B87 G75
Fees: (September 03) Day £1452–£6048

SE6

ST DUNSTAN'S COLLEGE
Stanstead Road, Catford, London SE6 4TY
Tel: (020) 8516 7200
Fax: (020) 8516 7300
Email: head@sdmail.org.uk
Head: Mrs Jane Davies
Type: Co-educational Day 4–18
No of pupils: B500 G422
Fees: (September 05) Day £7722–£10671

SE9

ST OLAVE'S PREPARATORY SCHOOL
106–110 Southwood Road, New Eltham, London SE9 3QS
Tel: (020) 8294 8930
Fax: (020) 8294 8939
Email: office@stolaves.org.uk
Head: Mrs C P Fisher
Type: Co-educational Day 3–11
No of pupils: B115 G88
Fees: (September 05)
Day £4140–£6600

SE12

COLFE'S SCHOOL
Horn Park Lane, London SE12 8AW
Tel: (020) 8852 2283
Fax: (020) 8297 1216
Email: head@colfes.com
Head: Mr R F Russell
Type: Co-educational Day 3–18
No of pupils: B677 G395
Fees: (September 05)
Day £7047–£10080

RIVERSTON SCHOOL
63–69 Eltham Road, London SE12 8UF
Tel: (020) 8318 4327
Fax: (020) 8297 0514
Email: info@riverston.greenwich.sch.uk
Head: Mrs S E Salathiel
Type: Co-educational Day 1–16
No of pupils: B245 G130
Fees: (September 04)
Day £4734–£6708

SE15

THE VILLA PRE-PREPARATORY SCHOOL
54 Lyndhurst Grove, London SE15 5AH
Tel: (0207) 7036216
Fax: (0207) 2526536
Email: thevillaschool@hotmail.com
Head: Mrs G Quinn
Type: Co-educational Day 4–7
No of pupils: B24 G24
Fees: (September 04) Day £6795

SE16

CAVENDISH SCHOOL
Surrey Docks Stadium, Salter Road, London SE16 5LH
Tel: (020) 7349 0088
Fax: (020) 7394 1015
Head: Mrs S D Craggs
Type: Co-educational Day 11–16
No of pupils: B25 G10
Fees: (September 05) Day £20000

SE19

VIRGO FIDELIS
147 Central Hill, Upper Norwood, London SE19 1RS
Tel: (020) 8653 2169
Fax: (020) 8766 8802
Email: virgofidelis@rmplc.co.uk
Head: Mrs J M Noronha
Type: Co-educational Day 3–11
No of pupils: B121 G142
Fees: (September 04)
Day £620–£1810

SE21

DULWICH COLLEGE
Dulwich Common, London SE21 7LD
Tel: (020) 8693 3601
Fax: (020) 8693 6319
Email: info@dulwich.org.uk
Head: Mr G G Able
Type: Boys Day and Boarding 7–18
No of boarders: F108 W20
Fees: (September 05) FB £22815 WB £21915 Day £11325

DULWICH COLLEGE PREPARATORY SCHOOL
42 Alleyn Park, Dulwich, London SE21 7AA
Tel: (020) 8670 3217
Fax: (020) 8766 7586
Email: registrar@dcpslondon.org
Head: Mr G Marsh
Type: Boys Day and Boarding 3–13 (Girls 3–5)
No of pupils: B785 G18
No of boarders: W30
Fees: (September 05)
WB £15513–£16761
Day £3522–£11409

OAKFIELD PREPARATORY SCHOOL
125–128 Thurlow Park Road, Dulwich, London SE21 8HP
Tel: (020) 8670 4206
Fax: (020) 8766 6744
Head: Mr B Wigglesworth
Type: Co-educational Day 2–11
No of pupils: B302 G243
Fees: (September 05)
Day £3849–£6138

ROSEMEAD PREPARATORY SCHOOL*
70 Thurlow Park Road, London SE21 8HZ
Tel: (020) 8670 5865
Fax: (020) 8761 9159
Email: admin@rosemeadprepschool.org.uk
Head: Mrs C Brown
Type: Co-educational Day 3–11
No of pupils: B157 G185
Fees: (September 05)
Day £5619–£6396

SE22

ALLEYN'S SCHOOL*
Townley Road, Dulwich, London SE22 8SU
Tel: (020) 8557 1500
Fax: (020) 8557 1462
Email: registrar@alleyns.org.uk
Head: Dr C Diggory
Type: Co-educational Day 4–18
No of pupils: B570 G588
Fees: (September 05)
Day £8790–£10680

JAMES ALLEN'S GIRLS' SCHOOL
East Dulwich Grove, London SE22 8TE
Tel: (020) 8693 1181
Fax: (020) 8693 7842
Email: postmaster@jags.org.uk
Head: Mrs M Gibbs
Type: Girls Day 11–18
No of pupils: 760
Fees: (September 05) Day £10305

JAMES ALLEN'S PREPARATORY SCHOOL
East Dulwich Grove, London SE22 8TE
Tel: (020) 8693 0374
Fax: (020) 8693 8031
Email: debbieh@jags.org.uk
Head: Mr P Heyworth
Type: Co-educational Day 4–11
No of pupils: B39 G261
Fees: (September 05) Day £8838

SE24

HERNE HILL SCHOOL
The Old Vicarage, 127 Herne Hill, London SE24 9LY
Tel: (020) 7274 6336
Fax: (020) 7924 9510
Email: enquiries@hernehillschool.co.uk
Head: Mrs V Tabone
Type: Co-educational Day 3–7
No of pupils: B125 G125
Fees: (September 05) Day £3360–£8355

EATON HOUSE SCHOOL BELGRAVIA*
3–5 Eaton Gate, Eaton Square, London SW1W 9BA
Tel: (020) 7730 9343
Fax: (020) 7730 1798
Email: llawrence@eatonhouseschools.com
Head: Miss L Watts
Type: Boys Day 4–8
No of pupils: 250
Fees: (September 05) Day £9150

SE26

SYDENHAM HIGH SCHOOL GDST
19 Westwood Hill, London SE26 6BL
Tel: (020) 8768 8000
Fax: (020) 8768 8002
Email: info@syd.gdst.net
Head: Mrs K Pullen
Type: Girls Day 4–18
No of pupils: 678
Fees: (September 04) Day £6729–£8649

SW1

EATON SQUARE SCHOOLS
79 Eccleston Square, London SW1V 1PP
Tel: (020) 7931 9469
Fax: (020) 7828 0164
Email: admissions@eatonsquare.westminster.sch.uk
Head: Mr Paul David
Type: Co-educational Day Boys 2–13 Girls 2–11
No of pupils: B245 G225
Fees: (September 05) Day £3820–£3975

FRANCIS HOLLAND SCHOOL
39 Graham Terrace, London SW1W 8JF
Tel: (020) 7730 2971
Fax: (020) 7823 4066
Email: office@fhs-sw1.org.uk
Head: Miss S Pattenden
Type: Girls Day 4–18
No of pupils: 475
Fees: (September 04) Day £8985–£10725

HELLENIC COLLEGE OF LONDON
67 Pont Street, Knightsbridge, London SW1X 0BD
Tel: (020) 7581 5044
Fax: (020) 7589 9055
Email: office@hellenic.org.uk
Head: Mrs F Bayliss
Type: Co-educational Day 3–16
No of pupils: B49 G45
Fees: (September 05) Day £7950–£10455

HILL HOUSE INTERNATIONAL JUNIOR SCHOOL
17 Hans Place, London SW1X 0EP
Tel: (020) 7584 1331
Fax: (020) 7591 3938
Head: Mr R Townend
Type: Co-educational Day 4–13
No of pupils: B610 G395
Fees: (September 05) Day £7000–£8600

MORE HOUSE*
22–24 Pont Street, Chelsea, London SW1X 0AA
Tel: (020) 7235 2855
Fax: (020) 7259 6782
Email: office@morehouse.org.uk
Head: Mrs L Falconer
Type: Girls Day 11–18
No of pupils: 220
Fees: (September 04) Day £9780

SUSSEX HOUSE SCHOOL
68 Cadogan Square, Chelsea, London SW1X 0EA
Tel: (020) 7584 1741
Fax: (020) 7589 2300
Head: Mr N P Kaye
Type: Boys Day 8–13
No of pupils: 180
Fees: (September 03) Day £10380

THOMAS'S KINDERGARTEN
14 Ranelagh Grove, London SW1W 8PD
Tel: (020) 7730 3596
Fax: (020) 7730 3596
Email: tspierenburg@thomas-s.co.uk
Head: Miss T Spierenburg
Type: Co-educational Day 2–4
No of pupils: B27 G27
Fees: (September 04) Day £950–£1195

WESTMINSTER ABBEY CHOIR SCHOOL
Dean's Yard, London SW1P 3NY
Tel: (020) 7222 6151
Fax: (020) 7222 1548
Email: headmaster@westminster-abbey.org
Head: Mr J Milton
Type: Boys Boarding 8–13 Flexi-boarding available
No of pupils: 32 *No of boarders:* F32
Fees: (September 04) FB £4293

WESTMINSTER CATHEDRAL CHOIR SCHOOL
Ambrosden Avenue, London SW1P 1QH
Tel: (020) 7798 9081
Fax: (020) 7630 7209
Email: office@choirschool.com
Head: Mr J Browne
Type: Boys Boarding and Day 8–13
No of pupils: 109
No of boarders: F31
Fees: (September 04) FB £5574 Day £10950

WESTMINSTER SCHOOL
17 Dean's Yard, Westminster, London SW1P 3PB
Tel: (020) 7963 1042
Fax: (020) 7963 1043
Email: registrar@westminster.org.uk
Head: Dr S Spurr
Type: Co-educational Boarding and Day Boys 13–18 Girls 16–18
No of pupils: B617 G117
No of boarders: F10 W168
Fees: (September 05)
F/WB £ £23046
Day £15693–£17313

WESTMINSTER UNDER SCHOOL
Adrian House, 27 Vincent Square, London SW1P 2NN
Tel: (020) 7821 5788
Fax: (020) 7821 0458
Email: under.school@westminster.org.uk
Head: Mr J P Edwards
Type: Boys Day 7–13
Flexi-boarding available
No of pupils: 267
Fees: (September 03) Day £9942

SW3

CAMERON HOUSE SCHOOL*
4 The Vale, Chelsea, London SW3 6AH
Tel: (020) 7352 4040
Fax: (020) 7352 2349
Email: info@cameronhouseschool.org
Head: Miss F N Stack
Type: Co-educational Day 4–11
No of pupils: B53 G67
Fees: (September 05) Day £10785

GARDEN HOUSE SCHOOL
Turks Row, London SW3 4TW
Tel: (020) 7730 1652
Fax: (020) 7730 0470
Email: info@gardenhouseschool.co.uk
Head: Mrs W Challen and Mr M Giles
Type: Co-educational Day 4–11 (Co-ed nursery)
No of pupils: B134 G287
Fees: (September 04)
Day £5625–£12267

JAMAHIRIYA SCHOOL
Glebe Place, London SW3 5JP
Tel: (020) 7352 6642
Fax: (020) 7352 6642
Head: Mr Alkawash
Type: Co-educational Day 5–17
No of pupils: B200 G200
Fees: (September 03)
Day £250–£1000

SW4

EATON HOUSE THE MANOR*
58 Clapham Common Northside, London SW4 9RU
Tel: (020) 7924 6000
Fax: (020) 7924 1530
Email: llawrence@eatonhouseschools.com
Head: Mr S Hepher and Mrs S Segrave
Type: Girls Day 2–4
No of pupils: B495 G25
Fees: (September 05)
Day £3750–£11040

PARKGATE HOUSE SCHOOL
80 Clapham Common North Side, London SW4 9SD
Tel: (020) 7350 2452
Fax: (020) 7738 1633
Email: office@parkgate-school.co.uk
Head: Ms C Shanley and Mrs T Masterson
Type: Co-educational Day 2–11
No of pupils: B100 G100
Fees: (September 05)
Day £3375–£9300

SW5

COLLINGHAM COLLEGE
23 Collingham Gardens, London SW5 0HL
Tel: (020) 7244 7414
Fax: (020) 7370 7312
Email: london@collingham.co.uk
Head: Mr G Hattee
Type: Co-educational Day 14–20
No of pupils: B120 G110
Fees: (September 05)
Day £11280–£14430

SW6

AL-MUNTADA ISLAMIC SCHOOL
7 Bridges Place, Parsons Green, London SW6 4HW
Tel: (020) 7471 8283
Fax: (020) 7371 7318
Head: Mr Z Chehimi
Type: Co-educational Day 4–11
No of pupils: B83 G93
Fees: (September 04) Day £2100

ERIDGE HOUSE
1 Fulham Park Road, Fulham, London SW6 4LJ
Tel: (020) 7471 4816
Email: office@eridgehouse.co.uk
Head: Mrs L Waring
Type: Co-educational Day 2–11
No of pupils: B50 G50
Fees: (September 05)
Day £4750–£8550

FULHAM PREP SCHOOL (PRE-PREP)
47A Fulham High Street, London SW6 3JJ
Tel: (020) 7371 9911
Fax: (020) 7371 9922
Email: admin@fulhamprep.co.uk
Head: Ms Di Steven
Type: Co-educational Day 4–7
No of pupils: B132 G92
Fees: (September 05) Day £9450

KENSINGTON PREP SCHOOL
596 Fulham Road, London SW6 5PA
Tel: (020) 7731 9300
Fax: (020) 7731 9301
Email: enquiries@kenprep.gdst.net
Head: Mrs P J F Lynch
Type: Girls Day 4–11
No of pupils: 285
Fees: (September 05) Day £8751

L'ECOLE DES PETITS
2 Hazlebury Road, London SW6 2NB
Tel: (020) 7371 8350
Fax: (020) 7736 9522
Email: ecolespetits@aol.com
Head: Mrs M Otten
Type: Co-educational Day 2–6 (Bilingual)
No of pupils: B65 G75
Fees: (September 04)
Day £3840–£5940

SINCLAIR HOUSE SCHOOL
159 Munster Road, Fulham, London SW6 6AD
Tel: (020) 7736 9182
Fax: (020) 7371 0295
Email: info@sinclairhouseschool.co.uk
Head: Mrs C T M O'Sullivan
Type: Co-educational Day 2–8
No of pupils: B28 G23
Fees: (September 04) Day £1400–£6900

SW7

DUFF MILLER
59 Queen's Gate, London SW7 5JP
Tel: (020) 7225 0577
Fax: (020) 7589 5155
Head: Mr C Denning
Type: Co-educational Day 14–18
No of pupils: B85 G85

EATON HOUSE THE VALE*
2 Elvaston Place, London SW7 5QH
Tel: (020) 7584 9151
Fax: (020) 7584 8368
Email: llawrence@eatonhouseschools.com
Head: Miss S Calder
Type: Co-educational Day Boys 4–8 Girls 4–11
No of pupils: B37 G56
Fees: (September 05) Day £9150

FALKNER HOUSE
19 Brechin Place, London SW7 4QB
Tel: (020) 7373 4501
Fax: (020) 7835 0073
Email: falknerhs@aol.com
Head: Mrs A Griggs
Type: Girls Day 3–11 (Co-ed 3–4)
No of pupils: B10 G170
Fees: (September 05) Day £5400–£10800

GLENDOWER PREPARATORY SCHOOL*
87 Queen's Gate, South Kensington, London SW7 5JX
Tel: (020) 7370 1927
Fax: (020) 7244 8308
Email: office@glendower.kensington.sch.uk
Head: Mrs R Bowman
Type: Girls Day 4–11
No of pupils: 187
Fees: (September 05) Day £9690

THE HAMPSHIRE SCHOOLS (KNIGHTSBRIDGE UNDER SCHOOL)
5 Wetherby Place, London SW7 4NX
Tel: (020) 7584 3297
Fax: (020) 7584 9733
Email: hampshire@indschool.org
Head: Mr A G Bray
Type: Co-educational Day 3–6
No of pupils: B45 G45
Fees: (September 04) Day £5280–£7530

THE HAMPSHIRE SCHOOLS (KNIGHTSBRIDGE UPPER SCHOOL)
63 Ennismore Gardens, London SW7 1NH
Tel: (020) 7584 3297
Fax: (020) 7584 9733
Email: hampshire@indschool.org
Head: Mr A G Bray
Type: Co-educational Day 5–8
No of pupils: B48 G48
Fees: (September 04) Day £8145–£9420

LYCEE FRANCAIS CHARLES DE GAULLE
35 Cromwell Road, London SW7 2DG
Tel: (020) 7584 6322
Fax: (020) 7823 7684
Email: proviseur@lyceefrancais.org.uk
Head: Mr A Becherand
Type: Co-educational Day 4–19
No of pupils: B1684 G1718
Fees: (September 04) Day £2292–£4935

MANDER PORTMAN WOODWARD
90–92 Queen's Gate, London SW7 5AB
Tel: (020) 7835 1355
Fax: (020) 7259 2705
Email: london@mpw.co.uk
Head: Mr S D Boyes
Type: Co-educational Day 14+
No of pupils: B207 G170
Fees: (September 05) Day £2102–£55796

QUEEN'S GATE SCHOOL*
133 Queen's Gate, Kensington, London SW7 5LE
Tel: (020) 7589 3587
Fax: (020) 7584 7691
Email: registrar@queensgate.org.uk
Head: Mrs A M Holyoak
Type: Girls Day 4–18
Fees: (September 05) Day £8700–£10875

ST NICHOLAS PREPARATORY SCHOOL*
23 Prince's Gate, London SW7 1PT
Tel: (020) 7225 1277
Fax: (020) 7823 7557
Email: stnicholas@mailbox.co.uk
Head: Mr D Wilson
Type: Co-educational Day 3–11
No of pupils: B125 G125
Fees: (September 05) Day £6060–£9735

ST PHILIP'S SCHOOL
6 Wetherby Place, London SW7 4ND
Tel: (020) 7373 3944
Fax: (020) 7244 9766
Email: info@stphilipschool.co.uk
Head: Mr H Biggs-Davison
Type: Boys Day 7–13
No of pupils: 111
Fees: (September 04) Day £9300

WESTMINSTER TUTORS
86 Old Brompton Road, London SW7 3LQ
Tel: (020) 7584 1288
Fax: (020) 7584 2637
Email: info@westminstertutors.co.uk
Head: Mr James Layland
Type: Co-educational Day Flexi-boarding available
No of pupils: B30 G30
Fees: (September 05) Day £12900–£16800

SW8

NEWTON PREP
149 Battersea Park Road, London SW8 4BX
Tel: (020) 7720 4091
Fax: (020) 7498 9052
Email: admin@newtonprep.london.sch.uk
Head: Mr R G Dell
Type: Co-educational Day 3–13
No of pupils: B290 G282
Fees: (September 05) Day £9150–£10530

THE WILLOW SCHOOL
c/o Clapham Baptist Church,
823–825 Wandsworth Road,
London SW8 3JL
Tel: (020) 7498 0319
Email: harriet@thewillownursery.com
Head: Mrs H Baring
Type: Co-educational Day 2–5
No of pupils: 38
Fees: (September 03)
Day £2865–£3000

SW10

REDCLIFFE SCHOOL*
47 Redcliffe Gardens, London
SW10 9JH
Tel: (020) 7352 9247
Fax: (020) 7352 6936
Email: admissions@redcliffeschool.com
Head: Miss R E Cunnah
Type: Co-educational Day Boys 3–8 Girls 3–11
No of pupils: B19 G73
Fees: (September 05) Day £8400

SW11

DOLPHIN SCHOOL (INCLUDING NOAH'S ARK NURSERY SCHOOLS)*
Northcote Road Baptist Church,
106 Northcote Road, London
SW11 6QW
Tel: (020) 7924 3472
Fax: (020) 8265 8700
Email: admissions@dolphinschool.org.uk
Head: Mrs S Rogers
Type: Co-educational Day 2–11
No of pupils: B84 G94
Fees: (September 05)
Day £3780–£6975

THE DOMINIE†
142 Battersea Park Road, London
SW11 4NB
Tel: (020) 7720 8783
Fax: (020) 7720 8783
Email: lrdominie@aol.com
Head: Mrs L Robertson
Type: Co-educational Day 6–12
No of pupils: B15 G15
Fees: (September 05) Day £15600

EMANUEL SCHOOL
Battersea Rise, London SW11 1HS
Tel: (020) 8870 4171
Fax: (020) 8877 1424
Email: enquiries@emanuel.org.uk
Head: Mr M D Hanley-Browne
Type: Co-educational Day 10–18
No of pupils: B501 G185
Fees: (September 05) Day £10974

NORTHCOTE LODGE SCHOOL
26 Bolingbroke Grove, London
SW11 6EL
Tel: (020) 8682 8888
Fax: (020) 8682 8890
Email: info@northwoodschool.com
Head: Mr P Cheeseman
Type: Boys Day 8–13
No of pupils: 183
Fees: (September 05)
Day £10560–£11325

THAMES CHRISTIAN COLLEGE
Wye Street, London SW11 2HB
Tel: (020) 7228 3933
Fax: (020) 7924 1112
Email: info@thameschristiancollege.org.uk
Head: Mr Timothy Rogers
Type: Co-educational Day 11–16
No of pupils: B50 G40
Fees: (September 04)
Day £1500–£8550

THOMAS'S KINDERGARTEN, BATTERSEA
The Crypt, Saint Mary's Church,
Battersea Church Road, London
SW11 3NA
Tel: (020) 7738 0400
Head: Miss I Jennings
Type: Co-educational Day 2–5
No of pupils: B24 G24
Fees: (September 03) Day £3600

THOMAS'S PREPARATORY SCHOOL
28–40 Battersea High Street,
London SW11 3JB
Tel: (020) 7978 0900
Fax: (020) 7978 0901
Email: Battersea@thomas-s.co.uk
Head: Mr B V R Thomas
Type: Co-educational Day 4–13
No of pupils: B270 G215
Fees: (September 05)
Day £10365–£11715

THOMAS' PREPARATORY SCHOOL CLAPHAM
Broomwood Road, London
SW11 6JZ
Tel: (020) 7326 9300
Fax: (020) 7326 9301
Email: clapham@thomas-s.co.uk
Head: Mrs P Evelegh
Type: Co-educational Day 4–13
No of pupils: B245 G276
Fees: (September 05)
Day £9825–£11115

SW12

BALHAM PREPARATORY SCHOOL
47a Balham High Road, London
SW12 9AW
Tel: (020) 8675 7747
Fax: (020) 8675 7912
Head: Mr K Bahauddin
Type: Co-educational Day 3–16
No of pupils: 500

BROOMWOOD HALL SCHOOL
74 Nightingale Lane, London
SW12 8NR
Tel: (020) 8682 8800
Fax: (020) 8675 0136
Email: broomwood@northwoodschools.com
Head: Mrs K A H Colquhoun
Type: Co-educational Day Boys 4–8 Girls 4–13
No of pupils: B165 G225
Fees: (September 03)
Day £7500–£9700

HORNSBY HOUSE SCHOOL
Hearnville Road, London
SW12 8RS
Tel: (020) 8673 7573
Fax: (020) 8673 6722
Email: school@hornsby-house.co.uk
Head: Mrs J Strong
Type: Co-educational Day 4–11
No of pupils: B161 G128
Fees: (September 04)
Day £7509–£8232

THE WHITE HOUSE PREP & WOODENTOPS KINDERGARTEN
24 Thornton Road, Clapham Park, London SW12 0LF
Tel: (020) 8674 9514
Email: office@whitehouseschool.com
Head: Mrs E Davies
Type: Co-educational Day 2–11
No of pupils: B60 G60
Fees: (September 05) Day £2625–£7485

SW13

THE HARRODIAN
Lonsdale Road, London SW13 9QN
Tel: (020) 8748 6117
Fax: (020) 8563 7327
Email: admin@harrodian.com
Head: Mr J R Hooke
Type: Co-educational Day 5–18
Fees: (September 05) Day £9357–£13053

ST PAUL'S PREPARATORY SCHOOL
Colet Court, Lonsdale Road, London SW13 9JT
Tel: (020) 8748 3461
Fax: (020) 8563 7361
Email: HMCC@stpaulsschool.org.uk
Head: Mr G J Thompson
Type: Boys Day 7–13
Fees: (September 05) Day £10920

ST PAUL'S SCHOOL
Lonsdale Road, Barnes, London SW13 9JT
Tel: (020) 8748 9162
Fax: (020) 8746 5353
Email: hmcc@stpaulsschool.org.uk
Head: Dr Martin Stephen
Type: Boys Day and Boarding 13–18 Flexi-boarding available
No of pupils: 830
No of boarders: F40 W40
Fees: (September 03) F/WB £ £19131 Day £12861

SW14

TOWER HOUSE SCHOOL
188 Sheen Lane, London SW14 8LF
Tel: (020) 8876 3323
Fax: (020) 8876 3321
Head: Mrs J Compton-Howlett
Type: Boys Day 4–13
No of pupils: 186
Fees: (September 04) Day £6804–£6996

SW15

HURLINGHAM PRIVATE SCHOOL
122 Putney Bridge Road, Putney, London SW15 2NQ
Tel: (020) 8874 7186
Fax: (020) 8875 0372
Email: admissions@hurlinghamschool.co.uk
Head: Mrs D Baker
Type: Co-educational Day 4–11
No of pupils: B95 G135
Fees: (September 05) Day £8145–£8745

IBSTOCK PLACE SCHOOL
Clarence Lane, Roehampton, London SW15 5PY
Tel: (020) 8876 9991
Fax: (020) 8878 4897
Email: registrar@ibstockplaceschool.co.uk
Head: Mrs A Sylvester Johnson
Type: Co-educational Day 3–18
No of pupils: B400 G355
Fees: (September 05) Day £4500–£11610

LION HOUSE SCHOOL
The Old Methodist Hall, Gwendolen Avenue, London SW15 6EH
Tel: (020) 8780 9446
Fax: (020) 8789 3331
Email: Lionhsp@yahoo.com
Head: Miss H J Luard
Type: Co-educational Day 3–8
No of pupils: B51 G54
Fees: (September 03) Day £2415–£6600

THE MERLIN SCHOOL
4 Carlton Drive, Putney Hill, London SW15 2BZ
Tel: (020) 8788 2769
Fax: (020) 8789 5227
Email: secretary@merlinschool.net
Head: Mrs K Prest
Type: Co-educational Day 4–8
No of pupils: 170
Fees: (September 03) Day £7270

PROSPECT HOUSE SCHOOL*
75 Putney Hill, London SW15 3NT
Tel: (020) 8780 0456
Fax: (020) 8780 3010
Email: info@prospecths.org.uk
Head: Mrs D Barratt
Type: Co-educational Day 3–11
No of pupils: B100 G100
Fees: (September 05) Day £4500–£9800

PUTNEY HIGH SCHOOL GDST
35 Putney Hill, London SW15 6BH
Tel: (020) 8788 4886
Fax: (020) 8789 8068
Email: putneyhigh@put.gdst.net
Head: Dr D V Lodge
Type: Girls Day 4–18
No of pupils: 877
Fees: (September 05) Day £7560–£9600

PUTNEY PARK SCHOOL
11 Woodborough Road, Putney, London SW15 6PY
Tel: (020) 8788 8316
Fax: (020) 8780 2376
Email: office@putneypark.london.sch.uk
Head: Mrs J Irving
Type: Co-educational Day Boys 4–8 Girls 4–16
No of pupils: B57 G222
Fees: (September 05) Day £7776–£8886

SW16

STREATHAM AND CLAPHAM HIGH SCHOOL
42 Abbotswood Road, London SW16 1AW
Tel: (020) 8677 8400
Fax: (020) 8677 2001
Email: enquiry@shc.gdst-net
Head: Mrs S Mitchell
Type: Girls Day 3–18 (Boys 3–5)
No of pupils: B1 G808
Fees: (September 04) Day £5187–£8649

WALDORF SCHOOL OF SOUTH WEST LONDON
Woodfields, Abbotswood Road, London SW16 1AP
Tel: (020) 8769 6587
Fax: (020) 8677 5334
Email: info@waldorf-swlondon.org
Head: Mr E Ladaga
Type: Co-educational Day 4–14
No of pupils: B55 G45
Fees: (September 05) Day £3090–£4414

SW17

EVELINE DAY SCHOOL
14 Trinity Crescent, Upper Tooting, London SW17 7AE
Tel: (020) 8672 4673
Fax: (020) 8672 7259
Head: Ms E Drut
Type: Co-educational Day 3–11
No of pupils: B34 G41
Fees: (September 04) Day £6761–£7956

FINTON HOUSE SCHOOL
171 Trinity Road, London SW17 7HL
Tel: (020) 8682 0921
Fax: (020) 8767 5017
Email: admissions@fintonhouse.org.uk
Head: Mr A Floyd
Type: Co-educational Day 4–11
No of pupils: B130 G180
Fees: (September 05) Day £8700–£9675

SW18

HIGHFIELD SCHOOL
256 Trinity Road, Wandsworth Common, London SW18 3RQ
Tel: (020) 8874 2778
Fax: (020) 88265 5262
Email: highfield@cmcl.dircon.co.uk
Head: Mrs V-J Lowe
Type: Co-educational Day 2–11
No of pupils: B39 G25
Fees: (September 04) Day £3300–£6585

THE ROCHE SCHOOL
11 Frogmore, Wandsworth, London SW18 1HW
Tel: (020) 8877 0823
Fax: (020) 8875 1156
Email: office@therocheschool.co.uk
Head: Dr J Roche
Type: Co-educational Day 3–11
No of pupils: B100 G105
Fees: (September 05) Day £4260–£8490

SW19

DONHEAD WIMBLEDON COLLEGE PREP SCHOOL
Donhead, 33 Edge Hill, Wimbledon, London SW19 4NP
Tel: (020) 8946 7000
Fax: (020) 8947 1219
Email: donheadoffice@btconnect.com
Head: Mr G C McGrath
Type: Boys Day 7–11
No of pupils: 160
Fees: (September 05) Day £5940

KING'S COLLEGE JUNIOR SCHOOL
Southside, Wimbledon Common, London SW19 4TT
Tel: (020) 8255 5335
Fax: (020) 8255 5339
Email: jsadmissions@kcs.org.uk
Head: Mr J A Evans
Type: Boys Day 7–13
No of pupils: 460
Fees: (September 04) Day £9855–£11085

KING'S COLLEGE SCHOOL
Wimbledon Common, London SW19 4TT
Tel: (020) 8255 5352
Fax: (020) 8255 5357
Email: admissions@kcs.org.uk
Head: Mr A C V Evans
Type: Boys Day 13–18
No of pupils: 752
Fees: (September 05) Day £13050

THE STUDY PREPARATORY SCHOOL
Camp Road, Wimbledon Common, London SW19 4UN
Tel: (020) 8947 6969
Fax: (020) 8944 5975
Email: wilberforce@thestudyprep.co.uk
Head: Mrs J Nicol
Type: Girls Day 4–11
No of pupils: 320
Fees: (September 04) Day £8385

WILLINGTON SCHOOL
Worcester Road, Wimbledon, London SW19 7QQ
Tel: (020) 8944 7020
Fax: (020) 8944 9596
Email: office@willingtonschool.co.uk
Head: Mr Graham Hill
Type: Boys Day 4–13
No of pupils: 210
Fees: (September 05) Day £6825–£8025

WIMBLEDON COMMON PREPARATORY SCHOOL
113 Ridgway, Wimbledon, London SW19 4TA
Tel: (020) 8946 1001
Fax: (020) 8946 1001
Email: info@wimbledoncommonprep.co.uk
Head: Mr N J Worsey
Type: Boys Day 4–8
No of pupils: 130
Fees: (September 05) Day £4770–£5220

WIMBLEDON HIGH SCHOOL GDST
Mansel Road, London SW19 4AB
Tel: (020) 8971 0900
Fax: (020) 8971 0901
Email: info@wim.gdst.net
Head: Mrs P H Wilkes
Type: Girls Day 4–18
No of pupils: 900
Fees: (September 04) Day £6729–£8649

HALL SCHOOL WIMBLEDON
17 The Downs (Senior School), Wimbledon, London SW20 8HF
Tel: (020) 8879 9200
Fax: (020) 8946 0864
Email: enquiries@hallschoolwimbledon.co.uk
Head: Mr T Hobbs and Mr J Hobbs
Type: Co-educational Day 4–16
No of pupils: B320 G280
Fees: (September 05)
Day £7317–£9315

SW20

THE NORWEGIAN SCHOOL
28 Arterberry Road, Wimbledon, London SW20 8AH
Tel: (020) 8947 6617/6627
Fax: (020) 8944 7345
Email: dnslondon@aol.com
Head: Mr A Larsen
Type: Co-educational Day 3–16
No of pupils: 101
Day £5600–£7450

THE ROWANS SCHOOL
19 Drax Avenue, Wimbledon, London SW20 0EG
Tel: (020) 8946 8220
Fax: (020) 8944 0822
Email: therowansschool@btinternet.com
Head: Mrs J Anderson
Type: Co-educational Day 3–8
No of pupils: B75 G50
Fees: (September 05)
Day £2805–£5445

URSULINE PREPARATORY SCHOOL
18 The Downs, London SW20 8HR
Tel: (020) 8947 0859
Fax: (020) 8947 0885
Email: ursulineprpsch@aol.com
Head: Mrs C Grogan
Type: Girls Day 3–11 (Boys 3–7)
No of pupils: B76 G172
Fees: (September 03)
Day £2415–£4095

W1

ALBEMARLE INDEPENDENT COLLEGE
18 Dunraven Street, London W1K 7FE
Tel: (020) 7409 7273
Fax: (020) 7629 9146
Email: admin@albemarle.org.uk
Head: Mr J Eytle and Miss B Mellon
Type: Co-educational Day 14–19 Flexi-boarding available
No of pupils: B76 G62
Fees: (September 05)
Day £11250–£12780

DAVIES LAING AND DICK*
100 Marylebone Lane, London W1U 2QB
Tel: (020) 7935 8411
Fax: (020) 7935 0755
Email: dld@dld.org
Head: Ms E Rickards
Type: Co-educational Day 14–19
No of pupils: B211 G174
Fees: (September 05)
Day £4876–£16250

GREAT BEGINNINGS MONTESSORI SCHOOL
82a Chiltern Street, Marylebone, London W1U 5AQ
Tel: (020) 7486 2276
Head: Mrs W Innes
Type: Co-educational Day 2–6
No of pupils: B30 G30
Day £1050–£1750

PORTLAND PLACE
56–58 Portland Place, London W1B 1NJ
Tel: (020) 7307 8700
Fax: (020) 7436 2676
Email: admin@portland-place.co.uk
Head: Mr R Walker
Type: Co-educational Day 11–18
No of pupils: B239 G83
Fees: (September 05) Day £10950

QUEEN'S COLLEGE
43–49 Harley Street, London W1G 8BT
Tel: (020) 7291 7000
Fax: (020) 7291 7099
Email: queens@qcl.org.uk
Head: Miss M M Connell
Type: Girls Day 11–18
No of pupils: 372
Fees: (September 05) Day £11400

QUEEN'S COLLEGE PREP SCHOOL
61 Portland Place, London W1B 1QP
Tel: (0207) 2910660
Fax: (0207) 2910669
Email: tbrook@qcps.org.uk
Head: Mrs J Davies
Type: Girls Day 4–11
No of pupils: 135

SOUTHBANK INTERNATIONAL SCHOOL, WESTMINSTER*
63–65 Portland Place, London W1B 1QR
Tel: (020) 7243 3803
Fax: (020) 7727 3290
Email: admissions@southbank.org
Head: Mr N Hughes and Ms C Thearle
Type: Co-educational Day 11–18
No of pupils: B128 G137
Fees: (September 05)
Day £16050–£17700

W2

CONNAUGHT HOUSE
47 Connaught Square, London W2 2HL
Tel: (020) 7262 8830
Fax: (020) 7262 0781
Head: Mr & Mrs F Hampton
Type: Co-educational Day Boys 4–8 Girls 4–11
No of pupils: B35 G35
Fees: (September 04)
Day £6525–£9750

THE HAMPSHIRE SCHOOLS (KENSINGTON GARDENS)
9 Queensborough Terrace, London W2 3TB
Tel: (020) 7584 3297
Fax: (020) 7584 9733
Email: hampshire@indschool.org
Head: Mr A G Bray
Type: Co-educational Day 4–13
No of pupils: B80 G80
Fees: (September 03)
Day £7005–£8625

LANSDOWNE COLLEGE*
40–44 Bark Place, London W2 4AT
Tel: (020) 7616 4400
Fax: (020) 7616 4401
Email: education@lansdownecollege.com
Head: Mr H Templeton
Type: Co-educational Day Boys 14–19 Girls 14–19
No of pupils: B100 G95
Fees: (September 05) Day £2500–£13350

PEMBRIDGE HALL
18 Pembridge Square, London W2 4EH
Tel: (020) 7229 0121
Fax: (020) 7792 1086
Head: Mrs E Marsden
Type: Girls Day 4–11
No of pupils: 250
Fees: (September 05) Day £11001

RAVENSTONE HOUSE PRE-PREPARATORY AND NURSERY
The Long Garden, Albion Street, Marble Arch, London W2 2AX
Tel: (020) 7262 1190
Fax: (020) 7724 6980
Email: info@ravenstonehouse.co.uk
Head: Mrs A Saunders
Type: Co-educational Day 0–7
No of pupils: B50 G50

WETHERBY SCHOOL*
11 Pembridge Square, London W2 4ED
Tel: (020) 7727 9581
Fax: (020) 7221 8827
Email: learn@WetherbySchool.co.uk
Head: Mrs J Aviss
Type: Boys Day 4–8
No of pupils: 235
Fees: (September 05) Day £10560

W3

BARBARA SPEAKE STAGE SCHOOL
East Acton Lane, London W3 7EG
Tel: (020) 8743 1306
Fax: (020) 8743 1306
Email: cpuk@aol.com or speakekids3@aol.com
Head: Miss B M Speake and Mr D R Speake
Type: Co-educational Day 3–16
No of pupils: B46 G94
Fees: (September 05) Day £4200–£4500

INTERNATIONAL SCHOOL OF LONDON*
139 Gunnersbury Avenue, London W3 8LG
Tel: (020) 8992 5823
Fax: (020) 8993 7012
Email: mail@islondon.com
Head: Mr A Makarem
Type: Co-educational Day Boys 3–19 Girls 4–18
No of pupils: B165 G123
Fees: (September 05) Day £11500–£15900

THE JAPANESE SCHOOL
87 Creffield Road, Acton, London W3 9PU
Tel: (020) 8993 7145
Fax: (020) 8992 1224
Head: Mr F Fudo
Type: Co-educational Day 6–15
No of pupils: B320 G260
Fees: (September 02) Day £1560

KING FAHAD ACADEMY
Bromyard Avenue, East Acton, London W3 7HD
Tel: (020) 8743 0131
Fax: (020) 8749 7085
Email: headmaster@thekfa.org.uk
Head: Mr Mansour Ghazali
Type: Co-educational Day 5–18
No of pupils: B300 G350
Fees: (September 04) Day £1000–£1200

W4

THE ARTS EDUCATIONAL SCHOOL*
Cone Ripman House, 14 Bath Road, Chiswick, London W4 1LY
Tel: (020) 8987 6600
Fax: (020) 8987 6601
Email: head@artsed.co.uk
Head: Mr R Luckham
Type: Co-educational Day 11–18
No of pupils: B51 G99
Fees: (September 05) Day £8472–£9471

CHISWICK AND BEDFORD PARK PREPARATORY SCHOOL
Priory House, Priory Avenue, Bedford Park, London W4 1TX
Tel: (020) 8994 1804
Fax: (020) 8995 3603
Email: cbpschool@aol.com
Head: Mrs C A Sunderland
Type: Co-educational Day Boys 4–8 Girls 4–11
No of pupils: B70 G115
Fees: (September 03) Day £5520–£6570

THE FALCONS SCHOOL FOR BOYS*
2 Burnaby Gardens, Chiswick, London W4 3DT
Tel: (020) 8747 8393
Fax: (020) 8995 3903
Email: admin@falconschool.com
Head: Mr B H Evans
Type: Boys Day 3–8
No of pupils: 200
Fees: (September 05) Day £4575–£8985

ORCHARD HOUSE SCHOOL*
16 Newton Grove, Bedford Park, London W4 1LB
Tel: (020) 8742 8544
Fax: (020) 8742 8522
Email: info@orchardhs.org.uk
Head: Mrs S A B Hobbs
Type: Co-educational Day Boys 3–8 Girls 3–11
No of pupils: B80 G140
Fees: (September 05) Day £4860–£10080

W5

ASTON HOUSE SCHOOL
1 Aston Road, Ealing, London W5 2RL
Tel: (020) 8566 7300
Fax: (020) 8566 7499
Email: ahs@happychild.co.uk
Head: Mrs P Seabrook
Type: Co-educational Day 3–11
No of pupils: B75 G75
Fees: (September 05) Day £5700–£7110

CLIFTON LODGE PREPARATORY SCHOOL
8 Mattock Lane, Ealing, London W5 5BG
Tel: (020) 8579 3662
Fax: (020) 8810 1332
Email: cliftonlodge@btinternet.com
Head: Mr D A P Blumlein
Type: Boys Day 4–13
No of pupils: 180
Fees: (September 04) Day £7140–£7800

DURSTON HOUSE
12–14 & 26 Castlebar Road, Ealing, London W5 2DR
Tel: (020) 8991 6532
Fax: (020) 8991 6547
Email: info@durstonhouse.ealing.sch.uk
Head: Mr N I Kendrick
Type: Boys Day 4–13
No of pupils: 400
Fees: (September 05) Day £7440–£9960

EALING INDEPENDENT COLLEGE
83 New Broadway, Ealing, London W5 5AL
Tel: (020) 8579 6668
Fax: (020) 8567 8688
Email: ealingcollege@btconnect.com
Head: Dr I Moores
Type: Co-educational Day 14–20
No of pupils: B45 G45
Fees: (September 05) Day £1580–£10650

THE FALCONS SCHOOL FOR GIRLS
15 Gunnersbury Avenue, Ealing, London W5 3XD
Tel: (020) 8992 5189
Fax: (020) 8752 1635
Email: cheath@falconsgirls.co.uk
Head: Mr B H Evans
Type: Girls Day 4–11
No of pupils: 120
Fees: (September 04) Day £7825

HARVINGTON SCHOOL
20 Castlebar Road, Ealing, London W5 2DS
Tel: (020) 8997 1583
Fax: (020) 8810 4756
Email: admin@harvingtonschool.com
Head: Dr F Meek
Type: Girls Day 3–16 (Boys 3–5)
No of pupils: B14 G210
Fees: (September 05) Day £5925–£7710

ST AUGUSTINE'S PRIORY
Hillcrest Road, Ealing, London W5 2JL
Tel: (020) 8997 2022
Fax: (020) 8810 6501
Email: admin@saintaugustinespriory.org.uk
Head: Mrs F Gumley-Mason
Type: Girls Day 4–18
No of pupils: 510
Fees: (September 04) Day £5475–£7635

ST BENEDICT'S JUNIOR SCHOOL
5 Montpelier Avenue, Ealing, London W5 2XP
Tel: (020) 8862 2050
Fax: (020) 8862 2058
Email: jssecretary@stbenedicts.org.uk
Head: Mr D A McSweeney
Type: Boys Day 3–11
No of pupils: 240
Fees: (September 04) Day £8010

ST BENEDICT'S SCHOOL
54 Eaton Rise, Ealing, London W5 2ES
Tel: (020) 8862 2000
Fax: (020) 8862 2199
Email: headmaster@stbenedicts.org.uk
Type: Boys Day 11–18 (Co-ed VIth Form)
No of pupils: B600 G21
Fees: (September 04) Day £9120

W6

BUTE HOUSE PREPARATORY SCHOOL FOR GIRLS
Luxemburg Gardens, London W6 7EA
Tel: (020) 7603 7381
Fax: (020) 7371 3446
Email: mail@butehouse.co.uk
Head: Mrs S Salvidant
Type: Girls Day 4–11
Fees: (September 05) Day £9228

ECOLE FRANCAISE JACQUES PREVERT
59 Brook Green, London W6 7BE
Tel: (020) 7602 6871
Fax: (020) 7602 3162
Email: info@ecoleprevert.org.uk
Head: Mr R Salva
Type: Co-educational Day 4–11
No of pupils: B136 G128
Fees: (September 03) Day £3075–£3300

THE GODOLPHIN AND LATYMER SCHOOL
Iffley Road, Hammersmith, London W6 0PG
Tel: (020) 8741 1936
Fax: (020) 8746 3352
Email: registrar@godolphinandlatymer.com
Head: Miss M Rudland
Type: Girls Day 11–18
No of pupils: 707
Fees: (September 03) Day £9345

LATYMER PREP SCHOOL*
36 Upper Mall, Hammersmith, London W6 9TA
Tel: (020) 8748 0303
Fax: (020) 8741 4916
Email: mlp@latymerprep.org
Head: Mr S P Dorrian
Type: Co-educational Day 7–11
Fees: (September 05) Day £10875

LATYMER UPPER SCHOOL*
King Street, Hammersmith, London W6 9LR
Tel: (020) 8741 1851
Fax: (020) 8748 5212
Email: registrar@latymer-upper.org
Head: Mr P J Winter
Type: Co-educational Day 11–18
No of pupils: B841 G204
Fees: (September 05) Day £11985

LE HERISSON
c/o The Methodist Church, Rivercourt Road, Hammersmith, London W6 9JT
Tel: (020) 8563 7664
Fax: (020) 8563 7664
Email: administration@leherissonschool.co.uk
Head: Ms B Rios
Type: Co-educational Day 2–6
No of pupils: 64
Fees: (September 04) Day £3360–£4560

RAVENSCOURT PARK PREPARATORY SCHOOL
16 Ravenscourt Avenue, London W6 0SL
Tel: (020) 8846 9153
Fax: (020) 8846 9413
Email: secretary@rpps.co.uk
Head: Mr R Relton
Type: Co-educational Day 4–11
No of pupils: B128 G134
Fees: (September 04) Day £8628

RAVENSCOURT THEATRE SCHOOL
Tandy House, 30–40 Dalling Road, London W6 0JB
Tel: (020) 8741 0707
Fax: (020) 8741 1786
Head: Mr J Roper
Type: Co-educational Day 7–16
No of pupils: B39 G56
Fees: (September 02) Day £4650

ST PAUL'S GIRLS' SCHOOL
Brook Green, London W6 7BS
Tel: (020) 7603 2288
Fax: (020) 7602 9932
Email: admissions@spgs.org
Head: Miss E Diggory
Type: Girls Day 11–18
Fees: (September 03) Day £10590

W8

ABINGDON HOUSE SCHOOL
4–6 Abingdon Road, London W8 6AF
Tel: (0845) 230 0426
Fax: (020) 7361 0751
Email: ahs@abingdonhouseschool.co.uk
Head: Mr N Rees
Type: Co-educational Day 4–9
No of pupils: B15 G2
Fees: (September 04) Day £17850

ASHBOURNE INDEPENDENT SIXTH FORM COLLEGE*
17 Old Court Place, Kensington, London W8 4PL
Tel: (020) 7937 3858
Fax: (020) 7937 2207
Email: admin@ashbournecollege.co.uk
Head: Mr M J H Kirby
Type: Co-educational Day and Boarding Boys 14–19 Girls 16–19
No of pupils: B80 G75
Fees: (September 04) FB £18500 Day £12450

ASHBOURNE MIDDLE SCHOOL*
17 Old Court Place, Kensington, London W8 4PL
Tel: (020) 7937 3858
Fax: (020) 7937 2207
Email: admin@ashbournecollege.co.uk
Head: Mr M J A Kirby and Ms C S Brahams
Type: Co-educational Day 13–16
No of pupils: B15 G10
Fees: (September 04) Day £12450

HAWKESDOWN HOUSE SCHOOL*
27 Edge Street, Kensington, London W8 7PN
Tel: (020) 7727 9090
Fax: (020) 7727 9988
Email: admin@hawkesdown.co.uk
Head: Mrs C J Leslie
Type: Boys Day 3–8
No of pupils: 125
Fees: (September 05) Day £8700–£10200

THOMAS'S PREPARATORY SCHOOL
17–19 Cottesmore Gardens, London W8 5PR
Tel: (020) 7361 6500
Fax: (020) 7361 6501
Email: Dmaine@thomas-s.co.uk
Head: Mrs D Maine
Type: Co-educational Day 4–11
No of pupils: B146 G164
Fees: (September 04) Day £9795–£10680

W10

BALES COLLEGE
742 Harrow Road, London W10 4AA
Tel: (020) 8960 5899
Fax: (020) 8960 8269
Email: info@balescollege.co.uk
Head: Mr W B Moore
Type: Co-educational Day and Boarding 11–19
No of pupils: B50 G50
No of boarders: F18 W2
Fees: (September 05) F/WB £ £13500 Day £6150–£6855

BASSETT HOUSE SCHOOL*
60 Bassett Road, London W10 6JP
Tel: (020) 8969 0313
Fax: (020) 8960 9624
Email: info@bassetths.org.uk
Head: Mrs A Harris
Type: Co-educational Day Girls 3–11 (Boys 3–8)
Fees: (September 05) Day £4820–£10080

THE LLOYD WILLIAMSON SCHOOL
12 Telford Road, London W10 5SH
Tel: (020) 8962 0345
Fax: (020) 8962 0345
Email: office@lloydwilliamson.demon.co.uk
Head: Miss L J L Williamson
Type: Co-educational Day 1–13
No of pupils: B60 G60
Fees: (September 04) Day £900–£7500

W11

DAVID GAME COLLEGE
69 Notting Hill Gate, London W11 3JS
Tel: (020) 7221 6665
Fax: (020) 7243 1730
Email: nhg@davidgame-group.com
Head: Mr D Game
Type: Co-educational Day and Boarding 15–25
No of pupils: B230 G220
No of boarders: F150

NORLAND PLACE SCHOOL
162–166 Holland Park Avenue, London W11 4UH
Tel: (020) 7603 9103
Fax: (020) 7603 0648
Email: office@norlandplace.com
Head: Mr P Mattar
Type: Co-educational Day Boys 4–8 Girls 4–11
No of pupils: B90 G150
Fees: (September 05) Day £8313–£10491

NOTTING HILL PREPARATORY SCHOOL
95 Lancaster Road, London W11 1QQ
Tel: (020) 7221 0727
Fax: (020) 7221 0332
Email: admin@nottinghillprep.com
Head: Mrs J Cameron
Type: Co-educational Day 5–13
No of pupils: B73 G83
Fees: (September 05) Day £3450

SOUTHBANK INTERNATIONAL SCHOOL, KENSINGTON*
36–38 Kensington Park Road, London W11 3BU
Tel: (020) 7243 3803
Fax: (020) 7727 3290
Email: admissions@southbank.org
Head: Mr N Hughes and Mr G Winning
Type: Co-educational Day 3–11
No of pupils: B100 G95
Fees: (September 05) Day £12600–£14850

WETHERBY PREPARATORY SCHOOL*
19 Pembridge Villas, London W11 3EP
Tel: (020) 7243 0243
Fax: (020) 7313 5244
Email: admin@wetherbyprep.co.uk
Head: Mr R Greenwood
Type: Boys Day 8–13
No of pupils: 46
Fees: (September 05) Day £11130

W13

AVENUE HOUSE SCHOOL*
70 The Avenue, Ealing, London W13 8LS
Tel: (020) 8998 9981
Fax: (020) 8991 1533
Email: avenuehouseschool@btinternet.com
Head: Mrs C Self
Type: Co-educational Day 3–11
No of pupils: B65 G75
Fees: (September 05) Day £3900–£6900

EALING COLLEGE UPPER SCHOOL
83 The Avenue, Ealing, London W13 8JS
Tel: (020) 8248 2312
Fax: (020) 8248 3765
Head: Mr B Webb
Type: Boys Day 11–18 (Co-ed VIth Form)
No of pupils: B136 G2
Fees: (September 03) Day £5720

NOTTING HILL AND EALING HIGH SCHOOL GDST
2 Cleveland Road, Ealing, London W13 8AX
Tel: (020) 8799 8400
Fax: (020) 8810 6891
Email: enquiries@nhehs.gdst.net
Head: Mrs S Whitfield
Type: Girls Day 5–18
No of pupils: 820
Fees: (September 05) Day £7149–£9189

W14

FULHAM PREP SCHOOL (PREP DEPT)*
Prep Department, 200 Greyhound Road, London W14 9RY
Tel: (020) 7386 2444
Fax: (020) 7386 2449
Email: prepadmin@fulhamprep.co.uk
Head: Mrs J Emmett
Type: Co-educational Day 7–13
No of pupils: B121 G85
Fees: (September 05) Day £10500

HOLLAND PARK PRE-PREPARATORY SCHOOL
5 & 9Holland Road, London W14 8HJ
Tel: (020) 7602 9066
Head: Miss K Mason and Ms E Tsakanika
Type: Co-educational Day 0–8

ST JAMES INDEPENDENT SCHOOL FOR BOYS
Earsby Street, Nr. Kensington Olympia, London W14 8SH
Tel: (020) 7348 1777
Fax: (020) 7348 1790
Email: juniorschools@stjamesschools.co.uk
Head: Mr P Moss
Type: Boys Day 4–10
No of pupils: 119
Fees: (September 05) Day £7050–£7680

ST JAMES INDEPENDENT SCHOOL FOR SENIOR GIRLS
Earsby Street, London W14 8SH
Tel: (020) 7348 1777
Fax: (020) 7348 1749
Email: enquiries@stjamessengirls.org.uk
Head: Mrs L A Hyde
Type: Girls Day 10–18
No of pupils: 247
Fees: (September 05) Day £8745–£9135

ST JAMES INDEPENDENT SCHOOL FOR GIRLS (JUNIORS)
Earsby Street, Olympia, London W14 8SH
Tel: (020) 7348 1777
Fax: (020) 7348 1790
Email: juniorschools@stjamesschools.co.uk
Head: Mr P Moss
Type: Girls Day 4–10
No of pupils: 138
Fees: (September 05) Day £7050–£7680

WC2

ROYAL BALLET SCHOOL

46 Floral Street, London
WC2E 9DA
Tel: (020) 7836 8899
Fax: (020) 7845 7080
Email: johnm@royalballetschool.co.uk
Head: Mr N Foster
Type: Co-educational Boarding and Day 11–18
No of pupils: B93 G109
No of boarders: F125
Fees: (September 04) FB £21516 Day £15930

THE URDANG ACADEMY OF BALLET

20–22 Shelton Street, London
WC2H 9JJ
Tel: (020) 7836 5709
Fax: 020 7836 7010
Email: info@theurdangacademy.com
Head: Miss S Goumain
Type: Co-educational Day 16–23
No of pupils: B27 G114
Fees: (September 03) Day £9960

GREATER MANCHESTER

AUDENSHAW

JOSEPH RAYNER INDEPENDENT SCHOOL

Red Hall, Audenshaw Road, Audenshaw, Greater Manchester
M34 5HT
Tel: (0161) 355 1434
Head: Mr G Hopkinson
Type: Co-educational Day 3–11
No of pupils: B2 G12

ECCLES

BRANWOOD PREPARATORY SCHOOL

Stafford Road, Monton, Eccles, Greater Manchester M30 9HN
Tel: (0161) 789 1054
Fax: (0161) 789 0561
Email: mail@branwoodschool.co.uk
Head: Mr W M Howard
Type: Co-educational Day 3–11
No of pupils: B95 G95
Fees: (September 05) Day £2955–£4044

CLARENDON COTTAGE SCHOOL

Ivy Bank House, Half Edge Lane, Eccles, Greater Manchester
M30 9BJ
Tel: (0161) 950 7868
Fax: (0161) 661 3822
Email: clarendon.cottage@dial.pipex.com
Head: Mrs E Bagnall
Type: Co-educational Day 1–11
No of pupils: B120 G100
Fees: (September 04) Day £1377–£5854

MONTON PREP SCHOOL WITH MONTESSORI NURSERIES

The School House, Francis Street, Monton, Eccles, Greater Manchester M30 9PR
Tel: (0161) 789 0472
Head: Miss D S Bradburn
Type: Co-educational Day 2–13
No of pupils: B74 G80

MANCHESTER

ABBEY COLLEGE

Cheapside, King Street, Manchester, Greater Manchester
M2 4WG
Tel: (0161) 817 2700
Fax: (0161) 817 2705
Email: admin@abbeymanchester.co.uk
Head: Mrs J Thomas
Type: Co-educational Day 15–21 Flexi-boarding available
No of pupils: B90 G90

ABBOTSFORD PREPARATORY SCHOOL

211 Flixton Road, Urmston, Manchester, Greater Manchester
M41 5PR
Tel: (0161) 748 3261
Fax: (0161) 748 7961
Email: secretary@abbotsford-prep.trafford.sch.uk
Head: Mr C J Davies
Type: Co-educational Day 3–11
No of pupils: B60 G64
Fees: (September 05) Day £4056–£4314

BRIDGEWATER SCHOOL
Drywood Hall, Worsley Road, Worsley, Manchester, Greater Manchester M28 2WQ
Tel: (0161) 794 1463
Fax: (0161) 794 3519
Email: admin@bridgewater.school.org.uk
Head: Ms G A Shannon-Little
Type: Co-educational Day 3–18
No of pupils: B268 G248
Fees: (September 04)
Day £4770–£6423

CHETHAM'S SCHOOL OF MUSIC
Long Millgate, Manchester, Greater Manchester M3 1SB
Tel: (0161) 834 9644
Fax: (0161) 839 3609
Head: Mrs C J Hickman
Type: Co-educational Boarding and Day 8–18
No of pupils: B140 G150
No of boarders: F229
Fees: (September 03) FB £21000
Day £17000

KASSIM DARWISH GRAMMAR SCHOOL FOR BOYS
Hartley Hall, Alexandra Road South, Chorlton-cum-Hardy, Manchester, Greater Manchester M16 8NH
Tel: (0161) 860–7676
Fax: (0161) 860–0011
Email: kdgb_ad@hotmail.com
Head: Mrs M Mohamed
Type: Boys Day 11–16
No of pupils: 166
Fees: (September 05) Day £4820

KING OF KINGS SCHOOL
142 Dantzic Street, Manchester, Greater Manchester M4 4DN
Tel: (0161) 834 4214
Head: Mrs B Lewis
Type: Co-educational Day 3–16
No of pupils: B14 G10

THE MANCHESTER GRAMMAR SCHOOL
Old Hall Lane, Manchester, Greater Manchester M13 0XT
Tel: (0161) 224 7201
Fax: (0161) 257 2446
Email: general@mgs.org
Head: Dr C Ray
Type: Boys Day 11–18
No of pupils: 1440
Fees: (September 05) Day £7239

MANCHESTER HIGH SCHOOL FOR GIRLS
Grangethorpe Road, Manchester, Greater Manchester M14 6HS
Tel: (0161) 224 0447
Fax: (0161) 224 6192
Email: administration@mhsg.manchester.sch.uk
Head: Mrs C Lee-Jones
Type: Girls Day 4–18
No of pupils: 936
Fees: (September 05)
Day £5154–£7236

MANCHESTER ISLAMIC HIGH SCHOOL
55 High Lane, Manchester, Greater Manchester M21 9FA
Tel: (0161) 881 2127
Fax: (0161) 861 0534
Head: Mrs M Mohamed
Type: Girls Day 11–16
Fees: (September 03) Day £2845

MANCHESTER MUSLIM PREPARATORY SCHOOL
551 Wilmslow Road, Withington, Manchester, Greater Manchester M20 4BA
Tel: (0161) 445 5452
Fax: (0161) 445 2283
Email: muslimprepschool@aol.com
Head: Mrs T Amin
Type: Co-educational Day 3–11
No of pupils: B79 G104
Fees: (September 03)
Day £2616–£2954

MOOR ALLERTON SCHOOL
131 Barlow Moor Road, Manchester, Greater Manchester M20 2PW
Tel: (0161) 445 4521
Fax: (0161) 434 5294
Email: office@moorallertonschool.manchester.sch.uk
Head: Mr P S Millard
Type: Co-educational Day 3–11
No of pupils: B80 G60
Fees: (September 03)
Day £4095–£5298

ST BEDE'S COLLEGE
Alexandra Park, Manchester, Greater Manchester M16 8HX
Tel: (0161) 226 3323
Fax: (0161) 226 3813
Email: enquiries@stbedescollege.co.uk
Head: Mr J Byrne
Type: Co-educational Day 4–18
Fees: (September 05)
Day £4446–£6780

WILLIAM HULME'S GRAMMAR SCHOOL
Spring Bridge Road, Manchester, Greater Manchester M16 8PR
Tel: (0161) 226 2054
Fax: (0161) 232 5544
Email: enquiries@whgs.co.uk
Head: Mr S R Patriarca
Type: Co-educational Day 3–18
No of pupils: B340 G168
Fees: (September 05)
Day £5219–£7472

WITHINGTON GIRLS' SCHOOL
Wellington Road, Fallowfield, Manchester, Greater Manchester M14 6BL
Tel: (0161) 224 1077
Fax: (0161) 248 5377
Email: office@withington.manchester.sch.uk
Head: Mrs J D Pickering
Type: Girls Day 7–18
No of pupils: 650
Fees: (September 05)
Day £5280–£7110

PRESTWICH

PRESTWICH PREPARATORY SCHOOL
400 Bury Old Road, Prestwich, Greater Manchester M25 1PZ
Tel: (0161) 773 1223
Head: Miss Shiels and Mr D R Sheldon
Type: Co-educational Day 2–11
No of pupils: B60 G60
Fees: (September 03) Day £3096

SALFORD

JEWISH HIGH SCHOOL FOR GIRLS
10 Radford Street, Salford, Greater Manchester M7 4NT
Tel: (0161) 792 2118
Head: Rabbi Y Goldblatt
Type: Girls Day 11–18
No of pupils: 165

TASHBAR PRIMARY SCHOOL
20 Upper Park Rd, Salford, Greater Manchester M7 4HL
Tel: (0161) 720 8254
Fax: (0161) 720 8146
Head: Mr A Pinczewski
Type: Boys Day 3–11
No of pupils: 270
Fees: (September 02)
Day £1020–£1620

MERSEYSIDE

BIRKENHEAD

HIGHFIELD SCHOOL
96 Bidston Road, Oxton, Birkenhead, Merseyside CH43 6TW
Tel: (0151) 652 3708
Fax: (0151) 652 3708
Email: highfield.school@btinternet.com
Head: Mrs S Morris
Type: Co-educational Day 2–16
No of pupils: B20 G100
Fees: (September 03)
Day £2400–£4170

FORMBY

CLARENCE HIGH SCHOOL*
West Lane, Freshfield, Formby, Merseyside L37 7AZ
Tel: (01704) 872151
Fax: (01704) 831001
Head: Mr D McKillop
Type: Co-educational Boarding and Day 9–17
No of pupils: B45 G15
No of boarders: F30
Fees: (September 05)
WB £49890–£74010
Day £36020–£40560

LIVERPOOL

ATHERTON HOUSE SCHOOL
6 Alexandra Road, Crosby, Liverpool, Merseyside L23 7TF
Tel: (0151) 924 5578
Fax: (0151) 924 0421
Email: head@athertonhouse.ndo.co.uk
Head: Mrs A Apel
Type: Co-educational Day 2–11
No of pupils: B35 G40
Fees: (September 03)
Day £999–£3012

BEECHENHURST PREPARATORY SCHOOL
145 Menlove Avenue, Liverpool, Merseyside L18 3EE
Tel: (0151) 722 3279
Fax: (0151) 722 0697
Head: Mrs C Wright
Type: Co-educational Day 3–11
No of pupils: B55 G55
Fees: (September 04) Day £3600

THE BELVEDERE SCHOOL GDST
17 Belvidere Road, Princes Park, Liverpool, Merseyside L8 3TF
Tel: (0151) 727 1284
Fax: (0151) 727 0602
Email: enquiries@belvedere.gdst.net
Head: Mrs G Richards
Type: Girls Day 3–18
No of pupils: 544
Fees: (September 03)
Day £3495–£5835

CARLETON HOUSE PREPARATORY SCHOOL
Lyndhurst Road, Mossley Hill, Liverpool, Merseyside L18 8AQ
Tel: (0151) 724 4880
Fax: (0151) 724 6086
Email: carleton@carletonhouse.fsbusiness.co.uk
Head: Mr P Andrew
Type: Co-educational Day 4–11
No of pupils: B88 G62
Fees: (September 05) Day £4485

LIVERPOOL COLLEGE
Queens's Drive, Mossley Hill, Liverpool, Merseyside L18 8BG
Tel: (0151) 724 4000
Fax: (0151) 729 0105
Email: admin@liverpoolcollege.org.uk
Head: Mr J D B Christian
Type: Co-educational Day 3–18
No of pupils: B518 G355
Fees: (September 04)
Day £4650–£7320

MERCHANT TAYLORS' SCHOOL
Liverpool Road, Crosby, Liverpool, Merseyside L23 0QP
Tel: (0151) 928 3308
Fax: (0151) 949 9300
Email: info@merchanttaylors.sefton.sch.uk
Head: Mr David Cook
Type: Boys Day 7–18
No of pupils: 830
Fees: (September 05)
Day £4707–£6552

MERCHANT TAYLORS' SCHOOL FOR GIRLS
Liverpool Road, Crosby, Liverpool, Merseyside L23 5SP
Tel: (0151) 924 3140
Fax: (0151) 932 1461
Email: office@mtgs.co.uk
Head: Mrs J C Moon
Type: Girls Day 4–18 (Boys 4–7)
No of pupils: B76 G817
Fees: (September 05)
Day £4941–£6876

NEWBOROUGH SCHOOL
Quarry Street, Woolton, Liverpool, Merseyside L25 6HD
Tel: (0151) 428 1838
Fax: (0151) 428 1838
Email: dorothyprior@supanet.com
Head: Miss D Prior
Type: Co-educational Day Boys 3–11 Girls 3–16
No of pupils: B50 G80
Fees: (September 04)
Day £2175–£2625

RUNNYMEDE ST EDWARD'S SCHOOL
North Drive, Sandfield Park, Liverpool, Merseyside L12 1LE
Tel: (0151) 281 2300
Fax: (0151) 281 4900
Email: contact@runnymede-school.org.uk
Head: Miss S Carter
Type: Co-educational Day 3–11
No of pupils: B190 G140
Fees: (September 03)
Day £4290–£4522

ST MARY'S COLLEGE
Crosby, Liverpool, Merseyside L23 5TW
Tel: (0151) 924 3926
Fax: (0151) 932 0363
Email: office@stmarys.lpool.sch.uk
Head: Mrs J Marsh
Type: Co-educational Day 0–18
No of pupils: B641 G423
Fees: (September 05)
Day £4587–£6768

STREATHAM HOUSE SCHOOL
Victoria Road West, Blundellsands, Liverpool, Merseyside L23 8UQ
Tel: (0151) 924 1514
Fax: (0151) 931 2780
Head: Mrs C Baxter
Type: Girls Day 2–16 (Boys 2–11)
No of pupils: B22 G139
Fees: (September 04)
Day £3000–£4800

NEWTON-LE-WILLOWS

NEWTON BANK SCHOOL
34 High Street, Newton-Le-Willows, Merseyside WA12 9SN
Tel: (01925) 225979
Head: Mrs J Butler
Type: Co-educational Day 2–10
No of pupils: B25 G38
Fees: (September 04) Day £2940

PRESCOT

TOWER COLLEGE
Mill Lane, Rainhill, Prescot, Merseyside L35 6NE
Tel: (0151) 426 4333
Fax: (0151) 426 3338
Email: towercollege@lineone.net
Head: Miss R J Oxley
Type: Co-educational Day 3–16
No of pupils: B312 G324
Fees: (September 04)
Day £3825–£4500

SOUTHPORT

SUNNYMEDE SCHOOL
4 Westcliffe Road, Birkdale, Southport, Merseyside PR8 2BN
Tel: (01704) 568593
Fax: (01704) 551745
Email: sunnymedeschool@btinternet.com
Head: Mr S J Pattinson
Type: Co-educational Day 3–11
No of pupils: B67 G63
Fees: (September 05)
Day £3870–£5550

TOWER DENE PREPARATORY SCHOOL
59–76 Cambridge Road, Southport, Merseyside PR9 9RH
Tel: (01704) 228556
Fax: (01704) 228556
Email: towerdeneschool@aol.com
Head: Mr J Preston
Type: Co-educational Day 0–11
No of pupils: B48 G52
Fees: (September 04)
Day £3060–£3660

WALLASEY

WESTBOURNE PREPARATORY SCHOOL
45 Penkett Road, Wallasey, Merseyside CH45 7QG
Tel: (0151) 639 2722
Head: Mrs H S Hamilton
Type: Co-educational Day 4–11
No of pupils: B30 G30
Fees: (September 04)
Day £1470–£1545

WIRRAL

AVALON PREPARATORY SCHOOL
Caldy Road, West Kirby, Wirral, Merseyside CH48 2HE
Tel: (0151) 625 6993
Fax: (0151) 625 0332
Email: schooloffice@avalon-school.co.uk
Head: Dr B Scott
Type: Co-educational Day 2–11
No of pupils: B104 G102
Fees: (September 04)
Day £3630–£4356

BIRKENHEAD HIGH SCHOOL GDST
86 Devonshire Place, Prenton, Wirral, Merseyside CH43 1TY
Tel: (0151) 652 5777
Fax: (0151) 670 0639
Email: admissionssec@birkhs.gdst.net
Head: Mrs C H Evans
Type: Girls Day 3–18
No of pupils: 800
Fees: (September 05)
Day £4410–£7365

BIRKENHEAD SCHOOL
58 Beresford Road, Oxton, Wirral, Merseyside CH43 2JD
Tel: (0151) 652 4014
Fax: (0151) 651 3091
Email: enquire@birkenheadschool.co.uk
Head: Mr D J Clark
Type: Boys Day 3–18
No of pupils: B669 G10
Fees: (September 05)
Day £5544–£7647

HESWALL PREPARATORY SCHOOL
Carberry, 28 Quarry Road East, Heswall, Wirral, Merseyside CH60 6RB
Tel: (0151) 342 7851
Fax: (0151) 342 7851
Email: hesprep@aol.com
Head: Mrs M Hannaford
Type: Co-educational Day 3–11
No of pupils: B25 G25
Fees: (September 04)
Day £870–£3750

KINGSMEAD SCHOOL
Bertram Drive, Hoylake, Wirral, Merseyside CH47 0LL
Tel: (0151) 632 3156
Fax: (0151) 632 0302
Email: kingsmeadschool@compuserve.com
Head: Mr J F Perry
Type: Co-educational Boarding and Day 2–16 Flexi-boarding available
No of pupils: B142 G241
No of boarders: F38 W4
Fees: (September 05)
FB £10650–£12390
WB £10260–£12000
Day £4605–£7290

PRENTON PREPARATORY SCHOOL
Mount Pleasant, Oxton, Wirral, Merseyside
Tel: (0151) 652 3182
Fax: (0151) 653 7428
Email: enquiry@prentonprep.co.uk
Head: Mrs N M Aloe
Type: Co-educational Day 2–11
No of pupils: B65 G87
Fees: (September 04)
Day £3435–£3585

MIDDLESEX

ASHFORD

ST DAVID'S SCHOOL
Church Road, Ashford, Middlesex TW15 3DZ
Tel: (01784) 252494
Fax: (01784) 248652
Email: office@stdavidsschool.com
Head: Ms P Bristow
Type: Girls Day and Boarding 3–18 Flexi-boarding available
No of pupils: 400
No of boarders: F33 W7
Fees: (September 04) FB £16023 WB £14817 Day £5112–£8673

EDGWARE

HOLLAND HOUSE
1 Broadhurst Avenue, Edgware, Middlesex HA8 8TP
Tel: (020) 8958 6979
Fax: (020) 8958 3591
Email: schooloffice@hollandhouse.org.uk
Head: Mrs I Tyk
Type: Co-educational Day 4–11
No of pupils: B70 G70
Fees: (September 03) Day £3705

MENORAH GRAMMAR SCHOOL
Abbots Road, Edgware, Middlesex HA8 0QS
Tel: (020) 8906 9756
Email: menorah@wowmail.com
Head: Rabbi A M Goldblatt
Type: Boys Day 11–18
No of pupils: 225

NORTH LONDON COLLEGIATE
Canons Drive, Edgware, Middlesex HA8 7RJ
Tel: (020) 8952 0912
Fax: (020) 8951 1391
Email: office@nlcs.org.uk
Head: Mrs B McCabe
Type: Girls Day 4–18
No of pupils: 1080
Fees: (September 05)
Day £8496–£10017

ENFIELD

ST JOHN'S SENIOR SCHOOL
North Lodge, The Ridgeway, Enfield, Middlesex EN2 8BE
Tel: (020) 8366 0035
Fax: (020) 8363 4439
Email: StJohnsSc@aol.com
Head: Mr A Tardios
Type: Co-educational Day 10–18
No of pupils: B98 G77
Fees: (September 05)
Day £6600–£7700

HAMPTON

ATHELSTAN HOUSE SCHOOL
36 Percy Road, Hampton, Middlesex TW12 2LA
Tel: (020) 8979 1045
Email: admin@athelstanhouseschool.co.uk
Head: Mrs E M Woolf
Type: Co-educational Day 3–7
No of pupils: B25 G32
Fees: (September 04)
Day £1817–£5451

DENMEAD SCHOOL
41–43 Wensleydale Road,
Hampton, Middlesex TW12 2LP
Tel: (020) 8979 1844
Fax: (020) 8941 8773
Email: secretary@
denmead.richmond.sch.uk
Head: Mr M T McKaughan
Type: Boys Day 2–11 (Girls 2–7)
No of pupils: B160 G18
Fees: (September 05)
Day £3330–£7695

HAMPTON SCHOOL
Hanworth Road, Hampton,
Middlesex TW12 3HD
Tel: (020) 8979 5526
Fax: (020) 8941 7368
Email: headmaster@
hampton.richmond.sch.uk
Head: Mr B R Martin
Type: Boys Day 11–18
No of pupils: 1098
Fees: (September 05) Day £3530

JACK AND JILL SCHOOL
30 Nightingale Road, Hampton,
Middlesex TW12 3HX
Tel: (020) 8979 3195
Fax: (020) 8979 3195
Email: jackandjillschool@
btconnect.com
Head: Miss K S Papirnik
Type: Girls Day 3–7 (Boys 3–5)
No of pupils: B21 G124
Fees: (September 04)
Day £3180–£6585

THE LADY ELEANOR HOLLES SCHOOL
102 Hanworth Road, Hampton,
Middlesex TW12 3HF
Tel: (020) 8979 1601
Fax: (020) 8941 8291
Email: office@lehs.org.uk
Head: Mrs G Low
Type: Girls Day 7–18
No of pupils: 860
Fees: (September 05)
Day £7695–£10203

TWICKENHAM PREPARATORY SCHOOL
Beveree, 43 High Street,
Hampton, Middlesex TW12 2SA
Tel: (020) 8979 6216
Fax: (020) 8979 1596
Email: office@twickenham-
prep.richmond.sch.uk
Head: Mr D Malam
Type: Co-educational Day Boys
4–13 Girls 4–11
No of pupils: B136 G134
Fees: (September 05)
Day £6810–£7290

HANWORTH

LITTLE EDEN SDA SCHOOL & EDEN HIGH SDA SCHOOL
Fortescue House, Park Road,
Hanworth, Middlesex TW13 6PN
Tel: (020) 8751 1844
Fax: (020) 8751 1844
Email: littleedensch@aol.com
Head: Mrs L A Osei
Type: Co-educational Day 3–16
No of pupils: B37 G27
Fees: (September 04)
Day £2550–£3525

HARROW

ALPHA PREPARATORY SCHOOL
Hindes Road, Harrow, Middlesex
HA1 1SH
Tel: (020) 8427 1471
Fax: (020) 8424 9324
Email: sec@alpha.harrow.sch.uk
Head: Mr P J Wylie
Type: Co-educational Day 4–11
No of pupils: B90 G70
Fees: (September 03)
Day £5850–£6450

BUCKINGHAM COLLEGE SCHOOL
15 Hindes Road, Harrow,
Middlesex HA1 1SH
Tel: (020) 8427 1220
Fax: (020) 8863 0816
Email: enquiries@buckcoll.org
Head: Mr D F Bell
Type: Boys Day 11–18 (Co-ed
VIth Form)
No of pupils: B175 G1
Fees: (September 04)
Day £6405–£7440

THE JOHN LYON SCHOOL
Middle Road, Harrow, Middlesex
HA2 0HN
Tel: (020) 8872 8400
Fax: (020) 8872 8455
Email: enquiries@johnlyon.org
Head: Mr K J Riley
Type: Boys Day 11–18
No of pupils: 580
Fees: (September 05) Day £10755

ORLEY FARM SCHOOL
South Hill Avenue, Harrow,
Middlesex HA1 3NU
Tel: (020) 8869 7600
Fax: (020) 8869 7601
Email: office@
orleyfarm.harrow.sch.uk
Head: Mr I S Elliott
Type: Co-educational Day 4–13
No of pupils: B380 G90
Fees: (September 04)
Day £7830–£9030

QUAINTON HALL SCHOOL
91 Hindes Road, Harrow,
Middlesex HA1 1RX
Tel: (020) 8427 1304
Fax: (020) 8861 8861
Email: admin@
quaintonhall.harrow.sch.uk
Head: Mr D P Banister
Type: Boys Day 4–13
No of pupils: 220
Fees: (September 04)
Day £5760–£7158

ROXETH MEAD SCHOOL
25 Middle Road, Harrow,
Middlesex HA2 0HW
Tel: (020) 8422 2092
Fax: (020) 8422 2092
Head: Mrs A J Isaacs
Type: Co-educational Day 3–7
No of pupils: B26 G35
Fees: (September 04) Day £4815

HARROW ON THE HILL

HARROW SCHOOL
1 High Street, Harrow on the Hill,
Middlesex HA1 3HT
Tel: (020) 8872 8003
Fax: (020) 8872 8012
Email: hm@harrowschool.org.uk
Head: Mr B J Lenon
Type: Boys Boarding 13–18
No of pupils: 800
No of boarders: F800
Fees: (September 04) FB £22350

HILLINGDON

ACS HILLINGDON INTERNATIONAL SCHOOL*

Hillingdon Court, 108 Vine Lane, Hillingdon, Middlesex UB10 0BE
Tel: (01895) 818402
Fax: (01895) 818404
Email: hillingdonadmissions@acs-england.co.uk
Head: Mrs G Apple
Type: Co-educational Day 4–18
No of pupils: B259 G236
Fees: (September 05)
Day £7250–£15650

ST HELEN'S COLLEGE

Parkway, Hillingdon, Middlesex UB10 9JX
Tel: (01895) 234371
Fax: (01895) 619818
Email: sthelenscoll@easymail.rmplc.co.uk
Head: Mr D A Crehan and Mrs G R Crehan
Type: Co-educational Day 3–11
No of pupils: B164 G178
Fees: (September 05)
Day £3255–£5580

ISLEWORTH

ASHTON HOUSE SCHOOL

50/52 Eversley Crescent, Isleworth, Middlesex TW7 4LW
Tel: (020) 8560 3902
Fax: (020) 8568 1097
Email: principal@ashtonhouse.com
Head: Miss M Regan
Type: Co-educational Day 3–11
No of pupils: B70 G80
Fees: (September 05)
Day £5091–£6906

NORTHWOOD

MERCHANT TAYLORS' SCHOOL

Sandy Lodge, Northwood, Middlesex HA6 2HT
Tel: (01923) 820644
Fax: (01923) 835110
Email: admissions@mtsn.org.uk
Head: Mr S N Wright
Type: Boys Day 11–18
No of pupils: 815
Fees: (September 05) Day £11990

NORTHWOOD COLLEGE

Maxwell Road, Northwood, Middlesex HA6 2YE
Tel: (01923) 825446
Fax: (01923) 836526
Email: davjem@northwoodcollege.co.uk
Head: Mrs R Mercer
Type: Girls Day 3–18
No of pupils: 796
Fees: (September 05)
Day £3018–£9873

ST HELEN'S SCHOOL*

Eastbury Road, Northwood, Middlesex HA6 3AS
Tel: (01923) 843210
Fax: (01923) 843211
Email: enquiries@sthn.co.uk
Head: Mrs M Morris
Type: Girls Day and Boarding 3–18 Flexi-boarding available
No of pupils: 1142
No of boarders: F24 W1
Fees: (September 05) FB £17958 WB £17322 Day £9690

ST JOHN'S NORTHWOOD

Potter Street Hill, Northwood, Middlesex HA6 3QY
Tel: (020) 8866 0067
Fax: (020) 8868 8770
Email: office@st-johns.org.uk
Head: Mr C R Kelly
Type: Boys Day 3–13
No of pupils: 390
Fees: (September 05)
Day £5964–£9050

ST MARTIN'S SCHOOL

40 Moor Park Road, Northwood, Middlesex HA6 2DJ
Tel: (01923) 825740
Fax: (01923) 835452
Email: office@stmartins.org.uk
Head: Mr D T Tidmarsh
Type: Boys Day 3–13
Fees: (September 05)
Day £2955–£9135

PINNER

BUCKINGHAM COLLEGE PREPARATORY SCHOOL

458 Rayners Lane, Pinner, Middlesex HA5 5DT
Tel: (020) 8866 2737
Fax: (020) 8868 3228
Email: enquiries@buckprep.org
Head: Mr L Smith
Type: Boys Day 4–11
No of pupils: 125
Fees: (September 05)
Day £5535–£7245

HEATHFIELD SCHOOL

Beaulieu Drive, Pinner, Middlesex HA5 1NB
Tel: (020) 8868 2346
Fax: (020) 8868 4405
Email: enquiries@hea.gdst.net
Head: Miss C Juett
Type: Girls Day 3–18
Fees: (September 05)
Day £5514–£9189

INNELLAN HOUSE SCHOOL

44 Love Lane, Pinner, Middlesex HA5 3EX
Tel: (020) 8866 1855
Fax: (020) 8866 1855
Email: innellan.house@virgin.net
Head: Ms J Watkins
Type: Co-educational Day 3–7
No of pupils: B27 G41
Fees: (September 04)
Day £4250–£4545

REDDIFORD

36–38 Cecil Park, Pinner, Middlesex HA5 5HH
Tel: (020) 8866 0660
Fax: (020) 8866 4847
Email: office@reddiford.org.uk
Head: Mr B Hembry
Type: Co-educational Day 2–11
No of pupils: B179 G122
Fees: (September 05)
Day £2880–£7080

SHEPPERTON

HALLIFORD SCHOOL

Russell Road, Shepperton,
Middlesex TW17 9HX
Tel: (01932) 223593
Fax: (01932) 229781
Email: registrar@hallifordschool.com
Head: Mr P V Cottam
Type: Boys Day 11–19 (Co-ed VIth Form)
No of pupils: 365
Fees: (September 05) Day £8700

STAINES

STAINES PREPARATORY SCHOOL

3 Gresham Road, Staines,
Middlesex TW18 2BT
Tel: (01784) 450909
Fax: (01784) 464424
Email: registrar@stainesprep.co.uk
Head: Mr P Roberts
Type: Co-educational Day 3–11
No of pupils: B206 G128
Fees: (September 05)
Day £1836–£6390

STANMORE

PETERBOROUGH & ST MARGARET'S SCHOOL

Common Road, Stanmore,
Middlesex HA7 3JB
Tel: (020) 8950 3600
Fax: (020) 8421 8946
Email: psm@psmschool.org
Head: Mrs S R Watts
Type: Girls Day 4–16
Fees: (September 05)
Day £5490–£8160

TWICKENHAM

THE MALL SCHOOL

185 Hampton Road, Twickenham,
Middlesex TW2 5NQ
Tel: (020) 8977 2523
Fax: (020) 8977 8771
Email: admissions@mall.richmond.sch.uk
Head: Dr J G Jeanes
Type: Boys Day 4–13
No of pupils: 300
Fees: (September 05)
Day £6975–£8085

NEWLAND HOUSE SCHOOL

Waldegrave Park, Twickenham,
Middlesex TW1 4TQ
Tel: (020) 8892 7479
Fax: (020) 8744 0399
Email: school@newlandhouse.co.uk
Head: Mr D J Ott
Type: Co-educational Day Boys 4–13 Girls 4–11
No of pupils: B267 G134
Fees: (September 05)
Day £5532–£8205

ST CATHERINE'S SCHOOL

Cross Deep, Twickenham,
Middlesex TW1 4QJ
Tel: (020) 8891 2898
Fax: (020) 8744 9629
Email: info@stcatherineschool.com
Head: Mrs Z Braganza
Type: Girls Day 3–16 (Sixth form in 2006)
No of pupils: 350
Fees: (September 05)
Day £6150–£8460

ST JAMES INDEPENDENT SCHOOL FOR BOYS (SENIOR)

Pope's Villa, 19 Cross Deep,
Twickenham, Middlesex
TW1 4QG
Tel: (020) 8892 2002
Fax: (020) 8892 4442
Email: admissions@stjamesboys.co.uk
Head: Mr David Boddy
Type: Boys Day and Boarding 10–18
No of pupils: 300
No of boarders: W28
Fees: (September 05)
WB £12345–£12735
Day £8745–£9135

SUNFLOWER MONTESSORI SCHOOL

8 Victoria Road, Twickenham,
Middlesex TW1 3HW
Tel: (020) 8891 2675
Fax: (020) 8891 1204
Head: Mrs J Yandell
Type: Co-educational Day 2–7
No of pupils: B25 G33
Fees: (September 04)
Day £1800–£4650

WEMBLEY

BUXLOW PREPARATORY SCHOOL

5/6 Castleton Gardens, Wembley,
Middlesex HA9 7QJ
Tel: (020) 8904 3615
Fax: (020) 8904 3606
Head: Mrs A Baines
Type: Co-educational Day 4–11
No of pupils: B72 G56
Fees: (September 04) Day £4644

ST CHRISTOPHER'S SCHOOL

71 Wembley Park Drive,
Wembley, Middlesex HA9 8HE
Tel: (020) 8902 5069
Fax: (020) 8903 5939
Email: stchris@happychild.co.uk
Head: Mr J M B Edwards
Type: Co-educational Day 4–11
No of pupils: B54 G56
Fees: (September 05)
Day £1750–£1850

NORFOLK

CROMER

BEESTON HALL SCHOOL
West Runton, Cromer, Norfolk
NR27 9NQ
Tel: (01263) 837324
Fax: (01263) 838177
Email: office@beestonhall.co.uk
Head: Mr I K MacAskill
Type: Co-educational Boarding and Day 7–13 Flexi-boarding available
No of pupils: B100 G65
No of boarders: F100
Fees: (September 05) FB £15075 Day £11265

DISS

RIDDLESWORTH HALL†
Diss, Norfolk IP22 2TA
Tel: (01953) 681246
Fax: (01953) 688124
Email: enquiries@riddlesworthhall.com
Head: Mr C Campbell
Type: Co-educational Day and Boarding Boys 2–11 Girls 2–13 (Girls' only boarding) Flexi-boarding available
No of pupils: B38 G123
No of boarders: F23 W15
Fees: (September 05) FB £14805 WB £13860 Day £5850–£8705

HOLT

GRESHAM'S PREPARATORY SCHOOL
Cromer Road, Holt, Norfolk
NR25 6EY
Tel: (01263) 714600
Fax: (01263) 714060
Email: prep@greshams.com
Head: Mr J H W Quick
Type: Co-educational Day and Boarding 3–13 Flexi-boarding available
No of pupils: B173 G163
No of boarders: F35
Fees: (September 05) FB £15075 Day £5715–£11565

GRESHAM'S SCHOOL
Cromer Road, Holt, Norfolk
NR25 6EY
Tel: (01263) 713271
Fax: (01263) 712028
Email: headmaster@greshams.com
Head: Mr A R Clark
Type: Co-educational Boarding and Day 13–18
No of pupils: B249 G210
No of boarders: F96 W178
Fees: (September 04) FB £19515 WB £19425 Day £15135

HUNSTANTON

GLEBE HOUSE SCHOOL
2 Cromer Road, Hunstanton, Norfolk PE36 6HW
Tel: (01485) 532809
Fax: (01485) 533900
Email: enquiries@glebehouseschool.co.uk
Head: Mr J Crofts
Type: Co-educational Boarding and Day 0–13 Flexi-boarding available
No of pupils: B72 G64
No of boarders: W40
Fees: (September 05) WB £599

KINGS LYNN

DOWNHAM PREP SCHOOL AND MONTESSORI NURSERY
The Old Rectory, Stow Bardolph, Kings Lynn, Norfolk PE34 3HT
Tel: (01366) 388066
Fax: (01366) 388066
Email: secretary@dpsmn.norfolk.sch.uk
Head: Mrs E J Laffeaty-Sharpe
Type: Co-educational Day 2–11
No of pupils: B72 G68
Fees: (September 05) Day £966–£5460

NORTH WALSHAM

ST NICHOLAS HOUSE KINDERGARTEN & PREP SCHOOL
Yarmouth Road, North Walsham, Norfolk NR28 9AT
Tel: (01692) 403143
Fax: (01692) 403143
Email: stnicholas@yarmouth47.fsnet.co.uk
Head: Mr C Wardle
Type: Co-educational Day 3–11
No of pupils: B50 G60
Fees: (September 04) Day £2760

NORWICH

ALL SAINTS SCHOOL
School Road, Lessingham, Norwich, Norfolk NR12 0DJ
Tel: (01692) 584999
Fax: (01692) 582083
Head: Mrs J Gardiner
Type: Co-educational Day 2–16
No of pupils: B40 G40
Fees: (September 04) Day £1860–£3045

HETHERSETT OLD HALL SCHOOL
Hethersett, Norwich, Norfolk
NR9 3DW
Tel: (01603) 810390
Fax: (01603) 812094
Email: enquiries@hohs.co.uk
Head: Mrs J M Mark
Type: Girls Boarding and Day 4–18 (Boys 4–7) Flexi-boarding available
No of pupils: B11 G228
No of boarders: F28
Fees: (September 05) FB £14250–£17700 Day £5595–£8985

LANGLEY PREPARATORY SCHOOL & NURSERY
Beech Hill, 11 Yarmouth Road, Thorpe St Andrew, Norwich, Norfolk NR7 0EA
Tel: (01603) 433861
Fax: (01603) 702639
Email: headmaster@langleyprep.norfolk.sch.uk
Head: Mr S B Marfleet
Type: Co-educational Day 2–11 Flexi-boarding available
No of pupils: B100 G65
Fees: (September 04)
Day £4335–£6300

LANGLEY SCHOOL*
Langley Park, Loddon, Norwich, Norfolk NR14 6BJ
Tel: (01508) 520210
Fax: (01508) 528058
Email: administration@langleyschool.co.uk
Head: Mr J G Malcolm
Type: Co-educational Boarding and Day 10–18 Flexi-boarding available
No of pupils: B295 G180
No of boarders: F105 W30
Fees: (September 05)
FB £13905–£16770
WB £12060–£13905
Day £6480–£8430

THE NEW ECCLES HALL SCHOOL
Quidenham, Norwich, Norfolk NR16 2NZ
Tel: (01953) 887217
Fax: (01953) 887397
Email: admin@neweccleshall.com
Head: Mr R W Allard
Type: Co-educational Day and Boarding 3–16 Flexi-boarding available
No of boarders: F72
Fees: (September 05)
F/WB £ £11775–£13965
Day £4500–£7470

NORWICH HIGH SCHOOL FOR GIRLS GDST
Eaton Grove, 95 Newmarket Road, Norwich, Norfolk NR2 2HU
Tel: (01603) 453265
Fax: (01603) 259891
Email: admissions@nor.gdst.net
Head: Mrs V C Bidwell
Type: Girls Day 4–18
No of pupils: 897
Fees: (September 05)
Day £5337–£7365

NORWICH SCHOOL
70 The Close, Norwich, Norfolk NR1 4DD
Tel: (01603) 728430
Fax: (01603) 627036
Email: head.sec@norwich-school.org.uk
Head: Mr J B Hawkins
Type: Boys Day 7–18 (Co-ed VIth Form)
No of pupils: B757 G84
Fees: (September 05)
Day £8316–£8640

NOTRE DAME PREPARATORY SCHOOL
147 Dereham Road, Norwich, Norfolk NR2 3TA
Tel: (01603) 625593
Fax: (01603) 444139
Email: notredameprepschool@norwich147.fsnet.co.uk
Head: Mrs V Short
Type: Co-educational Day 3–11
No of pupils: B66 G66
Fees: (September 05)
Day £2940–£4185

ST CHRISTOPHER'S SCHOOL
George Hill, Old Catton, Norwich, Norfolk NR6 7DE
Tel: (01603) 425179
Head: Mrs J Higgins
Type: Co-educational Day 2–9
No of pupils: B80 G60
Fees: (September 04)
Day £672–£4131

STRETTON SCHOOL
1 Albermarle Road, Norwich, Norfolk NR2 2DF
Tel: (01603) 451285
Fax: (01603) 458842
Email: enquiries@strettonschool.com
Head: Mrs Y D Barnett
Type: Co-educational Day 1–8
No of pupils: B43 G35

TAVERHAM HALL
Taverham, Norwich, Norfolk NR8 6HU
Tel: (01603) 868206
Fax: (01603) 861061
Email: enquire@taverhamhall.co.uk
Head: Mr W D Lawton
Type: Co-educational Boarding and Day 1–13 Flexi-boarding available
No of pupils: B130 G94
No of boarders: W25
Fees: (September 05) WB £11340
Day £1500–£9200

THORPE HOUSE SCHOOL
7 Yarmouth Road, Norwich, Norfolk NR7 0EA
Tel: (01603) 433055
Fax: (01603) 436323
Email: office@thorpehouseschool.com
Head: Mr A Todd
Type: Girls Day 3–16
No of pupils: 280
Fees: (September 04)
Day £3390–£5190

TOWN CLOSE HOUSE PREPARATORY SCHOOL
14 Ipswich Road, Norwich, Norfolk NR2 2LR
Tel: (01603) 620180
Fax: (01603) 618256
Email: admissions@townclose.com
Head: Mr Graeme Lowe
Type: Co-educational Day 3–13
No of pupils: B298 G168
Fees: (September 05)
Day £5070–£7920

WOOD DENE SCHOOL
Aylmerton Hall, Holt Road, Aylmerton, Norwich, Norfolk NR11 8QA
Tel: (01263) 837224
Fax: (01263) 835837
Email: mail@wood-dene.co.uk
Head: Mrs D M Taylor
Type: Co-educational Day 2–17
No of pupils: B80 G120
Fees: (September 05)
Day £2700–£5568

SWAFFHAM

SACRED HEART CONVENT SCHOOL
17 Mangate Street, Swaffham, Norfolk PE37 7QW
Tel: (01760) 721330
Fax: (01760) 725557
Email: info@sacredheartschool.co.uk
Head: Sister F Ridler
Type: Co-educational Day and Boarding Boys 3–11 Girls 3–16
No of pupils: B26 G194
No of boarders: W30
Fees: (September 03) FB £12420 WB £9225 Day £4275–£5850

THETFORD

THETFORD GRAMMAR SCHOOL
Bridge Street, Thetford, Norfolk IP24 3AF
Tel: (01842) 752840
Fax: (01842) 750220
Email: enquiries@thetfordgrammarschool.fsnet.co.uk
Head: Mr G J Price
Type: Co-educational Day 4–18
No of pupils: B170 G130
Fees: (September 04) Day £6096–£7365

NORTHAMPTONSHIRE

BLACKTHORN

ST PETER'S INDEPENDENT SCHOOL
Lingswood Park, Blackthorn, Northamptonshire NN3 8TA
Tel: (01604) 411745
Head: Mr G J Smith
Type: Co-educational Day 4–18
No of pupils: 170
Fees: (September 03) Day £2970

BRACKLEY

BEACHBOROUGH SCHOOL
Westbury, Brackley, Northamptonshire NN13 5LB
Tel: (01280) 700071
Fax: (01280) 704839
Email: office@beachborough.com
Head: Mr J Whybrow
Type: Co-educational Day and Boarding 2–13 Flexi-boarding available
No of pupils: B132 G95
No of boarders: W49
Fees: (September 05) Day £3744

WINCHESTER HOUSE SCHOOL
Brackley, Northamptonshire NN13 7AZ
Tel: (01280) 702483
Fax: (01280) 706400
Email: office@winchester-house.org
Head: Mr M S Seymour
Type: Co-educational Boarding and Day 3–13 Flexi-boarding available
No of pupils: B232 G134
No of boarders: F15 W54
Fees: (September 05) FB £16065 WB £12750–£16065 Day £5565–£12150

KETTERING

ST PETER'S SCHOOL
52 Headlands, Kettering, Northamptonshire NN15 6DJ
Tel: (01536) 512066
Fax: (01536) 416469
Email: info@st-peters.org.uk
Head: Mrs M Chapman
Type: Co-educational Day 2–11
No of pupils: B57 G78
Fees: (September 05) Day £4416–£5874

NORTHAMPTON

BOSWORTH INDEPENDENT COLLEGE
Nazareth House, Barrack Road, Northampton, Northamptonshire NN2 6AF
Tel: (01604) 239995
Fax: (01604) 239996
Email: info@bosworthcollege.com
Head: Mr M McQuin
Type: Co-educational Boarding and Day 14–22
No of pupils: B171 G149
No of boarders: F251 W5
Fees: (September 05) FB £15510–£18250 Day £6990–£8225

GREAT HOUGHTON PREPARATORY SCHOOL
Great Houghton Hall, Northampton, Northamptonshire NN4 7AG
Tel: (01604) 761907
Fax: (01604) 761251
Email: office@northamptonschool.com
Head: Mr R O Barnes
Type: Co-educational Day 3–13
No of pupils: B165 G75
Fees: (September 05) Day £4695–£8985

MAIDWELL HALL
Northampton, Northamptonshire NN6 9JG
Tel: (01604) 686234
Fax: (01604) 686659
Email: headmaster@maidwellhall.co.uk
Head: Mr R A Lankester
Type: Boys Boarding and Day 7–13 (Girls day only)
No of pupils: 104
No of boarders: F92
Fees: (September 05) FB £16800 Day £13440

NORTHAMPTON HIGH SCHOOL
Newport Pagnell Road, Hardingstone, Northampton, Northamptonshire NN4 6UU
Tel: (01604) 765765
Fax: (01604) 709418
Email: admin@northamptonhigh.northants.sch.uk
Head: Mrs L A Mayne
Type: Girls Day 3–18
No of pupils: 830
Fees: (September 05)
Day £6120–£7980

OVERSTONE PARK SCHOOL
Overstone Park, Overstone, Northampton, Northamptonshire NN6 0DT
Tel: (01604) 643787
Fax: (01604) 670445
Head: Mrs M F Brown
Type: Co-educational Day 0–16
No of pupils: 160

PARKSIDE SCHOOL
1–5 Vigo Crescent, Browns Way, Bedford Road, Northampton, Northamptonshire NN1 5NL
Tel: (01604) 637124
Fax: (01604) 637124
Head: Miss K M Madden
Type: Co-educational Day 2–16
No of pupils: B115 G135

QUINTON HOUSE SCHOOL*
Upton Hall, Upton, Northampton, Northamptonshire NN5 4UX
Tel: (01604) 752050
Fax: (01604) 581707
Email: quinton.house@lineone.net
Head: Mr J O'Leary
Type: Co-educational Day 3–18
No of pupils: B163 G162
Fees: (September 05)
Day £4125–£6804

ST MATTHEWS SCHOOL
100 Park Avenue North, Northampton, Northamptonshire NN3 2JB
Tel: (01604) 712647
Email: principal@st-matthewsschool.co.uk
Head: Mrs L Burgess
Type: Co-educational Day 2–9
No of pupils: B30 G30
Fees: (September 05)
Day £612–£5610

SPRATTON HALL
Spratton, Northampton, Northamptonshire NN6 8HP
Tel: (01604) 847292
Fax: (01604) 820844
Email: office@sprattonhall.demon.co.uk
Head: Mr S Player
Type: Co-educational Day 4–13
No of pupils: B213 G153
Fees: (September 04)
Day £4770–£7740

OUNDLE

LAXTON JUNIOR SCHOOL*
East Road, Oundle, Nr Peterborough, Northamptonshire PE8 4BX
Tel: (01832) 277275
Fax: (01832) 277271
Email: laxtonjunior@oundle.co.uk
Head: Miss S C Thomas
Type: Co-educational Day 4–11
No of pupils: B118 G103
Fees: (September 05)
Day £7365–£7734

OUNDLE SCHOOL
The Great Hall, New Street, Oundle, Nr Peterborough, Northamptonshire PE8 4GH
Tel: (01832) 277125
Fax: (01832) 277128
Email: registrar@oundle.co.uk
Head: Mr C M P Bush
Type: Co-educational Boarding and Day 11–19
No of pupils: B642 G409
No of boarders: F828
Fees: (September 05)
FB £16593–£21725
Day £10785–£13185

PITSFORD

NORTHAMPTONSHIRE GRAMMAR SCHOOL
Pitsford Hall, Pitsford, Northamptonshire NN6 9AX
Tel: (01604) 880306
Fax: (01604) 882212
Email: office@ngs-school.com
Head: Mr N R Toone
Type: Co-educational Day 3–18
No of pupils: B215 G139
Fees: (September 05)
Day £5067–£8940

NORTHUMBERLAND

ALNWICK

ROCK HALL SCHOOL

Rock, Alnwick, Northumberland NE66 3SB
Tel: (01665) 579224
Fax: (01665) 579467
Email: rockhallschool@btinternet.com
Head: Mrs L A Bosanquet
Type: Co-educational Day 3–13
No of pupils: B18 G26
Fees: (September 05)
Day £2430–£5499

ST OSWALD'S SCHOOL

Spring Gardens, South Road, Alnwick, Northumberland NE66 2NU
Tel: (01665) 602739
Fax: (01665) 602817
Email: st-oswalds@alnwick.fsnet.co.uk
Head: Mr R Croft
Type: Co-educational Day 3–16
No of pupils: B52 G58
Fees: (September 03)
Day £3885–£5220

BERWICK-UPON-TWEED

LONGRIDGE TOWERS SCHOOL

Berwick-upon-Tweed, Northumberland TD15 2XQ
Tel: (01289) 307584
Fax: (01289) 302581
Email: admissions@lts.org.uk
Head: Dr M J Barron
Type: Co-educational Day and Boarding 4–18 Flexi-boarding available
No of pupils: B165 G160
No of boarders: F21 W12
Fees: (September 04)
FB £13800–£14850
WB £12525–£13575
Day £4350–£7170

STOCKSFIELD

MOWDEN HALL SCHOOL

Newton, Stocksfield, Northumberland NE43 7TP
Tel: (01661) 842147
Fax: (01661) 842529
Email: lb@mowdenhall.co.uk
Head: Mr P Meadows
Type: Co-educational Boarding and Day 3–13
No of pupils: B136 G102
No of boarders: F110 W8
Fees: (September 03)
F/WB £ £13650 Day £3000–£9900

NOTTINGHAMSHIRE

EAST LEAKE

ARLEY HOUSE PNEU SCHOOL

8 Station Road, East Leake, Nottinghamshire LE12 6LQ
Tel: (01509) 852229
Fax: (01509) 852229
Email: office@arley-pneu.eastlake.sch.uk
Head: Mrs E A Gibbs
Type: Co-educational Day 3–11
No of pupils: B45 G37
Fees: (September 05)
Day £1365–£5235

MANSFIELD

MANSFIELD PREPARATORY SCHOOL

Welbeck Road, Mansfield, Nottinghamshire NG19 9LA
Tel: (01623) 420940
Head: Miss J Sparrow
Type: Co-educational Day 3–11
No of pupils: B50 G39
Fees: (September 03) Day £2070

SAVILLE HOUSE SCHOOL

11 Church Street, Mansfield Woodhouse, Mansfield, Nottinghamshire NG19 8AH
Tel: (01623) 625068
Fax: (01623) 420940
Email: cherubsnurseries@aol.com
Head: Mrs J Nutter
Type: Co-educational Day 3–13
No of pupils: B90 G75
Fees: (September 05) Day £2340

NEWARK

HIGHFIELDS SCHOOL

London Road, Newark, Nottinghamshire NG24 3AL
Tel: (01636) 704103
Fax: (01636) 680919
Email: office@highfieldsschool.co.uk
Head: Mr D R Wood
Type: Co-educational Day 3–11
No of pupils: B92 G90
Fees: (September 05) Day £4899

RODNEY SCHOOL
Kirklington, Newark,
Nottinghamshire NG22 8NB
Tel: (01636) 813281
Fax: (01636) 813281
Email: rodney@proweb.co.uk
Head: Miss G R T Howe
Type: Co-educational Boarding and Day 8–18 Flexi-boarding available
No of pupils: B53 G34
No of boarders: F32
Fees: (September 04)
FB £11985–£12585
Day £5775–£7485

WELLOW HOUSE SCHOOL
Wellow, Newark,
Nottinghamshire NG22 0EA
Tel: (01623) 861054
Fax: (01623) 836665
Email: wellowhouse@btinternet.com
Head: Dr M D W Tozer
Type: Co-educational Day and Boarding 2–13 Flexi-boarding available
No of pupils: B88 G76
No of boarders: W17
Fees: (September 03) WB £8775

NOTTINGHAM

ATTENBOROUGH PREPARATORY SCHOOL
The Strand, Attenborough,
Beeston, Nottingham,
Nottinghamshire NG9 6AU
Tel: (0115) 943 6725
Email: attprepschl@hotmail.com
Head: Mrs J Howarth
Type: Co-educational Day 4–11
No of pupils: B40 G40
Fees: (September 05)
Day £2370–£3400

COTESWOOD HOUSE SCHOOL
19 Thackeray's Lane,
Woodthorpe, Nottingham,
Nottinghamshire NG5 4HT
Tel: (0115) 967 6551
Type: Co-educational Day 3–11
No of pupils: B20 G20
Fees: (September 02)
Day £2460–£2520

DAGFA HOUSE SCHOOL
57 Broadgate, Beeston,
Nottingham, Nottinghamshire
NG9 2FU
Tel: (0115) 913 8330
Fax: (0115) 913 8331
Email: headmaster@dagfahouse.notts.sch.uk
Head: Mr A Hampton
Type: Co-educational Day 2–16
No of pupils: B145 G105
Fees: (September 05)
Day £5100–£6180

GREENHOLME SCHOOL
392 Derby Road, Nottingham,
Nottinghamshire NG7 2DX
Tel: (0115) 978 7329
Fax: (0115) 978 1160
Email: enquiries@greenholmeschool.co.uk
Head: Mrs M J Nicholson
Type: Co-educational Day 3–11
No of pupils: B124 G53
Fees: (September 05)
Day £5835–£6150

GROSVENOR SCHOOL
Edwalton, Nottingham,
Nottinghamshire NG12 4BS
Tel: (0115) 923 1184
Fax: (0115) 923 5184
Email: office@grosvenorschool.co.uk
Head: Mr C G J Oldershaw
Type: Co-educational Day 4–13
No of pupils: B109 G62
Fees: (September 04)
Day £5250–£5820

HAZEL HURST SCHOOL
400 Westdale Lane, Mapperley,
Nottingham, Nottinghamshire
NG3 6DG
Tel: (0115) 960 6759
Fax: (0115) 960 6759
Email: hazelhurst@onetel.com
Head: Mrs S Beak
Type: Co-educational Day 2–8
No of pupils: B25 G25
Fees: (September 05)
Day £3390–£3660

HOLLYGIRT SCHOOL
Elm Avenue, Nottingham,
Nottinghamshire NG3 4GF
Tel: (0115) 958 0596
Fax: (0115) 989 7929
Email: info@hollygirt.co.uk
Head: Mrs M Connolly
Type: Girls Day 3–16
No of pupils: 307
Fees: (September 05)
Day £5250–£6945

THE KING'S SCHOOL
Collygate Road, The Meadows,
Nottingham, Nottinghamshire
NG2 2EJ
Tel: (0115) 953 9194
Fax: (0115) 955 1148
Email: office@thekingsschool.info
Head: Mr R Southey
Type: Co-educational Day 4–16
No of pupils: B64 G53
Fees: (September 04) Day £3036

MOUNTFORD HOUSE SCHOOL
373 Mansfield Road, Nottingham,
Nottinghamshire NG5 2DA
Tel: (0115) 960 5676
Email: enquiries@mountfordhouse.nottingham.sch.uk
Head: Mrs D Williams
Type: Co-educational Day 3–11
No of pupils: B54 G30
Fees: (September 04)
Day £1500–£4556

NOTTINGHAM HIGH SCHOOL
Waverley Mount, Nottingham,
Nottinghamshire NG7 4ED
Tel: (0115) 978 6056
Fax: (0115) 924 9716
Email: info@notthigh.rmplc.co.uk
Head: Mr C S Parker
Type: Boys Day 11–18
No of pupils: 847
Fees: (September 05) Day £8394

NOTTINGHAM HIGH SCHOOL FOR GIRLS GDST
9 Arboretum Street, Nottingham,
Nottinghamshire NG1 4JB
Tel: (0115) 941 7663
Fax: (0115) 924 0757
Email: enquiries@not.gdst.net
Head: Mrs S M Gorham
Type: Girls Day 4–18
No of pupils: 1078
Fees: (September 05)
Day £5337–£7365

NOTTINGHAM HIGH JUNIOR SCHOOL
Waverley Mount, Nottingham,
Nottinghamshire NG7 4ED
Tel: (0115) 845 2214
Fax: (0115) 845 2298
Email: philpallant@rmplc.co.uk
Head: Mr P M Pallant
Type: Boys Day 7–11
No of pupils: 142
Fees: (September 05) Day £6813

PLUMTREE SCHOOL
Church Hill, Plumtree,
Nottingham, Nottinghamshire
NG12 5ND
Tel: (0115) 937 5859
Fax: (0115) 937 5859
Email: plumtreeschool@tiscali.co.uk
Head: Mr N White
Type: Co-educational Day 3–11
No of pupils: B70 G50
Fees: (September 05)
Day £2685–£4635

ST JOSEPH'S SCHOOL
33 Derby Road, Nottingham,
Nottinghamshire NG1 5AW
Tel: (0115) 941 8356
Fax: (0115) 941 8356
Email: office@st-josephs.nottingham.sch.uk
Head: Mr J Crawley
Type: Co-educational Day 1–11
No of pupils: B115 G72

SALTERFORD HOUSE SCHOOL
Salterford Lane, Calverton,
Nottingham, Nottinghamshire
NG14 6NZ
Tel: (0115) 965 2127
Fax: (0115) 9655627
Email: office@salterfordhouseschool.co.uk
Head: Mrs M Venables
Type: Co-educational Day 2–11
No of pupils: B86 G77
Fees: (September 05)
Day £4200–£4275

TRENT COLLEGE
Long Eaton, Nottingham,
Nottinghamshire NG10 4AD
Tel: (0115) 849 4949
Fax: (0115) 849 4997
Email: enquiry@trentcollege.net
Head: Mr J S Lee
Type: Co-educational Boarding and Day 3–18 Flexi-boarding available
No of pupils: B631 G452
No of boarders: F4 W124
Fees: (September 05)
WB £4063–£5644

WAVERLEY HOUSE PNEU SCHOOL
13 Waverley Street, Nottingham,
Nottinghamshire NG7 4DX
Tel: (0115) 978 3230
Fax: (0115) 978 3230
Email: wavhousepneu@btconnect.com
Head: Mrs H Dawes
Type: Co-educational Day 3–11
No of pupils: B33 G26
Fees: (September 05)
Day £2070–£5625

RETFORD

AL KARAM SECONDARY SCHOOL
Eaton Hall, Retford,
Nottinghamshire DN22 0PR
Tel: (01777) 706441
Fax: (01777) 711538
Email: info@alkaram.org
Head: Mr M I H Pirzada
Type: Boys Boarding 11–16 Flexi-boarding available
No of pupils: 140
No of boarders: F140
Fees: (September 04)
FB £3600–£6000

BRAMCOTE LORNE SCHOOL
Gamston, Retford,
Nottinghamshire DN22 0QQ
Tel: (01777) 838636
Fax: (01777) 838633
Email: headmaster@bramcote-lorne.notts.sch.uk
Head: Mr J H Gibson
Type: Co-educational Boarding and Day 3–13 Flexi-boarding available
No of pupils: B151 G149
No of boarders: F45 W30

RANBY HOUSE
Retford, Nottinghamshire
DN22 8HX
Tel: (01777) 703138
Fax: (01777) 702813
Email: office@ranbyhouseschool.co.uk
Head: Mr A C Morris
Type: Co-educational Day and Boarding 3–13 Flexi-boarding available
No of pupils: B174 G153
No of boarders: F64
Fees: (September 05)
F/WB £ £11985 Day £5250–£9150

SUTTON IN ASHFIELD

LAMMAS SCHOOL
Lammas Road, Sutton in Ashfield,
Nottinghamshire NG17 2AD
Tel: (01623) 516879
Fax: (01623) 516879
Email: information@lammas.co.uk
Head: Mr C M Peck
Type: Co-educational Day 4–16
No of pupils: B90 G70
Fees: (September 03)
Day £3000–£3375

WORKSOP

WORKSOP COLLEGE
Worksop, Nottinghamshire
S80 3AP
Tel: (01909) 537127
Fax: (01909) 537102
Email: headmaster@worksopcollege.notts.sch.uk
Head: Mr R A Collard
Type: Co-educational Boarding and Day 13–18 Flexi-boarding available
No of pupils: B287 G128
No of boarders: F87 W78
Fees: (September 04)
F/WB £ £17295 Day £11835

OXFORDSHIRE

ABINGDON

ABINGDON SCHOOL
Park Road, Abingdon, Oxfordshire OX14 IDE
Tel: (01235) 849041
Fax: (01235) 849085
Email: admissions@abingdon.org.uk
Head: Mr M Turner
Type: Boys Day and Boarding 11–18
No of pupils: 800
No of boarders: F70 W60
Fees: (September 05) FB £19644 WB £19002 Day £10767

COTHILL HOUSE PREPARATORY SCHOOL
Cothill, Abingdon, Oxfordshire OX13 6JL
Tel: (01865) 390800
Fax: (01865) 390205
Email: office@cothill.oxon.sch.uk
Head: Mr N R Brooks
Type: Boys Boarding 8–13
No of boarders: F250
Fees: (September 05) FB £17400

JOSCA'S PREPARATORY SCHOOL
Kingston Road, Frilford, Abingdon, Oxfordshire OX13 5NX
Tel: (01865) 391570
Fax: (01865) 391042
Email: enquiries@Joscas.org.uk
Head: Mr C J Davies
Type: Boys Day 4–13 (Girls 4–7) Flexi-boarding available
No of pupils: B210 G1
No of boarders: W1
Fees: (September 05) Day £8850

THE MANOR PREPARATORY SCHOOL*
Faringdon Road, Abingdon, Oxfordshire OX13 6LN
Tel: (01235) 523789
Fax: (01235) 559593
Email: registrar@manorprep.org
Head: Mrs D A Robinson
Type: Co-educational Day Boys 3–7 Girls 3–11
No of pupils: B20 G307
Fees: (September 05) Day £3600–£8100

OUR LADY'S CONVENT JUNIOR SCHOOL
St John's Road, Abingdon, Oxfordshire OX14 2HB
Tel: (01235) 523147
Fax: (01235) 530387
Email: office@ourladys-jun.oxon.sch.uk
Head: Sister J Frances
Type: Co-educational Day 3–11
No of pupils: B60 G90
Fees: (September 05) Day £1600

OUR LADY'S CONVENT SENIOR SCHOOL
Radley Road, Abingdon, Oxfordshire OX14 3PS
Tel: (01235) 524658
Fax: (01235) 535829
Email: office@olcss.org.uk
Head: Mrs L Renwick
Type: Girls Day 11–18
No of pupils: 397
Fees: (September 05) Day £7980

RADLEY COLLEGE
Abingdon, Oxfordshire OX14 2HR
Tel: (01235) 543000
Fax: (01235) 543106
Head: Mr A W McPhail
Type: Boys Boarding 13–18
No of boarders: F625
Fees: (September 05) FB £22740

SCHOOL OF ST HELEN & ST KATHARINE
Faringdon Road, Abingdon, Oxfordshire OX14 1BE
Tel: (01235) 520173
Fax: (01235) 532934
Email: info@shsk.org.uk
Head: Mrs C Hall
Type: Girls Day 9–18
No of pupils: 631
Fees: (September 05) Day £8511

BANBURY

BLOXHAM SCHOOL†
Bloxham, Banbury, Oxfordshire OX15 4PE
Tel: (01295) 720222
Fax: (01295) 721897
Email: marketing@bloxhamschool.com
Head: Mr M E Allbrook
Type: Co-educational Boarding and Day 11–18 Flexi-boarding available
No of pupils: B274 G152
No of boarders: F215 W17
Fees: (September 05) FB £21995 WB £14285 Day £11475–£16985

THE CARRDUS SCHOOL
Overthorpe Hall, Banbury, Oxfordshire OX17 2BS
Tel: (01295) 263733
Fax: (01295) 263733
Email: cardusschool@overthorpe.fsnet.co.uk
Head: Miss S Carrdus
Type: Girls Day 3–11 (Boys 3–8)
No of pupils: B26 G112
Fees: (September 04) Day £1287–£6630

ST JOHN'S PRIORY SCHOOL
St John's Road, Banbury, Oxfordshire OX16 5HX
Tel: (01295) 259607
Fax: (01295) 273326
Email: enquiries@stjohnspriory.com
Head: Mrs J M Walker
Type: Co-educational Day 2–11
No of pupils: B70 G64
Fees: (September 04) Day £1590–£5595

SIBFORD SCHOOL†
Sibford Ferris, Banbury,
Oxfordshire OX15 5QL
Tel: (01295) 781200
Fax: (01295) 781204
Email: sibfordschool@dial.pipex.com
Head: Mr M Goodwin
Type: Co-educational Boarding and Day 4–18 Flexi-boarding available
No of pupils: B247 G142
No of boarders: F33 W41
Fees: (September 05)
FB £16407–£16737
WB £11634–£15585
Day £5319–£8451

TUDOR HALL SCHOOL
Wykham Park, Banbury,
Oxfordshire OX16 9UR
Tel: (01295) 263434
Fax: (01295) 253264
Email: abrauer@tudorhallschool.com
Head: Miss W Griffiths
Type: Girls Boarding and Day 11–18
No of pupils: 276
No of boarders: F230
Fees: (September 05) FB £19545
Day £12600

CHIPPING NORTON

KINGHAM HILL SCHOOL*†
Kingham, Chipping Norton,
Oxfordshire OX7 6TH
Tel: (01608) 658999
Fax: (01608) 658658
Email: admissions@kingham-hill.oxon.sch.uk
Head: Mr M J Morris
Type: Co-educational Boarding and Day 11–18 Flexi-boarding available
No of pupils: B168 G61
No of boarders: F184
Fees: (September 05)
FB £16439–£18676
Day £10773–£12624

WINDRUSH VALLEY SCHOOL
The Green, London Lane,
Ascott-U-Wychwood, Chipping
Norton, Oxfordshire OX7 6AN
Tel: (01993) 831793
Fax: (01993) 831793
Email: windrushvalley@aol.com
Head: Mr G A Wood
Type: Co-educational Day 3–11
No of pupils: B60 G60
Fees: (September 05)
Day £3900–£4260

FARINGDON

FERNDALE PREPARATORY SCHOOL
5–7 Bromsgrove, Faringdon,
Oxfordshire SN7 7JF
Tel: (01367) 240618
Fax: (01367) 241429
Email: ferndaleprep.school@talk21.com
Head: Mr Andrew Mersh
Type: Co-educational Day 3–11
No of pupils: B55 G55
Fees: (September 05)
Day £5580–£6270

ST HUGH'S SCHOOL
Carswell Manor, Faringdon,
Oxfordshire SN7 8PT
Tel: (01367) 870700
Fax: (01367) 870707
Email: registrar@st-hughs.co.uk
Head: Mr D Cannon
Type: Co-educational Boarding and Day 4–13 Flexi-boarding available
No of pupils: B165 G110
No of boarders: W40
Fees: (September 05)
WB £13260–£14130
Day £6960–£11790

HENLEY-ON-THAMES

RUPERT HOUSE
90 Bell Street, Henley-on-Thames,
Oxfordshire RG9 2BN
Tel: (01491) 574263
Fax: (01491) 573988
Email: office@ruperthouse.oxon.sch.uk
Head: Mrs G M Crane
Type: Co-educational Day Boys 4–7 Girls 4–11
No of pupils: B54 G173
Fees: (September 03)
Day £2880–£6900

ST MARY'S SCHOOL
13 St Andrew's Road,
Henley-on-Thames, Oxfordshire
RG9 1HS
Tel: (01491) 573118
Email: stmarys.henley@btinternet.com
Head: Mrs S Bradley
Type: Co-educational Day 3–11
No of pupils: B72 G67
Fees: (September 05)
Day £1200–£6210

SHIPLAKE COLLEGE
Henley-on-Thames, Oxfordshire
RG9 4BW
Tel: (0118) 940 2455
Fax: (0118) 940 5204
Email: info@shiplake.org.uk
Head: Mr A G S Davies
Type: Boys Day and Boarding 13–18 (Day girls 16–18)
No of pupils: B285 G15
No of boarders: F171 W45
Fees: (September 04) FB £18840
Day £12705

OXFORD

ABACUS COLLEGE
Threeways House, George Street,
Oxford, Oxfordshire OX1 2BJ
Tel: (01865) 240111
Fax: (01865) 247259
Email: principal@abacuscollege.co.uk
Head: Dr R Carrington and Mrs J Wasilewski
Type: Co-educational Boarding and Day 16–19
No of pupils: B68 G52
No of boarders: F119
Fees: (September 05)
FB £10680–£12630
Day £6500–£8450

CHANDLINGS MANOR SCHOOL
Bagley Wood, Kennington,
Oxford, Oxfordshire OX1 5ND
Tel: (01865) 730771
Fax: (01865) 735194
Email: office@chandlings.com
Head: Mrs J Forrest
Type: Co-educational Day 4–11
No of pupils: B242 G138
Fees: (September 05)
Day £7080–£9300

CHERWELL COLLEGE*
Greyfriars, Paradise Street, Oxford, Oxfordshire OX1 1LD
Tel: (01865) 242670
Fax: (01865) 791761
Email: secretary@cherwell-college.co.uk
Head: Mr A Thompson
Type: Co-educational Boarding and Day 16+
No of pupils: B75 G75
No of boarders: F90 W10
Fees: (September 05)
F/WB £ £19500 Day £13000

CHRIST CHURCH CATHEDRAL SCHOOL
3 Brewer Street, Oxford, Oxfordshire OX1 1QW
Tel: (01865) 242561
Fax: (01865) 202945
Email: schooloffice@cccs.org.uk
Head: Mr M Bruce
Type: Boys Day and Boarding 2–13 (Girls 2–4)
No of pupils: B126 G8
No of boarders: F20
Fees: (September 05)
FB £5790–£6390
Day £2820–£9405

D'OVERBROECK'S COLLEGE*
The Swan Building, 111 Banbury Road, Oxford, Oxfordshire OX2 6JX
Tel: (01865) 310000
Fax: (01865) 552296
Email: mail@doverbroecks.com
Head: Mr S Cohen and Mr R Knowles
Type: Co-educational Day and Boarding 11–19
No of pupils: B170 G110
No of boarders: F100
Fees: (September 05)
FB £18150–£21795
Day £10110–£14550

DRAGON SCHOOL
Bardwell Road, Oxford, Oxfordshire OX2 6SS
Tel: (01865) 315405
Fax: (01865) 311664
Email: admissions@dragonschool.org
Head: Mr J R Baugh
Type: Co-educational Boarding and Day 8–13
No of boarders: F260
Fees: (September 05) FB £18300
Day £6930–£12780

GREENE'S TUTORIAL COLLEGE
45 Pembroke Street, Oxford, Oxfordshire OX1 1BP
Tel: (01865) 248308
Fax: (01865) 240700
Email: registrar@edward-greene.ac.uk
Head: Mr E P C Greene
Type: Co-educational Day and Boarding Boys 7–70 Girls 13–30 (Boarding (host families)) Flexi-boarding available
No of pupils: B40 G40
No of boarders: F20
Fees: (September 05)
F/WB £ £7595–£25375
Day £4095–£20475

EMMANUEL CHRISTIAN SCHOOL
Sandford Road, Littlemore, Oxford, Oxfordshire OX4 4PU
Tel: (01865) 395236
Fax: (01865) 395236
Email: jean@jpandy.fsnet.co.uk
Head: Miss J P Dandy
Type: Co-educational Day 3–11
No of pupils: B23 G32
Fees: (September 04) Day £3300

HEADINGTON SCHOOL
Oxford, Oxfordshire OX3 7TD
Tel: (01865) 759113
Fax: (01865) 760268
Email: admissions@headington.org
Head: Mrs A Coutts
Type: Girls Day and Boarding 3–18 (Co-ed 3–4) Flexi-boarding available
No of pupils: B8 G955
No of boarders: F115 W62
Fees: (September 05)
FB £16920–£18450
WB £16320–£17760
Day £4980–£9690

IQRA SCHOOL
Lawn Upton House, David Nicholls Close, Littlemore, Oxford, Oxfordshire OX4 4PU
Tel: (01865) 777254
Email: iqraschooloxford@yahoo.co.uk
Head: Mr H Ramzy and Mrs F Tenvir
Type: Girls Day 10–16
No of pupils: 60
Fees: (September 05) Day £1500

LECKFORD PLACE SCHOOL
c/o Beechlawn House, 1 Park Town, Oxford, Oxfordshire OX2 6SN
Tel: (01865) 310000
Fax: (01865) 552296
Email: mail@doverbroecks.oxon.sch.uk
Type: Co-educational Day 11–16

MAGDALEN COLLEGE SCHOOL
Cowley Place, Oxford, Oxfordshire OX4 1DZ
Tel: (01865) 242191
Fax: (01865) 240379
Email: admissions@mcsoxford.org
Head: Mr A D Halls
Type: Boys Day 7–18
No of pupils: 675
Fees: (September 05)
Day £8018–£9880

NEW COLLEGE SCHOOL
2 Savile Road, Oxford, Oxfordshire OX1 3UA
Tel: (01865) 243657
Fax: (01865) 201277
Head: Mrs P Hindle
Type: Boys Day 4–13
No of pupils: 158
Fees: (September 04)
Day £4665–£7530

OXFORD HIGH SCHOOL GDST
Belbroughton Road, Oxford, Oxfordshire OX2 6XA
Tel: (01865) 559888
Fax: (01865) 552343
Email: oxfordhigh@oxf.gdst.net
Head: Miss O F S Lusk
Type: Girls Day 3–18 (Boys 3–6)
No of pupils: B34 G890
Fees: (September 05)
Day £2205–£7365

OXFORD MONTESSORI SCHOOLS
Forest Farm, Elsfield, Oxford, Oxfordshire OX3 9UW
Tel: (01865) 358210
Fax: (01865) 358390
Email: oms.schools@btconnect.co.uk
Type: Co-educational Day 2–12
No of pupils: B60 G50
Fees: (September 05)
Day £4770–£6188

OXFORD TUTORIAL COLLEGE
12 King Edward Street, Oxford, Oxfordshire OX1 4HT
Tel: (01865) 793333
Fax: (01865) 793233
Email: info@otc.ac.uk
Head: Mrs F Pocock
Type: Co-educational Boarding and Day 16+
No of pupils: B70 G66
No of boarders: F45 W1

RYE ST ANTONY SCHOOL
Pullen's Lane, Oxford, Oxfordshire OX3 0BY
Tel: (01865) 762802
Fax: (01865) 763611
Email: headmistress@ryestantony.co.uk
Head: Miss A M Jones
Type: Girls Boarding and Day 3–18 (Boys 3–8) Flexi-boarding available
No of pupils: B20 G380
No of boarders: F60 W20
Fees: (September 05) FB £13200–£15570 WB £12285–£14670 Day £5640–£9165

ST CLARE'S, OXFORD*
139 Banbury Road, Oxford, Oxfordshire OX2 7AL
Tel: (01865) 552031
Fax: (01865) 513359
Email: admissions@stclares.ac.uk
Head: Mrs P Holloway
Type: Co-educational Boarding and Day 15–20 Flexi-boarding available
No of pupils: B82 G114
No of boarders: F183 W1
Fees: (September 04) FB £22715 Day £14000

ST EDWARD'S SCHOOL
Woodstock Road, Oxford, Oxfordshire OX2 7NN
Tel: (01865) 319200
Fax: (01865) 319202
Email: registrar@stedwards.oxon.sch.uk
Head: Mr A Trotman
Type: Co-educational Boarding and Day 13–18
No of pupils: B425 G232
No of boarders: F481
Fees: (September 05) FB £22710 Day £18168

SUMMER FIELDS
Mayfield Road, Oxford, Oxfordshire OX2 7EN
Tel: (01865) 454433
Fax: (01865) 459200
Email: schoolsec@summerfields.org.uk
Head: Mr R F Badham-Thornhill
Type: Boys Boarding and Day 7–13
No of pupils: 240
No of boarders: F230
Fees: (September 05) FB £16755 Day £12615

WYCHWOOD SCHOOL
74 Banbury Road, Oxford, Oxfordshire OX2 6JR
Tel: (01865) 557976
Fax: (01865) 556806
Email: admin@wychwood-school.org.uk
Head: Mrs S M P Wingfield Digby
Type: Girls Boarding and Day 11–18 Flexi-boarding available
No of pupils: 150
No of boarders: F27 W31
Fees: (September 04) FB £12450 WB £12150 Day £7860

WALLINGFORD

CRANFORD HOUSE SCHOOL
Moulsford, Wallingford, Oxfordshire OX10 9HT
Tel: (01491) 651218
Fax: (01491) 652557
Email: admissions@cranfordhouse.oxon.sch.uk
Head: Mrs C Hamilton
Type: Girls Day 3–16 (Boys 3–7)
No of pupils: B58 G246
Fees: (September 04) Day £5250–£8445

MOULSFORD PREPARATORY SCHOOL
Moulsford, Wallingford, Oxfordshire OX10 9HR
Tel: (01491) 651438
Fax: (01491) 651868
Email: secretary@moulsford.com
Head: Mr M J Higham
Type: Boys Boarding and Day 5–13
No of pupils: 220
No of boarders: W51
Fees: (September 04) WB £12150

WANTAGE

ST ANDREW'S
Wallingford Street, Wantage, Oxfordshire OX12 8AZ
Tel: (01235) 762345
Fax: (01235) 768274
Email: admin@St-Andrews-Wantage.oxon.sch.uk
Head: Mrs M Parkes
Type: Co-educational Day 3–11
No of pupils: B57 G43
Fees: (September 05) Day £1539–£1720

ST MARY'S SCHOOL
Newbury Street, Wantage, Oxfordshire OX12 8BZ
Tel: (01235) 773800
Fax: (01235) 760467
Email: admin@stmarys.oxon.sch.uk
Head: Mrs S Sowden
Type: Girls Boarding and Day 11–18
No of pupils: 200
No of boarders: F180
Fees: (September 05) FB £21990 Day £14700

WITNEY

COKETHORPE*
Witney, Oxfordshire OX29 7PU
Tel: (01993) 703921
Fax: (01993) 773499
Email: admin@cokethorpe.org.uk
Head: Mr D J Ettinger
Type: Co-educational Day 5–18
No of pupils: B416 G185
Fees: (September 05) Day £7320–£11820

THE KING'S SCHOOL
12 Wesley Walk, High Street, Witney, Oxfordshire OX8 6ZJ
Tel: (01993) 709985
Fax: (01993) 709986
Email: tks@occ.org.uk
Head: Mr K Elmitt
Type: Co-educational Day 11–16
No of pupils: B60 G50
Fees: (September 04) Day £5142

THE KING'S SCHOOL, PRIMARY
New Yatt Road, Witney,
Oxfordshire OX29 6TA
Tel: (01993) 778463
Fax: (01993) 778463
Head: Mrs A Gibbon
Type: Co-educational Day 5–11
No of pupils: B60 G60
Fees: (September 03) Day £3720

RUTLAND

OAKHAM

BROOKE PRIORY SCHOOL
Station Approach, Oakham,
Rutland LE15 6QW
Tel: (01572) 724778
Fax: (01572) 724969
Email: info@brooke.rutland.sch.uk
Head: Mrs E Bell
Type: Co-educational Day 3–11
No of pupils: B128 G112
Fees: (September 04)
Day £3936–£4920

OAKHAM SCHOOL*
Chapel Close, Oakham, Rutland
LE15 6DT
Tel: (01572) 758758
Fax: (01572) 758595
Email: admissions@oakham.rutland.sch.uk
Head: Dr J A F Spence
Type: Co-educational Boarding and Day 10–18
No of pupils: B520 G520
No of boarders: F620
Fees: (September 05)
FB £18330–£21420
Day £11640–£12810

UPPINGHAM

UPPINGHAM SCHOOL
Uppingham, Rutland LE15 9QE
Tel: (01572) 822216
Fax: (01572) 822332
Email: admissions@uppingham.co.uk
Head: Dr S C Winkley
Type: Co-educational Boarding and Day 13–18
No of pupils: B482 G268
No of boarders: F726
Fees: (September 05) FB £22500
Day £15750

WINDMILL HOUSE SCHOOL
22 Stockerston Road, Uppingham,
Rutland LE15 9UD
Tel: (01572) 823593
Fax: (01572) 822220
Head: Mrs J Taylor
Type: Co-educational Day 4–11
No of pupils: B40 G40
Fees: (September 04)
Day £3060–£4575

SHROPSHIRE

BRIDGNORTH

DOWER HOUSE SCHOOL
Quatt, Bridgnorth, Shropshire WV15 6QW
Tel: (01746) 780309
Email: info@dowerhouseschool.co.uk
Head: Mr A R T Ellis
Type: Co-educational Day Boys 2–11 Girls 3–11
No of pupils: B30 G35
Fees: (September 04)
Day £4590–£4950

BUCKNELL

BEDSTONE COLLEGE
Bedstone, Bucknell, Shropshire SY7 0BG
Tel: (01547) 530303
Fax: (01547) 530740
Email: admissions@bedstone.org
Head: Mr M S Symonds
Type: Co-educational Boarding and Day 3–18 Flexi-boarding available
No of pupils: B128 G108
No of boarders: F117
Fees: (September 05)
FB £12345–£17994
Day £7050–£9750

ELLESMERE

ELLESMERE COLLEGE†
Ellesmere, Shropshire SY12 9AB
Tel: (01691) 622321
Fax: (01691) 623286
Email: admin@ellesmere.biblio.net
Head: Mr B J Wignall
Type: Co-educational Boarding and Day 8–18 Flexi-boarding available
No of pupils: B351 G143
No of boarders: F65 W101
Fees: (September 05)
FB £15330–£18870
WB £15027–£15729
Day £7470–£12168

LUDLOW

MOOR PARK SCHOOL
Moor Park, Richard's Castle, Ludlow, Shropshire SY8 4DZ
Tel: (01584) 876061
Fax: (01584) 877311
Email: head@moorpark.org.uk
Head: Mr M R Piercy
Type: Co-educational Boarding and Day 3–13 Flexi-boarding available
No of pupils: B115 G115
No of boarders: F8 W40
Fees: (September 05)
F/WB £ £11310–£13770
Day £4095–£10080

NEWPORT

CASTLE HOUSE SCHOOL
Chetwynd End, Newport, Shropshire TF10 7JE
Tel: (01952) 811035
Fax: (01952) 811035
Email: ali@castlehouse.indschools.co.uk
Head: Mr R M Walden
Type: Co-educational Day 3–11
No of pupils: B55 G55
Fees: (September 04)
Day £2475–£5187

OSWESTRY

BELLAN HOUSE PREPARATORY SCHOOL
Bellan House, Church Street, Oswestry, Shropshire SY11 2ST
Tel: (01691) 653453
Fax: (01691) 680552
Email: enquiries@oswestryschool.co.uk
Head: Mrs S L Durham
Type: Co-educational Day 2–9 Flexi-boarding available
No of pupils: B91 G92
Fees: (September 03)
Day £940–£5100

MORETON HALL*
Weston Rhyn, Oswestry, Shropshire SY11 3EW
Tel: (01691) 776020
Fax: (01691) 778552
Email: admin@moretonhall.com
Head: Mr J Forster
Type: Co-educational Boarding and Day Boys 4–8 Girls 4–18
No of pupils: B8 G318
No of boarders: F233
Fees: (September 05)
FB £13500–£21255
Day £5700–£16050

OSWESTRY SCHOOL
Upper Brook Street, Oswestry, Shropshire SY11 2TL
Tel: (01691) 655711
Fax: (01691) 671194
Email: enquiries@oswestryschool.org.uk
Head: Mr P D Stockdale
Type: Co-educational Day and Boarding 2–18 Flexi-boarding available
No of pupils: B238 G181
No of boarders: F105 W6
Fees: (September 05) FB £17550 WB £15450 Day £4890–£10350

SHREWSBURY

ADCOTE SCHOOL FOR GIRLS
Little Ness, Shrewsbury, Shropshire SY4 2JY
Tel: (01939) 260202
Fax: (01939) 261300
Email: secretary@adcoteschool.co.uk
Head: Ms D J Hammond
Type: Girls Boarding and Day 4–18 Flexi-boarding available
No of pupils: 105
No of boarders: F35 W8
Fees: (September 05)
FB £13080–£18090
WB £11505–£16515
Day £5505–£10185

CONCORD COLLEGE
Acton Burnell Hall, Shrewsbury, Shropshire SY5 7PF
Tel: (01694) 731631
Fax: (01694) 731389
Email: theprincipal@concordcollegeuk.com
Head: Mr N G Hawkins
Type: Co-educational Boarding and Day 12–18
No of pupils: B160 G149
No of boarders: F290
Fees: (September 04) FB £17334 Day £6332

KINGSLAND GRANGE
Old Roman Road, Shrewsbury, Shropshire SY3 9AH
Tel: (01743) 232132
Fax: (01743) 352665
Email: mcjames@talk21.com
Head: Mr M C James
Type: Boys Day 4–13
No of pupils: 130
Fees: (September 05) Day £5280–£8400

PACKWOOD HAUGH SCHOOL
Ruyton XI Towns, Shrewsbury, Shropshire SY4 1HX
Tel: (01939) 260217
Fax: (01939) 262077
Email: head@packwood-haugh.co.uk
Head: Mr N T Westlake
Type: Co-educational Boarding and Day 4–13
No of pupils: B159 G111
No of boarders: F130
Fees: (September 05) FB £14340 Day £4935–£11475

PRESTFELDE PREPARATORY SCHOOL
London Road, Shrewsbury, Shropshire SY2 6NZ
Tel: (01743) 245400
Fax: (01743) 241434
Email: office@prestfelde.net
Head: Mr J R Bridgeland
Type: Co-educational Day and Boarding 3–13 Flexi-boarding available
No of pupils: B250 G85
No of boarders: F35 W10
Fees: (September 03) FB £10800 Day £2700–£8430

ST WINEFRIDE'S CONVENT SCHOOL
Belmont, Shrewsbury, Shropshire SY1 1TE
Tel: (01743) 369883
Fax: (01743) 341650
Head: Sister M Felicity
Type: Co-educational Day 3–11
No of pupils: B65 G86
Fees: (September 04) Day £2250–£2475

SHREWSBURY HIGH SCHOOL GDST
32 Town Walls, Shrewsbury, Shropshire SY1 1TN
Tel: (01743) 362872
Fax: (01743) 364942
Email: enquiries@shr.gdst.net
Head: Mrs M L R Cass
Type: Girls Day 2–18
No of pupils: 654
Fees: (September 05) Day £5337–£7365

SHREWSBURY SCHOOL
The Schools, Shrewsbury, Shropshire SY3 7BA
Tel: (01743) 280500
Fax: (01743) 243107
Email: enquiry@shrewsbury.org.uk
Head: Mr J Goulding
Type: Boys Boarding and Day 13–18
No of boarders: F558
Fees: (September 05) FB £22590 Day £15870

TELFORD

THE OLD HALL SCHOOL
Holyhead Road, Wellington, Telford, Shropshire TF1 2DN
Tel: (01952) 223117
Fax: (01952) 222674
Email: enq@oldhall.co.uk
Head: Mr R J Ward
Type: Co-educational Day 3–11 Flexi-boarding available
No of pupils: B136 G118
Fees: (September 04) Day £4860–£7650

WREKIN COLLEGE
Wellington, Telford, Shropshire TF1 3BH
Tel: (01952) 240131/242305
Fax: (01952) 240338
Email: info@wrekincollege.ac.uk
Head: Mr S G Drew
Type: Co-educational Boarding and Day 11–19 Flexi-boarding available
No of pupils: B269 G184
No of boarders: F114
Fees: (September 04) FB £16170–£18585 Day £9294–£11235

WHITCHURCH

WHITE HOUSE SCHOOL
Heath Road, Whitchurch, Shropshire SY13 2AA
Tel: (01948) 662730
Email: whitehouseschool@btconnect.com
Head: Mrs H Clarke
Type: Co-educational Day 3–11
No of pupils: B85 G85
Fees: (September 05) Day £1845–£2700

SOMERSET

BRUTON

BRUTON SCHOOL FOR GIRLS

Sunny Hill, Bruton, Somerset BA10 0NT
Tel: (01749) 814400
Fax: (01749) 812537
Email: info@brutonschool.co.uk
Head: Mrs B C Bates
Type: Girls Day and Boarding 3–18 Flexi-boarding available
No of pupils: B6 G380
No of boarders: F80 W20
Fees: (September 05)
FB £14235–£17490
WB £12900–£15285
Day £5475–£9675

KING'S BRUTON *

Bruton, Somerset BA10 0ED
Tel: (01749) 814200
Fax: (01749) 813426
Email: registrar@kingsbruton.com
Head: Mr N M Lashbrook
Type: Co-educational Boarding and Day 13–18
No of pupils: B243 G90
No of boarders: F248
Fees: (September 05) FB £20100
Day £14730

BURNHAM-ON-SEA

SOUTHLEIGH KINDERGARTEN

11 Rectory Road, Burnham-on-Sea, Somerset TA8 2BY
Tel: (01278) 783999
Head: Mrs L Easton
Type: Co-educational Day 2–7
No of pupils: B40 G40

CHARD

CHARD SCHOOL

Fore Street, Chard, Somerset TA20 1QA
Tel: (01460) 63234
Fax: (01460) 68988
Email: johnstotesbury@hotmail.com
Head: Mr J G Stotesbury
Type: Co-educational Day 2–11
No of pupils: B60 G60
Fees: (September 05)
Day £3618–£3897

CREWKERNE

PERROTT HILL SCHOOL

North Perrott, Crewkerne, Somerset TA18 7SL
Tel: (01460) 72051
Fax: (01460) 78246
Email: headmaster@perrotthill.com
Head: Mr M J Davies
Type: Co-educational Boarding and Day 3–13 Flexi-boarding available
No of pupils: B100 G80
No of boarders: F10 W25
Fees: (September 05) FB £14412
WB £13200 Day £4100

SHEPTON MALLET

ALL HALLOWS

Cranmore Hall, East Cranmore, Shepton Mallet, Somerset BA4 4SF
Tel: (01749) 880227
Fax: (01749) 880709
Email: info@allhallows.somerset.sch.uk
Head: Mr Ian Murphy
Type: Co-educational Boarding and Day 4–13 Flexi-boarding available
No of pupils: B160 G105
No of boarders: F70
Fees: (September 05) FB £14970
Day £4905–£9990

STREET

MILLFIELD PREPARATORY SCHOOL

Street, Somerset BA16 0YD
Tel: (01458) 832446
Fax: (01458) 833679
Email: admissions@millfieldschool.com
Head: Mr K Cheney
Type: Co-educational Boarding and Day 2–13
No of pupils: B299 G220
No of boarders: F174
Fees: (September 04) FB £15180
Day £4290–£10245

MILLFIELD SCHOOL

Street, Somerset BA16 0YD
Tel: (01458) 442291
Fax: (01458) 447276
Email: admissions@millfield.somerset.sch.uk
Head: Mr P M Johnson
Type: Co-educational Boarding and Day 13–18
No of pupils: B795 G468
No of boarders: F923

TAUNTON

KING'S COLLEGE

Taunton, Somerset TA1 3DX
Tel: (01823) 328200
Fax: (01823) 328202
Email: admissions@kings-taunton.co.uk
Head: Mr C D Ramsey
Type: Co-educational Boarding and Day 13–18
No of pupils: B267 G148
No of boarders: F278
Fees: (September 05) FB £19980
Day £13650

KING'S HALL SCHOOL

Kingston Road, Taunton, Somerset TA2 8AA
Tel: (01823) 285920
Fax: (01823) 285922
Email: kingshall@aol.com
Head: Mr J K Macpherson
Type: Co-educational Boarding and Day 3–13 Flexi-boarding available
No of pupils: B237 G182
No of boarders: F46 W12
Fees: (September 05)
F/WB £ £3650–£4750
Day £1200–£3365

QUEEN'S COLLEGE
Trull Road, Taunton, Somerset TA1 4QS
Tel: (01823) 340830
Fax: (01823) 338430
Email: admissions@queenscollege.org.uk
Head: Mr C J Alcock
Type: Co-educational Day and Boarding 3–18 Flexi-boarding available
No of pupils: B405 G365
No of boarders: F175
Fees: (September 05)
FB £7857–£17172
Day £3600–£11376

QUEEN'S COLLEGE JUNIOR AND PRE-PREPARATORY SCHOOLS
Trull Road, Taunton, Somerset TA1 4QP
Tel: (01823) 272990
Fax: (01823) 323811
Email: junior.head@queenscollege.org.uk
Head: Mr J M Backhouse and Mrs E Gibbs
Type: Co-educational Day and Boarding 3–11
No of pupils: B117 G107
No of boarders: F33
Fees: (September 03)
FB £7893–£10872
Day £3906–£7209

TAUNTON INTERNATIONAL STUDY CENTRE (TISC)
Taunton School, Taunton, Somerset TA2 6AD
Tel: (01823) 348100
Fax: (01823) 349206
Email: tisc@tauntonschool.co.uk
Head: Mrs C G Nixon
Type: Co-educational Boarding 12–17
No of pupils: B38 G21
No of boarders: F59
Fees: (September 05)
FB £22050–£24075

TAUNTON PREPARATORY SCHOOL
Staplegrove Road, Taunton, Somerset TA2 6AE
Tel: (01823) 349250
Fax: (01823) 349202
Email: tps.enquiries@tauntonschool.co.uk
Head: Mr M Anderson
Type: Co-educational Day and Boarding 3–13 Flexi-boarding available
No of pupils: B251 G193
No of boarders: F39
Fees: (September 05)
FB £8295–£15045
Day £4575–£9945

TAUNTON SCHOOL
Taunton, Somerset TA2 6AD
Tel: (01823) 349200/349223
Fax: (01823) 349201
Email: enquiries@tauntonschool.co.uk
Head: Dr J Newton
Type: Co-educational Boarding and Day 13–18
No of pupils: B256 G194
No of boarders: F177
Fees: (September 05) FB £19200
Day £12345

WATCHET

BUCKLAND SCHOOL
7 St Decumans Road, Watchet, Somerset TA23 0HR
Tel: (01984) 631314
Head: Mrs Pirt
Type: Co-educational Day 3–10
No of pupils: 40
Fees: (September 02) Day £1845

WELLINGTON

WELLINGTON SCHOOL
South Street, Wellington, Somerset TA21 8NT
Tel: (01823) 668800
Fax: (01823) 668844
Email: admin@wellington-school.org.uk
Head: Mr A J Rogers
Type: Co-educational Boarding and Day 10–18 Flexi-boarding available
No of pupils: B456 G357
No of boarders: F155 W7
Fees: (September 05)
FB £12660–£15612
WB £9948–£12270
Day £6450–£8382

WELLS

WELLS CATHEDRAL JUNIOR SCHOOL
8 New Street, Wells, Somerset BA5 2LQ
Tel: (01749) 834400
Fax: (01749) 834401
Email: juniorschool@wells-cathedral-school.com
Head: Mr N M Wilson
Type: Co-educational Boarding and Day 3–11 Flexi-boarding available
No of pupils: B94 G93
No of boarders: F4 W4
Fees: (September 04) FB £15750
WB £13311 Day £4995–£9450

WELLS CATHEDRAL SCHOOL
Wells, Somerset BA5 2ST
Tel: (01749) 834200
Fax: (01749) 834201
Email: admissions@wells-cathedral-school.com
Head: Mrs E C Cairncross
Type: Co-educational Boarding and Day 3–18 Flexi-boarding available
No of pupils: B342 G310
No of boarders: F205
Fees: (September 04)
FB £15750–£18690
Day £4995–£11190

YEOVIL

CHILTON CANTELO SCHOOL
Chilton Cantelo, Yeovil, Somerset BA22 8BG
Tel: (01935) 850555
Fax: (01935) 850482
Email: ccs@pavilion.co.uk
Head: Mr D S von Zeffman
Type: Co-educational Boarding and Day 7–18 Flexi-boarding available
No of pupils: B200 G160
No of boarders: F210
Fees: (September 04)
FB £11010–£14250
Day £5535–£7095

HAZLEGROVE (KING'S BRUTON PREPARATORY SCHOOL)†
Hazlegrove House, Sparkford, Yeovil, Somerset BA22 7JA
Tel: (01963) 440314
Fax: (01963) 440569
Email: office@hazlegrove.co.uk
Head: Mr R Fenwick
Type: Co-educational Day and Boarding 3–13 Flexi-boarding available
No of pupils: B193 G107
No of boarders: F55
Fees: (September 05)
FB £13650–£15465
Day £5550–£11265

THE PARK SCHOOL
The Park, Yeovil, Somerset BA20 1DH
Tel: (01935) 423514
Fax: (01935) 411257
Email: admin@parkschool.com
Head: Mr P W Bate
Type: Co-educational Day and Boarding 3–18 Flexi-boarding available
No of pupils: B104 G156
No of boarders: F29 W1
Fees: (September 05) FB £13785
WB £12285–£13185
Day £3930–£7065

BATH & NORTH EAST SOMERSET

BATH

BATH ACADEMY
27 Queen Square, Bath, Bath & North East Somerset BA1 2HX
Tel: (†44(0)1225) 334577
Fax: (01225) 482414
Email: principal@bathacademy.co.uk
Head: Mrs L H Brown
Type: Co-educational Boarding 16–20 Flexi-boarding available
No of pupils: B70 G70
No of boarders: F150
Fees: (September 05) FB £13450

DOWNSIDE SCHOOL*
Stratton-on-the-Fosse, Radstock, Bath, Somerset BA3 4RJ
Tel: (01761) 235100
Fax: (01761) 235105
Email: registrar@downside.co.uk
Head: Dom Leo Maidlow Davis
Type: Co-educational Boarding and Day 9–18
No of pupils: B367 G60
No of boarders: F229
Fees: (September 05)
FB £15558–£19590
Day £9192–£10224

KING EDWARD'S JUNIOR SCHOOL
North Road, Bath, Bath & North East Somerset BA2 6JA
Tel: (01225) 463218
Fax: (01225) 442178
Email: juniorschhead@kesbath.biblio.net
Head: Mr J Croker
Type: Co-educational Day 7–11
Fees: (September 05) Day £6954

KING EDWARD'S PRE-PREP SCHOOL
Weston Lane, Bath, Bath & North East Somerset BA1 4AQ
Tel: (01225) 421681
Fax: (01225) 428006
Email: kespp@btopenworld.com
Head: Mrs J A Siderfin
Type: Co-educational Day 3–7
No of pupils: B63 G24
Fees: (September 04)
Day £5082–£6213

KING EDWARD'S SCHOOL, BATH
North Road, Bath, Bath & North East Somerset BA2 6HU
Tel: (01225) 464313
Fax: (01225) 481363
Email: headmaster@kesbath.biblio.net
Head: Mr Crispin Rowe
Type: Co-educational Day 3–18
No of pupils: B486 G177
Fees: (September 04)
Day £5082–£8496

KINGSWOOD PREPARATORY SCHOOL
College Road, Lansdown, Bath, Bath & North East Somerset BA1 5SD
Tel: (01225) 734460
Fax: (01225) 464434
Email: enquiries@kingswood.bath.sch.uk
Head: Mr Marcus Cornah
Type: Co-educational Day and Boarding 3–11 Flexi-boarding available
No of pupils: B173 G145
No of boarders: F7 W7
Fees: (September 05)
FB £14112–£14910 WB £11856
Day £5958–£6894

KINGSWOOD SCHOOL*
Lansdown, Bath, Bath & North East Somerset BA1 5RG
Tel: (01225) 734210
Fax: (01225) 734305
Email: enquiries@kingswood.bath.sch.uk
Head: Mr G M Best
Type: Co-educational Boarding and Day 11–18 Flexi-boarding available
No of pupils: B350 G286
No of boarders: F138 W39
Fees: (September 05)
FB £16374–£19611
WB £14304–£17721 Day £8754

MONKTON COMBE JUNIOR SCHOOL
Combe Down, Bath, Bath & North East Somerset BA2 7ET
Tel: (01225) 837912
Fax: (01225) 840312
Email: admin@monktonjunior.org.uk
Head: Mr C J Stafford
Type: Co-educational Day and Boarding 2–13 Flexi-boarding available
No of pupils: B221 G151
No of boarders: F19 W41
Fees: (September 04)
FB £12210–£12810 WB £12570
Day £5490–£9675

MONKTON COMBE SCHOOL†
Bath, Bath & North East Somerset BA2 7HG
Tel: (01225) 721133
Fax: (01225) 721181
Email: admissions@monkton.org.uk
Head: Mr R P Backhouse
Type: Co-educational Boarding and Day 2–19 Flexi-boarding available
No of pupils: B452 G271
No of boarders: F261
Fees: (September 05)
FB £14898–£21306
WB £13017–£14262
Day £9570–£14949

PARAGON SCHOOL, PRIOR PARK COLLEGE JUNIOR
Lyncombe House, Lyncombe Vale, Bath, Bath & North East Somerset BA2 4LT
Tel: (01225) 310837
Fax: (01225) 427980
Email: office@paragonschool.co.uk
Head: Mr D J Martin
Type: Co-educational Day 3–11
No of pupils: B116 G86
Fees: (September 05)
Day £5010–£5580

PRIOR PARK COLLEGE*
Ralph Allen Drive, Bath, Bath & North East Somerset BA2 5AH
Tel: (01225) 831000
Fax: (01225) 835753
Email: admissions@priorpark.co.uk
Head: Dr G Mercer
Type: Co-educational Boarding and Day 11–18 (Boarding from 13) Flexi-boarding available
No of pupils: B300 G250
No of boarders: F124
Fees: (September 05) FB £19068
Day £9492–£10575

THE ROYAL HIGH SCHOOL*
Lansdown Road, Bath, Bath & North East Somerset BA1 5SZ
Tel: (01225) 313877
Fax: (01225) 465446
Email: royalhigh@bat.gdst.net
Head: Mr J Graham-Brown
Type: Girls Boarding and Day 3–18 Flexi-boarding available
No of pupils: 858
No of boarders: F98
Fees: (September 05) FB £14442
Day £4410–£7365

NORTH SOMERSET

WESTON-SUPER-MARE

ASHBROOKE HOUSE
9 Ellenborough Park North, Weston-Super-Mare, North Somerset BS23 1XH
Tel: (01934) 629515
Fax: (01934) 629685
Head: Mrs R Thomas
Type: Co-educational Day 3–11
No of pupils: B60 G50
Fees: (September 04)
Day £1554–£3159

LANCASTER HOUSE SCHOOL
38 Hill Road, Weston-Super-Mare, North Somerset BS23 2RY
Tel: (01934) 624116
Email: susanlewisbrent@supanet.com
Head: Mrs S Lewis
Type: Co-educational Day 4–11 Flexi-boarding available
No of pupils: B23 G23
Fees: (September 04)
Day £1800–£1950

WINSCOMBE

SIDCOT SCHOOL*†
Oakridge Lane, Winscombe, North Somerset BS25 1PD
Tel: (01934) 843102
Fax: (01934) 844181
Email: admissions@sidcot.org.uk
Head: Mr J Walmsley
Type: Co-educational Boarding and Day 3–18 Flexi-boarding available
No of pupils: B279 G221
No of boarders: F117 W29
Fees: (September 05)
FB £14550–£21600 WB £16050
Day £3750–£9990

WRAXALL

THE DOWNS SCHOOL
Wraxall, North Somerset BS48 1PF
Tel: (01275) 852008
Fax: (01275) 855840
Email: office@thedownsschool.co.uk
Head: Mr M A Gunn
Type: Co-educational Day and Boarding 4–13 Flexi-boarding available
No of pupils: B152 G67
No of boarders: W6
Fees: (September 05) WB £12900 Day £5850–£9990

STAFFORDSHIRE

ABBOTS BROMLEY

ABBOTS BROMLEY SCHOOL FOR GIRLS
Abbots Bromley, Staffordshire WS15 3BW
Tel: (01283) 840232
Fax: (01283) 840988
Email: registar@abbotsbromley.net
Head: Mrs P Woodhouse
Type: Girls Boarding and Day 4–18 Flexi-boarding available
No of pupils: 290
No of boarders: F50 W13
Fees: (September 05)
FB £14550–£18585
WB £14550–£17280
Day £4950–£10860

BREWOOD

VERNON LODGE PREPARATORY SCHOOL
School Lane, Stretton, Brewood, Staffordshire ST19 9LJ
Tel: (01902) 850568
Fax: (01902) 850568
Email: info@vernonlodge.co.uk
Head: Mrs P Sills
Type: Co-educational Day 2–11
No of pupils: B58 G35
Fees: (September 05)
Day £5040–£5760

CANNOCK

CHASE ACADEMY
Lyncroft House, St John's Road, Cannock, Staffordshire WS11 0UR
Tel: (01543) 501800
Fax: (01543) 501801
Email: info@chaseacademy.com
Head: Mr M D Ellse
Type: Co-educational Day and Boarding 3–18
No of pupils: B109 G82
No of boarders: F6
Fees: (September 05)
FB £8400–£13350
Day £2004–£6900

HANBURY

HANBURY PREP SCHOOL
New Lodge, Hanbury, Staffordshire DE13 8TG
Tel: (01283) 820236
Head: Mrs S Hall
Type: Co-educational Day 3–12

LICHFIELD

LICHFIELD CATHEDRAL SCHOOL
The Palace, Lichfield, Staffordshire WS13 7LH
Tel: (01543) 306170
Fax: (01543) 306176
Email: reception@lichfieldcathedralschool.com
Head: Mr P Allwood
Type: Co-educational Day and Boarding 3–13 Flexi-boarding available
No of pupils: 273
No of boarders: F18 W6
Fees: (September 04)
FB £11250–£11385
WB £9870–£10440
Day £4740–£7560

ST JOHN'S PREPARATORY SCHOOL
Green Gables, Longdon Hall, Longdon Green, Lichfield, Staffordshire WS15 4PT
Tel: (01543) 492782
Email: sjsann@aol.com
Head: Mrs A Watson
Type: Co-educational Day 3–11
No of pupils: B50 G34
Fees: (September 05)
Day £2775–£5400

NEWCASTLE-UNDER-LYME

EDENHURST SCHOOL
Westlands Avenue, Newcastle-under-Lyme, Staffordshire ST5 2PU
Tel: (01782) 619348
Fax: (01782) 662402
Email: headmaster@edenhurst.co.uk
Head: Mr N H F Copestick
Type: Co-educational Day 3–14
No of pupils: B118 G122
Fees: (September 04)
Day £4680–£6480

NEWCASTLE-UNDER-LYME SCHOOL
Mount Pleasant, Newcastle-under-Lyme, Staffordshire ST5 1DB
Tel: (01782) 631197
Fax: (01782) 632582
Email: info@nuls.org.uk
Head: Mr R S Dillow
Type: Co-educational Day 3–18
No of pupils: B550 G550
Fees: (September 05)
Day £5340–£6984

STAFFORD

BROOKLANDS SCHOOL
167 Eccleshall Road, Stafford, Staffordshire ST16 1PD
Tel: (01785) 251399
Fax: (01785) 244379
Email: enquiries@brooklandsschool.com
Head: Mr D R Williams
Type: Co-educational Day 0–11
No of pupils: B78 G75
Fees: (September 05)
Day £504–£6465

ST BEDE'S SCHOOL
Bishton Hall, Wolseley Bridge, Stafford, Staffordshire ST17 0XN
Tel: (01889) 881277
Fax: (01889) 882749
Email: admin@saintbedes.com
Head: Mr M E A McLuckie
Type: Co-educational Boarding and Day 2–13 Flexi-boarding available
No of pupils: B68 G50
No of boarders: F10 W15
Fees: (September 04) F/WB £ £8400
Day £4050–£6900

ST DOMINIC'S SCHOOL
32 Bargate Street, Brewood, Stafford, Staffordshire ST19 9BA
Tel: (01902) 850248
Fax: (01902) 851154
Email: enquiries@st-dominics-brewood.co.uk
Head: Mrs S White
Type: Girls Day 2–16 (Co-ed 2–7)
No of pupils: B5 G292
Fees: (September 04)
Day £2435–£8730

STAFFORD GRAMMAR SCHOOL
Burton Manor, Stafford, Staffordshire ST18 9AT
Tel: (01785) 249752
Fax: (01785) 255005
Email: headsec@staffordgs.plus.com
Head: Mr M R Darley
Type: Co-educational Day 11–18
No of pupils: B197 G160
Fees: (September 03) Day £6696

YARLET SCHOOL
Yarlet, Near Stafford, Stafford, Staffordshire ST18 9SU
Tel: (01785) 286568
Fax: (01785) 286569
Email: headmaster@yarletschool.co.uk
Head: Mr R S Plant
Type: Co-educational Day and Boarding 2–13 Flexi-boarding available
No of pupils: B112 G53
Fees: (September 05)
Day £4950–£7785

STOKE-ON-TRENT

ST DOMINIC'S INDEPENDENT JUNIOR SCHOOL
Hartshill Road, Stoke-on-Trent, Staffordshire ST4 7LY
Tel: (01782) 848588
Fax: (01782) 413778
Email: saintdominics@btconnect.com
Head: Mr J.F. Butler
Type: Co-educational Day 3–11
No of pupils: B64 G50
Fees: (September 05)
Day £3090–£3885

ST JOSEPH'S PREPARATORY SCHOOL
London Road, Trent Vale, Stoke-on-Trent, Staffordshire ST4 5RF
Tel: (01782) 417533
Fax: (01782) 849327
Email: enquiries@stjosephprepschool.co.uk
Head: Mrs S D Hutchinson
Type: Co-educational Day 3–11
No of pupils: 120
Fees: (September 04)
Day £3570–£4395

STONE

ST DOMINIC'S PRIORY SCHOOL
21 Station Road, Stone, Staffordshire ST15 8EN
Tel: (01785) 814181
Fax: (01785) 819361
Head: Mr A Egan
Type: Girls Day 3–18 (Boys 3–11)
No of pupils: B22 G350
Fees: (September 03)
Day £3967–£6088

UTTOXETER

ABBOTSHOLME SCHOOL
Rocester, Uttoxeter, Staffordshire ST14 5BS
Tel: (01889) 590217
Fax: (01889) 591001
Email: admissions@abbotsholme.co.uk
Head: Mr S Fairclough
Type: Co-educational Boarding and Day 5–18 (Boarders from 10) Flexi-boarding available
No of pupils: B171 G97
No of boarders: F55 W76
Fees: (September 05)
FB £17850–£21000
WB £13650–£17400
Day £7650–£14400

DENSTONE COLLEGE
Uttoxeter, Staffordshire ST14 5HN
Tel: (01889) 591415
Fax: (01889) 591295
Email: admissions@denstonecollege.org
Head: Mr D M Derbyshire
Type: Co-educational Boarding and Day 11–18
No of pupils: B325 G172
No of boarders: F138
Fees: (September 05)
F/WB £ £13950–£15300
Day £7200–£9480

SMALLWOOD MANOR PREPARATORY SCHOOL
Uttoxeter, Staffordshire ST14 8NS
Tel: (01889) 562083
Fax: (01889) 568682
Email: headmaster@smallwoodmanor.co.uk
Head: Revd C J Cann
Type: Co-educational Day 2–11
No of pupils: B88 G63
Fees: (September 04)
Day £5055–£6360

STOCKTON-ON-TEES

EAGLESCLIFFE

TEESSIDE PREPARATORY AND HIGH SCHOOL
The Avenue, Eaglescliffe, Stockton-on-Tees TS16 9AT
Tel: (01642) 782095
Fax: (01642) 791207
Email: info@teessidehigh.co.uk
Head: Mrs H J French
Type: Girls Day 3–18
No of pupils: 450
Fees: (September 05)
Day £4740–£7707

NORTON

RED HOUSE SCHOOL
36 The Green, Norton, Stockton-on-Tees TS20 1DX
Tel: (01642) 553370
Fax: (01642) 361031
Email: headmaster@r-h-s.com
Head: Mr C M J Allen
Type: Co-educational Day 3–16
No of pupils: B256 G182
Fees: (September 04)
Day £4380–£5580

YARM

YARM SCHOOL
The Friarage, Yarm, Stockton-on-Tees TS15 9EJ
Tel: (01642) 786023/781447
Fax: (01642) 789216
Email: dmd@yarmschool.org
Head: Mr D M Dunn
Type: Co-educational Day 3–18
No of pupils: B650 G300
Fees: (September 05)
Day £3837–£8391

England

SUFFOLK

BECCLES

THE OLD SCHOOL
Henstead, Beccles, Suffolk NR34 7LG
Tel: (01502) 741150
Fax: (01502) 741150
Email: oldschool@btclick.com
Head: Mr M J Hewett
Type: Co-educational Day 4–11
No of pupils: B68 G47
Fees: (September 04)
Day £3900–£4875

BRANDESTON

FRAMLINGHAM COLLEGE PREPARATORY SCHOOL
Brandeston Hall, Brandeston, Suffolk IP13 7AH
Tel: (01728) 685331
Fax: (01728) 685437
Email: office@brandestonhall.co.uk
Head: Mr N Woolnough
Type: Co-educational Boarding and Day 3–13 Flexi-boarding available
No of pupils: B136 G100
No of boarders: F37 W10
Fees: (September 05)
F/WB £ £14598 Day £5220–£9078

BURY ST EDMUNDS

CHERRY TREES SCHOOL
Flempton Road, Risby, Bury St Edmunds, Suffolk IP28 6QJ
Tel: (01284) 760531
Fax: (01284) 750177
Email: cherrytrees@cherrytrees-school.co.uk
Head: Ms W Compson
Type: Co-educational Day 0–11
No of pupils: B130 G126
Fees: (September 03)
Day £5040–£6000

CULFORD SCHOOL*
Bury St Edmunds, Suffolk IP28 6TX
Tel: (01284) 728615
Fax: (01284) 729146
Email: admissions@culford.co.uk
Head: Mr J Johnson-Munday
Type: Co-educational Boarding and Day 2–18 Flexi-boarding available
No of pupils: B323 G253
No of boarders: F116 W58
Fees: (September 05)
FB £15204–£19698
WB £13527–£19698
Day £7131–£12837

MORETON HALL PREPARATORY SCHOOL
Mount Road, Bury St Edmunds, Suffolk IP32 7BJ
Tel: (01284) 753532
Fax: (01284) 769197
Email: office@moretonhall.net
Head: Mr B Dunhill
Type: Co-educational Boarding and Day 3–13 Flexi-boarding available
No of pupils: B66 G48
No of boarders: F6 W7
Fees: (September 05) FB £14880
WB £12510 Day £5775–£9840

SOUTH LEE PREPARATORY SCHOOL
Nowton Road, Bury St Edmunds, Suffolk IP33 2BT
Tel: (01284) 754654
Fax: (01284) 706178
Email: office@southlee.co.uk
Head: Mr D Whipp
Type: Co-educational Day 2–13
No of pupils: B141 G150
Fees: (September 05)
Day £5175–£7575

FELIXSTOWE

FELIXSTOWE INTERNATIONAL COLLEGE
Felixstowe, Suffolk IP11 7NA
Tel: (01394) 282388
Fax: (01394) 276926
Email: felixc@rmplc.co.uk
Head: Mrs J S Lee
Type: Co-educational Boarding 9–17
No of pupils: B8 G17
No of boarders: F15
Fees: (September 04) FB £19500

HAVERHILL

BARNARDISTON HALL PREPARATORY SCHOOL
Barnardiston, Haverhill, Suffolk CB9 7TG
Tel: (01440) 786316
Fax: (01440) 786355
Email: registrar@barnardiston-hall.co.uk
Head: Lt Col K A Boulter
Type: Co-educational Day and Boarding 2–13 Flexi-boarding available
No of pupils: B121 G128
No of boarders: F30 W16
Fees: (September 05)
FB £11655–£13500 WB £12450
Day £6900–£8850

IPSWICH

AMBERFIELD SCHOOL
Nacton, Ipswich, Suffolk IP10 0HL
Tel: (01473) 659265
Fax: (01473) 659843
Email: registrar@amberfield.suffolk.sch.uk
Head: Mrs H Kay
Type: Girls Day 3–16 (Boys 3–7)
No of pupils: B16 G276
Fees: (September 05)
Day £5205–£7305

IPSWICH HIGH SCHOOL GDST
Woolverstone, Ipswich, Suffolk IP9 1AZ
Tel: (01473) 780201
Fax: (01473) 780985
Email: admissions@ihs.gdst.net
Head: Miss V C MacCuish
Type: Girls Day 3–18
No of pupils: 680
Fees: (September 05)
Day £5397–£7365

IPSWICH PREPARATORY SCHOOL
Henley Road, Ipswich, Suffolk IP1 3SQ
Tel: (01473) 408301
Fax: (01473) 400067
Email: prepregistrar@ipswich.suffolk.sch.uk
Head: Mrs J M Jones
Type: Co-educational Day 3–11
No of pupils: B187 G117
Fees: (September 05)
Day £5859–£6663

IPSWICH SCHOOL
Henley Road, Ipswich, Suffolk IP1 3SG
Tel: (01473) 408300
Fax: (01473) 400058
Email: registrar@ipswich.suffolk.sch.uk
Head: Mr I G Galbraith
Type: Co-educational Day and Boarding 11–18 Flexi-boarding available
No of pupils: B510 G225
No of boarders: F24 W14
Fees: (September 05)
FB £13665–£15774
WB £13029–£14850
Day £8187–£9057

OLD BUCKENHAM HALL SCHOOL
Brettenham Park, Ipswich, Suffolk IP7 7PH
Tel: (01449) 740252
Fax: (01449) 740955
Email: registrar@obh.co.uk
Head: Mr M A Ives
Type: Co-educational Day and Boarding 2–13
No of pupils: B173 G95
No of boarders: F75 W37
Fees: (September 05)
F/WB £ £15900
Day £6060–£12750

ORWELL PARK
Nacton, Ipswich, Suffolk IP10 0ER
Tel: (01473) 659225
Fax: (01473) 659822
Email: headmaster@orwellpark.co.uk
Head: Mr A H Auster
Type: Co-educational Boarding and Day 3–13 Flexi-boarding available
No of pupils: B210 G89
No of boarders: F78 W77
Fees: (September 05)
FB £14745–£16395
Day £4515–£12780

ROYAL HOSPITAL SCHOOL
Holbrook, Ipswich, Suffolk IP9 2RX
Tel: (01473) 326210
Fax: (01473) 326213
Email: admissions@royalhospitalschool.org
Head: Mr H W Blackett
Type: Co-educational Boarding and Day 11–18 (VIth Form day pupils)
No of pupils: B374 G257
No of boarders: F631
Fees: (September 05) FB £16908

ST JOSEPH'S COLLEGE
Belstead Road, Birkfield, Ipswich, Suffolk IP2 9DR
Tel: (01473) 690281
Fax: (01473) 602409
Email: registrar@stjos.co.uk
Head: Mrs S Grant
Type: Co-educational Day and Boarding 3–18 Flexi-boarding available
No of pupils: B423 G171
No of boarders: F61 W15
Fees: (September 02)
FB £11520–£12555
WB £10995–£12030
Day £4458–£7230

LEISTON

SUMMERHILL SCHOOL
Leiston, Suffolk IP16 4HY
Tel: (01728) 830540
Fax: (01728) 830540
Email: office@summerhillschool.co.uk
Head: Mrs Z S Readhead
Type: Co-educational Boarding and Day 6–17 Flexi-boarding available
No of pupils: B42 G41
No of boarders: F76
Fees: (September 04)
FB £8887–£10863
Day £5332–£6517

NEWMARKET

FAIRSTEAD HOUSE SCHOOL
Fordham Road, Newmarket, Suffolk CB8 7AA
Tel: (01638) 662318
Fax: (01638) 561685
Email: secretary@fairsteadhouse.co.uk
Head: Mrs D J Buckenham
Type: Co-educational Day 3–11
No of pupils: B64 G61
Fees: (September 05)
Day £5502–£5940

SOUTHWOLD

SAINT FELIX SCHOOLS*
Southwold, Suffolk IP18 6SD
Tel: (01502) 722175
Fax: (01502) 722641
Email: schooladmin@stfelix.suffolk.sch.uk
Head: Mr David Ward
Type: Co-educational Boarding and Day 1–18 (Boarding (girls only) 6–18) Flexi-boarding available
No of pupils: B100 G211
No of boarders: F49 W8

STOWMARKET

FINBOROUGH SCHOOL†
The Hall, Great Finborough, Stowmarket, Suffolk IP14 3EF
Tel: (01449) 773600
Fax: (01449) 773601
Email: admin@finborough.suffolk.sch.uk
Head: Mr J Sinclair
Type: Co-educational Boarding and Day 2–18 Flexi-boarding available
No of pupils: B107 G65
No of boarders: F108 W9
Fees: (September 04)
FB £11535–£14430
WB £9090–£11280
Day £4230–£6945

HILLCROFT PREPARATORY SCHOOL†
Walnutree Manor, Haughley Green, Stowmarket, Suffolk IP14 3RQ
Tel: (01449) 673003
Fax: (01449) 613072
Email: office@hillcroft.suffolk.sch.uk
Head: Mr F Rapsey and Mrs G Rapsey
Type: Co-educational Day 2–13
No of pupils: B46 G44
Fees: (September 04)
Day £1485–£7650

SUDBURY

STOKE COLLEGE
Stoke by Clare, Sudbury, Suffolk CO10 8JE
Tel: (01787) 278141
Fax: (01787) 277904
Email: office@stokecollege.co.uk
Head: Mr J Gibson
Type: Co-educational Day and Boarding 3–16 Flexi-boarding available
No of pupils: B155 G90
No of boarders: W16
Fees: (September 03)
WB £11052–£12711

WOODBRIDGE

THE ABBEY
The Prep School for Woodbridge School, Church Street, Woodbridge, Suffolk IP12 1DS
Tel: (01394) 382673
Fax: (01394) 383880
Email: office@theabbeyschool-suffolk.org.uk
Head: Mr N J Garrett
Type: Co-educational Day 4–11
No of pupils: B157 G154
Fees: (September 05)
Day £5644–£8562

FRAMLINGHAM COLLEGE
Framlingham, Woodbridge, Suffolk IP13 9EY
Tel: (01728) 723789
Fax: (01728) 724546
Email: admissions@framcollege.co.uk
Head: Mrs G M Randall
Type: Co-educational Boarding and Day 3–18 Flexi-boarding available
No of pupils: B400 G270
No of boarders: F325
Fees: (September 05)
FB £14598–£18516
Day £5220–£11901

WOODBRIDGE SCHOOL
Woodbridge, Suffolk IP12 4JH
Tel: (01394) 615000
Fax: (01394) 380944
Email: office@woodbridge.suffolk.sch.uk
Head: Mr S Cole and Mr Nick Garrett
Type: Co-educational Day and Boarding 11–18 Flexi-boarding available
No of pupils: B317 G265
No of boarders: F40 W3
Fees: (September 05)
F/WB £ £18066
Day £9746–£10374

SURREY

ASHTEAD

CITY OF LONDON FREEMEN'S SCHOOL
Ashtead Park, Ashtead, Surrey KT21 1ET
Tel: (01372) 277933
Fax: (01372) 276165
Email: headmaster@clfs.surrey.sch.uk
Head: Mr D C Haywood
Type: Co-educational Day and Boarding 7–18 Flexi-boarding available
No of pupils: B429 G397
No of boarders: F39
Fees: (September 05)
F/WB £ £17600
Day £8586–£11502

DOWNSEND SCHOOL, ASHTEAD LODGE
22 Oakfield Road, Ashtead, Surrey KT21 2RE
Tel: (01372) 273778
Fax: (01372) 273816
Email: ashteadlodge@downsend.co.uk
Head: Mrs K Barrett
Type: Co-educational Day 2–6
No of pupils: B38 G18
Fees: (September 04)
Day £540–£2130

PARSONS MEAD*
Ottways Lane, Ashtead, Surrey KT21 2PE
Tel: (01372) 276401
Fax: (01372) 278796
Email: parsonsmead@parsonmead.co.uk
Head: Mrs P M Taylor
Type: Girls Day 2–18 Flexi-boarding available
Fees: (September 04)
Day £3280–£10995

BAGSHOT

HALL GROVE SCHOOL
London Road, Bagshot, Surrey GU19 5HZ
Tel: (01276) 473059
Fax: (01276) 452003
Email: registrar@hallgrove.surrey.sch.uk
Head: Mr A R Graham
Type: Co-educational Day and Boarding 4–13 Flexi-boarding available
No of pupils: B255 G31
No of boarders: W20
Fees: (September 04)
WB £10545–£11175

BANSTEAD

GREENACRE SCHOOL FOR GIRLS*
Sutton Lane, Banstead, Surrey SM7 3RA
Tel: (01737) 352114
Fax: (01737) 373485
Email: admin@greenacre.surrey.sch.uk
Head: Mrs P M Wood
Type: Girls Day 3–18
No of pupils: 410
Fees: (September 05)
Day £2850–£9120

PRIORY SCHOOL
Bolters Lane, Banstead, Surrey SM7 2AJ
Tel: (01737) 366920
Fax: (01737) 366921
Email: office@priory-banstead.surrey.sch.uk
Head: Mr G D Malcolm
Type: Boys Day 2–13
No of pupils: 180
Fees: (September 03)
Day £2955–£7425

CAMBERLEY

HAWLEY PLACE SCHOOL
Fernhill Road, Blackwater, Camberley, Surrey GU17 9HU
Tel: (01276) 32028
Fax: (01276) 609695
Email: office@hawleyplace.com
Head: Mr T G Pipe and Mrs M L PIPE
Type: Co-educational Day Boys 2–11 Girls 2–16
No of pupils: B115 G265
Fees: (September 05) Day £5865–£7332

LYNDHURST SCHOOL
36 The Avenue, Camberley, Surrey GU15 3NE
Tel: (01276) 22895
Fax: (01276) 709186
Email: office@lyndhurstschool.com
Head: Mr S G Yeo
Type: Co-educational Day 2–12
No of pupils: B92 G80
Fees: (September 05) Day £4845–£6330

CATERHAM

CATERHAM PREPARATORY SCHOOL
Harestone Valley Road, Caterham, Surrey CR3 6YB
Tel: (01883) 342097
Fax: (01883) 341230
Email: howard.tuckett@caterhamschool.co.uk
Head: Mr H W G Tuckett
Type: Co-educational Day 3–11
No of pupils: B141 G131
Fees: (September 05) Day £3423–£8817

CATERHAM SCHOOL*
Harestone Valley Road, Caterham, Surrey CR3 6YA
Tel: (01883) 343028
Fax: (01883) 347795
Email: admissions@caterhamschool.co.uk
Head: Mr R A E Davey
Type: Co-educational Day and Boarding 3–18 Flexi-boarding available
No of pupils: B309 G437
No of boarders: F129 W2
Fees: (September 05) FB £19431–£20481 Day £10485–£10980

ESSENDENE LODGE SCHOOL
Essendene Road, Caterham, Surrey CR3 5PB
Tel: (01883) 348349
Fax: (01883) 348349
Email: office@essendenelodge.surrey.sch.uk
Head: Mr S.J. Haydock
Type: Co-educational Day 2–11
No of pupils: B71 G86
Fees: (September 05) Day £1575–£4125

OAKHYRST GRANGE SCHOOL
160 Stanstead Road, Caterham, Surrey CR3 6AF
Tel: (01883) 343344
Fax: (01883) 342021
Email: office@oakhyrstgrangeschool.co.uk
Head: Mrs E A Stanford
Type: Co-educational Day 3–11
No of pupils: B62 G66
Fees: (September 05) Day £1023–£5511

CHERTSEY

SIR WILLIAM PERKINS'S SCHOOL
Guildford Road, Chertsey, Surrey KT16 9BN
Tel: (01932) 574900
Fax: (01932) 574901
Email: reg@swps.org.uk
Head: Miss S Ross
Type: Girls Day 11–18
No of pupils: 570
Fees: (September 05) Day £9333

COBHAM

ACS COBHAM INTERNATIONAL SCHOOL*
Heywood, Portsmouth Road, Cobham, Surrey KT11 1BL
Tel: (01932) 867251
Fax: (01932) 869789
Email: cobhamadmissions@acs-england.co.uk
Head: Mr T J Lehman
Type: Co-educational Boarding and Day 2–18
No of pupils: B737 G571
No of boarders: F99 W15
Fees: (September 05) FB £22250–£26200 Day £4900–£15650

FELTONFLEET SCHOOL
Cobham, Surrey KT11 1DR
Tel: (01932) 862264
Fax: (01932) 860280
Email: p.ward@feltonfleet.co.uk
Head: Mr P Ward
Type: Co-educational Boarding and Day 3–13 Flexi-boarding available
No of pupils: B228 G102
No of boarders: W22
Fees: (September 04) WB £14250

NOTRE DAME PREPARATORY SCHOOL
Burwood House, Cobham, Surrey KT11 1HA
Tel: (01932) 869991
Fax: (01932) 589480
Email: headmaster@notredame.co.uk
Head: Mr D Plummer
Type: Girls Day 2–11 (Boys 2–5)
No of pupils: B10 G340
Fees: (September 05) Day £3105–£8070

NOTRE DAME SENIOR SCHOOL
Burwood House, Cobham, Surrey KT11 1HA
Tel: (01932) 869990
Fax: (01932) 589481
Email: headmistress@notredame.co.uk
Head: Mrs B Williams
Type: Girls Day 11–18
No of pupils: 375
Fees: (September 04) Day £8910

PARKSIDE SCHOOL
The Manor, Stoke D'Abernon, Cobham, Surrey KT11 3PX
Tel: (01932) 862749
Fax: (01932) 860251
Email: enquiries@parkside-school.co.uk
Head: Mr D Aylward
Type: Boys Day 4–13 (Co-ed 2–4)
No of pupils: B390 G20
Fees: (September 04) Day £690–£9405

REED'S SCHOOL*
Sandy Lane, Cobham, Surrey
KT11 2ES
Tel: (01932) 869001
Fax: (01932) 869046
Email: admissions@reeds.surrey.sch.uk
Head: Mr D W Jarrett
Type: Boys Boarding and Day 11–18 (Co-ed VIth Form)
No of pupils: B500 G50
No of boarders: F86
Fees: (September 04)
FB £15981–£19641
Day £11985–£14847

YEHUDI MENUHIN SCHOOL
Stoke D'Abernon, Cobham, Surrey
KT11 3QQ
Tel: (01932) 864739
Fax: (01932) 864633
Email: admin@yehudimenuhinschool.co.uk
Head: Mr N Chisholm
Type: Co-educational Boarding 8–18 Flexi-boarding available
No of pupils: B29 G37
No of boarders: F66
Fees: (September 05)
F/WB £ £31410 Day £30594

CRANLEIGH

CRANLEIGH PREPARATORY SCHOOL
Horseshoe Lane, Cranleigh, Surrey
GU6 8QH
Tel: (01483) 274199
Fax: (01483) 277136
Head: Mr M W Roulston
Type: Co-educational Boarding and Day 7–13
No of pupils: 231
No of boarders: F40

CRANLEIGH SCHOOL
Horseshoe Lane, Cranleigh, Surrey
GU6 8QQ
Tel: (01483) 273666
Fax: (01483) 267398
Email: enquiry@cranleigh.org
Head: Mr G de W Waller
Type: Co-educational Boarding and Day 13–18
No of pupils: B400 G205
No of boarders: F426
Fees: (September 05) FB £22350
Day £18105

CROYDON

CAMBRIDGE TUTORS COLLEGE
Water Tower Hill, Croydon, Surrey CR0 5SX
Tel: (020) 8688 5284
Fax: (020) 8686 9220
Email: admin@ctc.ac.uk
Head: Mr D A Lowe
Type: Co-educational Boarding and Day 15–22
No of pupils: B160 G150
No of boarders: F250
Fees: (September 05) FB £17500
Day £12150–£13050

NEW LIFE CHRISTIAN SCHOOL
Cairo New Road, Croydon, Surrey
CR0 1XP
Tel: (020) 8680 7671
Head: Mrs E Parker
Type: Co-educational Day 4–11
No of pupils: 140
Fees: (September 03)
Day £1098–£5490

OLD PALACE SCHOOL OF JOHN WHITGIFT
Old Palace Road, Croydon, Surrey
CR0 1AX
Tel: (020) 8688 2027
Fax: (020) 8680 5877
Email: info@oldpalace.croydon.sch.uk
Head: Ms J Harris
Type: Girls Day 4–18
Fees: (September 05)
Day £6507–£8703

ROYAL RUSSELL SCHOOL
Coombe Lane, Croydon, Surrey
CR9 5BX
Tel: (020) 8657 4433
Fax: (020) 8657 9555
Email: headmaster@royalrussell.croydon.sch.uk
Head: Dr J R Jennings
Type: Co-educational Boarding and Day 3–18 Flexi-boarding available
No of pupils: B485 G336
No of boarders: F115 W10
Fees: (September 05)
F/WB £ £15270–£20775
Day £6300–£10440

TRINITY SCHOOL
Shirley Park, Croydon, Surrey
CR9 7AT
Tel: (020) 8656 9541
Fax: (020) 8655 0522
Email: admissions@trinity.croydon.sch.uk
Head: Mr C J Tarrant
Type: Boys Day 10–18
No of pupils: 890
Fees: (September 05) Day £9975

WARLINGHAM PARK SCHOOL
Chelsham Common, Warlingham, Croydon, Surrey CR6 9PB
Tel: (01883) 626844
Fax: (01883) 625501
Email: info@warlinghamparkschool.com
Head: Mr M R Donald
Type: Co-educational Day 2–11
No of pupils: B64 G66
Fees: (September 05)
Day £2700–£5400

DORKING

ABINGER HAMMER VILLAGE SCHOOL
Hackhurst Lane, Abinger Hammer, Dorking, Surrey RH5 6SE
Tel: (01306) 730343
Head: Mrs C R Stansfeld
Type: Co-educational Day 4–8
No of pupils: B4 G8

BELMONT SCHOOL†
Feldemore, Holmbury St Mary, Dorking, Surrey RH5 6LQ
Tel: (01306) 730852/730829
Fax: (01306) 731220
Email: schooloffice@belmont-school.org
Head: Mr D Gainer
Type: Co-educational Boarding and Day 4–13 Flexi-boarding available
No of pupils: B194 G80
No of boarders: W40
Fees: (September 03) WB £11985

BOX HILL SCHOOL*†
Mickleham, Dorking, Surrey
RH5 6EA
Tel: (01372) 373382
Fax: (01372) 363942
Email: enquiries@
boxhillschool.org.uk
Head: Mr M Eagers
Type: Co-educational Boarding and Day 11–18
No of pupils: B249 G113
No of boarders: F107 W63
Fees: (September 05)
FB £18450–£20835
WB £15600–£17970
Day £9300–£11325

HURTWOOD HOUSE*
Holmbury St Mary, Dorking, Surrey RH5 6NU
Tel: (01483) 279000
Fax: (01483) 267586
Email: Info@hurtwood.net
Head: Mr K R B Jackson
Type: Co-educational Boarding and Day 16–18 Flexi-boarding available
No of pupils: B140 G150
No of boarders: F140 W140
Fees: (September 05)
F/WB £ £24600–£28290
Day £16400–£18860

NEW LODGE SCHOOL
Chichester Road, Dorking, Surrey
RH4 1LR
Tel: (01306) 882151
Fax: (01306) 882656
Email: www.newlodgeschool@
supanet.com
Head: Mrs S Watt
Type: Co-educational Day 3–11
No of pupils: B95 G75
Fees: (September 05)
Day £6450–£7440

ST TERESA'S SCHOOL*
Effingham Hill, Dorking, Surrey
RH5 6ST
Tel: (01372) 452037
Fax: (01372) 450311
Email: info@stteresas.surrey.sch.uk
Head: Mrs M Prescott
Type: Girls Boarding and Day 11–18 Flexi-boarding available
No of pupils: 330
No of boarders: F72 W15
Fees: (September 05)
FB £18105–£18855
WB £16725–£17457
Day £10350–£11100

EAST MOLESEY

HAMPTON COURT HOUSE
Hampton Court Road, East Molesey, Surrey KT8 9BS
Tel: (020) 8943 0889
Fax: (020) 8977 5357
Email: office@
hamptoncourthouse.com
Head: Lady Houston-Boswall
Type: Co-educational Boarding and Day Boys 3–16 Girls 3–13 Flexi-boarding available
No of pupils: B75 G65
No of boarders: W6
Fees: (September 05)
WB £14151–£15231
Day £7470–£9540

EFFINGHAM

ST TERESA'S PREPARATORY SCHOOL
Grove House, Guildford Road, Effingham, Surrey KT24 5QA
Tel: (01372) 453456
Fax: (01372) 451562
Email: prep@
st-teresas.demon.co.uk
Head: Mrs A Stewart
Type: Girls Day and Boarding 2–11 Flexi-boarding available
No of pupils: 160
No of boarders: F3
Fees: (September 04) FB £15020
WB £13725 Day £2640–£7680

EGHAM

ACS EGHAM INTERNATIONAL SCHOOL*
Woodlee, London Road (A30), Egham, Surrey TW20 0HS
Tel: (01784) 430611
Fax: (01784) 430626
Email: eghamadmissions@
acs-england.co.uk
Head: Ms M Hadley
Type: Co-educational Day Boys 0–18 Girls 2–18
No of pupils: B254 G230
Fees: (September 05)
Day £4900–£15650

BISHOPSGATE SCHOOL
Englefield Green, Egham, Surrey
TW20 0YJ
Tel: (01784) 432109
Fax: (01784) 430460
Email: admissions@
bishopsgate.surrey.sch.uk
Head: Mr M Dunning
Type: Co-educational Day and Boarding 2–13 Flexi-boarding available
No of pupils: B190 G103
No of boarders: W14
Fees: (September 04)
WB £11400–£12600

EPSOM

EPSOM COLLEGE
College Road, Epsom, Surrey
KT17 4JQ
Tel: (01372) 821004
Fax: (01372) 821237
Email: admissions@
epsomcollege.org.uk
Head: Mr S R Borthwick
Type: Co-educational Boarding and Day 13–18
No of pupils: B498 G222
No of boarders: F99 W232
Fees: (September 05) FB £22389
WB £21477 Day £15798

EWELL CASTLE SCHOOL
Church Street, Ewell, Epsom, Surrey KT17 2AW
Tel: (020) 8393 1413
Fax: (020) 8786 8218
Email: admissions@
ewellcastle.co.uk
Head: Mr A J Tibble
Type: Boys Day 3–18 (Co-ed 3–11)
No of pupils: B480 G65
Fees: (September 05)
Day £2445–£8925

KINGSWOOD HOUSE SCHOOL†
56 West Hill, Epsom, Surrey
KT19 8LG
Tel: (01372) 723590
Fax: (01372) 749081
Email: office@
kingswoodhouse.org
Head: Mr P Brooks
Type: Boys Day 2–13
No of pupils: 210
Fees: (September 03)
Day £5580–£7425

ST CHRISTOPHER'S SCHOOL
6 Downs Road, Epsom, Surrey
KT18 5HE
Tel: (01372) 721807
Fax: (01372) 726 717
Email: office@
st-christophers.surrey.sch.uk
Head: Mrs M V Evans
Type: Co-educational Day 3–7
No of pupils: B76 G75
Fees: (September 05)
Day £2970–£5745

ESHER

CLAREMONT FAN COURT SCHOOL*
Claremont Drive, Esher, Surrey
KT10 9LY
Tel: (01372) 467841
Fax: (01372) 471109
Email: mprentis@
claremont.surrey.sch.uk
Head: Mrs P B Farrar
Type: Co-educational Day 3–18
No of pupils: B300 G300
Fees: (September 05)
Day £2839–£10290

EMBERHURST
94 Ember Lane, Esher, Surrey
KT10 8EN
Tel: (020) 8398 2933
Email: emberhurstschool@
ntlworld.com
Head: Mrs P Chadwick
Type: Co-educational Day 2–8
No of pupils: B40 G35
Fees: (September 04)
Day £2500–£6000

GRANTCHESTER HOUSE
5 Hinchley Way, Hinchley Wood,
Esher, Surrey KT10 0BD
Tel: (020) 8398 1157
Fax: (020) 8398 1157
Email: enquiries@
grantchesterhouseschool.com
Head: Mrs A E Fry
Type: Co-educational Day 3–7
No of pupils: B49 G37
Fees: (September 04)
Day £3150–£5295

MILBOURNE LODGE SCHOOL
43 Arbrook Lane, Esher, Surrey
KT10 9EG
Tel: (01372) 462737
Fax: (01372) 471164
Email: headmaster@
milbournelodge.co.uk
Head: Mr P MacLarnon
Type: Co-educational Day 8–13
No of pupils: B165 G35
Fees: (September 02)
Day £6270–£6420

ROWAN PREPARATORY SCHOOL
6 Fitzalan Road, Claygate, Esher,
Surrey KT10 0LX
Tel: (01372) 462627
Fax: (01372) 470782
Email: office@rowan.surrey.sch.uk
Head: Mrs K Kershaw
Type: Girls Day 3–11
No of pupils: 300
Fees: (September 04)
Day £2675–£8295

EWHURST

DUKE OF KENT SCHOOL*
Peaslake Road, Ewhurst, Surrey
GU6 7NS
Tel: (01483) 277313
Fax: (01483) 273862
Email: dok.school@virgin.net
Head: Dr A Cameron
Type: Co-educational Boarding
and Day 4–13 Flexi-boarding
available
No of pupils: B121 G60
No of boarders: F6 W50
Fees: (September 05)
FB £12165–£14565
WB £9390–£11970
Day £4545–£10725

FARNHAM

BARFIELD SCHOOL
Runfold, Farnham, Surrey
GU10 1PB
Tel: (01252) 782271
Fax: (01252) 781480
Email: admin@barfieldschool.com
Head: Mr B Hoar
Type: Co-educational Day 3–13
No of pupils: B190 G130
Fees: (September 05)
Day £6510–£9636

EDGEBOROUGH
Frensham, Farnham, Surrey
GU10 3AH
Tel: (01252) 792495
Fax: (01252) 795156
Email: office@edgeborough.co.uk
Head: Mrs M A Jackson and Mr R
A Jackson
Type: Co-educational Day and
Boarding 3–13 Flexi-boarding
available
No of pupils: B206 G121
No of boarders: W50
Fees: (September 04)
WB £11805–£12885

FRENSHAM HEIGHTS SCHOOL*
Rowledge, Farnham, Surrey
GU10 4EA
Tel: (01252) 792561
Fax: (01252) 794335
Email: admissions@
frensham-heights.org.uk
Head: Mr A Fisher
Type: Co-educational Boarding
and Day 3–18
No of pupils: B240 G230
No of boarders: F100
Fees: (September 05)
FB £18855–£20160
Day £12240–£13545

MORE HOUSE SCHOOL†
Moons Hill, Frensham, Farnham,
Surrey GU10 3AP
Tel: (01252) 792303
Fax: (01252) 797601
Head: Mr B G Huggett
Type: Boys Boarding and Day
9–18
No of pupils: 225
No of boarders: F16 W76

GODALMING

ALDRO SCHOOL
Lombard Street, Shackleford,
Godalming, Surrey GU8 6AS
Tel: (01483) 409020
Fax: (01483) 409010
Email: hmsec@aldro.org
Head: Mr D W N Aston
Type: Boys Boarding and Day
7–13
No of pupils: 220
No of boarders: F52
Fees: (September 05) FB £16545
Day £12810

BARROW HILLS SCHOOL
Roke Lane, Witley, Godalming, Surrey GU8 5NY
Tel: (01428) 683639
Fax: (01428) 681906
Email: info@barrowhills.org.uk
Head: Mr M Connolly
Type: Co-educational Day 3–13
No of pupils: B175 G101
Fees: (September 05)
Day £5865–£9330

CHARTERHOUSE
Godalming, Surrey GU7 2DJ
Tel: (01483) 291501
Fax: (01483) 291507
Email: admissions@charterhouse.org.uk
Head: Rev J S Witheridge
Type: Boys Boarding and Day 13–18 (Co-ed VIth Form)
No of pupils: B635 G104
No of boarders: F720
Fees: (September 05) FB £23995
Day £19803

KING EDWARD'S SCHOOL WITLEY
Petworth Road, Wormley, Godalming, Surrey GU8 5SG
Tel: (01428) 682572
Fax: (01428) 682850
Email: admissions@kesw.surrey.sch.uk
Head: Mr P Kerr Fulton-Peebles
Type: Co-educational Boarding and Day 11–18 Flexi-boarding available
No of pupils: B295 G180
No of boarders: F260
Fees: (September 05) FB £18960
Day £14440

PRIOR'S FIELD SCHOOL*
Priorsfield Road, Hurtmore, Godalming, Surrey GU7 2RH
Tel: (01483) 810551
Fax: (01483) 810180
Email: admin@priorsfield.surrey.sch.uk
Head: Mrs J Dwyer
Type: Girls Boarding and Day 11–18
No of pupils: 324
No of boarders: F38 W80
Fees: (September 05)
F/WB £ £17850 Day £11085

ST HILARY'S SCHOOL*
Holloway Hill, Godalming, Surrey GU7 1RZ
Tel: (01483) 416551
Fax: (01483) 418325
Email: registrar@sthilarysschool.com
Head: Mrs S Bailes
Type: Co-educational Day Boys 2–7 Girls 2–11
No of pupils: B88 G177
Fees: (September 05)
Day £6270–£9060

GUILDFORD

DRAYTON HOUSE SCHOOL
35 Austen Road, Guildford, Surrey GU1 3NP
Tel: (01483) 504707
Email: ask@draytonhouse.co.uk
Head: Mrs J Tyson-Jones
Type: Co-educational Day 3–8 (Nursery 1–3)
No of pupils: 90
Fees: (September 03)
Day £2400–£8400

GUILDFORD HIGH SCHOOL
London Road, Guildford, Surrey GU1 1SJ
Tel: (01483) 561440
Fax: (01483) 306516
Email: alex.kearney@church-schools.com
Head: Mrs F J Boulton
Type: Girls Day 4–18
No of pupils: 930
Fees: (September 05)
Day £5937–£10005

LANESBOROUGH
Maori Road, Guildford, Surrey GU1 2EL
Tel: (01483) 880652
Fax: (01483) 880651
Email: secretary@lanesborough.surrey.sch.uk
Head: Mr M Shere
Type: Boys Day 3–13
No of pupils: 350
Fees: (September 05)
Day £5940–£8010

LONGACRE SCHOOL
Hullbrook Lane, Shamley Green, Guildford, Surrey GU5 0NQ
Tel: (01483) 893225
Fax: (01483) 893501
Email: office@longacre.surrey.sch.uk
Head: Mr M Beach
Type: Co-educational Day 2–11
No of pupils: B113 G106
Fees: (September 05)
Day £4398–£8274

PEASLAKE SCHOOL
Colmans Hill, Peaslake, Guildford, Surrey GU5 9ST
Tel: (01306) 730411
Fax: (01306) 730411
Email: info@peaslake.surrey.sch.uk
Head: Mrs J George
Type: Co-educational Day
No of pupils: B26 G25

ROYAL GRAMMAR SCHOOL
High Street, Guildford, Surrey GU1 3BB
Tel: (01483) 880600
Fax: (01483) 306127
Email: tmsyoung@rgs.guildford.co.uk
Head: Mr T M S Young
Type: Boys Day 11–18
No of pupils: 890
Fees: (September 05) Day £9888

RYDES HILL PREPARATORY SCHOOL
Aldershot Road, Guildford, Surrey GU2 8BP
Tel: (01483) 563160
Fax: (01483) 306714
Email: enquiries@rydeshill.com
Head: Mrs J Lenahan
Type: Co-educational Day Boys 3–7 Girls 3–11
No of pupils: B10 G150
Fees: (September 05)
Day £4470–£7485

ST CATHERINE'S SCHOOL
Station Road, Bramley, Guildford, Surrey GU5 0DF
Tel: (01483) 899609
Fax: (01483) 899608
Email: admissions@stcatherines.info
Head: Mrs A M Phillips
Type: Girls Day and Boarding 4–18 Flexi-boarding available
No of boarders: F24 W96
Fees: (September 05)
F/WB £ £17700
Day £5295–£10755

SURREY COLLEGE*
Admin Centre, Abbot House, Sydenham Road, Guildford, Surrey GU1 3RL
Tel: (01483) 565887
Fax: (01483) 534777
Email: mail@surrey-college.co.uk
Head: Ms L Cody
Type: Co-educational Day 15+ Flexi-boarding available
No of pupils: B60 G40
Fees: (September 05)
Day £2500–£11000

TORMEAD SCHOOL
27 Cranley Road, Guildford, Surrey GUI 2JD
Tel: (01483) 575101
Fax: (01483) 450592
Email: registrar@tormeadschool.org.uk
Head: Mrs S Marks
Type: Girls Day 4–18
No of pupils: 765
Fees: (September 05)
Day £4500–£9435

HASLEMERE

HASLEMERE PREPARATORY SCHOOL
The Heights, Hill Road, Haslemere, Surrey GU27 2JP
Tel: (01428) 642350
Fax: (01428) 645314
Email: office@haslemere-prep.surrey.sch.uk
Head: Mr K J Merrick
Type: Boys Day 2–14
No of pupils: B235 G13
Fees: (September 04)
Day £5769–£8256

THE ROYAL SCHOOL
Farnham Lane, Haslemere, Surrey GU27 1HQ
Tel: (01428) 605805
Fax: (01428) 603028
Email: admissions@royal.surrey.sch.uk
Head: Mrs L Taylor-Gooby
Type: Girls Day and Boarding 3–18 (Boys 2–4) Flexi-boarding available
No of pupils: B5 G353
No of boarders: F45 W45
Fees: (September 05)
F/WB £ £14919–£18843
Day £6384–£11868

ST IVES SCHOOL
Three Gates Lane, Haslemere, Surrey GU27 2ES
Tel: (01428) 643734
Fax: (01428) 644788
Email: admin@stiveshaslemere.com
Head: Mrs S E Cattaneo
Type: Girls Day 3–11 (Boys 3–5)
No of pupils: B5 G140
Fees: (September 05)
Day £6270–£8760

WISPERS SCHOOL FOR GIRLS
High Lane, Haslemere, Surrey GU27 1AD
Tel: (01428) 643646
Fax: (01428) 641120
Email: head@wispers.org.uk
Head: Mr L H Beltran
Type: Girls Boarding and Day 11–18
No of pupils: 125
No of boarders: F34 W3
Fees: (September 03)
F/WB £ £16464 Day £10395

HINDHEAD

AMESBURY
Hazel Grove, Hindhead, Surrey GU26 6BL
Tel: (01428) 604322
Fax: (01428) 607715
Email: enquiries@amesburyschool.co.uk
Head: Mr N Taylor
Type: Co-educational Day 3–13 Flexi-boarding available
No of pupils: B210 G115
No of boarders: W10
Fees: (September 05)
Day £6420–£10200

ST EDMUND'S SCHOOL
Portsmouth Road, Hindhead, Surrey GU26 6BH
Tel: (01428) 609875
Fax: (01428) 607898
Email: registrar@saintedmunds.co.uk
Head: Mr A J Walliker
Type: Boys Boarding and Day 2–13 (Co-ed day 2–7) Flexi-boarding available
No of pupils: B185 G5
No of boarders: W25
Fees: (September 05)
WB £9750–£14877
Day £1665–£11577

HORLEY

REDEHALL PREPARATORY SCHOOL
Redehall Road, Smallfield, Horley, Surrey RH6 9QA
Tel: (01342) 842987
Fax: (01342) 842987
Email: enquiries@redehallprep.org.uk
Head: Mrs E Boak
Type: Co-educational Day 4–11
No of pupils: B50 G53
Fees: (September 05)
Day £2415–£2535

KINGSTON-UPON-THAMES

CANBURY SCHOOL
Kingston Hill, Kingston-upon-Thames, Surrey KT2 7LN
Tel: (020) 8549 8622
Fax: (020) 8974 6018
Email: head@canburyschool.co.uk
Head: Mr R Metters
Type: Co-educational Day Boys 10–16 Girls 11–16
No of pupils: B45 G25
Fees: (September 05) Day £9675

HOLY CROSS PREPARATORY SCHOOL
George Road,
Kingston-upon-Thames, Surrey
KT2 7NU
Tel: (020) 8942 0729
Fax: (020) 8336 0764
Email: admissions@holycrossprep.co.uk
Head: Mrs K Hayes
Type: Girls Day 4–11
No of pupils: 250
Fees: (September 05) Day £6765

KINGSTON GRAMMAR SCHOOL*
London Road,
Kingston-upon-Thames, Surrey
KT2 6PY
Tel: (020) 8546 5875
Fax: (020) 8547 1499
Email: registar@kingston-grammar.surrey.sch.uk
Head: Mr C D Baxter
Type: Co-educational Day 10–18
No of pupils: B416 G293
Fees: (September 05)
Day £10503–£10785

MARYMOUNT INTERNATIONAL SCHOOL*
George Road,
Kingston-upon-Thames, Surrey
KT2 7PE
Tel: (020) 8949 0571
Fax: (020) 8336 2485
Email: admissions@marymountlondon.com
Head: Sister K Fagan
Type: Girls Day and Boarding 11–18 Flexi-boarding available
No of pupils: 230
No of boarders: F90 W12
Fees: (September 05)
FB £21750–£23150
WB £20650–£22050
Day £12350–£13750

PARK HILL SCHOOL
8 Queens Road,
Kingston-upon-Thames, Surrey
KT2 7SH
Tel: (020) 8546 5496
Fax: (020) 8546 4558
Email: admin@parkhillschool.com
Head: Mrs M D Christie
Type: Co-educational Day Boys 3–8 Girls 3–11
No of pupils: B45 G75
Fees: (September 04)
Day £3255–£6360

ROKEBY SCHOOL
George Road,
Kingston-upon-Thames, Surrey
KT2 7PB
Tel: (020) 8942 2247
Fax: (020) 8942 5707
Email: hmsec@rokeby.org.uk
Head: Mr M K Seigel
Type: Boys Day 4–13
No of pupils: 370
Fees: (September 05)
Day £6588–£9471

SURBITON HIGH SCHOOL
Surbiton Crescent,
Kingston-upon-Thames, Surrey
KT1 2JT
Tel: (020) 8546 5245
Fax: (020) 8547 0026
Email: surbiton.high@church-schools.com
Head: Dr J Longhurst
Type: Girls Day 4–18 (Boys 4–11)
No of pupils: B139 G1120
Fees: (September 05)
Day £5787–£9597

LEATHERHEAD

CRANMORE SCHOOL
West Horsley, Leatherhead, Surrey
KT24 6AT
Tel: (01483) 280340
Fax: (01483) 280341
Email: office@cranmoreprep.co.uk
Head: Mr A J Martin
Type: Boys Day 3–13
No of pupils: 520
Fees: (September 05)
Day £3300–£8850

DANES HILL SCHOOL†
Leatherhead Road, Oxshott,
Leatherhead, Surrey KT22 0JG
Tel: (01372) 842509
Fax: (01372) 844452
Email: registrar@daneshillschool.co.uk
Head: Mr R Parfitt
Type: Co-educational Day 3–13
No of pupils: B477 G395
Fees: (September 04)
Day £462–£9597

DOWNSEND SCHOOL
1 Leatherhead Road, Leatherhead,
Surrey KT22 8TJ
Tel: (01372) 372197
Fax: (01372) 363367
Email: admin@downsend.co.uk
Head: Mr A D White
Type: Co-educational Day 6–13
No of pupils: B300 G230

DOWNSEND SCHOOL, LEATHERHEAD LODGE
13 Epsom Road, Leatherhead,
Surrey KT22 8ST
Tel: (01372) 372123
Fax: (01372) 372123
Email: admin@downsend.co.uk
Head: Mrs G Brooks
Type: Co-educational Day 2–6
No of pupils: B77 G63
Fees: (September 04)
Day £1545–£5925

GLENESK SCHOOL
Ockham Road North, East
Horsley, Leatherhead, Surrey
KT24 6NS
Tel: (01483) 282329
Fax: (01483) 281489
Email: info@glenesk.co.uk
Head: Mrs S J Christie-Hall
Type: Co-educational Day 2–7
No of pupils: B74 G57
Fees: (September 05)
Day £1821–£7323

MANOR HOUSE SCHOOL
Manor House Lane, Little
Bookham, Leatherhead, Surrey
KT23 4EN
Tel: (01372) 458538
Fax: (01372) 450414
Email: admin@manorhouse.surrey.sch.uk
Head: Mrs A Morris
Type: Girls Day 2–16
No of pupils: 355
Fees: (September 05)
Day £2700–£10185

ST JOHN'S SCHOOL
Epsom Road, Leatherhead, Surrey
KT22 8SP
Tel: (01372) 373000
Fax: (01372) 386606
Email: secretary@stjohns.surrey.sch.uk
Head: Mr N J R Haddock
Type: Boys Boarding and Day 13–18 (Co-ed VIth Form) Flexi-boarding available
No of pupils: B417 G60
No of boarders: F131
Fees: (September 05) FB £20850
Day £15150

LINGFIELD

LINGFIELD NOTRE DAME SCHOOL
St Piers Lane, Lingfield, Surrey RH7 6PH
Tel: (01342) 833176
Fax: (01342) 836048
Email: office@lingfieldnotredame.co.uk
Head: Mrs N E Shepley
Type: Co-educational Day 2–18
No of pupils: B335 G375
Fees: (September 05)
Day £4575–£7695

NEW MALDEN

THE STUDY SCHOOL
57 Thetford Road, New Malden, Surrey KT3 5DP
Tel: (020) 8942 0754
Fax: (020) 8942 0754
Email: info@study.kingston.sch.uk
Head: Mrs S Mallin
Type: Co-educational Day 3–11
No of pupils: B66 G59
Fees: (September 05)
Day £3085–£7194

WESTBURY HOUSE SCHOOL
80 Westbury Road, New Malden, Surrey KT3 5AS
Tel: (020) 8942 5885
Fax: (020) 8942 5885
Email: info@westburyhouse.surrey.sch.uk
Head: Mrs M T Morton
Type: Co-educational Day 3–11
No of pupils: B68 G68
Fees: (September 05)
Day £1075–£2280

OXTED

HAZELWOOD SCHOOL
Wolf's Hill, Limpsfield, Oxted, Surrey RH8 0QU
Tel: (01883) 712194
Fax: (01883) 716135
Email: registrar@hazelwoodschool.com
Head: Mr Roger McDuff
Type: Co-educational Day 2–13
Flexi-boarding available
No of pupils: B218 G120
Fees: (September 05)
Day £3135–£9660

LAVEROCK SCHOOL
19 Bluehouse Lane, Oxted, Surrey RH8 0AA
Tel: (01883) 714171
Fax: (01883) 722206
Email: office@laverock.fsnet.co.uk
Head: Mrs A C Paterson
Type: Girls Day 3–11
No of pupils: 145
Fees: (September 05)
Day £3060–£8235

PURLEY

LALEHAM LEA SCHOOL
29 Peaks Hill, Purley, Surrey CR8 3JJ
Tel: (020) 8660 3351
Fax: (020) 8763 0901
Email: bursar@lalehamlea.co.uk
Head: Mrs M E McGaughrin
Type: Co-educational Day 3–11
No of pupils: B100 G50
Fees: (September 04) Day £4125

LODGE SCHOOL
11 Woodcote Lane, Purley, Surrey CR8 3HB
Tel: (020) 8660 3179
Fax: (020) 8660 1385
Email: principal@lodgeschool.co.uk
Head: Miss P Maynard
Type: Girls Day 3–18 (Boys 3–11)
No of pupils: B81 G175
Fees: (September 05)
Day £4920–£8970

OAKWOOD SCHOOL & NURSERY
Godstone Road, Purley, Surrey CR8 2AN
Tel: (020) 8668 8080
Fax: (020) 8668 2895
Email: enquiries@oakwoodschool.org.uk
Head: Mr C Candia
Type: Co-educational Day 2–11
No of pupils: B57 G48
Fees: (September 05)
Day £5205–£5670

ST DAVID'S SCHOOL
23 Woodcote Valley Road, Purley, Surrey CR8 3AL
Tel: (020) 8660 0723
Fax: (020) 8645 0426
Email: office@stdavidsschool.co.uk
Head: Mrs L Nash
Type: Co-educational Day 3–11
No of pupils: B84 G85
Fees: (September 05)
Day £2850–£5685

WEST DENE SCHOOL
167 Brighton Road, Purley, Surrey CR8 4HE
Tel: (020) 8660 2404
Fax: (020) 8660 1189
Email: head@westdeneschool.fsnet.co.uk
Head: Mr P Kelly
Type: Co-educational Day 2–11
No of pupils: B52 G62
Fees: (September 04)
Day £4575–£4710

REDHILL

THE HAWTHORNS SCHOOL
Pendell Court, Bletchingley, Redhill, Surrey RH1 4QJ
Tel: (01883) 743048
Fax: (01883) 744256
Email: office@hawthorns.com
Head: Mr T R Johns
Type: Co-educational Day 2–13
No of pupils: B319 G184
Fees: (September 04)
Day £1140–£7755

REIGATE

BURYS COURT SCHOOL
Flanchford Road, Leigh, Reigate, Surrey RH2 8RE
Tel: (01306) 611372
Email: enquiries@buryscourtschool.co.uk
Head: Mrs Berry Baker
Type: Co-educational Day 3–13
No of pupils: B50 G20
Fees: (September 05)
Day £4620–£6450

DUNOTTAR SCHOOL
High Trees Road, Reigate, Surrey RH2 7EL
Tel: (01737) 761945
Fax: (01737) 779450
Email: info@dunottar.surrey.sch.uk
Head: Mrs J Hobson
Type: Girls Day 3–18
No of pupils: 418
Fees: (September 04)
Day £5925–£9150

MICKLEFIELD SCHOOL
10/12 Somers Road, Reigate, Surrey RH2 9DU
Tel: (01737) 242615
Fax: (01737) 248889
Email: office@micklefieldschool.co.uk
Head: Mrs C Belton
Type: Co-educational Day 2–11
No of pupils: B112 G168
Fees: (September 05)
Day £960–£6810

REIGATE GRAMMAR SCHOOL
Reigate Road, Reigate, Surrey RH2 0QS
Tel: (01737) 222231
Fax: (01737) 224201
Email: info@reigategrammar.org
Head: Mr D S Thomas
Type: Co-educational Day 11–18
No of pupils: B526 G328
Fees: (September 05) Day £9909

REIGATE ST MARY'S PREPARATORY AND CHOIR SCHOOL
Chart Lane, Reigate, Surrey RH2 7RN
Tel: (01737) 244880
Fax: (01737) 221540
Email: hmsec@reigatestmarys.org
Head: Mr M Culverwell
Type: Co-educational Day 3–13
No of pupils: B156 G57
Fees: (September 05)
Day £1686–£7866

ROYAL ALEXANDRA AND ALBERT SCHOOL*
Gatton Park, Reigate, Surrey RH2 0TD
Tel: (01737) 649001
Fax: (01737) 649002
Email: admissions@gatton-park.org.uk
Head: Mr P Spencer Ellis
Type: Co-educational Boarding and Day 7–18 Flexi-boarding available
No of pupils: B359 G329
No of boarders: F389
Fees: (September 05)
FB £9780–£10050 Day £3150

RICHMOND

BROOMFIELD HOUSE SCHOOL
10 Broomfield Road, Kew Gardens, Richmond, Surrey TW9 3HS
Tel: (020) 8940 3884
Fax: (020) 8332 6485
Email: office@broomfieldschool.com
Head: Mr N O York
Type: Co-educational Day 3–11
No of pupils: B73 G87
Fees: (September 05)
Day £3315–£9177

THE GERMAN SCHOOL
Douglas House, Petersham Road, Richmond, Surrey TW10 7AH
Tel: (020) 8940 2510
Fax: (020) 8332 7446
Email: gerd.koehncke@dsLondon.org.uk
Head: Mr G Koehncke
Type: Co-educational Day 5–19
No of pupils: B320 G310
Fees: (January 04)
Day £2610–£3537

KEW COLLEGE
24/26 Cumberland Road, Kew, Richmond, Surrey TW9 3HQ
Tel: (020) 8940 2039
Fax: (020) 8332 9945
Email: KewCollege@aol.com
Head: Mrs D E Lyness
Type: Co-educational Day 3–11
No of pupils: B126 G141
Fees: (September 05)
Day £3255–£6120

KEW GREEN PREPARATORY SCHOOL*
Layton House, Ferry Lane, Richmond, Surrey TW9 3AF
Tel: (020) 8948 5999
Fax: (020) 8948 4774
Email: secretary@kgps.co.uk
Head: Mrs M Gardener
Type: Co-educational Day 4–11
No of pupils: B140 G140
Fees: (September 05) Day £3450

KING'S HOUSE SCHOOL
68 Kings Road, Richmond, Surrey TW10 6ES
Tel: (020) 8940 1878
Fax: (020) 8939 2501
Email: secretary1@kingshouse.richmond.sch.uk
Head: Mrs S Piper
Type: Boys Day 4–13
No of pupils: 380
Fees: (September 05)
Day £7095–£9585

OLD VICARAGE SCHOOL
48 Richmond Hill, Richmond, Surrey TW10 6QX
Tel: (020) 8940 0922
Fax: (020) 8948 6834
Email: office@oldvicarage-richmond.co.uk
Head: Mrs J Harrison
Type: Girls Day 4–11
No of pupils: 170
Fees: (September 05)
Day £6420–£7125

ROYAL BALLET SCHOOL
White Lodge, Richmond Park, Richmond, Surrey TW10 5HR
Tel: (020) 8392 8000
Fax: (020) 8392 8037
Email: enquiries@royalballetschool.co.uk
Head: Mrs P Hogg
Type: Co-educational Day and Boarding 11–16
No of pupils: B101 G106
No of boarders: F115

UNICORN SCHOOL
238 Kew Road, Kew, Richmond, Surrey TW9 3JX
Tel: (020) 8948 3926
Fax: (020) 8332 6814
Email: enquiries@unicornschool.org.uk
Head: Mrs R Linehan
Type: Co-educational Day 3–11
No of pupils: B83 G89
Fees: (September 05)
Day £4395–£8040

SOUTH CROYDON

CROHAM HURST SCHOOL*
79 Croham Road, South Croydon, Surrey CR2 7YN
Tel: (020) 8680 3064
Fax: (020) 8681 2490
Email: head@croham.surrey.sch.uk
Head: Mrs E J Abbotts
Type: Girls Day 3–18
No of pupils: 496
Fees: (September 05) Day £5160–£9285

CROYDON HIGH SCHOOL GDST
Old Farleigh Road, Selsdon, South Croydon, Surrey CR2 8YB
Tel: (020) 8651 5020
Fax: (020) 8657 5413
Email: info2@cry.gdst.net
Head: Miss L M Ogilvie
Type: Girls Day 3–18
No of pupils: 828
Fees: (September 05) Day £5514–£9189

CUMNOR HOUSE SCHOOL
168 Pampisford Road, South Croydon, Surrey CR2 6DA
Tel: (020) 8660 3445
Fax: (020) 8660 3445
Email: admin@cumnorhouse.com
Head: Mr P Clare-Hunt
Type: Boys Day 4–13
No of pupils: 350
Fees: (September 04) Day £5805–£6975

ELMHURST SCHOOL
44–48 South Park Hill Road, South Croydon, Surrey CR2 7DW
Tel: (020) 8688 0661
Fax: (020) 8686 7675
Email: office@elmhurstschool.net
Head: Mr B K Dighton
Type: Boys Day 4–11
No of pupils: 254
Fees: (September 04) Day £5355–£6390

SANDERSTEAD JUNIOR SCHOOL
29 Purley Oaks Road, Sanderstead, South Croydon, Surrey CR2 0NW
Tel: (020) 8660 0801
Fax: (020) 8763 2243
Email: aburrell26@aol.com
Head: Mrs A Barns
Type: Co-educational Day 3–12
No of pupils: B50 G50
Fees: (September 03) Day £3900–£5550

WHITGIFT SCHOOL
Haling Park, South Croydon, Surrey CR2 6YT
Tel: (020) 8688 9222
Fax: (020) 8760 0682
Email: office@whitgift.co.uk
Head: Dr C A Barnett and Dr J M Cox
Type: Boys Day 10–18
No of pupils: 1152
Fees: (September 05) Day £11259

SURBITON

LINLEY HOUSE
6 Berrylands Road, Surbiton, Surrey KT5 8RA
Tel: (020) 8399 4979
Fax: (020) 8399 4979
Head: Mrs S Mallin
Type: Co-educational Day 3–7
No of pupils: B18 G17
Fees: (September 04) Day £2916–£5910

SHREWSBURY HOUSE SCHOOL
107 Ditton Road, Surbiton, Surrey KT6 6RL
Tel: (020) 8399 3066
Fax: (020) 8339 9529
Email: office@shspost.co.uk
Head: Mr C M Ross
Type: Boys Day 7–13
No of pupils: 290
Fees: (September 05) Day £9750

SURBITON PREPARATORY SCHOOL
3 Avenue Elmers, Surbiton, Surrey KT6 4SP
Tel: (020) 8546 5245
Fax: (020) 8390 6640
Email: surbiton.prep@church-schools.com
Head: Mr S J Pryce
Type: Boys Day 4–11
No of pupils: 139
Fees: (September 05) Day £5787–£7884

SUTTON

HOMEFIELD SCHOOL*
Western Road, Sutton, Surrey SM1 2TE
Tel: (020) 8642 0965
Fax: (020) 8642 0965
Email: administration@homefield.sutton.sch.uk
Head: Mr P R Mowbray
Type: Boys Day 2–13
No of pupils: 380
Fees: (September 05) Day £3420–£7995

STOWFORD COLLEGE†
95 Brighton Road, Sutton, Surrey SM2 5SJ
Tel: (020) 8661 9444
Fax: (020) 8661 6136
Email: stowfordsch@btinternet.com
Head: Mr R J Shakespeare
Type: Co-educational Day 6–16 Flexi-boarding available
No of pupils: B55 G28
Fees: (September 04) Day £6300–£7200

SUTTON HIGH SCHOOL GDST
55 Cheam Road, Sutton, Surrey SM1 2AX
Tel: (020) 8642 0594
Fax: (020) 8642 2014
Email: office@sut.gdst.net
Head: Mr S Callaghan
Type: Girls Day 4–18
No of pupils: 751
Fees: (September 05) Day £7149–£9189

TADWORTH

ABERDOUR SCHOOL
Brighton Road, Burgh Heath, Tadworth, Surrey KT20 6AJ
Tel: (01737) 354119
Fax: (01737) 363044
Email: admin@aberdour.surrey.sch.uk
Head: Dr G Silverlock
Type: Co-educational Day 3–13
No of pupils: B200 G120
Fees: (September 05)
Day £3270–£8760

BRAMLEY SCHOOL
Chequers Lane, Walton-on-the-Hill, Tadworth, Surrey KT20 7ST
Tel: (01737) 812004
Fax: (01737) 819945
Email: office@bramleyschool.surrey.sch.uk
Head: Mrs P Burgess
Type: Girls Day 3–11
No of pupils: 120
Fees: (September 05)
Day £3300–£7245

CHINTHURST SCHOOL
Tadworth Street, Tadworth, Surrey KT20 5QZ
Tel: (01737) 812011
Fax: (01737) 814835
Email: enquiries@chinthurst.surrey.sch.uk
Head: Mr T J Egan
Type: Boys Day 3–13
No of pupils: 340
Fees: (September 05)
Day £2775–£7785

THAMES DITTON

WESTON GREEN SCHOOL
Weston Green Road, Thames Ditton, Surrey KT7 0JN
Tel: (020) 8398 2778
Fax: (020) 8398 2778
Email: info@westongreenschool.org.uk
Head: Mrs L Harvey
Type: Co-educational Day 2–8
No of pupils: 180
Fees: (September 03)
Day £3300–£5400

THORPE

TASIS THE AMERICAN SCHOOL IN ENGLAND*
Coldharbour Lane, Thorpe, Surrey TW20 8TE
Tel: (01932) 565252
Fax: (01932) 564644
Email: ukadmissions@tasis.com
Head: Dr J A Doran
Type: Co-educational Boarding and Day 3–18
No of pupils: B362 G354
No of boarders: F165
Fees: (September 05) FB £23600
Day £5200–£15300

WALLINGTON

COLLINGWOOD SCHOOL
3 Springfield Road, Wallington, Surrey SM6 0BD
Tel: (020) 8647 4607
Fax: (020) 8669 2884
Email: headmaster@collingwood.sutton.sch.uk
Head: Mr G M Barham
Type: Co-educational Day 2–11
No of pupils: B112 G64
Fees: (September 05)
Day £2700–£5085

WALTON-ON-THAMES

DANESFIELD MANOR SCHOOL
Rydens Avenue, Walton-on-Thames, Surrey KT12 3JB
Tel: (01932) 220930
Fax: (01932) 225640
Head: Mrs L A Muggleton and Mrs L Fidler
Type: Co-educational Day 1–11
No of pupils: B84 G85
Fees: (September 03)
Day £4050–£4191

WESTWARD PREPARATORY SCHOOL
47 Hersham Road, Walton-on-Thames, Surrey KT12 1LE
Tel: (01932) 220911
Fax: (01932) 220911
Head: Mrs P Robertson
Type: Co-educational Day 3–11
No of pupils: B70 G70
Fees: (September 03)
Day £3324–£4086

WEYBRIDGE

ST GEORGE'S COLLEGE
Weybridge Road, Addlestone, Weybridge, Surrey KT15 2QS
Tel: (01932) 839300
Fax: (01932) 839301
Email: info@st-georges-college.co.uk
Head: Mr J A Peake
Type: Co-educational Day 11–18
No of pupils: B525 G325
Fees: (September 04)
Day £7905–£9120

ST GEORGE'S COLLEGE JUNIOR SCHOOL
Thames Street, Weybridge, Surrey KT13 8NL
Tel: (01932) 839400
Fax: (01932) 839401
Email: jshead@st-georges-college.co.uk
Head: Mr A Hudson
Type: Co-educational Day 3–11
No of pupils: B346 G262
Fees: (September 04)
Day £2910–£7500

WINDLESHAM

WOODCOTE HOUSE SCHOOL
Snows Ride, Windlesham, Surrey GU20 6PF
Tel: (01276) 472115
Fax: (01276) 472890
Email: info@woodcotehouseschool.co.uk
Head: Mr N H K Paterson
Type: Boys Boarding and Day 7–14
No of pupils: 100
No of boarders: F75
Fees: (September 05) FB £13725
Day £9825

WOKING

COWORTH-FLEXLANDS SCHOOL
Valley End, Chobham, Woking, Surrey GU24 8TE
Tel: (01276) 855707
Fax: (01276) 856043
Email: admissions@coworthpark.co.uk
Head: Mrs S O E Stephen and Mrs A Green
Type: Co-educational Day Boys 3–7 Girls 3–11
No of pupils: B25 G199
Fees: (September 04)
Day £2970–£6915

GREENFIELD SCHOOL
Brooklyn Road, Woking, Surrey GU22 7TP
Tel: (01483) 772525
Fax: (01483) 728907
Email: principal@greenfield.surrey.sch.uk
Head: Ms Janis Radcliffe
Type: Co-educational Day 3–11
No of pupils: B105 G115
Fees: (September 03)
Day £3195–£5880

HALSTEAD PREPARATORY SCHOOL
Woodham Rise, Woking, Surrey GU21 4EE
Tel: (01483) 772682
Fax: (01483) 757611
Email: registrar@halstead-school.org.uk
Head: Mrs S Fellows
Type: Girls Day 3–11
No of pupils: 208
Fees: (September 05)
Day £3168–£8640

HOE BRIDGE SCHOOL*
Hoe Place, Old Woking Road, Woking, Surrey GU22 8JE
Tel: (01483) 760018
Fax: (01483) 757560
Email: enquiriesprep@hoebridgeschool.co.uk
Head: Mr R W K Barr
Type: Co-educational Day 2–13
No of pupils: B362 G112
Fees: (September 05)
Day £1404–£10185

OAKFIELD SCHOOL
Coldharbour Road, Pyrford, Woking, Surrey GU22 8SJ
Tel: (01932) 342465
Fax: (01932) 342745
Email: education@oakfieldschool.co.uk
Head: Mrs S H Goddard
Type: Co-educational Day Boys 3–7 Girls 3–16
No of pupils: B30 G150
Fees: (September 04)
Day £1000–£3200

PRINS WILLEM-ALEXANDER SCHOOL
Old Woking Road, Woking, Surrey GU22 8HY
Tel: (01483) 750409
Fax: (01483) 730962
Email: pwas@prinswillem-alexander.surrey.sch.uk
Head: Mr M Meines and Mr M Damhuis
Type: Co-educational Day 4–12
No of pupils: B70 G76
Fees: (September 05)
Day £6960–£10920

RIPLEY COURT SCHOOL
Rose Lane, Ripley, Woking, Surrey GU23 6NE
Tel: (01483) 225217
Fax: (01483) 223854
Email: rcshead@btconnect.com
Head: Mr A J Gough
Type: Co-educational Day 3–13
No of pupils: B170 G72
Fees: (September 05)
Day £5775–£8540

ST ANDREW'S (WOKING) SCHOOL TRUST*
Church Hill House, Wilson Way, Horsell, Woking, Surrey GU21 4QW
Tel: (01483) 760943
Fax: (01483) 740314
Email: admin@st-andrews.woking.sch.uk
Head: Mr J R Evans
Type: Co-educational Day 3–13
No of pupils: B217 G62
Fees: (September 05)
Day £3885–£9975

WOLDINGHAM

WOLDINGHAM SCHOOL*
Marden Park, Woldingham, Surrey CR3 7YA
Tel: (01883) 349431
Fax: (01883) 348653
Email: registrar@woldingham.surrey.sch.uk
Head: Miss D Vernon
Type: Girls Boarding and Day 11–18 Flexi-boarding available
No of pupils: 500
No of boarders: W400
Fees: (September 05) WB £21240
Day £12690

EAST SUSSEX

BATTLE

BATTLE ABBEY SCHOOL*

High Street, Battle, East Sussex TN33 0AD
Tel: (01424) 772385
Fax: (01424) 773573
Email: office@battleabbeyschool.com
Head: Mr R Clark
Type: Co-educational Boarding and Day 2–18 Flexi-boarding available
No of pupils: B144 G140
No of boarders: F48 W2
Fees: (September 05)
F/WB £ £14322–£17805
Day £5412–£10896

BRIGHTON

BRIGHTON AND HOVE HIGH SCHOOL GDST

Montpelier Road, Brighton, East Sussex BN1 3AT
Tel: (01273) 734112
Fax: (01273) 737120
Email: enquiries@bhhs.gdst.net
Head: Mrs A Greatorex
Type: Girls Day 3–18
No of pupils: 780
Fees: (September 03)
Day £4695–£6477

BRIGHTON COLLEGE

Eastern Road, Brighton, East Sussex BN2 0AL
Tel: (01273) 704200
Fax: (01273) 704204
Email: registrar@brightoncollege.net
Head: Dr A Seldon
Type: Co-educational Day and Boarding 13–18 Flexi-boarding available
No of pupils: B470 G240
No of boarders: F55 W68
Fees: (September 05) FB £20466
WB £17976 Day £13203

BRIGHTON COLLEGE PRE-PREPARATORY SCHOOL

Sutherland Road, Brighton, East Sussex BN2 0EQ
Tel: (01273) 704259
Fax: (01273) 704318
Email: registrar@brightoncollege.net
Head: Mrs S P Wicks
Type: Co-educational Day 3–8
No of pupils: B110 G85
Fees: (September 04)
Day £2607–£6918

BRIGHTON COLLEGE PREP SCHOOL

Walpole Lodge, Walpole Road, Brighton, East Sussex BN2 0EU
Tel: (01273) 704201
Fax: (01273) 704286
Email: prepsch@brightoncollege.org.uk
Head: Mr B Melia
Type: Co-educational Day 8–13
No of pupils: B180 G119
Fees: (September 03)
Day £8028–£10293

BRIGHTON STEINER SCHOOL LIMITED

Roedean Road, Brighton, East Sussex BN2 5RA
Tel: (01273) 386300
Fax: (01273) 386313
Head: Ms J Firth
Type: Co-educational Day 2–16
No of pupils: 200
Fees: (September 04) Day £2070

DHARMA SCHOOL

White House, Ladies Mile Road, Patcham, Brighton, East Sussex BN1 8TB
Tel: (01273) 502055
Fax: (01273) 556580
Head: Mr P Murdock
Type: Co-educational Day 3–11
No of pupils: B34 G36
Fees: (September 03) Day £3500

ROEDEAN SCHOOL

Roedean Way, Brighton, East Sussex BN2 5RQ
Tel: (01273) 603181
Fax: (01273) 680791
Email: admissions@roedean.co.uk
Head: Mrs C Shaw
Type: Girls Boarding and Day 11–18 Flexi-boarding available
No of pupils: 377
No of boarders: F316
Fees: (September 04)
FB £22200–£24450 Day £12390

ST AUBYNS SCHOOL

76 High Street, Rottingdean, Brighton, East Sussex BN2 7JN
Tel: (01273) 302170
Fax: (01273) 304004
Email: office@staubyns-school.org.uk
Head: Mr A G Gobat
Type: Co-educational Day and Boarding 3–13 Flexi-boarding available
No of pupils: B114 G76
No of boarders: W8
Fees: (September 05) WB £14925
Day £4425–£11925

ST MARY'S HALL*

Eastern Road, Brighton, East Sussex BN2 5JF
Tel: (01273) 606061
Fax: (01273) 620782
Email: registrar@stmaryshall.co.uk
Head: Mrs S M Meek
Type: Girls Day and Boarding 3–18 (Boys 3–8) Flexi-boarding available
No of pupils: B10 G295
No of boarders: F75 W5
Fees: (September 05)
FB £13218–£17475
WB £12594–£16755
Day £2178–£10584

EASTBOURNE

EASTBOURNE COLLEGE
Old Wish Road, Eastbourne, East Sussex BN21 4JX
Tel: (01323) 452323
Fax: (01323) 452354
Email: EDeacon@eastbourne-college.co.uk
Head: Mr S P Davies
Type: Co-educational Boarding and Day 13–18
No of pupils: B382 G227
No of boarders: F293
Fees: (September 05) FB £20685 Day £13695

MOIRA HOUSE SCHOOL
Upper Carlisle Road, Eastbourne, East Sussex BN20 7TE
Tel: (01323) 636800
Fax: (01323) 649720
Email: lyoung@moirahouse.e-sussex.sch.uk
Head: Mrs L Young
Type: Girls Day and Boarding 2–11 Flexi-boarding available
No of boarders: F4
Fees: (September 05) FB £15525–£19875 WB £14175–£17700 Day £4980–£11550

MOIRA HOUSE GIRLS SCHOOL
Upper Carlisle Road, Eastbourne, East Sussex BN20 7TE
Tel: (01323) 644144
Fax: (01323) 649720
Email: info@moirahouse.co.uk
Head: Mrs A Harris
Type: Girls Boarding and Day 3–19 Flexi-boarding available
No of pupils: 420
No of boarders: F110 W12
Fees: (September 05) FB £15525–£19875 WB £14175–£17700 Day £4980–£11550

ST ANDREW'S SCHOOL
Meads, Eastbourne, East Sussex BN20 7RP
Tel: (01323) 733203
Fax: (01323) 646860
Email: office@androvian.biblio.net
Head: Mr J Griffith
Type: Co-educational Boarding and Day 3–13 Flexi-boarding available
No of pupils: B236 G128
No of boarders: F16 W4
Fees: (September 05) FB £15390 WB £13650 Day £6210–£10815

ST BEDE'S PREP SCHOOL*†
Duke's Drive, Eastbourne, East Sussex BN20 7XL
Tel: (01323) 734222
Fax: (01323) 746437
Email: prep.school@stbedesschool.org
Head: Mr C P Pyemont
Type: Co-educational Boarding and Day 2–13 Flexi-boarding available
No of pupils: B250 G168
No of boarders: F60 W7
Fees: (September 05) FB £15030 Day £10470

FOREST ROW

ASHDOWN HOUSE SCHOOL
Forest Row, East Sussex RH18 5JY
Tel: (01342) 822574
Fax: (01342) 824380
Email: secretary@ashdownhouse.com
Head: Mr A R Taylor
Type: Co-educational Boarding 8–13
No of pupils: B90 G52
No of boarders: F142
Fees: (September 05) FB £17100

GREENFIELDS SCHOOL
Priory Road, Forest Row, East Sussex RH18 5JD
Tel: (01342) 822189
Fax: (01342) 825289
Email: grnflds@aol.com
Head: Mrs V Tupholme
Type: Co-educational Day and Boarding 2–19 Flexi-boarding available
No of pupils: B85 G70
No of boarders: F30
Fees: (September 05) F/WB £ £14000–£16000 Day £3300–£10000

MICHAEL HALL (STEINER WALDORF SCHOOL)*
Kidbrooke Park, Forest Row, East Sussex RH18 5JA
Tel: (01342) 822275
Fax: (01342) 826593
Email: info@michaelhall.co.uk
Type: Co-educational Day and Boarding 0–19 Flexi-boarding available
No of pupils: B300 G328
No of boarders: F15 W10
Fees: (September 05) FB £13880 WB £12820 Day £7890

HAILSHAM

ST BEDE'S SCHOOL*†
The Dicker, Hailsham, East Sussex BN27 3QH
Tel: (01323) 843252
Fax: (01323) 442628
Email: school.office@stbedesschool.org
Head: Mr S W Cole
Type: Co-educational Boarding and Day 11–19 Flexi-boarding available
No of pupils: B480 G320
No of boarders: F320
Fees: (September 05) FB £19785 Day £12165

HASTINGS

BUCKSWOOD SCHOOL*
Broomham Hall, Rye Road, Guestling, Hastings, East Sussex TN35 4LT
Tel: (01424) 813813
Fax: (01424) 812100
Email: achieve@buckswood.co.uk
Head: Mr T Fish
Type: Co-educational Day and Boarding 10–19 Flexi-boarding available
No of pupils: B150 G100
No of boarders: F150
Fees: (September 05) FB £17175 Day £8190

HOVE

BELLERBYS COLLEGE
44 Cromwell Road, Hove,
East Sussex BN3 3ER
Tel: (01273) 323374
Fax: (01273) 749322
Email: hove@bellerbys.com
Head: Mr N Addison
Type: Co-educational Boarding and Day 14+
No of pupils: B270 G210
No of boarders: F390
Fees: (September 03)
FB £15300–£18900

DEEPDENE SCHOOL
Hove, East Sussex BN3 4ED
Tel: (01273) 418984
Fax: (01273) 415543
Email: info@deepdeneschool.com
Head: Mrs L V Clark-Darby and Mrs N K Gane
Type: Co-educational Day 1–8
No of pupils: B108 G122
Fees: (September 04)
Day £2760–£7500

THE DRIVE PREP SCHOOL
101 The Drive, Hove, East Sussex
BN3 6GE
Tel: (01273) 738444
Fax: (01273) 738444
Email: enquiries@driveprep.brighton-hove.sch.uk
Head: Mrs S Parkinson
Type: Co-educational Day 3–16
No of pupils: 109
Fees: (September 04)
Day £3000–£6000

THE FOLD SCHOOL
201 New Church Road, Hove,
East Sussex BN3 4ED
Tel: (01273) 410901
Email: thefoldschool@ntlworld.com
Head: Dr C J Drake
Type: Co-educational Day 3–11
No of pupils: B37 G38
Fees: (September 04)
Day £3600–£4500

LANCING COLLEGE PREPARATORY SCHOOL AT MOWDEN
The Droveway, Hove, East Sussex
BN3 6LU
Tel: (01273) 503452
Fax: (01273) 503457
Email: info@lancingprep.co.uk
Head: Mr A Laurent
Type: Co-educational Day 3–13
No of pupils: B107 G21
Fees: (September 05)
Day £2550–£10155

ST CHRISTOPHER'S SCHOOL
33 New Church Road, Hove,
East Sussex BN3 4AD
Tel: (01273) 735404
Fax: (01273) 747956
Email: office@stchristophershove.org.uk
Head: Mrs H Beeby
Type: Co-educational Day 4–14
No of pupils: B166 G54
Fees: (September 04)
Day £4938–£5337

STONELANDS SCHOOL OF BALLET & THEATRE ARTS
170A Church Road, Hove,
East Sussex BN3 2DJ
Tel: (01273) 770445
Fax: (01273) 770444
Email: dianacarteur@stonelandsschool.co.uk
Head: Mrs D Carteur
Type: Co-educational Boarding and Day 5–16 Flexi-boarding available
No of pupils: B6 G44
No of boarders: F10 W10
Fees: (September 04) FB £13497
Day £3300–£5997

LEWES

LEWES OLD GRAMMAR SCHOOL
140 High Street, Lewes, East Sussex
BN7 1XS
Tel: (01273) 472634
Fax: (01273) 476948
Email: bursar@logs.uk.com
Head: Mr R Blewitt
Type: Co-educational Day 3–18
No of pupils: B210 G120
Fees: (September 05)
Day £4500–£8730

MAYFIELD

ST LEONARDS-MAYFIELD SCHOOL
The Old Palace, Mayfield,
East Sussex TN20 6PH
Tel: (01435) 874600
Fax: (01435) 872627
Email: admiss@stlm.e-sussex.sch.uk
Head: Mrs J Dalton
Type: Girls Boarding and Day 11–18 Flexi-boarding available
No of pupils: 400
No of boarders: F120 W40
Fees: (September 04)
F/WB £ £18510 Day £12060

SKIPPERS HILL MANOR PREPARATORY SCHOOL
Five Ashes, Mayfield, East Sussex
TN20 6HR
Tel: (01825) 830234
Fax: (01825) 831040
Email: info@skippershill.com
Head: Mr T W Lewis
Type: Co-educational Day 3–13
No of pupils: B80 G57
Fees: (September 04)
Day £2940–£9525

ROBERTSBRIDGE

BODIAM MANOR SCHOOL†
Bodiam, Robertsbridge, East Sussex
TN32 5UJ
Tel: (01580) 830225
Fax: (01580) 830227
Email: headmaster@bodiammanorschool.fsnet.co.uk
Head: Mr S Flutter
Type: Co-educational Day 2–13
No of pupils: B73 G72
Fees: (September 04)
Day £5337–£8319

DARVELL SCHOOL
Darvell Bruderhof, Robertsbridge,
East Sussex TN32 5DR
Tel: (01580) 883300
Fax: (01580) 883317
Head: Mr A Meier
Type: Co-educational Day 2–14
No of pupils: B55 G55

VINEHALL SCHOOL
Robertsbridge, East Sussex
TN32 5JL
Tel: (01580) 880413
Fax: (01580) 882119
Email: office@vinehallschool.com
Head: Mrs J L Robinson
Type: Co-educational Boarding and Day 2–13
No of pupils: B226 G147
No of boarders: F50
Fees: (September 05) FB £14880
Day £11445

SEAFORD

NEWLANDS INTERNATIONAL COLLEGE
Newlands Court, Sutton Avenue, Seaford, East Sussex BN25 4LF
Tel: (01323) 490000
Fax: (01323) 898420
Email: info@newlands-isc.com
Head: Mrs W Jarvis
Type: Co-educational Boarding and Day 11–18
Fees: (September 05) FB £17850
Day £10875

NEWLANDS SCHOOL*†
Eastbourne Road, Seaford,
East Sussex BN25 4NP
Tel: (01323) 892334 / 490000
Fax: (01323) 898420
Email: newlands1@msn.com
Head: Mr O T Price
Type: Co-educational Boarding and Day 0–18 (nursery & pre-prep)
Flexi-boarding available
No of pupils: B269 G182
No of boarders: F111
Fees: (September 05)
FB £14985–£17850
WB £14835–£17700
Day £4950–£10875

ST LEONARDS-ON-SEA

CLAREMONT SCHOOL
Baldslow, St Leonards-on-Sea,
East Sussex TN37 7PW
Tel: (01424) 751555
Fax: (01424) 754310
Email: enquiries@claremontschool.co.uk
Head: Mr M Beaumont and Mr I Culley
Type: Co-educational Day 1–14
No of pupils: B200 G200
Fees: (September 05)
Day £3900–£6750

WADHURST

BRICKLEHURST MANOR PREPARATORY
Stonegate, Wadhurst, East Sussex
TN5 7EL
Tel: (01580) 200448
Fax: (01580) 200998
Email: bricklehurst@btconnect.com
Head: Mrs C Flowers
Type: Co-educational Day 3–11
No of pupils: 124
Fees: (September 04)
Day £2550–£5925

SACRED HEART RC PRIMARY SCHOOL
Mayfield Lane, Durgates,
Wadhurst, East Sussex TN5 6DQ
Tel: (01892) 783414
Fax: (01892) 783510
Email: admin@wadhurstsacredheart.freeserve.co.uk
Head: Mrs H Castle
Type: Co-educational Day 3–11
No of pupils: B60 G60
Fees: (September 05)
Day £2400–£4350

WEST SUSSEX

ARUNDEL

SLINDON COLLEGE†
Slindon, Arundel, West Sussex
BN18 0RH
Tel: (01243) 814320
Fax: (01243) 814702
Email: registrar@slindoncollege.fsnet.co.uk
Head: Mr I P Graham
Type: Boys Boarding and Day 9–16 Flexi-boarding available
No of pupils: 100
No of boarders: F20 W30
Fees: (September 05)
F/WB £ £19470–£20070
Day £11190–£12540

BURGESS HILL

BURGESS HILL SCHOOL FOR GIRLS*
Keymer Road, Burgess Hill,
West Sussex RH15 0EG
Tel: (01444) 241050
Fax: (01444) 870314
Email: registrar@burgesshill-school.com
Head: Mrs J A Aughwane
Type: Girls Boarding and Day 3–18 Flexi-boarding available
No of pupils: B60 G636
No of boarders: F48 W50
Fees: (September 05) FB £17655
Day £4860–£10170

ST PETER'S SCHOOL
Upper St John's Road, Burgess Hill, West Sussex RH15 8HB
Tel: (01444) 235880
Fax: (01444) 258081
Head: Mr H G Stevens
Type: Co-educational Day 2–13
No of pupils: B98 G84
Fees: (September 03)
Day £624–£5640

CHICHESTER

GREAT BALLARD SCHOOL
Eartham, Chichester, West Sussex PO18 0LR
Tel: (01243) 814236
Fax: (01243) 814586
Email: gbschool@breathemail.net
Head: Mr R E Jennings
Type: Co-educational Boarding and Day 2–13 Flexi-boarding available
No of pupils: B104 G116
No of boarders: W29
Fees: (September 04) FB £11985 WB £11100 Day £2415–£8970

LAVANT HOUSE
West Lavant, Chichester, West Sussex PO18 9AB
Tel: (01243) 527211
Fax: (01243) 530490
Email: office@lavanthouse.org.uk
Head: Mrs M Scott
Type: Girls Day and Boarding 3–18 Flexi-boarding available
No of pupils: 145
No of boarders: F7 W7
Fees: (September 05) F/WB £ £13335–£15990 Day £5010–£10095

THE LITTLEMEAD SCHOOL
Tangmere Road, Tangmere, Chichester, West Sussex PO20 6EU
Tel: (01243) 787551
Fax: (01243) 527249
Head: Mrs S Carter
Type: Co-educational Day 0–14 Flexi-boarding available
No of pupils: B16 G26

OAKWOOD SCHOOL
Oakwood, Chichester, West Sussex PO18 9AN
Tel: (01243) 575209
Fax: (01243) 575433
Email: office@oakwoodschool.co.uk
Head: Mr A H Cowell
Type: Co-educational Day 2–11
No of pupils: B140 G140
Fees: (September 05) Day £920–£8880

THE PREBENDAL SCHOOL
54 West Street, Chichester, West Sussex PO19 1RT
Tel: (01243) 782026/784828
Fax: (01243) 771821
Email: secretary.prebendal@btconnect.com
Head: Rev Canon G C Hall
Type: Co-educational Day and Boarding 3–14 Flexi-boarding available
No of pupils: B167 G121
No of boarders: F18 W12
Fees: (September 04) FB £11652 WB £11148 Day £8604

PREBENDAL SCHOOL (NORTHGATE HOUSE)
38 North Street, Chichester, West Sussex PO19 1LX
Tel: (01243) 784828
Email: secretary.prebendal@btconnect.com
Head: Mrs L M Greenall
Type: Co-educational Day 3–7
No of pupils: B53 G42
Fees: (September 05) Day £2280–£5436

WESTBOURNE HOUSE SCHOOL
Shopwyke, Chichester, West Sussex PO20 2BH
Tel: (01243) 782739
Fax: (01243) 770759
Email: whouseoffice@rmplc.co.uk
Head: Mr B G Law
Type: Co-educational Boarding and Day 3–13 Flexi-boarding available
No of pupils: B203 G161
No of boarders: F73
Fees: (September 05) FB £13470 Day £5670–£10860

COPTHORNE

COPTHORNE PREP SCHOOL
Effingham Lane, Copthorne, West Sussex RH10 3HR
Tel: (01342) 712311
Fax: (01342) 714014
Email: office@copthorneprep.co.uk
Head: Mr C Jones
Type: Co-educational Day and Boarding 2–13 Flexi-boarding available
No of pupils: B127 G88
No of boarders: W10
Fees: (September 05) WB £11930 Day £6000–£10500

CRAWLEY

WILLOW TREE MONTESSORI SCHOOL
Charlwood House, Charlwood Road, Lowfield Heath, Crawley, West Sussex RH11 0QA
Tel: (01293) 565544
Fax: (01293) 611705
Head: Mrs G Kerfante
Type: Co-educational Day 1–8
No of pupils: B84 G66
Fees: (September 02) Day £2310–£3600

EAST GRINSTEAD

BRAMBLETYE SCHOOL*
Lewes Road, Brambletye, East Grinstead, West Sussex RH19 3PD
Tel: (01342) 321004
Fax: (01342) 317562
Email: admin@brambletye.com
Head: Mr H D Cocke
Type: Co-educational Boarding and Day 3–13
No of pupils: B164 G93
No of boarders: F71
Fees: (September 05) FB £15600 Day £11850–£14850

FONTHILL LODGE
Coombe Hill Road, East Grinstead, West Sussex RH9 4LY
Tel: (01342) 321635
Fax: (01342) 326844
Email: enquiries@fonthill-lodge.co.uk
Head: Mrs J Griffiths
Type: Co-educational Day 2–11 (Single-sex ed 8–11)
No of pupils: B91 G99
Fees: (September 05) Day £6060–£9390

STOKE BRUNSWICK
Ashurstwood, East Grinstead, West Sussex RH19 3PF
Tel: (01342) 828200
Fax: (01342) 828201
Email: headmaster@stokebrunswick.co.uk
Head: Mr R Taylor
Type: Co-educational Boarding and Day 3–13 Flexi-boarding available
No of pupils: B100 G55
No of boarders: W10
Fees: (September 04) WB £12675

HAYWARDS HEATH

ARDINGLY COLLEGE
Haywards Heath, West Sussex
RH17 6SQ
Tel: (01444) 893000
Fax: (01444) 893001
Email: registrar@ardingly.com
Head: Mr J R Franklin
Type: Co-educational Boarding and Day 3–18 Flexi-boarding available
No of pupils: B470 G286
No of boarders: F243
Fees: (September 05)
FB £14160–£20520
Day £1660–£5120

ARDINGLY COLLEGE JUNIOR SCHOOL
Haywards Heath, West Sussex
RH17 6SQ
Tel: (01444) 892279
Fax: (01444) 892169
Email: head.acjs@virgin.net
Head: Mr M Groome
Type: Co-educational Boarding and Day 7–13 (and pre-prep) Flexi-boarding available
No of pupils: B129 G94
No of boarders: F17
Fees: (September 04) FB £13500
Day £7275–£9150

CUMNOR HOUSE SCHOOL
Danehill, Haywards Heath,
West Sussex RH17 7HT
Tel: (01825) 790347
Fax: (01825) 790910
Email: office@cumnor.co.uk
Head: Mr C St J Heinrich
Type: Co-educational Boarding and Day 4–13
No of pupils: B182 G150
No of boarders: F26
Fees: (September 05) FB £14745
Day £6540–£12330

GREAT WALSTEAD
East Mascalls Lane, Lindfield,
Haywards Heath, West Sussex
RH16 2QL
Tel: (01444) 483528
Fax: (01444) 482122
Email: admin@greatwalstead.co.uk
Head: Mr H J Lowries
Type: Co-educational Day and Boarding 2–13 Flexi-boarding available
No of pupils: B245 G166
No of boarders: W30
Fees: (September 05) WB £10635
Day £4800–£9885

HANDCROSS PARK SCHOOL
Handcross, Haywards Heath,
West Sussex RH17 6HF
Tel: (01444) 400526
Fax: (01444) 400527
Email: whilton@handxpark.com
Head: Mr W J Hilton
Type: Co-educational Day and Boarding 3–13 Flexi-boarding available
No of pupils: B180 G120
No of boarders: W10
Fees: (September 05) WB £13527
Day £2802–£11544

TAVISTOCK & SUMMERHILL SCHOOL
Summerhill Lane, Haywards
Heath, West Sussex RH16 1RP
Tel: (01444) 450256
Fax: (01444) 458251
Email: info@tavistockandsummerhill.co.uk
Head: Mr M Barber
Type: Co-educational Day 3–13
No of pupils: B99 G53
Fees: (September 05)
Day £4455–£8190

HORSHAM

CHRIST'S HOSPITAL
Horsham, West Sussex RH13 0YP
Tel: (01403) 211293
Fax: (01403) 211580
Email: enquiries@christs-hospital.org.uk
Head: Dr P C D Southern
Type: Co-educational Boarding 11–18
No of pupils: B493 G348
No of boarders: F841
Fees: (September 03) FB £17050

FARLINGTON SCHOOL*
Strood Park, Horsham, West Sussex
RH12 3PN
Tel: (01403) 254967
Fax: (01403) 272258
Email: office@farlingtonschool.net
Head: Mrs P M Mawer
Type: Girls Boarding and Day 4–18 Flexi-boarding available
No of pupils: 500
No of boarders: F28 W13
Fees: (September 05)
FB £13800–£16815
WB £13455–£16470
Day £5115–£10575

PENNTHORPE SCHOOL
Church Street, Rudgwick,
Horsham, West Sussex RH12 3HJ
Tel: (01403) 822391
Fax: (01403) 822438
Email: pennthorpe@lineone.net
Head: Mr S Moll
Type: Co-educational Day 2–14
No of pupils: B194 G108
Fees: (September 05)
Day £1098–£9990

HURSTPIERPOINT

HURSTPIERPOINT COLLEGE
College Lane, Hurstpierpoint,
West Sussex BN6 9JS
Tel: (01273) 833636
Fax: (01273) 835257
Email: Info@hppc.co.uk
Head: Mr T J Manly
Type: Co-educational Boarding and Day 7–18 Flexi-boarding available
No of pupils: B404 G212
No of boarders: F53 W248
Fees: (September 05)
FB £13800–£19785
WB £13140–£18945
Day £10260–£15105

LANCING

ARDMORE MONTESSORI SCHOOL
Wembley Gardens, Lancing,
West Sussex BN15 9LA
Tel: (01903) 755583
Head: Mr N Peck
Type: Co-educational Day 2–12
No of pupils: 60

LANCING COLLEGE
Lancing, West Sussex BN15 0RW
Tel: (01273) 452213
Fax: (01273) 464720
Email: admissions@lancing.dialnet.com
Head: Mr P M Tinniswood
Type: Co-educational Boarding and Day 13–18 Flexi-boarding available
No of pupils: B316 G122
No of boarders: F278
Fees: (September 05) FB £21885 Day £15225

MIDHURST

CONIFERS SCHOOL
Egmont Road, Midhurst, West Sussex GU29 9BG
Tel: (01730) 813243
Fax: (01730) 813382
Email: admin@conifersschool.com
Head: Mrs L R Fox
Type: Co-educational Day Boys 3–8 Girls 3–11
No of pupils: B30 G70
Fees: (September 05) Day £504–£6945

ST MARGARET'S SCHOOL CONVENT OF MERCY
Petersfield Road, Midhurst, West Sussex GU29 9JN
Tel: (01730) 813956
Fax: (01730) 810829
Email: smsadmin@conventofmercy.org
Head: Mr V Fox
Type: Co-educational Day 2–11
No of pupils: B86 G151
Fees: (September 05) Day £1380–£5685

PEASE POTTAGE

COTTESMORE SCHOOL*
Buchan Hill, Pease Pottage, West Sussex RH11 9AU
Tel: (01293) 520648
Fax: (01293) 614784
Email: schooloffice@cottesmoreschool.com
Head: Mr I J Tysoe
Type: Co-educational Boarding 8–13
No of pupils: B100 G50
No of boarders: F150
Fees: (September 05) FB £15900

PETWORTH

SEAFORD COLLEGE*
Lavington Park, Petworth, West Sussex GU27 0NB
Tel: (01798) 867392
Fax: (01798) 867606
Email: seaford@clara.co.uk
Head: Mr T J Mullins
Type: Co-educational Boarding and Day 10–18 Flexi-boarding available
No of pupils: B310 G141
No of boarders: F45 W82
Fees: (September 05)
FB £14760–£19110
WB £12870–£16200
Day £10050–£12540

PULBOROUGH

ARUNDALE PREPARATORY SCHOOL
Lower Street, Pulborough, West Sussex RH20 2BX
Tel: (01798) 872520
Fax: (01798) 875202
Email: arundale@easynet.co.uk
Head: Miss K Lovejoy
Type: Co-educational Day 2–11
No of pupils: B31 G79
Fees: (September 05) Day £2652–£7605

DORSET HOUSE SCHOOL
The Manor, Church Lane, Bury, Pulborough, West Sussex RH20 1PB
Tel: (01798) 831456
Fax: (01798) 831141
Email: headmaster@dorsethouse.w-sussex.sch.uk
Head: Mr E J D Clarke
Type: Boys Boarding and Day 3–13 Flexi-boarding available
No of pupils: 130
No of boarders: W30
Fees: (September 04) WB £10470–£13389

WINDLESHAM HOUSE*
Washington, Pulborough, West Sussex RH20 4AY
Tel: (01903) 874700
Fax: (01903) 874702
Email: office@windlesham.com
Head: Mr P Lough
Type: Co-educational Boarding 7–13 (Day pre-prep 4–7)
No of pupils: B164 G91
No of boarders: F242
Fees: (September 05) FB £15675

SHOREHAM-BY-SEA

SHOREHAM COLLEGE
St Julian's Lane, Shoreham-by-Sea, West Sussex BN43 6YW
Tel: (01273) 592681
Fax: (01273) 591673
Email: info@shorehamcollege.co.uk
Head: Mr R K Iremonger
Type: Co-educational Day 3–16
No of pupils: B280 G144
Fees: (September 05) Day £5400–£8850

SOMPTING

SOMPTING ABBOTTS SCHOOL*
Church Lane, Sompting, West Sussex BN15 0AZ
Tel: (01903) 235960
Fax: (01903) 210045
Email: office@somptingabbotts.com
Head: Mrs P M Sinclair and Mr T R Sinclair
Type: Co-educational Day and Boarding 3–13 Flexi-boarding available
No of pupils: B125 G55
No of boarders: W12
Fees: (September 05) WB £9600 Day £5400–£7200

STEYNING

THE TOWERS CONVENT SCHOOL
Henfield Road, Upper Beeding, Steyning, West Sussex BN44 3TF
Tel: (01903) 812185
Fax: (01903) 813858
Email: admin@towers.w-sussex.sch.uk
Head: Mrs C Baker
Type: Girls Day and Boarding 4–16 (Boys 3–11) Flexi-boarding available
No of pupils: 249
No of boarders: F44 W1
Fees: (September 05)
FB £9150–£11100
WB £8700–£9150
Day £5250–£5796

TURNERS HILL

WORTH SCHOOL
Paddockhurst Road, Turners Hill, West Sussex RH10 4SD
Tel: (01342) 710200
Fax: (01342) 710230
Email: registry@worth.org.uk
Head: Mr P Armstrong
Type: Boys Boarding and Day 11–18
No of pupils: 445
No of boarders: F295
Fees: (September 05)
FB £19047–£21165
Day £14115–£15678

WORTHING

BROADWATER MANOR SCHOOL
Broadwater Road, Worthing, West Sussex BN14 8HU
Tel: (01903) 201123
Fax: (01903) 821777
Email: info@broadwatermanor.com
Head: Mrs E K Woodley
Type: Co-educational Day 2–13
No of pupils: B192 G147
Fees: (September 03)
Day £480–£5685

OUR LADY OF SION SCHOOL
Gratwicke Road, Worthing, West Sussex BN11 4BL
Tel: (01903) 204063
Fax: (01903) 214434
Email: enquiries@sionschool.org.uk
Head: Mr M Scullion
Type: Co-educational Day 2–18
No of pupils: B229 G250
Fees: (September 05)
Day £5160–£8055

SANDHURST SCHOOL
101 Brighton Road, Worthing, West Sussex BN11 2EL
Tel: (01903) 201933
Fax: (01903) 824752
Email: enquiries@sandhurst-school.co.uk
Head: Mrs S A Hale
Type: Co-educational Day 2–13
No of pupils: B50 G82
Fees: (September 03)
Day £2499–£3129

TYNE AND WEAR

NEWCASTLE UPON TYNE

AKHURST PREPARATORY SCHOOL
The Grove, Jesmond, Newcastle upon Tyne, Tyne and Wear NE2 2PN
Tel: (0191) 281 2116
Fax: (0191) 281 3964
Email: akhurst@rmplc.co.uk
Head: Mr & Mrs R J Derham
Type: Co-educational Day 1–12
No of pupils: B130 G70
Fees: (September 03)
Day £4590–£5025

NEWCASTLE SCHOOL FOR BOYS
30 West Avenue, Gosforth, Newcastle upon Tyne, Tyne and Wear NE3 4ES
Tel: (0191) 285 1619
Fax: (0191) 213 1105
Email: office@newcastleschool.co.uk
Head: Mr P M Garner
Type: Boys Day 3–13
No of pupils: 392
Fees: (September 05) Day £6855

CENTRAL NEWCASTLE HIGH SCHOOL GDST
Eskdale Terrace, Newcastle upon Tyne, Tyne and Wear NE2 4DS
Tel: (0191) 281 1768
Fax: (0191) 281 3267
Email: general@cnw.gdst.net
Head: Mrs L J Griffin
Type: Girls Day 3–18
No of pupils: 967
Fees: (September 04)
Day £4149–£6930

DAME ALLAN'S BOYS SCHOOL
Fowberry Crescent, Fenham, Newcastle upon Tyne, Tyne and Wear NE4 9YJ
Tel: (0191) 275 0608
Fax: (0191) 275 1502
Email: enquiries@dameallans.co.uk
Head: Dr J R Hind
Type: Boys Day 8–18 (Co-ed VIth Form)
No of pupils: 510
Fees: (September 05)
Day £5697–£7239

DAME ALLAN'S GIRLS SCHOOL
Fowberry Crescent, Fenham, Newcastle upon Tyne, Tyne and Wear NE4 9YJ
Tel: (0191) 275 0708
Fax: (0191) 275 1502
Email: enquiries@dameallans.co.uk
Head: Dr J R Hind
Type: Girls Day 8–18 (Co-ed VIth Form)
No of pupils: 422
Fees: (September 05)
Day £5697–£7239

LA SAGESSE SCHOOL
North Jesmond, Newcastle upon Tyne, Tyne and Wear NE2 3RJ
Tel: (0191) 281 3474
Fax: (0191) 281 2721
Email: office@lsh.org.uk
Head: Miss L Clark
Type: Girls Day 3–18
Fees: (September 03)
Day £4050–£6885

LINDEN SCHOOL
72 Station Road, Forest Hall,
Newcastle upon Tyne,
Tyne and Wear NE12 9BQ
Tel: (0191) 266 2943
Fax: (0191) 266 2943
Head: Mr A J Edge
Type: Co-educational Day 3–11
No of pupils: B60 G58

NEWCASTLE PREPARATORY SCHOOL
6 Eslington Road, Jesmond,
Newcastle upon Tyne,
Tyne and Wear NE2 4RH
Tel: (0191) 281 1769
Fax: (0191) 281 5668
Email: enquiries@newcastleprepschool.org.uk
Head: Mrs M Coates
Type: Co-educational Day 3–11
No of pupils: B160 G60
Fees: (September 05)
Day £5784–£6600

NEWCASTLE UPON TYNE CHURCH HIGH SCHOOL
Tankerville Terrace, Jesmond,
Newcastle upon Tyne,
Tyne and Wear NE2 3BA
Tel: (0191) 281 4306
Fax: (0191) 281 0806
Email: info@churchhigh.com
Head: Mrs L G Smith
Type: Girls Day 2–18
No of pupils: 609
Fees: (September 03)
Day £4692–£6699

ROYAL GRAMMAR SCHOOL
Eskdale Terrace, Newcastle upon Tyne, Tyne and Wear NE2 4DX
Tel: (0191) 281 5711
Fax: (0191) 212 0392
Email: hm@rgs.newcastle.sch.uk
Head: Mr J F X Miller
Type: Boys Day 8–18 (Co-ed VIth form)
No of pupils: B1067 G74
Fees: (September 05)
Day £6141–£7329

WESTFIELD SCHOOL
Oakfield Road, Gosforth,
Newcastle upon Tyne,
Tyne and Wear NE3 4HS
Tel: (0191) 285 1948
Fax: (0191) 213 0734
Email: westfield@westfield.newcastle.sch.uk
Head: Mrs M Farndale
Type: Girls Day 3–18
No of pupils: 370
Fees: (September 04)
Day £2667–£7152

SUNDERLAND

ARGYLE HOUSE SCHOOL
19/20 Thornhill Park, Sunderland,
Tyne and Wear SR2 7LA
Tel: (0191) 510 0726
Fax: (0191) 567 2209
Email: info@argylehouseschool.co.uk
Head: Mr C Johnson
Type: Co-educational Day 3–16
No of pupils: B156 G81
Fees: (September 03)
Day £3570–£4750

GRINDON HALL CHRISTIAN SCHOOL
Nookside, Sunderland,
Tyne and Wear SR4 8PG
Tel: (0191) 534 4444
Fax: (0191) 534 4111
Email: info@grindonhall.com
Head: Mr C J Gray
Type: Co-educational Day 3–18
(VIth Form from Sept 2005)
Fees: (September 05)
Day £2715–£4725

SUNDERLAND HIGH SCHOOL
Mowbray Road, Sunderland,
Tyne and Wear SR2 8HY
Tel: (0191) 567 4984
Fax: (0191) 510 3953
Email: info@sunderlandhigh.co.uk
Head: Dr A Slater
Type: Co-educational Day 2–18
No of pupils: B318 G257
Fees: (September 04)
Day £4365–£6255

TYNEMOUTH

THE KING'S SCHOOL
Huntington Place, Tynemouth,
Tyne and Wear NE30 4RF
Tel: (0191) 258 5995
Fax: (0191) 296 3826
Email: hm@kings-tynemouth.co.uk
Head: Mr P J S Cantwell
Type: Co-educational Day 4–18
No of pupils: B552 G294
Fees: (September 04)
Day £5298–£6978

WHICKHAM

CHASE SCHOOL
Rectory Lane, Whickham,
Tyne and Wear NE16 4PD
Tel: (0191) 488 9432
Fax: (0191) 488 8855
Head: Mrs A Nelson
Type: Co-educational Day 4–11
No of pupils: B22 G19

WARWICKSHIRE

ATHERSTONE

TWYCROSS HOUSE SCHOOL
Twycross, Atherstone,
Warwickshire CV9 3PL
Tel: (01827) 880651
Head: Mr R V Kirkpatrick
Type: Co-educational Day 8–19
No of pupils: B143 G169

KENILWORTH

ABBOTSFORD SCHOOL
Bridge Street, Kenilworth,
Warwickshire CV8 1BP
Tel: (01926) 852826
Fax: (01926) 852753
Email: office@abbotsfordschool.co.uk
Head: Mrs J Jarvis
Type: Co-educational Day 3–11
No of pupils: B75 G58
Fees: (September 05)
Day £3780–£4830

LEAMINGTON SPA

ARNOLD LODGE SCHOOL
Kenilworth Road, Leamington Spa,
Warwickshire CV32 5TW
Tel: (01926) 778050
Fax: (01926) 743311
Email: info@arnoldlodge.com
Head: Mrs E M Hickling
Type: Co-educational Day 3–13
No of pupils: B231 G95
Fees: (September 05)
Day £4710–£7311

EMSCOTE HOUSE SCHOOL AND NURSERY
46 Warwick Place, Leamington
Spa, Warwickshire CV32 5DE
Tel: (01926) 425067
Email: headteacher@emscotehouse.demon.co.uk
Head: Mrs G J Andrews
Type: Co-educational Day 2–7
No of pupils: B34 G27
Fees: (September 05)
Day £1380–£5575

THE KINGSLEY SCHOOL
Beauchamp Avenue, Leamington
Spa, Warwickshire CV32 5RD
Tel: (01926) 425127
Fax: (01926) 831691
Email: admin@kingsley.warwickshire.sch.uk
Head: Mrs C Mannion Watson
Type: Girls Day 3–18 (Boys 2–7)
No of pupils: B2 G500
Fees: (September 04)
Day £4350–£6435

NUNEATON

MILVERTON HOUSE SCHOOL
Holman Way, Park Street,
Attleborough, Nuneaton,
Warwickshire CV11 4EL
Tel: (024) 7664 1722
Fax: (024) 76641722
Email: reception@milvertonhsch.co.uk
Head: Mr C D Badham
Type: Co-educational Day 0–11
No of pupils: B150 G150
Fees: (September 04)
Day £4167–£4284

THE WOLSTAN PREPARATORY SCHOOL
Temple Hall, Wellsborough,
Nuneaton, Warwickshire
CV13 6PA
Tel: (01455) 293024
Fax: (01455) 293040
Email: info@wolstan.org.uk
Head: Mr S Barnett
Type: Co-educational Day 3–10
No of pupils: B85 G67
Fees: (September 04)
Day £4665–£6570

RUGBY

BILTON GRANGE
Rugby Road, Dunchurch, Rugby,
Warwickshire CV22 6QU
Tel: (01788) 810217
Fax: (01788) 816922
Email: headmaster@biltongrange.co.uk
Head: Mr J P Kirk
Type: Co-educational Boarding and Day 4–13 Flexi-boarding available
No of pupils: B189 G136
No of boarders: F40 W15
Fees: (September 04)
F/WB £ £13950
Day £5043–£11490

THE CRESCENT SCHOOL
Bawnmore Road, Bilton, Rugby,
Warwickshire CV22 7QH
Tel: (01788) 521595
Fax: (01788) 816185
Email: admin@crescentschool.co.uk
Head: Mr R H Marshall
Type: Co-educational Day 3–11
No of pupils: B70 G87
Fees: (September 05)
Day £1350–£5835

PRINCETHORPE COLLEGE
Princethorpe, Rugby,
Warwickshire CV23 9PX
Tel: (01926) 634200
Fax: (01926) 633365
Email: post@princethorpe.co.uk
Head: Mr J M Shinkwin
Type: Co-educational Day 11–18
No of pupils: B393 G270
Fees: (September 05) FB £7275

RUGBY SCHOOL
Rugby, Warwickshire CV22 5EH
Tel: (01788) 556276
Fax: (01788) 556277
Email: registry@rugbyschool.net
Head: Mr P S J Derham
Type: Co-educational Boarding and Day 11–18
No of pupils: B442 G338
No of boarders: F654
Fees: (September 04) FB £21750
Day £13800

STRATFORD-UPON-AVON

THE CROFT PREPARATORY SCHOOL
Alveston Hill, Loxley Road,
Stratford-upon-Avon,
Warwickshire CV37 7RL
Tel: (01789) 293795
Fax: (01789) 414960
Email: office@croftschool.co.uk
Head: Dr P Thompson
Type: Co-educational Day 2–11
No of pupils: B223 G190
Fees: (September 05)
Day £1080–£7305

ELFIN PRE-PREP & NURSERY SCHOOL
26 Evesham Place,
Stratford-upon-Avon,
Warwickshire CV37 6HT
Tel: (01789) 292571
Fax: (01789) 292450
Email: elfinschool@btinternet.com
Head: Mrs B A Buczacki
Type: Co-educational Day 2–8
No of pupils: B16 G16
Fees: (September 05)
Day £2874–£3732

STRATFORD PREPARATORY SCHOOL
Church House, Old Town,
Stratford-upon-Avon,
Warwickshire CV37 6BG
Tel: (01789) 297993
Fax: (01789) 263993
Head: Mrs C Quinn
Type: Co-educational Day 2–11
No of pupils: B58 G56
Fees: (September 04)
Day £5355–£5550

WARWICK

THE KING'S HIGH SCHOOL FOR GIRLS
Smith Street, Warwick,
Warwickshire CV34 4HJ
Tel: (01926) 494485
Fax: (01926) 403089
Email: kings@khsw.warwks.sch.uk
Head: Mrs E Surber
Type: Girls Day 10–18
No of pupils: 570
Fees: (September 05) Day £8019

WARWICK PREPARATORY SCHOOL
Bridge Field, Banbury Road,
Warwick, Warwickshire CV34 6PL
Tel: (01926) 491545
Fax: (01926) 403456
Email: info@warwick-prep.warwickshire.sch.uk
Head: Mrs D M Robinson
Type: Co-educational Day Boys 3–7 Girls 3–11
No of pupils: B99 G346
Fees: (September 04)
Day £2427–£7341

WARWICK SCHOOL
Myton Road, Warwick,
Warwickshire CV34 6PP
Tel: (01926) 776400
Fax: (01926) 401259
Email: enquiries@warwickschool.org
Head: Mr E B Halse
Type: Boys Day and Boarding 7–18 Flexi-boarding available
No of pupils: 1090
No of boarders: F35 W11
Fees: (September 02)
FB £12003–£13307
WB £11076–£12480
Day £5508–£7080

WEST MIDLANDS

BIRMINGHAM

ABBEY COLLEGE
10 St Pauls Square, Birmingham,
West Midlands B3 1QU
Tel: (0121) 236 7474
Fax: (0121) 236 3937
Email: adminbir@abbeycollege.co.uk
Head: Dr C Devine
Type: Co-educational Day 13+ Flexi-boarding available
No of pupils: B95 G61
No of boarders: F1

AL HIJRAH SCHOOL
Cherrywood Centre, Burbidge Road, Bordesley Green,
Birmingham, West Midlands
B9 4US
Tel: (0121) 773 7979
Head: Mr M A K Saqib
Type: Co-educational Day 4–11 (Single sex ed)
No of pupils: B128 G128

BIRCHFIELD INDEPENDENT GIRLS SCHOOL
Beacon House, 30 Beacon Hill,
Aston, Birmingham,
West Midlands B6 6JU
Tel: (0121) 327 7707
Fax: (0121) 327 6888
Head: Mrs K Chawdhry
Type: Girls Day 11–16
No of pupils: 170
Fees: (September 03) Day £1050

THE BLUE COAT SCHOOL
Somerset Road, Edgbaston,
Birmingham, West Midlands
B17 0HR
Tel: (0121) 410 6800
Fax: (0121) 454 7757
Email: admissions@bluecoat.bham.sch.uk
Head: Mr A D J Browning
Type: Co-educational Day and Boarding 2–11 Flexi-boarding available
No of pupils: B309 G202
No of boarders: F5 W12
Fees: (September 04) FB £12906
WB £11664 Day £4980–£7554

DARUL ULOOM ISLAMIC HIGH SCHOOL & COLLEGE
521–527 Coventry Road,
Smallheath, Birmingham,
West Midlands B10 0LL
Tel: (0121) 772 6408
Fax: (0121) 773 4340
Head: Dr A A Rahim
Type: Co-educational Day and Boarding (Single-sex ed)
No of pupils: B77 G13
No of boarders: F14

EASTBOURNE HOUSE SCHOOL
111 Yardley Road, Acocks Green,
Birmingham, West Midlands
B27 6LL
Tel: (0121) 706 2013
Fax: (0121) 706 2013
Email: admin@eastbournehouse.bham.sch.uk
Head: Mr P J Moynihan
Type: Co-educational Day 3–11
No of pupils: B66 G58
Fees: (September 05)
Day £2709–£3990

EDGBASTON HIGH SCHOOL FOR GIRLS
Westbourne Road, Edgbaston,
Birmingham, West Midlands
B15 3TS
Tel: (0121) 454 5831
Fax: (0121) 454 2363
Email: genoffice@edgbastonhigh.bham.sch.uk
Head: Dr R Weeks
Type: Girls Day 2–18
No of pupils: 922
Fees: (September 05)
Day £3279–£7368

ELMHURST SCHOOL FOR DANCE
247–249 Bristol Road, Edgbaston,
Birmingham, West Midlands
B5 7UH
Tel: (0121) 472 6655
Fax: (0121) 472 6654
Email: elmhurst@cableol.co.uk
Head: Mr J McNamara
Type: Co-educational Boarding and Day 11–19
No of pupils: B26 G159
No of boarders: F158
Fees: (September 05)
FB £16536–£17172
Day £12879–£13356

HALLFIELD SCHOOL
48 Church Road, Edgbaston,
Birmingham, West Midlands
B15 3SJ
Tel: (0121) 454 1496
Fax: (0121) 454 9182
Email: admissions@hallfield.bham.sch.uk
Head: Mr C T O'Donnell
Type: Co-educational Day 2–11
No of pupils: B327 G130
Fees: (September 04)
Day £5160–£7800

HIGHCLARE SCHOOL
10 Sutton Road, Erdington,
Birmingham, West Midlands
B23 6QL
Tel: (0121) 373 7400
Fax: (0121) 373 7445
Email: abbey@highclareschool.co.uk
Head: Mrs M Viles
Type: Girls Day 1–18 (Boys 1–11 & 16–18)
No of pupils: B223 G507
Fees: (September 05)
Day £4650–£7905

HONEYBOURNE SCHOOL
621 Fox Hollies Road, Hall Green,
Birmingham, West Midlands
B28 9DW
Tel: (0121) 777 3778
Email: hbsinfo@hotmail.com
Head: Mr R J Croucher
Type: Co-educational Day 2–11
No of pupils: B30 G35
Fees: (September 04)
Day £989–£1049

KING EDWARD VI HIGH SCHOOL FOR GIRLS
Edgbaston Park Road,
Birmingham, West Midlands
B15 2UB
Tel: (0121) 472 1834
Fax: (0121) 471 3808
Email: admissions@kehs.co.uk
Head: Miss S H Evans
Type: Girls Day 11–18
No of pupils: 540
Fees: (September 04) Day £6990

KING EDWARD'S SCHOOL
Edgbaston Park Road,
Birmingham, West Midlands
B15 2UA
Tel: (0121) 472 1672
Fax: (0121) 415 4327
Email: office@kes.bham.sch.uk
Head: Mr J A Claughton
Type: Boys Day 11–18
No of pupils: 840
Fees: (September 05) Day £7749

MANDER PORTMAN WOODWARD
38 Highfield Road, Edgbaston,
Birmingham, West Midlands
B15 3ED
Tel: (0121) 454 9637
Fax: (0121) 454 6433
Email: enq@birmingham.mpw.co.uk
Head: Mrs D J Jewell
Type: Co-educational Day 14+
No of pupils: B50 G50
Fees: (September 05)
Day £2292–£12792

NORFOLK HOUSE SCHOOL
4 Norfolk Road, Edgbaston,
Birmingham, West Midlands
B15 3PS
Tel: (0121) 454 7021
Fax: (0121) 454 7021
Email: office@norfolkhouseschool.org.uk
Head: Mrs Helen Maresca
Type: Co-educational Day 3–11
No of pupils: B80 G78
Fees: (September 04)
Day £2487–£4311

PRIORY SCHOOL
39 Sir Harry's Road, Edgbaston,
Birmingham, West Midlands
B15 2UR
Tel: (0121) 440 0256
Fax: (0121) 440 3639
Email: enquiries@prioryschool.net
Head: Mrs E Brook
Type: Girls Day 1–18 (Co-ed 1–11)
No of pupils: B70 G230
Fees: (September 04)
Day £4500–£7605

RATHVILLY SCHOOL
119 Bunbury Road, Birmingham, West Midlands B31 2NB
Tel: (0121) 475 1509
Head: Mrs D P Edwards
Type: Co-educational Day 3–11
No of pupils: B55 G65
Fees: (September 04) Day £2055–£3720

ROSSLYN SCHOOL
1597 Stratford Road, Hall Green, Birmingham, West Midlands B28 9JB
Tel: (0121) 744 2743
Fax: (0121) 744 2743
Email: office@rosslynschool.co.uk
Head: Mrs P J Scott
Type: Co-educational Day 2–11
No of pupils: B49 G55
Fees: (September 04) Day £2580–£3255

ST GEORGE'S SCHOOL, EDGBASTON
31 Calthorpe Road, Birmingham, West Midlands B15 1RX
Tel: (0121) 625 0398
Fax: (0121) 625 3340
Email: admin@sgse.co.uk
Head: Miss H J Phillips
Type: Co-educational Day 3–18
No of pupils: B280 G140
Fees: (September 05) Day £3900–£7680

WEST HOUSE SCHOOL
24 St James's Road, Edgbaston, Birmingham, West Midlands B15 2NX
Tel: (0121) 440 4097
Fax: (0121) 440 5839
Email: secretary@westhouseschool.demon.co.uk
Head: Mr A Lyttle
Type: Boys Day 1–11 (Girls 1–4)
No of pupils: B185 G15
Fees: (September 05) Day £1689–£7668

WOODSTOCK GIRLS' SCHOOL
11–15 Woodstock Road, Moseley, Birmingham, West Midlands B13 9BB
Tel: (0121) 449 9640
Head: Mrs T Anees
Type: Girls Day 11–15
No of pupils: 120
Fees: (September 05) Day £540–£2430

COVENTRY

BABLAKE SCHOOL
Coundon Road, Coventry, West Midlands CV1 4AU
Tel: (024) 7627 1200
Fax: (024) 7627 1290
Email: hmsec@bablake.coventry.sch.uk
Head: Mr J Watson
Type: Co-educational Day 11–19
No of pupils: B450 G450
Fees: (September 05) Day £7035

CHESHUNT PRE-PREPARATORY SCHOOL
8 Park Road, Coventry, West Midlands CV1 2LH
Tel: (024) 7622 1677
Fax: (024) 7623 1630
Head: Mrs F Ward
Type: Co-educational Day 3–8
No of pupils: 100
Fees: (September 03) Day £1133–£1196

COVENTRY MUSLIM SCHOOL
643 Foleshill Road, Coventry, West Midlands CV6 5JQ
Tel: (024) 7626 1803
Fax: (024) 7626 1803
Email: admin@coventrymuslimschool.freeserve.co.uk
Head: Mrs M Ashique
Type: Girls Day 4–16
No of pupils: B8 G52

COVENTRY PREP SCHOOL
Kenilworth Road, Coventry, West Midlands CV3 6PT
Tel: (024) 7627 1307
Fax: (024) 7627 1308
Email: headmaster@coventryprep.co.uk
Head: Mr N Lovell
Type: Co-educational Day 3–13
No of pupils: B127 G76
Fees: (September 04) Day £4585–£7131

DAVENPORT LODGE SCHOOL
21 Davenport Road, Earlsdon, Coventry, West Midlands CV5 6QA
Tel: (024) 7667 5051
Email: principal@davenportlodge.coventry.sch.uk
Head: Mrs M D Martin
Type: Co-educational Day 2–8
Fees: (September 04) Day £1260–£4200

KING HENRY VIII SCHOOL
Warwick Road, Coventry, West Midlands CV3 6AQ
Tel: (024) 7672 1111
Fax: (024) 7672 1188
Email: info@khviii.com
Head: Mr G D Fisher
Type: Co-educational Day 7–18
No of pupils: B422 G434
Fees: (September 04) Day £6636

PATTISON COLLEGE
90 Binley Road, Coventry, West Midlands CV3 1FQ
Tel: (024) 7645 5031
Email: pattisonsinfo@btconnect.com
Head: Mrs E A P Connell and Mrs J A Satchell
Type: Co-educational Day 3–16
No of pupils: B38 G108
Fees: (September 03) Day £3630–£4620

SOLIHULL

EVERSFIELD PREPARATORY SCHOOL
Warwick Road, Solihull, West Midlands B91 1AT
Tel: (0121) 705 0354
Fax: (0121) 709 0168
Email: enquiries@eversfield.co.uk
Head: Mr K U Madden
Type: Co-educational Day 2–11
No of pupils: B191 G54
Fees: (September 04) Day £2010–£6609

KINGSWOOD SCHOOL
St James Place, Shirley, Solihull, West Midlands B90 2BA
Tel: (0121) 744 7883
Fax: (0121) 744 1282
Email: kingswoodhm@aol.com
Head: Mr P Callaghan
Type: Co-educational Day 2–11
No of pupils: B50 G30
Fees: (September 04) Day £308–£5101

RUCKLEIGH SCHOOL
17 Lode Lane, Solihull,
West Midlands B91 2AB
Tel: (0121) 705 2773
Fax: (0121) 704 4883
Email: admin@ruckleigh.co.uk
Head: Mrs B M Forster
Type: Co-educational Day 2–11
No of pupils: B122 G84
Fees: (September 04)
Day £1935–£5565

SAINT MARTIN'S SCHOOL
Malvern Hall, Brueton Avenue,
Solihull, West Midlands B91 3EN
Tel: (0121) 705 1265
Fax: (0121) 711 4529
Email: mail@saintmartins-school.com
Head: Mrs J Carwithen
Type: Girls Day 3–18
No of pupils: 520
Fees: (September 05)
Day £2970–£7875

SOLIHULL SCHOOL
Warwick Road, Solihull,
West Midlands B91 3DJ
Tel: (0121) 705 4273
Fax: (0121) 711 4439
Email: enquiries@solsch.org.uk
Head: Mr P J Griffiths
Type: Co-educational Day 7–18
No of pupils: B990 G162
Fees: (September 05)
Day £6150–£7905

SUTTON COLDFIELD

THE SHRUBBERY SCHOOL
Walmley Ash Road, Walmley,
Sutton Coldfield, West Midlands
B76 1HY
Tel: (0121) 351 1582
Fax: (0121) 351 1124
Head: Mrs H Cook
Type: Co-educational Day 3–11
No of pupils: B152 G118
Fees: (September 03)
Day £2067–£4329

WALSALL

HYDESVILLE TOWER SCHOOL*
25 Broadway North, Walsall,
West Midlands WS1 2QG
Tel: (01922) 624374
Fax: (01922) 746169
Email: info@hydesville.com
Head: Dr Leslie Fox
Type: Co-educational Day 3–16
No of pupils: B184 G167
Fees: (September 05)
Day £4452–£7767

MAYFIELD PREPARATORY SCHOOL
Sutton Road, Walsall,
West Midlands WS1 2PD
Tel: (01922) 624107
Fax: (01299) 746908
Email: info@mayfieldprep.co.uk
Head: Mrs C M Jones
Type: Co-educational Day 3–11
No of pupils: B110 G91
Fees: (September 03) Day £4950

WOLVERHAMPTON

BIRCHFIELD SCHOOL
Albrighton, Wolverhampton,
West Midlands WV7 3AF
Tel: (01902) 372534
Fax: (01902) 373516
Email: office@birchfieldschool.co.uk
Head: Mr R P Merriman
Type: Boys Boarding and Day 4–13 Flexi-boarding available
No of pupils: 156
No of boarders: W19
Fees: (September 05) WB £12420
Day £5775–£9240

THE DRIVE PREPARATORY SCHOOL
Wood Road, Tettenhall,
Wolverhampton, West Midlands
WV6 8RX
Tel: (01902) 751125
Fax: (01902) 741940
Head: Mr P Cochrane
Type: Co-educational Day 2–7
No of pupils: 142

NEWBRIDGE PREPARATORY SCHOOL
51 Newbridge Crescent,
Tettenhall, Wolverhampton,
West Midlands WV6 0LH
Tel: (01902) 751088
Fax: (01902) 751333
Email: office@newbridge.wolverhampton.sch.uk
Head: Mrs B Pring
Type: Girls Day 3–11
No of pupils: 148
Fees: (September 03)
Day £3327–£5067

THE ROYAL WOLVERHAMPTON JUNIOR SCHOOL
Penn Road, Wolverhampton,
West Midlands WV3 0EF
Tel: (01902) 349100
Fax: (01902) 344496
Head: Mrs M Saunders
Type: Co-educational Day and Boarding 2–11
No of pupils: B92 G87
No of boarders: F4
Fees: (September 05) FB £17220
Day £5115–£7485

THE ROYAL WOLVERHAMPTON SCHOOL
Penn Road, Wolverhampton,
West Midlands WV3 0EG
Tel: (01902) 341230
Fax: (01902) 349119
Email: mo@royal.wolverhampton.sch.uk
Head: Mr T L Waters
Type: Co-educational Boarding and Day 2–18 Flexi-boarding available
No of pupils: B262 G211
No of boarders: F134 W10
Fees: (September 05)
FB £17220–£19800
WB £17040–£17220
Day £5115–£9945

TETTENHALL COLLEGE†
Wood Road, Tettenhall, Wolverhampton, West Midlands WV6 8QX
Tel: (01902) 751119
Fax: (01902) 741940
Email: head@tettcoll.wolverhants.sch.uk
Head: Dr P C Bodkin
Type: Co-educational Boarding and Day 2–18 Flexi-boarding available
No of pupils: B293 G195
No of boarders: F56 W25
Fees: (September 05)
FB £13728–£16722
WB £11139–£13914
Day £4656–£9621

WOLVERHAMPTON GRAMMAR SCHOOL
Compton Road, Wolverhampton, West Midlands WV3 9RB
Tel: (01902) 421326
Fax: (01902) 421819
Email: wgs@wgs.org.uk
Head: Dr B Trafford
Type: Co-educational Day 10–18
No of pupils: B395 G272
Fees: (September 05) Day £8682

WILTSHIRE

CALNE

ST MARGARET'S PREPARATORY SCHOOL
Curzon Street, Calne, Wiltshire SN11 0DF
Tel: (01249) 857220
Fax: (01249) 857227
Email: admin@stmargaretsprep.org.uk
Head: Mrs K E Cordon
Type: Co-educational Day 3–11
No of pupils: B70 G105
Fees: (September 05)
Day £2850–£6870

ST MARY'S SCHOOL
Calne, Wiltshire SN11 0DF
Tel: (01249) 857200
Fax: (01249) 857207
Email: admissions@stmaryscalne.org
Head: Dr H M Wright
Type: Girls Boarding and Day 11–18
No of pupils: 300
No of boarders: F250
Fees: (September 04) FB £21300
Day £14400

CHIPPENHAM

GRITTLETON HOUSE SCHOOL*
Grittleton, Chippenham, Wiltshire SN14 6AP
Tel: (01249) 782434
Fax: (01249) 782669
Email: secretary@grittletonhouseschool.org
Head: Mrs C Whitney
Type: Co-educational Day 2–16
No of pupils: B154 G137
Fees: (September 05)
Day £4620–£7455

CORSHAM

HEYWOOD PREPARATORY SCHOOL
The Priory, Priory Street, Corsham, Wiltshire SN13 0AP
Tel: (01249) 713379
Fax: (01249) 701757
Email: principal@heywood.wilts.sch.uk
Head: Mrs P Hall and Mr M Hall
Type: Co-educational Day 3–11
No of pupils: B103 G75
Fees: (September 05)
Day £4335–£4995

CRICKLADE

MEADOWPARK NURSERY & PRE-PREP SCHOOL
Calcutt Street, Cricklade, Wiltshire SN6 6BA
Tel: (01793) 752600
Fax: (01793) 752600
Email: mpschoffice@aol.com
Head: Mrs R Kular
Type: Co-educational Day 0–7
No of pupils: B122 G105
Fees: (September 04)
Day £660–£4950

PRIOR PARK PREPARATORY SCHOOL†
Calcutt Street, Cricklade, Wiltshire SN6 6BB
Tel: (01793) 750275
Fax: (01793) 750910
Email: officepriorparkprep@priorpark.co.uk
Head: Mr G B Hobern
Type: Co-educational Boarding and Day 7–13 Flexi-boarding available
No of pupils: B112 G70
No of boarders: F26 W23
Fees: (September 05)
F/WB £ £11901–£12714
Day £8190–£9150

England

DEVIZES

DAUNTSEY'S SCHOOL*
High Street, West Lavington, Devizes, Wiltshire SN10 4HE
Tel: (01380) 814500
Fax: (01380) 814501
Email: information@dauntseys.wilts.sch.uk
Head: Mr S B Roberts
Type: Co-educational Boarding and Day 11–18
No of pupils: B396 G351
No of boarders: F275
Fees: (September 05) FB £20160 Day £11940

THE MILL SCHOOL
Whistley Road, Potterne, Devizes, Wiltshire SN10 5TE
Tel: (01380) 723011
Fax: (01380) 736530
Email: office@mill.wilts.sch.uk
Head: Mrs L Gill
Type: Co-educational Day 4–11
No of pupils: B37 G47
Fees: (September 05)
Day £4440–£5520

MARLBOROUGH

MARLBOROUGH COLLEGE
Marlborough, Wiltshire SN8 1PA
Tel: (01672) 892300
Fax: (01672) 892307
Email: admissions@marlboroughcollege.org
Head: Mr N A Sampson
Type: Co-educational Boarding 13–18
No of pupils: B554 G318
No of boarders: F872
Fees: (September 05) FB £23160 Day £17370

ST ANDREW SCHOOL
Ogbourne St Andrew, Marlborough, Wiltshire SN8 1SB
Tel: (01672) 841291
Head: Miss S Platt
Type: Co-educational Day 3–11
No of pupils: B18 G23
Fees: (September 02)
Day £1920–£3600

STEPPING STONES NURSERY AND PRE-PREPARATORY SCHOOL
Oakhill Farm, Froxfield, Marlborough, Wiltshire SN8 3JT
Tel: (01488) 681067
Fax: (01488) 681067
Head: Miss S Corfield and Miss A Harron
Type: Co-educational Day 2–8
No of pupils: B89 G80
Fees: (September 03)
Day £1330–£3390

MELKSHAM

STONAR SCHOOL*
Cottles Park, Atworth, Melksham, Wiltshire SN12 8NT
Tel: (01225) 701740
Fax: (01225) 790830
Email: admissions@stonarschool.com
Head: Mrs S Shayler
Type: Girls Boarding and Day 2–18 Flexi-boarding available
No of pupils: B17 G401
No of boarders: F190 W80
Fees: (September 05)
F/WB £ £14250–£16650
Day £4800–£9375

PEWSEY

ST FRANCIS SCHOOL
Marlborough Road, Pewsey, Wiltshire SN9 5NT
Tel: (01672) 563228
Fax: (01672) 564323
Email: admissions@st-francis.wilts.sch.uk
Head: Mr P W Blundell
Type: Co-educational Day 2–13
No of pupils: B156 G140
Fees: (September 05)
Day £540–£8025

SALISBURY

APPLEFORD SCHOOL†
Shrewton, Salisbury, Wiltshire SP3 4HL
Tel: (01980) 621020
Fax: (01980) 621366
Email: secretary@appleford.wilts.sch.uk
Head: The Revd B Clarke
Type: Co-educational Boarding and Day 7–13
No of pupils: B66 G17
No of boarders: F14 W40

AVONDALE SCHOOL
High Street, Bulford, Salisbury, Wiltshire SP4 9DR
Tel: (01980) 632387
Email: avondale.school@tiscali.co.uk
Head: Mr R McNeall and Mrs S McNeall
Type: Co-educational Day 3–11
No of pupils: B50 G50
Fees: (September 05)
Day £2610–£4410

CHAFYN GROVE SCHOOL
Bourne Avenue, Salisbury, Wiltshire SP1 1LR
Tel: (01722) 333423
Fax: (01722) 323114
Email: info@chafyngrove.co.uk
Head: Mr E J Newton
Type: Co-educational Boarding and Day 3–13 Flexi-boarding available
No of pupils: B204 G76
No of boarders: F44
Fees: (September 05)
FB £12435–£15345
Day £5565–£11460

GODOLPHIN PREPARATORY SCHOOL
Laverstock Road, Salisbury, Wiltshire SP1 2RB
Tel: (01722) 430652
Fax: (01722) 430651
Email: prep@godolphin.wilts.sch.uk
Head: Mrs P White
Type: Girls Day 3–11
Fees: (September 05)
Day £4389–£8622

THE GODOLPHIN SCHOOL
Milford Hill, Salisbury, Wiltshire SP1 2RA
Tel: (01722) 430500
Fax: (01722) 430501
Email: admissions@godolphin.wilts.sch.uk
Head: Miss M J Horsburgh
Type: Girls Boarding and Day 11–18 Flexi-boarding available
No of pupils: 410
No of boarders: F186
Fees: (September 05) FB £19800 Day £12885

LA RETRAITE SWAN
Campbell Road, Salisbury, Wiltshire SP1 3BQ
Tel: (01722) 333094
Fax: (01722) 330868
Email: admissions@laraswan.co.uk
Head: Mrs R A Simmons
Type: Co-educational Day 2–16
No of pupils: B178 G165
Fees: (September 05)
Day £5145–£8745

LEADEN HALL
70 The Close, Salisbury, Wiltshire SP1 2EP
Tel: (01722) 439269
Fax: (01722) 410575
Email: admin@leaden-hall.com
Head: Mrs D Watkins
Type: Girls Day and Boarding 3–11 (Boys 3–4) Flexi-boarding available
No of pupils: B2 G237
No of boarders: F29
Fees: (September 05) FB £12522
Day £3435–£8850

NORMAN COURT PREPARATORY SCHOOL
West Tytherley, Salisbury, Wiltshire SP5 1NH
Tel: (01980) 862345
Fax: (01980) 862082
Email: office@normancourt.co.uk
Head: Mr K N Foyle
Type: Co-educational Boarding and Day 3–13 Flexi-boarding available
No of pupils: B197 G110
No of boarders: F22 W46
Fees: (September 05)
F/WB £ £15450
Day £5760–£11445

SALISBURY CATHEDRAL SCHOOL
1 The Close, Salisbury, Wiltshire SP1 2EQ
Tel: (01722) 555300
Fax: (01722) 410910
Email: admissions@salisburycathedralschool.com
Head: Mr R M Thackray
Type: Co-educational Day and Boarding 3–13 Flexi-boarding available
No of pupils: B126 G86
No of boarders: F43
Fees: (September 05) FB £15180
Day £3420–£10380

SANDROYD SCHOOL
Rushmore, Tollard Royal, Salisbury, Wiltshire SP5 5QD
Tel: (01725) 516264
Fax: (01725) 516441
Email: enquiries@sandroyd.com
Head: Mr Martin Harris
Type: Co-educational Boarding and Day Boys 7–13 Girls 7–10 Flexi-boarding available
No of pupils: B151 G12
No of boarders: F71
Fees: (September 04)
FB £12450–£15450
Day £9450–£12900

SOUTH HILLS SCHOOL
Home Farm Road, Wilton, Salisbury, Wiltshire SP2 8PJ
Tel: (01722) 744971
Fax: (01722) 744971
Email: southhillsschool@btinternet.com
Head: Mrs A Proctor
Type: Co-educational Day 0–7
No of pupils: B80 G80
Fees: (September 04)
Day £778–£3402

SHRIVENHAM

PINEWOOD SCHOOL*
Bourton, Shrivenham, Wiltshire SN6 8HZ
Tel: (01793) 782205
Fax: (01793) 783476
Email: office@pinewoodschool.co.uk
Head: Mr P J Hoyland
Type: Co-educational Boarding and Day 3–13 Flexi-boarding available
No of pupils: B147 G149
No of boarders: W30
Fees: (September 05) FB £14310
WB £13800 Day £5775–£11070

SWINDON

MARANATHA CHRISTIAN SCHOOL
Queenlaines Farm, Sevenhampton, Swindon, Wiltshire SN6 7SQ
Tel: (01793) 762075
Fax: (01793) 783783
Head: Mr P Medlock
Type: Co-educational Day 3–18
No of pupils: B20 G20
Fees: (September 03)
Day £850–£2145

TROWBRIDGE

ROUNDSTONE PREPARATORY SCHOOL
Courtfield House, Polebarn Road, Trowbridge, Wiltshire BA14 7EG
Tel: (01225) 752847
Head: Mrs M E Pearce
Type: Co-educational Day 4–11
No of pupils: B54 G50
Fees: (September 04)
Day £2775–£3075

WARMINSTER

STOURBRIDGE HOUSE SCHOOL
Castle Street, Mere, Warminster, Wiltshire BA12 6JQ
Tel: (01747) 860165
Fax: (01747) 861945
Email: office@stourbridgehouse.wilts.sch.uk
Head: Mrs E Coward
Type: Co-educational Day 2–9
No of pupils: B33 G38
Fees: (September 05)
Day £4080–£4290

WARMINSTER SCHOOL
Church Street, Warminster, Wiltshire BA12 8PJ
Tel: (01985) 210100
Fax: (01985) 214129
Email: admin@warminsterschool.org.uk
Head: Mr D Dowdles
Type: Co-educational Boarding and Day 3–18 Flexi-boarding available
No of pupils: B400 G250
No of boarders: F234
Fees: (September 05)
FB £13635–£16800
Day £5100–£9660

WORCESTERSHIRE

BEWDLEY

MOFFATS SCHOOL*
Kinlet Hall, Kinlet, Bewdley, Worcestershire DY12 3AY
Tel: (01299) 841230
Fax: (01299) 841444
Email: office@moffats.co.uk
Head: Mr M H Daborn
Type: Co-educational Boarding and Day 4–13 Flexi-boarding available
No of pupils: B46 G39
No of boarders: F43
Fees: (September 05)
F/WB £ £11385 Day £988–£2382

BROMSGROVE

BROMSGROVE PRE-PREPARATORY AND NURSERY SCHOOL
Avoncroft House, Hanbury Road, Bromsgrove, Worcestershire B60 4JS
Tel: (01527) 873007
Fax: (01527) 873007
Email: preprep@bromsgrove-school.co.uk
Head: Mrs S Pickering
Type: Co-educational Day 2–7
No of pupils: B100 G79

BROMSGROVE PREPARATORY SCHOOL
Old Station Road , Bromsgrove, Worcestershire B60 2BU
Tel: (01527) 579600
Fax: (01527) 579571
Email: admissions@bromsgrove-school.co.uk
Head: Mr Peter Lee-Smith
Type: Co-educational Boarding and Day 7–13 Flexi-boarding available
No of pupils: B203 G161
No of boarders: F52
Fees: (September 05)
FB £13695–£17025
Day £7305–£9585

BROMSGROVE SCHOOL*
Worcester Road, Bromsgrove, Worcestershire B61 7DU
Tel: (01527) 579679
Fax: (01527) 576177
Email: admissions@bromsgrove-school.co.uk
Head: Mr C Edwards
Type: Co-educational Boarding and Day 13–18
No of pupils: B451 G290
No of boarders: F367
Fees: (September 05) FB £18990
Day £10560

DROITWICH

WHITFORD HALL & DODDERHILL SCHOOL
Crutch Lane, Droitwich, Worcestershire WR9 0BE
Tel: (01905) 778290
Fax: (01905) 790623
Email: admin@whitford-dodderhill.worcs.sch.uk
Head: Mrs J Mumby
Type: Girls Day 3–16 (Boys 3–9)
No of pupils: B20 G200
Fees: (September 03)
Day £4290–£7260

EVESHAM

GREEN HILL SCHOOL
Evesham, Worcestershire WR11 4NG
Tel: (01386) 442364
Fax: (01386) 442364
Email: oliverlister@greenhillschool.co.uk
Head: Mr O Lister
Type: Co-educational Day 3–13
No of pupils: B55 G50
Fees: (September 04)
Day £4050–£5310

KIDDERMINSTER

HARTLEBURY SCHOOL
Hartlebury, Kidderminster, Worcestershire DY11 7TE
Tel: (01299) 250258
Fax: (01299) 250379
Email: enquiries@hartleburyschool.com
Head: Miss C Coles
Type: Co-educational Day 4–16
No of pupils: B72 G38
Fees: (September 03)
Day £3000–£7650

HEATHFIELD SCHOOL
Wolverley, Kidderminster, Worcestershire DY10 3QE
Tel: (01562) 850204
Fax: (01562) 852609
Head: Mr Ian Wilson
Type: Co-educational Day 3–16
No of pupils: B156 G106
Fees: (September 04)
Day £1188–£7420

HOLY TRINITY SCHOOL
Birmingham Road, Kidderminster, Worcestershire DY10 2BY
Tel: (01562) 822929
Fax: (01562) 865137
Email: office@holytrinity.co.uk
Head: Mrs Y L Wilkinson
Type: Co-educational Day Boys 0–11 Girls 0–18
No of pupils: B38 G312
Fees: (September 05)
Day £3975–£7785

WINTERFOLD HOUSE
Chaddesley Corbett, Kidderminster, Worcestershire DY10 4PW
Tel: (01562) 777234
Fax: (01562) 777078
Email: head@winterfoldhouse.co.uk
Head: Mr W C R Ibbetson-Price
Type: Co-educational Day 3–13
No of pupils: B220 G116
Fees: (September 05)
Day £4350–£8775

MALVERN

THE DOWNS SCHOOL
Colwall, Malvern, Worcestershire WR13 6EY
Tel: (01684) 540277
Fax: (01684) 540094
Email: downshm@aol.com
Head: Mr A Ramsay
Type: Co-educational Boarding and Day 3–13 Flexi-boarding available
No of pupils: B70 G70
No of boarders: F20 W30
Fees: (September 05) FB £14400 Day £4400–£9600

THE ELMS
Colwall, Malvern, Worcestershire WR13 6EF
Tel: (01684) 540344
Fax: (01684) 571174
Email: office@elmsschool.co.uk
Head: Mr L A C Ashby
Type: Co-educational Boarding and Day 3–13 Flexi-boarding available
No of pupils: B111 G81
No of boarders: F86
Fees: (September 05) FB £16200 Day £5550–£14850

MALVERN COLLEGE PREPARATORY AND PRE-PREP SCHOOL†
Abbey Road, Malvern, Worcestershire WR14 3HF
Tel: (01684) 581600
Fax: (01684) 581601
Email: prep@malcol.org.uk
Head: Mr P H Moody
Type: Co-educational Boarding and Day 2–13 Flexi-boarding available
No of pupils: B97 G91
No of boarders: F50
Fees: (September 05) FB £9111–£14565 Day £4374–£11004

MADRESFIELD EARLY YEARS CENTRE
Hayswood Farm, Madresfield, Malvern, Worcestershire WR13 5AA
Tel: (01684) 574378
Fax: (01684) 567772
Email: meyc1to8yrs@aol.com
Head: Mrs B J Bennett
Type: Co-educational Day 1–8
No of pupils: B117 G102
Fees: (September 05) Day £4370–£4864

MALVERN COLLEGE*
College Road, Malvern, Worcestershire WR14 3DF
Tel: (01684) 581500
Fax: (01684) 581617
Email: srj@malcol.org
Head: Mr H C K Carson
Type: Co-educational Boarding and Day 13–18
No of pupils: B356 G213
No of boarders: F450
Fees: (September 05) FB £22056–£23532 Day £14619–£15072

MALVERN GIRLS' COLLEGE*
Avenue Road, Malvern, Worcestershire WR14 3BA
Tel: (01684) 892288
Fax: (01684) 566204
Email: registrar@mgc.worcs.sch.uk
Head: Mrs P M C Leggate
Type: Girls Boarding and Day 11–18
No of pupils: 330
No of boarders: F270
Fees: (September 05) FB £20340 WB £18300 Day £9900

ST JAMES'S SCHOOL†
West Malvern, Malvern, Worcestershire WR14 4DF
Tel: (01684) 560851
Fax: (01684) 569252
Email: admissions@st-james-school.fsnet.co.uk
Head: Mrs R Hayes
Type: Girls Day and Boarding 7–18 Flexi-boarding available
No of pupils: 150
No of boarders: F35 W12
Fees: (September 05) FB £19740–£20880 WB £19740 Day £5868–£11985

MALVERN WELLS

THE ABBEY COLLEGE
253 Wells Road, Malvern Wells, Worcestershire WR14 4JF
Tel: (01684) 892300
Fax: (01684) 892757
Email: enquiries@abbeycollege.co.uk
Head: Mr P Moere
Type: Co-educational Boarding and Day 13+ Flexi-boarding available
No of pupils: B70 G50
No of boarders: F116 W4
Fees: (September 05) FB £15950 WB £11771 Day £7975

PERSHORE

BOWBROOK HOUSE SCHOOL
Peopleton, Pershore, Worcestershire WR10 2EE
Tel: (01905) 841242
Fax: (01905) 840716
Email: bowbrookhouse@school73.freeserve.co.uk
Head: Mr C D Allen
Type: Co-educational Day 3–16
No of pupils: B118 G53
Fees: (September 05) Day £3480–£6450

TENBURY WELLS

SAINT MICHAEL'S COLLEGE
Oldwood Road, St Michaels, Tenbury Wells, Worcestershire WR15 8PH
Tel: (01584) 811300
Fax: (01584) 811221
Email: info@st-michaels.uk.com
Head: Mr S Higgins
Type: Co-educational Day and Boarding 14–19
No of pupils: B85 G75
No of boarders: F95
Fees: (September 05) FB £14500–£15700

WORCESTER

ABBERLEY HALL
Worcester, Worcestershire WR6 6DD
Tel: (01299) 896275
Fax: (01299) 896875
Email: john.walker@abberleyhall.co.uk
Head: Mr J G W Walker
Type: Co-educational Boarding and Day 2–13 Flexi-boarding available
No of pupils: B179 G93
No of boarders: F111
Fees: (September 04) FB £14130 Day £11325

THE ALICE OTTLEY SCHOOL
Britannia House, Upper Tything, Worcester, Worcestershire WR1 1HW
Tel: (01905) 27061
Fax: (01905) 724626
Email: enquiries@thealiceottleyschool.co.uk
Head: Mrs M E Chapman
Type: Girls Day 3–19
No of pupils: 543
Fees: (September 05) Day £4398–£8685

KING'S HAWFORD
Worcester, Worcestershire WR3 7SE
Tel: (01905) 451292
Fax: (01905) 756502
Email: office@Kingshawford.org.uk
Head: Mr R Middleton
Type: Co-educational Day 2–11
No of pupils: B168 G118
Fees: (September 03) Day £4470–£7959

THE KING'S SCHOOL
Worcester, Worcestershire WR1 2LL
Tel: (01905) 721700
Fax: (01905) 721710
Email: info@ksw.org.uk
Head: Mr T H Keyes
Type: Co-educational Day 7–18
No of pupils: B552 G438
Fees: (September 03) Day £5349–£8304

RGS THE GRANGE
Grange Lane, Claines, Worcester, Worcestershire WR3 7RR
Tel: (01905) 451205
Fax: (01905) 757917
Email: grange@rgsw.org.uk
Head: Mr R E Hunt
Type: Co-educational Day 2–11
No of pupils: B265 G105
Fees: (September 05) Day £1410–£6850

RIVER SCHOOL
Oakfield House, Droitwich Road, Worcester, Worcestershire WR3 7ST
Tel: (01905) 457047
Fax: (01905) 754492
Head: Mr G Coyle
Type: Co-educational Day 5–16
No of pupils: B67 G82
Fees: (September 04) Day £3084

ROYAL GRAMMAR SCHOOL WORCESTER
Upper Tything, Worcester, Worcestershire WR1 1HP
Tel: (01905) 613391
Fax: (01905) 726892
Email: office@rgsw.org.uk
Head: Mr A R Rattue
Type: Co-educational Day 11–18
No of pupils: B604 G88
Fees: (September 05) Day £7992

ST MARY'S CONVENT SCHOOL
Mount Battenhall, Worcester, Worcestershire WR5 2HP
Tel: (01905) 357786
Fax: (01905) 351718
Email: head@stmarys.org.uk
Head: Mrs S K Cookson
Type: Girls Day 2–18 (Boys 2–8)
No of pupils: B5 G304
Fees: (September 04) Day £4215–£7410

SUNNYSIDE SCHOOL
Barbourne Terrace, Worcester, Worcestershire WR1 3JR
Tel: (01905) 23973
Email: info@sunnysideschool.co.uk
Head: Mrs P A Lewis
Type: Co-educational Day 1–9
No of pupils: B70 G70
Fees: (September 05) Day £3960–£4335

EAST RIDING OF YORKSHIRE

ANLABY

HULL HIGH SCHOOL
Tranby Croft, Anlaby, East Riding of Yorkshire HU10 7EH
Tel: (01482) 657016
Fax: (01482) 655389
Email: jean.phillips@church-schools.com
Head: Mrs A V Wood
Type: Girls Day 3–18 (Boys 3–11)
No of pupils: B142 G339
Fees: (September 04) Day £4290–£6720

DRIFIELD

ST FRANCIS PREPARATORY SCHOOL
25 High Street, Nafferton, Drifield, East Riding of Yorkshire YO25 0HR
Tel: (01377) 254628
Head: Mr A J Phillips
Type: Co-educational Day 3–16
No of pupils: B50 G40
Fees: (September 02) Day £415–£1300

HESSLE

HESSLE MOUNT SCHOOL
Jenny Brough Lane, Hessle, East Riding of Yorkshire HU13 0JX
Tel: (01482) 643371/641948
Fax: (01482) 643371
Email: info@hesslemountschool.org.uk
Head: Mrs Cutting
Type: Co-educational Day 3–8
No of pupils: 160
Fees: (September 03) Day £3180–£3390

HULL

FROEBEL HOUSE SCHOOL
5 Marlborough Avenue, Princes Avenue, Hull, East Riding of Yorkshire HU5 3JP
Tel: (01482) 342272
Fax: (01482) 342272
Email: froebel@froebel.karoo.co.uk
Head: Mrs L A Roberts
Type: Co-educational Day 4–11
No of pupils: B56 G51
Fees: (September 04) Day £2829

HYMERS COLLEGE
Hymers Avenue, Hull, East Riding of Yorkshire HU3 1LW
Tel: (01482) 343555
Fax: (01482) 472854
Email: enquiries@hymers.hull.sch.uk
Head: Mr J C Morris
Type: Co-educational Day 8–18
No of pupils: B539 G440
Fees: (September 05) Day £6705

KINGSTON-UPON-HULL

HULL GRAMMAR SCHOOL
Cottingham Road, Kingston-Upon-Hull, East Riding of Yorkshire HU5 2DL
Tel: (01482) 440144
Fax: (01482) 441312
Email: hgs@church-schools.com
Head: Mr R Haworth
Type: Co-educational Day 11–18 Flexi-boarding available
No of pupils: B196 G114
Fees: (September 04) Day £6525–£6720

POCKLINGTON

POCKLINGTON MONTESSORI SCHOOL
Bielby Lane, Pocklington, East Riding of Yorkshire YO42 1NT
Tel: (01759) 305436
Fax: (01759) 321421
Email: info@montessoriandmore.co.uk
Head: Ms R Pressland
Type: Co-educational Day 0–7
No of pupils: B162 G138
Fees: (September 02) Day £1372–£1445

POCKLINGTON SCHOOL
West Green, Pocklington, East Riding of Yorkshire YO42 2NJ
Tel: (01759) 321200
Fax: (01759) 306366
Email: enquiry@www.pocklingtonschool.com
Head: Mr N Clements
Type: Co-educational Boarding and Day 7–18 Flexi-boarding available
No of pupils: B453 G352
No of boarders: F122 W20
Fees: (September 05)
FB £13995–£16332
WB £13125–£15549
Day £6192–£9213

NORTH YORKSHIRE

BEDALE

AYSGARTH PREPARATORY SCHOOL
Bedale, North Yorkshire DL8 1TF
Tel: (01677) 450240
Fax: (01677) 450736
Email: enquiry@aysgarthschool.co.uk
Head: Mr C A A Goddard
Type: Boys Boarding 3–13 (Co-ed day 3–8) Flexi-boarding available
No of pupils: B148 G19
No of boarders: F67 W20
Fees: (September 04)
F/WB £ £14325
Day £1160–£11325

HARROGATE

ASHVILLE COLLEGE
Green Lane, Harrogate, North Yorkshire HG2 9JP
Tel: (01423) 566358
Fax: (01423) 505142
Email: ashville@ashville.co.uk
Head: Mr A Fleck
Type: Co-educational Day and Boarding 4–18 Flexi-boarding available
No of pupils: B500 G330
No of boarders: F133 W7
Fees: (September 05)
FB £15195–£17340
WB £14430–£15795
Day £5085–£8835

BELMONT GROSVENOR SCHOOL
Swarcliffe Hall, Birstwith, Harrogate, North Yorkshire HG3 2JG
Tel: (01423) 771029
Fax: (01423) 772600
Email: belmontgrosvenor@pobox.com
Head: Miss J Merriman
Type: Co-educational Day 2–13
No of pupils: B183 G162
Fees: (September 03)
Day £1296–£6360

BRACKENFIELD SCHOOL
128 Duchy Road, Harrogate,
North Yorkshire HG1 2HE
Tel: (01423) 508558
Fax: (01423) 524841
Email: admin@brackenfield.n-yorks.sch.uk
Head: Mrs J Skillington
Type: Co-educational Day 2–11
No of pupils: B81 G80
Fees: (September 05)
Day £2175–£5625

HARROGATE LADIES' COLLEGE
Clarence Drive, Harrogate,
North Yorkshire HG1 2QG
Tel: (01423) 504543
Fax: (01423) 568893
Email: enquire@hlc.org.uk
Head: Dr M J Hustler
Type: Girls Boarding and Day 10–18 Flexi-boarding available
No of pupils: 320
No of boarders: F160 W15
Fees: (September 05)
F/WB £ £17700 Day £10500

HARROGATE TUTORIAL COLLEGE
2 The Oval, Harrogate,
North Yorkshire HG2 9BA
Tel: (01423) 501041
Fax: (01423) 531110
Email: study@htcuk.org
Head: Mr K W Pollard
Type: Co-educational Day and Boarding 15–20 Flexi-boarding available
No of pupils: B36 G34
No of boarders: F20 W20
Fees: (September 05)
FB £12950–£14450
WB £11750–£13250
Day £3500–£11850

HIGHFIELD PREPARATORY SCHOOL
Clarence Drive, Harrogate,
North Yorkshire HG1 2QG
Tel: (01423) 504543
Fax: (01423) 568893
Email: enquire@hlc.org.uk
Head: Mrs C Cameron
Type: Co-educational Day and Boarding 4–11 Flexi-boarding available
No of pupils: B61 G136
Fees: (September 05)
Day £5625–£6105

MALTON

WOODLEIGH SCHOOL†
Langton, Malton, North Yorkshire
YO17 9QN
Tel: (01653) 658215
Fax: (01653) 658423
Head: Mr D M England
Type: Co-educational Boarding and Day 3–13 Flexi-boarding available
No of pupils: B69 G49
No of boarders: F10 W25
Fees: (September 03)
F/WB £ £7494–£9024
Day £2931–£6894

RIPON

RIPON CATHEDRAL CHOIR SCHOOL
Whitcliffe Lane, Ripon,
North Yorkshire HG4 2LA
Tel: (01765) 602134
Fax: (01765) 608760
Email: admin@choirschool.demon.co.uk
Head: Mr C R E Pepys
Type: Co-educational Boarding and Day 3–13
No of pupils: B62 G46
No of boarders: F19 W4
Fees: (September 05) FB £11880
WB £10965 Day £2220–£8760

SCARBOROUGH

BRAMCOTE SCHOOL
Filey Road, Scarborough,
North Yorkshire YO11 2TT
Tel: (01723) 373086
Fax: (01723) 364186
Email: office@bramcoteschool.com
Head: Mr A G W Lewin
Type: Co-educational Boarding and Day 7–13 Flexi-boarding available
No of pupils: B53 G50
No of boarders: F54 W33
Fees: (September 05) FB £14310
Day £9375–£10275

LISVANE, SCARBOROUGH COLLEGE JUNIOR SCHOOL
Filey Road, Scarborough,
North Yorkshire YO11 3BA
Tel: (01723) 380606
Fax: (01723) 380607
Email: lisvane@scarboroughcoll.co.uk
Head: Mr G S Twist
Type: Co-educational Day and Boarding 3–11 Flexi-boarding available
No of pupils: B66 G69
Fees: (September 05)
F/WB £ £12411 Day £5400–£6939

SCARBOROUGH COLLEGE & LISVANE SCHOOL
Filey Road, Scarborough,
North Yorkshire YO11 3BA
Tel: (01723) 360620
Fax: (01723) 377265
Email: admin@scarboroughcollege.co.uk
Head: Mr T L Kirkup
Type: Co-educational Boarding and Day 3–18 Flexi-boarding available
No of pupils: B289 G228
No of boarders: F41 W20
Fees: (September 05)
F/WB £ £12411 Day £5400–£8136

SELBY

READ SCHOOL
Drax, Selby, North Yorkshire
YO8 8NL
Tel: (01757) 618248
Fax: (01757) 617432
Email: richard.hadfield@virgin.net
Head: Mr R A Hadfield
Type: Co-educational Day and Boarding 4–18 Flexi-boarding available
No of pupils: B198 G135
No of boarders: F70 W2
Fees: (September 05)
FB £12600–£14490
WB £11814–£13590
Day £4710–£6696

SETTLE

CATTERAL HALL SCHOOL
Giggleswick, Settle,
North Yorkshire BD24 0DG
Tel: (01729) 893100
Fax: (01729) 893158
Email: catteralhall@giggleswick.org.uk
Head: Mr R Hunter
Type: Co-educational Boarding and Day 7–13 Flexi-boarding available
No of pupils: B69 G43
No of boarders: F54
Fees: (September 05)
FB £12420–£14730
Day £10200–£11505

GIGGLESWICK SCHOOL
Giggleswick, Settle,
North Yorkshire BD24 0DE
Tel: (01729) 893000
Fax: (01729) 893150
Email: enquiries@giggleswick.org.uk
Head: Mr G P Boult
Type: Co-educational Boarding and Day 13–18
No of pupils: B199 G119
No of boarders: F203
Fees: (September 05) FB £20970
Day £14100

SKIPTON

MALSIS SCHOOL
Cross Hills, Skipton,
North Yorkshire BD20 8DT
Tel: (01535) 633027
Fax: (01535) 630571
Email: admin@malsis.com
Head: Mr C J Lush
Type: Co-educational Boarding and Day 3–13
No of pupils: B129 G57
No of boarders: F39
Fees: (September 05) FB £14100
Day £5760–£10800

THIRSK

QUEEN MARY'S SCHOOL
Baldersby Park, Topcliffe, Thirsk,
North Yorkshire YO7 3BZ
Tel: (01845) 575000
Fax: (01845) 575001
Email: admin@queenmarys.org
Head: Mr R A McKenzie Johnson
Type: Girls Boarding and Day 3–16 (Boys 3–7) Flexi-boarding available
No of pupils: B15 G230
No of boarders: F16 W45
Fees: (September 04)
F/WB £ £11925–£13680
Day £4350–£9720

WHITBY

BOTTON VILLAGE SCHOOL
Danby, Whitby, North Yorkshire
YO21 2NJ
Tel: (01287) 661206
Type: Co-educational Day 4–14
No of pupils: B53 G41

FYLING HALL SCHOOL
Robin Hood's Bay, Whitby,
North Yorkshire YO22 4QD
Tel: (01947) 880353
Fax: (01947) 881097
Email: office@fylinghall.org
Head: Dr G K Horridge
Type: Co-educational Boarding and Day 4–19
No of pupils: B98 G88
No of boarders: F101 W9
Fees: (September 05)
FB £10335–£13650
WB £9900–£10980
Day £4185–£5685

YORK

AMPLEFORTH COLLEGE
York, North Yorkshire YO62 4EY
Tel: (01439) 766000
Fax: (01439) 788330
Email: admissions@ampleforth.org.uk
Head: Rev C G E Everitt
Type: Co-educational Boarding and Day 13–18
No of pupils: B474 G87
No of boarders: F502
Fees: (September 05) FB £21450

BOOTHAM SCHOOL
Bootham, York, North Yorkshire
YO30 7BU
Tel: (01904) 623261
Fax: (01904) 652106
Email: enquiries@bootham.york.sch.uk
Head: Mr J Taylor
Type: Co-educational Boarding and Day 11–18 Flexi-boarding available
No of pupils: B270 G166
No of boarders: F80 W40
Fees: (September 04)
F/WB £ £11340–£17025
Day £10425–£10980

CLIFTON PREPARATORY SCHOOL
York, North Yorkshire YO30 6AB
Tel: (01904) 623716
Fax: (01904) 640974
Email: enquiries@cliftonprep.york.sch.uk
Head: Mrs P Arkley
Type: Co-educational Day 3–8
No of pupils: B102 G76
Fees: (September 04)
Day £4450–£5145

CUNDALL MANOR SCHOOL
Helperby, York, North Yorkshire
YO6 2RW
Tel: (01423) 360200
Fax: (01423) 360754
Email: headmaster@cundallmanor.co.uk
Head: Mr P Phillips
Type: Co-educational Boarding and Day 2–13
No of boarders: F30 W35
Fees: (September 05) FB £10500
Day £3489–£8997

EBOR PREPARATORY SCHOOL
Rawcliffe Lane, York,
North Yorkshire YO30 6NP
Tel: (01904) 655021
Fax: (01904) 651666
Email: office@eborschool.york.sch.uk
Head: Ms S Ratcliffe
Type: Co-educational Day 3–11
No of pupils: B70 G60
Fees: (September 03)
Day £1725–£4500

HOWSHAM HALL
York, North Yorkshire YO60 7PJ
Tel: (01653) 618374
Fax: (01653) 618295
Email: howsham@simonknock.freeserve.co.uk
Head: Mr S J Knock
Type: Co-educational Boarding and Day 5–14 Flexi-boarding available
No of pupils: B60 G15
No of boarders: F40
Fees: (September 04) FB £8100 Day £3300–£5700

THE MINSTER SCHOOL
Deangate, York, North Yorkshire YO1 7JA
Tel: (01904) 557230
Fax: (01904) 557232
Email: school@yorkminster.org
Head: Mr R Moore
Type: Co-educational Day 3–13
No of pupils: B100 G80
Fees: (September 04) Day £3780–£5820

TREGELLES
The Mount Junior School, Dalton Terrace, York, North Yorkshire YO24 4DD
Tel: (01904) 667513
Fax: (01904) 667524
Email: registrar@mount.n-yorks.sch.uk
Head: Mr M Andrews
Type: Co-educational Day 3–11
No of pupils: B59 G135
Fees: (September 03) Day £4560–£6075

THE MOUNT SCHOOL
Dalton Terrace, York, North Yorkshire YO24 4DD
Tel: (01904) 667500
Fax: (01904) 667524
Email: registrar@mount.n-yorks.sch.uk
Head: Mrs D J Gant
Type: Girls Boarding and Day 11–18 Flexi-boarding available
No of pupils: 374
No of boarders: F72 W30
Fees: (September 04) F/WB £ £16605 Day £10695

QUEEN ETHELBURGA'S COLLEGE*
Thorpe Underwood Hall, Ouseburn, York, North Yorkshire YO26 9SS
Tel: (0870) 742 3300
Fax: (0870) 742 3310
Email: remember@compuserve.com
Head: Mr P Dass
Type: Co-educational Boarding and Day 2–20
No of pupils: B150 G260
No of boarders: F270 W30
Fees: (September 04) FB £14955–£23100 Day £3225–£7110

QUEEN MARGARET'S SCHOOL
Escrick Park, York, North Yorkshire YO19 6EU
Tel: (01904) 728261
Fax: (01904) 728150
Email: enquiries@queenmargaretsschool.co.uk
Head: Dr G A H Chapman
Type: Girls Boarding and Day 11–18
No of pupils: 362
No of boarders: F249 W85
Fees: (September 05) F/WB £ £18675 Day £11835

ST MARTIN'S AMPLEFORTH
Gilling Castle, Gilling East, York, North Yorkshire YO62 4HP
Tel: (01439) 766600
Fax: (01439) 788538
Email: headmaster@stmartins.ampleforth.org.uk
Head: Mr N J Higham
Type: Co-educational Boarding and Day 3–13 Flexi-boarding available
No of pupils: B135 G55
No of boarders: F80
Fees: (September 05) FB £14655 Day £4335–£8055

ST PETER'S SCHOOL
York, North Yorkshire YO30 6AB
Tel: (01904) 527 300
Fax: (01904) 527 302
Email: enquiries@st-peters.york.sch.uk
Head: Mr R I Smyth
Type: Co-educational Boarding and Day 13–18
No of pupils: B318 G202
No of boarders: F142
Fees: (September 04) FB £16986–£17439 Day £9891–£10386

TERRINGTON HALL
Terrington, York, North Yorkshire YO60 6PR
Tel: (01653) 648227
Fax: (01653) 648458
Email: enquiries@terringtonhall.com
Head: Mr J Glen
Type: Co-educational Boarding and Day 3–13 Flexi-boarding available
No of pupils: B120 G88
No of boarders: F35 W5
Fees: (September 05) F/WB £ £13050 Day £4500–£8800

SOUTH YORKSHIRE

BARNSLEY

BARNSLEY CHRISTIAN SCHOOL

Hope House, Blucher Street,
Barnsley, South Yorkshire S70 1AP
Tel: (01226) 211011
Fax: (01226) 211011
Email: admin@barnsleyfellowship.fsnet.co.uk
Head: Mr G-J Barnes
Type: Co-educational Day 5–16
No of pupils: B49 G45
Fees: (September 05)
Day £2829–£3420

DONCASTER

HILL HOUSE ST MARY'S SCHOOL

65 Bawtry Road, Doncaster,
South Yorkshire DN4 7AD
Tel: (01302) 535926
Fax: (01302) 534675
Email: jharrington@hillhousestmarys.co.uk
Head: Mr J Cusworth
Type: Co-educational Day 2–16
No of pupils: B224 G237
Fees: (September 05)
Day £5550–£7929

SYCAMORE HALL PREPARATORY SCHOOL

1 Hall Flat Lane, Balby, Doncaster,
South Yorkshire DN4 8PT
Tel: (01302) 856800
Email: sycamorehall@tiscali.co.uk
Head: Miss J Spencer
Type: Co-educational Day 3–11
No of pupils: B41 G43

ROTHERHAM

RUDSTON PREPARATORY SCHOOL

59–63 Broom Road, Rotherham,
South Yorkshire S60 2SW
Tel: (01709) 837774
Fax: (01709) 837975
Email: office@rudstonschool.com
Type: Co-educational Day 2–11
No of pupils: B114 G101
Fees: (September 05) Day £4740

SHEFFIELD

ASHDELL PREPARATORY SCHOOL

266 Fulwood Road, Sheffield,
South Yorkshire S10 3BL
Tel: (0114) 266 3835
Fax: (0114) 267 1762
Email: headteacher@ashdell-prep.sheffield.sch.uk
Head: Mrs S Williams
Type: Girls Day 4–11
No of pupils: 123
Fees: (September 05)
Day £5850–£6750

BIRKDALE SCHOOL

Oakholme Road, Sheffield,
South Yorkshire S10 3DH
Tel: (0114) 266 8409
Fax: (0114) 267 1947
Email: admissions@birkdale.sheffield.sch.uk
Head: Mr R J Court
Type: Boys Day 4–18 (Co-ed VIth Form)
No of pupils: B730 G50
Fees: (September 05)
Day £5856–£8388

BRANTWOOD SCHOOL FOR GIRLS

1 Kenwood Bank, Sheffield,
South Yorkshire S7 1NU
Tel: (0114) 258 1747
Fax: (0114) 258 1847
Email: enquiries@brantwoodschool.co.uk
Head: Mrs V Fairbairn Barnes
Type: Girls Day 3–16
No of pupils: 200
Fees: (September 05)
Day £5079–£7158

HANDSWORTH CHRISTIAN SCHOOL

231 Handsworth Road,
Handsworth, Sheffield,
South Yorkshire S13 9BJ
Tel: (0114) 243 0276
Head: Mrs P Arnott
Type: Co-educational Day 4–16
No of pupils: 144
Fees: (September 04)
Day £1920–£2160

MYLNHURST RC SCHOOL & NURSERY

Button Hill, Sheffield,
South Yorkshire S11 9HJ
Tel: (0114) 236 1411
Fax: (0114) 236 1411
Email: cp_emmott@hotmail.com
Head: Mr C Emmott
Type: Co-educational Day 3–11
No of pupils: B95 G89
Fees: (September 04)
Day £1380–£4917

SHEFFIELD HIGH SCHOOL GDST

10 Rutland Park, Broomhill,
Sheffield, South Yorkshire S10 2PE
Tel: (0114) 266 0324
Email: enquiries@she.gdst.net
Head: Mrs V A Dunsford
Type: Girls Day 4–18
No of pupils: 974
Fees: (September 05)
Day £5337–£7365

WESTBOURNE SCHOOL

50–54 Westbourne Road,
Sheffield, South Yorkshire
S10 2QQ
Tel: (0114) 266 0374
Fax: (0114) 267 0862
Email: jbatty@westbourneschool.co.uk
Head: Mr J Hicks
Type: Co-educational Day 4–16
No of pupils: B214 G44
Fees: (September 03)
Day £4950–£7390

WEST YORKSHIRE

APPERLEY BRIDGE

WOODHOUSE GROVE SCHOOL

Apperley Bridge, West Yorkshire BD10 0NR
Tel: (0113) 250 2477
Fax: (0113) 250 5290
Email: enquiries@woodhousegrove.co.uk
Head: Mr D C Humphreys
Type: Co-educational Boarding and Day 11–18 Flexi-boarding available
No of pupils: B412 G259
No of boarders: F83 W20
Fees: (September 05) FB £15600
WB £14250–£14475
Day £8430–£8625

BATLEY

BATLEY GRAMMAR SCHOOL

Carlinghow Hill, Batley, West Yorkshire WF17 0AD
Tel: (01924) 474980
Fax: (01924) 471960
Email: hmsec@batleygrammar.co.uk
Head: Mr B Battye
Type: Co-educational Day 3–18
No of pupils: B224 G158
Fees: (September 05)
Day £4770–£7098

DALE HOUSE SCHOOL

Ruby Street, Carlinghow, Batley, West Yorkshire WF17 8HL
Head: Mrs S M G Fletcher
Type: Co-educational Day 2–11
No of pupils: B40 G43
Fees: (September 05)
Day £4050–£4350

BINGLEY

LADY LANE PARK SCHOOL

Lady Lane, Bingley, West Yorkshire BD16 4AP
Tel: (01274) 551168
Fax: (01274) 569732
Email: secretary@ladylanepark.co.uk
Head: Mrs G Wilson
Type: Co-educational Day 2–11
No of pupils: B99 G87
Fees: (September 05)
Day £1541–£1636

BRADFORD

BRADFORD CHRISTIAN SCHOOL

Livingstone Road, Bolton Woods, Bradford, West Yorkshire BD2 1BT
Tel: (01274) 595819
Fax: (01274) 620738
Email: bchristians@btconnect.com
Head: Mr P J Moon
Type: Co-educational Day 4–16
No of pupils: 197
Fees: (September 04)
Day £4788–£10476

BRADFORD GIRLS' GRAMMAR SCHOOL

Squire Lane, Bradford, West Yorkshire BD9 6RB
Tel: (01274) 545395
Fax: (01274) 482595
Email: headsec@bggs.com
Head: Mrs L J Warrington
Type: Girls Day 2–18
No of pupils: B4 G670
Fees: (September 05)
Day £5283–£8640

BRADFORD GRAMMAR SCHOOL

Keighley Road, Bradford, West Yorkshire BD9 4JP
Tel: (01274) 553702
Fax: (01274) 548129
Email: hmsec@bradfordgrammar.com
Head: Mr S R Davidson
Type: Co-educational Day 6–18
No of pupils: B802 G305
Fees: (September 05)
Day £6455–£8666

BRONTE HOUSE SCHOOL

Apperley Bridge, Bradford, West Yorkshire BD10 0PQ
Tel: (0113) 250 2811
Fax: (0113) 250 0666
Email: general.enquiries@brontehouse.org.uk
Head: Mr C B F Hall
Type: Co-educational Boarding and Day 3–11 Flexi-boarding available
No of pupils: B170 G110
No of boarders: F5
Fees: (September 04)
FB £12870–£12900
WB £10170–£10200
Day £4980–£7200

NETHERLEIGH AND ROSSEFIELD SCHOOL

Parsons Road, Heaton, Bradford, West Yorkshire BD9 4AY
Tel: (01274) 543162
Fax: (01274)493011
Head: Mrs M Midgley
Type: Co-educational Day 3–11
No of pupils: B110 G65
Fees: (September 03)
Day £2010–£3360

SHAW HOUSE SCHOOL

150–152 Wilmer Road, Heaton, Bradford, West Yorkshire BD9 4AH
Tel: (01274) 496299
Fax: (01274) 496299
Email: shawcoll@aol.com
Head: Mr H R Williams
Type: Co-educational Day 11–18
No of pupils: B75 G45
Fees: (September 03)
Day £4500–£4800

BRIGHOUSE

THE RASTRICK INDEPENDENT SCHOOL

Ogden Lane, Rastrick, Brighouse, West Yorkshire HD6 3HF
Tel: (01484) 400344
Fax: 01484 718318
Head: Mrs S A Vaughey
Type: Co-educational Day 0–16 Flexi-boarding available
No of pupils: B93 G99
Fees: (September 04)
Day £4395–£7335

HALIFAX

THE GLEDDINGS SCHOOL
Birdcage Lane, Halifax,
West Yorkshire HX3 0JB
Tel: (01422) 354605
Email: TheGleddings@aol.com
Head: Mrs Wilson
Type: Co-educational Day 3–11
No of pupils: B80 G80
Fees: (September 03)
Day £3810–£3840

HIPPERHOLME GRAMMAR SCHOOL
Bramley Lane, Hipperholme,
Halifax, West Yorkshire HX3 8JE
Tel: (01422) 202256
Fax: (01422) 204592
Email: headmaster@hipperholmegrammar.org.uk
Head: Dr J Scarth
Type: Co-educational Day 11–18
No of pupils: B160 G145
Fees: (September 04) Day £6510

LIGHTCLIFFE PREPARATORY
Wakefield Road, Halifax,
West Yorkshire HX3 8AQ
Tel: (01422) 201330
Fax: (01422) 204845
Email: thesecretary@lightcliffepreparatoryschool.co.uk
Head: Mrs J A Pickersgill
Type: Co-educational Day 2–11
No of pupils: B85 G85
Fees: (September 05)
Day £2850–£4800

HEBDEN BRIDGE

GLEN HOUSE MONTESSORI SCHOOL
Cragg Vale, Hebden Bridge,
West Yorkshire HX7 5SQ
Tel: (01422) 884682
Email: glenhouseschool@3-c.coop
Head: Ms M Scaife
Type: Co-educational Day 3–15
No of pupils: B11 G16
Fees: (September 04)
Day £684–£3420

HUDDERSFIELD

HUDDERSFIELD GRAMMAR SCHOOL
Royds Mount, Luck Lane, Marsh,
Huddersfield, West Yorkshire
HD1 4QX
Tel: (01484) 424549
Fax: (01484) 531835
Email: admin@huddersfield-grammarschool.co.uk
Head: Mrs E J Jackson and
Mrs J L Straughan
Type: Co-educational Day 3–16
No of pupils: B194 G156
Fees: (September 05)
Day £4590–£5754

ISLAMIA GIRLS HIGH SCHOOL
Thornton Lodge Road, Thornton
Lodge, Huddersfield,
West Yorkshire HD1 3JQ
Tel: (01484) 432928
Head: Mr I Meer
Type: Girls Day 11–16
No of pupils: 77

MOUNT SCHOOL
3 Binham Road, Edgerton,
Huddersfield, West Yorkshire
HD2 2AP
Tel: (01484) 426432
Fax: (01484) 426432
Email: info@themount.org.uk
Head: Mr N M Smith
Type: Co-educational Day 3–11
No of pupils: B75 G75
Fees: (September 05) Day £4494

MOUNTJOY HOUSE SCHOOL
63 New North Road,
Huddersfield, West Yorkshire
HD1 5ND
Tel: (01484) 429967
Fax: (01484) 362653
Email: mjhhuddersfield@aol.com
Head: Mrs C Rogers
Type: Co-educational Day 3–11
No of pupils: B43 G43
Fees: (September 02)
Day £1800–£3400

ROSEMEADE SCHOOL
12 Bank End Lane, Almondbury,
Huddersfield, West Yorkshire
HD5 8ES
Tel: (01484) 421076
Fax: (01484) 652025
Email: rosemeadeschool@uk2.net
Head: Mrs H M Hebblethwaite
and Mrs C M Howson
Type: Co-educational Day 3–11
No of pupils: B40 G38
Fees: (September 05)
Day £4150–£4360

ILKLEY

GHYLL ROYD SCHOOL
Greystone Manor, Ilkley Road,
Burley in Wharfedale, Ilkley,
West Yorkshire LS29 7HW
Tel: (01943) 865575
Fax: (01943) 865574
Email: information@ghyllroydschool.co.uk
Head: Mrs I Connor
Type: Boys Day 2–11
No of pupils: 90
Fees: (September 04)
Day £4440–£5412

MOORFIELD SCHOOL
Wharfedale Lodge, Ben Rhydding
Road, Ilkley, West Yorkshire
LS29 8RL
Tel: (01943) 607285
Fax: (01943) 603186
Email: enquiries@moorfield-school.yorks.com
Head: Mrs J E Disley
Type: Girls Day 2–11
No of pupils: 130
Fees: (September 05)
Day £900–£5385

WESTVILLE HOUSE PREPARATORY SCHOOL
Carter's Lane, Middleton, Ilkley,
West Yorkshire LS29 0DQ
Tel: (01943) 608053
Fax: (01943) 817410
Email: westville@epals.com
Head: Mr C A Holloway
Type: Co-educational Day 3–11
No of pupils: B90 G61
Fees: (September 05)
Day £3600–£6255

LEEDS

ALCUIN SCHOOL
64 Woodland Lane, Leeds,
West Yorkshire LS7 4PD
Tel: (0113) 269 1173
Email: alcuin@legend.co.uk
Head: Mr J Hipshon
Type: Co-educational Day 4–11
No of pupils: B20 G26
Fees: (September 05)
Day £3675–£4800

THE FROEBELIAN SCHOOL
Clarence Road, Horsforth, Leeds,
West Yorkshire LS18 4LB
Tel: (0113) 258 3047
Fax: (0113) 258 0173
Email: office@froebelian.co.uk
Head: Mr J Tranmer
Type: Co-educational Day 3–11
No of pupils: B92 G77
Fees: (September 05)
Day £3285–£4950

GATEWAYS SCHOOL
Harewood, Leeds, West Yorkshire
LS17 9LE
Tel: (0113) 288 6345
Fax: (0113) 288 6148
Email: gateways@gatewayschool.co.uk
Head: Mrs D Davidson
Type: Girls Day 3–18 (Boys 3–7)
No of pupils: B24 G503
Fees: (September 05)
Day £4392–£7965

LEEDS GIRLS' HIGH SCHOOL
Headingley Lane, Leeds,
West Yorkshire LS6 1BN
Tel: (0113) 274 4000
Fax: (0113) 275 2217
Email: enquiries@lghs.org
Head: Ms S Fishburn
Type: Girls Day 3–19
No of pupils: 990
Fees: (September 02)
Day £4926–£7365

LEEDS GRAMMAR SCHOOL
Alwoodley Gates, Harrogate
Road, Leeds, West Yorkshire
LS17 8GS
Tel: (0113) 229 1552
Fax: (0113) 228 5111
Email: info@lgs.leeds.sch.uk
Head: Dr M Bailey
Type: Boys Day 4–18
No of pupils: 1380
Fees: (September 04)
Day £4545–£8055

NEW HORIZON COMMUNITY SCHOOL
Newton Hill House, Newton Hill
Road, Leeds, West Yorkshire
LS7 4JE
Tel: (0113) 262 4001
Fax: (0113) 262 4912
Email: nhcsleeds@newtonhillhouse.wanadoo.co.uk
Head: Mrs S Dambatta
Type: Girls Day 11–16
No of pupils: 100
Fees: (September 05) Day £500

MOORLANDS SCHOOL
Foxhill, Weetwood Lane, Leeds,
West Yorkshire LS16 5PF
Tel: (0113) 278 5286
Fax: (0113) 230 6548
Email: headmaster@moorlands-school.co.uk
Head: Mr J Johnson
Type: Co-educational Day 3–13
No of pupils: B150 G59
Fees: (September 03)
Day £2595–£5820

RICHMOND HOUSE SCHOOL
170 Otley Road, Leeds,
West Yorkshire LS16 5LG
Tel: (0113) 275 2670
Fax: (0113) 230 4868
Email: enquiries@rhschool.org
Head: Mr G Milne
Type: Co-educational Day 3–11
No of pupils: B163 G127
Fees: (September 05)
Day £3549–£5568

ST AGNES PNEU SCHOOL
25 Burton Crescent, Leeds,
West Yorkshire LS6 4DN
Tel: (0113) 278 6722
Email: info@st-agnes.demon.co.uk
Head: Mrs S McMeeking
Type: Co-educational Day 2–7
No of pupils: B22 G24
Fees: (September 02)
Day £2362–£4328

WAKEFIELD TUTORIAL PREPARATORY SCHOOL
Commercial Street, Morley, Leeds,
West Yorkshire LS27 8HY
Tel: (0113) 253 4033
Fax: (0113) 253 3581
Email: Headteacher@wtschool.co.uk
Head: Mrs J A Tanner
Type: Co-educational Day 4–11
No of pupils: B25 G25
Fees: (September 04)
Day £3291–£3651

PONTEFRACT

ACKWORTH SCHOOL*
Ackworth, Pontefract,
West Yorkshire WF7 7LT
Tel: (01977) 611401
Fax: (01977) 616225
Email: admissions@ackworthschool.com
Head: Mr P Simpson
Type: Co-educational Boarding and Day 4–18
No of pupils: B290 G271
No of boarders: F83
Fees: (September 05) FB £15498
Day £9354

INGLEBROOK SCHOOL
Northgate Close, Pontefract,
West Yorkshire WF8 1HJ
Tel: (01977) 700120
Head: Mrs J Bellamy
Type: Co-educational Day 2–11
No of pupils: B90 G90
Fees: (September 02)
Day £534–£2400

THE INTERNATIONAL CENTRE, ACKWORTH SCHOOL
Ackworth, Pontefract,
West Yorkshire WF7 7LT
Tel: (01977) 611401
Fax: (01977) 616225
Email: admissions@ackworthschool.com
Head: Mr P J Simpson
Type: Co-educational Day and Boarding 2–18 Flexi-boarding available
No of pupils: B280 G288
No of boarders: F93
Fees: (September 05) FB £15498
Day £9354

PUDSEY

FULNECK SCHOOL†
Fulneck, Pudsey, West Yorkshire LS28 8DS
Tel: (0113) 257 0235
Fax: (0113) 255 7316
Email: general@fulneckschool.co.uk
Head: Mr T Kernohan
Type: Co-educational Day and Boarding 3–18 Flexi-boarding available
No of pupils: B228 G159
No of boarders: F38 W9
Fees: (September 05)
FB £12585–£15285
WB £11640–£13920
Day £2895–£8325

RISHWORTH

RISHWORTH SCHOOL
Rishworth, West Yorkshire HX6 4QA
Tel: (01422) 822217
Fax: (01422) 820911
Email: admin@rishworth-school.co.uk
Head: Mr R A Baker
Type: Co-educational Day and Boarding 3–18 Flexi-boarding available
No of pupils: B290 G280
No of boarders: F78 W14
Fees: (September 05)
FB £14925–£16275
WB £13575–£14850
Day £4290–£8370

WAKEFIELD

CLIFF SCHOOL
St John's Lodge, 2 Leeds Road, Wakefield, West Yorkshire WF1 3JT
Tel: (01924) 373597
Fax: (01924) 211137
Email: info@cliffschool.com
Head: Miss A D Gleave
Type: Co-educational Day 0–11
No of pupils: B40 G100
Fees: (September 05)
Day £5967–£8528

QUEEN ELIZABETH GRAMMAR SCHOOL
154 Northgate, Wakefield, West Yorkshire WF1 3QX
Tel: (01924) 373943
Fax: (01924) 231603
Email: admissions@qegsss.org.uk
Head: Mr M R Gibbons
Type: Boys Day 7–18
Fees: (September 05) Day £7896

ST HILDA'S SCHOOL
Dovecote Lane, Horbury, Wakefield, West Yorkshire WF4 6BB
Tel: (01924) 260706
Fax: (01924) 272516
Head: Mrs J Sharpe
Type: Co-educational Day Boys 3–7 Girls 3–11
No of pupils: B44 G89
Fees: (September 04)
Day £4498–£4798

SILCOATES SCHOOL
Wrenthorpe, Wakefield, West Yorkshire WF2 0PD
Tel: (01924) 291614
Fax: (01924) 368693
Email: hmsilcoates@aol.com
Head: Mr A P Spillane
Type: Co-educational Day 7–18
No of pupils: B377 G339
Fees: (September 04)
Day £5244–£8856

SUNNY HILL HOUSE SCHOOL
Wrenthorpe Lane, Wrenthorpe, Wakefield, West Yorkshire WF2 0QB
Tel: (01924) 291717
Fax: (01924) 291717
Email: shhschool@aol.com
Head: Mrs H K Cushing
Type: Co-educational Day 2–7
No of pupils: B54 G49
Fees: (September 05) Day £4722

WAKEFIELD GIRLS' HIGH SCHOOL
Wentworth Street, Wakefield, West Yorkshire WF1 2QS
Tel: (01924) 372490
Fax: (01924) 231601
Email: admissions@wghsss.org.uk
Head: Mrs P A Langham
Type: Girls Day 11–18
No of pupils: 734
Fees: (September 04) Day £7491

WAKEFIELD INDEPENDENT SCHOOL
The Nostell Centre, Doncaster Road, Nostell, Wakefield, West Yorkshire WF4 1QG
Tel: (01924) 865757
Fax: (01924) 865757
Email: headatwis@fsmail.net
Head: Ms K E Caryl
Type: Day
No of pupils: B120 G100
Fees: (September 04)
Day £3540–£5280

2.3
Northern Ireland

COUNTY ANTRIM

BELFAST

BELFAST ROYAL ACADEMY
Belfast, County Antrim BT14 6JL
Tel: (028) 9074 0423
Fax: (028) 9075 0607
Email: enquiries@bfsra.belfast.ni.sch.uk
Head: Mr W S F Young
Type: Co-educational Day 4–19
No of pupils: B772 G819
Fees: (September 03) Day £230

CABIN HILL SCHOOL
562–594 Upper Newtownards Road, Knock, Belfast, County Antrim BT4 3HJ
Tel: (028) 9065 3368
Fax: (028) 9065 1966
Email: info@cabinhill.belfast.ni.sch.uk
Head: Mrs H M Rowan
Type: Boys Day and Boarding 3–13 (Co-ed kindergarten) Flexi-boarding available
No of pupils: B284 G8
No of boarders: F6 W21

CAMPBELL COLLEGE
Belfast, County Antrim BT4 2ND
Tel: (028) 9076 3076
Fax: (028) 9076 1894
Email: hmoffice@campbellcollege.co.uk
Head: Mr W D A Gribson
Type: Boys Boarding and Day 11–18 Flexi-boarding available
No of pupils: 800
No of boarders: F16 W24
Fees: (September 03)
FB £7098–£8109
WB £6998–£8009
Day £1146–£1674

METHODIST COLLEGE
1 Malone Road, Belfast, County Antrim BT9 6BY
Tel: (028) 9020 5205
Fax: (028) 9020 5230
Email: school@methody.org
Head: Dr T W Mulryne
Type: Co-educational Day and Boarding 4–19
No of pupils: B1300 G1100
No of boarders: F170
Fees: (September 03)
FB £5350–£10280 Day £385–£470

ROYAL BELFAST ACADEMICAL INSTITUTION
College Square East, Belfast, County Antrim BT1 6DL
Tel: (028) 9024 0461
Fax: (028) 9023 7464
Email: prinsec@rbai.belfast.ni.sch.uk
Head: Mr R M Ridley
Type: Boys Day 4–18
No of pupils: 1300
Fees: (September 05)
Day £690–£3100

VICTORIA COLLEGE BELFAST
Cranmore Park, Belfast, County Antrim BT9 6JA
Tel: (028) 9066 1506
Fax: (028) 9066 6898
Email: vcbinfo@aol.com
Head: Ms P Slevin
Type: Girls Day and Boarding 4–18 Flexi-boarding available
No of pupils: 1029
No of boarders: F47
Fees: (September 05) F/WB £ £6750
Day £310

COUNTY ARMAGH

ARMAGH

THE ROYAL SCHOOL
College Hill, Armagh, County Armagh BT61 9DH
Tel: (028) 3752 2807
Fax: (028) 3752 5014
Head: Mr P Crute
Type: Co-educational Boarding and Day 10–19 Flexi-boarding available
No of pupils: B333 G336
No of boarders: F16 W65
Fees: (September 05)
FB £5500–£8300
WB £3700–£7500 Day £220–£230

COUNTY DOWN

BANGOR

BANGOR GRAMMAR SCHOOL
13 College Avenue, Bangor, County Down BT20 5HJ
Tel: (028) 9147 3734
Fax: (028) 9127 3245
Email: info@bgs.bangor.ni.sch.uk
Head: Mr S D Connolly
Type: Boys Day 11–18
No of pupils: 888
Fees: (September 04)
Day £80–£270

HOLYWOOD

THE HOLYWOOD RUDOLF STEINER SCHOOL
The Highlands, 34 Croft Road, Holywood, County Down BT18 0PR
Tel: (028) 9042 8029
Fax: (028) 9042 8029
Email: info@holywood-steiner.co.uk
Type: Co-educational Day 4–17
Fees: (September 05) Day £2520

ROCKPORT SCHOOL
15 Rockport Road, Craigavad, Holywood, County Down BT18 0DD
Tel: (028) 9042 8372
Fax: (028) 9042 2608
Email: info@rockportschool.com
Head: Mrs C A Osborne
Type: Co-educational Boarding and Day 3–16 (Boarding 7–13) Flexi-boarding available
No of pupils: B111 G112
No of boarders: W16
Fees: (September 05)
WB £7395–£10245
Day £3525–£8400

COUNTY LONDONDERRY

COLERAINE

COLERAINE ACADEMICAL INSTITUTION
Castlerock Road, Coleraine,
County Londonderry BT51 3LA
Tel: (028) 7034 4331
Fax: (028) 7035 2632
Email: cai@
colerainai.demon.co.uk
Head: Mr L Quigg
Type: Boys Day 11–19
No of pupils: 720
Fees: (September 03) Day £100

COUNTY TYRONE

DUNGANNON

THE ROYAL SCHOOL DUNGANNON
1 Ranfurly Road, Dungannon,
County Tyrone BT71 6EG
Tel: (028) 8772 2710
Fax: (028) 8775 2845
Email: hmsec@
rsd.dungannon.ni.sch.uk
Head: Mr P D Hewitt
Type: Co-educational Day and Boarding 11–19 Flexi-boarding available
No of pupils: B320 G337
No of boarders: F35 W10
Fees: (September 05)
F/WB £ £5250–£9500
Day £100–£150
Fees: (September 04)
Day £3540–£5280

2.4 Scotland

ABERDEENSHIRE

ABERDEEN

ABERDEEN WALDORF SCHOOL
Craigton Road, Cults, Aberdeen, Aberdeenshire AB15 9QD
Tel: (01224) 869932
Fax: (01224) 868366
Email: aws@talk21.com
Head: Mr P Hansmann
Type: Co-educational Day 3–16
No of pupils: B70 G55
Fees: (September 05)
Day £1500–£6700

ALBYN SCHOOL*
17–23 Queens Road, Aberdeen, Aberdeenshire AB15 4PB
Tel: (01224) 322408
Fax: (01224) 209173
Email: information@albynschool.co.uk
Head: Dr J D Halliday
Type: Co-educational Day Boys 2–10 Girls 2–18
No of pupils: B60 G350
Fees: (September 05)
Day £4900–£7900

THE HAMILTON SCHOOL
55–57 & 80–84 Queens Road, Aberdeen, Aberdeenshire AB15 4YE
Tel: (01224) 317295
Fax: (01224) 317165
Email: hamilton.admin@virgin.net
Head: Ms K Taylor
Type: Co-educational Day 0–12

INTERNATIONAL SCHOOL OF ABERDEEN
'Fairgirth', 296 North Deeside Road, Milltimber, Aberdeen, Aberdeenshire AB13 OAB
Tel: (01224) 732267
Fax: (01224) 735648
Email: admin@isa.aberdeen.sch.uk
Head: Dr D A Hovde
Type: Co-educational Day 3–18
No of pupils: B180 G153
Fees: (September 05)
Day £13125–£14700

ROBERT GORDONS COLLEGE
Schoolhill, Aberdeen, Aberdeenshire AB10 1FE
Tel: (01224) 646346
Fax: (01224) 630301
Email: h.ouston@rgc.aberdeen.sch.uk
Head: Mr Hugh Ouston
Type: Co-educational Day 4–18
No of pupils: B910 G558
Fees: (September 05)
Day £4840–£7600

ST MARGARET'S SCHOOL FOR GIRLS
17 Albyn Place, Aberdeen, Aberdeenshire AB10 1RU
Tel: (01224) 584466
Fax: (01224) 585600
Email: info@st-margaret.aberdeen.sch.uk
Head: Mrs L Mckay
Type: Girls Day 3–18 (Boys 3–5)
No of pupils: B2 G365
Fees: (September 05)
Day £4386–£7653

TOTAL FINA ELF FRENCH SCHOOL
1–5 Whitehall Place, Aberdeen, Aberdeenshire AB25 4RH
Tel: (01224) 645545
Fax: (01224) 645565
Head: Mr J Albert
Type: Co-educational Day 4–18
No of pupils: 97

ANGUS

DUNDEE

THE HIGH SCHOOL OF DUNDEE
Euclid Crescent, Dundee, Angus DD1 1HU
Tel: (01382) 202921
Fax: (01382) 229822
Email: admissions@dundeehigh.dundeecity.sch.uk
Head: Mr A M Duncan
Type: Co-educational Day 5–18
No of pupils: B533 G495
Fees: (September 05)
Day £5550–£7890

MONTROSE

LATHALLAN SCHOOL
Brotherton Castle, Johnshaven, Montrose, Angus DD10 0HN
Tel: (01561) 362220
Fax: (01561) 361695
Email: office@lathallan.com
Head: Mr Andrew Giles
Type: Co-educational Boarding and Day 5–13 Flexi-boarding available
No of pupils: B54 G44
No of boarders: W35
Fees: (September 05)
WB £9687–£12651

ARGYLL AND BUTE

HELENSBURGH

LOMOND SCHOOL
10 Stafford Street, Helensburgh, Argyll and Bute G84 9JX
Tel: (01436) 672476
Fax: (01436) 678320
Email: admin@lomond-school.demon.co.uk
Head: Mr A D Macdonald
Type: Co-educational Day and Boarding 3–19
No of pupils: B280 G282
No of boarders: F64
Fees: (September 05)
FB £15915–£16140
Day £3690–£7545

SOUTH AYRSHIRE

AYR

WELLINGTON SCHOOL
Carleton Turrets, Craigweil Road, Ayr, South Ayrshire KA7 2XH
Tel: (01292) 269321
Fax: (01292) 272161
Email: info@wellingtonschool.org
Head: Mrs G Leask
Type: Co-educational Day 3–18
No of pupils: B270 G315
Fees: (September 05)
Day £2460–£8265

CLACKMANNANSHIRE

DOLLAR

DOLLAR ACADEMY
Dollar, Clackmannanshire FK14 7DU
Tel: (01259) 742511
Fax: (01259) 742867
Email: rector@dollaracademy.org.uk
Head: Mr J S Robertson
Type: Co-educational Day and Boarding 5–18 Flexi-boarding available
No of pupils: B621 G579
No of boarders: F85 W9
Fees: (September 03)
FB £13761–£15462
WB £12942–£14643
Day £5157–£6858

FIFE

KIRKCALDY

SEA VIEW PRIVATE SCHOOL

102 Loughborough Road,
Kirkcaldy, Fife KY1 3DD
Tel: (01592) 652244
Fax: (01592) 655929
Email: seaviewkdy@sol.co.uk
Head: Mr Andrew Moss and Mrs Louise Moss
Type: Co-educational Day 3–12
No of pupils: B32 G25
Fees: (September 04)
Day £3954–£4284

ST ANDREWS

ST LEONARDS SCHOOL & VITH FORM COLLEGE

St Andrews, Fife KY16 9QJ
Tel: (01334) 472126
Fax: (01334) 476152
Email: info@stleonards-fife.org
Head: Mr R Tims
Type: Co-educational Boarding and Day 3–19 Flexi-boarding available
No of pupils: B81 G231
No of boarders: F136
Fees: (September 03)
FB £13941–£18384
Day £5730–£10305

GLASGOW

GLASGOW

CRAIGHOLME SCHOOL

72 St Andrews Drive, Glasgow
Glasgow G41 4HS
Tel: (0141) 427 0375
Fax: (0141) 427 6396
Email: principal@craigholme.co.uk
Head: Mrs G Stobo
Type: Girls Day 3–18 (Boys 3–5)
No of pupils: B10 G537
Fees: (September 05)
Day £3615–£7500

THE GLASGOW ACADEMY DAIRSIE HOUSE

54 Newlands Road, Glasgow
Glasgow G43 2JG
Tel: (0141) 632 0736
Fax: (0141) 632 0736
Email: admin@dairsiehouse.glasgow.sch.uk
Head: Mrs S S McKnight
Type: Co-educational Day 3–9
No of pupils: B47 G27
Fees: (September 05)
Day £2595–£4695

THE GLASGOW ACADEMY

Colebrooke Street, Glasgow
Glasgow G12 8HE
Tel: (0141) 334 8558
Fax: (0141) 337 3473
Email: enquiries@tga.org.uk
Head: Mr P J Brodie
Type: Co-educational Day 3–18
No of pupils: B580 G520
Fees: (September 05)
Day £2595–£7680

GLASGOW STEINER SCHOOL

52 Lumsden Street, Glasgow
Glasgow G3 8RH
Tel: (0141) 334 8855
Fax: (0141) 334 8855
Email: admin@glasgowsteinerschool.org
Head: Ms C Rocher
Type: Co-educational Day 3–14
No of pupils: B53 G38
Fees: (September 05)
Day £1140–£4380

THE HIGH SCHOOL OF GLASGOW

637 Crow Road, Glasgow
Glasgow G13 1PL
Tel: (0141) 954 9628
Fax: (0141) 435 5708
Email: rector@hsog.co.uk
Head: Mr C D R Mair
Type: Co-educational Day 3–18
No of pupils: B535 G524
Fees: (September 05)
Day £2547–£7848

HUTCHESONS' GRAMMAR SCHOOL

21 Beaton Road, Glasgow
Glasgow G41 4NW
Tel: (0141) 423 2933
Fax: (0141) 424 0251
Email: admissions@hutchesons.org
Head: Mr G W A MacAllister
Type: Co-educational Day 3–18
No of pupils: B1002 G947
Fees: (September 04)
Day £3894–£7050

HUTCHESONS' LILYBANK JUNIOR SCHOOL
4 Lilybank Terrace, Glasgow
Glasgow G12 8RX
Tel: (0141) 339 9127
Fax: (0141) 357 5530
Head: Mr J G Knowles
Type: Co-educational Day 3–11
No of pupils: 130
Fees: (September 03)
Day £2508–£5888

KELVINSIDE ACADEMY
33 Kirklee Road, Glasgow
Glasgow G12 0SW
Tel: (0141) 357 3376
Fax: (0141) 357 5401
Email: rector@kelvinsideacademy.org.uk
Head: Mr J L Broadfoot
Type: Co-educational Day 3–18
No of pupils: B408 G220
Fees: (September 03)
Day £4500–£7380

ST ALOYSIUS' COLLEGE
45 Hill Street, Glasgow Glasgow
G3 6RJ
Tel: (0141) 332 3190
Fax: (0141) 353 0426
Email: mail@staloysius.org
Head: Mr J E Stoer
Type: Co-educational Day 3–18
No of pupils: B700 G600
Fees: (September 05)
Day £5385–£6940

ST ALOYSIUS JUNIOR SCHOOL
56–58 Hill Street, Glasgow
Glasgow G3 6RH
Tel: (0141) 331 9200
Head: Mrs F Davidson
Type: Co-educational Day 5–12
No of pupils: 431
Fees: (September 04)
Day £6200–£6400

LANARKSHIRE

HAMILTON

HAMILTON COLLEGE
Bothwell Road, Hamilton,
Lanarkshire ML3 0AY
Tel: (01698) 282700
Fax: (01698) 281589
Email: principal@hamiltoncollege.co.uk
Head: Mr A J Leach
Type: Co-educational Day 3–18
No of pupils: B400 G400

SOUTH LANARKSHIRE

RUTHERGLEN

FERNHILL SCHOOL
Fernbrae Avenue, Rutherglen,
South Lanarkshire G73 4SG
Tel: (0141) 634 2674
Fax: (0141) 631 4343
Email: info@fernhillschool.co.uk
Head: Mrs A Crammond
Type: Girls Day 4–18 (Boys 4–11)
No of pupils: B61 G270
Fees: (September 05)
Day £5250–£6750

LOTHIAN

DUNBAR

BELHAVEN HILL
Dunbar, Lothian EH42 1NN
Tel: (01368) 862785
Fax: (01368) 865225
Email: headmaster@belhavenhill.com
Head: Mr I M Osborne
Type: Co-educational Boarding and Day 7–13
No of pupils: B68 G54
No of boarders: F95
Fees: (September 05) FB £14775 Day £10245

EDINBURGH

BASIL PATERSON TUTORIAL COLLEGE*
66 Queen Street, Edinburgh, Lothian EH2 4NA
Tel: (0131) 225 3802
Fax: (0131) 226 6701
Email: info@basilpaterson.co.uk
Head: Mr C Smith
Type: Co-educational Boarding and Day 15+
No of pupils: B15 G15
No of boarders: F7
Fees: (September 05) FB £3360 Day £2200–£12000

CARGILFIELD
Barnton Avenue West, Edinburgh, Lothian EH4 6HU
Tel: (0131) 336 2207
Fax: (0131) 336 3179
Email: admin@cargilfield.com
Head: Mr J Elder
Type: Co-educational Boarding and Day 3–13 Flexi-boarding available
No of pupils: B127 G53
No of boarders: F21
Fees: (September 05) FB £4400 WB £4200 Day £2150–£3450

CLIFTON HALL SCHOOL
Newbridge, Edinburgh, Lothian EH28 8LQ
Tel: (0131) 333 1359
Fax: (0131) 333 4609
Email: office@cliftonhall.org.uk
Head: Mr R Grant
Type: Co-educational Day 3–11
No of pupils: B70 G70
Fees: (September 05) Day £2850–£7500

DUNEDIN SCHOOL
5 Gilmerton Road, Edinburgh, Lothian EH16 5TY
Tel: (0131) 664 1328
Email: staff@dunedin.edin.sch.uk
Head: Mrs S Peck and Mrs S Ford
Type: Co-educational Day 10–17
No of pupils: B10 G10
Fees: (September 04) Day £9345

THE EDINBURGH ACADEMY
42 Henderson Row, Edinburgh, Lothian EH3 5BL
Tel: (0131) 556 4603
Fax: (0131) 624 4994
Email: rector@edinburghacademy.org.uk
Head: Mr J V Light
Type: Boys Day and Boarding 5–18 (Co-ed VIth Form) Flexi-boarding available
No of pupils: B451 G25
No of boarders: F17 W2

THE EDINBURGH RUDOLF STEINER SCHOOL
60 Spylaw Road, Edinburgh, Lothian EH10 5BR
Tel: (0131) 337 3410
Fax: (0131) 538 6066
Email: steinersch@aol.com
Head: Mr A Farquharson
Type: Co-educational Day 3–18 Flexi-boarding available
No of pupils: B150 G150
No of boarders: F8 W1
Fees: (September 04) Day £969–£5217

FETTES COLLEGE
Carrington Road, Edinburgh, Lothian EH4 1QX
Tel: (0131) 311 6701
Fax: (0131) 311 6714
Email: enquiries@fettes.com
Head: Mr M C B Spens
Type: Co-educational Boarding and Day 7–18
No of pupils: B349 G250
No of boarders: F362
Fees: (September 05) FB £15360–£21210 Day £9810–£14859

GEORGE HERIOT'S SCHOOL
Lauriston Place, Edinburgh, Lothian EH3 9EQ
Tel: (0131) 229 7263
Fax: (0131) 229 6363
Email: admissions@george-heriots.com
Head: Mr A G Hector and Mr C D Wyllie
Type: Co-educational Day 4–18
No of pupils: B907 G691
Fees: (September 05) Day £4896–£7386

GEORGE WATSON'S COLLEGE
Colinton Road, Edinburgh, Lothian EH10 5EG
Tel: (0131) 446 6000
Fax: (0131) 446 6090
Email: admissions@gwc.org.uk
Head: Mr G H Edwards
Type: Co-educational Day 3–18
No of pupils: B1215 G1088
Fees: (September 05) Day £2265–£7818

MANNAFIELDS CHRISTIAN SCHOOL
170 Easter Road, Edinburgh, Lothian EH7 5QE
Tel: (0131) 659 5602
Email: head@mannafields.org.uk
Head: Mr G S Ackerman
Type: Co-educational Day 5–14
Fees: (September 04) Day £200–£3600

THE MARY ERSKINE SCHOOL
Ravelston, Edinburgh, Lothian EH4 3NT
Tel: (0131) 347 5700
Fax: (0131) 347 5799
Email: schoolsecretary@esmgc.com
Head: Mr J N D Gray
Type: Girls Day and Boarding 12–18 (Co-ed VIth Form)
No of boarders: F20
Fees: (September 05) FB £15045 Day £7929

MERCHISTON CASTLE SCHOOL*†
Colinton, Edinburgh, Lothian EH13 0PU
Tel: (0131) 312 2200
Fax: (0131) 441 6060
Email: admissions@merchiston.co.uk
Head: Mr A R Hunter
Type: Boys Boarding and Day 8–18
No of pupils: 426
No of boarders: F288
Fees: (September 05) FB £13980–£20775 Day £9525–£14850

ST GEORGE'S SCHOOL FOR GIRLS
Garscube Terrace, Edinburgh, Lothian EH12 6BG
Tel: (0131) 311 8000
Fax: (0131) 311 8120
Email: head@st-georges.edin.sch.uk
Head: Dr J McClure
Type: Girls Day and Boarding 2–18 (Boys 2–5) Flexi-boarding available
No of pupils: B19 G965
No of boarders: F40
Fees: (September 05) FB £15630–£17550 Day £2790–£8775

ST MARGARET'S SCHOOL
East Suffolk Road, Edinburgh, Lothian EH16 5PJ
Tel: (0131) 668 1986
Fax: (0131) 667 9814
Email: admissions@st-margarets.sch.uk
Head: Mrs E M Davis
Type: Girls Day 1–18 (Boys 1–8)
No of pupils: B68 G472
Fees: (September 04) Day £5712–£6981

ST MARY'S MUSIC SCHOOL
Coates Hall, 25 Grosvenor Crescent, Edinburgh, Lothian EH12 5EL
Tel: (0131) 538 7766
Fax: (0131) 467 7289
Email: info@st-marys-music-school.co.uk
Head: Mrs J J Rimer
Type: Co-educational Boarding and Day 9–19
No of pupils: B36 G33
No of boarders: F25

ST SERF'S SCHOOL
5 Wester Coates Gardens, Edinburgh, Lothian EH12 5LT
Tel: (0131) 337 1015
Fax: (0131) 346 7829
Email: office@stserfsschool.freeserve.co.uk
Head: Mrs K D Hume
Type: Co-educational Day 5–18
No of pupils: B65 G50
Fees: (September 05) Day £4560–£6360

STEWART'S MELVILLE COLLEGE
Queensferry Road, Edinburgh, Lothian EH4 3EZ
Tel: (0131) 311 1000
Fax: (0131) 311 1099
Email: secretary@esmgc.com
Head: Mr J N D Gray
Type: Boys Day and Boarding 12–18 (Co-ed VIth Form) Flexi-boarding available
No of boarders: F21
Fees: (September 05) FB £15045 Day £7929

HADDINGTON

THE COMPASS SCHOOL
West Road, Haddington, Lothian EH41 3RD
Tel: (01620) 822642
Fax: (01620) 822144
Email: office@thecompassschool.co.uk
Head: Mr M Becher
Type: Co-educational Day 4–11
No of pupils: B58 G64
Fees: (September 04) Day £3480–£5550

MUSSELBURGH

LORETTO JUNIOR SCHOOL
North Esk Lodge, 1 North High Street, Musselburgh, Lothian EH21 6JA
Tel: (0131) 653 4570
Fax: (0131) 653 4571
Email: juniorschool@loretto.com
Head: Mr R G Selley
Type: Co-educational Boarding and Day 3–13 Flexi-boarding available
No of pupils: B122 G65
No of boarders: F16 W4
Fees: (September 05) FB £14865–£15858 Day £9825–£10521

LORETTO SCHOOL
Musselburgh, Lothian EH21 7RE
Tel: (0131) 653 4455
Fax: (0131) 653 4456
Email: admissions@loretto.com
Head: Mr M B Mavor
Type: Co-educational Boarding and Day 3–18 Flexi-boarding available
No of pupils: B236 G190
No of boarders: F202 W30
Fees: (September 04) F/WB £ £14147–£20028 Day £4410–£13365

MORAYSHIRE

ELGIN

GORDONSTOUN SCHOOL*
Elgin, Morayshire IV30 5RF
Tel: (01343) 837837
Fax: (01343) 837808
Email: admissions@gordonstoun.org.uk
Head: Mr M C Pyper
Type: Co-educational Boarding and Day 8–18
No of pupils: B307 G235
No of boarders: F474
Fees: (September 05)
FB £14644–£21789
Day £8170–£14703

ROSEBRAE SCHOOL
Spynie, Elgin, Morayshire IV30 8XT
Tel: (01343) 544841
Fax: (01343) 544841
Email: enquiries@rosebrae.moray.sch.uk
Head: Mrs B MacPherson
Type: Co-educational Day 2–8
No of pupils: B32 G32
Fees: (September 05)
Day £405–£3840

PERTH AND KINROSS

CRIEFF

ARDVRECK SCHOOL
Gwydyr Road, Crieff, Perthshire PH7 4EX
Tel: (01764) 653112
Fax: (01764) 654920
Email: headmaster@ardvreck.org.uk
Head: Mr P Watson
Type: Co-educational Day and Boarding 3–13
No of pupils: B80 G70
No of boarders: F105
Fees: (September 03) FB £13110
Day £8112

MORRISON'S ACADEMY
Ferntower Road, Crieff, Perth and Kinross PH7 3AN
Tel: (01764) 653885
Fax: (01764) 655411
Email: principal@morrisonsacademy.org
Head: Mr S Pengelley
Type: Co-educational Day and Boarding 3–18 Flexi-boarding available
No of pupils: B256 G222
No of boarders: F18 W10
Fees: (September 05)
FB £17868–£18822
WB £13758–£14712
Day £2050–£7719

DUNBLANE

QUEEN VICTORIA SCHOOL
Dunblane, Perth and Kinross FK15 0JY
Tel: (01786) 822288
Fax: (0131) 310 2926
Email: enquiries@qvs.org.uk
Head: Mr B Raine
Type: Co-educational Boarding 11–18
No of pupils: B137 G127
No of boarders: F264
Fees: (September 05) FB £1024

PERTH

CRAIGCLOWAN PREPARATORY SCHOOL
Edinburgh Road, Perth, Perth and Kinross PH2 8PS
Tel: (01738) 626310
Fax: (01738) 440349
Email: mbeale@btconnect.com
Head: Mr M E Beale
Type: Co-educational Day 3–13
No of pupils: B160 G145
Fees: (September 05)
Day £4500–£7200

GLENALMOND COLLEGE*
Perth, Perth and Kinross PH1 3RY
Tel: (01738) 842056
Fax: (01738) 842063
Email: registrar@glenalmondcollege.co.uk
Head: Mr G Woods
Type: Co-educational Boarding and Day 12–18
No of pupils: 385
No of boarders: F326
Fees: (September 05)
FB £15975–£21300
Day £10905–£14520

KILGRASTON (A SACRED HEART SCHOOL)†
Bridge of Earn, Perth, Perth and Kinross PH2 9BQ
Tel: (01738) 812257
Fax: (01738) 813410
Email: registrar@kilgraston.pkc.sch.uk
Head: Mr M Farmer
Type: Girls Boarding and Day 2–18 (Boys day 2–9) Flexi-boarding available
No of pupils: B10 G239
No of boarders: F100
Fees: (September 05)
FB £15600–£20835
Day £6360–£11025

STRATHALLAN SCHOOL*
Forgandenny, Perth, Perth and Kinross PH2 9EG
Tel: (01738) 812546
Fax: (01738) 812549
Email: admissions@strathallan.co.uk
Head: Mr B K Thompson
Type: Co-educational Boarding and Day 10–18
No of pupils: B263 G188
No of boarders: F296
Fees: (September 05)
FB £14760–£20685
Day £9210–£14025

RENFREWSHIRE

KILMACOLM

ST COLUMBA'S SCHOOL
Duchal Road, Kilmacolm, Renfrewshire PA13 4AU
Tel: (01505) 872238
Fax: (01505) 873995
Email: secretary@st-columbas.org
Head: Mr D Girdwood
Type: Co-educational Day 3–18
No of pupils: B349 G374
Fees: (September 05)
Day £1900–£7410

NEWTON MEARNS

BELMONT HOUSE
Sandringham Avenue, Newton Mearns, Renfrewshire G77 5DU
Tel: (0141) 639 2922
Fax: (0141) 639 9860
Email: admin@belmontschool.co.uk
Head: Mr M D Shanks
Type: Co-educational Day 3–18
No of pupils: B271 G54
Fees: (September 05)
Day £3375–£7659

ROXBURGHSHIRE

MELROSE

ST MARY'S PREPARATORY SCHOOL
Abbey Park, Melrose, Roxburghshire TD6 9LN
Tel: (01896) 822517
Fax: (01896) 823550
Email: enquiries@stmarys.newnet.co.uk
Head: Mr J Brett
Type: Co-educational Day and Boarding 2–13 Flexi-boarding available
No of pupils: B57 G80
No of boarders: W21
Fees: (September 05) WB £11970
Day £7350–£10200

STIRLING

STIRLING

BEACONHURST SCHOOL
52 Kenilworth Road, Bridge of Allan, Stirling Stirling FK9 4RR
Tel: (01786) 832146
Fax: (01786) 833415
Email: secretary@beaconhurst.stirling.sch.uk
Head: Mr I W Kilpatrick
Type: Co-educational Day 3–18
No of pupils: B178 G160
Fees: (September 04)
Day £1792–£7200
Fees: (September 04)
Day £3540–£5280

2.5
Wales

BRIDGEND

PORTHCAWL

ST CLARE'S SCHOOL
Newton, Porthcawl, Bridgend
CF36 5NR
Tel: (01656) 782509
Fax: (01656) 785818
Email: info@stclares-school.co.uk
Head: Mrs C M Barnard
Type: Co-educational Day 3–18
No of pupils: B156 G222
Fees: (September 05)
Day £3225–£6150

ST JOHN'S SCHOOL
Newton, Porthcawl, Bridgend
CF36 5NP
Tel: (01656) 783404
Fax: (01656) 783535
Email: stjohns.school@virgin.net
Head: Mrs C A Clint
Type: Co-educational Day 3–16
Fees: (September 05)
Day £3750–£7920

CARDIFF

CARDIFF

THE CARDIFF ACADEMY
40–41 The Parade, Roath, Cardiff
Cardiff CF24 3AB
Tel: (02920) 409630
Fax: (02920) 455273
Email: 40–41@theparade.fsbusiness.co.uk
Head: Dr S R Wilson
Type: Co-educational Day 14–18
No of pupils: B25 G25
Fees: (September 05)
Day £6000–£9000

THE CATHEDRAL SCHOOL
Cardiff Road, Llandaff, Cardiff
Cardiff CF5 2YH
Tel: (029) 2056 3179
Fax: (029) 2056 7752
Email: Registrar@cathedral-school.co.uk
Head: Mr P L Gray
Type: Co-educational Day 3–16
No of pupils: B428 G192
Fees: (September 05)
Day £5385–£7785

ELM TREE HOUSE
Clive Road, Llandaff, Cardiff
Cardiff CF5 1GN
Tel: (029) 2022 3388
Fax: (029) 2022 3388
Head: Mrs C M Thomas
Type: Co-educational Day 2–11
No of pupils: B25 G95

HOWELL'S SCHOOL, LLANDAFF GDST
Cardiff Road, Llandaff, Cardiff Cardiff CF5 2YD
Tel: (029) 2056 2019
Fax: (029) 2057 8879
Email: mail@how.gdst.net
Head: Mrs J Fitz
Type: Co-educational Day Boys 16–18 Girls 3–18
No of pupils: B25 G805
Fees: (September 05)
Day £4605–£7413

KINGS MONKTON SCHOOL
6 West Grove, Cardiff Cardiff CF24 3XL
Tel: (029) 2048 2854
Fax: (029) 2049 0484
Email: mail@kingsmonkton.org.uk
Head: Mr R N Griffin
Type: Co-educational Day 3–18
No of pupils: B230 G160
Fees: (September 05)
Day £4605–£6090

ST JOHN'S COLLEGE
College Green, Newport Road, Old St Mellons, Cardiff Cardiff CF3 5YX
Tel: (029) 2077 8936
Fax: (029) 20779099
Head: Dr D Neville
Type: Co-educational Day 3–18
No of pupils: B240 G200

WESTBOURNE SCHOOL
4 Hickman Road, Penarth, Cardiff Cardiff CF64 2AJ
Tel: (029) 2070 5705
Fax: (029) 2070 9988
Email: info@westbourneschool.com
Head: Mr A Swain and Mr K Underhill
Type: Co-educational Day 1–11
No of pupils: B110 G70
Fees: (September 03)
Day £2940–£6150

CARMARTHENSHIRE

LLANDOVERY

LLANDOVERY COLLEGE
Llandovery, Carmarthenshire SA20 0EE
Tel: (01550) 723000
Fax: (01550) 723002
Email: mail@llandoverycollege.com
Head: Mr P A Hogan
Type: Co-educational Boarding and Day 4–18 Flexi-boarding available
No of pupils: B206 G127
No of boarders: F135 W20
Fees: (September 05)
FB £10350–£17460
Day £4995–£10050

LLANELLI

ST MICHAEL'S SCHOOL
Bryn, Llanelli, Carmarthenshire SA14 9TU
Tel: (01554) 820325
Fax: (01554) 821716
Head: Mr D T Sheehan
Type: Co-educational Day 3–18
No of pupils: B210 G179
No of boarders: F19
Fees: (September 03)
Day £3198–£6105

CONWY

COLWYN BAY

LYNDON PREPARATORY SCHOOL
Pwllycrochan Avenue, Colwyn Bay, Conwy LL29 7BP
Tel: (01492) 530381
Fax: (01492) 539720
Email: lyndon@rydal-penrhos.co.uk
Head: Mr M Collins
Type: Co-educational Boarding and Day 2–11 Flexi-boarding available
No of pupils: B125 G112
Fees: (September 05)
FB £11400–£13200
WB £10260–£11880
Day £3930–£5880

RYDAL PENRHOS SENIOR SCHOOL
Pwllycrochan Avenue, Colwyn Bay, Conwy LL29 7BT
Tel: (01492) 530155
Fax: (01492) 534072
Email: info@rydal-penrhos.com
Head: Mr M S James
Type: Co-educational Boarding and Day 11–18 (Single-sex ed 11–16) Flexi-boarding available
No of pupils: B220 G174
No of boarders: F150
Fees: (September 03)
FB £14541–£16485
Day £9216–£9813

LLANDUDNO

ST DAVID'S COLLEGE†
Llandudno, Conwy LL30 1RD
Tel: (01492) 875974
Fax: (01492) 870383
Email: headmaster@stdavidscollege.co.uk
Head: Mr W Seymour
Type: Co-educational Boarding and Day 11–18 Flexi-boarding available
No of pupils: B200 G60
No of boarders: F160 W5
Fees: (September 05)
F/WB £ £15780–£16395
Day £10260–£10659

DENBIGHSHIRE

DENBIGH

HOWELL'S SCHOOL
Denbigh, Denbighshire LL16 3EN
Tel: (01745) 813631
Fax: (01745) 814443
Email: enquiries@howells.org
Head: Mrs L Robinson
Type: Girls Boarding and Day 2–18 Flexi-boarding available
No of pupils: 300
No of boarders: F100 W30
Fees: (September 05)
F/WB £ £9054–£14955
Day £4185–£9570

RHYL

NORTHGATE PREPARATORY
57 Russell Road, Rhyl, Denbighshire LL18 3DD
Tel: (01745) 342510
Email: northgateschool@btinternet.com
Head: Mr P G Orton
Type: Co-educational Day 4–11
No of pupils: B23 G23
Fees: (September 02)
Day £2250–£2400

RUTHIN

RUTHIN SCHOOL
Mold Road, Ruthin, Denbighshire LL15 1EE
Tel: (01824) 702543
Fax: (01824) 707141
Email: secretary@ruthinschool.co.uk
Head: Mr J S Rowlands
Type: Co-educational Boarding and Day 3–18 Flexi-boarding available
No of pupils: B141 G55
No of boarders: F53 W8
Fees: (September 05) FB £16260 WB £13560 Day £5250–£10020

ST ASAPH

FAIRHOLME PREPARATORY SCHOOL
Mount Road, St Asaph, Denbighshire LL17 0DH
Tel: (01745) 583505
Fax: (01745) 584332
Email: success@fairholmeschool.com
Head: Mrs M Cashman
Type: Co-educational Day 3–11
No of pupils: B70 G60
Fees: (September 04)
Day £3360–£3660

GWYNEDD

BANGOR

HILLGROVE SCHOOL
Ffriddoedd Road, Bangor,
Gwynedd LL57 2TW
Tel: (01248) 353568
Fax: (01248) 353971
Email: headmaster@
hillgrove.gwynedd.sch.uk
Head: Mr J G Porter
Type: Co-educational Day 3–16
No of pupils: B72 G82
Fees: (September 05)
Day £2040–£3480

ST GERARD'S SCHOOL
Ffriddoedd Road, Bangor,
Gwynedd LL57 2EL
Tel: (01248) 351656
Fax: (01248) 351204
Head: Miss A Parkinson
Type: Co-educational Day 3–18
No of pupils: B169 G184
Fees: (September 03)
Day £3285–£4965

MONMOUTHSHIRE

CHEPSTOW

ST JOHN'S-ON-THE-HILL
Tutshill, Chepstow,
Monmouthshire NP16 7LE
Tel: (01291) 622045
Fax: (01291) 623932
Email: registrar@
stjohnsonthehill.co.uk
Head: Mr I K Etchells
Type: Co-educational Boarding and Day 2–13 (Nursery from 3 months) Flexi-boarding available
No of pupils: B192 G133
No of boarders: F35 W2
Fees: (September 04)
F/WB £ £11235 Day £4995–£8265

MONMOUTH

HABERDASHERS' MONMOUTH SCHOOL FOR GIRLS
Hereford Road, Monmouth,
Monmouthshire NP25 5XT
Tel: (01600) 711100
Fax: (01600) 711233
Email: admissions@hmsg.co.uk
Head: Dr B Despontin
Type: Girls Day and Boarding 7–18 Flexi-boarding available
No of pupils: 681
No of boarders: F100
Fees: (September 04)
F/WB £ £14382–£14874
Day £6537–£7827

MONMOUTH SCHOOL
Almshouse Street, Monmouth,
Monmouthshire NP25 3XP
Tel: (01600) 713143
Fax: (01600) 772701
Email: admissions@
monmouthschool.org
Head: Dr S G Connors
Type: Boys Boarding and Day 7–18 (Boarding 11–18) Flexi-boarding available
No of pupils: 680
No of boarders: F135
Fees: (September 05)
F/WB £ £15846 Day £6660–£9504

NEWPORT

NEWPORT

ROUGEMONT SCHOOL
Llantarnam Hall, Malpas Road,
Newport Newport NP20 6QB
Tel: (01633) 820800
Fax: (01633) 855598
Email: registrar@rsch.co.uk
Head: Dr J Tribbick
Type: Co-educational Day 3–18
No of pupils: B369 G336
Fees: (September 05)
Day £4950–£7650

PEMBROKESHIRE

SAUNDERSFOOT

NETHERWOOD SCHOOL
Saundersfoot, Pembrokeshire
SA69 9BE
Tel: (01834) 811057
Fax: (01834) 811023
Email: netherwood.school@virgin.net
Head: Mr D H Morris
Type: Co-educational Day and Boarding 3–18 Flexi-boarding available
No of pupils: B76 G59
No of boarders: F24 W4
Fees: (September 04)
FB £9150–£12750
WB £7950–£8850
Day £3600–£6750

POWYS

BRECON

CHRIST COLLEGE
Brecon, Powys LD3 8AG
Tel: (01874) 615440
Fax: (01874) 615475
Email: enquiries@christcollegebrecon.com
Head: Mr D P Jones
Type: Co-educational Boarding and Day 11–18 Flexi-boarding available
No of pupils: B185 G115
No of boarders: F172 W55
Fees: (September 05)
F/WB £ £13950–£17820
Day £10470–£11925

SWANSEA

SWANSEA

CRAIG-Y-NOS SCHOOL
Clyne Common, Bishopston, Swansea Swansea SA3 3JB
Tel: (01792) 234288
Fax: (01792) 233813
Email: craigynos.school@btinternet.com
Head: Mr G W Fursland
Type: Co-educational Day 2–11
No of pupils: B84 G60
Fees: (September 05)
Day £3075–£4080

FFYNONE HOUSE SCHOOL
36 St James' Crescent, Swansea Swansea SA1 6DR
Tel: (01792) 464967
Fax: (01792) 455202
Head: Mrs Edwina Jones
Type: Co-educational Day 9–18
No of pupils: B120 G129
Fees: (September 04)
Day £4344–£6210

OAKLEIGH HOUSE
38 Penlan Crescent, Uplands, Swansea Swansea SA2 0RL
Tel: (01792) 298537
Fax: (01792) 280371
Head: Mrs R Ferriman
Type: Co-educational Boarding and Day 3–9
No of pupils: B57 G81
Fees: (September 05)
Day £3516–£7062
Fees: (September 04)
Day £3540–£5280

2.6
Overseas Schools

FRANCE

L'ERMITAGE – INTERNATIONAL SCHOOL OF FRANCE*
46 Avenue Egle, Maisons Laffitte, 78600, France
Tel: (+33) 1 39 62 0402
Fax: (+33) 1 39 62 5402
Email: ermitage@ermitage.fr
Head: Mr C Hunter
Type: Co-educational Boarding and Day 2–18
No of pupils: B457 G447
No of boarders: F14 W101
Fees: Fees vary according to the choice of programme: French national, bilingual or IGCSE/A-Level

MOUGINS SCHOOL*
615 Avenue Dr Maurice Donat, Font de l'Orme, BP 401, 06251 Mougins Cedex, France
Tel: (+33) 4 93 90 15 47
Fax: (+33) 4 93 75 3140
Email: information@mougins-school.com
Head: Mr B G Hickmore
Type: Co-educational Day 3–18
No of pupils: B239 G183

PHILIPPINES

THE BRITISH SCHOOL*
36th Street University Park,
Bonifacio, Global City, Taguig,
Metro Manila, 1634, Philippines
Tel: (+632) 840 15 70
Fax: (+632) 840 15 20
Email: admissions@britishschoolmanila.org
Head: Mr Chris Mantz
Type: Co-educational Day 3–18
No of pupils: B279 G338
Fees: Fees per annum (day) £7,555–£8,333

SPAIN

KING'S COLLEGE MADRID*
Paseo de los Andes, 35, 28761
Soto de Vinuelas, Madrid, Spain
Tel: (+34) 918 034 800
Fax: (+34) 918 036 557
Email: info@kingscollege.es
Head: Mr D Johnson
Type: Co-educational Boarding and Day 1–18
No of pupils: B760 G720
No of boarders: F20
Fees: Fees per term (full boarding) €2,222 additional; (day) €1,390 – €2,837

SWITZERLAND

AIGLON COLLEGE*
Rue Centrale, 1885 Chesières,
Switzerland
Tel: (+41) 24 496 6126
Fax: (+41) 24 496 6162
Email: admissions@aiglon.ch
Head: The Revd Dr J Long
Type: Co-educational Boarding and Day 9–18
No of pupils: B185 G165
Fees: (full boarding) SFr65200; (day) SFr45600

JOHN F KENNEDY INTERNATIONAL SCHOOL*
CH 3792 Saanen-Gstaad,
Switzerland, Switzerland
Tel: (+41) 33 744 1372
Fax: (+41) 33 7448982
Email: lovell@jfk.ch
Type: Co-educational Boarding and Day 4–14
No of pupils: B30 G30
No of boarders: F26

Part 3

School Profiles

COUNTIES OF ENGLAND, SCOTLAND AND WALES

SCOTLAND
Highland
Moray
Aberdeenshire
Aberdeen City
Perth and Kinross
Angus
Fife
Argyll and Bute
Stirling
Borders
South Lanarkshire
East Ayrshire
South Ayrshire
Dumfries and Galloway
1. Inverclyde
2. North Ayrshire
3. Renfrewshire
4. West Dunbartonshire
5. East Dunbartonshire
6. North Lanarkshire
7. Falkirk
8. Clackmannanshire
9. West Lothian
10. City of Edinburgh
11. Midlothian
12. East Lothian
NORTHERN ENGLAND
Northumberland
Newcastle upon Tyne
Hartlepool
Stockton-on-Tees
Middlesbrough
Durham
Cumbria
North Yorkshire
York
East Riding of Yorkshire
North Lincolnshire
North East Lincolnshire
Lancashire
West Yorkshire
Merseyside
G. M.
South Yorkshire
Cheshire
Derbyshire
Nottinghamshire
Staffordshire
Isle of Man
WALES
Denbighshire
Flintshire
Conwy
Wrexham
Gwynedd
Ceredigion
Powys
Carmarthenshire
Pembrokeshire
1. Monmouthshire
2. Torfean
3. Newport
4. Blaenau Gwent
5. Caerphilly
6. Cardiff
7. Merthyr Tydfil
8. Cynon Taff
9. Vale of Glamorgan
10. Bridgend
11. Neath Port Talbot
12. Swansea
CENTRAL ENGLAND
Shropshire
W.M
Worcestershire
Warwickshire
Herefordshire
Gloucestershire
Oxfordshire
EASTERN ENGLAND
Lincolnshire
Rutland
Leicestershire
Norfolk
Northamptonshire
Cambridgeshire
Suffolk
HOME COUNTIES (North)
Bedfordshire
Buckinghamshire
Hertfordshire
Essex
Berkshire
LONDON
Greater London
13. South Gloucestershire
14. Bath and North East Somerset
15. City of Bristol
16. North Somerset
Wiltshire
Somerset
Hampshire
Devon
Dorset
Cornwall
Isle of Wight
SOUTH WEST ENGLAND
HOME COUNTIES (South)
Surrey
Kent
West Sussex
East Sussex

3.1 England

MAP OF NORTHERN ENGLAND

PROFILED SCHOOLS IN NORTHERN ENGLAND

(Incorporating the counties of Cheshire, Cumbria, Derbyshire, Durham, Hartlepool, Lancashire, North East Lincolnshire, North Lincolnshire, Greater Manchester, Merseyside, Middlesbrough, Northumberland, Nottinghamshire, Staffordshire, Stockton-on-Tees, East Riding of Yorkshire, North Yorkshire, South Yorkshire, West Yorkshire)

Casterton School

Kirkby Lonsdale, Cumbria LA6 2SG
Tel: (01524) 279200 Fax: (01524) 279208 E-mail: admissions@castertonschool.co.uk
Website: www.castertonschool.co.uk www.gabbitas.net

Headmaster Dr P McLaughlin BA Hons PhD
Founded 1823
School status Co-educational boarding and day. Day boys 3–11. Flexi-boarding available. Co-educational independent pre-prep and prep, girls' senior boarding and day.
Religious denomination Church of England
Member of AGBIS, BSA, GSA
Accredited by GSA
Learning difficulties DYS
Age range 3–18; *boarders from* 8
No of pupils 370; *(full boarding)* 281; *Girls* 355; *Boys* 15
Fees per annum *(full boarding)* £13,257–£16,587; *(weekly)* £12,909–£13,854; *(day)* £4,578–£9,924

Beautifully bordering on the three counties of North Yorkshire and the Dales, Cumbria and Lancashire, Casterton School is a leading academic girls boarding and day school. Examination results are consistently outstanding. In 2005, the A level pass rate was 100 per cent, with 84 per cent achieving grades A or B. At GCSE, 66 per cent at A* or A grades. Almost all girls remain at Casterton for their A levels, with many new girls choosing Casterton for their Sixth Form and all expect to go on to Russell Group universities as well as Oxbridge. Casterton offers a wide choice of sports and activities. Full use is made of the school's unique environment and the fact that it is a boarding school. Great emphasis is placed upon extra-curricular activities; hockey, netball and lacrosse, athletics, tennis and rounders are played on a new all-weather pitch, there is an indoor heated swimming pool and riding stables, and most girls take part in the Duke of Edinburgh's Award scheme. There are very strong traditions in the arts, music and drama, with many opportunities for performance and competition in sports regionally and nationally. In addition to a continuous programme of improvements, new buildings in recent years have included an arts centre, a science/maths building, a sports pavilion and the all-weather pitch.

There is an 11+ house for boarders joining the Senior School; they have access to all of the Senior School facilities and an exciting programme of activities operates every weekend. Between the ages of 12 and 16, girls live in small and friendly senior boarding houses. There are three separate, highly individual Sixth Form houses with study-bedroom accommodation. There is greater freedom at this stage in order to prepare girls for future working or university life. Visitors often comment upon the happy and positive atmosphere in the school.

Casterton is eight miles from the M6, 20 minutes from mainline stations and within close proximity of Manchester Airport, Leeds/ Bradford, Blackpool for the Isle of Man, and a comprehensive escort system is provided. The schools is accessible from the M6, with Edinburgh in the North and Cheshire and Shropshire and London in the South, all using the M6. York, Leeds and Harrogate are close by on the A59 and A65 respectively.

Chetwynde School

Croslands, Rating Lane, Barrow-in-Furness, Cumbria LA13 0NY
Tel: (01229) 824210 Fax: (01229) 871440
E-mail: info@chetwynde.cumbria.sch.uk
Website: www.chetwynde.cumbria.sch.uk www.gabbitas.net

Head Mrs I Nixon
Founded 1938
School status Co-educational day only
Religious denomination Inter-denominational
Age range 3–18
Fees per annum *(day)* £4,245–£4,599

Chetwynde School occupies an attractive site situated near the Lake District. It has grown into a substantial and successful school with an excellent academic and outstanding sporting reputation.

The school prides itself on high academic standards based on good teaching and individual attention. The GCSE pass rate for five Grades A to C has been at or above 97 per cent for over three years and the A level pass rate stands at or above 99 per cent over the same period. All our Sixth Form pupils go on to higher education. The curriculum is broad and challenging, with an emphasis on music and sport.

Lime House School

Holm Hill, Dalston, Carlisle, Cumbria CA5 7BX Tel: (01228) 710225 Fax: (01228) 710508
E-mail: lhsoffice@aol.com Website: www.limehouseschool.co.uk

Headmaster Mr N A Rice MA BA CertEd
Bursar Mrs J Fisher **Founded** 1809
School status Co-educational independent boarding and day
Religious denomination Non-denominational
Learning difficulties SNU/DYS MLD
Age range 4–18; *boarders from* 9
No of pupils 210; *(full boarding)* 140; *(weekly boarding)* 10; *Girls* 80; *Boys* 130
Average class size 20
Fees per annum *(full boarding)* £12,000; *(day)* £6,000

Lime House School aims to ensure that each pupil achieves his or her potential both academically and socially, with each child treated individually. Our pupils are cared for in a safe rural environment and every possible attempt is made to ensure that they develop confidence and self-esteem.

Boarding is available to all pupils, with the majority being full boarders. Each pupil's pastoral care is the shared responsibility of a residential member of staff who lives in their boarding area, a residential matron and the pupil's form teacher.

Foreign students whose first language is not English add to the cosmopolitan atmosphere of the school. They are prepared for Cambridge English examinations and follow the same curriculum as all other students.

Games and sport form an important part of school life. All students participate and a wide range of team and individual sports is offered. Most pupils take games to GCSE level, with many continuing to A level.

We would welcome a visit to our school to see it in action. Simply contact the school and we will arrange a time convenient for you.

St Bees School

St Bees, Cumbria CA27 0DS Tel: (01946) 828010 Fax: (01946) 828011
E-mail: helen.miller@st-bees-school.co.uk Website: www.st-bees-school.org

Head Mr P J Capes BSc MA **Founded** 1583
School status Co-educational boarding and day. Flexi-boarding available.
Religious denomination Church of England
Member of BSA, HMC; **Accredited by** HMC
Learning difficulties SNU/DYC DYP DYS MLD
Behavioural and emotional disorders TS/ADD ADHD
Physical and medical conditions RA SM/EPI HEA HI
Age range 11–18
No of pupils 308; *(full boarding)* 88; *(weekly boarding)* 38; *(day)* 182; *Girls* 119; *Boys* 189
Teacher:pupil ratio 1:10
Average class size 20
Fees per annum *(full boarding)* £14,568–£20,088; *(weekly)* £11,955–£17,139; *(day)* £9,321–£12,039

Curriculum Very broad during the first three years: drama, music, information technology and outdoor pursuits. Sixteen GCSE and 17 A level courses offered; over 95 per cent of leavers go on to higher education.

Entrance Own examinations; Common Entrance. Sixth Form entrance requires minimum of 5 GCSEs at grade C or higher.

Scholarships Academic and music at 11+, 13+ and at 16+. Art, music and sport into Sixth Form.

Sport and extra-curricular activities Outstanding sporting record and facilities. Lake District nearby used for outdoor pursuits.

Boarding Weekly, full and flexi.

Windermere St Anne's

Windermere, Cumbria LA23 1NW
Tel: (01539) 446164 Fax: (01539) 488414
E-mail: office@wsaschool.com
Website: www.wsaschool.com www.gabbitas.net

Headmistress Miss W A Ellis BA (Hons) PGCE
Founded 1863
School status Co-educational boarding and day
Religious denomination Non-denominational
Member of BSA, Round Square, SHMIS
Age range 2–18; *boarders from* 8
No of pupils 274; *(full boarding)* 83; *(weekly boarding)* 44; *(day)* 147; *Girls* 145; *Boys* 129
Teacher:pupil ratio 1:6
Average class size 15
Fees per annum *(full boarding)* £16,005–£18,000; *(weekly)* £15,120–£17,100; *(day)* £9,000–£9,966

Windermere St Anne's is an independent boarding and day school with facilities for over 300 senior school pupils. For over 130 years the school has created a strong reputation for the individual development of pupils, from the UK and overseas, based on academic, cultural and sporting achievement, supported by close pastoral care and an international perspective.

The philosophy of the school centres around development of the individual through a balanced, fully rounded approach to education. The aim is to ensure that all pupils are able to fulfil their potential. Targets are set not for the school but for each pupil and success is judged by personal achievement. This allows pupils to progress academically and develop their self-confidence and self-awareness at the same time.

A nurturing environment exists, with extremely supportive staff. This helps create a lively, caring, family atmosphere and mutual trust and respect within the school. Among the pupils, the ethos produces independence, individual responsibility, and a sense of adventure towards discovery and learning.

Windermere St Anne's has probably one of the most enviable locations for a school. In the heart of the Lake District, with views over Windermere to the fells beyond, the school is set in 80 acres of wooded parkland, with landscaped gardens and has a private lakeshore water sports centre.

The school policy is to provide equal opportunities for all pupils and each year group is divided into forms with sets in the main subjects. Class sizes are currently around 15 pupils. The curriculum comprises English, business studies, history, geography, French, mathematics, physics, chemistry, biology, music, art, drama, dance, home economics, information technology, design and technology, religious studies and physical education and games. Spanish and German are taken in Year 8. A number of scholarships are available to boys and girls for entry into all years for academic and creative disciplines.

The co-educational Junior Department, Elleray, has close links with the senior school. The children study a full range of subjects and enjoy a full activity programme after school.

Mount St Mary's College

Spinkhill, Derbyshire S21 3YL
Tel: (01246) 433388 Fax: (01246) 435511
E-mail: headmaster@msmcollege.com
Website: www.msmcollege.com www.gabbitas.net

Headmaster Mr P G MacDonald
Founded 1842
College status Co-educational independent boarding and day. Flexi-boarding available.
Religious denomination Roman Catholic
Learning difficulties CA SC SNU/DYC DYP DYS
Behavioural and emotional disorders ADD ADHD ASP AUT
Physical and medical conditions IT SM WA3/EPI HEA HI
Age range 11–18; *boarders from* 11
No of pupils 390; *(full boarding)* 65; *(weekly boarding)* 11; *(day)* 314; *Senior* 310; *Sixth Form* 80; *Girls* 142; *Boys* 248
Teacher:pupil ratio 1:9
Average class size 15
Fees per annum *(full boarding)* £11,865–£15,660; *(weekly)* £10,065–£13,545; *(day)* £7,470–£8,685. Private music lessons £25 per hour; EAL lessons £1170 per annum or £390 per term

Mount St Mary's College, established in 1842, is a co-educational Catholic school welcoming children of all denominations. The school is situated in beautiful surroundings close to the M1 junction 30, with minibus service to local areas.

The school offers:

- Excellent teacher:pupil ratio and high standards (100 per cent pass rate at A2).
- Specialist science block, new ICT centre, new music school, new resources centre and excellent sports facilities.
- Scholarships, bursaries and Mount assisted places scheme available.

Entry 11+ via entrance examination (February); 13+ via Common Entrance or interview; 16+ by interview and GCSE results.

Stonyhurst College

Stonyhurst, Clitheroe, Lancashire BB7 9PZ Tel: (01254) 827073 Fax: (01254) 827135
E-mail: admissions@stonyhurst.ac.uk Website: www.stonyhurst.ac.uk

Headmaster Mr A J F Aylward MA (Oxon)
Founded 1593
College status Co-educational boarding and day. Flexi-boarding available.
Religious denomination Roman Catholic
Member of ISBA, SATIPS
Accredited by HMC, ISC
Learning difficulties SNU/DYC DYP DYS MLD
Behavioural and emotional disorders CO ST/ADD ADHD ASP
Physical and medical conditions SM WA3/EPI HEA HI; **Teacher:pupil ratio** 1:8
Age range 13–18; *boarders from* 13
No of pupils 440; *Girls* 134; *Boys* 306
Fees per annum *(full boarding)* £21,303; *(weekly)* £18,225; *(day)* £12,456

Stonyhurst College is a Catholic, co-educational boarding and day school but warmly invites applications from other denominations. We also have an international school roll, delivering a broadly-based curriculum sensitive to others and the needs of the wider world.

A tutor system means that each pupil's progress is carefully monitored, and a programme of 25 AS/A levels ensures that the brightest are challenged, while not losing sight of the needs of those less gifted. A networked ICT system means that all pupils have e-mail and controlled internet access.

Sporting and recreational facilities are outstanding, and this is reflected in Stonyhurst's national reputation for its sporting excellence.

Academic, music, art and design, Sixth Form and all-rounder scholarships (supported by bursaries where appropriate) at 11+ (for entry to St Mary's Hall), 13+ and for Sixth Form entry.

England

Clarence High School

West Lane, Freshfield, Formby, Merseyside L37 7AZ Tel: (01704) 872151 Fax: (01704) 831001

Principal Mr D McKillop
School status Co-educational boarding and day
Learning difficulties BESD
Behavioural and emotional disorders CO ST TS/ADD ADHD ASP ASD SNU CB TOU
Age range 9–17
No of pupils 60; *(full boarding)* 30; *(day)* 30; *Girls* 15; *Boys* 45
Fees per annum *(weekly)* £49,890–£74,010; *(day)* £36,020–£40,560

Clarence High School (formerly Clarence House) is a day and residential special school catering for the needs of pupils with severe emotional and/or behavioural difficulties

Our success has been achieved in providing an open, honest environment where pupils feel valued, supported, respected and cared for.

Clarence High School is set in leafy Freshfield near Formby Point nature reserve, our school provides a secure, open environment for both boys and girls from 7 to 17 years. It seeks to meet the educational, spiritual, social and welfare needs of the children in a supportive, caring atmosphere. Where possible, the school encourages and promotes the facilitation of a reintegration into mainstream education.

Our emphasis is on a good learning environment, with a broad and balanced curriculum, teaching a wide range of subjects. We offer college links programmes and work experience placements, and our flexible Key Stage Four curriculum provides access to formal qualifications. Independent counsellors are also available and work with the young people on an individual basis.

Close contact with home is maintained via telephone, visits and home leave on a regular, planned basis.

- DfES approved special school.
- Very good Ofsted report 2004 (November)
- Excellent CSCI Inspection report 2004 (December)
- Good learning environment, which has a broad and well-balanced curriculum offering a wide range of subjects.
- Good residential accommodation with singe room occupancy.
- Comprehensive assessment of individual needs and excellent programmes of education, therapy and care.
- Well-qualified and very experienced staff team.
- Access to formal qualifications through an extremely flexible Key Stage 4 curriculum.
- Access to college links programmes and work experience placements.
- Quality Award for Careers Education and Guidance.
- Member of the Institute of Career Guidance.
- FA Charter Standard Award – North-West

We value and care for pupils and staff. We listen and act on the views of parents and carers. We offer value for money to placing authorities

Clarence High School is a 'special school' in all senses of the word.

Ackworth School

Ackworth, Pontefract, West Yorkshire WF7 7LT
Tel: (01977) 611401 Fax: (01977) 616225 E-mail: admissions@ackworthschool.com
Website: www.ackworthschool.com www.gabbitas.net

Headmaster Mr P Simpson
Founded 1779
School status Co-educational boarding and day
Religious denomination Quaker
Accredited by HMC, SHMIS
Age range 4–18
No of pupils 561; *(full boarding)* 83; *Girls* 271; *Boys* 290
Fees per annum *(full boarding)* £15,498; *(day)* £9,354

Ackworth is a boarding and day school for boys and girls aged 4 to 18. Boarding starts at 11 and boarders have well-presented accommodation in rooms for two or three. A major refurbishment of boarding accommodation has recently been completed. Ackworth has superb teaching facilities (the refurbished theatre is the latest addition), and a stable, devoted, staff who have established a tradition of excellence in academic results. Each year more than 95 per cent of Sixth Form leavers go to university. Music, drama and sporting facilities are outstanding leading to first rate sporting achievement and a fine musical and theatrical tradition. The school is friendly and welcoming.

Entry is by academic test. Academic, music and art scholarships are available.

Queen Ethelburga's College

Thorpe Underwood Hall, Ouseburn, York, North Yorkshire YO26 9SS
Tel: (0870) 742 3300 Fax: (0870) 742 3310
E-mail: remember@compuserve.com
Website: www.queenethelburgas.edu www.gabbitas.net

Headmaster Mr P Dass BA MA
Provost Mr Brian Martin
Head of Senior School Mr Stephen Jandrell
Founded 1912
College status Co-educational boarding and day
Religious denomination Church of England
Age range 2–20
No of pupils 410; *(full boarding)* 270; *(weekly boarding)* 30; *Girls* 260; *Boys* 150
Teacher:pupil ratio 1:10
Average class size 20
Fees per annum *(full boarding)* £14,955–£23,100; *(day)* £3,225–£7,110

Broad-based curriculum following National Curriculum in key subject areas. Entry to Preparatory School by assessment and interview. Students move through to Senior School. External entry to Senior School is by test and interview. Senior students are prepared for GCSE, A levels and advanced vocational courses. Recent heavy investment in living accommodation, equestrian centre, business and computing suite, cookery area, purpose-built laboratories and lecture theatre.

MAP OF EASTERN ENGLAND

PROFILED SCHOOLS IN EASTERN ENGLAND

(Incorporating the counties of Cambridgeshire, Leicestershire, Lincolnshire, Norfolk, Northamptonshire, Suffolk)

Map Number **Page Number**

Cambridge Arts & Sciences (CATS)

Round Church Street, Cambridge, Cambridgeshire CB5 8AD
Tel: (01223) 314431 Fax: (01223) 467773 E-mail: enquiries@catscollege.com
Website: www.ceg-uk.com www.gabbitas.net

Director & Principal Mrs E Armstrong BA (Hons) Dip Psych MSc
Director of Studies Mr D Shah BA (Hons) PhD
Registrar Mrs J Mullan **Founded** 1985
School status Co-educational boarding and day
Member of ISA
Accredited by BAC, British Council, ISA
Learning difficulties SC SNU/DYC DYP DYS
Behavioural and emotional disorders CO/ADD ADHD ASP BESD
Physical and medical conditions AT RA/EPI HEA
Age range 14–19; *boarders from* 14
No of pupils 247; *(full boarding)* 220; *(weekly boarding)* 5; *(day)* 22; *Girls* 133; *Boys* 114
Teacher:pupil ratio 1:3; **Average class size** 5
Fees per annum *(full boarding)* £15,610–£19,155; *(day)* £12,640–£14,465

Our campus, surrounding the Cambridge Union, includes science and computer labs, photography, video and art studios, and music and drama facilities. All students are members of the Cambridge Union Society and they attend its lectures and debating workshops. Over 40 A level subjects may be studied. Class sizes are limited to seven and the staff:student ratio is 1:3. A premium is placed on individual attention and students have a personal tutor who monitors well-being and progress. A range of sports, extra-curricular activities and study trips are offered. Entry is by interview and school reference.

Cambridge Centre for Sixth Form Studies

1 Salisbury Villas, Station Road, Cambridge, Cambridgeshire CB1 2JF
Tel: (01223) 716890 Fax: (01223) 517530 E-mail: enquiries@ccss.co.uk
Website: www.ccss.co.uk www.ccss.uk.tt (student website)

Principal Mr Neil Roskilly
Founded 1981
School status Co-educational independent Sixth Form college boarding and day
Religious denomination Non-denominational
Member of CIFE, ISA, ISCis
Accredited by ISA Registered charity. Member of the European Council of International Schools (ECIS).
Learning difficulties WI/DYP DYS
Behavioural and emotional disorders CO/ADD ASP; **Physical and medical conditions** RA
Age range 15–19; *boarders from* 15
No of pupils 160; *(full boarding)* 106; *(day)* 54; *Sixth Form* 160; *Girls* 70; *Boys* 90
Teacher:pupil ratio 1:3; **Average class size** 4–5
Fees per annum *(boarding)* £16,791–£21,915; *(day)* £8,643–£13,767

CCSS is one of the UK's leading independent Sixth Form colleges, specializing in A level and GCSE courses for entry into the best British universities. We are an educational charity and student-centred in all we do.

Because the college is small it is easy for new students to settle in and make friends. Two-thirds of our students are boarders and the rest come from Cambridge and the surrounding area. Just over half of our students live outside the UK, from over 25 different countries.

There is a wide range of subjects to choose from, and we help students decide on the right subjects for university entrance. Although most of our students take A levels over two years, we accept some for intensive one-year courses if they have the right academic background.

We also provide a specialized and very effective one-year GCSE programme aimed at students who have completed Year 10 (or equivalent), and those who need to improve results.

The King's School Ely

Ely, Cambridgeshire CB7 4DB
Tel: (01353) 660702 Fax: (01353) 667485 E-mail: admissions@kings-ely.cambs.sch.uk
Website: www.kings-ely.cambs.sch.uk www.gabbitas.net

Head Mrs S E Freestone GRSM, MEd, LRAM, ARCM
Founded 970
School status Co-educational independent boarding and day. Flexi-boarding available.
Religious denomination Church of England, Inter-denominational
Member of HMC, IAPS, ISCis, SHMIS
Accredited by HMC, IAPS, ISC, SHMIS
Learning difficulties WI/DYS
Age range 2–18; *boarders from* 8
No of pupils 907; *(full boarding)* 163; *(weekly boarding)* 61; *(day)* 683; *Nursery* 54; *Pre-prep* 112; *Prep* 349; *Senior* 242; *Sixth Form* 150; *Girls* 365; *Boys* 542
Teacher:pupil ratio 1:9; **Average class size** 20
Fees per annum *(full boarding)* £14,175–£19,410; *(weekly)* £14,175–£19,410; *(day)* £5,835–£13,410

The King's School, Ely is a friendly, well-balanced and caring community known for getting the best from a broad range of abilities. Founded over 1,000 years ago, the school enjoys an exceptional setting next to Ely Cathedral. The equivalent of a whole working-day each week is devoted to sports, creative and performing arts and a unique outdoor pursuits programme: the Ely Scheme. Team sports and a range of alternatives, including golf, are offered. There is a strong rowing tradition. Everyone is encouraged to take up a musical instrument. New developments over the past six years include a technology centre, library, art school, all-weather pitch and a £1 million Senior Music School. A £1 million Junior School development to provide seven new classrooms and a science laboratory for Years 7 and 8 opened at the start of the 2003 school year. Boarding is increasingly popular and facilities have been upgraded throughout the school.

St Mary's School

Bateman Street, Cambridge, Cambridgeshire CB2 1LY
Tel: (01223) 353253 Fax: (01223) 357451 E-mail: enquiries@stmaryscambridge.co.uk
Website: www.stmaryscambridge.co.uk www.gabbitas.net

Headmistress Mrs J Triffitt MA
Founded 1898
School status Girls' boarding and day. Flexi-boarding available.
Religious denomination Roman Catholic
Member of GSA; **Accredited by** GSA
Age range 11–18
No of pupils *(full boarding)* 46; *(weekly boarding)* 7
Average class size 20 in Senior School, fewer in Sixth Form
Fees per annum *(full boarding)* £19,650; *(weekly)* £17,370; *(day)* £9,870

St Mary's is a purposeful and happy school. Founded in 1898 we provide an all-round education in a welcoming Christian community that encourages all girls to reach their full potential. We are situated in the centre of the beautiful university city of Cambridge, close to the railway

station, 50 miles from London and within easy reach of four major airports. St Mary's offers an excellent academic education (one of the UK's top 300 schools), a strong tradition of excellent pastoral care, and a lively programme of extra-curricular activities, including rowing, yoga, a thriving Duke of Edinburgh's Award scheme and over 85 trips outside the classroom.

Brooke House College

Leicester Road, Market Harborough, Leicestershire LE16 7AU
Tel: (01858) 462452 Fax: (01858) 462487 E-mail: enquiries@brookehouse.com
Website: www.brookehouse.com www.gabbitas.net

Director Mr G E I Williams MA(Oxon)
Founded 1967
College status Co-educational independent boarding and day
Religious denomination Non-denominational
Member of CIFE; **Accredited by** BAC
Learning difficulties CA SC/DYS
Behavioural and emotional disorders CO
Physical and medical conditions RA
Age range 14–19; *boarders from* 14
No of pupils 180; *(full boarding)* 175; *(day)* 5; *Senior* 30; *Sixth Form* 150; *Girls* 80; *Boys* 100
Teacher:pupil ratio 1:5; **Average class size** 1:8
Fees per annum *(full boarding)* £16,950; *(day)* £9,900

Brooke House is a fully residential, international college. Intensive, small-group tuition is provided by GCSE, A level and pre-university foundation courses. The college possesses excellent academic facilities including science laboratories, an art and design studio and two recently developed computer rooms. A comprehensive programme of extra-curricular activities is organized for students' free time. Personal tutors cater for every student's pastoral needs. The college's full-time Universities Admissions Adviser gives advice and guidance. Brooke House has an enviable tradition of assisting international and UK students to gain places at the most prestigious of universities in the UK and the USA.

Loughborough Grammar School

Burton Walks, Loughborough, Leicestershire LE11 2DU Tel: (01509) 233233
Fax: (01509) 218436 E-mail: registrar@loughgs.leics.sch.uk Website: www.loughgs.leics.sch.uk

Head Mr P B Fisher MA **Founded** 1495
School status Boys' independent boarding and day. Flexi-boarding available.
Religious denomination Non-denominational
Member of BSA, HMC, ISCis, SHA
Accredited by HMC
Learning difficulties RA/DYP DYS
Physical and medical conditions RA
Age range 10–18; **Teacher:pupil ratio** 1:12
No of pupils 1010; *(full boarding)* 38; *(weekly boarding)* 10; *Boys* 1010
Average class size (Year 6) 15; (Years 7–11) 20; (Sixth Form) 12
Fees per annum *(full boarding)* £14,472; *(weekly)* £12,780; *(day)* £8,145

Loughborough Grammar School was founded in 1495 and is among the oldest and academically successful schools in the country. It is part of a larger 'family' known as the Loughborough Endowed Schools. Situated in the same spacious and attractive grounds surrounding the Grammar School, are Loughborough High School for Girls and Fairfield School, the co-educational Preparatory School.

The school prides itself on having a family atmosphere and very active house system. The boarding houses are an integral part of the school, and cater for weekly and termly boarders. Academic results are consistently good or excellent with 98 per cent going to university each year, many to Oxford/Cambridge. Music and drama are very strongly supported, most orchestras and productions being run jointly with our sister girls' High School, as well as joint Sixth Form lessons in certain subjects. A wide range of sports and games is available, as well as numerous clubs and societies, including outdoor pursuits, a large CCF, Scouts and the Duke of Edinburgh's Award Scheme.

Entry is at 10+, 11+, 13+ and Sixth Form. Scholarships are available as well as School Assisted Places.

Oakham School

Chapel Close, Oakham, Rutland LE15 6DT
Tel: (01572) 758758 Fax: (01572) 758595
E-mail: admissions@oakham.rutland.sch.uk
Website: www.oakham.rutland.sch.uk www.gabbitas.net

Headmaster Dr J A F Spence BA PhD
Founded 1584
School status Co-educational independent boarding and day
Religious denomination Church of England
Member of BSA, HMC, ISCis
Accredited by HMC, ISC
Learning difficulties SNU/DYC DYP DYS
Behavioural and emotional disorders CO/ADD ADHD ASP
Age range 10–18; *boarders from* 10
No of pupils 1040; *(full boarding)* 620; *(day)* 420; *Prep* 351; *Senior* 515; *Sixth Form* 174; *Girls* 520; *Boys* 520
Average class size 15
Fees per annum *(full boarding)* £18,330–£21,420; *(day)* £11,640–£12,810

Founded in 1584, Oakham is a fully co-educational boarding and day school. A pioneer of full co-education over 30 years ago and one of the first schools to offer the International Baccalaureate as an alternative to AS/A2, Oakham is committed to innovation and opportunity in an atmosphere that inspires enthusiasm, self-confidence and intellectual curiosity. There are 16 houses and each pupil belongs to a small tutor group so that his or her progress can be carefully monitored, thereby ensuring that each child receives expert tuition, care and guidance.

High academic standards are achieved. In 2005, 156 candidates took GCSEs gaining a 98.4 per cent pass rate with 59 per cent gaining grades A* or A. 130 candidates took 405 A levels with 100 per cent pass rate and 74.1 per cent gaining grades A or B. IB students also gained 100 per cent pass with a record breaking 33 per cent gaining 40 or more points out of the possible 45. Oakham has an excellent reputation for the quality of its musical and dramatic activities. The Art, Design & Technology department includes as part of its staff an 'artist in residence'. Musicians and actors have performed in the United States, Germany and South Africa. Participation in the Edinburgh Fringe Festival is an annual event. Social and cultural visits to Russia, Peru, North Africa, New Guinea, Israel and the Arctic Circle have also taken place.

Games teams compete successfully in local and national competitions. The principal games are rugby football, association football, cricket, hockey, tennis, athletics, lacrosse, swimming, shooting, squash and netball, and teams have toured Japan, Canada, the United States, Australia, New Zealand and France. Oakham has an established reputation in chess.

A modern Information and Communication Technology department is readily available to all and a magnificent library and study centre opened in 1994. Oakham is at the forefront of curriculum development in science.

Normal points of entry to Oakham are at 10, 11, 13 or 16 years. The scholarship examinations to the Sixth Form are held in November and Junior entry exams and scholarships in January and February. Common Entrance is in June and the Oakham School entry examination for 13-year-olds is held in March. Students entering the Sixth Form will normally be offered a conditional place, pending GCSE results. A full programme of the International Baccalaureate is available as an alternative to AS/A2.

Oakham is well served by the national rail network, and motorway and trunk-road system. Co-education and the school's proximity to both London and Midland airports (there is a direct rail link to Stansted) make Oakham particularly well suited to families living abroad.

Langley School

Langley Park, Loddon, Norwich, Norfolk NR14 6BJ Tel: (01508) 520210 Fax: (01508) 528058
E-mail: administration@langleyschool.co.uk Website: www.langleyschool.co.uk www.gabbitas.net

Headmaster Mr J G Malcolm BSc MA Cert Ed
Founded 1910
School status Co-educational boarding and day. Flexi-boarding available.
Religious denomination Non-denominational
Member of AGBIS, IAPS, ISCis, SHA, SHMIS;
Accredited by IAPS, SHMIS
Learning difficulties SNU/DYC DYP DYS
Behavioural and emotional disorders RA/ADD
Physical and medical conditions BL CA IT SM TW WA1/CP HEA IM VI W
Age range 10–18; *boarders from* 10
No of pupils 475; *(full boarding)* 105; *(weekly boarding)* 30; *Nursery* 50; *Prep* 80; *Senior* 215; *Sixth Form* 130; *Girls* 180; *Boys* 295
Teacher:pupil ratio 1:8; **Average class size** 15
Fees per annum *(full boarding)* £13,905–£16,770; *(weekly)* £12,060–£13,905; *(day)* £64,80–£8,430

General Situated in some 100 acres of playing fields and wooded parkland landscaped by Capability Brown, Langley is approximately 100 miles from London and close to Norwich Airport for international connections.

A programme of continuous investment has ensured that students benefit from the latest technology and learning opportunities whilst enjoying the heritage and history of a delightful country house. The impressive facilities include a large sports hall, artificial hockey pitch, indoor activity centre, lecture/film theatre, performing arts centre, new studios for art, sculpture and ceramics, new 11-laboratory science complex, workshops for technology and electronics, and separate computer centres for the teaching of ICT.

Curriculum An experienced graduate staff employ formal teaching methods with an emphasis on good manners, high standards of academic work and encouraging students to partake in as wide a range of experience as possible. With a staff:student ratio of 1:8, classes are small and there are currently 28 GCSE, A2 and AS level subjects to choose from including all the sciences, four modern languages, business studies, information technology, psychology, philosophy, law, media studies and drama, as well as the more traditional subjects. Entry to the Sixth Form is selective and the majority of students take four or five subjects to AS level in L6 and three to A2 in U6 for entry to university or the professions. Students with specific learning difficulties or whose first language is not English can receive additional help from specialist staff.

Games and activities Activities cannot be described as extra-curricular as they take place within the normal school day. All students are expected to take part but they can choose from a list of over 80 alternatives each week. The daily programme has options for those interested in drama, music, art, science, technology, academic pursuits, creative activities and many more. Within the programme the school also operates an active Combined Cadet Force and Duke of Edinburgh's Award Scheme as avenues for adventure training and service.

Sport also plays a major part in the activity programme with opportunities for aerobics, athletics, badminton, basketball, canoeing, climbing, croquet, cross-country, fencing, golf, gymnastics, judo, orienteering, sailing, shooting, squash, swimming, table-tennis, tennis, volleyball and windsurfing as well as the major games of rugby, soccer, hockey, cricket, netball and rounders.

Performing arts The drama, music and art departments offer a termly programme of studio events featuring workshops, professional artistes as well as numerous performances by Langley students. In addition, the Arts Umbrella programme offers the opportunity for parents and students to experience the theatrical and musical productions in London and other centres.

Admission and Scholarships At 10, 11, and 13 it is normal for a student to be offered a place based on interview and satisfactory reports from their previous school or through the Common Entrance examination. At Sixth Form candidates must have completed a satisfactory GCSE course. Competitive Entrance Scholarships are offered in music, drama, art, sport, technology and for academic ability. The auditions, interviews and examination take place in late February and details can be obtained from the school.

Laxton Junior School

East Road, Oundle, Near Peterborough, Northamptonshire PE8 4BX
Tel: (01832) 277275 Fax: (01832) 277271 E-mail: laxtonjunior@oundle.co.uk
Website: www.laxtonjunior.org.uk www.gabbitas.net

Headmistress Miss S C Thomas
Founded 1973
School status Co-educational independent day only
Religious denomination Church of England
Member of IAPS, ISCis; **Accredited by** IAPS
Learning difficulties SNU/DYS
Physical and medical conditions TW WA1
Age range 4–11
No of pupils 221; *(day)* 221; *Pre-prep* 92; *Prep* 129; *Girls* 103; *Boys* 118
Average class size Max 20
Fees per annum *(day)* £7,365–£7,734

Founded in 1973, Laxton Junior School is a co-educational day school, which is housed in new premises, located in the picturesque market town of Oundle, Northamptonshire. The school offers a broad and well-balanced curriculum where children are encouraged to fulfil their potential in a happy and secure environment, supported by a dedicated team of professionals.

Through the academic curriculum and caring pastoral system, the school aims to lay solid foundations in the development of well-motivated, confident and happy individuals who are always willing to give of their best on the road to high achievement.

England

Quinton House School

Upton Hall, Upton, Northampton, Northamptonshire NN5 4UX
Tel: (01604) 752050 Fax: (01604) 581707 E-mail: quinton.house@lineone.net
Website: www.quintonhouseschool.net www.cognitaschools.co.uk

Headmaster Mr J O'Leary
Founded 1946
School status Co-educational independent. Pre-prep referred to as Nursery.
Religious denomination Non-denominational
Learning difficulties SNU/DYS
Physical and medical conditions RA/HI
Age range 3–18
No of pupils 325; *Girls* 162; *Boys* 163
Teacher:pupil ratio 1:12; **Average class size** 20
Fees per annum *(day)* £4,125–£6,804

Located amidst 30 acres of beautiful parkland on the edge of Northampton, Quinton House is a thriving, well-balanced and caring community where every student is provided with positive encouragement and support to help them develop academically and emotionally. It is proud of its special 'family atmosphere' and of its long-standing reputation for producing well-rounded and considerate individuals who perform well academically. The facilities are impressive and the school is renowned for its success in preparing students exceptionally well for the challenges of higher education and adult life. The school also operates an 'open door' policy enabling parents to have access to the Headmaster and form tutors at any time.

Culford School

Bury St Edmunds, Suffolk IP28 6TX Tel: (01284) 728615 Fax: (01284) 729146
E-mail: admissions@culford.co.uk Website: www.culford.co.uk

Headmaster Mr J Johnson-Munday MA MBA
Founded 1881
School status Co-educational independent boarding and day. Flexi-boarding available.
Religious denomination Methodist
Member of AGBIS, HMC, IAPS
Accredited by HMC, IAPS
Learning difficulties WI/DYC DYP DYS
Physical and medical conditions RA
Age range 2–18; *boarders from* 8
No of pupils 576; *(full boarding)* 120; *(weekly boarding)* 58; *(day)* 398; *Nursery* 12; *Pre-prep* 66; *Prep* 176; *Senior* 195; *Sixth Form* 127; *Girls* 253; *Boys* 323
Teacher:pupil ratio 1:9; **Average class size** 18
Fees per annum *(full boarding)* £15,204–£19,698; *(weekly)* £13,527–£19,698; *(day)* £7,131–£12,837

Culford aims to provide an inspiring environment in which pupils will want to live, study and learn.

We are predominantly a boarding school where all pupils benefit from the extended school day and a rich programme of weekend activities.

Our focus is on finding ways in which we can stretch pupils to enable them to achieve – to delight both themselves and their parents with the people they turn out to be. We are passionate about an academic curriculum that seeks to inspire pupils to achieve more than they think possible. We are passionate, too, about what goes on outside the classroom, believing that academic success is only part of the measure of a well-educated adult.

Saint Felix Schools

Southwold, Suffolk IP18 6SD
Tel: (01502) 722175 Fax: (01502) 722641
E-mail: schooladmin@stfelix.suffolk.sch.uk
Website: www.stfelix.co.uk

Headmaster Mr David Ward
School status Co-educational boarding and day. Flexi-boarding available.
Religious denomination Non-denominational
Age range 1–18; *boarders from* 6–18
No of pupils 311; *(full boarding)* 49; *(weekly boarding)* 8; *Girls* 211; *Boys* 100

Saint Felix is set in 75 acres of glorious grounds on the edge of the seaside town of Southwold. Small classes enable pupils to achieve high academic results at all levels.

Facilities include an impressive sports hall complex, squash courts, indoor swimming pool and an equestrian course. Pupils gain gold medals in National Schools Swimming events.

Saint Felix has a strong Arts and Music tradition: the school holds the Artsmark Gold Award.

The Duke of Edinburgh's Award Scheme is encouraged: the Prep school operates its own award scheme. Emphasis is placed on extra-curricular activities after school and at weekends. Extended day arrangements for working parents. English as a Foreign Language (EFL) is offered on the curriculum.

MAP OF CENTRAL ENGLAND

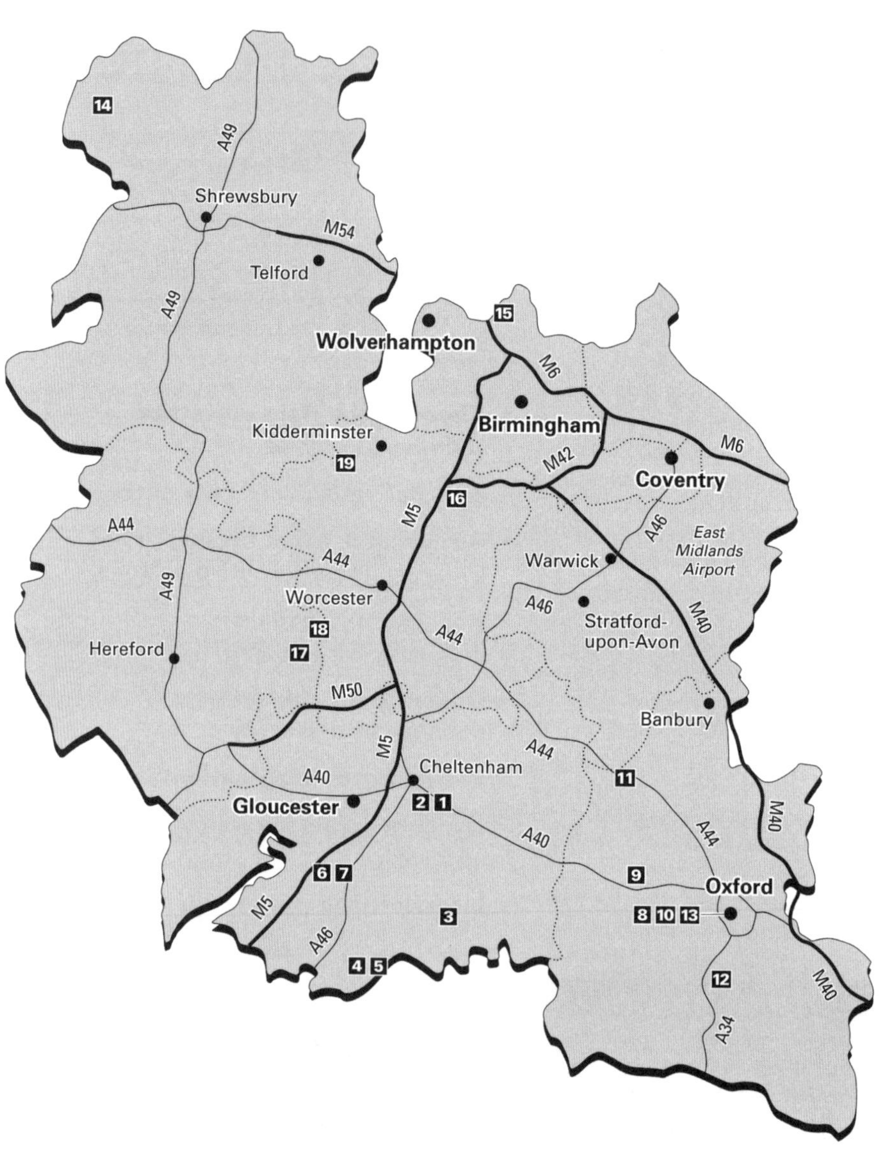

PROFILED SCHOOLS IN CENTRAL ENGLAND

(Incorporating the counties of Gloucestershire, Herefordshire, Oxfordshire, West Midlands, Shropshire, Warwickshire, Worcestershire)

Dean Close Preparatory School

Lansdown Road, Cheltenham, Gloucestershire GL51 6QS
Tel: (01242) 512217 Fax: (01242) 258005 E-mail: dcpsoffice@deanclose.org.uk
Website: www.deancloseprep.co.uk/prep www.gabbitas.net

Head Rev L Browne **Founded** 1886
School status Co-educational boarding and day. Flexi-boarding available.
Religious denomination Church of England
Member of IAPS; **Accredited by** IAPS
Learning difficulties SNU/DYC DYP DYS MLD
Behavioural and emotional disorders CA/ADHD **Age range** 2–13; *boarders from* 7
No of pupils 369; *(full boarding)* 60; *Girls* 174; *Boys* 195
Teacher:pupil ratio 1:8; **Average class size** 15
Fees per annum *(full boarding)* £12,585–£15,885; *(weekly)* £8,670–£12,225; *(day)* £7,545–£11,100

Dean Close Preparatory School is a Christian family school committed to the development of the individual child in all aspects of education.

The school follows the Common Entrance base but firmly embraces the National Curriculum.

An entry test in English, mathematics and verbal reasoning appropriate for the pupil's age is set and most children spend a day in the school.

Academic and music scholarships and exhibitions, and sports awards are offered at 11+.

There are three boarding houses run by house parents. The number of day boarders in each house is limited to ensure a large full-time boarding community. There are also three day houses offering pastoral care of the highest order. The modern classrooms include two science laboratories, a Computer Centre and an Art and Technology Department. Other facilities include a swimming pool, and theatre in the Senior School.

Dean Close School

Shelburne Road, Cheltenham, Gloucestershire GL51 6HE
Tel: (01242) 258044 Fax: (01242) 258003
E-mail: registrar@deanclose.org.uk Website: www.deanclose.org.uk www.gabbitas.net

Headmaster Rev T M Hastie-Smith MA Cert Theol **Founded** 1886
School status Co-educational independent boarding and day
Religious denomination Christian
Member of HMC; **Accredited by** HMC
Learning difficulties WI/DYC DYP DYS
Behavioural and emotional disorders RA/ADD ADHD ASP
Physical and medical conditions RA SM
Age range 13–18
No of pupils 472; *(full boarding)* 264; *Girls* 205; *Boys* 267
Fees per annum *(full boarding)* £22,485; *(day)* £15,885

Dean Close is truly co-educational, with over 30 years' experience and almost equal numbers of girls and boys. The school aims to broaden the opportunities of each and every pupil through an

exceptional array of facilities and coaching in sport, music, theatre and art, and offers almost 100 extra-curricular clubs and societies. Facilities include a 25-metre indoor pool, a brand new sports hall, two AstroTurf pitches, an impressive 550-seat theatre/concert hall, a purpose-built arts centre and a music school. A level results in 2005 generated over 72 per cent of passes at grade A or B, and at GCSE every pupil gained a minimum of six passes, 96 per cent achieving at least eight.

Rendcomb College

Rendcomb, Cirencester, Gloucestershire GL7 7HA Tel: (01285) 831213 Fax: (01285) 831121
E-mail: info@rendcomb.gloucs.sch.uk Website: www.rendcombcollege.co.uk

Headmaster Mr Gerry Holden MA St Andrews PGCE FRSA
College status Co-educational boarding and day. Flexi-boarding available.
Religious denomination Church of England
Member of HMC, ISCis, SHMIS
Accredited by HMC, SHMIS
Learning difficulties WI
Age range 3–18
No of pupils 375; *(full boarding)* 150; *Girls* 176; *Boys* 199
Fees per annum *(full boarding)* £14,190–£18,765; *(weekly)* £14,190–£18,765; *(day)* £4,530–£14,580

Set in over 200 acres of beautiful Cotswold countryside, Rendcomb College and Junior School combines the friendliness of a small school with a long tradition of academic achievement. Committed to nurturing the individual; small class sizes and a three-weekly academic grading system ensure that every pupil achieves their full potential. Boarding accommodation is superb and every pupil from the fourth form upwards has a single, spacious study bedroom. Nearly every Sixth Form pupil goes on to university, including Oxbridge. Rendcomb has excellent facilities for sport, drama, music, art and ICT and the extensive choice of extra-curricular activities, from riding to shooting, cookery to expedition training, develops pupils' self-confidence and motivation. Rendcomb is conveniently situated for the M4 and M5 and most major airports.

Querns Westonbirt School

Tetbury, Gloucestershire GL8 8QG Tel: (01666) 881390 Fax: (01666) 881391
E-mail: querns@westonbirt.gloucs.sch.uk Website: www.querns.gloucs.sch.uk

Headmistress Miss V James BA (Hons), PGCE
School status Co-educational day only
Religious denomination Church of England
Age range 4–11
No of pupils 90; *Girls* 50; *Boys* 40
Fees per annum *(day)* £5,115–£7,050

In our beautiful rural setting, the children of Querns Westonbirt enjoy a happy and positive experience of primary education in which they are truly nurtured as individuals. Within our caring family atmosphere, they quickly develop a love of learning and of all aspects of school life.

Academic success is just one of our aims. We value achievement in extra-curricular activities such as sport, art, music and drama. We also encourage personal qualities such as kindness and good manners.

By the time children leave Querns Westonbirt, they will have acquired not only a firm academic foundation but also the study skills, self-knowledge and self-confidence to make the very best of their opportunities, wherever they go.

Westonbirt School

Tetbury, Gloucestershire GL8 8QG Tel: (01666) 880333 Fax: (01666) 880364
E-mail: office@westonbirt.gloucs.sch.uk Website: www.westonbirt.gloucs.sch.uk

Headmistress Mrs M Henderson MA (Hons), PGCE
School status Girls' boarding and day. Flexi-boarding available.
Religious denomination Church of England
Member of GSA, ISCis; **Accredited by** ISCis
Age range 11–18
No of pupils 230; *(full boarding)* 155; *(day)* 75; *Sixth Form* 70
Fees per annum *(full boarding)* £19,905–£20,580; *(day)* £13,740–£14,280

Providing all the advantages of a small rural girls' school, Westonbirt will enable your daughter to fulfil her potential both academically and in extra-curricular activities, whether academic work comes naturally to her or if she needs more encouragement and coaching.

Westonbirt is among the top 5 per cent of schools nationally for 'value added', ie in the level of improvement achieved by its pupils from age 11 to 16. Pupils typically pass at least nine GCSEs and three A levels with the grades required to secure a place at a good university.

There is also the chance to study for non-academic qualifications such as the popular Leith's Certificate in Food and Wine and the Duke of Edinburgh's Award. Extensive facilities within the school's 250 acre, Grade I listed estate include a new sports centre from September 2005 and a nine-hole golf course.

Wycliffe College and Preparatory School

Bath Road, Stonehouse, Gloucestershire GL10 2JQ Tel: (01453) 822432 Fax: (01453) 827634
E-mail: senior@wycliffe.co.uk Website: www.wycliffe.co.uk

Head Mrs M E Burnet Ward MA
Second Master Mr P Woolley BA
Founded 1882
College status Co-educational boarding and day. Flexi-boarding available.
Religious denomination Inter-denominational
Member of GSA, HMC, IAPS, SHA
Learning difficulties SNU/DYP DYS
Behavioural and emotional disorders RA/ASP TOU
Physical and medical conditions RA
Age range 13–18; *boarders from* 8
No of pupils 421; *(full boarding)* 252; *(day)* 169; *Sixth Form* 200; *Girls* 150; *Boys* 271
Teacher:pupil ratio 1:12; **Average class size** 16
Fees per annum *(full boarding)* £19,545–£23,775; *(day)* £12,225–£13,395

Wycliffe is situated in sixty acres of parkland on the edge of the Cotswolds. There has been much investment over the last five years and these new facilities enable pupils to achieve the very best results. The focus is on individual learning and there is a wide range of AS courses including psychology, media studies, theatre studies, Japanese and ICT as well as the traditional subjects. Music and drama play a large part in school life and a wide variety of sport is available, including rowing, squash and basketball. Pastoral care is excellent and pupils each have their own tutor. A warm and friendly welcome awaits visitors.

Wycliffe Preparatory School

Ryeford Hall, Stonehouse, Gloucestershire GL10 2LD Tel: (01453) 820471 Fax: (01453) 825604
E-mail: prep@wycliffe.co.uk Website: www.wycliffe.co.uk www.gabbitas.net

Head Mr A P Palmer BEd MA
Founded 1927
School status Co-educational Pre-Prep and Prep boarding and day. Flexi-boarding available.
Religious denomination Inter-denominational
Member of ISIS; **Accredited by** ISIS, IAPS
Learning difficulties DYS DYP
Age range 2½–13; *boarders from* 7
No of pupils *(full boarding)* 50; *(day)* 215; *Girls* 100; *Boys* 165
Fees per annum *(full boarding)* £10,860–£13,635; *(day)* £4,605–£9,420

At Wycliffe Preparatory School our aim is to educate pupils to become confident and capable of dealing with the challenges that lie ahead of them; to achieve academically in a happy and caring environment, but also to contribute to sport, music, art and drama, as well as other activities which make the school such a special place.

Academic achievements at Wycliffe Preparatory School are also high and the school prides itself on enabling every child to reach his or her full academic and personal potential. Scholarships, both academic and non-academic, are available for entry at 11+. Forces bursaries are also offered.

Morning and afternoon créche in the Pre-Prep and an extended day with supervised prep and evening activities in the Prep School enable the necessary flexibility for working parents.

An excellent pastoral care system ensures that the academic progress and welfare of the children are monitored very carefully.

Cherwell College

Greyfriars, Paradise Street, Oxford, Oxfordshire OX1 1LD
Tel: (01865) 242670 Fax: (01865) 791761 E-mail: secretary@cherwell-college.co.uk
Website: www.cherwell-college.co.uk www.gabbitas.net

Principal Mr A Thompson
Founded 1973
College status Co-educational boarding and day
Member of CIFE
Accredited by BAC
Learning difficulties SC WI/DYC DYP DYS MLD
Behavioural and emotional disorders CO
Physical and medical conditions RA/HEA IM
Age range 16+
No of pupils 150; *(full boarding)* 90; *(weekly boarding)* 10; *(day)* 50; *Senior* 30; *Sixth Form* 120; *Girls* 75; *Boys* 75
Teacher:pupil ratio 1:1
Fees per annum *(full boarding)* £19,500; *(weekly)* £19,500; *(day)* £13,000

Cherwell is a well-established, fully co-educational day and residential college that prepares students under close personal supervision for their GCSE and A level examinations.

Cherwell's distinction is that of tuition geared to the needs of the individual, where tutorials are supported by interactive seminars and trials held weekly, lectures, revision classes and practicals for those studying natural sciences and art.

Accommodation arrangements are made. Students may live in a hall of residence, with a family or self-cater in a flat or bedsit. Provision is made for all sports at Cherwell.

Cokethorpe

Witney, Oxfordshire OX29 7PU Tel: (01993) 703921 Fax: (01993) 773499
E-mail: admin@cokethorpe.org.uk Website: www.cokethorpe.org.uk www.gabbitas.net

Headmaster Mr D J Ettinger BA, MA, PGSE
Registrar Mrs F M Rutland MA
Founded 1957
School status Co-educational independent day only
Religious denomination Inter-denominational
Member of AGBIS, ISBA, ISCis, SHMIS
Learning difficulties SNU/DYS MLD
Physical and medical conditions AT RA TW/EPI HEA HI VI
Age range 5–18
No of pupils 601; *(day)* 601; *Prep* 142; *Senior* 379; *Sixth Form* 80; *Girls* 185; *Boys* 416
Teacher:pupil ratio 1:10; **Average class size** 17
Fees per annum *(day)* £7,320–£11,820

Set in 150 acres of stunningly beautiful Oxfordshire parkland, just south of Witney, Cokethorpe offers a broad and exciting education to girls and boys aged from 5 to 18. The school is centred around an elegant Queen Anne Mansion House (the Junior School), with a series of courtyards housing a range of modern teaching and sporting facilities for the Senior School. A network of buses brings pupils from a wide area, classes are small and there is an unparalleled range of extra-curricular activities. Expectations and aspirations are high, with many academic, sporting and other achievements, notably a recent meteoric rise in GCSE and A level results, which has established Cokethorpe among the best independent schools in the area. Its growing reputation reflects the inspirational teaching, safe and tranquil environment, recent results and dynamic leadership.

d'Overbroeck's College

The Swan Building, 111 Banbury Road, Oxford, Oxfordshire OX2 6JX
Tel: (01865) 310000 Fax: (01865) 552296 E-mail: mail@doverbroecks.com
Website: www.doverbroecks.com www.gabbitas.net

Principal Mr S Cohen **Founded** 1977
College status Co-educational independent boarding and day. Day only 11–16.
Religious denomination Non-denominational
Member of ISA, ISCis, SHMIS
Accredited by ISA, SHMIS
Learning difficulties DYS MLD
Behavioural and emotional disorders CO/ADD
Physical and medical conditions RA/HEA VI
Age range 11–19
No of pupils 300; *(full boarding)* 105; *(day)* 195; *Girls* 130; *Boys* 170
Teacher:pupil ratio 1:8; **Average class size** 8
Fees per annum *(full boarding)* £18,150–£21,795; *(day)* £10,110–£14,550

The d'Overbroeck's Sixth Form is a co-educational college in Oxford offering Sixth Form education in a Sixth Form environment. Teachers are A level specialists and the approach suits students who are ready to move on from school at age 16. It is an excellent transition to university for students seeking interactive teaching, managed independence and an approach that gets the best out of every individual. Flexible, personal and highly stimulating, d'Overbroeck's provides an enriching Sixth Form experience enabling students to develop the skills needed for university and beyond. Studies are complemented by a full and busy extra-curricular programme.

Below Sixth Form pupils may join Leckford Place School at 11+ or 13+, Oxford's newest fully co-educational independent school for 11 to 16-year-olds.

England

Kingham Hill School

Kingham, Chipping Norton, Oxfordshire OX7 6TH Tel: (01608) 658999 Fax: (01608) 658658
E-mail: admissions@kingham-hill.oxon.sch.uk Website: www.kingham-hill.oxon.sch.uk
www.gabbitas.net Open Morning: 4 February 2006; 20 May 2006 Assessment day: 3 March 2006

Headmaster Mr M J Morris BEd (Hons), BA
Founded 1886
School status Co-educational independent boarding and day. Flexi-boarding available.
Religious denomination Christian
Member of AGBIS, BSA, CReSTeD, ISBA, SHA, SHMIS; **Accredited by** ISC, SHMIS
Membership of AEGIS
Learning difficulties CA SNU/DYC DYP DYS
Behavioural and emotional disorders CO RA/ADD ASP
Physical and medical conditions RA SM WA3/HEA
Age range 11–18; *boarders from* 11
No of pupils 229; *(full boarding)* 184; *(day)* 45; *Sixth Form* 48; *Girls* 61; *Boys* 168
Teacher:pupil ratio 1:7; **Average class size** 16
Fees per annum *(full boarding)* £16,439–£18,676; *(day)* £10,773–£12,624

Set in 92 acres of spectacular Cotswold countryside, the school is just 80 minutes train journey from London. Many parents are attracted by the family atmosphere and pastoral care which supports the Christian ethos of the school. Each student receives individual attention and is given the opportunity to explore their talents and gain the knowledge and skills that will prepare them for life. In June 2005 a new Dance and Drama Studio and a Fitness Suite opened – linked to our indoor swimming pool and Sports Hall. Our outdoor pursuits programme, famed assault course and sporting activities are exceptional!

The Manor Preparatory School

Faringdon Road, Abingdon, Oxfordshire OX13 6LN
Tel: (01235) 523789 Fax: (01235) 559593
E-mail: registrar@manorprep.org Website: www.manorprep.org

Headmistress Mrs D A Robinson BA PGCE MBA
Deputy Head Mrs A G Barnes BEd, ISI inspector
Founded 1947
School status Co-educational day only
Religious denomination Church of England
Member of AGBIS, IAPS, ISBA, ISCis, SATIPS
Accredited by IAPS, ISC Nursery also Ofsted accredited
Learning difficulties CA WI/DYC DYP DYS
Behavioural and emotional disorders CA
Physical and medical conditions AT CA SM TW WA2/HI VI
Age range Boys 3–7; Girls 3–11
No of pupils 327; *Girls* 307; *Boys* 20
Teacher:pupil ratio Between 1:9 and 1:12
Average class size Pre-prep 18, Prep 24
Fees per annum *(day)* £3,600–£8,100

Renowned for academic excellence and with a broad curriculum The Manor has superb facilities, including award-winning classrooms and three IT suites, set in extensive grounds. A thriving music department boasts two orchestras, 4 choirs, various ensembles and a jazz band. The Manor holds the 'Gold Activemark' award from Sport England for its 'commitment to promoting the benefits of physical activity and sport'.

Extra-curricular clubs and before and after school care are available. There are also sessions for pre-nursery children and a MiniMum's Club for mothers with babies and toddlers.

Lively, experienced staff encourage all pupils to contribute positively to the school community, to show consideration towards other people, to have a disciplined approach to work – and above all to have fun! They leave us happy, fully prepared and confident to take the next step in their education.

St Clare's, Oxford

139 Banbury Road, Oxford, Oxfordshire OX2 7AL
Tel: (01865) 552031 Fax: (01865) 513359
E-mail: admissions@stclares.ac.uk
Website: www.stclares.ac.uk www.gabbitas.net

Principal Mrs P Holloway MSc (Oxon) BSc, PGCE, Dip PM
Founded 1953
School status Co-educational independent Sixth Form college boarding and day. Flexi-boarding available.
Religious denomination Non-denominational
Member of English UK, CASE, CIFE, CIS, IBO, LISA
Age range 15⁺–20
No of pupils 196; *(full boarding)* 183; *(weekly boarding)* 1; *(day)* 12; *Girls* 114; *Boys* 82
Teacher:pupil ratio 1:8
Average class size 9
Fees per annum *(full boarding)* £22,715; *(day)* £14,000

St Clare's is a co-educational day and residential college in Oxford. Founded in 1953, it has grown out of a scheme to establish links between British and European students after the war. The college is a registered charity that aims to promote international understanding and high academic standards in its students.

Around 360 students from over 40 countries study during the academic year, with around 20 per cent British students. The minimum age is 15, and the atmosphere is informal and friendly, encouraging personal responsibility. The college is located in a pleasant residential area about 1½ km from Oxford city centre, and occupies 25 Victorian houses to which purpose-built facilities have been added. These include an outstanding library (35,000 volumes, audio-visual centre and computer suite), four science laboratories, art studio, hall, music suite, dining room and student café. Students live in college houses under the care of a resident warden.

Courses are offered at pre-university and university levels, and in English language. The pre-university courses are taught at a separate site. The 2-year pre-university course leads to the International Baccalaureate (IB) Diploma, designed to educate the whole person and to qualify for entry to the world's most demanding universities. Students choose six subjects, providing a programme balancing in depth and breadth. They also complete a research project, follow a course in critical thinking and take part in extra-curricular activities.

A one-year university foundation course preparing students for entry to British universities is also offered. A new development is the IB Institute, which offers tailored revision courses during Easter and Summer vacations.

Teaching staff are selected for their strong academic background and teaching skills. Many are involved in IB curriculum development and examining, and the college (which has offered the IB since 1977), regularly assists schools introducing the programme, and runs training workshops for experienced IB teachers. The staff:student ratio is around 1:8.

Students are assigned a personal tutor who oversees welfare and progress, meeting students individually each week.

There is an extensive programme of social, cultural, service and sporting activities, and students are encouraged to take full advantage of all the opportunities that Oxford provides.

Entry is on the basis of academic results, interview and school reports. Scholarships and bursaries are available.

Almost all IB Diploma students proceed to higher education in Britain or elsewhere and are assisted by two higher education advisers.

Moreton Hall

Weston Rhyn, Oswestry, Shropshire SY11 3EW
Tel: (01691) 776020 Fax: (01691) 778552
E-mail: admin@moretonhall.com
Website: www.moretonhall.org www.gabbitas.net

Principal Mr J Forster BA
Founded 1913
School status Co-educational boarding and day
Religious denomination Church of England
Member of AGBIS, BSA, GSA, ISCis, SHA
Learning difficulties SNU/DYC DYP DYS
Behavioural and emotional disorders CO ST
Physical and medical conditions DS IT SL TW WA3/EPI HEA
Age range Boys 4–8; Girls 4–18; *boarders from* 8
No of pupils 326; *(full boarding)* 233; *(day)* 93; *Nursery* 21; *Pre-prep* 30; *Prep* 36; *Senior* 137; *Sixth Form* 102; *Girls* 318; *Boys* 8
Teacher:pupil ratio 1:8
Average class size 15
Fees per annum *(full boarding)* £13,500–£21,255; *(day)* £5,700–£16,050

Curriculum Going well beyond the National Curriculum, some 20 subjects are available at GCSE, ranging from the traditional academic subjects such as Latin and the sciences, to practical subjects such as drama, dance and physical education. Modern languages available include French, German and Spanish. A levels in history of art, human biology, business studies and theatre studies extend the range of the curriculum. Information technology is a compulsory subject up to Sixth Form, optional thereafter.

Entry requirements Girls are admitted to the school, normally in September, at the age of 11, either by Common Entrance or by the school's entrance examination, which is held at the end of January each year. Sixth Form entrance is by examination and interview, and numbers are limited. Since September 2005 girls from the age of 4 have been admitted to Moreton First and boys can attend between the ages of 4 and 8.

Academic and leisure facilities Moreton Hall has recently completed an ambitious building and refurbishment programme. The new laboratories, information technology rooms and Art Design Centre are housed within a short distance of the central classroom, careers and library complex. An exceptionally well-equipped sports centre comprising a sports hall and floodlit tennis courts, along with heated swimming pool, nine-hole golf course and playing fields, are set in one hundred acres of beautiful parkland at the foot of the Berwyn Hills. The school offers a wide range of sporting options, including lacrosse, netball, hockey, cricket, tennis and athletics. Sailing and riding are also popular. Moreton Enterprises, a Sixth Form managed company, offers the girls real business experience. A new radio station and recording studio were opened in 1997.

Scholarships A number of scholarships and bursaries are awarded to girls entering the Lower Sixth or to assist a pupil in the school to complete her education. Awards for music, drama, art and for outstanding sporting talent are made at 11+, 12+, 13+ and 16+.

Boarding facilities Younger girls are housed in the Norton-Roberts building under the supervision of resident houseparents. Boarding houses at Moreton Hall are all linked informally with houses at Shrewsbury School, meeting regularly for musical, dramatic and social occasions. A new Sixth Form boarding house opened in September 2003.

Hydesville Tower School

25 Broadway North, Walsall, West Midlands WS1 2QG
Tel: (01922) 624374 Fax: (01922) 746169
E-mail: info@hydesville.com Website: www.hydesville.com www.cognitaschools.co.uk

Headmaster Dr Leslie Fox BSc(Eng) MA EdD PGCE
Founded 1952
School status Co-educational day only
Religious denomination Christian
Member of ISA
Learning difficulties WI/DYP DYS
Physical and medical conditions IT TW WA2
Age range 3–16
No of pupils 351; *Girls* 167; *Boys* 184
Average class size 14
Fees per annum *(day)* £4,452–£7,767

Hydesville is a family day school. In addition to those from Walsall, pupils travel on supervised coaches from Cannock, Lichfield, Sutton Coldfield, North Birmingham and West Bromwich. The three separate sections of the school cater for pupils from Nursery and Pre-Prep through the Juniors to Seniors. A high proportion of Junior School children gain places at the local grammar schools. The Senior School regularly achieves over 90 per cent GCSE pass rate. Music, drama and sport are key elements in Hydesville's extracurricular programme. Altogether, a very friendly school with happy children who do well.

Bromsgrove School

Worcester Road, Bromsgrove, Worcestershire B61 7DU Tel: (01527) 579679 Fax: (01527) 576177
E-mail: admissions@bromsgrove-school.co.uk Website: www.bromsgrove-school.co.uk
www.gabbitas.net

Headmaster Mr C Edwards MA Oxon
Founded 1553
School status Co-educational independent Pre-Prep, Prep and Senior School
Religious denomination Church of England
Member of BSA, HMC, IAPS, ISCis
Accredited by HMC, IAPS
Learning difficulties WI/DYP DYS
Behavioural and emotional disorders RA
Physical and medical conditions RA
Age range 2–18; *boarders from 7*
No of pupils 741; *(full boarding)* 367; *(day)* 374; *Girls* 290; *Boys* 451
Teacher:pupil ratio 1:9; **Average class size** 20
Fees per annum *(full boarding)* £18,990; *(day)* £10,560

Situated in a leafy 100-acre, self-contained campus, Bromsgrove School provides a very wide range of academic, extra-curricular and sporting activities. With over £22 million invested in buildings and development, there are excellent facilities for both study and recreation. While the school offers both boarding and day education, the ethos is that of a vibrant boarding community.

Bromsgrove School is not as selective at 13 as its very high league table position suggests. The value added is what makes us special. Our own entry papers are used more frequently than Common Entrance to identify late-blossoming potential.

Entry between ages 7 and 11 is based on assessment tests and at 13 on interview and tests, or Common Entrance. Entry into the Sixth Form is dependent on results at GCSE.

Malvern College

College Road, Malvern, Worcestershire WR14 3DF Tel: (01684) 581500 Fax: (01684) 581617
E-mail: srj@malcol.org Website: www.malcol.org www.gabbitas.net

Head Mr H C K Carson **Founded** 1865
College status Co-educational boarding and day
Religious denomination Church of England
Member of CASE, HMC
Accredited by HMC, ISC
Learning difficulties SNU/DYP DYS MLD
Physical and medical conditions RA/EPI HEA
Age range 13–18; **Teacher:pupil ratio** 1:8
No of pupils 569; *(full boarding)* 450; *(day)* 119; *Girls* 213; *Boys* 356
Fees per annum *(full boarding)* £22,056–£23,532; *(day)* £14,619–£15,072. Pre-prep (boarding) £8,595; (day) £4,125–£5,460. Prep (boarding) £11,415–£13,740; (day) £8,130–£10,380. Senior (boarding) £21,015–£21,990; (day) £13,935–£16,080

Malvern College is a thriving co-educational boarding and day school that respects and nurtures a child's individuality in a friendly, safe, environment. The college has an excellent reputation for pastoral care and pupils leave the school as confident, mature young men and women. The school is ranked in the top 20 in Britain in the academic league tables and offers a choice between the International Baccalaureate and A levels in the Sixth Form. While retaining the best traditional values, Malvern College is modern and innovative in its approach.

Malvern Girls' College

Avenue Road, Malvern, Worcestershire WR14 3BA
Tel: (01684) 892288 Fax: (01684) 566204 E-mail: registrar@mgc.worcs.sch.uk
Website: www.mgc.worcs.sch.uk www.gabbitas.net

Head Mrs P M C Leggate BA, MEd, PGCE
Founded 1893
College status Girls' boarding and day
Religious denomination Church of England
Member of BSA, CIS, GSA, ISBA, ISCis, NAHT, SHA; **Accredited by** GSA
Learning difficulties WI/DYS MLD
Age range 11–18; *boarders from* 11
No of pupils 330; *(full boarding)* 270
Teacher:pupil ratio 1:7
Average class size 14
Fees per annum *(full boarding)* £20,340; *(weekly)* £18,300; *(day)* £9,900

In a class of its own, Malvern Girls' College offers a high-quality academic programme in a friendly boarding environment. With an emphasis on care for the individual, each girl is encouraged actively to develop her own talents and personality. The college offers extensive opportunities for participation in sport and a wide range of extra-curricular activities, which help to develop confident and independent young women. The college is situated in one of the most beautiful areas of Britain, at the foot of the Malvern Hills. Founded in 1893, it enjoys a deserved reputation for excellent academic results.

The college is committed to providing for the education of the whole person, so when every girl leaves she is well equipped to fulfil her own individual potential with a sense of social commitment, responsibility and enthusiasm. The Head emphasizes that the college caters for a wide range of ability on entry.

At Malvern Girls' College we recognize that greater flexibility and choice is essential today to meet the different needs of parents and girls. Accordingly the college offers several options for day girls and boarders, including from September 2006 a year 6 entry.

With a broad-based curriculum girls can select from more than 20 subjects offered at GCSE, AS and A2 level. Academic staff are well qualified, lively and enthusiastic. Teaching in small groups encourages quality discussion, analysis and problem solving.

The college is committed to promoting facilities that support a forward-looking curriculum. This is evident in the state-of-the-art science centre and the multimedia language centre, which provides 21st-century teaching facilities. There is also considerable investment in information technology. There is a strong musical tradition in the college, with more than three-quarters of pupils playing at least one instrument.

Boarding life revolves around the five Houses, including a Lower Middle School House for 11 to 13-year-olds, and two Sixth Form houses. Day boarders are regarded as full members of the Houses and take part in all House activities. Pastoral care is excellent, supported by dedicated House staff.

Girls are encouraged to take part in community service. Every year, members of the Lower Sixth undertake a week's community service placement.

The college has been awarded Sport England's Sportsmark Gold award for its physical education provision in teaching more than 21 sports. Facilities include an indoor swimming pool, floodlit AstroTurf pitches and squash courts.

There is a varied weekend programme of activities for all age groups, including abseiling, canoeing, dry-slope skiing, rock climbing, photography, water sports and expeditions leading to the Duke of Edinburgh's Award.

Admission is through the college's own examinations, or through Common Entrance examination, together with an interview with the Head. The college offers Academic Entrance Scholarships and Exhibitions, as well as entrance awards for excellence in art, music, and physical education.

Moffats School

Kinlet Hall, Kinlet, Bewdley, Worcestershire DY12 3AY Tel: (01299) 841230
Fax: (01299) 841444 E-mail: office@moffats.co.uk Website: www.moffats.co.uk

Head Mr M H Daborn **Founded** 1934
School status Co-educational boarding and day. Flexi-boarding available.
Member of BSA, ISA, ISCis
Accredited by ISA, ISC; **Age range** 4–13
No of pupils 85; *(full boarding)* 43; *Girls* 39; *Boys* 46
Teacher:pupil ratio 1:7; **Average class size** 12
Fees per annum *(full boarding)* £11,385; *(weekly)* £11,385; *(day)* £988–£2,382

Set in a beautiful Georgian house on the Shropshire–Worcestershire border, Moffats provides a happy, safe environment valuing childhood. This family-run school has an ethos that children should receive unlimited encouragement in all they do, and that high academic standards are maintained without expecting more than each child's natural capacity. Good manners, kindness and respect for others are greatly valued. Small classes ensure high attention, so that each individual, whether a bright pupil or one needing more assistance, progresses at the right pace, receiving as much help as is needed.

The school's 108-acre grounds provide space not only for daily sports but also for riding, a popular option. The school carefully maintains a balance between class work and other activities, promoting cultural awareness, strengthening self-confidence and ensuring a sense of fun. Prime importance is given to the development of communication skills. Pupils regularly gain distinctions in annual ESB examinations. The school runs two choirs.

MAP OF THE HOME COUNTIES (NORTH)

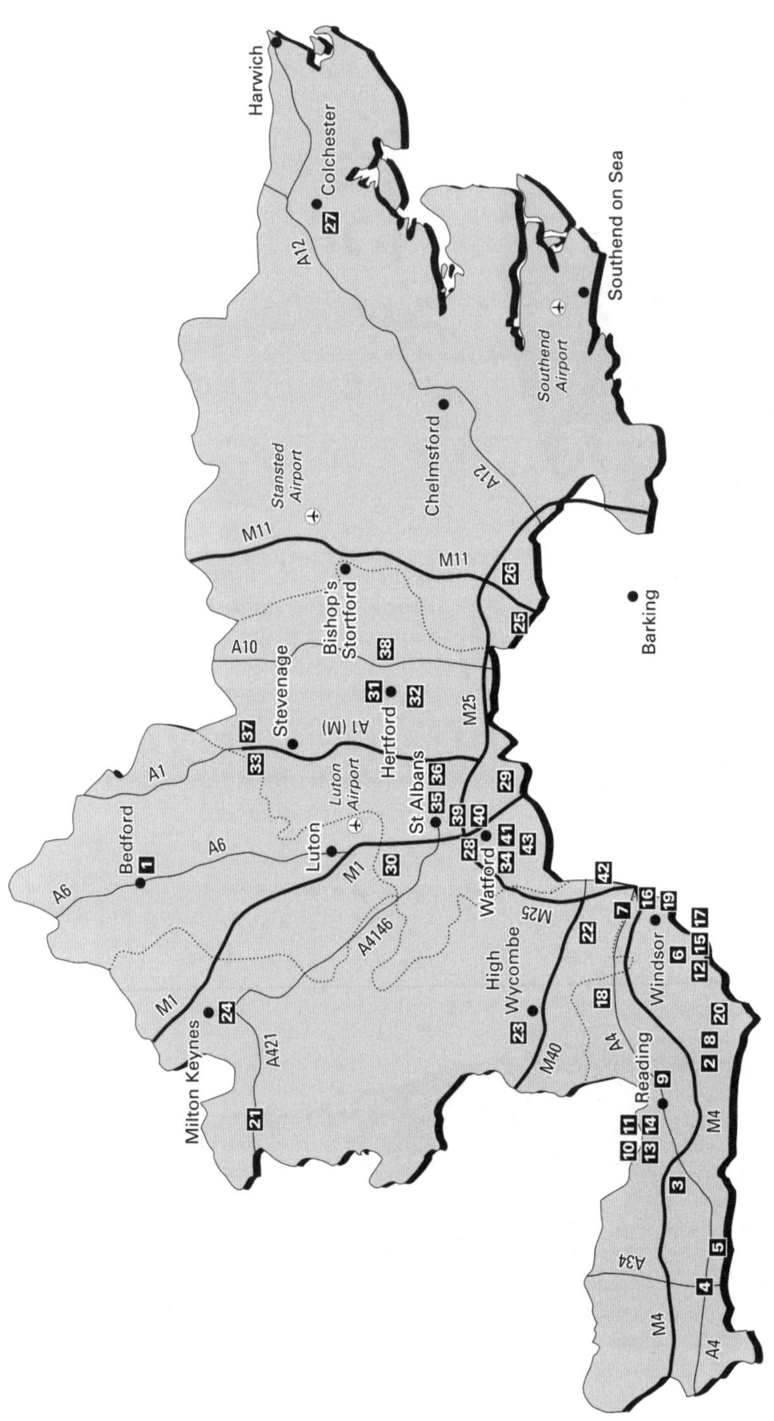

PROFILED SCHOOLS IN THE HOME COUNTIES (NORTH)

(Incorporating the counties of Bedfordshire, Berkshire, Buckinghamshire, Essex, Hertfordshire, Middlesex)

Polam School

45 Lansdowne Road, Bedford, Bedfordshire MK40 2BY
Tel: (01234) 261864 Fax: (01234) 261194 E-mail: polam@supanet.com
Website: www.polamschool.co.uk www.cognitaschools.co.uk

Principal Mr A R Brown
School status Co-educational day only
Religious denomination Non-denominational
Learning difficulties WI/DYS
No of pupils 220; *Girls* 110; *Boys* 110
Fees per annum *(day)* £2,691–£5,190

Enjoying outstanding modern facilities, including a purpose-built sports hall and indoor swimming pool, Polam has an unparalleled record as a successful feeder school for 7+, 8+ and 9+ entry to the academically highly selective Harpur Trust Schools in Bedford.

Starting from the nursery, through to transfer age, boys and girls are provided with a wealth of experiences, academic, sporting and cultural in small classes with expert tuition in a friendly and secure environment.

Always forward looking, Polam nevertheless places emphasis on the traditional values of consideration, good manners and self-discipline and no visitor to the school could fail to be impressed with the happy and purposeful atmosphere which prevails.

Bearwood College

Bearwood Road, Wokingham, Berkshire RG41 5BG Tel: (0118) 974 8300 Fax: (0118) 977 3186
E-mail: headmaster@bearwoodcollege.berks.sch.uk registrar@bearwoodcollege.berks.sch.uk
Website: www.bearwoodcollege.berks.sch.uk www.gabbitas.net

Headmaster Mr S Aiano MA (Cantab) PGCE
Founded 1827
College status Co-educational boarding and day. Flexi-boarding available.
Religious denomination Church of England
Member of BSA, ISCis, SHA, SHMIS
Accredited by British Council, SHMIS
Learning difficulties SNU/DYS MLD
Behavioural and emotional disorders ADD ASP CB
Physical and medical conditions AT SM TW/EPI HEA VI
Age range 11–18
No of pupils 318; *(full boarding)* 65; *(weekly boarding)* 44; *(day)* 209; *Prep* 61; *Senior* 183; *Sixth Form* 74; *Girls* 68; *Boys* 250
Teacher:pupil ratio 1:8; **Average class size** 18
Fees per annum *(full boarding)* £17,910–£20,640; *(weekly)* £17,910–£20,640; *(day)* £11,160–£13,020

All pupils are positively encouraged to perform to their best, both academically and outside the classroom. The academic programme culminates in a full range of GCSEs and a choice of over 20 A level subject choices. A generous staff:pupil ratio ensures small classes, allowing real focus on each pupil.

Pupils engage in a wide selection of games, both team and individual sports, and other extra-curricular activities. Drama and music are important features of college life, based in the renowned Bearwood College Theatre and Music School.

Pastoral care is given a high priority. Every pupil is a member of one of the seven houses, under a housemaster or housemistress, an assistant and a body of pastoral tutors.

Access to Bearwood College is easy. We are close to the motorway network, and within easy reach of Heathrow and Gatwick airports, and 35 minutes from London by train.

England

Bradfield College

Bradfield, Reading, Berkshire RG7 6AR Tel: (0118) 964 4510 Fax: (0118) 964 4511
E-mail: headmaster@bradfieldcollege.org.uk Website: www.bradfieldcollege.org.uk

Head Mr P J M Roberts
Founded 1850
College status Fully co-educational independent boarding and day
Religious denomination Church of England
Member of BSA, HMC, ISCis
Accredited by HMC
Learning difficulties SNU/DYS
Age range 13–18; *boarders from* 13
No of pupils 630; *(full boarding)* 550; *(day)* 80 *Junior* 300; *Sixth Form* 330; *Girls* 150; *Boys* 480
Teacher:pupil ratio 1:8
Average class size 16
Fees per annum *(full boarding)* £21,750; *(day)* £17,400

Curriculum A wide selection of subjects at GCSE is extended at A level with exciting additions such as economics, business studies, film studies, textiles, music technology and PE. All pupils in the Sixth Form go on to university.

Entry requirements and procedures Entrance at 13+ by Common Entrance. Scholarships, exhibitions and Art/Music/DT awards at 13+. Sixth Form entry is by our own internal assessments, which lead to the offer of places in the December preceding the year of entry. The College is effectively the village and is situated close to Junction 12 of the M4 and within easy reach of Reading Station and Heathrow Airport. The College offers an all-round education based on superb facilities and a young and dynamic staff. The boarding houses offer single and double bedsits.

Cheam School

Headley, Newbury, Berkshire RG19 8LD Tel: (01635) 268381 Fax: (01635) 269345
E-mail: registrar@cheamschool.co.uk Website: www.cheamschool.co.uk www.gabbitas.net

Head Mr M R Johnson BEd **Founded** 1645
School status Co-educational boarding and day. Flexi-boarding available.
Religious denomination Church of England
Member of AGBIS, BSA, IAPS, ISBA
Accredited by ISC
Learning difficulties SC SNU/DYP DYS MLD
Behavioural and emotional disorders CO
Physical and medical conditions RA SM WA2/HEA
Age range 3–13; *boarders from* 8
No of pupils 371; *(full boarding)* 19; *(weekly boarding)* 74; *(day)* 278; *Nursery* 13; *Pre-prep* 75; *Prep* 283; *Girls* 153; *Boys* 218
Fees per annum *(full boarding)* £17,325; *(day)* £7,335–£12,825

Curriculum For the 21st century your child needs the best possible preparation: communication, adaptability and confidence will be vitally important. Children are prepared in small classes (maximum 18) for Common Entrance and scholarships to all major public schools. The syllabus covers and exceeds National Curriculum requirements. Those with special needs are well catered for.

Entry requirements By interview. One scholarship is offered annually.

Academic and leisure facilities Excellent facilities set in a stimulating yet secure 80-acre estate. New classroom block, music school and refurbished chapel, completed September 2001. Modern science block (1996); dedicated IT, art and design departments; superb sporting facilities include squash court and 9-hole golf course. New indoor sports centre (completed September 2003).

Pastoral care and boarding facilities Each child is under the watchful eye of two house tutors and a form teacher; resident staff and matrons supervise boarders in comfortable dormitories. Separate girls' boarding accommodation. Nursery and pre-prep on site.

Downe House

Cold Ash, Thatcham, Berkshire RG18 9JJ Tel: (01635) 200286 Fax: (01635) 202026
E-mail: correspondence@downehouse.net Website: www.downehouse.net www.gabbitas.net

Headmistress Mrs E McKendrick BA
Founded 1907
School status Girls' boarding and day
Religious denomination Church of England
Learning difficulties SNU/DYP DYS
Behavioural and emotional disorders RA
Physical and medical conditions RA/HEA HI
Age range 11–18; **Teacher:pupil ratio** 1:7
No of pupils 561; *(full boarding)* 549; *(day)* 12
Fees per annum *(full boarding)* £22,875; *(day)* £16,560

Curriculum A wide selection of subjects is available at both GCSE and A level. Girls are also prepared for university entrance.

Entry requirements and procedures By Common Entrance and assessment. Seven passes at grade B or above for an A level course. Scholarships at 11+, 12+, 13+ and Sixth Form.

The School is only 5 miles from Newbury, with easy access to the motorway network, London

and Heathrow Airport. It has an excellent academic record, with nearly all pupils going on to university.

Academic and leisure facilities Sixth Form complex with study-bedrooms. Extensive refurbishment of all boarding houses. Significant expenditure on ICT, with voicemail and e-mail for every girl. New Sports Hall and Performing Arts Centre, and indoor swimming pool. One term spent in France in 12+ year.

Leith's Food and Wine Certificate is offered in the Sixth Form.

Heathfield School

London Road, Ascot, Berkshire SL5 8BQ
Tel: (01344) 898342 Fax: (01344) 890689 E-mail: registrar@heathfieldschool.net
Website: www.heathfieldschool.net www.gabbitas.net

Headmistress Mrs F King BA(Oxon) MA(London) MBA(Hull)
Founded 1899
School status Girls' boarding only
Member of ISCis, SHA
Accredited by GSA, HMC, IAPS, ISC
Age range 11–18
No of pupils 220
Fees per annum *(full boarding)* £22,890

Heathfield is a leading full boarding school for girls from the ages of 11 to 18, set in 35 acres renowned for modern teaching and recreational facilities, superb academic results and a strong family atmosphere.

At weekends, girls can relax after a hard week of studies through a vast choice of sports, activities, trips and social events.

As you would expect from a full boarding school, the accommodation is of the highest standards and older girls enjoy a single study bedroom. The Upper Sixth Form have their own centre.

Ascot is centrally placed in the South East of England, with excellent transport links to London (40 minutes), motorways (M4, M3) and major airports (Heathrow, Gatwick).

England

Long Close School

Upton Court Road, Upton, Berkshire SL3 7LU Tel: (01753) 520095 Fax: (01753) 821463
E-mail: info@longcloseschool.co.uk Web: www.longcloseschool.co.uk www.cognitaschools.co.uk

Headmistress Mrs W Holland LRAM ARCM GRSM Cer **Founded** 1940
School status Co-educational day only
Religious denomination Non-denominational
Member of IAPS; **Accredited by** IAPS
Learning difficulties CA SNU/DYP DYS MLD
Behavioural and emotional disorders ADD ADHD
Physical and medical conditions IT RA SM TW WA2/HEA
Age range 2–13; Nursery 2–4; Prep 4–11; Upper Prep 11–13
No of pupils: *(day)* 197
Fees per annum *(day)* £4,860–£8,580

Long Close provides a rich learning environment for boys and girls from nursery to age 13. It has a well-established reputation for friendliness and achievement. A strong emphasis is placed on individual attention in small classes, so each child has the greatest chance of success.

Children are prepared for Scholarship and Common Entrance exams to independent schools at 13, and for entry to grammar schools at 11. The broadly based curriculum, with emphasis on English, mathematics and science, aims to help all children fulfil their individual potential.

Children leave Long Close not only with academic skills and ability but also with a generally well-rounded education. They have learned to respect and care for others.

We invite you to visit Long Close and see this lively school in action.

Luckley-Oakfield School

Luckley Road, Wokingham, Berkshire RG40 3EU Tel: (0118) 978 4175 Fax: (0118) 977 0305
E-mail: registrar@luckley.wokingham.sch.uk
Website: www.luckley.wokingham.sch.uk www.gabbitas.net

Headmistress Miss V A Davis ARCS BSc
Founded 1918
School status Girls' independent boarding and day. Flexi-boarding available.
Religious denomination Church of England
Member of AGBIS, BSA, GSA
Accredited by GSA
Behavioural and emotional disorders RA/ ADHD
Age range 11–18
No of pupils 304; *(full boarding)* 24; *(weekly boarding)* 8; *(day)* 272; *Senior* 258; *Sixth Form* 46
Teacher:pupil ratio 1:8; **Average class size** 18
Fees per annum *(full boarding)* £17,604; *(weekly)* £16,236; *(day)* £10,314

Luckley-Oakfield provides a welcoming and comfortable setting for studies, recreation and friendships. It prides itself on excellent GCSE and A level results as well as successes in music, drama and the Duke of Edinburgh's Award Scheme and outstanding value-added results recognized nationally. Facilities include an IT centre, three art studios, sports hall, covered swimming pool, Sixth Form house and new Jubilee Library building. Pupils are backed by a high standard of pastoral care, which has long been synonymous with the name of the school. These values are encompassed within the Christian principles upon which life at Luckley is based.

The Oratory Preparatory School

Goring Heath, Reading, Berkshire RG8 7SF
Tel: (0118) 984 4511 Fax: (0118) 984 4806
E-mail: office@oratoryprep.co.uk
Website: www.oratoryprep.co.uk www.gabbitas.net

Headmaster Mr D L Sexon
Founded 1859
School status Co-educational boarding and day. Flexi-boarding available.
Religious denomination Roman Catholic
Learning difficulties CA WI/DYC DYP DYS
Behavioural and emotional disorders RA/ADD
Physical and medical conditions CA WA1/HEA HI
Age range 3–13
No of pupils 404; *(full boarding)* 23; *Girls* 122; *Boys* 282
Fees per annum *(full boarding)* £12,555; *(day)* £2,700–£9,105

The Oratory Preparatory School is a Roman Catholic school which prepares boys for the Oratory School and boys and girls for all independent senior schools. There is a well-qualified staff of 36 and visiting staff. There is a chaplain, a senior matron who is an SRN and two assistant matrons.

The school has an excellent record of achievement in recent years, gaining many scholarships for academic study, as well as for music, art and sport, for entry to a wide number of schools. Great opportunity is provided in music, art and drama and the school is proud of its success in all the major sports.

Padworth College

Padworth, Reading, Berkshire RG7 4NR Tel: (0118) 983 2644 Fax: (0118) 983 4515
E-mail: info@padworth.com Website: www.padworth.com

Principal Mr R Swan MA Oxon
Founded 1963
College status Co-educational independent boarding and day. Flexi-boarding available.
Religious denomination Non-denominational
Member of ARELS, CIFE, SHA
Accredited by BAC, British Council Member of English UK and CIFE
Age range 13–19; *boarders from* 13
No of pupils 95; *(full boarding)* 65; *(weekly boarding)* 10; *(day)* 20; *Senior* 30; *Sixth Form* 65; *Girls* 80; *Boys* 15
Teacher:pupil ratio 1:4; **Average class size** 5
Fees per annum *(full boarding)* £18,600; *(weekly)* £13,500; *(day)* £7,500

Padworth College is characterized by excellent academic results, small classes, individual attention and an informal tutorial atmosphere. Padworth is a truly international community with students drawn from more than 25 countries including a significant and increasing number of British students.

Padworth College provides a wide and flexible programme of academic courses leading to GCSE, A Level, AVCE and University Access/Foundation. Students are accepted throughout the academic year for any length of time from one term to five years. A strong emphasis is placed on pastoral care and helping every student to achieve his or her potential. Generous scholarships are available.

Housed in an 18th century country house in its own grounds, Padworth is conveniently located just 20 minutes from the university town of Reading and 45 minutes from Heathrow Airport by road.

England

Pangbourne College

Pangbourne, Berkshire RG8 8LA
Tel: (0118) 984 2101 Fax: (0118) 984 5443 E-mail: registrar@pangcoll.co.uk
Website: www.pangbournecollege.com www.gabbitas.net

Headmaster Mr T J C Garnier BSc, PGCE (Oxon)
Founded 1917
College status Co-educational boarding and day. Flexi-boarding available.
Religious denomination Church of England
Age range 11–18
No of pupils 394; *(full boarding)* 193; *Girls* 100; *Boys* 294
Teacher:pupil ratio 1:7
Fees per annum *(full boarding)* £14,955–£20,595; *(day)* £10,515–£14,445

Entry at 11, 13 and Sixth Form. Generous scholarship provision with academic, sport, music, art, technology and all-rounder awards available.

A modern friendly school with a distinctive history, an excellent system of caring for the development of each pupil and an ethos of courtesy and teamwork. Famous for sport, especially rowing, judo and rugby, the college encourages all pupils to be active and enjoy the outdoors. Widespread involvement in music and drama adds to the vibrant and exciting atmosphere. New junior and girls' boarding houses will open in 2005 and 2007. The buildings are set in fine grounds of 240 acres, ten minutes from Junction 12 of the M4.

Papplewick School

Windsor Road, Ascot, Berkshire SL5 7LH
Tel: (01344) 621488 Fax: (01344) 874639
E-mail: hm@papplewick.org.uk
Website: http://www.papplewick.org.uk www.gabbitas.net

Head Mr T W Bunbury BA(Hons) PGCE
Founded 1947
School status Boys' independent boarding and day
Religious denomination Church of England
Member of IAPS, ISCis, NAHT, SATIPS
Learning difficulties WI/DYP DYS MLD
Behavioural and emotional disorders RA/ADD
Physical and medical conditions RA
Age range 7–13; *boarders from 7*
No of pupils 203; *(full boarding)* 130
Teacher:pupil ratio 1:8
Average class size 14
Fees per annum *(full boarding)* £17,775; *(day)* £13,650

Curriculum All main subjects are studied. ICT is taught throughout the school, as are art, design and technology. One accelerated stream towards scholarships and two streams towards Common Entrance passes. Balance is maintained with music, PE and a wide range of competitive sports and games. Magnificent new sports hall, music school and indoor pool.

Boarders Year 3 to 5 boarders may go home on Saturday nights. Year 6 to 8 boarders may go home on Sundays.

Entry requirements Parental choice and interview followed by placing test. It is essential to register boys well in advance of their sixth birthday.

Papplewick enjoys a spacious rural location on the edge of Windsor Great Park. Convenient links with M4, M3, M25, Heathrow and Gatwick. The quality of care and the dedication of staff are outstanding and remain Papplewick's special hallmark.

Queen Anne's School

6 Henley Road, Caversham, Reading, Berkshire RG4 6DX
Tel: (0118) 918 7333 Fax: (0118) 918 7310
E-mail: admis@queenannes.reading.sch.uk Website: www.qas.org.uk www.gabbitas.net

Headmistress Mrs D Forbes
Founded 1894
School status Girls' boarding and day. Flexi-boarding available.
Religious denomination Church of England
Age range 11–18
No of pupils 340; *(full boarding)* 100; *(weekly boarding)* 80
Teacher:pupil ratio 1:7.4; **Ave class size** 16–18
Fees per annum *(full boarding)* £21,222; *(day)* £14,334

Situated on a 35-acre campus north of Reading with excellent road/rail links to London, Heathrow and the South East. Entry at 11, 12, 13 and Sixth Form, by Common Entrance or school's own examination. Academic, music, art, sport and Sixth Form scholarships available.

Facilities include: 250-seat performing arts centre, large music department, modern languages centre, ICT department and a new £3 million science block for 2006. Also excellent sports centre with squash courts, climbing wall and indoor swimming pool. Queen Anne's girls are able to grow and learn in the security of a single sex environment. A wide range of extra-curricular activities and excellent academic results prepare them well for university and successful careers.

Reading Blue Coat School

Holme Park, Sonning-on-Thames, Reading, Berkshire RG4 6SU
Tel: (0118) 944 1005 Fax: (0118) 944 2690 E-mail: vmf@blue-coat.reading.sch.uk
Website: www.blue-coat.reading.sch.uk www.gabbitas.net

Headmaster Mr S J W McArthur BSc MA FCollP **Founded** 1646
School status Boys' (11–18) Co-educational (Sixth Form) day only
Religious denomination Church of England
Member of AGBIS, HMC, SHMIS
No of pupils 669; *Senior* 454; *Sixth Form* 215; *Girls* 55; *Boys* 614
Fees per annum *(day)* £9,900

Richard Aldworth founded the school in 1646 for 'Scholars in Blue Coates'. Today the magnificent riverside setting at Sonning-on-Thames provides an excellent campus. The imaginative development programme has enhanced the fine facilities at this forward-looking school. Recent major projects are the science laboratories, library, dining hall and the exciting dimension of the sports centre, which provides courts for indoor sports, a climbing wall and an extensive fitness suite. Day places are available to boys from 11 to 18 with girls joining our co-educational Sixth Form.

The school is well known for its academic standards, for science, the humanities, arts, technology and ICT, and the fostering of sporting and artistic development in its pupils. We have a superb tradition of art, drama and music, with regular performances and exhibitions. The school has an international reputation for public speaking. Our activities programme offers a wide range from adventure training and the Duke of Edinburgh's Award to sailing, archery and community service.

The extensive grounds and sports fields provide superb facilities for a wide range of sports including rugby, tennis and rowing.

The school believes in each individual's contribution and in enabling pupils to reach their potential. While examination success is our goal, we also recognize the other facets to education and encourage sports and creativity.

England

St George's School

Ascot, Berkshire SL5 7DZ Tel: (01344) 629900 Fax: (01344) 629901
E-mail: office@stgeorges-ascot.org.uk Website: www.stgeorges-ascot.org.uk www.gabbitas.net

Headmistress Mrs C Jordan MA PGCE
Founded 1877
School status Girls' boarding and day. Flexi-boarding available.
Religious denomination Church of England
Member of GSA
Learning difficulties WI/DYC DYP DYS
Behavioural and emotional disorders RA/ADHD ASP
Physical and medical conditions HL RA SM/HEA VI
Age range 11–18
No of pupils 293; *(full boarding)* 143; *(day)* 150
Fees per annum *(full boarding)* £21,600; *(day)* £13,950

St George's School, Ascot, is an independent school for girls, located in the Berkshire countryside. It is situated between the M3, M4 and M25 motorways, allowing for easy access to London, Heathrow and Gatwick.

Entry is by examination at 11, 12 or 13 and, while broadstream, the academic results are outstanding. There are limited places at 16+.

Boarders and day girls benefit from the caring and personal attention of a dedicated teaching and pastoral staff. The main faith is Church of England, but girls from any denomination are welcome. Extra-curricular activities are many and include music, drama, debating, voluntary service, Duke of Edinburgh's Award and photography. Sport is excellent and includes lacrosse, tennis, swimming, gymnastics, squash and fitness exercising.

St George's, Ascot is committed to the development of the individual and her talents, to the best of her ability.

St John's Beaumont

Priest Hill, Old Windsor, Windsor, Berkshire SL4 2JN Tel: (01784) 432428 Fax: (01784) 494048
E-mail: admissions@stjohnsbeaumont.co.uk Website: www.stjohnsbeaumont.org.uk

Acting Headmaster Mr G Delaney
Founded 1888
School status Boys' boarding and day
Religious denomination Roman Catholic
Member of AGBIS, BSA, IAPS, ISCis;
Accredited by IAPS, ISC
Physical and medical conditions IT SM TW WA2
Age range 4–13
No of pupils 342; *(full boarding)* 30; *(weekly boarding)* 30; *(day)* 282; *Boys* 342
Teacher:pupil ratio 1:8; **Average class size** 17
Fees per annum *(full boarding)* £17,286; *(weekly)* £14,580; *(day)* £5,997–£11,046

St John's Beaumont is a Roman Catholic school founded in 1888 by the Society of Jesus. Set in grounds of over 100 acres on the edge of Old Windsor are the imposing, spacious, bright purpose-built premises designed by J F Bentley, architect of Westminster Cathedral. The school

has outstanding academic, creative and sporting facilities including a science and technology block, an art and craft block, a music school and drama centre and an ICT centre and library complex. In 2004 wireless technology was made available in classrooms, enabling access to individual laptops. The school has a well-equipped gymnasium, an indoor 25-metre swimming pool and four tennis courts. In addition a new sports complex is being built and should be completed within the next academic year. On top of the daily curriculum schedules, there are various extra activities after school. These include chess, bridge, art, drama and various sports. Games are played every day and the school particularly excels at rugby, cricket, tennis and swimming.

St Mary's School, Ascot

St Mary's Road, Ascot, Berkshire SL5 9JF Tel: (01344) 623721 Fax: (01344) 873281
E-mail: admissions@st-marys-ascot.co.uk Website: www.st-marys-ascot.co.uk www.gabbitas.net

Headmistress Mrs M Breen MSc BSc
Founded 1885
School status Girls' independent boarding and day
Religious denomination Roman Catholic
Learning difficulties WI/DYS
Physical and medical conditions HEA HI
Age range 11–18; *boarders from* 11
No of pupils 356; *(full boarding)* 340; *(day)* 16; *Senior* 250; *Sixth Form* 106
Teacher:pupil ratio 1:7; **Average class size** 15
Fees per annum *(full boarding)* £22,047; *(day)* £15,384

St Mary's is a selective independent Roman Catholic boarding school for girls aged 11 to 18 years. The school is situated in 55 acres close to the M3, M4 and M25 motorways and within easy access of London and the airports. Entry at 11+, 13+ and 16+ is subject to the school's own entry procedure. Facilities are excellent as are

examination results, with 85 per cent A to B grades at A level and 99 per cent A to C grades at GCSE (2005). The majority of pupils stay on for the Sixth Form and 99 per cent go on to university.

We are very proud of our outstanding facilities, which include a purpose-built language faculty, a state-of-the-art library with integrated IT, a purpose-built Upper Sixth house of single study bedrooms, a science centre, a music school, an art complex, a drama studio, a heated indoor swimming pool, an all-weather sports surface, a school intranet, and a new purpose-built sports complex.

St Piran's Preparatory School

Gringer Hill, Maidenhead, Berkshire SL6 7LZ Tel: (01628) 594300 Fax: (01628) 594301
E-mail: office@stpirans.co.uk Website: www.stpirans.co.uk www.gabbitas.net

Headmaster Mr J Carroll BA Hons BPhilEd PGCE **Founded** 1805
School status Co-educational day only
Religious denomination Church of England
Member of IAPS, ISBA, ISCis, NAHT, SATIPS;
Accredited by IAPS
Learning difficulties WI/DYC DYP DYS MLD
Behavioural and emotional disorders RA/ADD ADHD ASP
Physical and medical conditions AT RA SM WA3/EPI HEA HI VI
Age range 3–13; **Average class size** 18
No of pupils 328; *(day)* 328; *Nursery* 31; *Prep* 297; *Girls* 110; *Boys* 218
Fees per annum *(day)* £2,598–£8,790

Curriculum National Curriculum subjects up to Year 8. French is offered from Reception to Year 8. German and Spanish are options for seniors.

Sport A comprehensive range for all pupils. Facilities include a new sports hall, indoor swimming pool, all-weather pitch and dance studio.

Facilities Excellent facilities. Fully networked ICT department, PCs in classrooms and a new learning resource centre. We have three specialist teachers for those who need additional support. Trampolining, drama, games and crafts, among others, are activities for Year 5 to Year 8 at the end of the day.

Entry requirements Entry is by interview, school report and, where necessary, a short assessment if entry is higher up in the school. The school has expanded to a three-form entry at age 7+.

Upton House School

115 St Leonard's Road, Windsor, Berkshire SL4 3DF Tel: (01753) 862610 Fax: (01753) 621950
E-mail: info@uptonhouse.org.uk Website: www.uptonhouse.org.uk www.gabbitas.net

Headmistress Mrs M Collins BA (Hons) PGCE
Founded 1936
School status Co-educational independent day only
Religious denomination Church of England
Member of IAPS; **Accredited by** IAPS
Learning difficulties SNU/DYP DYS MLD
Behavioural and emotional disorders CA RA ST TS/ADD
Physical and medical conditions CA IT RA SM TW/EPI HEA
Age range Boys 2–7; Girls 2–11
No of pupils 210; *Girls* 160; *Boys* 50
Fees per annum *(day)* £1,160–£3,660

Upton House School is a thriving community of 220 children and 30 staff in the heart of historic Windsor. It is dedicated to a caring philosophy for all its children, allowing each to develop their talents and, at the same time, to learn the importance of helping others in the wider world.

A very full syllabus is offered and we take particular pride in making the whole learning process fun – with a range of extra-curricular activities, off-site visits, after-school clubs, dramatic productions, summer camps, etc.

For further information or a copy of our prospectus, please contact the Secretary, Mrs Jill Gilmour on (01753) 862610 or at info@uptonhouse.org.uk or www.uptonhouse.org.uk.

England

Wellington College

Duke's Ride, Crowthorne, Berkshire RG45 7PU Tel: (01344) 444012 Fax: (01344) 444005
E-mail: registrar@wellingtoncollege.org.uk Website: www.wellingtoncollege.org.uk

The Acting Master Mr R I H B Dyer
Founded 1853
College status Boys' (13–18) independent FE (Co-ed Sixth Form) boarding and day. Fully co-ed from September 2006. Boarders from age 13. Dr Anthony Seldon becomes Head in January 2006. He aims to make the school the best co-ed in the country.
Religious denomination Church of England
Accredited by HMC
No of pupils 757; *(full boarding)* 640; *(day)* 130; *Sixth Form* 335; *Girls* 50; *Boys* 707
Teacher:pupil ratio 1:8; **Average class size** 16
Fees per annum *(full boarding)* £22,995; *(day)* £18,396

Wellington College is one of the country's leading independent schools. It stands in an attractive 400-acre woodland estate.

A sensible priority is given to academic study (98 per cent of leavers go on to take degree courses), but the highest standards are also achieved in other aspects of school life, including sport, art, technology, writing, music and drama. Extra-curricular activities are important, as they develop self-confidence and provide experience in teamwork, initiative and leadership.

Wellington provides a well-disciplined, Christian framework within which pupils have a wide range of opportunities to fulfil their personal potential.

Akeley Wood School

Akeley Wood, Buckingham, Buckinghamshire MK18 5AE
Tel: (01280) 812000 Fax: (01280) 822945 E-mail: enquiries@akeleywoodschool.co.uk
Website: www.akeleywoodschool.co.uk www.cognitaschools.co.uk

Head Dr J Grundy
School status Co-educational day only
Religious denomination Non-denominational
Learning difficulties SNU/DYP DYS
Age range 3–18
No of pupils 888; *Girls* 367; *Boys* 521
Fees per annum *(day)* £2,880–£8,475

Akeley Wood is an independent co-educational day school for pupils aged 3 to 18 years. The school provides continuity of education for its pupils on three beautiful sites with specialist facilities located between Milton Keynes and Buckingham. It enjoys a high level of support and monitoring from belonging to Cognita Schools.

Akeley Wood's main aim is that pupils should continually develop their individual talents and personal qualities. It is a happy school where pupils are expected to respect, help and care for each other.

In academic terms, the school aims to help every individual fulfil his or her potential. This is achieved through skilled, dedicated and enthusiastic teaching in small classes, differentiating the expectation for every pupil.

The school believes in the education of the whole child – so music, art, drama and PE all play a vital part.

We welcome you to visit the school in action.

Caldicott School

Crown Lane, Farnham Royal, Buckinghamshire SL2 3SL
Tel: (01753) 649300 Fax: (01753) 649325 E-mail: office@caldicott.com
Website: www.caldicott.com www.gabbitas.net

The Headmaster Mr S J G Doggart
Founded 1904
School status Boys' independent boarding and day
Religious denomination Church of England
Learning difficulties SNU/DYC DYP DYS
Behavioural and emotional disorders ST/ADD
Physical and medical conditions RA SM TW WA2
Age range 7–13
No of pupils 240; *(full boarding)* 116; *(weekly boarding)* 124; *Boys* 240
Average class size 12
Fees per annum *(full boarding)* £15,966; *(day)* £11,970

Caldicott is a leading IAPS preparatory school for boys, with 240 pupils, situated in 40 acres, adjacent to Burnham Beeches, yet only 20 minutes from Heathrow Airport. All boys board during their last two years. Boarding facilities are comfortable and homely. Boys are prepared for Common Entrance/Scholarship examinations to Public Schools and achieve a high rate of success. Caldicott has well-equipped academic facilities, extensive sports facilities, excellent design workshops, a computer department, and a purpose-built Music School. The new Performing Arts Centre opened in September, providing a superb facility for music, art and drama. Entry is via interview and assessment. Prospectus available from Headmaster's office.

Pipers Corner School

Pipers Lane, Great Kingshill, High Wycombe, Buckinghamshire HP15 6LP
Tel: (01494) 718255 Fax: (01494) 719806
E-mail: school@piperscorner.co.uk
Website: www.gabbitas.net

Headmistress Mrs V M Stattersfield MA(Oxon) PGCE
Founded 1930
School status Girls' boarding and day. Flexi-boarding available.
Religious denomination Church of England
Age range 4–18
No of pupils 470; *(full boarding)* 25; *(weekly boarding)* 25; *(day)* 420
Fees per annum *(full boarding)* £13,035–£15,945; *(weekly)* £12,825–£15,735; *(day)* £4,350–£9,645

Set in 36 acres of the beautiful Chilterns, our spacious campus, with its outstanding facilities, is only half an hour from Heathrow and less than an hour from London.

Pipers is not only for girls with academic, artistic or sporting talent who hit the headlines or gain Oxbridge places (although ours do!), it is just as proud of students with average abilities who strive to do their best and achieve more than they ever thought they would. Every success is valued. We provide a challenging and well-balanced curriculum. Girls achieve high standards and are well prepared for higher education.

In boarding, the atmosphere is calm and relaxed, with the emphasis on family values and with friendly, well-ordered supervision. An exciting variety of weekend activities is organized for the girls.

Entry requirements Preparatory Department by interview and report; Senior School by entrance examination, interview and report.

Scholarships Academic and service bursaries and Sixth Form scholarships are available.

Swanbourne House School

Swanbourne, Milton Keynes, Buckinghamshire MK17 0HZ
Tel: (01296) 720264 Fax: (01296) 728089 E-mail: office@swanbourne.org
Website: www.swanbourne.org www.gabbitas.net

Joint Heads Mr S D Goodhart BEd (Hons) and Mrs J Goodhart BEd **Founded** 1920
School status Co-educational independent boarding and day. Flexi-boarding available.
Religious denomination Church of England
Member of IAPS; **Accredited by** IAPS
Age range 3–13
No of pupils 413; *(full boarding)* 28; *(flexi boarding)* 60; *(day)* 364; *Nursery* 45; *Pre-prep* 123; *Prep* 245; *Girls* 188; *Boys* 225
Fees per annum *(full boarding)* £14,580; *(weekly)* £14,580; *(day)* £3,000–£11,370

Swanbourne House is a successful IAPS preparatory school from which academic scholarships and awards in arts/sport and music are won each year. We have had three Kings Scholars to Eton in recent years and have strong Common Entrance results. There are many opportunities for personal development through activities, sport, the arts, holiday clubs and trips abroad.

Pupils have a form tutor in addition to a Housemaster and are prepared for Public School through leadership training, Public School Induction, socials, first aid, personal advice, taking responsibility and study skills. Pupils also take part in a French immersion programme for one week and attend an outdoor pursuits course.

Facilities Laboratory, computer rooms, bistro, AstroTurf, engineering workshop, comfortable boarding house, Design and Art Centre, language lab, library, amphitheatre, sports hall and a year-round swimming pool.

Entry is by a familiarization day and short assessment test.

Avon House

490 High Road, Woodford Green, Essex IG8 0PN
Tel: (020) 8504 1749
Avon House Dyslexia Centre
Tel: (020) 8559 0708

Principal Mrs S Ferrari
Head of Centre Mrs F Cookson
School status Co-educational independent day only
Religious denomination Christian
Member of CReSTeD
Avon House Dyslexia Centre
Assessment and Tuition
CReSTeD Reg. Corporate membership BDA
Learning difficulties SNU/DYS
Behavioural and emotional disorders CO ST
Age range 3–11
No of pupils 220; *(day)* 220; *Pre-prep* 144; *Prep* 75; *Girls* 102; *Boys* 117
Fees per annum *(day)* £5,280–£6,360

Chigwell School

High Road, Chigwell, Essex IG7 6QF
Tel: (020) 8501 5700 Fax: (020) 8500 6232 E-mail: hm@chigwell-school.org
Website: www.chigwell-school.org www.gabbitas.net

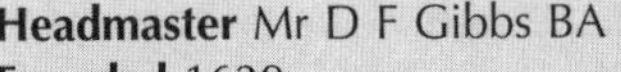

Headmaster Mr D F Gibbs BA
Founded 1629
School status Co-educational boarding and day. Flexi-boarding available.
Religious denomination Church of England
Member of HMC, IAPS
Accredited by HMC, IAPS, ISC
Age range 7–18; *boarders from* 15
No of pupils 730; *(full boarding)* 30; *(weekly boarding)* 10; *(day)* 690; *Girls* 291; *Boys* 439
Teacher:pupil ratio 1:3
Average class size 10 (Sixth Form); 20 (Junior School)
Fees per annum *(full boarding)* £16,866; *(weekly)* £15,042–£15,966; *(day)* £7,215–£11,097

Founded in 1629 by Samuel Harsnett, Archbishop of York and Vice Chancellor of Cambridge University, Chigwell School has been a centre of learning for over 375 years, from the days when William Penn was a pupil to modern times. The school stands in a superb green belt location, in 70 acres of its own grounds, playing fields and woodlands, between Epping and Hainault Forests and yet only 40 minutes away from central London by Underground. The original building has been in continuous use for over 370 years, but in the past 20 years there has been an extensive building programme, providing modern facilities which blend in with the original nucleus of the school.

Colchester High School

Wellesley Road, Colchester, Essex CO3 3HD Tel: (01206) 573389 Fax: (01206) 573114
E-mail: info@colchesterhighschool.co.uk
Website: www.colchesterhighschool.co.uk www.cognitaschools.co.uk

Principal Mr D E Wood MA Cert Ed
School status Co-educational independent day
Religious denomination Inter-denominational
Member of ISA, ISBA, ISCis
Learning difficulties CA RA/DYS
Behavioural and emotional disorders CO/ADD ADHD ASP AUT
Physical and medical conditions RA/CP HEA
Age range Boys 3–16; Girls 3–11
No of pupils 486; *Girls* 62; *Boys* 424
Fees per annum *(day)* £5,220–£7,080

Colchester High School ensures that each pupil achieves his or her personal best: we focus on the strengths of each individual child. Running in parallel with academic achievement is our emphasis on a secure and caring environment which encourages good manners, consideration for others and a strong sense of social responsibility.

Colchester High School aims to allow all its pupils to realize their full potential by ensuring the school offers a caring, friendly and calm environment in which learning can take place. Small class sizes and a stable and committed team of staff ensure a clear focus on the strengths of each child. This learning is not just academic but embraces a wide range of stimulating activities. It also encourages good manners, consideration for others and a strong sense of social responsibility.

Abbot's Hill School

Bunkers Lane, Hemel Hempstead, Hertfordshire HP3 8RP
Tel: (01442) 240333 Fax: (01442) 269981
E-mail: registrar@abbotshill.herts.sch.uk Website: www.abbotshill.herts.sch.uk

Headmistress Mrs K Lewis
Founded 1912
School status Girls' independent day only
Religious denomination Church of England
Member of AHIS, GSA, ISCis
Accredited by GSA, IAPS, ISC
Learning difficulties CA SNU/DYC DYP DYS
Behavioural and emotional disorders CO/ASP BESD
Physical and medical conditions IT SM/EPI HEA HI VI
Age range Girls 3–16; Boys 3–7
No of pupils 443; *Girls* 438; *Boys* 5
Average class size 15–18
Fees per annum *(day)* £6,180–£10,950

A thriving, vibrant, high-achieving school, Abbot's Hill is set in 76 acres of parkland on the edge of Hemel Hempstead, Hertfordshire.

We are justly proud of our academic record but never stray from our prime objective: to educate the whole person, to achieve his or her highest personal, social and educational potential. Every pupil benefits from being known personally by the Headmistress and teaching staff in a warm and enabling environment.

The school and its dedicated staff offer excellent facilities and a wide range of subjects and extra-curricular activities.

Aldenham School

Elstree, Hertfordshire WD6 3AJ Tel: (01923) 858122 Fax: (01923) 854410
E-mail: enquiries@aldenham.com Website: www.aldenham.com

Headmaster Mr JC Fowler
Founded 1597
School status Co-educational independent boarding and day. Flexi-boarding available.
Religious denomination Church of England, Inter-denominational
Member of AGBIS, BSA, CASE, HMC, IAPS, ISCis; **Accredited by** HMC, IAPS, ISA, ISC
Learning difficulties SNU/DYP DYS
Behavioural and emotional disorders CO/ADD ADHD ASP
Physical and medical conditions HEA VI
Age range 2–18
No of pupils 635; *(full boarding)* 100; *(weekly boarding)* 45; *Girls* 88; *Boys* 547
Teacher:pupil ratio 1:8; **Average class size** 20
Fees per annum *(full boarding)* £14,676–£20,664; *(weekly)* £12,294–£16,982; *(day)* £9,798–£14,223

Aldenham stands in a 100+ acre site with modern facilities including a new state-of-the-art classroom block for modern languages, English and media studies, plus a new design technology and computing centre, large sports hall, floodlit artificial turf pitch, refurbished science block and Music School.

The curriculum includes the arts, sciences and humanities, music technology, business studies, theatre studies and sports science. A personal tutor is provided for every pupil.

An extensive and highly successful games and activities programme includes football, hockey, basketball, squash, sailing and cricket. Strong Music and Drama departments stage regular productions. The Learning Support department encourages able pupils with dyslexia and dyscalculia and provides specialist English lessons for overseas students (ESL). Awards for academic potential, sport, music (including Organ Scholarship), art and technology are available.

The Arts Educational School

Tring Park, Tring, Hertfordshire HP23 5LX
Tel: (01442) 824255 Fax: (01442) 891069
E-mail: info@aes-tring.com
Website: www.aes-tring.com

The Headmaster Mr S Anderson MA, BMus, ARCM
Founded 1919
School status Co-educational boarding and day
Religious denomination Non-denominational
Member of BSA, ISA, SHA, SHMIS
Learning difficulties WI/DYS MLD
Physical and medical conditions SM
Age range 8–18
No of pupils 273; *(full boarding)* 205; *(day)* 68; *Prep* 10; *Senior* 157; *Sixth Form* 106; *Girls* 222; *Boys* 51
Fees per annum *(full boarding)* £16,380–£23,130; *(day)* £11,895–£18,600

Tring Park offers exciting educational opportunities for pupils who show talent in one or more of the Performing Arts and we are committed to ensuring that all pupils fulfil their potential.

The school is set in 17 acres of attractive and secluded parkland and the main house was formerly a Rothschild Mansion.

Today, the school accommodates up to 200 boarders and up to 95 day pupils and aims to provide an environment ideally suited to the teaching of the Performing Arts, combined with academic study to the highest level.

Tring Park is part of the Music and Dance Scheme, funded and administered by the DfES, and places are awarded annually under this scheme for talented classical dancers. A number of Dance and Drama Awards are available for the Sixth Form dance course.

Up to the age of 14 all pupils study dance, music and drama combined with a full and vigorous academic curriculum. The pupils all study eight or nine GCSE subjects combined with the Dance, Musical Theatre or Drama course. Academic study receives equal emphasis and the department provides a broad and balanced curriculum for all pupils. Following success in the A level examinations, many of our Sixth Form students proceed to higher vocational or academic studies at universities and colleges. For others, the opportunity to perform becomes a reality immediately.

For those entering the Dance course, we believe in training the whole dancer in body, mind and in artistic understanding. Dancers are encouraged to fulfil their own individual potential and each pupil's progress is monitored carefully.

Those senior pupils joining the Drama course will undertake an intensive and wide-ranging preparation for direct entry into the theatre, further training at drama school or, with appropriate A levels, higher education on a relevant degree course.

The Musical Theatre course is designed to extend the skills of the all-round performer and to focus them in this popular entertainment area.

Throughout the school, pupils have frequent opportunities to present work in the Markova Theatre and there are regular public shows given by all pupils. The range of work undertaken provides pupils with the opportunity to become versatile and able to communicate skilfully, whatever the chosen field.

Duncombe School

4 Warren Park Road, Bengeo, Hertford, Hertfordshire SG14 3JA
Tel: (01992) 414100 Fax: (01992) 414111 E-mail: admissions@duncombe-school.co.uk
Website: www.duncombe-school.co.uk www.cognitaschools.co.uk
Admissions enquiries tel: 01992 414109

Headmaster Mr D Baldwin MA BEd
Registrar Mrs D L Russell BSc **Founded** 1939
School status Co-educational independent day only
Religious denomination Church of England
Member of ISA, ISCis, NAHT
Accredited by ISA, ISC
Learning difficulties SNU/DYP DYS
Behavioural and emotional disorders CA ST/ADHD AUT
Physical and medical conditions HEA HI VI
Age range 2–11
No of pupils 305; *(day)* 305; *Nursery* 61; *Pre-prep* 107; *Prep* 137; *Girls* 149; *Boys* 156
Teacher:pupil ratio 1:8; **Average class size** 17
Fees per annum *(day)* £1,536–£8,040

Duncombe School provides the highest quality education, combining a proven record of academic achievement with sporting excellence.

The curriculum covers a wide range of subjects with specialist staff in many areas. Resources include two ICT suites, an extensive library, science and music rooms, art and craft studio and an AstroTurf pitch and athletics track. Breakfast club and after-school activities are very popular.

Haileybury

Hertford, Hertfordshire SG13 7NU Tel: (01992) 463353 Fax: (01992) 470663
E-mail: registrar@haileybury.com Website: www.haileybury.com www.gabbitas.net

The Master Mr S A Westley MA
Registrar Mrs E Alexander BA
Founded 1862
School status Co-educational independent boarding and day
Religious denomination Church of England
Member of HMC
Accredited by HMC
Learning difficulties RA SNU/DYC DYP DYS
Behavioural and emotional disorders CO/ASP AUT
Physical and medical conditions WA2 WA3/HEA W
Age range 11–18; *boarders from* 11
No of pupils 744; *(full boarding)* 469; *(day)* 275; *Girls* 315; *Boys* 429
Teacher:pupil ratio 1:7
Average class size 16
Fees per annum *(full boarding)* £15,735–£21,990; *(day)* £10,980–£16,515

Boys and girls, mostly boarding, admitted at 11 into the Lower School, at 13 into the Main School, and also into the Sixth Form.

Magnificent classical buildings are complemented by modern, state-of-the art developments. Set in 500 rural acres and situated 20 miles north of central London, Haileybury combines high academic standards with broad-ranging excellence in art, music, drama and sport. The school is pleased to offer International Baccalaureate alongside A levels. Please contact the Registrar for further details.

England

Kingshott School

St Ippolyts, Hitchin, Hertfordshire SG4 7JX Tel: (01462) 432009 Fax: (01462) 421652
E-mail: pi@kingshott.herts.sch.uk Website: www.kingshottschool.co.uk

Headmaster Mr P R Ilott BA **Founded** 1931
School status Co-educational day only
Religious denomination Church of England
Learning difficulties WI/DYP DYS
Physical and medical conditions RA SM/HEA
Age range 4–13
No of pupils 356; *Girls* 120; *Boys* 236
Teacher:pupil ratio 1:10; **Average class size** 20
Fees per annum *(day)* £6,600–£8,220

Kingshott is an independent co-educational day preparatory school for children aged between 4 and 13. Class sizes are around 20. The school is set in very pleasant surroundings just outside Hitchin with 14 acres of playing fields.

Kingshott has an excellent reputation for preparing children for the rapidly changing world of the 21st century without losing sight of traditional approaches and values. The school achieves outstanding academic results and caters for a broad range of ability. The overriding aims are to provide an all round education and to pursue excellence in a friendly, happy but structured environment. Kingshott's teaching staff is long-serving, enthusiastic and highly experienced.

In September 2004 the new Pre-Prep building (Reception to Year 2) opened. This consists of nine classrooms and a hall. Up to 50 places are now available in Reception. A recent Ofsted inspection report on the Reception classes was outstanding. The top grade was achieved in all areas inspected.

A new Prep School development will follow. This will include science laboratories, a Music School, Art and Design Centre, classrooms, completely revamped hall and swimming pool, and more. This will ensure unrivalled facilities in the area.

For more details and to arrange a visit to the school, contact the Registrar, Mrs Claire Day on 01462 432009. We look forward to hearing from you.

The Royal Masonic School for Girls

Rickmansworth Park, Rickmansworth, Hertfordshire WD3 4HF
Tel: (01923) 773168 Fax: (01923) 896729 E-mail: enquiries@royalmasonic.herts.sch.uk
Website: www.royalmasonic.herts.sch.uk www.gabbitas.net

The Headmistress Mrs D Rose MA (Cantab)
Founded 1788
School status Girls' boarding and day. Flexi-boarding available.
Religious denomination Non-denominational
Member of BSA, GSA
Age range 4–18
No of pupils 781; *(full boarding)* 110; *(weekly boarding)* 57; *(day)* 614; *Pre-prep* 54; *Prep* 140; *Senior* 417; *Sixth Form* 170
Teacher:pupil ratio 1:12; **Ave class size** 18–20
Fees per annum *(full boarding)* £9,675–£15,720; *(weekly)* £9,600–£15,645; *(day)* £5,445–£9,705

RMS offers an exceptionally wide-ranging curriculum in a supportive and friendly environment, where the highest standards prevail. Our girls receive individual attention and are given the confidence to succeed.

The school has outstanding facilities and occupies a stunning 315-acre site. An impressive sports hall, indoor swimming pool, squash, tennis and netball courts, and hockey pitches maintain sporting excellence.

Rickmansworth is close to the M25 and London is easily accessible.

Boarding pupils are cared for in well-appointed and spacious houses. In each house there is a balanced number of boarders and day pupils.

Admission is by the school's own entrance examination and interview. A number of generous scholarships are available.

St Albans High School for Girls

Townsend Avenue, St Albans, Hertfordshire AL1 3SJ Tel: (01727) 853800 Fax: (01727) 792516
E-mail: admissions@stalbans-high.herts.sch.uk Website: www.sahs.org.uk www.gabbitas.net

Headmistress Ms J C Pain MA MA MBA
Founded 1889
School status Girls' independent day only
Religious denomination Church of England
Member of GDST, GSA, ISCis
Accredited by GSA
Learning difficulties SNU/DYS MLD
Physical and medical conditions TW WA2/W
Age range 4–18
No of pupils 950; *Pre-prep* 124; *Prep* 188; *Senior* 470; *Sixth Form* 168
Fees per annum *(day)* £6,975–£8,865
Fees Lunch included for infants

Curriculum A broad and balanced academic education is provided to include National Curriculum subjects and others. Teaching methods are modern and extensive use is made of resources such as computers and audio-video equipment. Public examination results at GCSE and A level are of a consistently high standard and, for the vast majority, degree courses follow.

Entry requirements and examinations Entry is by examination at 4, 5, 7, 11 and 16, with intermediate ages being subject to vacancies.

Academic and leisure facilities A wide range of extra-curricular activities are offered, with sport, music and drama featuring strongly. Facilities for physical education include a sports hall (to which an indoor pool and leisure complex, operable from September 2006, are being added) and playing fields.

Scholarships/bursaries Academic and music scholarships are available on entry at 11. Further academic scholarships are available at 16.

St Albans School

Abbey Gateway, St Albans, Hertfordshire AL3 4HB
Tel: (01727) 855521 Fax: (01727) 843447
E-mail: hm@st-albans-school.org.uk
Website: www.st-albans.herts.sch.uk www.gabbitas.net

The Headmaster Mr A R Grant
Founded 948
School status Boys' (11–18) Co-educational (Sixth Form) day only
Religious denomination Non-denominational
No of pupils 778; *Girls* 38; *Boys* 740
Fees per annum *(day)* £10,542

Following the abolition of the Government's Assisted Places Scheme, the school is able to offer some assistance with fees in certain circumstances of proven need, from its own endowed bursary fund. All bursaries are means-tested. A variable number of academic scholarships worth up to 50 per cent of the annual fees are awarded on academic merit at 11+, 13+ and 16+. Scholarships for music and art are offered at 13+. Bursaries towards music tuition are provided for pupils from each year in the school. Further details of all awards are available from the Head.

The school is a registered charity and aims to provide an excellent education, enabling pupils to achieve the highest standard of academic success according to ability, and to develop their character and personality so as to become caring and self-disciplined adults.

St Christopher School

Barrington Road, Letchworth, Hertfordshire SG6 3JZ
Tel: (01462) 650850 Fax: (01462) 481578 E-mail: admissions@stchris.co.uk
Website: www.stchris.co.uk www.gabbitas.net Direct line for Admissions: 01462 650947

Headmaster Mr D Wilkinson MA MLitt FRSA
Registrar Mrs M McAlister **Founded** 1915
School status Co-educational independent boarding and day. Flexi-boarding available.
Religious denomination Non-denominational
Member of AGBIS, BSA, SHMIS
Accredited by ISC, SHMIS
Learning difficulties SNU/DYP DYS
Behavioural and emotional disorders ASP
Physical and medical conditions RA/EPI
Age range 2–19; *boarders from* 2
No of pupils 548; *(full boarding)* 67; *(day)* 481; *Nursery* 15; *Prep* 146; *Senior* 295; *Sixth Form* 93; *Girls* 234; *Boys* 314
Teacher:pupil ratio 1:9; **Average class size** 16
Fees per annum *(full boarding)* £16,242–£20,325; *(day)* £2,910–£11,565. Scholarships and bursaries are available for new entrants to Years 7, 9 and the Sixth Form.

St Christopher School is situated in Letchworth, 35 miles north of London on the A1(M), with easy access to the M25 and all major airports. The fast trains from Kings Cross take 30 minutes. There is a domestic village atmosphere, with most of the buildings in the 'Garden City' idiom and surrounded by attractive grounds.

The school provides a complete education from infancy to adulthood. Children of one family, whatever their ages, can attend the same school. The school provides day as well as boarding pupils with a wide range of opportunity throughout every day of the week.

Boarders live in family-style houses under the supervision of resident houseparents. The diet is vegetarian. There is a strong community feel and many staff live in or adjacent to the school with their own children attending.

The school has long been noted for the value it places on the individual and for the encouragement of self-confidence. It attracts children (and parents) with strong independent attitudes and many children who need to be valued for themselves flourish at St Christopher. There is no school uniform worn apart from in games and all are referred to by first names.

The teaching is of a high standard and academic results are creditable. Most Sixth Formers proceed to a degree course and the school gives careful advice on future plans. St Christopher does not believe in artificial competition in academic work; thus there are no subject or form orders.

The school is strong in the creative and performing arts as well as the core academic subjects such as science and maths. There are excellent, purpose-built music and technology facilities, a superb theatre and a 25-metre indoor swimming pool. A new ICT building was opened in September 2004.

There is a very wide range of sports, games and extra-curricular courses, with a special emphasis on outdoor pursuits such as climbing, walking, camping and orienteering. There are major expeditions for all in each year group and regular weekend trips.

The school has strong local support and pupils are involved in a range of ventures among the local community. There are strong international links and regular exchanges with schools in France, Germany and Spain, and visits by Sixth Formers to development projects in India and Kosovo.

St Edmund's College

Old Hall Green, Ware, Hertfordshire SG11 1DS Tel: (01920) 824247 Fax: (01920) 823011
E-mail: admissions@stedmundscollege.org Website: www.stedmundscollege.org www.gabbitas.net

Head Mr C P Long BA (Newcastle)
Founded 1568
College status Co-educational boarding and day. Flexi-boarding available.
Religious denomination Roman Catholic
Member of HMC, ISCis; **Accredited by** British Council, HMC, ISC Member of English UK
Learning difficulties CA WI/DYP DYS
Behavioural and emotional disorders RA/ASP
Physical and medical conditions IT SM TW WA2/EPI HEA HI VI
Age range 3–18; *boarders from* 11
No of pupils 705; *(full boarding)* 70; *(weekly boarding)* 27; *(day)* 608; *Nursery* 26; *Pre-prep* 17; *Prep* 132; *Senior* 530; *Sixth Form* 117; *Girls* 252; *Boys* 453
Teacher:pupil ratio 1:9; **Ave class size** 10–21
Fees per annum *(full boarding)* £16,200; *(weekly)* £14,700; *(day)* £7,290

Located on a beautiful 400 acre site in the Hertfordshire countryside, the college is within easy reach of central London, with London Stansted airport only 15 minutes away.

As England's oldest Catholic School we welcome students from all faiths and cultures who appreciate the benefits of a Catholic education.

As well as the impressive facade of the main building that resembles a large stately home, the College boasts excellent teaching and sports facilities including state-of-the art computer suites, art and design technology workshops, floodlit all-weather sports pitch, tennis courts, an indoor swimming pool and a dedicated Sixth Form centre.

Full English language support across the curriculum for overseas students and an international Summer School is held in July/August.

England

St Hilda's School

High Street, Bushey, Hertfordshire WD23 3DA Tel: (020) 8950 1751 Fax: (020) 8420 4523
E-mail: registrar@sthildasbushey.co.uk Website: www.sthildas-school.co.uk

Headmistress Mrs L Cavanagh MA Dip CE
School status Girls' (3–11) independent. Boys attend age 3 to 5.
Religious denomination Non-denominational
Member of IAPS, NAHT; **Accredited by** IAPS
IAPS School for girls ages 3 to 11 years. Co-ed Kindergarten dept. Boys prepared for Prep Schools.
Learning difficulties CA WI/DYP DYS
Behavioural and emotional disorders ST/ASP
Physical and medical conditions CA RA SM TW/EPI HEA HI
No of pupils 125; *Nursery* 12; *Pre-prep* 35; *Prep* 73; *Girls* 120; *Boys* 5
Fees per annum *(day)* £4,080–£7,500. Lower school £2,400 per term. Upper School £2,500 per term

St Hilda's School in Bushey has occupied its present 4-acre site between Bushey and Bushey Heath since 1928. Excellent facilities include tennis and netball courts; a heated, covered swimming pool; a large multi-purpose hall; art and design/technology rooms; well-equipped library; computer suite and science room. Open mornings will offer you an opportunity to experience the real strength of the school; the ethos; the teaching and learning. The Headmistress, Mrs Loraine Cavanagh, and her enthusiastic staff, value and encourage the 'community', family and caring side of the School. Children from the very youngest are introduced to a wide range of subjects, which includes French, Spanish and Latin, music, drama and swimming.

St Margaret's School

Merry Hill Road, Bushey, Hertfordshire WD23 1DT
Tel: (020) 8901 0870 Fax: (020) 8950 1677
E-mail: schooloffice@stmargarets.herts.sch.uk
Website: www.stmargaretsbushey.co.uk www.gabbitas.net

Headteacher Mr Mark Ferris
Founded 1749
School status Girls' independent boarding and day. Flexi-boarding available.
Religious denomination Church of England
Member of BSA, GSA
Age range 4–18; *boarders from* 11
No of pupils 400; *(full boarding)* 60; *(day)* 340; *Pre-prep* 36; *Prep* 61; *Senior* 225; *Sixth Form* 78
Fees per annum *(full boarding)* £18,885; *(weekly)* £18,885; *(day)* £7,005–£10,545; All fees include lunch for day girls

Established in 1749, St Margaret's School educates girls aged 4 to 18 years. We have an outstanding reputation as a caring and supportive community with an excellent record of success at all public examinations. Bursaries and scholarships are available. The original buildings have been extended and upgraded considerably in the past decade, including a £3 million sports centre, which opened in 2002. There is a wide range of sporting and cultural activities, with language exchange visits, choir, orchestra, speech and drama, ballet, judo, the Duke of Edinburgh's Award Scheme and World Challenge expeditions.

York House School

Redheath, Sarratt Road, Croxley Green, Rickmansworth, Hertfordshire WD3 4LW
Tel: (01923) 772395 Fax: (01923) 779231
E-mail: yhsoffice@aol.com
Website: www.york-house.com www.gabbitas.net

Headmaster Mr P R MacDougall BEd (Hons)
Founded 1910
School status Boys' (3–13) Co-educational (2–5) day only
Religious denomination Church of England
Member of IAPS, ISCis
Learning difficulties WI/DYS
Behavioural and emotional disorders RA
No of pupils 285; *Girls* 15; *Boys* 270
Average class size 16
Fees per annum *(day)* £8,130

York House is a well-established, innovative and forward-looking school. Pupils are encouraged to achieve maximum potential, both academically and socially, in a happy, caring environment.

Children are encouraged to enjoy learning, creativity, self-discipline and understanding of others. Music, art and drama play important roles in the school's wide curriculum, while a wide range of sports, clubs and societies round off the boys' development.

There is a multi-purpose sports hall/theatre, a library, music facilities and a state-of-the-art computer suite. A new nine-classroom block for 2 to 7-year-olds opened in 2001.

Phase III of the exciting school development plan is now complete. This excellent new building comprises large classrooms for the Junior School, Design Technology, Art and Science Laboratory.

American Community School

See page 368

St Helen's School

Eastbury Road, Northwood, Middlesex HA6 3AS Tel: (01923) 843210 Fax: (01923) 843211
E-mail: enquiries@sthn.co.uk Website: www.sthelensnorthwood.co.uk

Head Mrs M Morris BA **Founded** 1899
Deputy Heads Mrs J Roseblade & Mr P Tiley
School status Girls' independent boarding and day. Flexi-boarding available.
Religious denomination Christian
Member of GSA, ISCis
Learning difficulties WI/DYP DYS
Behavioural & emotional disorders CO
Physical & medical conditions TW/HEA HI VI
Age range 3–18; *boarders from* 11
No of pupils 1142; *(full boarding)* 24; *(weekly boarding)* 1; *(day)* 1117; *Nursery* 49; *Pre-prep* 57; *Prep* 354; *Senior* 498; *Sixth Form* 184
Teacher:pupil ratio 1:10; **Average class size** 21
Fees per annum *(full boarding)* £17,958; *(weekly)* £17,322; *(day)* £9,690

St Helen's School is a highly academic school. Pupils achieve outstanding GCSE and A level results and go on to excellent universities of their first choice. The International Baccalaureate

Diploma is offered alongside A levels in the Sixth Form. The curriculum enables every girl to achieve intellectual and personal fulfilment and to develop talents to the full. Staff are subject specialists who inspire a love of their subjects. Girls study two modern foreign languages together with Latin. Science is taught throughout as three separate subjects. Excellent specialist facilities exist for science, design and technology, art, drama, modern languages, music and ICT. Our grounds offer opportunities for a range of sporting activities, several of which are pursued to national standard. Each girl is encouraged to give of her best, be tolerant and caring of others, and make a positive contribution.

MAP OF LONDON

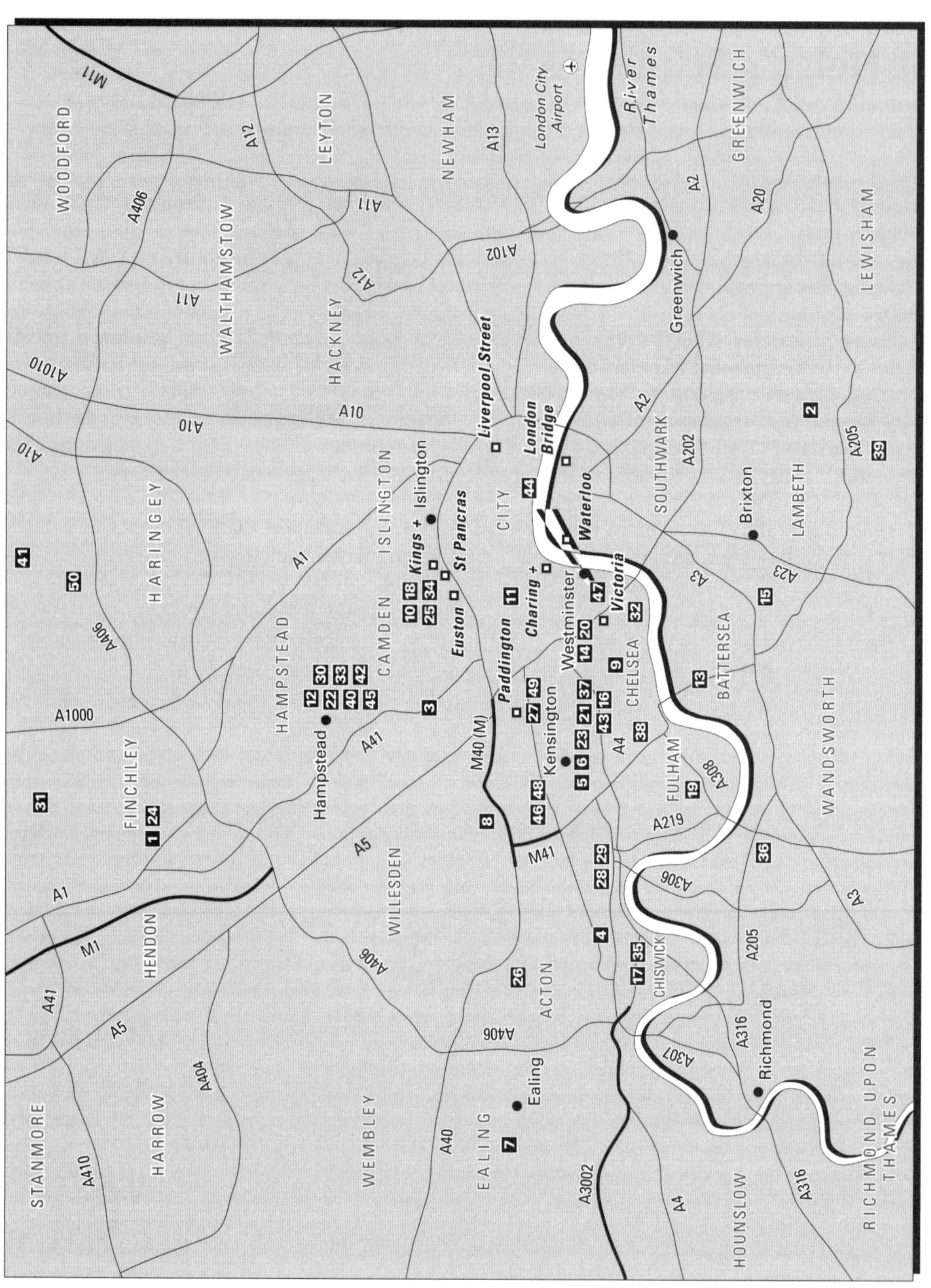

PROFILED SCHOOLS IN LONDON

Albany College

21/24 Queen's Road, Hendon, London NW4 2TL
Tel: (020) 8202 5965 Fax: (020) 8202 8460
E-mail: info@albany-college.co.uk
Website: www.albany-college.co.uk www.gabbitas.net

Principal Mr R J Arthy BSc MPhil
Founded 1974
College status Co-educational day only. First Independent College to gain registration under the Ofsted '163' inspections in 2003.
Age range 14–19
No of pupils 201; *Girls* 81; *Boys* 120
Teacher:pupil ratio 1:4
Average class size 10
Fees per annum *(day)* £10,500–£12,000

Albany is a highly successful, well-established, caring and cosmopolitan independent Fifth and Sixth Form College. Our teaching and academic counselling is extremely effective. In June 2001, 27 students gained at least 2 A-grade A level passes, and there were 45 perfect module scores, with the majority of students gaining places at traditional established universities. In February 2000, Albany was specially singled out by the *Daily Telegraph* for our high A level grade improvements for resit candidates.

Albany has a highly qualified and dedicated professional teaching and administrative team whose enthusiasm and commitment have enabled our students to attain outstanding results. Our aim is that students leave the college with the confidence and skills necessary to be happy and successful throughout life.

Alleyn's School

Townley Road, Dulwich, London SE22 8SU Tel: (020) 8557 1500 Fax: (020) 8557 1462
E-mail: registrar@alleyns.org.uk Website: www.alleyns.org.uk

Headmaster Dr C Diggory BSc, MA, EdD, CMath,FIMA, FRSA
Deputy Heads Mr MG Longmore MA and Mrs J M Helm BSc, FRSA
Founded 1619
School status Co-educational independent day only
Religious denomination Church of England
Member of HMC, IAPS, SHA
Accredited by HMC, IAPS
Learning difficulties WI/DYC DYP DYS
Behavioural and emotional disorders CO/ADD ADHD ASP TOU
Physical and medical conditions RA SM TW/EPI HEA HI VI
Age range 4–18
No of pupils 1158; *Girls* 588; *Boys* 570
Teacher:pupil ratio 1:9
Average class size Juniors (under 11) 21; Seniors (11–16) 20–25; Sixth Form 12
Fees per annum *(day)* £8,790–£10,680

The origins of the school can be traced back to 1619, when Edward Alleyn, the Elizabethan actor manager, founded his 'College of God's Gift' in Dulwich. Alleyn's School itself was established in 1883 by the College Governors and later became a Direct Grant School (from 1958–75). The school then became fully independent and the first HMC school in London to go fully co-educational. The Worshipful Company of Saddlers in the City of London has been a vital supporter and benefactor throughout this time, sponsoring scholarships and supporting the school.

The American School in London

1 Waverley Place, London NW8 0NP
Tel: (020) 7449 1200 Fax: (020) 7449 1350 E-mail: admissions@asl.org Website: www.asl.org

Head Dr W C Mules **Founded** 1951
School status Co-educational independent day only
Religious denomination Non-denominational
Member of CASE, CIS, ECIS, FRB, NAIS
Accredited by MSA (USA), ECIS
Behavioural and emotional disorders CO
Physical and medical conditions SM
Age range 4–18
No of pupils 1312; *Girls* 636; *Boys* 676
Fees per annum *(day)* £15,160–£18,570

The American School in London is a co-educational, non-profit institution which offers an outstanding American education. The curriculum leads to an American high school diploma, and a strong Advanced Placement programme enables students to enter the top universities in the United States, the UK and other countries.

The core curriculum of English, maths, science and social studies is enriched with courses in

modern languages, computing, fine arts and physical education. Small classes allow teachers to focus on individuals; students are encouraged to take an active role in learning to develop the skills necessary for independent critical thinking and expression. Many extra-curricular activities, including sports, music, drama and community service, are available for students of all ages.

The American School in London welcomes students of all nationalities, including non-English speakers below the age of 10, who meet the scholastic standards. Entry is at any time throughout the year.

The Arts Educational School

Cone Ripman House, 14 Bath Road, Chiswick, London W4 1LY
Tel: (020) 8987 6600 Fax: (020) 8987 6601 E-mail: head@artsed.co.uk
Website: www.artsed.co.uk www.gabbitas.net

Headmaster Mr R Luckham BSc (Hons), MBIM
Founded 1919
School status Co-educational day only. Specialize in performing arts but also strong on academics.
Religious denomination Inter-denominational
Member of ISA, ISCis, SHA
Accredited by ISA, ISC
Learning difficulties CA RA/DYS
Age range 11–18
No of pupils 150; *(day)* 150; *Senior* 110; *Sixth Form* 40; *Girls* 99; *Boys* 51
Teacher:pupil ratio 1:7; **Average class size** 12
Fees per annum *(day)* £8,472–£9,471

The Arts Educational School (London) provides a stimulating academic curriculum that prepares pupils for the full range of GCSE examinations. In addition, it is a leader in the provision of study and training for music, dance and drama. Pupils are taught in small groups in dedicated subject areas by highly trained specialist staff. To accommodate the arts training there is an extended timetable for all pupils in the senior school (8.30 am–5.30 pm).

The school shares excellent facilities including a proscenium arch theatre and studio theatre. In-house production and design teams service all major productions. Wide ranges of performance opportunities are available to all pupils.

The school is a caring, friendly environment in which young people are expected to take full responsibility for themselves and the vibrant learning community of which they are members. Self-esteem and confidence are nurtured, as is sensitivity and appreciation of the needs of others.

Many of the school's graduates go on to higher education, professional training and illustrious careers in the world of the performing and creative arts.

Ashbourne Independent Sixth Form College

17 Old Court Place, Kensington, London W8 4PL
Tel: (020) 7937 3858 Fax: (020) 7937 2207 E-mail: admin@ashbournecollege.co.uk
Website: www.ashbournecollege.co.uk www.gabbitas.net

Principal Mr M J H Kirby MSc
Vice Principal Ms C S R Brahams BA Hons (Durham) MA PGCE **Founded** 1981
College status Co-educational boarding and day
Religious denomination Non-denominational
Age range Boys 14–19; Girls 16–19; *boarders from* 16
No of pupils 155; *(day)* 155; *Girls* 75; *Boys* 80
Average class size 8
Fees per annum *(full boarding)* £18,500; *(day)* £12,450

Wonderfully situated near Kensington Gardens, Ashbourne is a few minutes away from many of London's greatest attractions.

The wide-ranging curriculum embraces both the traditional and the modern. Professor John Foreman, FRCP, oversees Ashbourne's flagship Medical School programme that has helped medical students achieve a 64 per cent success rate over the past three years. There is also an excellent programme for media, including drama, film, fashion, photography, art and graphics.

Class sizes are restricted to a maximum of ten, reflecting the importance placed on individual attention, communication and feedback. Ashbourne believes that high expectations are the key to academic achievement, and encourages and supports students accordingly.

It has recently implemented a system of Personal Tutors to enable students to be supported throughout their Sixth Form including their application to UCAS.

Ashbourne Middle School

17 Old Court Place, Kensington, London W8 4PL
Tel: (020) 7937 3858 Fax: (020) 7937 2207 E-mail: admin@ashbournecollege.co.uk
Website: www.ashbournecollege.co.uk www.gabbitas.net

Principal Mr M J A Kirby MSc, BApSc
Founded 1981
School status Co-educational day only
Religious denomination Non-denominational
Member of CIFE
Accredited by BAC, British Council
Age range 13–16
No of pupils 25; *Girls* 10; *Boys* 15
Average class size 8
Fees per annum *(day)* £12,450

Wonderfully situated near Kensington Gardens, Ashbourne is a few minutes away from many of London's greatest attractions. The school has an informal and friendly atmosphere which is conducive to learning.

Class sizes are restricted to a maximum of ten, reflecting the importance placed on individual attention, communication and feedback. Staff–student relations are personable and informal yet provide discipline and encourage independence and self-reliance.

Ashbourne believes that high expectations are the key to academic achievement, and encourages and supports students accordingly.

Avenue House School

70 The Avenue, Ealing, London W13 8LS Tel: (020) 8998 9981 Fax: (020) 8991 1533
E-mail: avenuehouseschool@btinternet.com Website: www.avenuehouse.com

Principal Mrs C Self
Admissions Mrs A Stacey
Founded 1995
School status Co-educational independent day only
Religious denomination Non-denominational
Member of IAPS, NAHT, SATIPS
Accredited by IAPS
Learning difficulties WI/DYS
Behavioural and emotional disorders RA
Physical and medical conditions RA SM/HEA VI
Age range 3–11
No of pupils 140; *(day)* 140; *Girls* 75; *Boys* 65
Average class size 20
Fees per annum *(day)* £3,900–£6,900

Avenue House is a small, happy, caring, academic school situated in a quiet leafy area of Ealing. Founded in January 1995, the aim of this co-educational pre-preparatory and preparatory school is to provide an environment where each child can realize his or her educational potential to the full. Pupils are encouraged to develop their own individual talents and personalities, enabling them to become self-confident, enthusiastic and caring children who learn to value the importance of diligent work from an early age.

Pupils are taught in small classes where they can achieve their full potential in academic subjects, music, drama and sport. A broad curriculum is taught where the emphasis is on understanding concepts so pupils can convey the fruits of their skills. Avenue House School does not test children on entry at Reception age as we feel that each child develops at their own individual rate. All pupils are monitored and assessed individually throughout the year and frequent meetings with parents and the school are actively encouraged. We believe a positive approach to learning leads to excellence.

Children in the Nursery are taught in a stimulating environment. They follow the Early Years Foundation stages, which includes Language & Literacy, Knowledge & Understanding of the World, French, Computers, Cooking, Drama, Music and Movement, PE, Art and Design Technology. Weekly swimming lessons are provided for the Nursery to Year 6.

The Preparatory School curriculum, while aware of the National Curriculum, is based on the need to prepare pupils for the relevant public examination of the parents' choice. In conjunction with the traditional academic subjects the children are taught French, music, PE, gymnastics, art and drama. The school has access to a purpose-built science laboratory and its own small library. We also have the latest in laptop computers for all classes, with a wireless broadband internet connection installed throughout the school.

Avenue House School offers an after-school care service for parental convenience as well as a variety of after-school clubs, including drama, football and art.

Educational visits play an important role in helping children relate their class work to the real world. For this reason pupils are taken on outings each term, where they can benefit from having first-hand knowledge of London and its surrounding area. In addition children from Years 5 and 6 have the opportunity to go on a residential activity trip to the Black Mountains and children from Year 6 have the opportunity to go to Paris or Brussels for the day.

At Avenue House we believe a happy child is most likely to succeed.

Bassett House School

60 Bassett Road, London W10 6JP
Tel: (020) 8969 0313 Fax: (020) 8960 9624
E-mail: info@bassetths.org.uk
Website: www.bassetths.org.uk

Head Mrs A Harris BEd(Lond) CEPLF(Caen)
School status Co-educational day only
Religious denomination Non-denominational
Member of IAPS
Accredited by IAPS
Age range Boys 3–8; Girls 3–11
Fees per annum *(day)* £4,820–£10,080

Bassett House School is situated in a large Victorian house in North Kensington, which was recently rebuilt to very high standards. Boys leave the school aged 8 for prep schools specializing in preparation for senior school examinations at 13+. Girls are prepared for senior school examinations at 11+. The school is equipped with a science and IT lab, gym/theatre and school hall, music room and art room.

Orchard House School

16 Newton Grove, Bedford Park, London W4 1LB
Tel: (020) 8742 8544 Fax: (020) 8742 8522
E-mail: info@orchardhs.org.uk Website: www.orchardhs.org.uk

Headmistress Mrs S A B Hobbs BA(Hons)(Exeter) PGCE MontDip
School status Co-educational day only
Religious denomination Non-denominational
Member of IAPS, ISBA
Accredited by IAPS
Age range Boys 3–8; Girls 3–11
No of pupils 220; *Girls* 140; *Boys* 80
Fees per annum *(day)* £4,860–£10,080

Orchard House School occupies a substantial Norman Shaw house in the conservation area of Bedford Park, Chiswick, with a large garden and recreational area. Boys leave the school at age 8+ for prep schools specializing in preparation for boys' senior school examinations at 13+. Girls are prepared for senior school examinations at 11+. The school has its own sports area and is equipped with a science and IT lab, music room and art room.

Prospect House School

75 Putney Hill, London SW15 3NT
Tel: (020) 8780 0456 Fax: (020) 8780 3010
E-mail: info@prospecths.org.uk Website: www.prospecths.org.uk

Headmistress Mrs D Barratt MEd (Newcastle)
Founded 1991
School status Co-educational day only
Religious denomination Non-denominational
Member of IAPS, ISBA
Age range 3–11
No of pupils 200; *Girls* 100; *Boys* 100
Teacher:pupil ratio 1:8
Average class size 18
Fees per annum *(day)* £4,500–£9,800

Prospect House School is a member of House Schools Group and has sister schools at Bassett House School in Kensington and Orchard House School in Chiswick. It is based in an imposing Victorian house opposite Putney Heath. Boys and girls are prepared for examinations at senior school at 11+. The school enjoys a large garden and all-weather sports area. It is also equipped with a maths and IT lab, gym/theatre and school hall, music rooms and art room. Music is a popular key option. The school is highly staffed and equipped. Academic results have been strong.

Cameron House School

4 The Vale, Chelsea, London SW3 6AH Tel: (020) 7352 4040 Fax: (020) 7352 2349
E-mail: info@cameronhouseschool.org Website: www.cameronhouseschool.org www.gabbitas.net

The Headmistress Miss F N Stack BA (Hons) PGCE Mont Dip
Founded 1985
School status Co-educational independent day
Religious denomination Church of England
Member of CReSTeD, IAPS, NAHT, SATIPS;
Accredited by IAPS, ISC
Learning difficulties CA SNU/DYC DYP DYS
Behavioural and emotional disorders ST/ADD
Physical and medical conditions CA RA
Age range 4–11
No of pupils 120; *(day)* 120; *Pre-prep* 58; *Prep* 62; *Girls* 67; *Boys* 53
Teacher:pupil ratio 1:9; **Average class size** 18
Fees per annum *(day)* £10,785

Cameron House aims to produce academically confident pupils who appreciate the virtues of courtesy, good manners and kindness, and are positive-minded and confident. Our highly qualified and dedicated teaching staff create a stimulating environment in which initiative and individual objectives can flourish.

The curriculum is broadly based and designed to cultivate a wide range of interests, though emphasis is placed on the core curriculum. Essential disciplines are balanced with our aesthetic and practical activities such as speech and drama, debating and French. The school is well equipped with its own class libraries, and a dedicated IT room with a bank of mobile laptops.

Pupils discover their talents through a wide variety of optional clubs after school. Children are encouraged to join the Junior Choir while Chamber Choir is more selective in developing classical singing talent.

The learning process necessarily focuses on public exams. For boys these can take place at any time after the age of seven. Girls are prepared for the entrance exam to independent London day or country boarding schools.

The Cavendish School

31 Inverness Street, London NW1 7HB
Tel: (020) 7485 1958 Fax: (020) 7267 0098
E-mail: admissions@cavendish-school.co.uk
Website: www.cavendishschool.co.uk www.gabbitas.net
For all enquiries please contact the Admissions Secretary, Mrs Frances Jones

Headmistress Mrs L D Hayes BA (Hons) Dip.Ed
Founded 1875
School status Girls' day only
Religious denomination Roman Catholic
Member of AGBIS, IAPS, ISBA, ISCis
Age range 3–11
No of pupils 160; *Nursery* 13; *Pre-prep* 22; *Prep* 135; *Girls* 160
Teacher:pupil ratio 1:8
Average class size 20
Fees per annum *(day)* £8,598; Nursery £4,326–£8,112. All fees include lunches and outings.

Parents seeking a happy, exceptionally well-resourced, academic girls' preparatory school should consider The Cavendish School – a Catholic preparatory school accepting all denominations, housed in spacious Victorian school buildings and a modern block with two secluded playgrounds. Founded in 1875, The Cavendish School specializes in providing a well-balanced curriculum in a caring, family atmosphere. A broad range of subjects and extra-curricular activities, ballet, BAYS, science, gymnastics and games is taught by highly qualified experienced staff. An after-school care facility is provided along with flexible nursery arrangements.

The school aims to stimulate the children's attainment of sound academic standards whilst also encouraging the development of their creative skills, confidence and happiness.

Davies Laing and Dick

100 Marylebone Lane, London W1U 2QB
Tel: (020) 7935 8411 Fax: (020) 7935 0755
E-mail: dld@dld.org
Website: www.dld.org www.gabbitas.net

Principal Ms E Rickards MA PGCE
Founded 1931
School status Co-educational independent Sixth Form college
Religious denomination Non-denominational
Accredited by BAC, ISA
Learning difficulties DYS
Age range 14–19; *boarders from* 16
No of pupils 370; *(day)* 367; *Sixth Form* 320; *Girls* 185; *Boys* 185
Average class size 5
Fees per annum *(day)* £5,490–£14,760

Davies Laing and Dick is housed in two adjoining buildings in central London: one in Marylebone Lane, the other in Bulstrode Street. The student roll is 370. Over three-quarters of the students are Sixth Formers preparing for A levels. There are 50 GCSE students taking intensive one-year or two-year courses. Others are retaking A levels with the aim of securing a place at a leading university.

Apart from the traditional school subjects, other subjects offered at A level include drama and theatre studies, photography, film and media studies, performance studies, philosophy and music technology. The Portfolio Course prepares students for Art School. Facilities are excellent: there is an 80 seat state-of-the-art theatre, an art block comprising fine art, sculpture/ceramics and textiles, photography studio and dark room. The music department includes a technology studio and a recording studio. There are two ICT classrooms. An additional student access ICT room with 16 computers adjoins the library. All three laboratories are newly equipped and have interactive white boards. The media/film suite has digital editing facilities.

Students are expected to be strongly committed to their studies. They are supported in this by excellent study facilities, an effective personal tutoring system which includes hourly attendance monitoring, a weekly meeting, three weekly and termly reports and, where necessary, compulsory supervised study/Saturday morning attendance. All students are given personal advice on their university applications. Prospective medical students and those applying to Oxford or Cambridge are given supplementary tuition in current affairs, ethics and critical thinking. Mock interviews are held for those applying for medicine/dentistry and Oxbridge. Tutors are highly qualified and chosen for their ability to encourage and inspire. Staff turnover is minimal.

There is a college canteen although A level students may go out for lunch if they wish. Extra-curricular activities include the DLD Youth Theatre, Philosophy Club, Duke of Edinburgh's Award scheme, Young Enterprise, music technology, vocal ensemble, film making, yoga, dance and *Planet DLD* – the college newspaper. There are football and basketball teams. Other sports include gym, rock climbing, tennis and swimming.

Devonshire House Preparatory School

2 Arkwright Road, Hampstead, London NW3 6AE
Tel: (020) 7435 1916 Fax: (020) 7431 4787
E-mail: enquiries@devonshirehouseprepschool.co.uk
Website: www.devonshirehouseschool.co.uk www.gabbitas.net

Headmistress Mrs S Alexander BA (Hons)
Founded 1989
School status Co-educational day only
Religious denomination Non-denominational
Learning difficulties SC WI/DYP DYS
Behavioural and emotional disorders RA
Physical and medical conditions RA
Age range Boys 2–13
No of pupils 528; *Girls* 240; *Boys* 288
Fees per annum *(day)* £9,300–£10,200

Curriculum Early literacy and numeracy are very important and the traditional academic subjects form the core curriculum. Specialist teaching and the combined sciences form an increasingly important part of the timetable as the children grow older. Expression in all forms of communication is encouraged, with classes also having lessons in art, music, drama, French, and information and design technology. Much encouragement is given to pupils to help to widen their horizons and broaden their interests. The school fosters a sense of responsibility amongst the pupils.

Entry requirements The offer of places is subject to availability and to an interview. Children wishing to enter the school over the age of 6 will normally be required to take a formal written test.

Academic and leisure facilities The school is situated in fine premises in the heart of Hampstead with their own walled grounds. The aim is to achieve high academic standards whilst developing enthusiasm and initiative throughout a wide range of interests. It is considered essential to encourage pupils to develop their own individual personalities and a good sense of personal responsibility.

Scholarships The school offers academic and music scholarships.

Dolphin School (Including Noah's Ark Nursery Schools)

Northcote Road Baptist Church, 106 Northcote Road, London SW11 6QW
Tel: (020) 7924 3472 Fax: (020) 8265 8700 E-mail: admissions@dolphinschool.org.uk
Website: www.dolphinschool.org.uk www.gabbitas.net

Headteacher Mrs S Rogers BA Dip Ed
Early Years Co-ordinator Miss A Miller TTC (NZ)
Deputy Principal Miss J Baker MA Education, Art & Design
Founded 1986
School status Co-educational day only
Religious denomination Christian
Member of Christian Schools Trust, NAHT Association of Christian Schools
Learning difficulties CA WI/DYP DYS
Behavioural and emotional disorders RA/AUT
Physical and medical conditions AT SM/HEA
Age range 2–11
No of pupils 178; *(day)* 178; *Nursery* 96; *Pre-prep* 46; *Prep* 36; *Girls* 94; *Boys* 84
Teacher:pupil ratio 1:18 in Pre-prep & Prep
Average class size 13 in Pre-prep & Prep

Fees per annum *(day)* £3,780–£6,975

Location 10 minutes walk from Clapham Junction; 4 minutes walk from Wandsworth Common.

We aim to develop the whole child within a secure, loving environment where children discover their unique gifts, reach their full potential and grow in confidence. We encourage and give children opportunities to develop their own personality and gifts. Parents who transfer children to Dolphin from other schools often notice an increased self-confidence and sense of security, fostered by our commitment to clear boundaries and unconditional love.

Dolphin School's vision is to educate children towards a Christian world view so that as adults they will be equipped to make a difference within their social and professional sphere.

Eaton House School Belgravia

3–5 Eaton Gate, Eaton Square, London SW1W 9BA
Tel: (020) 7730 9343 Fax: (020) 7730 1798
E-mail: llawrence@eatonhouseschools.com
Website: www.eatonhouseschools.com

Headmistress Miss L Watts
Founded 1897
School status Boys' independent day only
Religious denomination Non-denominational
Learning difficulties SNU/DYS
Behavioural and emotional disorders RA
Physical and medical conditions RA WA2
Age range 4–8
No of pupils 250; *(day)* 250; *Boys* 250
Teacher:pupil ratio 1:12
Average class size 20
Fees per annum *(day)* £9,150

The school is centrally located in a beautiful building in Eaton Square SW1. The children enjoy the advantages of being educated close to the centre of London with all its museums, art, sport and other educational amenities.

For over 100 years we have been producing well-balanced children who have a real enthusiasm for learning and an outgoing attitude – truly ready to take on the world with confidence. The academic standard reached by every one of our pupils is outstanding, as highlighted in our recent OFSTED report (view it in full at www.ofsted.gov.uk).

Eaton House Belgravia combines a traditional approach to teaching, with modern facilities and extremely experienced staff. The core curriculum focuses on English, mathematics and reading, but also introduces the boys to a wide range of other subjects. For instance, every pupil enjoys ICT lessons from the age of four, learning to find their way around a computer, then adding word-processing, spreadsheets and internet research to their skills.

Small class sizes ensure every pupil is both supported and stretched to achieve their highest potential. Cooperative effort is encouraged via an effective House System, but individual diligence is also valued and rewarded.

The premises combine history with the most modern facilities, such as the Centenary Science Laboratory and large gym where the boys can enjoy activities such as indoor hockey and climbing, in addition to the usual outdoor competitive sports. Music and drama play an important part in the life of the school, as does learning to help others. Throughout the year, the boys put on productions and concerts and organize events in support of their favourite charities.

Most Eaton House Belgravia boys go on to London day schools in the area, such as Colet Court, Westminster Under, Sussex House and Eaton House The Manor, our own Preparatory School in Clapham, at 7+ or 8+. Others are accepted at boarding schools such as Summer Fields, Ludgrove and The Dragon.

Like all the schools in the Eaton House Group, Eaton House Belgravia is a non-selective school. With its excellent academic record, early registration of interest is advisable.

Eaton House The Manor

58 Clapham Common Northside, London SW4 9RU
Tel: (020) 7924 6000 Fax: (020) 7924 1530
E-mail: llawrence@eatonhouseschools.com
Website: www.eatonhouseschools.com

Headmaster (Preparatory School) Mr S Hepher
Headmistress (Pre-preparatory School) Mrs S Seagrave
Founded 1993
School status Girls' independent day 2–4 Co-educational Nursery, boys' pre-prep and prep schools
Religious denomination Non-denominational
Member of NAHT, SATIPS
Learning difficulties SNU/DYC DYP DYS
Behavioural and emotional disorders CA RA/AUT
Physical and medical conditions WA1/CP IM
No of pupils 520; *(day)* 520; *Nursery* 80; *Pre-prep* 240; *Prep* 200; *Girls* 25; *Boys* 495
Teacher:pupil ratio 1:10
Average class size 20
Fees per annum *(day)* £3,750–£11,040

The quality of an Eaton House The Manor education means that all of the boys leaving the Prep School go on to their first choice of senior school, with several winning scholarships. Entrance to the Pre-Prep School is non-selective – our approach means that we succeed in bringing out the best in each child, fostering a lifelong enthusiasm for learning and striving for the highest academic results. Pupils go on to the most prestigious public schools including Westminster, St Paul's, Eton, Harrow, Radley, Charterhouse, Marlborough and Dulwich College.

The Nursery School takes both boys and girls from the age of 2½. It is expected that the boys will continue to enter the Pre-Prep and Preparatory Schools, while many girls may go on to our sister school, Eaton House The Vale.

The curriculum at Eaton House The Manor is traditional. Strong moral values and a concern for others are emphasized in the classroom and through the House system. Care is taken to develop each child's confidence, and instil a healthy pride in achieving personal goals as well as participating in team games and competitions. Every day, children at the Prep School enjoy a reading period after lunch and can attend a supervised homework club at the end of the day.

Pupils are taught in a vibrant environment on a spacious site opposite Clapham Common. A recent multi-million pound investment to extend and improve facilities means Pre-Prep pupils benefit from the latest computer technology in the new ICT lab, an extended library and extremely good music facilities. The Prep pupils are enjoying the new art and design studios.

The children enjoy many day and weekend trips and are encouraged to take part in a host of extra-curricular activities. Displays, concerts and dramatic performances in the school theatre and gym always prove popular, as do the many 'parent vs pupils' sporting events. Parents are encouraged to be closely involved in their children's education, and to take part in many of the school's activities.

Admittance to Eaton House The Manor Nursery and Pre-Preparatory Schools are on a first-come, first-served basis, and parents wishing to enrol their children in the Nursery School are advised to register them at birth. Entry to the Preparatory School is at 8 years of age by examination. Places are offered at 7+ and 8+.

Parental visits occur a year before the child's projected start date, backed up by a report from their current Pre-Preparatory School.

Eaton House The Vale

2 Elvaston Place, London SW7 5QH
Tel: (020) 7584 9151 Fax: (020) 7584 8368
E-mail: llawrence@eatonhouseschools.com
Website: www.eatonhouseschools.com

Headmistress Miss S Calder
Founded 1950
School status Co-educational independent day only
Religious denomination Non-denominational
Member of IAPS
Learning difficulties RA
Physical and medical conditions RA
Age range Boys 4–8; Girls 4–11
No of pupils 93; *Girls* 56; *Boys* 37
Teacher:pupil ratio 1:10
Average class size 12
Fees per annum *(day)* £9,150

Centrally situated in South Kensington, near Hyde Park, Eaton House The Vale offers a personalized education of exceptional quality to both boys and girls. The school is housed in a beautiful building and its pupils benefit from being near the centre of one of the most vibrant and exciting cities in the world. Pupils undertake a traditional curriculum that is brought alive by the many trips and visits they enjoy. A recent Ofsted report commented on the excellent teaching and pastoral care of the children (view it in full at www.ofsted.gov.uk).

Eaton House The Vale takes children from the age of 4 and from the beginning emphasizes the core subjects of maths and English. Intensive teaching methods mean that all pupils attain a high academic standard and receive a strong grounding in a whole range of subjects from a very early age. The high teacher:pupil ratio and amount of individual attention each child can therefore expect means Eaton House The Vale pupils are independent thinkers whose creativity and spirit are encouraged in a caring environment.

Boys take their Preparatory entrance examinations at 8 and are very successful in achieving their first choice of school. Many go on to our sister school, Eaton House The Manor Preparatory School, while others achieve places at London day schools such as Colet Court, Sussex House, Westminster Under and Westminster Cathedral Choir School, as well as notable boarding schools such as Ludgrove, The Dragon and Windlesham House.

Girls are thoroughly prepared for both the London day schools and Common Entrance exams at 11, with excellent results. Teaching is in classes of no more than 10, and a small number of places are available for girls to join at 9 and enjoy the advantage of our intensive preparation. Girls move on to highly-regarded academic institutions such as St Paul's Girls School, The Godolphin and Latymer School and Frances Holland School among the day schools and St Mary's Calne, Heathfield and Woldingham among boarding schools.

Eaton House The Vale is a non-selective school; admittance is on a first-come, first-served basis at the age of 4 and early application is advised. Girls wishing to join at 9 are assessed via a written paper.

The Falcons School for Boys

2 Burnaby Gardens, Chiswick, London W4 3DT Tel: (020) 8747 8393 Fax: (020) 8995 3903
E-mail: admin@falconschool.com Website: www.falconschool.com

Principal Mr B H Evans BEd
Founded 1956
School status Boys' independent day only
Religious denomination Inter-denominational
Accreditation inspection for IAPS scheduled November 2005
Learning difficulties CA WI
Physical and medical conditions RA/HEA
Age range 3–8
No of pupils 200; *(day)* 200; *Nursery* 27; *Pre-prep* 173; *Boys* 200
Teacher:pupil ratio 1:9; **Average class size** 18
Fees per annum *(day)* £4,575–£8,985

The school has a reputation for excellence within a friendly and caring atmosphere and enjoys an impressive record of entrance results to all the London day schools.

One of the only single sex pre-preparatory boy's schools in West London, our aim is for each boy to reach his full potential in a happy and stimulating environment, led by a talented and committed team of fully qualified staff. The school provides a safe outdoor space for play and sport, a well-equipped gym, a library, a music room and an ICT suite. Sport plays a large part in the life of the school, with the emphasis on participation and enjoyment for all. A variety of after-school activities are offered that enhance a varied and comprehensive curriculum.

Entry to the school is through the Nursery aged 3, Reception aged 4, or as occasional places become available in the different year groups. For further information please contact the school office, who will also be able to give you details of our Girls School (3–11 years) located in the same area at 15 Gunnersby Avenue, London W5 3XD Tel: (020) 8992 5189 Fax: (020) 8752 1635 E-mail: admin@falconsgirls.co.uk.

Francis Holland School

Clarence Gate, Ivor Place, London NW1 6XR
Tel: (020) 7723 0176 Fax: (020) 7706 1522
E-mail: admin@fhs-nw1.org.uk
Website: www.francisholland.org,uk

Headmistress Mrs V M Durham
School status Girls' day only
Religious denomination Church of England
Age range 11–18
Fees per annum *(day)* £10,875

Fulham Prep School

Prep Department, 200 Greyhound Road, London W14 9RY Tel: (020) 7386 2444
Fax: (020) 7386 2449 E-mail: prepadmin@fulhamprep.co.uk Website: www.fulhamprep.co.uk
Pre-Prep (4–7) based at: 47a Fulham High Street, London SW6 3JJ

Principal & Head of Prep School Mrs J Emmett
Head of Pre-Prep Ms D Steven
Founded 1996
School status Co-educational independent day only
Religious denomination Non-denominational
Learning difficulties WI/DYC DYP DYS
Physical and medical conditions WA2
Age range 7–13
No of pupils 206; *Prep* 206; *Girls* 85; *Boys* 121
Teacher:pupil ratio 1:9; **Average class size** 16
No of pupils 224 pupils in Pre-prep School
Fees per annum *(day)* £10,500

Curriculum In the Pre-prep School, the curriculum, though broadly based, lays particular emphasis on the early acquisition of the traditional basic skills of reading, writing and numeracy. We do not prepare children for 7+ and 8+ exams.

FULHAM PREP SCHOOL

Entry requirements The school is non-selective at the Reception stage, while entry into other years is by assessment in Maths and English. Siblings of current pupils are given priority.

Academic and other facilities Academic achievement is strong but we also put a lot of emphasis on all-round development, providing an extensive range of activities featuring sport, music, art and drama. The school has two choirs and an orchestra. A wide range of lunchtime and after-school clubs is offered each term.

Gatehouse School

Sewardstone Road, Victoria Park, London E2 9JG
Tel: (020) 8980 2978 Fax: (020) 8983 1642
E-mail: admin@gatehouse.towerhamlets.sch.uk
Website: www.gatehouse.towerhamlets.sch.uk

The Headmistress Mrs Belinda Canham JP BA(Hons) PGCE (Froebel)
School status Co-educational independent day only
Religious denomination Christian
Learning difficulties SNU
Age range 3–11
No of pupils 200; *(day)* 184; *Girls* 99; *Boys* 101
Fees per annum *(day)* £5,535–£6,765

Founded in May 1948 by Phyllis Wallbank, a pioneer of educational development, in the gatehouse of St Bartholomew of the Great Priory Church, West Smithfield. The school was then a pioneer of much that is now generally accepted in education.

Gatehouse's policy is: Children of any race, colour, creed, background and intellect shall be accepted as students and work side by side without streaming or any kind of segregation with the aim that each child shall get to know and love God, and to develop their own uniqueness of personality to enable them to appreciate the world and the world to appreciate them.

Gatehouse is now located in Sewardstone Road close to Victoria Park, where it continues to follow the education philosophy of Phyllis Wallbank.

Glendower Preparatory School

87 Queen's Gate, South Kensington, London SW7 5JX
Tel: (020) 7370 1927 Fax: (020) 7244 8308
E-mail: office@glendower.kensington.sch.uk www.gabbitas.net

Headmistress Mrs R Bowman BSc
Founded 1895
School status Girls' day only
Religious denomination Non-denominational
Age range 4–11
No of pupils 187
Average class size 16
Fees per annum *(day)* £9,690

Why choose Glendower for your daughter?

Our school is small in numbers, 187 pupils, aged between 4 and 11, but high in expectation and achievement. We aim to provide a stimulating environment in which each girl is valued and can enjoy developing her particular talents to the full, whether they be in art, music, sport, drama or other social activities. In the family atmosphere of Glendower, girls acquire the confidence to develop their talents to the utmost of their ability and gain the solid academic foundations necessary for competitive entry into a leading London day school or boarding school. We are a happy school!

For further details please contact the school office.

Hampstead Fine Arts, Independent College

24 Lambolle Place, Hampstead, London NW3 4PG
Tel: (020) 7586 0312 Fax: (020) 7483 0355
E-mail: mail@hampsteadfinearts.com
Website: www.hampsteadfinearts.com

Principal Ms C Cave CFA (Oxon) and Mr N Cochrane CFA (Oxon)
Founded 1978
College status Co-educational day only
Age range 14–19
No of pupils 105; *Girls* 45; *Boys* 60
Fees per annum *(day)* £12,750

Hampstead Fine Arts is a small college specializing in the arts and humanities at GCSE and A Level. We also offer a Fine Art Foundation course – a unique and intensive introduction to art and design. The college is situated in central yet leafy Belsize Park, and each of the three departments – GCSE, A Level and Art – has its own specially equipped building.

Hampstead Fine Arts has approximately one hundred students and provides high quality education at all levels in a supportive and stimulating atmosphere. Classes are small to give maximum attention and encourage proactive participation on the part of the student. Each student is allocated a personal tutor and has timetabled weekly meetings and fortnightly reports. The college consistently achieves excellent results, with students gaining high examination passes, a wide range of University and Art School places, and subsequent success in professional careers.

We provide an excellent opportunity to study in a friendly and supportive environment: a highly effective bridge between school and university.

Hawkesdown House School

27 Edge Street, Kensington, London W8 7PN
Tel: (020) 7727 9090 Fax: (020) 7727 9988
E-mail: admin@hawkesdown.co.uk
Website: www.hawkesdown.co.uk www.gabbitas.net

Headmistress Mrs C J Leslie BA Cert Ed
Founded 2001
School status Boys' independent day only
Member of IAPS
Accredited by IAPS, ISC
Age range 3–8
No of pupils 125; *Nursery* 14; *Pre-prep* 111
Fees per annum *(day)* £8,700–£10,200

Hawkesdown House is an independent school for boys from the ages of three to eight. In December 2003, the Headmistress was the first head of a freestanding pre-preparatory school to be elected to the IAPS (Incorporated Association of Preparatory Schools). Early literacy and numeracy are of prime importance and the traditional academic subjects form the core curriculum. A balanced education helps all aspects of learning and a wide range of interests is encouraged. The school finds and fosters individual talents in each pupil. Boys are prepared for entry at eight to the main London and other preparatory schools. The Headmistress places the greatest importance on matching boys happily and successfully to potential schools and spends time with parents ensuring that the transition is smooth and free of stress.

Sound and thorough early education is important for success, and also for self-confidence. The thoughtful and thorough teaching and care at Hawkesdown House ensure high academic standards and promote initiative, kindness and courtesy. Hawkesdown is a school with fun and laughter, where boys develop their own personalities together with a sense of personal responsibility.

The school provides an excellent traditional education, with the benefits of modern technology, in a safe, happy and caring atmosphere. Many of the boys coming to the school are from within walking distance and the school, although just four years old, is rapidly becoming an important part of the Kensington community.

There are clear expectations and the boys are encouraged by positive motivation and by recognition and praise for achievement, progress and effort. Individual attention and pastoral care for each of the boys is of great importance.

Hawkesdown House has a fine building in Edge Street, off Kensington Church Street.

Parents who would like further information or to visit the school and meet the Headmistress should contact the School Office for a prospectus or an appointment.

Hendon Preparatory School

20 Tenterden Grove, Hendon, London NW4 1TD Tel: (020) 8203 7727 Fax: (020) 8203 3465
E-mail: info@hendonprep.co.uk Website: www.hendonprep.co.uk www.cognitaschools.co.uk

Headmaster Mr D Weale
Founded 1874
School status Co-educational day only
Religious denomination Non-denominational
Member of IAPS; **Accredited by** IAPS
Learning difficulties SNU/DYS
Age range 4–13
No of pupils 130; *Prep* 130; *Girls* 40; *Boys* 90
Teacher:pupil ratio 1:15
Fees per annum *(day)* £7,245–£9,435

Hendon is a long-established co-educational prep school, providing high quality education for boys and girls from age four to thirteen. The school is located in a quiet, residential part of Hendon, conveniently close to the M1, A1 and North Circular Road.

Hendon is well equipped for ICT, DT and science and participates in a full programme of sports at various centres. Pupils enjoy educational visits and have the opportunity to go on residential trips as well as being encouraged to play a part in dramatic and musical productions.

The school is well known for its caring family atmosphere, small classes and a high proportion of specialist subject teachers. Although Hendon is a mixed ability school, pupils achieve considerable success in transfer examinations to secondary education, with a commendable number of scholarships at 11+ for girls and 13+ for boys.

International Community School

4 York Terrace East, Regent's Park, London NW1 4PT Tel: (020) 7935 1206 Fax: (020) 7935 7915
E-mail: admissions@ics.uk.net Website: www.ics.uk.net

Head of School Mr P Hurd BSc PGCSE
Founded 1979
School status Co-educational day only
Religious denomination Non-denominational
Member of ARELS, CIS, LISA
Accredited by British Council. Accredited by DfES.
Learning difficulties CA WI/DOW DYP DYS
Behavioural and emotional disorders ADD ASP AUT
Age range 3–18
No of pupils 240; *Girls* 120; *Boys* 120
Teacher:pupil ratio 1:8; **Average class size** 16
Fees per annum *(day)* £9,696–£12,708

ICS is a small friendly central London school. Children and faculty are from 65 countries (including the UK) and form a dynamic learning community.

Teaching and learning are driven by best practice utilizing aspects of the English and international curriculums. In September 2006, pending authorization, the International Baccalaureate Diploma will be launched for university bound students. The school has a strong pastoral care/welfare reputation and classes are kept to a maximum of 18 students. Environmental, sports and language visits to overseas destinations and to our outdoor education centre in Suffolk feature every holiday.

Throughout ICS there is a specialist English for Education department, providing intensive English for students year-round.

A strong Special Educational Needs department supports students in all areas of the school.

International School of London

139 Gunnersbury Avenue, London W3 8LG
Tel: (020) 8992 5823 Fax: (020) 8993 7012
E-mail: mail@islondon.com
Website: www.islondon.com

Director Mr A Makarem
Founded 1972
School status Co-educational independent day only
Religious denomination Non-denominational
Member of CIS, IBO, IBSCA, LISA
Accredited by CIS
Age range Boys 3–19; Girls 4–18
No of pupils 288; *Girls* 123; *Boys* 165
Fees per annum *(day)* £11,500–£15,900

The International School of London (ISL) accepts students of all nationalities from early childhood (3 years old) up to the International Baccalaureate Diploma (16–19).

ISL is implementing the IB Primary Years Programme (PYP) throughout all the primary classes, from early childhood to Year Six (10 years old). Using the PYP we provide students with an international curriculum which focuses on developing the whole child.

The secondary curriculum follows the IB Middle Years Programme and the full IB Diploma. Comprehensive and integrated English as a Second Language programmes are available at all ages. Students can also follow courses in 20 home languages including Arabic, Danish, Dutch, Hindi, Italian, Japanese, Portuguese and Spanish.

To join ISL parents will need to provide the Admissions Office with a completed application form and previous school records. Most students join ISL in September, but we admit students throughout the year, provided that we have places available.

We offer door-to-door transport covering west, central and south London.

Lansdowne College

40–44 Bark Place, London W2 4AT Tel: (020) 7616 4400 Fax: (020) 7616 4401
E-mail: education@lansdownecollege.com Web: www.lansdownecollege.com www.gabbitas.net

Principal Mr Hugh Templeton FCCA
Vice Principal Mr Gary Hunter BA FRSA
Founded 1976
College status Co-educational independent Sixth Form college day only
Religious denomination Non-denominational
Member of CIFE; **Accredited by** BAC, British Council
Learning difficulties RA/DYC DYP DYS
Behavioural and emotional disorders RA/ADD ADHD
Physical and medical conditions RA/EPI HEA
Age range Boys 14–19; Girls 14–19
No of pupils 195; *Senior* 20; *Sixth Form* 175; *Girls* 95; *Boys* 100
Teacher:pupil ratio 1:7; **Average class size** 8
Fees per annum *(day)* £2,500–£13,350. Scholarships and bursaries covering part fees are available

Lansdowne College is housed in a modern, spacious building with excellent facilities, including a 200-seater hall.

The College is renowned for the warm, supportive atmosphere provided by our staff and students together. Our students thrive on a mixture of expert tuition, hard work and pastoral care, and, as young adults, benefit from an environment that, while maintaining academic rigour and discipline, provides a relaxed and friendly atmosphere, allowing each student to achieve his or her full potential.

At Lansdowne we offer all the subjects on the school curriculum and many others that are not. Teaching is in small groups for both A level and GCSE students. We have an expanding GCSE department and we also offer one-term and one-year A level retake courses, alongside traditional A level courses.

Applications are welcome all year round and prospective students are welcome to visit the college at any time.

Latymer Prep School

36 Upper Mall, Hammersmith, London W6 9TA Tel: (020) 8748 0303 Fax: (020) 8741 4916
E-mail: mlp@latymerprep.org Website: www.latymerprep.org www.gabbitas.net

Principal Mr S P Dorrian BA
Founded 1995
School status Co-educational independent day only
Religious denomination Non-denominational
Member of IAPS, SATIPS
Age range 7–11
No of pupils 160; **Average class size** 20
Fees per annum *(day)* £10,875

Curriculum Children are taught the full range of subjects following National Curriculum guidelines, but to an advanced standard. Classes are small, which allows for close monitoring and evaluation of each pupil's progress and well-being.

Entry requirements and procedures The school is academically selective and entry to the school is by assessment in maths, English and verbal reasoning. Visits for prospective parents occur throughout the Autumn term and can be arranged by telephoning for an appointment.

Academic and leisure facilities Academic achievement is strong, but in addition there is an extensive range of activities featuring sport, music, art and drama. The school has a large choir and its own orchestra.

The school is well resourced, sharing catering, sport and theatre facilities with the Upper School.

Sports include contact and touch rugby, soccer, cricket, tennis, hockey, gymnastics and dance. There is also a thriving swimming club (the school has its own indoor pool). Karate, fencing and a whole range of clubs take place after school.

Latymer Upper School

King Street, Hammersmith, London W6 9LR Tel: (020) 8741 1851 Fax: (020) 8748 5212
E-mail: registrar@latymer-upper.org Website: www.latymer.org www.gabbitas.net

Head Mr P J Winter MA (Oxon)
Founded 1624
School status Co-educational day only
Religious denomination Non-denominational
Member of HMC; **Accredited by** HMC
Learning difficulties SNU/DYP DYS
Behavioural and emotional disorders ASP
Physical and medical conditions RA/CP HEA
Age range 11–18
No of pupils 1045; *Girls* 204; *Boys* 841
Teacher:pupil ratio 1:10; **Average class size** 22
Fees per annum *(day)* £11,985

Latymer conducts competitive examinations and interviews are held for entry at 7, 11 and 13, and at 16 for the Sixth Form. Scholarships of up to half fees are awarded each year for art, drama and sport in the Sixth Form. Scholarships of up to half fees are awarded annually at 11+, 13+ and 16+ for music. Exhibitions for art, drama, music and sport and fixed-sum awards are available at 11+, 13+ and 16+.

A full range of academic subjects is offered to GCSE and AS/A2 level. Science is taught as separate subjects by subject specialists.

The school has a strong tradition of excellent pastoral care. Teams of form tutors deliver a coherent programme promoting involvement in the community, charity work, and the personal, social and academic development of their form.

Music and drama play a large part in the life of the school. There are several orchestras and choirs and concerts are given each term. The £4 million Latymer Arts Centre (including a 300-seat theatre) opened in January 2000.

The school has a boathouse in the grounds with direct river access, a large sports hall and an indoor swimming pool on site.

The Duke of Edinburgh's Award Scheme flourishes in the school, with several boys and girls achieving the Gold Award each year.

Lyndhurst House Preparatory School

24 Lyndhurst Gardens, Hampstead, London NW3 5NW
Tel: (020) 7435 4936 E-mail: pmg@lyndhursthouse.co.uk Website: www.lyndhursthouse.co.uk
A large detached Victorian red-brick building with its own playground in a quiet side street.

Headmaster Mr M O Spilberg MA
Founded 1952
School status Boys' day only. A small, friendly school with an intimate feel and high expectations.
Religious denomination Non-denominational
Member of IAPS, ISCis, NAHT, SATIPS;
Accredited by IAPS, ISC
Learning difficulties CA
Age range 4–13
No of pupils 140; *(day)* 140; *Pre-prep* 20; *Prep* 120; *Boys* 140
Teacher:pupil ratio 1:8.4
Average class size 12
Fees per annum *(day)* £10,050–£11,520

With the opening of our new Pre-Prep department, there are now entry points at 4+, 5+, 6+, 7+, 8+ and 11+ subject to interview and availability.

England

Mill Hill School

The Ridgeway, Mill Hill, London NW7 1QS
Tel: (020) 8959 1221 Fax: (020) 8906 2614
E-mail: registrations@millhill.org.uk
Website: www.millhill.org.uk

Headmaster Mr W R Winfield
Founded 1807
School status Co-educational boarding and day
Age range 13–18
No of pupils 601; *(full boarding)* 170; *Girls* 160; *Boys* 441
Teacher:pupil ratio 1:8
Average class size 17–24
Fees per annum *(full boarding)* £20,715; *(day)* £13,206

Founded in 1807, Mill Hill School offers education to boys and girls aged 13 to 18 years. The schools occupy a magnificent parkland site of 120 acres, only 10 miles from central London and within easy reach of Heathrow Airport and other transport links. The boarders form the heart of a vibrant, open and cosmopolitan community where the contribution of every child is valued.

Curriculum Mill Hill School offers exciting teaching methods set against a traditional background. At age 13 pupils follow a broad curriculum in which the core subjects are separately streamed by ability. GCSE French may be taken in the second year but all other subjects are taken in the third year.

In the Lower Sixth, pupils take a one-year course to AS level in four subjects. In the Upper Sixth they continue with three of these to A level. Pupils are specially prepared in all subjects for Oxford and Cambridge.

Academic performance The school has achieved excellent public examination results year on year. Notable strengths are history, art, science, modern languages and business education. In 2004, the three-year average pass rate was another school record, with over 98 per cent of entries graded A to E and over 59 per cent graded A to B. The A to E pass rate for AS level was also a school record at over 95 per cent. At GCSE, 123 pupils achieved an A* to C pass rate, with 76 per cent A* to B and 41 per cent A* or A grades. Academic and careers guidance is provided throughout a pupil's career at the school, with particular care taken over AS and A level and university course choices. More than 95 per cent of our leavers go on to university.

Drama, art, multi-media and IT Mill Hill has an outstanding reputation for music, drama and art. Over the past four years the school has opened a new drama centre, along with new facilities for art/design and music. The school has over 200 computers and is a leader in IT and internet communication.

Sports and other extra-curricular activities Historically great sports achievers, we offer over 26 sporting disciplines, and are frequent participants in national and overseas inter-school contests. Extra-curricular activities include a Community Service group and a Combined Cadet Force, along with a wide range of other clubs and societies. Key developments for 2003/2004 include a new Sixth Form Centre, a new indoor swimming pool and a refurbishment programme for one of the classroom blocks.

European initiative We are leaders in developing an integrated European education policy.

Scholarships The school offers a range of academic, sports and music scholarships and bursary awards.

Entrance examinations Entrance at 13+ and 14+ is by tests and interviews and a head's confidential reference. Entrance at 16+ is by interview and school reference and is normally conditional on GCSE performance. Entrance and scholarship examinations are held in January.

For further information please contact the Admissions Office.

More House

22–24 Pont Street, Chelsea, London SW1X 0AA Tel: (020) 7235 2855 Fax: (020) 7259 6782
E-mail: office@morehouse.org.uk Website: www.morehouse.org.uk

Headmistress Mrs L Falconer BSc (Hons)
Founded 1953
School status Girls' day only
Religious denomination Roman Catholic
Member of GSA
Age range 11–18; **No of pupils** 220
Teacher:pupil ratio 1:6; **Average class size** 18
Fees per annum *(day)* £9,780
Fees Includes all meals and books and certain school trips

More House is a Catholic Foundation, which accepts pupils of all faiths.

We offer a full range of academic subjects up to GCSE and A level. Every girl takes a full and balanced programme of science up to GCSE. Theatre studies, history of art, classical civilisation, economics and textiles are added to the traditional academic choices at Sixth Form.

The combination of high quality of teaching throughout the school, excellent pastoral care for the girls and the generous provision of all the equipment a modern school needs for its pupils to succeed results in excellent examination results.

Sports fixtures occur regularly against local schools.

Music is a particular strength of More House and there are five choirs, including one for parents and friends.

Scholarships are awarded on entry to Year 7 and Sixth Form for academic and musical excellence.

North Bridge House School Nursery and Prep

33 Fitzjohn's Avenue, London NW3 5JY Tel: (020) 7435 9641 Fax: (020) 7431 7930
E-mail: nursery@northbridgehouse.com Website: www.cognitaschools.co.uk
Senior School: 1 Gloucester Avenue, London NW1 7AB Tel: (020) 7267 6266.

Headmistress Mrs R Allsopp
Lower Prep School Head Mr J Battye
Upper Prep School Head Mr B Bibby
Senior School Head A Ayre
Founded 1939
School status Co-educational day only
Religious denomination Non-denominational
Learning difficulties DYS
Age range 3–5
No of pupils 223; *Girls* 108; *Boys* 115
Fees per annum *(day)* £4,110–£10,035

North Bridge House provides a complete education for children aged from 2½ to 16 years. The school comprises two Victorian villas in Hampstead and a large Victorian building facing Regents Park.

North Bridge House offers a busy and happy environment where pupils are encouraged to develop a critical spirit, self-confidence, clarity of expression and social awareness. The school also promotes the adoption of good work habits in order to provide pupils with a sound foundation for their future development.

North Bridge House offers withdrawal tuition for pupils between 7 and 16 years who have special educational needs or who have been classified as dyslexic.

We have an outstanding record of success at Common Entrance and send 70 to 80 children annually to the London Public Day Schools.

North Bridge House Senior School

1 Gloucester Avenue, London NW1 7AB
Tel: (020) 7267 6266 Fax: (020) 7284 2508 E-mail: seniorschool@northbridgehouse.com
Website: www.nbhseniorschool.co.uk www.cognitaschools.co.uk

Head of Senior School Miss A Ayre
School status Co-educational day only
Religious denomination Non-denominational
Learning difficulties SNU/DYP DYS
Age range 11–16
Fees per annum *(day)* £10,035

North Bridge House Senior School for boys and girls aged 11 to 16 years, occupies a prominent three storey building at 1 Gloucester Avenue overlooking Parkway and Regent's Park. Our facilities include a large assembly hall, a purpose built art and science block, gymnasium, laboratories, art and music rooms, computer rooms, a photographic darkroom, a technology workshop and a media suite.

North Bridge House has a long history of academic success and provides a nurturing, supportive environment. The school:

- produces excellent academic results;
- offers a wide range of activities, sports and events;
- aims to help every individual fulfil his or her academic potential;
- provides skilled, dedicated and enthusiastic teaching in small classes.

Queen's Gate School

133 Queen's Gate, Kensington, London SW7 5LE Tel: (020) 7589 3587 Fax: (020) 7584 7691
E-mail: registrar@queensgate.org.uk Website: www.queensgate.org.uk

Principal Mrs A M Holyoak CertEd
Founded 1891
School status Girls' day only
Religious denomination Non-denominational
Member of GSA
Learning difficulties WI/DYS
Age range 4–18
No of pupils 422
Fees per annum *(day)* £8,700–£10,875

Curriculum and academic life The curriculum is rich, varied, well balanced and as wide as possible during the years leading to the GCSE examinations, and is frequently reviewed to take into account new approaches to teaching and scientific and technological change.

All girls sit GCSE examinations in English Language, English Literature, mathematics, a modern language, and a science, and have the option of taking courses in additional science subjects, the humanities, a range of modern languages, classics, business studies, computer studies, art and design, graphic design, music and drama. Decisions on options are made after full consultation with parents.

Small classes ensure maximum guidance with coursework and much individual attention. Each girl's work is frequently assessed and progress and achievement are carefully monitored. Detailed reports are written for parents.

Entry requirements and procedures Girls enter the preliminary form aged four without formal testing, but visit the school for a morning of assessment in the autumn term prior to the September entry. Girls wishing to enter after this take tests in maths and English. Girls in Year 6 are required to pass the London Day Schools Consortium 11+ Examination before moving up into the Senior School.

Senior School Girls sit the London Day Schools Consortium Examination at 11+ and the school's own entrance examinations at 12+, 13+ and 16+. All girls are interviewed.

Sixth Form Girls entering the Sixth Form are required to have at least five GCSE passes, grades A to C, with at least an A grade in those subjects they wish to pursue to A2. They are expected to study four or five A/S levels and to continue three of those subjects to A2.

Examinations offered Edexcel, OCR, AQA.

Academic and leisure facilities The school has well-equipped science and computer laboratories and is conveniently placed to take full advantage of the resources offered by a central London education. It is within easy walking distance of the Science Museum, Geological and Natural History Museums and the Victoria and Albert Museum, Hyde Park and Kensington Gardens.

The girls play netball, hockey, lacrosse and tennis and, as well as having their own gymnasium, enjoy the facilities of a local sports hall, athletics grounds and swimming pools.

Scholarships One 8+ scholarship (external and internal), two internal Sixth Form scholarships.

Queen's Gate School Trust is a registered charity which exists to provide high-quality education for girls in central London.

Redcliffe School

47 Redcliffe Gardens, London SW10 9JH
Tel: (020) 7352 9247 Fax: (020) 7352 6936
E-mail: admissions@redcliffeschool.com
Website: www.redcliffeschool.com www.gabbitas.net

Headmistress Miss R E Cunnah
Founded 1948
School status Co-educational independent day only
Religious denomination Christian
Member of IAPS
Age range Boys 3–8; Girls 3–11
No of pupils 92; *Nursery* 10; *Girls* 73; *Boys* 19
Fees per annum *(day)* £8,400

Redcliffe School is a small, friendly school. It caters for a range of abilities and enables children to reach a high academic standard whilst developing the potential of each individual. Basic skills are accentuated within a broad and balanced curriculum incorporating creative and practical activities.

Rosemead Preparatory School

70 Thurlow Park Road, London SE21 8HZ
Tel: (020) 8670 5865 Fax: (020) 8761 9159
E-mail: admin@rosemeadprepschool.org.uk
Website: www.rosemeadprepschool.org.uk www.gabbitas.net

Headteacher Mrs C Brown BA MBA (Ed) Cert Ed
Founded 1942
School status Co-educational day only
Religious denomination Non-denominational
Member of ISCis
Accredited by ISA
Age range 3–11
No of pupils 342; *Girls* 185; *Boys* 157
Fees per annum *(day)* £5,619–£6,396

Rosemead is a well-established preparatory school with a fine record of academic achievement. Children are prepared for entrance to independent London day schools at age 11 years, many gaining awards and scholarships. The school has a happy, family atmosphere with boys and girls enjoying a varied, balanced curriculum which includes maths, English, science, French, information and communication technology, arts and humanities. Music and drama are strong subjects with tuition available in most orchestral instruments and various music groups meeting frequently. A full programme of physical education includes gymnastics, most major games, dance and (from age 6) swimming. Classes make regular visits to places of interest. A residential field studies course is arranged for the junior pupils along with various school holidays. Main entry to the school is at Nursery (age 3), following informal assessment, and at National Curriculum Year 3, following a formal assessment. The school is administered by a board of governors elected annually by the parents.

The Royal School, Hampstead

65 Rosslyn Hill, Hampstead, London NW3 5UD
Tel: (020) 7794 7708 Fax: (020) 7431 6741
E-mail: admissions@royalschoolhampstead.net
Website: www.royalschoolhampstead.net www.gabbitas.net
Nursery website: www.royalschool-nursery.net

Principal Mrs C Hawkins BA
Founded 1855
School status Girls' boarding and day. Flexi-boarding available.
Religious denomination Non-denominational
Age range 3–18
No of pupils 246; *(full boarding)* 25; *(weekly boarding)* 13
Teacher:pupil ratio 1:8
Average class size 15
Fees per annum *(full boarding)* £11,520–£14,295; *(weekly)* £9,510–£11,880; *(day)* £5,760–£7,185

Curriculum Balanced curriculum, including two modern languages and three sciences, leading to GCSE, AS and A2. EFL is offered as required. There are a variety of sports, plus music, drama, ballet, Duke of Edinburgh's Award, Young Enterprise, self-defence, Japanese and art. The school has a low teacher to pupil ratio.

Entry requirements Entry is by interview and previous school reports. An entrance test is taken where applicable. Scholarships and bursaries are available.

The school is small, caring and happy, with a staff dedicated to the academic and personal development of each child as an individual. Its boarding options include 'flexi-boarding'.

The school is situated in pleasant surroundings only 250 metres from Hampstead tube station. It has comfortable, spacious and light classrooms, and a separate Sixth Form study centre with personal work stations, IT, common room and kitchen facilities. There is a large car park.

England

Salcombe Preparatory School

224–226 Chase Side, Southgate, London N14 4PL Tel: (020) 8441 5282 / 5356
Fax: (020) 8441 5282 E-mail: info@salcombeprep.co.uk
Website: www.salcombeprep.co.uk www.cognitaschools.co.uk

Headmaster Mr F Steadman
Founded 1918
School status Co-educational day only
Religious denomination Non-denominational
Member of IAPS, ISA; **Accredited by** IAPS, ISA
Learning difficulties SNU/DYS
Age range 4–11
No of pupils 300; *Girls* 115; *Boys* 185
Average class size 14
Fees per annum *(day)* £6,720

Salcombe enjoys an excellent local reputation for its academic success rate, sporting prowess and cultural activities, catering for boys and girls from age four to eleven. The Infant Department in Green Road, Southgate, opened in 1998 and occupies a modernized and extended Grade II listed building while the older pupils enjoy the adapted and greatly extended original site in Chase Side, a short walk away.

Small classes and largely specialist subject teaching for older pupils ensure high academic standards while the emphasis on art, music, drama and sport ensures that there is something for all to find success in.

The extended day option, originally intended for the convenience of working parents, is often taken up at pupils' request.

St Margaret's School

18 Kidderpore Gardens, London NW3 7SR Tel: (020) 7435 2439 Fax: (020) 7431 1308
E-mail: headmistress@st-margarets.co.uk Website: www.st-margarets.co.uk www.gabbitas.net

Headmistress Mrs S Meaden BA MBA PGCE
Founded 1884
School status Girls' day only
Religious denomination Church of England
Member of ISA; **Accredited by** ISA, ISC
Learning difficulties RA/DYC DYP DYS MLD
Age range 4–16; **No of pupils** 135
Average class size 14
Fees per annum *(day)* £7,665–£8,850

St Margaret's offers a high standard of teaching in small classes. Pupils follow the National Curriculum. French begins in the infant classes, and in the senior school Spanish, Russian and classical civilisation are offered in addition to the core National Curriculum subjects. All girls go on to full-time Sixth Form education. Recent leavers are now studying at St Paul's Girls' School, North London Collegiate School, Highgate School, Channing School, Camden School for Girls, Henrietta Barnett and Woodhouse Sixth Form College.

The girls frequently visit London theatres, art galleries and concert halls. Extra-curricular activities include netball, drama clubs, self-defence, batik classes, yoga, and junior and senior choirs. Girls may have individual instrumental and speech and drama lessons.

Entrance is by interview at ages 4, 5 and 6, and by interview and written test from the age of 7. A prospectus is available from the school and Suzanne Meaden is happy to see parents at any time.

St Nicholas Preparatory School

23 Prince's Gate, London SW7 1PT
Tel: (020) 7225 1277 Fax: (020) 7823 7557 E-mail: stnicholas@mailbox.co.uk
Website: www.stnicholas.kensington.sch.uk www.cognitaschools.co.uk

Headmaster Mr D Wilson BEd MA Dip TEFL
Founded 1968
School status Co-educational day only
Religious denomination Non-denominational
Learning difficulties WI/DYS
Age range 3–11
No of pupils 250; *Girls* 125; *Boys* 125
Fees per annum *(day)* £6,060–£9,735

St Nicholas Preparatory and Pre-Preparatory Schools are co-educational day schools for children aged 3 to 13 situated on two sites in the heart of London.

At Prince's Gate, overlooking Hyde Park, Nursery and Reception classes have been in existence since 1968, offering a child-centred approach to learning using the Montessori method in classes of around 20 children. In 1998 the school developed its facilities to offer a broad-based, traditional programme of education to prepare pupils for

entrance examinations to all the leading senior schools at 7+, 8+ and 11+. The school has a fully equipped science room, two networked suites of personal computers and 12 wireless laptops, an outstanding library, and also benefits from its own gymnasium and ballet floor. The academic programme is based on the National Curriculum of England and Wales, and includes a full range of sports, music and arts, providing a balanced and challenging curriculum. We take full advantage of being within walking distance of the Science Museum, the Natural History Museum, the V&A Museum and other famous places of interest.

St Paul's Cathedral School

2 New Change, London EC4M 9AD
Tel: (020) 7248 5156 Fax: (020) 7329 6568
E-mail: admissions@spcs.london.sch.uk Website: www.spcs.london.sch.uk

Headmaster Mr A H Dobbin
School status Co-educational boarding and day
Religious denomination Church of England
Age range 4–13
No of pupils 206; *(full boarding)* 40; *Girls* 66; *Boys* 140
Fees per annum *(full boarding)* £5,199; *(day)* £8,964

Governed by the Dean and Chapter, the original residential choir school now includes non-chorister day boys and girls from age 4–13.

Curriculum A broad curriculum leads to scholarship and Common Entrance examinations at 13 and the school has an excellent record in placing pupils in senior schools of their choice, many with scholarships. A wide variety of sport and musical instrument tuition is offered. Choristers receive an outstanding choral training as members of the renowned St Paul's Cathedral Choir.

Facilities The refurbishment of the school's facilities has provided a separate Pre-Preparatory Department, improved classrooms and new boarding facilities for the choristers.

Admission Children are interviewed and tested before September entry at 4+ or 7+ years old. Voice trials and tests for choristers are held three times a year for boys of nearly 7 years and upwards.

Southbank International Schools

Head Mr N Hughes
School status Co-educational day only

Member of CIS, IBO, IBSCA, ISCis, LISA
Accredited by CIS, ISC, MSA (USA)

Southbank International School, Westminster

63–65 Portland Place, London W1B 1QR Tel: (020) 7243 3803 Fax: (020) 7727 3290
E-mail: admissions@southbank.org Website: www.southbank.org

Learning difficulties WI/DYPS DYS MLD
Behavioural & emotional disorders RA/ADHD
Age range 11–18

No of pupils 265; *Girls* 137; *Boys* 128
Fees per annum *(day)* £16,050–£17,700
Curriculum IBMYP, IDP

Southbank International School, Kensington

36–38 Kensington Park Road, London W11 3BU Tel: (020) 7243 3803 Fax: (020) 7727 3290
E-mail: admissions@southbank.org Website: www.southbank.org

Learning difficulties WI/DYP DYS MLD
Behavioural and emotional disorders RA/ADD
Physical and medical conditions WA3
Age range 3–11

No of pupils 195; *Girls* 95; *Boys* 100
Fees per annum *(day)* £12,600–£14,850
Curriculum IBPYP

Southbank International School, Hampstead

16 Netherhall Gardens, Hampstead, London NW3 5TH Tel: (020) 7243 3803
Fax: (020) 7727 3290 E-mail: admissions@southbank.org Website: www.southbank.org

Learning difficulties WI/DYP DYS
Behavioural and emotional disorders RA/ADD
Physical and medical conditions CA IT RA WA2/CP HEA HI **Age range** 3–14
No of pupils 189; *(day)* 189; *Girls* 95; *Boys* 94

Average class size 16
Fees per annum *(day)* £12,600–£17,700
Curriculum IBPYP, IBMYP

Wetherby Preparatory School

19 Pembridge Villas, London W11 3EP
Tel: (020) 7243 0243 Fax: (020) 7313 5244
E-mail: admin@wetherbyprep.co.uk

Headteacher Mr R Greenwood BSc FTCL ARCM
Founded 2004
School status Boys' independent day only
Religious denomination Christian
Learning difficulties WI/DYS
Physical and medical conditions RA
Age range 8–13
No of pupils 46
Teacher:pupil ratio 1:16
Average class size 12–16
Fees per annum *(day)* £11,130

Wetherby Preparatory School is an independent school for boys aged 8 to 13 years and opened its doors in September 2004.

Entry is via assessment for external pupils, held in the January preceding entry. Pupils follow an academic curriculum, with Sports and the Arts playing a valuable balancing role. Please contact the School Administrator for registration forms or to book a visit.

Wetherby School

11 Pembridge Square, London W2 4ED Tel: (020) 7727 9581 Fax: (020) 7221 8827
E-mail: learn@wetherbyschool.co.uk Website: www.alphaplusgroup.co.uk
Wetherby Preparatory School, 11 Pembridge Villas W11 3EP
For boys aged 8–13, automatic entry for Wetherby Pre-Prep boys

Headmistress Mrs J Aviss MA London
Founded 1951
School status Boys' day only
Religious denomination Non-denominational
Learning difficulties WI/DYP DYS
Physical and medical conditions RA/HEA
Age range 4–8
No of pupils 235; *Pre-prep* 235; *Boys* 235
Teacher:pupil ratio 1:10; **Average class size** 21
Fees per annum *(day)* £10,560

Wetherby School is an independent school for boys aged 4 to 8½ years. The school is based in a freehold, double-fronted listed building of the Italian Ornate style dating back to 1849. It overlooks the beautiful Pembridge Square gardens, where the boys enjoy playtime each day.

There is no test on entry; places are offered on interview with the parents and the Head Teacher. Expectations of the boys are good social skills, discipline and the ability to interact with their peer group in a confident and caring manner. The school prides itself on attention to detail; each child is valued as an individual and this is implemented through a high teacher:pupil teaching ratio.

Wetherby is a traditional school; high academic standards prevail and the boys enjoy a healthy balance between this and many other curriculum activities that are offered during the school day. Sports and the Arts have a particularly high profile within the school. Wetherby offers excellent facilities for IT, library, indoor gym and individual specialist teaching if required. In addition, the school is well known for the home cooked healthy lunches it provides.

The school operates a sibling policy, though early registration is advised. Please contact the Administrator's office in the first instance.

Woodside Park International School

6 Friern Barnet Lane, London N11 3LX Tel: (020) 8920 0600 Fax: (020) 8368 3220
E-mail: admissions@wpis.org Website: www.wpis.org www.gabbitas.net

Head Mr D P Rose MA(Ed) BA Cert Ed LPSH
Founded 1995
School status Co-educational independent day only. IB World School.
Religious denomination Non-denominational
Member of CReSTeD, IBO, ISCis, LISA
Accredited by CIS, IAPS, ISA, ISC
Age range 2–19; *boarders from* 16
No of pupils 405; *Nursery* 40; *Pre-prep* 42; *Prep* 140; *Senior* 158; *Sixth Form* 25; *Girls* 144; *Boys* 261
Average class size 15
Fees per annum *(day)* £1,400–£5,100. English as an alternative language and musical instrument tuition available at extra cost.

Woodside Park International School provides a secure, well-ordered and happy environment. All areas of achievement are celebrated, and our students take pride in being members of a thriving school community.

The school offers the internationally acclaimed curriculum of the Primary Years, Middle Years and Diploma programmes of the highly respected International Baccalaureate Organization. Characterized by being exceptionally stimulating and interesting for students, strong emphasis is placed on developing intellectual rigour and high academic standards. The ideals of international understanding and responsible citizenship underpin an approach that is geared towards life beyond school: higher education, business, family, society; wherever in the world the student might be now, or might choose to go.

England

MAP OF THE HOME COUNTIES (SOUTH)

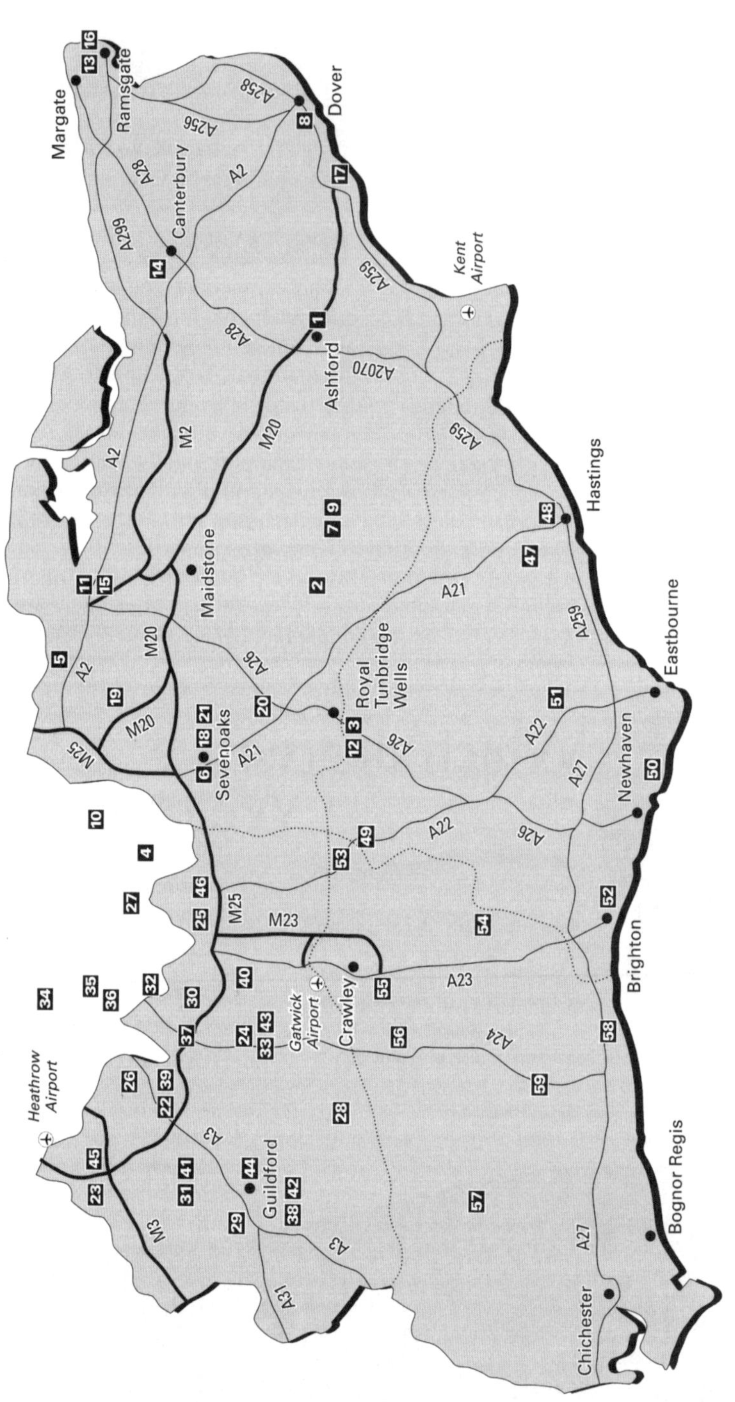

PROFILED SCHOOLS IN THE HOME COUNTIES (SOUTH)

(Incorporating the counties of Kent, Surrey, East Sussex, West Sussex)

Ashford School

East Hill, Ashford, Kent TN24 8PB Tel: (01233) 625171 Fax: (01233) 647185
E-mail: registrar@ashfordschool.co.uk Website: www.ashfordschool.co.uk

Head Mr M R Buchanan
School status Co-educational boarding and day. Flexi-boarding available.
Age range 3–18
No of pupils 665; *(full boarding)* 80; *(weekly boarding)* 10; *Girls* 522; *Boys* 143
Fees per annum *(full boarding)* £16,785–£20,190; *(weekly)* £15,105–£17,553; *(day)* £4,764–£11,088

A new chapter has begun in the long history of Ashford School as it opens its doors to boys as well as girls. Parents choose Ashford School for many reasons: high achievement leading to the best UK and overseas universities, close attention to the needs of the individual, an orderly, challenging and supportive environment, a wide range of co-curricular activities and energetic, specialist teachers that are supported by extensive resources and inventive leadership.

If boarding is what you are after there are two high quality boarding houses catering for children from 11–18 years. Both provide shared rooms of two or three children or in individual study bedrooms with en-suite bathrooms. An international flavour pervades the boarding houses and the diversity of cultures provides a stimulating term-time home. With no lessons on Saturday there is plenty of time to make use of the school facilities or participate in a variety of visits to London, Canterbury or elsewhere.

Bedgebury School

Goudhurst, Cranbrook, Kent TN17 2SH Tel: (01580) 878143 Fax: (01580) 879136
E-mail: registrar@bedgeburyschool.co.uk Website: www.bedgeburyschool.co.uk www.gabbitas.net

Head Mrs H Moriarty MA **Founded** 1920
School status Girls' boarding and day. Flexi-boarding available.
Religious denomination Church of England
Member of BHS, BSA, CReSTeD, GSA, ISCis;
Accredited by GSA
Learning difficulties CA SC SNU/DYP DYS MLD
Behavioural and emotional disorders CO/ADD ADHD ASP BESD CB
Physical and medical conditions HL RA/EPI HEA HI
Age range Girls 2–18; Boys 2–7; *boarders from 7*
No of pupils 297; *(full boarding)* 96; *(weekly boarding)* 49; *(day)* 152; *Nursery* 10; *Pre-prep* 44; *Prep* 46; *Senior* 149; *Sixth Form* 48; *Girls* 293; *Boys* 4
Teacher:pupil ratio 1:8; **Av. class size** 10–12
Fees per annum *(full boarding)* £13,035–£19,725; *(weekly)* £13,035–£19,725; *(day)* £490–£12,345

The broad education Bedgebury offers builds confidence, inspires enthusiasm and delivers achievement. The Senior School, set in 200 acres, is for girls aged from 11+; the Junior School is for children from 2½ to 11. Outstanding facilities include a new sports hall, a 22-acre lake for water sports, assault course and abseil tower. The art centre has studios for art, ceramics, jewellery, design technology and fashion. The riding centre, with stabling for 60 horses, has two indoor and two outdoor schools and a full cross-country course.

Beechwood Sacred Heart School

12 Pembury Road, Tunbridge Wells, Kent TN2 3QD Tel: (01892) 532747 Fax: (01892) 536164
E-mail: bsh@beechwood.org.uk Website: www.beechwood.org.uk www.gabbitas.net

Headmaster Mr N R Beesley MA (Oxon)
Founded 1915
School status Co-educational independent boarding and day. Flexi-boarding available.
Religious denomination Roman Catholic
Member of BSA, GSA, ISCis
Accredited by GSA GSA
Learning difficulties WI/DYC DYP DYS
Behavioural and emotional disorders ADD ASP AUT
Physical and medical conditions AT RA SM/EPI HEA
Age range Boys 3–11; Girls 3–18; *boarders from* 10
No of pupils 377; *(full boarding)* 50; *(weekly boarding)* 20; *Prep* 154; *Senior* 173; *Sixth Form* 50; *Girls* 302; *Boys* 75
Teacher:pupil ratio 1:9; **Average class size** 15
Fees per annum *(full boarding)* £18,225; *(weekly)* £16,230; *(day)* £11,250

Beechwood is an independent GSA day and boarding school for girls aged 11 to 18, with its own integral Preparatory School for boys and girls aged 3 to 11.

We are firmly committed to the single-sex education of girls at secondary level, as we believe that this provides for them a secure environment in which their educational and pastoral needs can be met most effectively. Selection for entry is based on interview and previous school report.

Facilities include a library, an up-to-date computer room, a modern well-equipped science building, and a language and business centre, heated outdoor swimming pool, a gymnasium and much more.

The extended day (activities until 6.00 pm) and flexi-boarding provide valuable support for working parents.

England

Breaside Preparatory School

41 Orchard Road, Bromley, Kent BR1 2PR
Tel: (020) 8460 0916 Fax: (020) 8466 5664
E-mail: info@breaside.co.uk Website: www.breaside.co.uk www.cognitaschools.co.uk

Headmaster Mr N D Kynaston
Founded 1950
School status Co-educational day only
Religious denomination Non-denominational
Member of IAPS; **Accredited by** IAPS
Learning difficulties CA SNU/DYP DYS
Behavioural and emotional disorders RA
Physical and medical conditions IT RA/HEA
Age range 3–11
No of pupils 249; *Girls* 107; *Boys* 142
Average class size 20
Fees per annum *(day)* £3,630–£7,185

Breaside is a co-educational school with a well-established reputation for friendliness and high achievement. On the Chislehurst side of Bromley, it is easily reached from many parts of South East London.

Curriculum A strong emphasis is placed on individual attention in small classes. Children are prepared for all senior schools and those with additional promise sit scholarships. The broadly based curriculum aims to help children fulfil their potential. French is taught from Reception and pupils are able to participate in the many games, clubs and activities. The school is well-resourced and enjoys the support of belonging to Cognita Schools Ltd.

Entry requirements Interview and test after five years of age. The school is well worth a visit to experience the busy, caring environment created by our dedicated staff.

Cobham Hall

Cobham, Gravesend, Kent DA12 3BL Tel: (01474) 823371 Fax: (01474) 825906
E-mail: enquiries@cobhamhall.com Website: www.cobhamhall.com www.gabbitas.net

Headmistress Mrs H Davy MA (Oxon)
Founded 1962
School status Girls' boarding and day. Flexi-boarding available.
Religious denomination Inter-denominational
Member of BSA, CReSTeD, GSA, ISCis, Round Square
Accredited by ISC
Age range 11–18
No of pupils 220; *(full boarding)* 104; *(weekly boarding)* 16; *Girls* 220
Fees per annum *(full boarding)* £17,400–£21,300; *(weekly)* £17,400–£21,300; *(day)* £10,400–£14,700

One of Britain's leading girls' schools, Cobham Hall promotes excellence in all subjects and enables the majority of students to proceed to higher education. Specialist help is provided for dyslexic students and our EFL department offers overseas students English language support.

The school is housed in a beautiful 16th century mansion set in landscaped parkland of 150 acres with a purpose-built classroom block, modern boarding houses, an indoor swimming pool and sports centre.

Membership of Round Square, an affiliation which unites schools around the world, provides the opportunity for international exchanges.

Cobham Hall is situated 25 miles from central London, with easy access to international airports.

Combe Bank School

Sundridge, Sevenoaks, Kent TN14 6AE Tel: (01959) 563720 Fax: (01959) 561997
E-mail: enquiries@combebank.kent.sch.uk Website: www.combebank.kent.sch.uk

Headmistress Mrs R Martin MEd NPQH FRSA
Founded 1924 **School status** Girls' day only
Religious denomination Roman Catholic
Member of GSA; **Accredited by** GSA
Learning difficulties RA/DYC DYP DYS
Behavioural and emotional disorders ASP
Physical and medical conditions SL TW/EPI HEA
Age range 3–18
No of pupils 349; *Nursery* 30; *Pre-prep* 15; *Prep* 121; *Senior* 146; *Sixth Form* 37; *Girls* 339; *Boys* 10
Fees per annum *(day)* £6,495–£11,640

At Combe Bank each student is recognized as an individual whose needs, hopes and ambitions have to be met. Our pupils are given the tools to succeed and the confidence required to embrace their future with enthusiasm.

This successful independent school offers a modern education with traditional values. In

addition to an excellent record of academic success there is an innovative enrichment programme designed to add value to the education of our students. Combe Bank is a school offering a nurturing environment with a strong Christian ethos. Our examination results are excellent and our facilities among the best in the area. The school is housed in a beautiful Palladian building set in 27 acres of parkland. In recent years a splendid sixth form centre has been added and a sports facility which includes a swimming pool and fitness suite.

Cranbrook School

Cranbrook, Kent TN17 3JD
Tel: (01580) 711800 Fax: (01580) 711828 E-mail: registrar@cranbrook.kent.sch.uk
Website: www.cranbrookschool.co.uk www.gabbitas.net

Head Mrs A Daly MA **Founded** 1518
School status Co-educational boarding and day. State (Voluntary-aided).
Religious denomination Non-denominational
Member of BSA, ISBA
Learning difficulties RA/DYP DYS
Behavioural and emotional disorders RA/ADD ASP
Physical and medical conditions RA
Age range 13–18; *boarders from* 13
No of pupils 751; *(full boarding)* 241; *(day)* 510; *Sixth Form* 300; *Girls* 359; *Boys* 392
Average class size 30
Fees per annum *(full boarding)* £8,025–£8,640

Cranbrook is a selective co-educational boarding and day school offering a superb all-round education at a very reasonable cost, with a wide range of extra-curricular activities, located in a small country town in the beautiful Kentish Weald. High academic standards of 99 per cent A to C grades at GCSE and 100 per cent pass rate (71 per cent A/B grades) at A level. Over 95 per cent of students go on to university. Cranbrook has been awarded Science Specialist and Training School status.

Music, art and drama thrive and teams compete at the highest levels in all major sports. Musical activities include an orchestra and choral society. Cranbrook has fine facilities for the creative arts, including a 400-seat theatre and new Performing Arts Centre, with a state-of-the-art recording studio. The school has plentiful playing fields, a swimming pool, a sports hall and AstroTurf pitches. Teams play at the highest levels locally and nationally.

Entry at 13+ and 16+ is by interview and examination. Details from the Registrar, Cranbrook School.

Dover College

Effingham Crescent, Dover, Kent CT17 9RH Tel: (01304) 205969 Fax: (01304) 242208
E-mail: registrar@dovercollege.org.uk Website: www.dovercollege.org.uk www.gabbitas.net

Headmaster Mr Stephen Jones MSc MLitt FRSA
Founded 1871
College status Co-educational independent boarding and day. Flexi-boarding available.
Religious denomination Church of England
Member of BSA, CReSTeD, ISCis, SHMIS
Accredited by GSA, ISC, SHMIS International Study Centre on site
Learning difficulties WI/DYP DYS
Behavioural and emotional disorders CO/ADD ADHD
Physical and medical conditions RA SM/EPI HEA HI
Age range 4–18; *boarders from* 11
No of pupils 360; *(full boarding)* 120; *(weekly boarding)* 13; *(day)* 227; *Pre-prep* 70; *Senior* 191; *Sixth Form* 99; *Girls* 154; *Boys* 206
Teacher:pupil ratio 1:8
Average class size GCSE 15–20; A level 10–15
Fees per annum *(full boarding)* £14,250–£19,065; *(weekly)* £13,260–£14,880; *(day)* £4,860–£9,525. Sibling/HM Forces bursaries available. International Study Centre on site.

Dover College is a small dynamic school, where pupils are given the opportunity to fulfil their potential within a happy, caring environment. Pupils benefit enormously from small classes, excellent teaching and from the breadth of education on offer. Music, art, drama and sport are an integral part of the curriculum. Scholarships are also available from 11+.

Dulwich Preparatory School, Cranbrook

Coursehorn, Cranbrook, Kent TN17 3NP Tel: (01580) 712179 Fax: (01580) 715322
E-mail: registrar@dcpskent.org Website: www.dcpskent.org www.gabbitas.net

Head Mr S L Rigby BA PGCE **Founded** 1939
School status Co-educational boarding and day. Flexi-boarding available.
Religious denomination Church of England
Learning difficulties CA SNU/DYP DYS
Behavioural and emotional disorders ADHD ASP; **Physical and medical conditions** IT RA/EPI HEA IM **Age range** 3–13; *boarders from* 9
No of pupils 523; *(full boarding)* 2; *(weekly boarding)* 8; *(day)* 513; *Nursery* 20; *Pre-prep* 120; *Prep* 383; *Girls* 231; *Boys* 292
Average class size 20
Fees per annum *(weekly)* £15,843; *(day)* £3,699–£10,836

The school is fully co-educational, taking pupils on a first come, first served basis. There is a strong academic tradition enabling children to achieve scholarships to top senior schools. The emphasis is on up-to-date teaching and the school has achieved notable successes in music and art. Entry is at 3+ and 4; by assessment from 7+ onwards.

Curriculum National Curriculum followed. Usual subjects taught, plus French, art, DT, drama, IT, music and physical education.

Examinations offered Pupils prepare for 11+, Common Entrance and scholarships.

Academic and leisure facilities Music School, IT & CDT centre and a new theatre/art room block. All-weather pitches, athletics track, playing fields, tennis courts, sports hall complex, two swimming pools.

Boarding facilities Weekly from age nine, in two houses. Six to eight pupils in each dormitory. Travel to/from airports arranged, plus train travel to/from London escorted by staff.

Special needs Gifted children catered for. Remedial and dyslexia help given. Several trained staff.

Farringtons School

Perry Street, Chislehurst, Kent BR7 6LR Tel: (020) 8467 0256 Fax: (020) 8467 5442
E-mail: admissions@farringtons.kent.sch.uk Website: www.farringtons.org.uk www.gabbitas.net

Headmistress Mrs C James MA
Registrar Mrs F Vail
Founded 1911
School status Co-educational independent boarding and day. Flexi-boarding available.
Religious denomination Methodist
Member of BSA, GSA, ISCis
Accredited by British Council, GSA, ISC
Learning difficulties SNU/DYP DYS MLD
Behavioural and emotional disorders RA
Physical and medical conditions RA/EPI HEA HI VI
Age range Boys 4–7; Girls 4–19; *boarders from* 7
No of pupils 526; *(full boarding)* 37; *(weekly boarding)* 5; *(day)* 484; *Nursery* 24; *Prep* 207; *Senior* 247; *Sixth Form* 48; *Girls* 516; *Boys* 10
Average class size 16 (juniors); 20 (seniors)
Fees per annum *(full boarding)* £14,850–£17,040; *(weekly)* £14,250–£16,020; *(day)* £6,480–£9,270

Our aims are numerous but very clear – to provide the best education for every student within a happy, safe, supportive Christian environment.

Visitors always comment on the atmosphere of warmth and friendliness which greets them and which is so apparent between children and staff. It is this special environment of care and support that encourages students to achieve their full potential, whether as academic high fliers or by excelling in sport, music, drama or any of the many other disciplines on offer. Nothing breeds confidence like success and no effort or achievement is considered too small to praise.

We offer an excellent extra-curricular programme, which helps to promote the healthy development of the whole student, so that when children leave us, they are confident, self-reliant, compassionate and responsible, equipped to take up the place to which they aspire amidst the challenges of higher education and employment in the 21st century.

Gad's Hill School

Higham, Rochester, Kent ME3 7PA Tel: (01474) 822366 Fax: (01474) 822977
E-mail: admissions@gadshillschool.co.uk Website: www.gadshill.org www.gabbitas.net

Headmaster Mr D G Craggs BSc, MA, NPQH
Founded 1924
School status Co-educational independent day
Religious denomination Non-denominational
Member of ISA; **Accredited by** ISA, ISC
Learning difficulties SNU/DYS
Physical and medical conditions RA SM WA3
Age range 3–16
No of pupils 340; *(day)* 340; *Nursery* 20; *Pre-prep* 60; *Prep* 80; *Senior* 180; *Girls* 170; *Boys* 170
Teacher:pupil ratio 1:10; **Average class size** 20
Fees per annum *(day)* £5,300–£6,300

Once the home of Charles Dickens, Gad's Hill School is surrounded by beautiful grounds, playing fields and countryside.

At Gad's we believe that education is primarily about 'learning for life' and that while academic success is a priority, it is only a part of what makes Gad's so successful. Excellent teaching, enthusiastic students and staff, and our friendly, close community all help to ensure that our children achieve success in life.

School days, according to perceived wisdom, are supposed to be 'the happiest days of your life'. Children who enjoy school are much more likely to learn productively and to achieve success, and therefore it will be no surprise that one of our priorities is to ensure that all of our pupils are happy. At Gad's Hill you will find that small classes, picturesque surroundings and a positive approach help to produce an environment where your child will thrive and succeed.

Holmewood House

Langton Green, Tunbridge Wells, Kent TN3 0EB Tel: (01892) 860000 Fax: (01892) 863970
E-mail: registrar@holmewood.kent.sch.uk Web: www.holmewood.kent.sch.uk www.gabbitas.net

Headmaster Mr A S R Corbett MA PGCE
Founded 1945
School status Co-educational boarding and day. Flexi-boarding available.
Religious denomination Inter-denominational
Member of IAPS, ISBA, ISCis
Accredited by IAPS
Learning difficulties SNU/DYP DYS MLD
Behavioural and emotional disorders CA CO ST TS/ASP
Physical and medical conditions CA SM/EPI HEA HI VI **Age range** 3–13
No of pupils 515; *(weekly boarding)* 6; *(day)* 509; *Nursery* 28; *Pre-prep* 148; *Prep* 339; *Girls* 193; *Boys* 322
Teacher:pupil ratio 1:8; **Average class size** 16
Fees per annum *(weekly)* £16,200; *(day)* £4,375–£12,855

The school follows a broad-based curriculum while covering all aspects of the National Curriculum, Common Entrance and scholarship examinations to independent schools by the age of 13. Holmewood consistently enjoys outstanding academic, art and music successes, with many scholarships won to top independent schools and through the Common Entrance examination.

We offer weekly and flexi-boarding. Boarders are cared for by experienced houseparents who live in a flat alongside the boarding areas.

Form teachers are responsible for pastoral care, and a tutor system for the older children ensures that each child is cared for and guided in all matters during their time at school.

Sports and facilities include: 25m indoor swimming pool, large sports hall, all-weather pitch and running track, hard tennis courts, squash courts and an indoor .22 shooting range.

The Jubilee Theatre is a showcase for our many excellent concerts and productions.

Entry requirements Non-selective but all children are assessed prior to entry.

The Junior School, St Lawrence College

College Road, Ramsgate, Kent CT11 7AF Tel: (01843) 572931 Fax: (01843) 572917
E-mail: ah@slcuk.com Website: www.slcuk.com

Head of the Junior School Mr R Tunnicliffe MA BEd (Liverpool) **Founded** 1886
College status Co-educational independent boarding and day. Flexi-boarding available.
Religious denomination Church of England
Member of IAPS; **Accredited by** IAPS
Age range 3–11; *boarders from* 7
No of pupils 132; *(full boarding)* 7; *Nursery* 18; *Pre-prep* 38; *Prep* 76; *Girls* 52; *Boys* 80
Teacher:pupil ratio 1:8; **Average class size** 12
No of pupils The Senior School has 300 pupils.
Fees per annum *(full boarding)* £16,029; *(weekly)* £16,029; *(day)* £4,653–£9,891

Ten-year-old, Sofia said: 'If I could, I would go back to being three and start again at St Lawrence College.' Our pupils really enjoy their time at school. The teachers see their role as building firm foundations for their pupils. This is true for their academic life and also for their development as people.

At the foundation stage work is based on the Early Learning Goals but these are extended by excellent teaching and facilities including an outdoor classroom equipped with a Pirate boat! The Junior School pupils perform very well at Key Stage 1 and 2 tests revealing high levels of 'value added'. A recent inspection particularly praised the top two years of our school in terms of teaching, academic progress and the maturity of our pupils. Why not come and see why Sofia wanted to do it all again?

Kent College

Whitstable Road, Canterbury, Kent CT2 9DT Tel: (01227) 763231 Fax: (01227) 787450
E-mail: enquiries@kentcollege.co.uk Website: www.kentcollege.com www.gabbitas.net
Junior School website: www.kentcollege.com/junior

Head Mr GG Carminati MA
Founded 1885
College status Co-educational independent boarding and day. Flexi-boarding available.
Religious denomination Methodist
Member of HMC, IAPS, ISCis
Accredited by HMC, IAPS, ISC
Learning difficulties SNU/DYP DYS
Age range 3–18; *boarders from* 7
No of pupils 687; *(full boarding)* 160; *(weekly boarding)* 4; *(day)* 523; *Nursery* 29; *Pre-prep* 193; *Senior* 314; *Sixth Form* 151; *Girls* 309; *Boys* 378
Teacher:pupil ratio 1:9; **Average class size** 15
Fees per annum *(full boarding)* £14,979–£20,535; *(weekly)* £14,979–£19,902; *(day)* £6,816–£12,015. Fees for attending the International Study Centre are £7,780 per term (boarding) and £4,940 (day)

Kent College is a vibrant co-educational boarding and day school, situated in semi-rural surroundings, yet only a few minutes walk from the centre of Canterbury. We offer small classes and a broad curriculum that allows all students to fulfil their potential. The visual and performing arts have a high profile, as does sport, and the school also has its own farm, and an International Study Centre and Dyslexic Unit.

A highly developed pastoral structure, based on the school's Christian tradition, ensures that student welfare and guidance are of the highest order. Various scholarships are available.

Rochester Independent College

Star Hill, Rochester, Kent ME1 1XF
Tel: (01634) 828115 Fax: (01634) 405667
E-mail: admissions@rochester-college.org
Website: www.rochester-college.org www.gabbitas.net

Co Principal Mr A Brownlow
Founded 1985
College status Co-educational boarding and day. Flexi-boarding available.
Accredited by BAC
Learning difficulties DYP DYS
Behavioural and emotional disorders RA
Age range 13–21
No of pupils 220; *(full boarding)* 70; *Girls* 110; *Boys* 110
Fees per annum *(full boarding)* £19,005; *(day)* £12,150

Rochester Independent College is one of the UK's leading alternatives to conventional secondary education. Accepting day and boarding students from the age of 13 we focus on examination success in a lively, supportive and informal atmosphere. Students are encouraged to be themselves and achieve A level and GCSE results that often exceed their expectations. No bells ring, there is no uniform and everybody is on first name terms. The average class size is eight.

St Lawrence College

College Road, Ramsgate, Kent CT11 7AE
Tel: (01843) 572931 Fax: (01843) 572917
E-mail: ah@slcuk.com Website: www.slcuk.com www.gabbitas.net

Headmaster Rev C W M Aitken BA Durham
Head of Junior School Mr Roy Tunnicliffe MA, BEd
Founded 1879
College status Co-educational independent boarding and day. Flexi-boarding available.
Religious denomination Church of England
Member of HMC, IAPS, ISCis
Accredited by HMC, IAPS
Learning difficulties SNU/DYC DYP DYS MLD
Behavioural and emotional disorders ST/ADD ADHD ASP
Physical and medical conditions RA WA3/EPI HEA VI
Age range 3–18; *boarders from 7*
No of pupils 433; *(full boarding)* 169; *(weekly boarding)* 2; *(day)* 262; *Nursery* 18; *Pre-prep* 38; *Prep* 76; *Senior* 205; *Sixth Form* 96; *Girls* 172; *Boys* 261
Teacher:pupil ratio 1:8
Average class size 15
Fees per annum *(full boarding)* £16,029–£21,780; *(weekly)* £16,029–£21,780; *(day)* £4,653–£12,963

Walk through the historic arch at St Lawrence College in Kent and you will immediately feel at home. The school welcomes students from all over the world and is a happy and caring international community. Recently modernized rooms and dormitories provide some of the best boarding accommodation in the country.

Outstanding results are achieved by the most academic students who progress to many of the top universities. The school is also highly regarded as a centre of excellence for 'value added'; students who need additional support perform well beyond expectation.

The school has stunningly beautiful surroundings and outstanding sports facilities. The buildings reflect the nature of the school: steeped in history and tradition, yet modern, creative and forward-thinking. The main building has a striking 19th century facade dating back to 1884 which sits alongside the glorious chapel which was completed in 1927. The new Middle School – opens September 2006 – is an imaginative design: architecturally striking, with a glass atrium, and a virtual library at its centre. Throughout the school, the lively, professional approach to education and an innovative curriculum provide a challenging and stimulating framework for teaching and learning, but most of all, the school really takes care of its pupils.

The school is close to the channel tunnel and the port of Dover and has excellent transport links to London and Europe. Gatwick airport is within easy reach.

Selecting a school can be one of the most important decisions we have to make and we therefore encourage parents to visit the school if at all possible The school is justifiably proud that St Lawrence students leave as confident, compassionate and capable adults.

St Mary's Westbrook

Ravenlea Road, Folkestone, Kent CT20 2JU
Tel: (01303) 854006 Fax: (01303) 249901 E-mail: hm@st-marys-westbrook.co.uk
Website: www.st-marys-westbrook.co.uk www.gabbitas.net

Headmistress (Senior School) Mrs L A Watson MA (Ed) **Founded** 1997
School status Co-educational independent boarding and day. Flexi-boarding available. One-year intensive English course offered in preparation for A levels.
Religious denomination Christian
Member of BSA, COBISEC, IAPS, ISA, ISBA, ISCis
Learning difficulties CA RA/DYS MLD
Age range 2–17; *boarders from* 11
No of pupils 190; *(full boarding)* 42; *(day)* 148; *Nursery* 62; *Pre-prep* 26; *Prep* 35; *Senior* 67; *Girls* 93; *Boys* 97
Teacher:pupil ratio 1:15; **Average class size** 15
Fees per annum *(full boarding)* £14,400; *(day)* £4,200–£9,750

St Mary's Westbrook Senior School is a co-educational boarding and day school for pupils aged 11 to 17. From September 2005 there is a separate Prep School with Kindergarten, known as Westbrook House Preparatory School.

The curriculum is broad and balanced. English as a Foreign Language is offered and the school has a comprehensive extra-curricular programme.

There are strong musical and sporting traditions. The school prepares students for GCSE examinations and accepts pupils of all ages.

England

Sevenoaks School

Sevenoaks, Kent TN13 1HU Tel: (01732) 455133 Fax: (01732) 456143
E-mail: regist@sevenoaksschool.org Website: www.sevenoaksschool.org www.gabbitas.net

Head Mrs C L Ricks MA **Founded** 1432
School status Co-educational independent boarding and day
Religious denomination Inter-denominational
Member of BSA, HMC, IBO, ISCis
Accredited by HMC
Learning difficulties WI/DYP DYS
Behavioural and emotional disorders CO
Physical and medical conditions WA2/W
Age range 11–18; *boarders from* 11
No of pupils 988; *(full boarding)* 340; *(day)* 648; *Senior* 567; *Sixth Form* 421; *Girls* 506; *Boys* 482
Teacher:pupil ratio 1:10; **Average class size** 15
Fees per annum *(full boarding)* £21,609–£23,430; *(day)* £13,413–£15,234

Sevenoaks is a co-educational, independent, boarding and day school, situated next to the 1,000 acres of Knole Park, 30 minutes from central London and Gatwick Airport, and an hour from Heathrow. Approximately one-third of the 988 students are boarders. Pupils worldwide enter at 11, 13 or 16, taking GCSEs and the International Baccalaureate. Sevenoaks aspires to high academic standards – all students proceed to Oxbridge and major universities – while providing excellent facilities for sport and co-curricular activities. More than 50 scholarships are awarded annually for academic excellence, art, music, sport and all-round ability. Prospectus and further details are available from the Registrar.

Steephill Independent School

Castle Hill, Fawkham, Longfield, Kent DA3 7BG Tel: (01474) 702107 Fax: (01474) 706011
E-mail: secretary@steephill.co.uk Website: www.steephill.co.uk

Headteacher Mrs C Birtwell BSc MBA PGCE
Bursar Mr Nicola Kiley
Founded 1935
School status Co-educational independent day only
Religious denomination Church of England
Interim list for ISA
Learning difficulties CA WI/DYS MLD
Behavioural and emotional disorders RA ST
Physical and medical conditions RA TW WA2
Age range 3–11
No of pupils 108; *Girls* 54; *Boys* 54
Teacher:pupil ratio 1:12; **Average class size** 14
Fees per annum *(day)* £4,941

Steephill is an independent day school which takes pupils from 3½ to 11 years old. It is situated in the beautiful Fawkham Valley countryside in a quiet lane overlooking the 13th century village church. The school was founded in 1935 by Miss Eileen Bignold, who established its excellent reputation for high academic standards. These have been continued by the Educational Trust, which was formed in 1990 to run the school through a Board of Governors. Our small classes bring out the best in young children, who receive all the help and encouragement they need from Steephill's qualified, dedicated teachers. With just 14 pupils in a class, each child benefits from the individual attention necessary to achieve his or her full potential. As a small school the staff, parents and children all know each other and this contributes to our happy, family atmosphere.

Tonbridge School

Tonbridge, Kent TN9 1JP Tel: (01732) 304297 Fax: (01732) 363424
E-mail: hmsec@tonbridge-school.org Website: www.tonbridge-school.co.uk www.gabbitas.net

Head Mr T H P Haynes **Founded** 1553
School status Boys' independent boarding and day
Religious denomination Church of England
Member of BSA, HMC; **Accredited by** ISC
Learning difficulties SNU/DYP DYS
Behavioural and emotional disorders CO
Physical and medical conditions AT SM WA3/HEA
Age range 13–18
No of pupils 754; *(full boarding)* 433; *(day)* 321; *Boys* 754
Fees per annum *(full boarding)* £23,784; *(day)* £16,806

Tonbridge School was founded in 1553 and today occupies an extensive site of about 150 acres on the northern edge of Tonbridge. Academic standards are high. Tonbridge was the 6th HMC school in the 2002 Financial Times league table. The 2005 Good Schools Guide says of Tonbridge School: 'One of the very best, outstanding in everything that really counts'. The 2005 A level results included 87 per cent A and B grades and a 100 per cent pass rate. Over 20 per cent of leavers go to Oxbridge. Facilities are outstanding for sport, music, drama, art and technology. Both boarders and day boys benefit from strong pastoral support based in the seven boarding houses and five day houses. Generous scholarships are available.

Walthamstow Hall

Hollybush Lane, Sevenoaks, Kent TN13 3UL
Tel: (01732) 451334 Fax: (01732) 740439 E-mail: registrar@walthamstow-hall.co.uk
Website: www.walthamstow-hall.co.uk www.gabbitas.net

Headmistress Mrs J Milner MA (Oxon)
Founded 1838
School status Girls' independent day only
Religious denomination Inter-denominational
Member of AGBIS, GSA, IAPS, ISCis
Accredited by GSA, IAPS, ISC
Learning difficulties WI
Physical and medical conditions SM TW/HEA
Age range 3–18
No of pupils 478; *Nursery* 14; *Pre-prep* 69; *Prep* 121; *Senior* 274; *Sixth Form* 60
Average class size 15
Fees per annum *(day)* £2,520–£3,920

We are a selective, independent day school for girls, offering excellent facilities with a caring and supportive environment from Kindergarten to Sixth Form. Set in beautiful grounds, with good transport links and minibus services, we offer a broad and varied curriculum with many extra-

curricular activities. The combination of first-class teachers and small class sizes means that each child is given a high level of personal attention, enabling them to reach their full potential. We have our own theatre, swimming pool and extensive sports grounds including tennis and squash courts. Girls have many opportunities to excel in music, art, drama and sport, with some of our teams competing at national and international level. Entry is at 3+, 4+, 7+, 11+, 13+ and 16+. In the Sixth Form there are over 23 subjects to choose from and girls benefit from small tutor groups with specialist staff, excellent careers and higher education advice. There are scholarships and bursaries available for entry into the Senior School.

England

ACS Cobham International School

Heywood, Portsmouth Road, Cobham, Surrey KT11 1BL Tel: (01932) 867251 Fax: (01932) 869789
E-mail: cobhamadmissions@acs-england.co.uk Website: www.acs-england.co.uk

Head Mr T J Lehman
Founded 1967
School status Co-educational boarding and day
Religious denomination Non-denominational
Physical and medical conditions HEA
Age range 2½–18; *boarders from* 12
No of pupils 1308; *Girls* 571; *Boys* 737
Teacher:pupil ratio 1:9; **Average class size** 20
Fees per annum *(boarding)* £22,500–£26,200; *(day)* £4,900–£15,650

ACS Cobham offers academic programmes, including the International Baccalaureate Diploma, and an America High School Diploma, including Advanced Placement (AP) courses.

ACS graduates attend leading universities including Cambridge, Imperial College London, and Oxford.

Premier sports facilities include a new Sports Centre which houses a basketball/volleyball show court, 25-metre swimming pool, dance studio, fitness suite and cafeteria.

Co-educational boarding with separate-wing accommodation for 110 students; two-person rooms with en suite facilities and internet connections.

ACS Egham International School

Woodlee, London Road, Egham, Surrey TW20 0HS Tel: (01784) 430611 Fax: (01784) 430626
E-mail: eghamadmissions@acs-england.co.uk Website: www.acs-england.co.uk

Head Ms M Hadley **Founded** 1967
School status Co-educational day only
Religious denomination Non-denominational
Age range Boys 2½–18; Girls 2½–18
No of pupils 484; *Girls* 230; *Boys* 254
Teacher:pupil ratio 1:9; **Average class size** 16
Fees per annum *(day)* £4,900–£15,650

Academic programmes at Egham include the International Baccalaureate (IB) Primary Years Programme, the IB Middle Years Programme, the IB Diploma and an American High School Diploma. ACS graduates attend leading universities around the world including Cambridge, Imperial College London, London School of Economics and Oxford.

Superb teaching, sports, and extra-curricular facilities. Promotes active participation in a wide range of extra-curricular activities including local and international community service projects.

ACS Hillingdon International School

Hillingdon Court, 108 Vine Lane, Hillingdon, Middlesex UB10 0BE
Tel: (01895) 818402 Fax: (01895) 818404 E-mail: hillingdonadmissions@acs-england.co.uk
Website: www.acs-england.co.uk

Head of School Mrs G Apple **Founded** 1967
School status Co-educational day only
Religious denomination Non-denominational
Member of BSA, CIS, IBO, ISA, LISA NEAS&C
Age range 4–18
No of pupils 495; *Girls* 236; *Boys* 259
Teacher:pupil ratio 1:9; **Average class size** 20
Fees per annum *(day)* £7,250–£15,000

ACS Hillingdon's academic programme includes the International Baccalaureate Diploma, and an American High School Diploma including Advanced Placement (AP) courses.

ACS graduates attend leading universities around the world including Cambridge, Imperial College London, London School of Economics, and Oxford.

Excellent facilities are augmented by a new music centre, complete with digital recording studio, rehearsal rooms, practice studios and a computer lab for music technology. On-site playing fields, tennis courts, and playgrounds with additional off-site soccer, rugby, track, baseball, softball, swimming and golf facilities.

Box Hill School

Mickleham, Dorking, Surrey RH5 6EA Tel: (01372) 373382 Fax: (01372) 363942
E-mail: enquiries@boxhillschool.org.uk Website: www.boxhillschool.org.uk www.gabbitas.net

Head Mr M Eagers MA **Founded** 1959
School status Co-educational boarding and day
Religious denomination Non-denominational
Member of AGBIS, BSA, ISBA, ISCis, Round Square, SHA, SHMIS
Accredited by British Council, ISC, SHMIS
Learning difficulties SNU/DYP DYS
Age range 11–18
No of pupils 362; *(full boarding)* 107; *(weekly boarding)* 63; *Girls* 113; *Boys* 249
Teacher:pupil ratio 1:8.5; **Ave class size** 18
Fees per annum *(full boarding)* £18,450–£20,835; *(weekly)* £15,600–£17,970; *(day)* £9,300–£11,325; (ISC per annum) £16,950–£19,650

Entry requirements and procedures Interview; written tests in maths and English; confidential report from previous school.

Subject specialties and academic track record Strong in maths and English, also art, PE, drama, computing, design/technology.

Examinations offered Wide choice at both GCSE and A level; no attempt to force pupils into a mould.

Termly exchanges and visits with sister schools in Germany, Australia, Switzerland, the USA and Canada offer unique opportunities, particularly for languages. Project work is undertaken in India, Kenya and Thailand.

Scholarships, exhibitions and bursaries There is a sliding scale of day fees. Scholarships are offered at 11+, 13+ and Year 12.

Caterham School

Harestone Valley Road, Caterham, Surrey CR3 6YA Tel: (01883) 343028 Fax: (01883) 347795
E-mail: admissions@caterhamschool.co.uk Website: www.caterhamschool.co.uk

Head Mr R A E Davey MA **Founded** 1811
School status Co-educational independent boarding and day. Flexi-boarding available.
Religious denomination URC
Member of AGBIS, BSA, HMC, IAPS, ISCis, SHA
Learning difficulties SNU/DYC DYP DYS MLD
Behavioural and emotional disorders CO ST/ADD ADHD ASP AUT
Physical and medical conditions AT SM TW WA2/EPI HEA HI IM VI W
Age range 3–18; *boarders from* 11
No of pupils *(full boarding)* 129; *(weekly boarding)* 2; *Prep* 272; *Senior* 746; *Sixth Form* 241; *Girls* 428; *Boys* 590
Teacher:pupil ratio 1:10; **Average class size** 20
Fees per annum *(full boarding)* £19,431–£20,481; *(day)* £10,485–£10,980

The essence of Caterham School derives from the quality of the teaching, the pastoral care and a personalized tutorial system. We encourage pupils to develop their own sense of worth and purpose and so achieve their full potential with a sense of responsibility and discipline.

Excellent academic results have firmly established the school in the First Division of UK Independent Schools. The majority of A level students go on to a Top Tier university.

A wide range of activities enable the students to develop their skills and interests. Over a year there are 18 different sports, 14 music groups and 17 various clubs.

Situated on a beautiful 80 acre campus the school is on the edge of London, 5 minutes from the M25 and 20 minutes from Gatwick airport.

Claremont Fan Court School

Claremont Drive, Esher, Surrey KT10 9LY
Tel: (01372) 467841 Fax: (01372) 471109
E-mail: mprentis@claremont.surrey.sch.uk
Website: www.claremont-school.co.uk www.gabbitas.net
Junior School: abutler@claremont.surrey.sch.uk

Principal Mrs P B Farrar
Founded 1922
School status Co-educational day only
Religious denomination Christian Science, all denominations welcome
Member of SHMIS
Learning difficulties CA SNU/DYP DYS
Behavioural and emotional disorders ST/ADHD
Physical and medical conditions AT CA RA SL TW WA2/HI IM W
Age range 3–18
No of pupils 600; *Girls* 300; *Boys* 300
Fees per annum *(day)* £2,839–£10,290

The school is situated in the Claremont Estate, one of the premier historic sites in the country. The original house and the famous landscape garden were first laid out by Sir John Vanbrugh for the Duke of Newcastle early in the 18th century. Later Capability Brown built the present Palladian mansion for Clive of India and landscaped the grounds in his typical manner. For over a century Claremont was a royal residence and played an important part in Queen Victoria's early years.

Aims An excellent academic programme with small class sizes provides the pupils with a wide and varied curriculum. High personal expectations and moral values are established and developed within small classes in a happy, positive environment free from the excessive pressures sometimes placed on young people today.

Curriculum The expectation of high academic achievement and personal growth is established in the junior years. The syllabus follows National Curriculum guidelines but our expectations of attainment are well beyond the national levels. Over the next three years there will be a phased development into e-learning through the introduction of laptops for every child from Year 4 to Year 10. Classrooms have been specially designed for collaborative, independent learning and most have been fitted with interactive white boards. The academic programme in Senior School ensures that all pupils attain the highest qualifications of which they are capable for entry into university or college.

Students also have a strong tradition of excellence in technology, drama, music, art and sport. Facilities include four ICT suites, a fully equipped design and technology studio, and a workshop. Major drama productions are performed in the Joyce Grenfell Centre for the Performing Arts. The music department benefits from excellent music technology facilities.

A fully equipped sports centre and gymnasium enhance sports at Claremont. Teams compete regularly with neighbouring schools, with individuals competing at county and national levels.

Entry to the school Applications for entry into the School are welcome at all levels. Main intakes are at 3+, 4+, 7+, 11+ and Sixth Form.

Scholarships Academic scholarships are available at Years 3, 7, 9 and Sixth Form. Music, art, drama and sport scholarships are also available.

Croham Hurst School

79 Croham Road, South Croydon, Surrey CR2 7YN Tel: (020) 8680 3064 Fax: (020) 8681 2490
E-mail: head@croham.surrey.sch.uk Website: www.crohamhurst.com www.gabbitas.net

Headmistress Mrs E J Abbotts BA MEd
Bursar Mr G M Flook BA PGCE
Founded 1899
School status Girls' independent day only
Religious denomination Non-denominational
Member of AGBIS, GSA, ISCis, SHA;
Accredited by GSA, ISC
Learning difficulties CA WI/DYC DYP DYS
Behavioural and emotional disorders RA/ADHD
Physical and medical conditions AT CA IT SM TW/HEA HI IM
Age range 3–18
No of pupils 496; *Nursery* 15; *Pre-prep* 12; *Prep* 142; *Senior* 270; *Sixth Form* 57
Teacher:pupil ratio 1:10; **Average class size** 16
Fees per annum *(day)* £5,160–£9,285

Croham Hurst occupies an attractive site close to green belt woodland, easily accessible by public transport. The extensive facilities include a superb design and technology centre as well as art and drama studios, a fine music suite and laboratories, PE facilities and a swimming pool. The school offers three fully equipped IT suites and a generous provision of computers for curriculum use. The school maintains a reputation for high achievement and is committed to developing the individual potential of each girl.

We have a proven record of excellent results at GCSE and A level and a tradition of university entrance, including Oxford and Cambridge.

Many girls begin their education in the stimulating environment of the onsite Junior School and continue to the Senior School, where learning is supported by small teaching groups and personalized timetables including classics and psychology. There is an exciting programme of extra-curricular activities.

Entrance is by interview and test relevant to age. Bursaries, scholarships and awards, including Sixth Form scholarships, are available.

England

Duke of Kent School

Peaslake Road, Ewhurst, Surrey GU6 7NS Tel: (01483) 277313 Fax: (01483) 273862
E-mail: dok.school@virgin.net Website: www.dukeofkentschool.org.uk www.gabbitas.net

Headmaster Dr A Cameron
Founded 1976
School status Co-educational independent boarding and day. Flexi-boarding available.
Religious denomination Non-denominational
Member of BSA, ISCis; **Accredited by** IAPS
Learning difficulties SNU/DYS
Physical and medical conditions RA/HEA
Age range 4–13
No of pupils 181; *(full boarding)* 6; *(weekly boarding)* 50; *(day)* 125; *Pre-prep* 37; *Prep* 144; *Girls* 60; *Boys* 121
Teacher:pupil ratio 1:8; **Average class size** 14
Fees per annum *(full boarding)* £12,165–£14,565; *(weekly)* £9,390–£11,970; *(day)* £4,545–£10,725

A happy and caring co-educational day and boarding school situated in a beautiful location in the Surrey hills with easy access to Gatwick, Heathrow and major stations. Pupils are prepared for entry to many leading public schools and a full range of music and sport are offered and played in the extensive facilities.

Curriculum All main subjects required for Common Entrance and public school scholarships plus art, music, drama, CDT, computer studies and a structured games and activity programme.

Entry Placement tests and interviews. Bursaries and scholarships available.

Frensham Heights School

Rowledge, Farnham, Surrey GU10 4EA
Tel: (01252) 792561 Fax: (01252) 794335
E-mail: admissions@frensham-heights.org.uk
Website: www.frensham-heights.org.uk www.gabbitas.net

Headmaster Mr A Fisher
Founded 1925
School status Co-educational independent boarding and day
Religious denomination Non-denominational
Age range 3–18
No of pupils 490; *(boarding)* 100; *Girls* 246; *Boys* 244
Fees per annum *(boarding)* £18,855–£20,160; *(day)* £12,240–£13,545

Frensham Heights is a fully co-educational HMC boarding (full or weekly) and day school of 490 pupils aged between 3 and 18. The school's philosophy endorses liberal values and promotes strong personal relationships and respect for the individual. It achieves distinguished results in the performing and creative arts. Classes are small and academic results are excellent. New facilities include a multi-award winning Performing Arts Centre, a Music School, an indoor sports hall, modern science laboratories, a fully equipped ICT Suite, a newly renovated library and an adventure centre for outdoor education. New sixth form boarding house opens September 2006. The school is situated in beautiful grounds near Farnham, 45 minutes from Heathrow and Gatwick airports.

Greenacre School for Girls

Sutton Lane, Banstead, Surrey SM7 3RA Tel: (01737) 352114 Fax: (01737) 373485 E-mail: admin@greenacre.surrey.sch.uk Website: www.greenacre.surrey.sch.uk www.gabbitas.net

Headmistress Mrs P M Wood BA
Founded 1933
School status Girls' independent day only
Religious denomination Non-denominational
Member of AGBIS, GSA, ISBA, ISCis, SHA
Learning difficulties DYS
Age range 3–18 **No of pupils** 410
Fees per annum *(day)* £2,850–£9,120

Greenacre is a lively school where pupils are encouraged to achieve the highest possible academic results, whilst maintaining an active extra-curricular interest. Pupils, staff and parents work co-operatively to support the girls in their aspirations.

The school maintains traditional values whilst providing modern facilities and resources for the ever-changing 21st century.

Facilities include bright classrooms with all subjects having specialist rooms, Sixth Form faculty designated learning resource centres, a library with a qualified librarian, a 'thin client' computer suite, swimming pool, sports hall, a science building incorporating a lecture theatre and interactive whiteboards throughout the whole school. The da Vinci Centre, opened in Spring 2004, incorporating a state-of-the-art recording studio. ICT is a major school focus, both pupils and staff have access to a very effective and secure computer system. A wide range of clubs allows sporting, dramatic and musical involvement at all levels. The Duke of Edinburgh's Award attracts large numbers, whilst the Model United Nations broadens outlook and instils awareness of the wider world. Extensive travel both at home and abroad

The school plays a major part in our local community, participating in community and parish events.

At Greenacre, we believe we are 'sailing' with confidence towards the challenges of the 21st century.

Hoe Bridge School

Hoe Place, Old Woking Road, Woking, Surrey GU22 8JE
Tel: (01483) 760018 Fax: (01483) 757560 E-mail: enquiriesprep@hoebridgeschool.co.uk
Website: www.hoebridgeschool.co.uk www.gabbitas.net

Head Mr R W K Barr
Pre-prep-Head Mrs L M Renfrew
Founded 1987
School status Co-educational day only
Religious denomination Non-denominational
Member of IAPS; **Accredited by** IAPS
Age range 2–13
No of pupils 474; *Girls* 112; *Boys* 362
Teacher:pupil ratio 1:10
Average class size 18
Fees per annum *(day)* £1,404–£10,185

The Pre-Preparatory Department is for children aged 2½ to 7. It is an attractive purpose-built school with its own play areas in landscaped grounds and with its own Nursery Unit.

The Prep School prepares boys and girls between the ages of 7 and 14 for the scholarship and Common Entrance requirements of all senior independent schools. The curriculum includes those subjects, games and activities necessary for a child's development.

The school stands in its own grounds of 20 acres. These afford facilities for all games and outdoor pursuits, including rugby, soccer, hockey, netball, basketball, cricket, athletics, tennis and swimming. It also has four new all-weather tennis courts providing ample space for all sports.

A 17th century mansion forms the heart of the school but extensive architect-designed buildings have been added over the past ten years. These include laboratories, changing rooms, classrooms and a multi-purpose Sports Hall.

The school has a Design and Music Centre set in a restored 17th century tower and stable block. This provides superb facilities for art, design technology, information technology and music. ICT is networked throughout the school and there are two computer suites.

England

Homefield School

Western Road, Sutton, Surrey SM1 2TE Tel: (020) 8642 0965 Fax: (020) 8642 0965
E-mail: administration@homefield.sutton.sch.uk Website: www.homefield.sutton.sch.uk

Headmaster Mr P R Mowbray MA Cant
Founded 1870
School status Boys' independent day only
Religious denomination Non-denominational
Member of IAPS, ISCis
Accredited by IAPS, ISC
Learning difficulties SNU/DYC DYP DYS MLD
Behavioural and emotional disorders RA
Physical and medical conditions RA SL WA2/HEA
Age range 2½–13; **No of pupils** 380; *Nursery* 30; *Pre-prep* 150; *Prep* 200
Teacher:pupil ratio 1:10; **Average class size** 17
Fees per annum *(day)* £3,420–£7,995
Fees Nursery vouchers accepted

Homefield is housed in an extensive purpose-built complex complemented by a spacious state-of-the-art Early Years' Unit and a 2-acre adjoining playing field.

The school is renowned for its intimacy and family atmosphere, the fulfilment of individual

potential, the openness of communication, the provision of specialist teaching, its commitment to best practice and its all-round academic, musical, dramatic, sporting and artistic achievements.

In the past ten years, it has continued to achieve a 100 per cent pass rate at Common Entrance.

The school is proud of its county and national representatives in table tennis, squash, athletics, swimming, football, rugby, cricket and chess. There are a multitude of clubs, such as fencing, judo, basketball, music bands and orchestras, as well as trips, both in the UK and abroad.

Academic scholarships and occasional bursaries are available.

Before and after-school care available.

Hurtwood House

Holmbury St Mary, Dorking, Surrey RH5 6NU Tel: (01483) 279000 Fax: (01483) 267586
E-mail: Info@hurtwood.net Website: www.hurtwoodhouse.com www.gabbitas.net

Headmaster Mr K R B Jackson MA
Founded 1970
School status Co-educational boarding and day. Flexi-boarding available.
Religious denomination Non-denominational
Age range 16–18

No of pupils 290; *(full boarding)* 140; *(weekly boarding)* 140; *(day)* 10; *Girls* 150; *Boys* 140
Fees per annum *(full boarding)* £24,600–£28,290; *(weekly)* £24,600–£28,290; *(day)* £16,400–£18,860

Kew Green Preparatory School

Layton House, Ferry Lane, Richmond, Surrey TW9 3AF Tel: (020) 8948 5999
Fax: (020) 8948 4774 E-mail: secretary@kgps.co.uk Website: www.kgps.co.uk

Head Mrs M Gardener PGCE
School status Co-educational day only
Religious denomination Non-denominational
Learning difficulties CA SNU WI/DYC DYP DYS MLD
Behavioural and emotional disorders CA CO/ADD ASP AUT
Age range 4–11
No of pupils 280; *Girls* 140; *Boys* 140
Fees per annum *(day)* £3,450

Kew Green Preparatory School provides an education of the highest quality. Unlike many private schools, LPS Ltd is owned by fully qualified and experienced teachers who understand that effective learning is achieved without pressure in a warm and nurturing environment. We are committed to co-education, opposed to 'cramming', and work on the basis of keeping pupils from age 4 to secondary transfer at 11 years. Within this timescale we are able to allow children to develop at their own pace whilst providing a rich curriculum. We strive to inculcate in our pupils a proper self-esteem and respect for others. Above all, we want our children to be clamouring at our gates every morning and to show a marked reluctance to leave at the end of the day!

Kingston Grammar School

London Road, Kingston-upon-Thames, Surrey KT2 6PY
Tel: (020) 8546 5875 Fax: (020) 8547 1499 E-mail: registar@kingston-grammar.surrey.sch.uk
Website: www.kingston-grammar.surrey.sch.uk www.gabbitas.net

Headmaster Mr C D Baxter MA (Oxon) FRSA
Founded 1561
School status Co-educational day only
Religious denomination Christian
Member of HMC
Age range 10–18
No of pupils 709; *Girls* 293; *Boys* 416
Average class size 24
Fees per annum *(day)* £10,503–£10,785

In Years 1 and 2 pupils follow a wide curriculum including Latin, French, German and technology. In the third year an option scheme introduces Spanish. Further options are undertaken in the fourth year, when the pupils select 10 subjects for GCSE. A number take mathematics in the fourth year. In the Sixth Form a comprehensive range of A2 levels and AS levels are available. At all levels pupils receive careers advice and have a timetable constructed based on their options. A major new development opens in September 2005.

Entry requirements Entry at 10+ and 11+ is by examination in January, at 13+ by Common Entrance or our own examination. At 16+ entrance is by interview and GCSE results. Academic, art, music and sports awards are available, together with means-tested bursaries.

Kingston Grammar School Foundation, a registered charity, exists to provide high-quality education for girls and boys.

Marymount International School

George Road, Kingston-upon-Thames, Surrey KT2 7PE Tel: (020) 8949 0571 Fax: (020) 8336 2485
E-mail: admissions@marymountlondon.com Web: www.marymountlondon.com www.gabbitas.net

Head Sister K Fagan RSHM **Founded** 1955
School status Girls' independent boarding and day. Flexi-boarding available.
Religious denomination Roman Catholic
Member of CIS, GSA, IBO, ISCis, LISA, MSA (USA), SHA; **Accredited by** CIS, GSA, ISC, MSA (USA)
Learning difficulties RA SC SNU/DYC DYS MLD
Behavioural and emotional disorders CO RA ST TS/ADD ADHD BESD
Physical and medical conditions AT RA SM TW WA2/HEA VI
Age range 11–18; *boarders from* 11
No of pupils 230; *(full boarding)* 90; *(weekly boarding)* 12; *(day)* 128; *Senior* 135; *Sixth Form* 95
Teacher:pupil ratio 1:8; **Ave class size** 10–12
Fees per annum *(full boarding)* £21,750–£23,150; *(weekly)* £20,650–£22,050; *(day)* £12,350–£13,750

Curriculum International Baccalaureate (IB). 98 per cent of our students enter university.

Entry requirements Application form and reports for previous three years.

Boarding facilities A new extension provides additional accommodation.

Facilities Computer centre, sports hall, theatre, music centre, modern science block. Marymount has students of over 49 nationalities and is conveniently situated for London and its airports.

Parsons Mead

Ottways Lane, Ashtead, Surrey KT21 2PE
Tel: (01372) 276401 Fax: (01372) 278796 E-mail: parsonsmead@parsonmead.co.uk
Website: www.parsonsmeadsurrey.co.uk www.gabbitas.net

Headmistress Mrs P M Taylor
Founded 1897
School status Girls' day only. Flexi-boarding available.
Religious denomination Church of England
Age range 2–18
Fees per annum *(day)* £3,280–£10,995

Parsons Mead provides an excellent all-round education for girls. The pupils enjoy a beautiful 12-acre site and flourish in a happy, caring environment. They are helped to achieve their best standard in KS1, KS2, GCSE, AS and A level examinations. Our recent results were excellent, often demonstrating superb value added. Sport, music, drama and art are particular strengths of the school.

Parsons Mead girls study at such universities as Cambridge, Manchester, Warwick, Durham and Southampton.

Facilities are continually upgraded. The Senior department recently benefited from a new Sixth Form centre and a pottery room, whilst the Junior department has a new IT Suite.

Day boarding operates from 7.30 am to 6.00 pm with occasional overnight boarding. A minibus service runs from Tadworth and to and from Kingston, Surbiton and Ashtead Station.

Prior's Field School

Priorsfield Road, Hurtmore, Godalming, Surrey GU7 2RH Tel: (01483) 810551 Fax: (01483) 810180
E-mail: admin@priorsfield.surrey.sch.uk Website: www.priorsfield.surrey.sch.uk www.gabbitas.net

Headmistress Mrs J Dwyer BEd (Hons) (Cantab)
Founded 1902
School status Girls' independent boarding and day
Religious denomination Non-denominational
Member of BSA, GSA; **Accredited by** GSA
Learning difficulties WI/DYC DYP DYS
Behavioural and emotional disorders CO/ADHD
Physical and medical conditions SM TW WA3/EPI HEA HI VI
Age range 11–18
No of pupils 324; *(full boarding)* 38; *(weekly boarding)* 80; *(day)* 206; *Girls* 324
Teacher:pupil ratio 1:7; **Average class size** 17
Fees per annum *(full boarding)* £17,850; *(weekly)* £17,850; *(day)* £11,085

Prior's Field is set in 25 acres of Surrey countryside and has a tradition of excellent examination results in a friendly atmosphere. A wide range of AS and A level subjects are offered and most leavers proceed to university.

The Duke of Edinburgh's Award and Young Enterprise schemes, as well as visits abroad, breed self-reliance. A new sports hall, dramatic arts centre, and an extension to the Sixth Form house have been completed. Sports include netball, hockey, athletics and regional standard tennis. There is a tradition of choral training and drama productions. Individual study bedrooms from Year 10. Entry at 11+, 13+ and Sixth Form. Academic, drama, art and music scholarships are awarded annually. Reduced fees for service daughters.

Reed's School

Sandy Lane, Cobham, Surrey KT11 2ES
Tel: (01932) 869001 Fax: (01932) 869046
E-mail: admissions@reeds.surrey.sch.uk
Website: www.reeds.surrey.sch.uk www.gabbitas.net

Headmaster Mr D W Jarrett
Founded 1813
School status Boys' (11–18) Co-educational (Sixth Form) boarding and day
Religious denomination Church of England
No of pupils 550; *(full boarding)* 86; *Girls* 50; *Boys* 500
Fees per annum *(full boarding)* £15,981–£19,641; *(day)* £11,985–£14,847

The Headmaster is assisted by a permanent full-time teaching staff of 60+, including a school chaplain, and pupils are prepared for GCSE, AS and A level examinations with a variety of boards. Up to the beginning of GCSE courses, the school broadly follows the National Curriculum. At GCSE all pupils take English, English Literature, maths, a modern language, ICT, science and 2–3 option subjects; most pupils take 10 subjects in all. A wide range of AS and A level options are available.

Registration and entry Pupils may be registered at any time but, for 13+, registrations must be received at least two years in advance of entry date. Entry is at ages 11+, 12+, 13+ and Sixth Form. Entry at 11+ and 12+ is by special examination, while at 13+ it is normally by Common Entrance or Common Scholarship. Sixth Form entry is determined by entry tests in November, school report and interview. Foundation bursaries are available to children who meet the specific criteria. For information on this please contact the school.

Scholarships Academic, music, art, drama, sport and all-round scholarships up to the value of half fees are offered each year for pupils entering at 11+, 13+ and Sixth Form. In addition Design Technology scholarships are available for 13+ and Sixth Form applicants.

Facilities Nine science laboratories and specialist classrooms for all subjects, including outstanding facilities for art, graphic design, photography and printing, music and music technology, technology and ICT. Full facilities for rugby, hockey, cricket, tennis, squash and swimming, including a sports hall, swimming pool, two artificial hockey pitches, nine tennis courts and an indoor tennis centre. A new Music School opened in 2001 and in 2005 four biology laboratories and five classrooms were opened together with extended Day Pupil facilities. There are three separate boarding houses: The Close for 11 and 12+, School House for 13–16 and a Sixth Form house.

There is an ongoing development programme with plans for, among other things, a performance hall, lecture theatre and enhanced girls' facilities and accommodation.

Ethos While the ethos of the school is directed towards academic achievement, Reed's offers an extensive range of opportunities to each pupil through its Activities Curriculum. Reed's is also distinctive in that the school has an international dimension through its partnership with the Rijnlands Lyceum for Dutch-speaking pupils. Pupils participate in the Duke of Edinburgh's Award Scheme, the CCF, major sports (rugby, hockey and cricket), and a whole host of options which extend from the martial arts to dance and archery. In addition, the school is developing partnerships with the Lawn Tennis Association and the British Ski Academy as a centre of excellence for tennis and skiing.

Through creating the highest quality of opportunities Reed's genuinely seeks to identify the talents of each individual, thereby enabling every pupil to leave the school with the qualities necessary to be high achievers in their chosen careers. The school is situated just off the A3 in 40 acres of Surrey heathland within easy reach of Heathrow and Gatwick airports. Application should be made to the Registrar/Admissions Secretary: admissions@reeds.surrey.sch.uk.

Royal Alexandra and Albert School

Gatton Park, Reigate, Surrey RH2 0TD Tel: (01737) 649001 Fax: (01737) 649002
E-mail: admissions@gatton-park.org.uk Website: www.gatton-park.org.uk

Headmaster Mr P Spencer Ellis BA MPhil NPQH
Founded 1758
School status Co-educational voluntary aided boarding and day. Flexi-boarding available.
Religious denomination Church of England
Member of BSA, SHA, SHMIS
Accredited by SHMIS SBSA (State Boarding Schools Association)
Age range 7–18; *boarders from* 7
No of pupils 688; *(full boarding)* 389; *(day)* 299; *Prep* 146; *Senior* 542; *Girls* 329; *Boys* 359
Average class size 24
Fees per annum *(full boarding)* £9,780–£10,050; *(day)* £3,150

This is a true boarding school in the sense that the majority of pupils are boarders. We have Saturday lessons and longer holidays, and run a vast range of sporting and other activities in the afternoons, evenings and at weekends.

Admission is by confidential reference from the current school and interview, together with some diagnostic tests, but is restricted to citizens of the UK and other EU countries and those with the right of residence in the UK.

Set in 260 acres of parkland, yet close to London, we have an excellent range of facilities including a sports hall, riding school, indoor swimming pool, drama studio, chapel, new music department and nine boarding houses, eight of which have been recently refurbished to a very high standard.

St Andrew's (Woking) School Trust

Church Hill House, Wilson Way, Horsell, Woking, Surrey GU21 4QW
Tel: (01483) 760943 Fax: (01483) 740314 E-mail: admin@st-andrews.woking.sch.uk
Website: www.st-andrews.woking.sch.uk www.gabbitas.net

Headmaster Mr J R Evans BEd (Hons) Ad Dip Ed Man
Deputy Head Mr A K Perks MSc BSc
Founded 1938
School status Co-educational independent day only
Religious denomination Church of England
Member of IAPS; **Accredited by** ISC
Learning difficulties CA WI/DYS MLD
Behavioural and emotional disorders RA/ADD ADHD
Physical and medical conditions RA SM
Age range 3–13
No of pupils 279; *Nursery* 31; *Pre-prep* 97; *Prep* 151; *Girls* 62; *Boys* 217
Teacher:pupil ratio 1:9
Average class size 14
Fees per annum *(day)* £3,885–£9,975
The above fees are per term.

Curriculum Children are prepared for Common Entrance and scholarships to a wide range of senior schools, with top awards won every year. Specialist teaching facilities for all subjects. The curriculum is broad and appropriate to children of all abilities. The school places great emphasis on music and the Arts.

Academic and leisure activities There is a sports hall, all-weather tennis and netball courts, heated pool and ample grounds for games. Major games are soccer, hockey, cricket, swimming, tennis, athletics, netball and rounders. In addition the children do rugby, cross-country and basketball.

Activities programme Children can be supervised at school from 8.00 am and, through our extensive after-school activities programme, until 6.00/6.30 pm most evenings during the week.

Entry requirements Entry test for children over 6. The school has a number of scholarships and bursaries available at 7+ and 11+.

St Hilary's School

Holloway Hill, Godalming, Surrey GU7 1RZ
Tel: (01483) 416551 Fax: (01483) 418325
E-mail: registrar@sthilarysschool.com
Website: www.sthilaryschool.com

Headmistress Mrs S Bailes BA (Hon) MA PGCE
School status Co-educational day only
Religious denomination Non-denominational
Age range Boys 2–7; Girls 2–11
No of pupils 265; *Girls* 177; *Boys* 88
Fees per annum *(day)* £6,270–£9,060

Visit St Hilary's and leave doors open for the future. As Headmistress Mrs Susan Bailes remarks: 'Our aim is to provide a happy, secure environment and to unlock a love of learning, which will last forever.' If you want the best for your child, where he or she is treated as an individual in small classes with dedicated staff, encouraged to grow in self-esteem while receiving a firm academic foundation, then choose St Hilary's School. We are proud of our independence and the successes of our pupils. Facilities include an all-weather pitch, superb ICT suite along with vibrant extra-curricular provision.

St Teresa's School

Effingham Hill, Dorking, Surrey RH5 6ST
Tel: (01372) 452037 Fax: (01372) 450311
E-mail: info@stteresas.surrey.sch.uk
Website: www.stteresas.surrey.sch.uk www.gabbitas.net

Senior School Head Mrs M Prescott
Prep School Head Mrs A M Stewart MA (Hons) PGCE
Founded 1928
School status Girls' independent boarding and day. Flexi-boarding available.
Religious denomination Roman Catholic
Learning difficulties SNU/DYC DYP DYS
Behavioural and emotional disorders CO/ADHD
Physical and medical conditions SM
Age range 11–18
No of pupils 330; *(full boarding)* 72; *(weekly boarding)* 15; *(day)* 243; *Senior* 255; *Sixth Form* 75
Fees per annum *(full boarding)* £18,105–£18,855; *(weekly)* £16,725–£17,457; *(day)* £10,350–£11,100

St Teresa's is a thriving girls' school situated in 45 acres of beautiful parkland in the Surrey Hills, with good road and rail links to London and the airports, and a network of coach services. Since its establishment in 1928, the school facilities have been continually expanded and updated. A new indoor swimming pool complex opened in 2004 and a magnificent £3 million Performing Arts Centre and Theatre Hall was completed in 2005. Over £5 million has been invested in the development of the education campus since the millennium.

St Teresa's is a community of about 450 girls, including some 87 boarders, who enjoy first class care in a flexible boarding system with a programme of weekend activities. Although a Catholic foundation, St Teresa's welcomes girls of all denominations and everyone is encouraged to respect one another in a happy, caring Christian environment. The school is particularly sensitive to the differing needs and latent talents of each individual girl and adopts a 'can do' attitude, stimulating, supporting and developing each girl's interests and talents.

Girls in the Preparatory School benefit from specialist subject teachers and assume responsibility in their last year through a School Council. They can take advantage of an extended day, including breakfast and homework supervision and the 19 extra-curricular activities and clubs on offer.

Entrance to the Senior School is at 11+, but girls are also warmly welcomed at 12+ and 13+. Scholarships are available at all these entry points and in the Sixth Form. There are 60+ extra-curricular activities on offer and girls are encouraged to develop their life skills through the Duke of Edinburgh's Award scheme, the Young Enterprise scheme, World Challenge and work experience.

St Teresa's offers a very broad curriculum with 27 subjects at A level. All girls go on to higher education: many to first rank universities, including Oxbridge, others to the best art schools, drama schools and music colleges.

Surrey College

Admin Centre, Abbot House, Sydenham Road, Guildford, Surrey GU1 3RL
Tel: (01483) 565887 Fax: (01483) 534777 E-mail: mail@surrey-college.co.uk
Website: www.surrey-college.co.uk www.gabbitas.net

Principal Ms L Cody BA MA PGCE DSA
Vice Principal Ms V Alexander BA PGCE CTESOL **Founded** 1982
College status Co-educational independent Fifth and Sixth Form College. Flexi-boarding available.
Religious denomination Non-denominational
Member of ARELS, CIFE; **Accredited by** BAC
Surrey College is registered with the DfES and is a member of BAC and CIFE.
Learning difficulties RA WI/DYP DYS
Behavioural and emotional disorders TS/CB
Physical and medical conditions RA
Age range 15+
No of pupils 100; *Girls* 40; *Boys* 60
Teacher:pupil ratio 1:4; **Average class size** 6
Fees per annum *(day)* £2,500–£11,000
Fees Host family accommodation available, fees £110 per week

Surrey College is an independent co-educational Fifth and Sixth Form college dedicated to the pursuit of academic excellence. We offer an extensive range of GCSE, AS and A level courses, delivered in a supportive atmosphere with high levels of personal attention. We also offer a fully accredited one-year International Foundation Programme, to prepare overseas students for entry to UK universities.

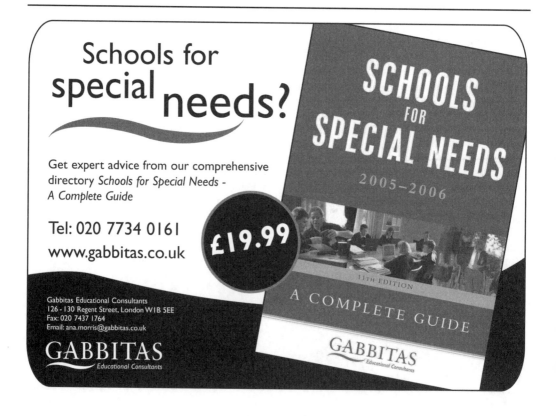

TASIS The American School in England

Coldharbour Lane, Thorpe, Surrey TW20 8TE Tel: (01932) 565252 Fax: (01932) 564644
E-mail: ukadmissions@tasis.com Website: www.tasis.com www.gabbitas.net

Ofsted inspected TASIS in 2004 and praised its programmes and the overall tone of the school.

Headmaster Dr J A Doran PhD
Director of Admissions Miss B Thorburn BSc MSc Dip RSA Grad CIPD
Founded 1976
School status Co-educational boarding and day
Religious denomination Non-denominational
Member of CASE, CIS, IBO, IBSCA, LISA, NAIS, NEASC; **Accredited by** CIS Also a member of The Association of Boarding Schools (TABS), an American organization.
Behavioural and emotional disorders CO
Physical and medical conditions SM TW WA2/W
Age range 3–18; *boarders from* 14
No of pupils 716; *(full boarding)* 165; *(day)* 551; *Nursery* 12; *Pre-prep* 242; *Prep* 153; *Senior* 128; *Sixth Form* 181; *Girls* 354; *Boys* 362
Teacher:pupil ratio 1:12; **Average class size** 15
Fees per annum *(full boarding)* £23,600; *(day)* £5,200–£15,300

TASIS England is located on a historic 35-acre campus just 18 miles from London, the cultural capital of the English-speaking world. TASIS fosters academic and personal growth for day students (3–18 years) and boarding students (14–18 years), in a quiet and safe village while providing a university preparatory curriculum with an international perspective. From the IB diploma, Advanced Placement classes, and English as a Second Language courses to exceptional European travel opportunities, fine sports and technology facilities, and an outstanding arts programme, the TASIS experience prepares young people to meet the challenges of a demanding world. Small classes and close to 100 dedicated, experienced faculty members provide individualized attention and an outstanding environment for learning. Believing in the worth of each individual and the importance of enduring relationships, TASIS seeks to embody and instil the values of personal responsibility, civility, compassion, justice and truth.

The school's international student enrolment is drawn from all corners of the world. TASIS England

embraces three divisions: Lower School (Nursery–Grade 5; ages 3–10), Middle School (Grades 6–8; ages 11–13), and Upper School (Grades 9–13; ages 14–18). Students in each division regularly benefit from the opportunity to work closely with visiting artists, actors, musicians and sports professionals. The comprehensive athletics programme includes intramurals in the Lower School and interscholastic games for Middle School, JV and varsity teams. Throughout the year, students enjoy numerous field trips, weekend activities and travel throughout the UK and abroad.

The combination of well-equipped facilities and a strong academic programme has given TASIS its valued reputation both here and abroad. Each year TASIS students are offered places at some of the finest universities within the UK, US, Canada and other parts of the world.

Admissions decisions for the academic school year are made on a rolling basis upon receipt of a completed application form together with the application fee, three teachers' recommendations, and three years of transcripts. Standardized test scores and a student questionnaire are required. An interview is recommended unless distance is a prohibiting factor. For additional information, please contact Miss Bronwyn Thorburn, Director of Admissions (ukadmissions@tasis.com).

TASIS England also offers summer programmes for day and boarding students from ages 12 to 18. Local and international students participate in intensive courses for high school credit, enrichment programmes, theatre workshops, Shakespeare, IB prep classes, ESL, TOEFL and SAT Review. Students also enjoy extensive sports activities and travel, both international and within the UK. For more information please contact Faie Gilbert, Director of Summer Admissions (uksummer@tasis.com).

Woldingham School

Marden Park, Woldingham, Surrey CR3 7YA
Tel: (01883) 349431 Fax: (01883) 348653 E-mail: registrar@woldingham.surrey.sch.uk
Website: www.woldinghamschool.co.uk www.gabbitas.net

Headmistress Miss D Vernon BA
Founded 1842
School status Girls' independent boarding and day. Flexi-boarding available.
Religious denomination Roman Catholic
Member of AGBIS, BSA, GSA, ISA
Accredited by GSA
Learning difficulties WI/DYC DYP DYS
Behavioural and emotional disorders RA/ADD
Physical and medical conditions SL TW WA1/EPI HI IM W
Age range 11–18
No of pupils 500; *(weekly boarding)* 400; *(day)* 100
Teacher:pupil ratio 1:7
Average class size 16 in senior school/ 7 in Sixth Form
Fees per annum *(weekly)* £21,240; *(day)* £12,690

Curriculum Most girls take nine or ten GCSEs. All acquire at least a 'working knowledge' of two European languages and take science to 16+ either on an integrated or separate subject basis. The aim is to provide 'breadth and balance' so that alternative academic pathways are available at 16+. The school offers academic excellence with an emphasis on value added performance. Sixth Formers study four AS level subjects in the Lower Sixth and continue with three or four to A2 level in the Upper Sixth. All Sixth Formers additionally follow a General Studies programme.

Entry requirements and procedures Woldingham is a caring community with a Catholic foundation which welcomes girls of all faiths. Girls enter at 11+ or 13+ having taken the Common Entrance Examination. This age group also attend the school for a one-day informal assessment during the previous autumn. Entry is also at 13+ and 16+ and some vacancies may be available in other years. Sixth Form entrants should be capable of taking at least four AS levels in Lower Sixth and three A2 levels in Upper Sixth. Academic, drama, art, sport and music scholarships are available.

Examinations and Boards offered GCSE Core Curriculum of seven or eight subjects with three options chosen from a further ten. Choice of four AS subjects from twenty-three in the Lower Sixth with three continued to A2 in the Upper Sixth. Sixth Form students prepared for entry to UK and American universities including Oxbridge.

Boarding facilities Girls are organized on a year group basis, pastoral supervision and support being provided by Heads of Years and assistants. The school's stunning 700-acre site provides an exceptional range of extra-curricular and study facilities, as well as excellent modern boarding accommodation. Senior House accommodates girls aged 13 to 16, with the majority in single study bedrooms. Berwick House provides outstanding facilities with single rooms for Lower Sixth girls and the very new Shanley House provides even better facilities in en suite single study bedrooms for the Upper Sixth. Other facilities include a state-of-the-art teaching centre for the Expressive Arts which comprises a dedicated Music Centre and 600-seat auditorium. An all-weather sports pitch was opened for use in March 2003, complementing the existing sports facilities which include a new Sports Hall, heated indoor swimming pool and indoor and outdoor tennis courts.

Battle Abbey School

High Street, Battle, East Sussex TN33 0AD Tel: (01424) 772385 Fax: (01424) 773573
E-mail: office@battleabbeyschool.com Website: www.battleabbeyschool.com www.gabbitas.net

Head Mr R Clark **Founded** 1922
School status Co-educational boarding and day. Flexi-boarding available.
Religious denomination Non-denominational
Learning difficulties CA SC WI/DYC DYP DYS
Behavioural and emotional disorders RA ST/ ADHD ASP AUT
Physical and medical conditions RA SM WA3/HEA VI
Age range 2–18; *boarders from* 8
No of pupils 288; *(full boarding)* 48; *(weekly boarding)* 2; *(day)* 238; *Nursery* 7; *Prep* 73; *Senior* 159; *Sixth Form* 49; *Girls* 144; *Boys* 144
Fees per annum *(full boarding)* £14,322–£17,805; *(weekly)* £14,322–£17,805; *(day)* £5,412–£10,896

Battle Abbey School, which occupies one of the most famous historical sites in the world – that of the 1066 Battle of Hastings – is an independent, co-educational school for pupils aged from 2½ to 18. Boarders are accepted from the age of 8. The school is large enough to encourage healthy competition and to develop the social skills and awareness of others, learnt by being part of a lively community, but it is small enough to have many of the attributes of a large family. Teaching classes are small throughout the school, allowing individual attention and the opportunity for all pupils to achieve their maximum potential. A new Performing Arts Centre opened at the school in the Summer of 2005.

England

Buckswood School

Broomham Hall, Rye Road, Guestling, Hastings, East Sussex TN35 4LT
Tel: (01424) 813813 Fax: (01424) 812100 E-mail: achieve@buckswood.co.uk
Website: www.buckswood.co.uk www.gabbitas.net

Director Mr T Fish
Registrar Miss Fiona Wratten
School status Co-educational independent boarding and day. Flexi-boarding available.
Religious denomination Non-denominational
Member of ARELS
Accredited by British Council
Learning difficulties WI/DYS MLD
Age range 10–19; *boarders from* 10
No of pupils 250; *(full boarding)* 150; *(day)* 100; *Senior* 190; *Sixth Form* 60; *Girls* 100; *Boys* 150
Teacher:pupil ratio 1:8; **Average class size** 14
Fees per annum *(full boarding)* £17,175; *(day)* £8,190

A truly international educational environment awaits your child at Buckswood. Parents select Buckswood because they know it is a school that contributes something special to their children's education. Its size allows the school to preserve a more home-like atmosphere, where the care and welfare of students is a priority.

Buckswood follows the National Curriculum, and small classes for GCSE and A levels ensure pupils receive more individual attention.

We have a large campus near the seaside town of Hastings with a swimming pool, horse riding, large sports grounds and new tennis courts – sports and activities play an important part of a Buckswood all-round education.

Michael Hall (Steiner Waldorf School)

Kidbrooke Park, Forest Row, East Sussex RH18 5JA
Tel: (01342) 822275 Fax: (01342) 826593
E-mail: info@michaelhall.co.uk Website: www.michaelhall.co.uk www.gabbitas.net

Founded 1925
School status Co-educational boarding and day. Flexi-boarding available.
Religious denomination Christian
Age range 0–19
No of pupils 628; *(full boarding)* 15; *(weekly boarding)* 10
Girls 328; *Boys* 300
Fees per annum *(full boarding)* £13,880; *(weekly)* £12,820; *(day)* £7,890

Protecting the right to childhood.
Creating abilities for life.

Offering a structured and imaginative approach and an international curriculum, Michael Hall has gained wide recognition as a creative and compassionate alternative to more traditional avenues of education.

* Full age-range from pre-school to university entrance.
* Unique international curriculum based on child development.
* Languages from age six.
* GCSE, AS and A level.
* Arts, crafts, sport, sciences and humanities.
* Intensive English courses for foreign students.
* Over 600 day and boarding pupils.
* Set in rural Sussex, within reach of main cultural centres.

Newlands School

Eastbourne Road, Seaford, East Sussex BN25 4NP Tel: (01323) 892334/490000 Fax: (01323) 898420
E-mail: newlands1@msn.com Website: www.newlands-school.com www.gabbitas.net

Headmaster Mr O T Price BEd (Hons)
Founded 1854
School status Co-educational independent boarding and day. Flexi-boarding available.
Religious denomination Inter-denominational
Member of CReSTeD, IAPS, ISA, ISCis, SATIPS;
Accredited by IAPS, ISA, ISC
Learning difficulties SNU/DYC DYP DYS
Age range 0–18
No of pupils 451; *(full boarding)* 111; *(day)* 340; *Nursery* 29; *Pre-prep* 45; *Prep* 203; *Senior* 128; *Sixth Form* 46; *Girls* 182; *Boys* 269
Teacher:pupil ratio 1:8; **Average class size** 15
Fees per annum *(full boarding)* £14,985–£17,850; *(weekly)* £14,835–£17,700; *(day)* £4,950–£10,875

Newlands is a friendly, happy school with a strong academic tradition. Classes are small and a pupil's progress is monitored carefully. A high quality teaching ensures the pupils achieve excellent examination results. The wide range of activities available make it possible for every pupil to achieve success and confidence in one field or another.

Location Newlands is situated on one 21-acre campus in a pleasant coastal town surrounded by an area of outstanding natural beauty. Good communication links exist with Gatwick (37 miles), Heathrow (78 miles) and London (65 miles).

High academic standards At Newlands, we expect pupils to attain optimum results in external examinations, as is evident by our strong academic record. A level and GCSE results show year-on-year improvement.

The arts flourish with thriving music, drama, dance and art departments. There is a strong choral tradition and annual dramatic productions. A Theatre Arts Course is available to students who wish to specialize in dance, drama, music and art within an academic environment.

Entry requirements Interview and school reports are required.

Scholarships Academic, drama, sport, music, art and theatre arts scholarships are available for the Preparatory and Manor parts of the school. We also prepare Preparatory pupils for scholarships to Newlands Manor at 13 years. There is a generous discount for service families as fees are in line with the BSA.

Academic and sports facilities Our facilities include five high-tech computer rooms, science laboratories, a large art studio, a language laboratory, a design technology workshop, an assembly hall/theatre and a music room.

There are the equivalent of eight football pitches, a heated indoor swimming pool, a hard playing surface for three tennis/netball courts, a gymnasium, and a .22 rifle range. There are many opportunities for sports, including soccer, hockey, rugby, netball, cricket, athletics, volleyball, basketball, squash, rounders, badminton, tennis, horse-riding and cross-country running. A new multi-purpose hall is appropriate for most indoor games as well as other activities.

Accelerated Learning Unit This nationally renowned centre has specialist teachers who provide one-to-one tuition for gifted pupils, dyslexic pupils and those learning English as a foreign language. All members of staff are fully qualified with diplomas in Special Education Needs or Certificate/Diplomas in Teaching English as a Foreign Language.

The centre is approved by CReSTeD, having a category B listing, supported by the British Dyslexia Association and the Dyslexia Institute.

Gifted pupils receive intensive tuition in their area of giftedness, so that they can achieve success at an earlier age.

Study skills and examination techniques are taught in order to prepare pupils for their GCSE and A level courses.

Newlands International College, a specialist language school for students whose first language is not English, was opened in September 2005 to prepare students for entry into the mainstream school or directly into higher education.

St Bede's School

The Dicker, Hailsham, East Sussex BN27 3QH
Tel: (01323) 843252 Fax: (01323) 442628
E-mail: school.office@stbedesschool.org
Website: www.stbedesschool.org www.gabbitas.net

Headmaster Mr S W Cole
Head (Prep School) Mr C Pyemont
Founded 1978 & 1895
School status Co-educational independent boarding and day. Flexi-boarding available.
Religious denomination Inter-denominational
Member of AGBIS, CReSTeD, IAPS, ISCis, SHMIS
Accredited by IAPS, SHMIS
Learning difficulties SNU/DYP DYS
Behavioural and emotional disorders CO/ADD ADHD ASP
Physical and medical conditions SM/EPI
Age range 11–19
No of pupils 800; *(full boarding)* 320; *(day)* 480; *Girls* 320; *Boys* 480
Teacher:pupil ratio 1:8
Fees per annum *(full boarding)* £19,785; *(day)* £12,165 (not including Pre-prep)

St Bede's is one of Britain's leading independent co-educational schools. The school is proudly and purposefully non-selective and the generous staffing ratio of 1:8 enables outstanding results to be achieved. The Senior School is located on a separate campus to the Pre-prep and Prep Schools, which gives students a change of teaching staff and environment as well as the opportunity to mature.

Location The Senior School is found at the heart of the village of Upper Dicker, based on a small country estate set in beautiful countryside. The Prep School is situated nearby on the seafront in Eastbourne. Both schools are easily accessible by road and rail from London's airports and Channel seaports. Transport to and from school can be arranged for boarders and a school bus service is available for day students.

Curriculum St Bede's provides an extremely wide-ranging and flexible programme. In the early years at the Prep School there is a strong emphasis on literacy and numeracy as well as skills such as

languages and computing. Academic standards are high and all students are prepared for Common Entrance and Scholarship exams.

Facilities Both schools have imaginatively converted and added to their original Edwardian buildings to provide excellent teaching and sporting facilities. Each site provides an indoor sports centre, indoor swimming pool, EFL centre, art, design and technology studios and an impressive computer network. In addition the Senior School has a drama studio, riding stables, a practice golf course, and ceramics and graphic design studios.

Sporting and club activities Both schools are particularly strong in football, tennis, cricket, squash and swimming. The Prep School has a very strong games-playing tradition and encourages students of all abilities to participate in sport. At the Senior School games are organized as part of an extensive club activities programme which takes place every day. In all there are over 140 club activities, ranging from all kinds of sport and outdoor pursuits to activities within the fields of art, drama, music, journalism, science, agriculture and technology.

Scholarships and bursaries A generous number of academic, art, music, dance, drama, and sports scholarships are available at both schools and scholarships may be awarded to those entering the Sixth Form.

St Mary's Hall

Eastern Road, Brighton, East Sussex BN2 5JF Tel: (01273) 606061 Fax: (01273) 620782
E-mail: registrar@stmaryshall.co.uk Website: www.stmaryshall.co.uk www.gabbitas.net

Head Mrs S M Meek MA
Founded 1836
School status Girls' independent boarding and day. Flexi-boarding available.
Religious denomination Church of Fngland
Member of AGBIS, BSA, GSA, IAPS, ISCis, SHA; **Accredited by** GSA, ISC
Learning difficulties CA/DYS MLD
Age range Girls 3–18; Boys 3–8
No of pupils 305; *(full boarding)* 75; *(weekly boarding)* 5; *(day)* 225; *Nursery* 6; *Pre-prep* 26; *Prep* 55; *Senior* 164; *Sixth Form* 54; *Girls* 295; *Boys* 10
Teacher:pupil ratio 1:15 average
Average class size 12–20
Fees per annum *(full boarding)* £13,218–£17,475; *(weekly)* £12,594–£16,755; *(day)* £2,178–£10,584

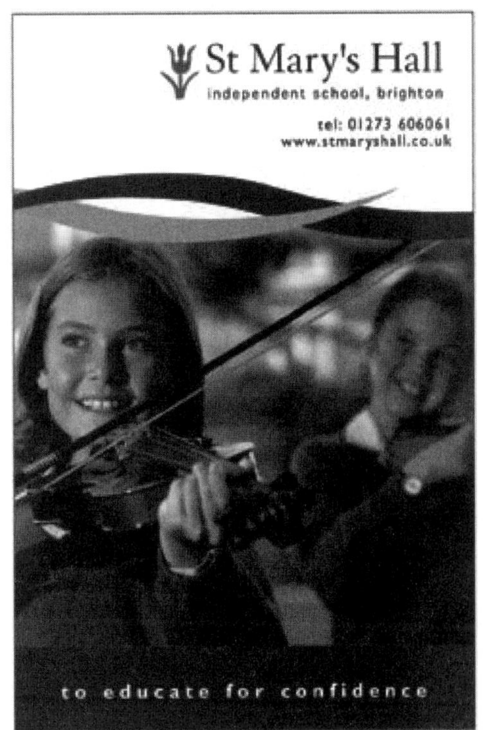

St Mary's Hall is one of the oldest schools for girls in Britain, and is proud of its tradition of respect for the individual and its capacity to provide the best of modern education in a caring family atmosphere.

The aim in the Pre-preparatory and the Preparatory is to take each pupil to their next stage of learning in a supportive and stimulating environment. Children work steadily towards literacy and numeracy goals, while subjects like music, French and swimming are gradually introduced into the curriculum.

In the Senior School students are taught by specialized subject teachers. Seventeen subjects are offered at GCSE; students normally sit between eight and ten. A wide variety of subjects are also available at A level, where the school has consistently good results: 100 per cent pass rate in 2003 and 99 per cent in 2004. The great majority of students obtain a place at their first choice of university.

Academic and leisure facilities There are two well-appointed technology rooms. The art block includes two pottery kilns and a darkroom. Drama studies take place in a studio theatre with a computerized stage-lighting system. The playing field, all-weather tennis courts and a 25-metre heated indoor swimming pool are all on site. The school has its own chapel. There are three boarding houses designed for the needs of different age groups, each with dedicated House staff. An International Study Centre was created specifically for overseas students, to allow them a seamless and rapid integration into the school. An expert and enthusiastic ESL (English as a second language) team runs the centre.

St Mary's Hall is a charity established to 'educate for confidence'. Entry is by assessment in the Junior Department and examination and interview in the Senior School. Academic, art, drama, music and sport scholarships are available on entry to years 7, 10 and 12. St Mary's Hall has a Clergy and Armed Forces bursary scheme, together with its own assisted places.

Prospective parents are welcome to visit the school during one of its regular open mornings (October, February and May) or indeed by individual appointment. Prospective pupils are welcome to spend a day at the school or, if boarding is being considered, to stay overnight.

Brambletye School

Lewes Road, Brambletye, East Grinstead, West Sussex RH19 3PD
Tel: (01342) 321004 Fax: (01342) 317562 E-mail: admin@brambletye.com
Website: www.brambletye.com www.gabbitas.net

Headmaster Mr H D Cocke **Founded** 1919
School status Co-educational boarding and day
Religious denomination Church of England
Member of AGBIS, BSA, IAPS, ISBA, ISCis, SATIPS; **Accredited by** IAPS
Learning difficulties WI/DYC DYP DYS
Behavioural and emotional disorders RA/ ADHD
Physical and medical conditions RA SM/HEA
Age range 3–13; *boarders from* 7
No of pupils 257; *(full boarding)* 71; *(day)* 186; *Nursery* 20; *Pre-prep* 76; *Prep* 181; *Girls* 93; *Boys* 164
Teacher:pupil ratio 1:7; **Average class size** 16
Fees per annum *(full boarding)* £15,600; *(day)* £11,850–£14,850
Fees Nursery £3,810–£5,325 Pre-Prep £6,090

Brambletye is situated in 140-acre grounds. It has a new sports hall and pre-preparatory building, theatre, art department, indoor swimming pool, hard tennis courts, 6-hole golf course, computer centre and library.

Children may start as boarders or day pupils, but there is an expectation that all pupils will board in their final three years. Our generous exeat system means that, on average, there is a leave-out weekend every fortnight.

Music awards are available each year in the spring, details of which, along with the School Prospectus, can be obtained on application to the Headmaster's Secretary.

Burgess Hill School for Girls

Keymer Road, Burgess Hill, West Sussex RH15 0EG
Tel: (01444) 241050 Fax: (01444) 870314 E-mail: registrar@burgesshill-school.com
Website: www.burgesshill-school.com www.gabbitas.net Junior School tel: 01444 233167

Headmistress Mrs JA Aughwane BSc (Hons) PGCE
Founded 1906
School status Girls' independent boarding and day. Flexi-boarding available.
Religious denomination Inter-denominational
Member of GSA
Accredited by GSA
Learning difficulties RA/DYP DYS
Physical and medical conditions HL TW WA3/HEA
Age range 2½–18; *boarders from* 11
No of pupils 696; *(full boarding)* 50; *(day)* 646; *Nursery* 105; *Prep* 201; *Senior* 298; *Sixth Form* 92; *Girls* 636; *Boys* 60
Teacher:pupil ratio 1:18
Average class size 20 max
Fees per annum *(full boarding)* £17,655; *(day)* £4,860–£10,170

Burgess Hill School stands in 14 acres of beautiful grounds close to the centre of the town and is a 20-minute drive from Gatwick Airport.

The excellent facilities include a fully equipped science block, a technology laboratory, a learning resources centre, an art and design studio, a textiles centre, a music centre and a drama studio. The Sixth Form have their own centre with individual study areas, common rooms and an HE centre holding extensive careers advice.

The main aim of the school is to challenge the students to achieve goals well beyond their own expectations in all the activities they pursue. We educate for life and develop consideration for others, a love of learning, self-esteem and self-discipline. The curriculum is broad and challenging and relevant to the needs of young people. There is a wide choice of subjects both at GCSE and at A level.

There are well-appointed boarding houses adjoining the school grounds. The rooms and common rooms are spacious, light and pleasantly furnished, and the atmosphere is informal and friendly.

The school also runs a daily bus service to and from a number of outlying districts, including Turners Hill, Henfield, Cowfold, Lewes, Uckfield, Newick, East Grinstead and Worthing.

For further details please contact the Registrar.

Cottesmore School

Buchan Hill, Pease Pottage, West Sussex RH11 9AU
Tel: (01293) 520648 Fax: (01293) 614784
E-mail: schooloffice@cottesmoreschool.com
Website: www.cottesmoreschool.com www.gabbitas.net

Head Mr I J Tysoe BA
PA to Headmaster Miss J A Scola
Founded 1894
School status Co-educational boarding only
Religious denomination Church of England
Member of IAPS, ISCis
Accredited by IAPS, ISC
Learning difficulties SNU/DYP DYS
Behavioural and emotional disorders RA ST
Physical and medical conditions AT RA SM TW WA3/HEA IM
Age range 8–13
No of pupils 150; *(full boarding)* 150; *Prep* 150; *Girls* 50; *Boys* 100
Teacher:pupil ratio 1:9
Average class size 12
Fees per annum *(full boarding)* £15,900

Cottesmore is the only all-boarding co-educational prep school in England, situated one mile from Exit 11 of the M23, ten minutes from Gatwick Airport and one hour from central London and Heathrow Airport.

Curriculum Boys and girls are taught together in classes averaging 14 in number. The teacher: pupil ratio is 1:9. Children are fully prepared for Common Entrance and scholarship examinations.

Music The musical tradition is strong, with more than 80 per cent of children learning a variety of instruments; there is a chapel choir, a school orchestra, and several musical ensembles.

Drama Several plays are produced every year, with major productions open to parents.

Sport The major games are association and rugby football, cricket, hockey, netball and rounders. Numerous other sports are taught and encouraged. They include tennis, squash, golf, riding, athletics, cross-country running, swimming (facilities include a 20-metre indoor pool), windsurfing, fishing, boating, shooting, judo, archery and trampolining. The school competes at a national level in several of these sports.

A new technology centre houses an ICT suite, design technology room, two science labs and art studios.

Hobbies and activities These include pottery, photography, stamp collecting, chess, bridge, model-making, model railway, tenpin bowling, roller hockey, gardening, ballet, modern dancing, drama, craft, carpentry, printing, cooking and debating.

The boys and girls lead a full and varied life and are encouraged to take part in as wide a variety of activities as possible. With a third of the children having parents living and working abroad, weekends-in are a vital part of school life and are made busy and fun for all.

Entry requirements Entry is by Headmaster's interview and a report from the previous school. For a prospectus and more information, please write to, or telephone, the Headmaster's Personal Assistant.

Farlington School

Strood Park, Horsham, West Sussex RH12 3PN Tel: (01403) 254967 Fax: (01403) 272258
E-mail: office@farlingtonschool.net Website: www.farlingtonschool.net www.gabbitas.net

Headmistress Mrs P M Mawer **Founded** 1896
School status Girls' boarding and day. Flexi-boarding available.
Religious denomination Church of England
Member of BSA, GSA, IAPS
Learning difficulties CA RA/DYP DYS
Behavioural and emotional disorders CO/ADHD
Physical and medical conditions CA RA TW/HEA IM
Age range 4–18
No of pupils 500; *(full boarding)* 28; *(weekly boarding)* 13
Average class size 15 (fewer in Sixth Form)
Fees per annum *(full boarding)* £13,800–£16,815; *(weekly)* £13,455–£16,470; *(day)* £5,115–£10,575

Curriculum Broadly-based academic curriculum. Wide range of subjects offered at GCSE; 19 subjects at A level and AS level.

Entry requirements and procedures Our own exam and interview.

Examination results 2004 100 per cent A level pass rate; 90 per cent A to C. GCSE: 98 per cent A* to C; 66 per cent A* to A.

Academic and leisure facilities New sports hall, new library, new Sixth Form Centre, new prep building, new computer facilities. Science building with five large laboratories, and interactive white boards. All-weather pitch, outdoor heated swimming pool and student-run farm.

Scholarships Music, art, drama, PE, academic, Sixth Form.

Boarding facilities Weekly, full and flexi in small, friendly boarding house.

England

Seaford College

Lavington Park, Petworth, West Sussex GU27 0NB Tel: (01798) 867392 Fax: (01798) 867606
E-mail: seaford@clara.co.uk Website: www.seaford.org www.gabbitas.net

Head Mr T J Mullins BA **Founded** 1884
College status Co-educational boarding and day. Flexi-boarding available.
Religious denomination Church of England
Member of SHMIS
Learning difficulties SNU/DYP DYS MLD
Physical and medical conditions SL TW WA2 WA3/CP HEA W
Age range 10–18; *boarders from* 10
No of pupils 451; *(full boarding)* 45; *(weekly boarding)* 82; *(day)* 324; *Senior* 352; *Sixth Form* 99; *Girls* 141; *Boys* 310
Teacher:pupil ratio 1:9
Average class size 15–20
Fees per annum *(full boarding)* £14,760–£19,110; *(weekly)* £12,870–£16,200; *(day)* £10,050–£12,540. Flexi-boarding available for day pupils.

Seaford College was founded in 1884 and is a fully co-educational school for boarding and day pupils aged 10 to 18. Situated within 400 acres at the foot of the South Downs, the college is close to the historic town of Petworth and just seven miles from the closest railway station. Heathrow and Gatwick airports are within an hour's drive. Pupils may board weekly or full-time and a bus service collects day pupils from a wide area.

Curriculum A wide range of subjects are offered at GCSE and a wide choice of A level options are available to the large Sixth Form. Ninety six per cent of leavers go on to university.

Entry requirements and procedures Entrance to the Junior House at 10+ and 11+ is based on ability tests, taster day and reference. Entrance to the senior school at 13+ is based on similar lines, along with Common Entrance Examination results. Sixth Form entry is dependent on GCSE results and an interview. Overseas pupils must pass an English exam set by the college and past academic achievements will also be taken into account.

Academic and leisure facilities The college boasts an impressive and successful Art, Design and Technology Centre. Outstanding sports facilities include six rugby pitches, an all-weather hockey pitch of international standard and a golf course and driving range. Our staff, who have coached at international level, have helped the college gain an excellent sporting record. The hockey and rugby teams have toured South Africa, Australia, Canada and New Zealand and our pupils have played at county and national level.

Music and drama feature strongly in the life of the college. The Chapel Choir enjoys an international reputation and they have sung for Her Majesty Queen Elizabeth, the Queen Mother as well as touring internationally.

Scholarships Academic, design and technology, music (instrumental or choral), sport or art scholarships to the value of £500 are offered, but must be accompanied by a good all-round academic standard. Parents who require further discount from the fees may apply for a bursary, which will be means-tested.

Bursaries Available to Forces families and siblings.

Boarding facilities Boys aged 13 to 17 are based in Johnson Hall boarding house and day accommodation. The older boys have individual studies and the younger boys sleep in rooms of two or three. Second-year A level students are accommodated in a separate house, offering more privileges and responsibility and helping with the transition from the protection of school life to the relative freedom of university. The girls' boarding house, comprising dormitories for pre-GCSE girls, and single and twin rooms for lower sixth is located in the Mansion House. Dormitory facilities are provided in the Junior House for girls and boys aged 10 to 13.

For further information and a prospectus please contact the Admissions Secretary.

Sompting Abbotts School

Church Lane, Sompting, West Sussex BN15 0AZ Tel: (01903) 235960 Fax: (01903) 210045
E-mail: office@somptingabbotts.com Website: www.somptingabbotts.com www.gabbitas.net

Principal Mrs P M Sinclair **Founded** 1921
School status Co-educational boarding and day. Flexi-boarding available.
Religious denomination Church of England
Accredited by IAPS
Learning difficulties WI/DYC DYS
Behavioural and emotional disorders RA
Physical and medical conditions HEA HI
Age range 3–13; **Average class size** 20
No of pupils 180; *(weekly boarding)* 12; *Girls* 55; *Boys* 125
Teacher:pupil ratio 1:15/1:20
Fees per annum *(weekly)* £9,600; *(day)* £5,400–£7,200. Sibling discounts available: 1st: 8 per cent 2nd: 10 per cent 3rd: 12 per cent

Sompting Abbots School is situated on the edge of the South Downs, set in 30 acres, facing the sea with views towards Beachy Head and the Isle of Wight. The aim of the school is to provide a well-balanced education in a caring environment

whilst developing the individual needs of each child.

The school has a vibrant Pre-Preparatory department, which includes lively and stimulating Early Years classes. In the Preparatory department, a well-equipped Computer Room and Science Laboratory is enjoyed by all ages. The Art and Drama departments offer wide scope for creativity, and peripatetic teachers provide tuition for a range of musical instruments.

Weekly boarding is available for the boys from Monday morning to Friday evening and flexi-boarding is also available.

England

Windlesham House

Washington, Pulborough, West Sussex RH20 4AY Tel: (01903) 874700 Fax: (01903) 874702
E-mail: office@windlesham.com Website: www.windlesham.com www.gabbitas.net

Head Mr P Lough MA (Oxon) **Founded** 1837
School status Co-educational boarding and day
Religious denomination Church of England
Member of BSA, IAPS, ISBA, ISCis, SATIPS;
Accredited by IAPS
Learning difficulties SNU/DYC DYP DYS MLD SLD
Behavioural and emotional disorders CO RA ST/ADD
Physical and medical conditions CA IT RA SM WA3/HI
Age range 4–13; *boarders from 7*
No of pupils 255; *(full boarding)* 242; *(day)* 13; *Pre-prep* 28; *Girls* 91; *Boys* 164
Teacher:pupil ratio 1:7; **Average class size** 16
Fees per annum *(full boarding)* £15,675

Curriculum Broad curriculum enables children to discover and develop their personal strengths and talents. Strong academic record and emphasis on creative arts, drama, music and sport.

Entrance requirements No entrance examination. Flexible entrance policy.

Academic/leisure facilities Recently upgraded science labs, ICT, dorms and classrooms. Theatre/sports hall, swimming pool (indoor), gymnasium, dance/drama studio, tennis and squash courts, AstroTurf pitch, extensive playing fields and grounds (60 acres).

Boarding This is very much a family school where all children board from 8 years old. Warm, friendly, child-centred atmosphere. Individuality is respected (dress code rather than uniform) and relationships between staff and children are excellent. We produce happy, rounded and confident children. Newly upgraded dormitory areas and Medical Centre.

Pre-prep Opened September 1997 offering a wide curriculum and making use of the excellent facilities of the main school.

MAP OF SOUTH WEST ENGLAND

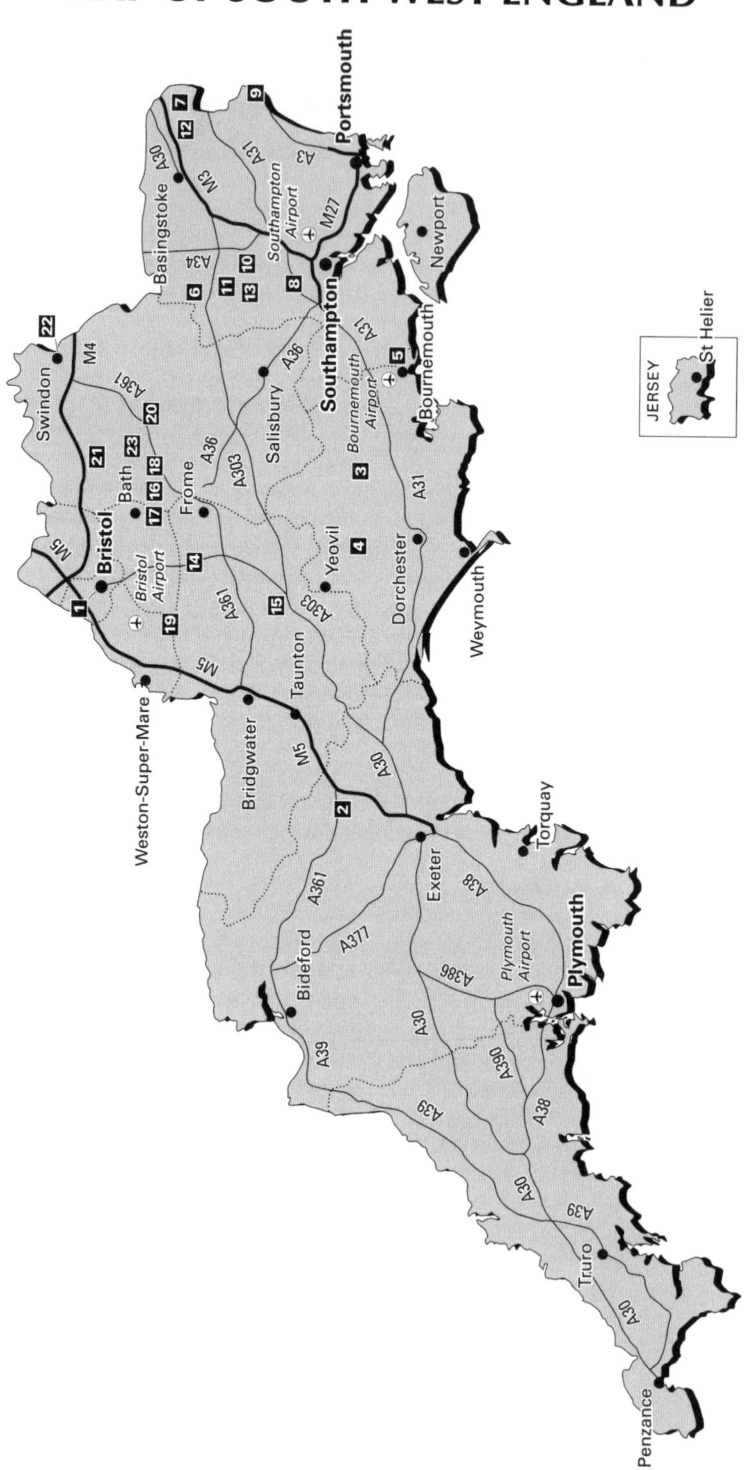

PROFILED SCHOOLS IN SOUTH WEST ENGLAND

(Incorporating the counties of Bath and North East Somerset, City of Bristol, Cornwall, Devon, Dorset, South Gloucestershire, Hampshire, Isle of Wight, Somerset, North Somerset, Wiltshire)

Map Number **Page Number**

Clifton College

32 College Road, Clifton, Bristol, Bristol BS8 3JH
Tel: (0117) 315 7000 Fax: (0117) 315 7101 E-mail: admissions@clifton-college.avon.sch.uk
Website: www.cliftoncollegeuk.com www.gabbitas.net

Headmaster Mr Mark Moore MA
Director of Admissions Mr Philip Hallworth MA MEd **Founded** 1862
College status Co-educational boarding and day. Flexi-boarding available.
Religious denomination Church of England
Member of HMC
Learning difficulties SNU/DYC DYP DYS
Behavioural and emotional disorders RA/ADD ASP
Physical and medical conditions WA3/HEA
Age range 13–18
No of pupils 653; *(full boarding)* 370; *Girls* 228; *Boys* 425
Teacher:pupil ratio 1:8; **Average class size** 20
Fees per annum *(full boarding)* £21,915; *(day)* £14,505

Clifton offers a broad and flexible curriculum with an unusually large number of subjects on offer. Entry at 13+ is by Common Entrance or ability tests. Scholarships are available at 11 (for prep school), 13 and 16 for academic, art, music, sport and all-round abilities. The school occupies a superb site in what has been described as 'the handsomest suburb in Europe'. Academic excellence, magnificent buildings and cultural facilities, a pioneering spirit and a high level of pastoral care in a caring and friendly atmosphere characterize the Clifton of today.

Blundell's School

Tiverton, Devon EX16 4DN Tel: (01884) 252543 Fax: (01884) 243232
E-mail: registrars@blundells.org Website: www.blundells.org www.gabbitas.net

Headmaster Mr I R Davenport BA
Founded 1604
School status Co-educational boarding and day. Flexi-boarding available.
Religious denomination Church of England
Member of BSA, HMC, ISCis
Accredited by HMC, ISC
Learning difficulties SNU/DYS
Behavioural and emotional disorders CO
Physical and medical conditions SM TW
Age range 11–18
No of pupils 565; *(full boarding)* 120; *(weekly boarding)* 280; *(day)* 165; *Senior* 390; *Sixth Form* 175; *Girls* 230; *Boys* 335
Teacher:pupil ratio 1:11; **Average class size** 14
Fees per annum *(full boarding)* £13,755–£20,475; *(weekly)* £12,435–£17,940; *(day)* £8,220–£13,200

Blundell's School, founded in 1604, remains Devon's oldest and most significant educational establishment. The 1990s saw an exciting period of renewal, with the introduction of co-education, a new 11–13 department (130 pupils) and the recent incorporation of St Aubyn's Preparatory School. Blundell's is, and should be viewed as being, an entire education. Having just celebrated its quatercentenary in 2004 Blundell's confirms its position as a premier West Country school accessing the wider world. Examinations show 75 per cent A/Bs at A level and traditional strengths at sports, music and drama.

Clayesmore School

Iwerne Minster, Blandford Forum, Dorset DT11 8LL Tel: (01747) 812122 Fax: (01747) 811343
E-mail: hmsec@clayesmore.com Website: www.clayesmore.com

Headmaster Mr M G Cooke BEd (Hons) FCollP
School status Co-educational independent boarding and day. Senior School, Prep School, Pre-Prep and Nursery for children aged 2½–18.
Religious denomination Church of England
Member of CReSTeD, HMC, IAPS, ISCis, SATIPS, SHMIS
Accredited by HMC, IAPS, SHMIS
Learning difficulties SNU/DYC DYS
Physical and medical conditions AT RA SM/HEA
Age range 2½–18; *boarders from* 8
No of pupils 376; *(full boarding)* 218; *(day)* 158; *Nursery* 15; *Pre-prep* 32; *Prep* 218; *Sixth Form* 111; *Girls* 135; *Boys* 241
Teacher:pupil ratio 1:10; **Av. class size** 18–20
Fees per annum *(full boarding)* £20,745; *(day)* £15,180

The abiding aim of Clayesmore School is to discover and develop the unique gifts of every girl and boy. Clayesmore is a small and closely knit community that is proud to be a truly family orientated school in which pupils have the space and freedom to grow in confidence and achieve the highest standards possible. The school has expanded significantly in recent years with major investment in academic buildings and facilities for the science, IT and humanities departments. Located in 62 acres of glorious parkland, Clayesmore is a vibrant, thriving boarding and day school full of creative, energetic and highly talented individuals. The aim is to harness these talents and motivate all our pupils to reach further, to gain valuable experience and achieve more success than they ever imagined possible.

International College, Sherborne School

Newell Grange, Sherborne, Dorset DT9 4EZ
Tel: (01935) 814743 Fax: (01935) 816863 E-mail: reception@sherborne-ic.net
Website: www.sherborne-ic.net www.gabbitas.net

Principal Dr C J Greenfield
Founded 1977
College status Co-educational boarding only
Member of BSA, COBISEC, ISA
Accredited by ISA
Physical and medical conditions SM TW WA2
Age range 11–17
No of pupils 130; *(full boarding)* 130; *Girls* 50; *Boys* 80
Teacher:pupil ratio 1:3
Average class size 6 students
Fees per annum *(full boarding)* £24,810–£27,060

The International College is unique. It was established in 1977 (as the International Study Centre) to prepare boys – and later girls – from non-British educational backgrounds so that they could function successfully in traditional British boarding schools. Typically these boys and girls spend one year at the International College before moving on to a traditional British boarding school where the majority of students are British. Those students who join in Year 10 (usually around 14 or 15 years old) and start a two-year course leading towards GCSE examinations must stay at the school for the duration of the course.

The college has three major aims:

- concentrated improvement in spoken and written English;
- academic preparation in English in the full range of curriculum subjects;
- a good introduction to British educational procedures and the British way of life.

The arrangements of the college are designed to achieve these tasks. Classes are small, usually between six and eight students to each teacher. All teachers are not only experienced specialists in their own subject, but also have additional training in teaching the English language.

Characteristics The teaching facilities at the International College include modern classrooms, eight science laboratories, a computer centre and a library with internet access. The college uses the extensive sporting, musical and theatre facilities at Sherborne School including a 25-metre indoor swimming pool. A new teaching building, containing 17 classrooms, was opened in September 2005.

The International College has gained an unrivalled reputation for providing the very best start to British independent education for children from overseas. Through a carefully supervised programme of study, students gain a sound working knowledge of the main British curriculum subjects such as mathematics, the sciences and humanities. The college has high standards of discipline and pastoral care. Most weekends there is a busy programme that ensures students are fully occupied on Saturday and Sunday.

Wentworth College

College Road, Bournemouth, Dorset BH5 2DY
Tel: (01202) 423266 Fax: (01202) 418030 E-mail: enquiries@wentworthcollege.com
Website: www.wentworthcollege.com www.gabbitas.net

Headmistress Miss S Coe BA Hons PGCE FRGS
Founded 1871
College status Girls' boarding and day. Flexi-boarding available.
Religious denomination Inter-denominational
Member of GSA; **Accredited by** GSA, ISC
Learning difficulties SNU/DYC DYP DYS
Behavioural and emotional disorders ADD ASP
Physical and medical conditions AT RA WA3/CP HEA
Age range 11–18; *boarders from* 11
No of pupils 220; *(full boarding)* 40; *(weekly boarding)* 20
Fees per annum *(full boarding)* £15,570; *(weekly)* £15,570; *(day)* £9,675

Wentworth College provides a stimulating and caring environment with committed teachers who respond to the needs of every girl, helping her to reach her full potential. We aim to develop happy, confident young women who are proud of their academic success and personal achievement, and who leave equipped for adult life.

Situated in beautiful grounds on a cliff top just 200 metres from Bournemouth's award-winning beaches and close to the New Forest, the school offers well-equipped teaching and excellent sports facilities. We have a dedicated Sixth Form study centre and offer numerous extra-curricular activities.

Farleigh School

Red Rice, Andover, Hampshire SP11 7PW
Tel: (01264) 710766 Fax: (01264) 710070 E-mail: office@farleighschool.co.uk
Website: www.farleighschool.com www.gabbitas.net

Head Father Simon Everson
Founded 1953
School status Co-educational independent boarding and day. Flexi-boarding available.
Religious denomination Roman Catholic
Member of BSA, IAPS, ISCis
Accredited by IAPS
Age range 3–13; *boarders from 7*
No of pupils 393; *(boarding)* 115; *Girls* 160; *Boys* 233
Fees per annum *(full boarding)* £16,155; *(weekly)* £16,155; *(day)* £3,360–£12,225

Farleigh School is a leading co-educational IAPS Catholic boarding and day Prep School of 400 children, aged 3 to 13 years.

Boarding and day pupils alike benefit from excellent pastoral care in a happy atmosphere, supported by a large number of resident staff. The school's Catholic ethos is given visible expression

by the Headmaster, who is also the resident Chaplain. Farleigh warmly welcomes children of other faiths.

The school has an excellent academic and sporting reputation, each year sending pupils to all the major senior schools via Common Entrance and 13+ scholarships. Up-to-date facilities include a new 22-metre heated indoor swimming pool, a spacious art and design technology building, a theatre, science laboratories, sports hall, well-equipped music department and state-of-the-art IT suites.

A wide range of clubs and activities are arranged after school and at weekends, giving students a full and varied life. A resident catering team provide healthy homemade food.

Farnborough Hill

Farnborough, Hampshire GU14 8AT Tel: (01252) 545197 Fax: (01252) 513037
E-mail: devdir@farnborough-hill.org.uk Website: www.farnborough-hill.org.uk

Headmistress Miss J Thomas MA PGCE
Development Director Mrs C Duffin BA MCIM
Founded 1889
School status Girls' independent day only
Religious denomination Roman Catholic
Member of AGBIS, GSA, ISCis
Accredited by GSA, ISC
Learning difficulties SNU/DYC DYP DYS
Behavioural and emotional disorders CO/ADD ADHD
Physical and medical conditions RA SM/EPI HEA HI
Age range 11–18
No of pupils 505
Teacher:pupil ratio 1:10; **Average class size** 22
Fees per annum *(day)* £8,280

Farnborough Hill is housed in the historic home of the Empress Eugenie. Facilities include a chapel, sports hall, gymnasium, indoor swimming pool, laboratories, technology workshops, and

extensive playing fields. The school is committed to the education of the whole person in a caring, Christian environment. Academic standards are high: GCSE and A level pass rates are always close to 100 per cent. Among the many extra-curricular activities there is particular emphasis on sport and the creative arts. Entry is by examination taken in January for the following September. The school offers bursaries and academic, sporting and musical scholarships. Excellent transport links and school coaches bring pupils from Hampshire, Berkshire and Surrey.

Hampshire Collegiate School, Embley Park

Embley Park, Romsey, Hampshire SO51 6ZE Tel: (01794) 512206 Fax: (01794) 518737
E-mail: info@hampshirecs.org.uk Website: www.hampshirecs.org.uk www.embleypark.org.uk

Principal Mr D F Chapman BA (Dunelm)
Founded 1946
School status Co-educational independent boarding and day. Flexi-boarding available.
Religious denomination Church of England
Member of AGBIS, BSA, IAPS, SHA, SHMIS
Learning difficulties SNU/DYP DYS
Behavioural & emotional disorders RA/ADD ADHD
Physical & medical conditions SM WA2/HEA W
Age range 3–18; *boarders from* 11
No of pupils 480; *(full boarding)* 30; *(weekly boarding)* 46; *Girls* 180; *Boys* 300
Teacher:pupil ratio 1:<20; (classes) 1:15
Average class size 18
Fees per annum *(full boarding)* £8,310–£16,620; *(weekly)* £8,310–£16,620; *(day)* £5,000–£10,005

HCS Embley Park has a wide ability range (100+ IQ), with some very bright, and some more average, pupils. Although its league table position has been enhanced greatly in past years, it has no further plans to become more selective and uses the yardstick of Cognitive Ability Tests at point of entry to evaluate its 'value-added' (average 155 per cent GCSE 2003–2005; that is, the average candidate performed 55 per cent above his or her potential). In 2005 the GCSE pass rate A*–C was 96 per cent and at A level 100 per cent, while 90 per cent of the Upper Sixth went on to university degree courses. In September 2006, HCS Embley Park and HCS Atherley will join at Embley and £13.75 million is to be spent on new facilities by that date.

Highfield School

Highfield Lane, Liphook, Hampshire GU30 7LQ
Tel: (01428) 728000 Fax: (01428) 728001
E-mail: office@highfieldschool.org.uk
Website: www.highfieldschool.org.uk www.gabbitas.net

Headmaster Mr P G S Evitt MA
Founded 1907
School status Co-educational boarding and day
Religious denomination Church of England
Member of IAPS, ISCis, NAHT
Accredited by IAPS, ISC
Learning difficulties CA SNU/DYP DYS
Physical and medical conditions RA SM/HEA
Age range 8–13
No of pupils 235; *(full boarding)* 79; *Girls* 113; *Boys* 122
Teacher:pupil ratio 1:9
Average class size 16
Fees per annum *(full boarding)* £14,100–£16,050; *(day)* £10,800–£14,100

Highfield is a co-educational day and boarding school founded in 1907 and set in 175 acres of superb grounds on the Hampshire/Sussex border. Highfield children are prepared for Common Entrance and scholarships to all the major senior schools. The broad curriculum includes ICT, PE and DT and the school's excellent tradition in music, drama and art is reflected in the number of scholarships gained recently. The school has built new facilities for Science, Maths, English and ICT. All the major sports are offered and over 50 activities take place in the evenings, lunchtimes and at weekends.

The Pilgrims' School

3 The Close, Winchester, Hampshire SO23 9LT
Tel: (01962) 854189 Fax: (01962) 843610 E-mail: info@pilgrims-school.co.uk
Website: www.pilgrims-school.co.uk www.gabbitas.net

Headmaster Dr B A Rees BA BD DipMin Phd
Founded 1931
School status Boys' prep boarding and day
Religious denomination Church of England
Member of IAPS
Learning difficulties WI/DYP DYS
Age range 7–13
No of pupils 203; *(full boarding)* 40; *(weekly boarding)* 25; *(day)* 138
Average class size 15
Fees per annum *(full boarding)* £14,790; *(day)* £11,790

Boys' selective preparatory school (IAPS) for weekly/full boarders and day boys, incorporating the Choristers of Winchester Cathedral and the Quiristers of Winchester College who attend the school with choral scholarships to the value of half the boarding fee. High academic standards and an enviable scholarship record are hallmarks of the school. There are excellent facilities for music, sport and academic study, with exceptional staff:pupil ratio and pastoral structure. The school is situated in beautiful buildings in the Cathedral Close with adjacent playing fields, and benefits additionally from the sporting and recreational facilities of Winchester College. For further information, please apply to the Headmaster.

England

Rookwood School

Weyhill Road, Andover, Hampshire SP10 3AL Tel: (01264) 325900 Fax: (01264) 325909
E-mail: office@rookwood.hants.sch.uk Website: www.rookwood.hants.sch.uk www.gabbitas.net

Headmistress Mrs M P Langley BSc (Hons)
Founded 1934
School status Co-educational independent boarding and day. Flexi-boarding available.
Religious denomination Non-denominational
Member of BSA, ISA, ISCis, SHA
Accredited by ISA
Learning difficulties CA WI/DYP DYS
Behavioural & emotional disorders RA/ADHD ASP
Physical & medical conditions CA RA/HEA HI
Age range 3–16; *boarders from* 8
No of pupils 307; *(full boarding)* 26; *(day)* 281; *Nursery* 25; *Pre-prep* 48; *Prep* 128; *Senior* 106; *Girls* 187; *Boys* 120; **Ave class size** 14
Fees per annum *(full boarding)* £14,040–£16,479; *(day)* £5,625–£9,240

Rookwood School offers an excellent education for children from Nursery to GCSE.

Both the co-educational Nursery and Pre-Preparatory School and the Preparatory School are housed in purpose-built quarters on the main school site. The disciplined and happy environment encourages all the children to give of their personal best. We prepare pupils for the Common Entrance examination.

The school is non-selective, yet the Senior School's excellent GCSE results (100 per cent gained at least 7 A* to C grades in 2005) are testament to the high academic standards achieved in small classes.

A wide range of sports and extra-curricular activities cater for all abilities and interests.

Pupils working hard and playing hard are evident everywhere, including at the small boarding houses with their unique family atmosphere and excellent programme of weekend activities.

St Nicholas' School

Redfields House, Redfields Lane, Church Crookham, Fleet, Hampshire GU52 0RF
Tel: (01252) 850121 Fax: (01252) 850718 E-mail: registrar@st-nicholas.hants.sch.uk
Website: www.st-nicholas.hants.sch.uk www.gabbitas.net

Headmistress Mrs A V Whatmough BA(Hons) Cert Ed
Founded 1935
School status Co-educational independent day only
Religious denomination Church of England
Age range Boys 3–7; Girls 3–16
No of pupils 370; *Girls* 350; *Boys* 20
Fees per annum *(day)* £3,150–£8,520

At St Nicholas' School we believe that the best education is a partnership between teachers, pupils and parents. By creating a supportive environment, the personal and academic potential of each pupil can be developed. Classes are small and facilities are excellent. The personal and academic progress of each individual is monitored carefully and should any help be needed, it is available. The secure base laid at St Nicholas' gives students a wide range of choice for the next stage of their education. The fact that they are welcome wherever they go is a tribute to the work of the school.

Winchester College

College Street, Winchester, Hampshire SO23 9NA
Tel: (01962) 621247 Fax: (01962) 621106
E-mail: admissions@winchestercollege.co.uk
Website: www.winchestercollege.org www.gabbitas.net

Headmaster Dr R D Townsend MA DPhil
Registrar Dr A P Wolters BSc PhD CChem MRSC
Bursar Mr J E Hynam MPhil BEd ACP
Founded 1382
College status Boys' independent boarding and day
Religious denomination Church of England
Member of AGBIS, HMC, ISCis, SHA
Learning difficulties DYS
Age range 13–18
No of pupils 689; *(full boarding)* 667; *(day)* 22; *Boys* 689
Teacher:pupil ratio 1:8
Fees per annum *(full boarding)* £23,500; *(day)* £22,325

Winchester College is a boarding school for boys aged 13–18. It was founded in 1382 by William of Wykeham, Bishop of Winchester and Chancellor to Richard II, and has the longest unbroken history of any school in the country. Its setting is one of unrivalled beauty and spaciousness.

Winchester enjoys an international reputation for its outstanding academic record. This can be seen not just in its excellent examination results but also in the quality of the intellectual training it provides. Nearly all of it pupils go on to good universities and about 45 each year win places at Oxford or Cambridge.

The high academic standards are matched by similar achievements in music, art, drama and a wide range of sporting activities. The school has extensive playing fields and generous provision for pupils to develop their cultural and athletic interests.

There are about 700 boys in the school, most of whom are boarders, but day boys are accepted.

Generous academic and music awards are offered annually to boys entering the school at age 13 and 16. Financial help with the fees is available to all candidates on a means-tested basis.

13+ academic scholarships and exhibitions The examination of candidates for scholarships and exhibitions is held at the college in early May; about 15 scholarships and about 6 exhibitions are offered. Scholarships have a basic value of 25 per cent of the full fee. Exhibitions are also awarded on the same exam. Candidates must be under 14 and at least 12 on 1 September in the year in which they sit the exam. Entry forms, which must be returned by April, are available from the Master in College, Winchester College, College Street, Winchester SO23 9NA.

Sixth Form academic awards The entrance examination for both awards and places takes place at the college early in the Spring term. Up to four scholarships with a maximum value of 25 per cent of the full fee are offered. Entry forms, which must be returned by mid-November the previous year, are obtainable from the Registrar (address as above).

Details of music awards can also be obtained from Winchester College Music School, Culver Road, Winchester SO23 9JF; Tel: (01962) 621122.

Downside School

Stratton-on-the-Fosse, Radstock, Bath, Somerset BA3 4RJ
Tel: (01761) 235100 Fax: (01761) 235105 E-mail: registrar@downside.co.uk
Website: www.downside.co.uk www.gabbitas.net
For a prospectus and admissions information please contact the registrar on (01761) 235103

Headmaster Dom Leo Maidlow Davis MA BD STL
Founded 1604
School status Co-educational independent boarding and day
Religious denomination Roman Catholic
Member of HMC, ISCis
Learning difficulties SNU/DYS
Age range 9–18
No of pupils 427; *(full boarding)* 229; *(day)* 98; *Prep* 86; *Senior* 239; *Sixth Form* 102; *Girls* 60; *Boys* 367
Average class size 20
Fees per annum *(full boarding)* £15,558–£19,590; *(day)* £9,192–£10,224

Downside is undergoing major redevelopment as it establishes itself as a leading Catholic fully co-educational boarding and day school from 2005. The school offers a demanding but balanced academic education to GCSE and A level, with many pupils going on to leading universities. Entry is at 9+, 11+, 13+ or 16+ but can be at other stages depending upon assessment, report and interview. Day pupils benefit from the many opportunities available in a busy boarding school, while having the flexibility to return home after classes or after prep.

Downside has a strong sporting and musical tradition. Facilities include a theatre, recently upgraded ICT facilities, design, art and ceramics centres, sports hall and indoor pool. Flagship developments for co-education include a performing arts complex and a Learning Resource Centre.

Scholarships and bursaries are also available.

King's Bruton

Bruton, Somerset BA10 0ED Tel: (01749) 814200 Fax: (01749) 813426
E-mail: registrar@kingsbruton.com Website: www.kingsbruton.com www.gabbitas.net

Headmaster Mr N M Lashbrook BA
Founded 1519
School status Co-educational independent boarding and day
Religious denomination Church of England
Member of CReSTeD, HMC, ISCis
Accredited by HMC
Learning difficulties SNU/DYC DYP DYS
Behavioural and emotional disorders ADD ADHD ASP
Physical and medical conditions EPI HEA HI VI
Age range 13–18
No of pupils 333; *(full boarding)* 248; *(day)* 85; *Senior* 187; *Sixth Form* 146; *Girls* 90; *Boys* 243
Teacher:pupil ratio 1:8; **Average class size** 15
Fees per annum *(full boarding)* £20,100; *(day)* £14,730

The King's Senior School is situated in the small Somerset town of Bruton. Founded in the early 16th century, the school combines historic buildings with more recent development. The Preparatory School lies in 220 acres of parkland at Sparkford, 8 miles away. Both schools foster a close community within which all members are given the opportunity to achieve their academic, spiritual, social, aesthetic and physical potential. The schools have a lively, purposeful and friendly atmosphere where everyone is able to flourish within a supportive and disciplined framework.

Kingswood School

Lansdown, Bath, Bath & North East Somerset BA1 5RG Tel: (01225) 734210 Fax: (01225) 734305
E-mail: enquiries@kingswood.bath.sch.uk Web: www.kingswood.bath.sch.uk www.gabbitas.net

Head Mr G M Best MA **Founded** 1748
School status Co-educational boarding and day. Flexi-boarding available.
Religious denomination Methodist
Member of BSA
Accredited by British Council, HMC, IAPS, ISC
Learning difficulties WI/DYC DYP DYS
Behavioural & emotional disorders ADHD ASP
Physical & medical conditions RA/HEA HI
Age range 11–18; **Teacher:pupil ratio** 1:9
No of pupils 636; *(full boarding)* 138; *(weekly boarding)* 39; *(day)* 459; *Nursery* 40; *Pre-prep* 36; *Prep* 97; *Senior* 282; *Sixth Form* 181; *Girls* 286; *Boys* 350
Average class size 22 (Senior School)
Fees per annum *(full boarding)* £16,374–£19,611; *(weekly)* £14,304–£17,721; *(day)* £8,754

Making a smooth transition from primary to secondary education is something Kingswood School

takes very seriously and it therefore provides a special Junior House so that pupils easily adapt to the new routines. At HMC Inspection the school was judged to provide 'exceptional pastoral care'.

The boarding and day pupils are integrated throughout all ages and both benefit from the opportunity of learning alongside children of different nationalities and cultures. The school has a significant number of boarding pupils from HM Forces families and is experienced at looking after the needs of these particular children.

While attaining high academic standards, Kingswood has a range of superb facilities in science and technology, sport, music and the arts. Over 70 different extracurricular activities are offered, in addition to weekend entertainment for boarders.

England

Prior Park College

Ralph Allen Drive, Bath, Bath & North East Somerset BA2 5AH
Tel: (01225) 831000 Fax: (01225) 835753 E-mail: admissions@priorpark.co.uk
Website: www.priorpark.co.uk www.gabbitas.net

Headmaster Dr G Mercer
Founded 1831
College status Co-educational boarding and day. Flexi-boarding available.
Religious denomination Inter-denominational, Roman Catholic
Member of CIS, HMC, ISCis
Accredited by CIS, HMC
Learning difficulties RA/DYP DYS
Physical and medical conditions WA3/VI
Age range 11–18; *boarders from* 13
No of pupils 550; *(full boarding)* 124; *Girls* 250; *Boys* 300
Teacher:pupil ratio 1:9; **Average class size** 20
Fees per annum *(full boarding)* £19,068; *(day)* £9,492–£10,575

Prior Park is a friendly, well-established co-educational, Christian community encouraging academic confidence and all-round success. The

wonderful setting of Prior Park lends itself to the encouragement of artistic and creative talent. The outstanding performances of our pupils in our 22 music, drama and dance productions have earned the college an enviable reputation. The Combined Cadet Force, Duke of Edinburgh's Award scheme and Prior Concern, our own community service programme, sporting excellence and sport for all offer further opportunities.

The Royal High School

Girls' Day School Trust

Lansdown Road, Bath, Bath & North East Somerset BA1 5SZ
Tel: (01225) 313877 Fax: (01225) 465446
E-mail: royalhigh@bat.gdst.net Website: www.gdst.net/royalhighbath www.gabbitas.net

Headmaster Mr J Graham-Brown BA (Hons) M.Phil.
Head of Junior School Mrs Helen Fathers BA (Hons)
School status Girls' independent boarding and day. Flexi-boarding available. GDST school.
Religious denomination Non-denominational
Member of GDST, GSA
Learning difficulties DYP DYS
Age range 3–18; *boarders from* 11
No of pupils 858; *(full boarding)* 98
Average class size 22
Fees per annum *(full boarding)* £14,442; *(day)* £4,410–£7,365

As one of the 25 Girls' Day School Trust schools, we belong to an organization that is renowned for providing high-quality all-round education at an affordable cost to girls of academic promise. We are unique among Trust schools in offering the enriching experience of boarding, giving parents more flexibility as circumstances and preferences change. Recent developments include fully refurbished boarding accommodation, and a new sports hall, science laboratories and ICT suites. We are proud of our strong academic tradition and our girls' achievements.

Sidcot School

Oakridge Lane, Winscombe, North Somerset BS25 1PD
Tel: (01934) 843102 Fax: (01934) 844181 E-mail: admissions@sidcot.org.uk
Website: www.sidcot.org.uk www.gabbitas.net

Head Mr J Walmsley BSc **Founded** 1699
School status Co-educational independent boarding and day. Flexi-boarding available.
Religious denomination Quaker
Member of BSA, CReSTeD, ISA, ISBA, ISCis, SHA, SHMIS; **Accredited by** British Council
Learning difficulties CA SNU/DYS
Behavioural and emotional disorders RA/ADD ADHD ASP BESD CB
Physical and medical conditions SM TW WA2/EPI HEA
Age range 3–18
No of pupils 500; *(full boarding)* 117; *(weekly boarding)* 29; *(day)* 354; *Nursery* 34; *Pre-prep* 66; *Prep* 50; *Senior* 232; *Sixth Form* 118; *Girls* 221; *Boys* 279
Teacher:pupil ratio 1:15; **Average class size** 15
Fees per annum *(full boarding)* £14,550–£21,600; *(weekly)* £16,050; *(day)* £3,750–£9,990

Sidcot School is a thriving independent co-educational day and boarding school situated in 150 acres of beautiful countryside.

Sidcot offers a blend of excellent traditional and state-of-the-art facilities. It is well equipped with academic facilities, a new learning resource and Sixth Form centre, excellent computer facilities, sports hall complex with heated swimming pool, extensive playing fields and a riding centre.

Our Quaker philosophy means that we value all children whatever their abilities. Our students gain excellent exam results but also develop as caring and confident individuals. Happy children learn, and small classes and good working relationships between staff and students make for a positive and inclusive atmosphere.

Academic, music, sports and Sixth Form scholarships are available. Quaker bursaries are available for members of the Society of Friends. We welcome pupils of all faiths or none.

England

Dauntsey's School

High Street, West Lavington, Devizes, Wiltshire SN10 4HE
Tel: (01380) 814500 Fax: (01380) 814501
E-mail: information@dauntseys.wilts.sch.uk Website: www.dauntseys.wilts.sch.uk

Head Mr S B Roberts MA **Founded** 1542
School status Co-educational boarding and day
Religious denomination Inter-denominational
Member of BSA, HMC
Learning difficulties WI/DYS
Behavioural and emotional disorders CO
Physical and medical conditions SL SM TW WA1/W
Age range 11–18
No of pupils 747; *(full boarding)* 275; *(day)* 472; *Sixth Form* 246; *Girls* 351; *Boys* 396
Teacher:pupil ratio 1:9
Average class size Maximum of 20 up to GCSE, 8–12 in Sixth Form
Fees per annum *(full boarding)* £20,160; *(day)* £11,940

Dauntsey's is a very happy and successful co-educational independent school. Excellent facilities are available for academic work, music, drama, art and sport. There are several new buildings: a new five-studio art school, a new library and IT suite, a major science development and a brand new senior girls' boarding house.

Outward-bound activities flourish and include a very active sailing club, which sails the famous Jolie Brise (winner of the Tall Ships' Race in both 2000 and 2002).

There is an emphasis on pastoral care and Christian values, though worship is not narrowly denominational. There is a flexible system of exeats for boarders.

Careers advice is thorough and there is a programme of work experience. Virtually all the pupils go on to university and each year several go to Oxbridge.

Visitors are always welcome. Please contact the Registrar for a prospectus and details of the entry procedure.

Grittleton House School

Grittleton, Chippenham, Wiltshire SN14 6AP Tel: (01249) 782434 Fax: (01249) 782669
E-mail: secretary@grittletonhouseschool.org Website: www.grittletonhouseschool.org

Head Mrs C Whitney **Founded** 1951
School status Co-educational independent day
Religious denomination Non-denominational
Learning difficulties WI/DYS
Age range 2–16
No of pupils 291; *Nursery* 18; *Pre-prep* 56; *Prep* 73; *Senior* 144; *Girls* 137; *Boys* 154
Teacher:pupil ratio 1:14; **Average class size** 15
Fees per annum *(day)* £4,620–£7,455

Grittleton House School was founded more than fifty years ago, and for the last 36 years has occupied its present premises, an impressive Victorian manor house which has been sympathetically converted to provide for all the needs of pupils from Nursery school to GCSE.

The Nursery and Infant occupy their own specialized area; older children benefit by being able to use the science labs, the ICT suite, specialist art, HE and music rooms, the heated swimming pool, and the excellent studio theatre.

Grittleton House staff provide specialist teaching and the curriculum is broad and varied; all pupils are encouraged to reach the highest goals. Pupils may choose from a large variety of subjects offered in addition to the core at GCSE level and Grittleton House is consistently at the top of the league tables for this area.

The school offers 'Twilight Club' for those who need to stay for a light tea. Here they can quietly do their homework, supervised by a member of staff, or join in the many after-school activities which vary each term. Many children also take piano, woodwind, string or guitar lessons and the Grittleton House rock group, Long Way Down, has played to enthusiastic audiences!

Pinewood School

Bourton, Shrivenham, Wiltshire SN6 8HZ Tel: (01793) 782205 Fax: (01793) 783476
E-mail: office@pinewoodschool.co.uk Website: www.pinewood.oxon.sch.uk www.gabbitas.net

Head Mr P J Hoyland **Founded** 1875
School status Co-educational independent boarding and day. Flexi-boarding available.
Religious denomination Church of England
Member of IAPS; **Accredited by** IAPS
Learning difficulties SNU/DYP DYS MLD
Behavioural and emotional disorders RA
Physical and medical conditions WA3
Age range 3–13
No of pupils 296; *(weekly boarding)* 30; *(day)* 266; *Nursery* 22; *Pre-prep* 73; *Prep* 201; *Girls* 149; *Boys* 147
Fees per annum *(full boarding)* £14,310; *(weekly)* £13,800; *(day)* £5,775–£11,070

Pinewood offers a quality, family-based, co-educational environment where children are encouraged to think for themselves and a strong emphasis is placed on self-reliance, manners, trust and a regard for others. Resources include a purpose-built Music School and Junior Forms' wing, a flourishing Pre-prep and Nursery, art and design workshops, research and reference library and ICT rooms. Excellent academic results are achieved through a mixture of traditional and forward-thinking. Outside trips are frequent and visiting speakers prominent. Music and drama are encouraged. Sport is keenly coached, and matches are played at all levels on our picturesque playing fields, which incorporate a nine-hole golf course. There is a wide range of activities and clubs both for day-children and, in the evenings, for boarders.

Stonar School

Cottles Park, Atworth, Melksham, Wiltshire SN12 8NT Tel: (01225) 701740 Fax: (01225) 790830
E-mail: admissions@stonarschool.com Website: www.stonarschool.com www.gabbitas.net

Head Mrs S Shayler **Founded** 1895
School status Girls' boarding and day. Flexi-boarding available.
Religious denomination Inter-denominational
Member of BSA, GSA, ISCis, SHA
Accredited by GSA, ISC
Learning difficulties CA WI/DYP DYS MLD
Behavioural and emotional disorders CA CO
Physical and medical conditions AT CA RA SM/EPI HEA VI
Age range 2–18; *boarders from* 8
No of pupils 418; *(full boarding)* 190; *(weekly boarding)* 18; *(day)* 210; *Nursery* 45; *Pre-prep* 28; *Prep* 64; *Senior* 217; *Sixth Form* 64; *Girls* 401; *Boys* 17
Teacher:pupil ratio 1:9; **Average class size** 14
Fees per annum *(full boarding)* £14,250–£16,650; *(weekly)* £14,250–£16,650; *(day)* £4,800–£9,375

Stonar School is set in over 80 acres of parkland within easy reach of the city of Bath.

The emphasis is on challenging and developing the individual with high expectations for achievement across the board.

Facilities are excellent and modern with an on-site equestrian centre, swimming pool, theatre, sports hall and AstroTurf as well as a purpose-built music suite and art studio.

The school has a highly qualified, talented and dedicated staff who also offer a wide range of extra-curricular activities. The Duke of Edinburgh's Award scheme and trips run by the geography department to exotic locations such as Ecuador are also on offer.

There is a thriving Sixth Form with modern accommodation encouraging a degree of independence as an excellent preparation for life beyond school.

3.2 Scotland

MAP OF SCOTLAND

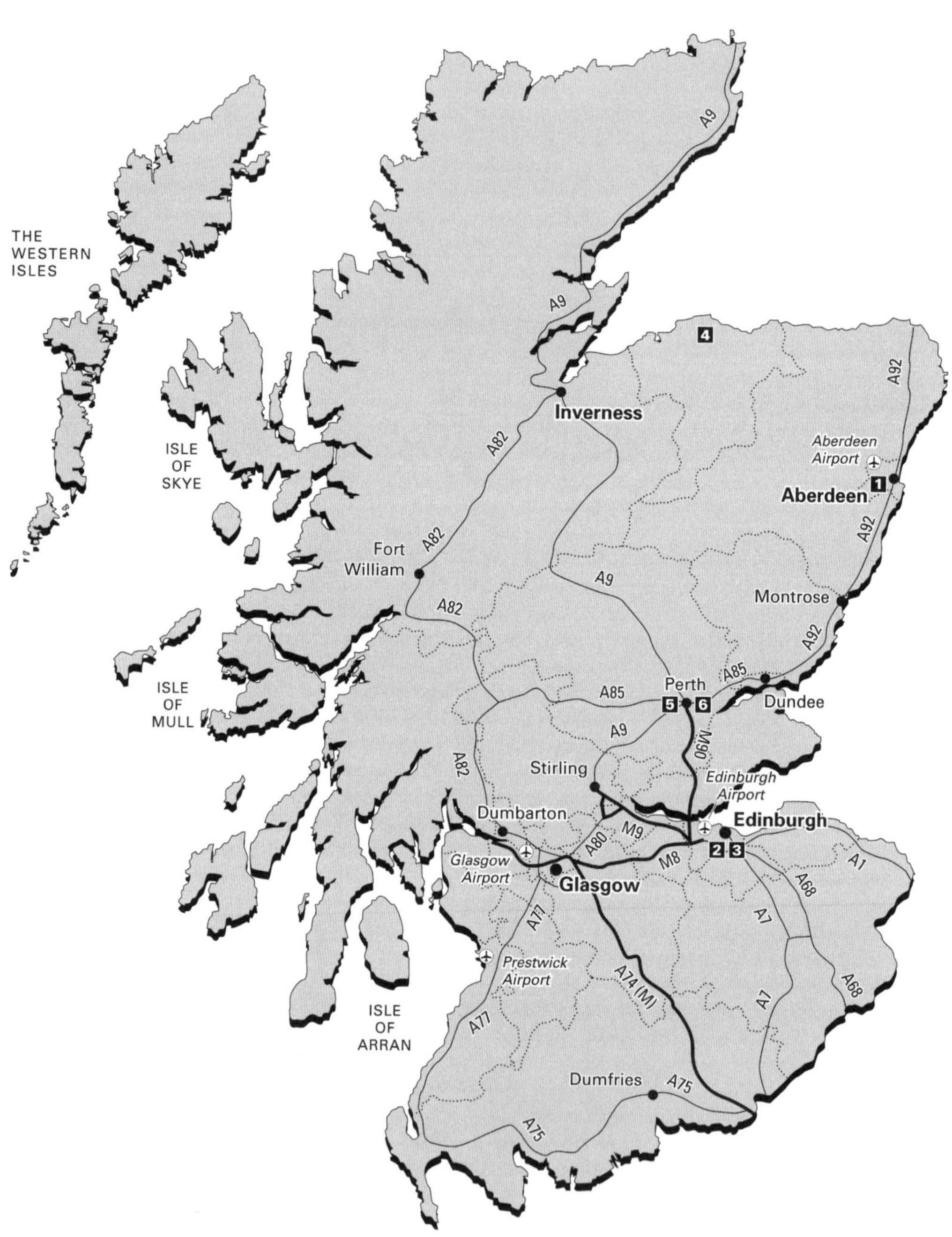

PROFILED SCHOOLS IN SCOTLAND

(Incorporating the counties of Aberdeen City, Aberdeenshire, Angus, Argyll and Bute, East Ayrshire, North Ayrshire, South Ayrshire, Borders, City of Edinburgh, Dumfries and Galloway, East Dunbartonshire, West Dunbartonshire, Falkirk, Fife, Highland, Inverclyde, East Lothian, Midlothian, Moray, Perth and Kinross, Renfrewshire, Stirling, South Lanarkshire, West Lothian)

Albyn School

17–23 Queens Road, Aberdeen, Aberdeenshire AB15 4PB
Tel: (01224) 322408 Fax: (01224) 209173 E-mail: information@albynschool.co.uk
Website: www.albynschool.co.uk www.gabbitas.net

Headmaster Dr JD Halliday BA PhD
Founded 1867
School status Co-educational independent day only. Co-educational nurseries for children aged 12 weeks to 5 years.
Religious denomination Non-denominational
Member of GSA, HAS, ISBA, SCIS, SHA
Learning difficulties SNU/DYP DYS
Physical and medical conditions CA IT RA TW/EPI HEA HI
Age range Boys 2–10; Girls 2–18
No of pupils 410; *Nursery* 80; *Pre-prep* 60; *Prep* 100; *Senior* 105; *Sixth Form* 65; *Girls* 350; *Boys* 60
Teacher:pupil ratio 1:8; **Average class size** 15
Fees per annum *(day)* £4,900–£7,900

Albyn School is characterized by small classes, high academic standards and a very friendly, supportive environment. We also believe in the key role of extra-curricular activities. Each individual pupil is nurtured in a happy, caring, and purposeful environment. Consequently, our academic results are always among the very best in Scotland and 95 per cent of girls go on to Higher Education. Music, art and design, French, ICT and PE are taught in primary by secondary specialists. Recently we have invested in a new baby and toddler nursery, an ICT suite, a Business Education Centre, two science labs and a geography room. After 140 years as a girls' school we are going co-educational, with boys enrolled up to Year 6 in 2006.

Basil Paterson College

66 Queen Street, Edinburgh, Lothian EH2 4NA Tel: (0131) 225 3802 Fax: (0131) 226 6701
E-mail: info@basilpaterson.co.uk Website: www.basilpaterson.co.uk www.gabbitas.net

Principal Mr C Smith MA(Hons), PGCE
Founded 1929
College status Co-educational boarding and day. Basil Paterson College offers full- and part-time tuition. It is also an EFL College.
Religious denomination Inter-denominational
Member of SCIS; **Accredited by** BAC, British Council Basil Paterson College is inspected by the British Council as well as BAC.
Learning difficulties RA/DYP DYS
Behavioural and emotional disorders RA
Physical and medical conditions TW WA2
Age range 15–19; *boarders from* 15
No of pupils 30; *(full boarding)* 2; *(day)* 28; *Senior* 2; *Sixth Form* 28; *Girls* 15; *Boys* 15
Teacher:pupil ratio 1:4; **Average class size** 4
Fees per annum *(day)* £2,200–£12,000. The cost is per subject studied and there is a discount for the 3rd subject at the same level.

Basil Paterson Tutorial College combines academic excellence and tuition flexibility to provide success for all its clients in the heart of Edinburgh's famous Georgian New Town.

The building contains a student common room with wireless internet access as well as modern PCs for email, a student study centre with 10 state-of-the-art PCs and a cafe area.

The college has two schools, combining academic studies with the teaching of English as a foreign language.

The college offers part-time as well as flexible tuition (evenings/weekends) as well as a wide range of courses for British and overseas students in preparation for A levels, AS levels, Scottish Highers and GCSE or Standard Grade examinations.

Classes are small, thus allowing students individual attention. A student adviser is present to monitor progress, offer advice and assist with careers, academic and personal matters.

Merchiston Castle School

Colinton, Edinburgh, Lothian EH13 0PU Tel: (0131) 312 2200 Fax: (0131) 441 6060
E-mail: admissions@merchiston.co.uk Website: www.merchiston.co.uk www.gabbitas.net

Head Mr A R Hunter BA **Founded** 1833
School status Boys' independent boarding and day
Religious denomination Inter-denominational
Member of BSA, CReSTeD, HMC, ISBA, ISCis, SCIS; **Accredited by** HMC, ISC
Learning difficulties SNU/DYP DYS MLD
Age range 8–18; *boarders from* 8
No of pupils 426; *(full boarding)* 288; *(day)* 138; *Prep* 104; *Senior* 173; *Sixth Form* 149; *Boys* 426; **Teacher:pupil ratio** 1:9
Average class size (under 11) 15; (11–16) 16; (Sixth Form) 9
Fees per annum *(full boarding)* £13,980–£20,775; *(day)* £9,525–£14,850

Set in 100 acres of parkland Merchiston is a school renowned for academic and sporting excellence.

Merchiston offers a full range of GCSEs, A levels and Highers. In 2005, 74 per cent of A level

candidates gained A and B grades, while at GCSE 53 per cent of grades were awarded at A and A*; 87 per cent of pupils achieved a place at their first choice of university. Regular winners of national engineering, electronic and mathematics prizes. Sporting achievements include 7 pupils participating at international level. Strongly featured music department with prestigious school choir and pipe band.

Integral Junior department (8–12 years). Strong links with two girls' schools. Junior teaching centre, refurbished science labs, modern IT suite, Music School and library. Indoor pool and sports hall. Extensive co-curricular activities. Admission though school's own exam. Scholarships and bursaries available.

Scotland

Gordonstoun School

Elgin, Morayshire IV30 5RF Tel: (01343) 837837 Fax: (01343) 837808
E-mail: admissions@gordonstoun.org.uk Website: www.gordonstoun.org.uk www.gabbitas.net

Principal Mr M C Pyper BA **Founded** 1934
School status Co-educational independent boarding and day
Religious denomination Non-denominational
Member of Round Square, SCIS
Learning difficulties SC SNU/DYC DYP DYS MLD
Behavioural and emotional disorders CO RA/ADD
Physical and medical conditions RA SM/HEA
Age range 8–18; *boarders from* 8
No of pupils 542; *(full boarding)* 474; *(day)* 68; *Prep* 83; *Senior* 185; *Sixth Form* 274; *Girls* 235; *Boys* 307
Teacher:pupil ratio 1:7
Average class size 12–15 at GCSE level
Fees per annum *(full boarding)* £14,644–£21,789; *(weekly)* £11,977 (Prep only); *(day)* £8,170–£14,703

Set in a magnificent 150-acre estate, Gordonstoun lies between the mountains and the sea in beautiful Morayshire countryside. The campus is well located for easy access to the international airports of Aberdeen and Inverness, as well as mainline railway stations.

The school's distinctive, holistic ethos is based on internationalism, challenge, responsibility and service and aims to prepare students to make a positive contribution to society in the 21st century. Offering a broad, integrated curriculum, Gordonstoun combines study for GCSE and AS/A level with sporting, creative and outdoor education, including the school's unique sail training programme, to help students encompass the school motto, *Plus Est En Vous* (There is more to you).

Glenalmond College

Perth, Perth and Kinross PH1 3RY
Tel: (01738) 842056 Fax: (01738) 842063 E-mail: registrar@glenalmondcollege.co.uk
Website: www.glenalmondcollege.co.uk www.gabbitas.net

Warden Mr G Woods
Registrar Mr J M B Poulter **Founded** 1847
College status Co-educational boarding and day
Religious denomination Episcopelian
Member of HMC, SCIS
Age range 12–18; *boarders from* 12
No of pupils 385; *(full boarding)* 326; *(day)* 59; *Senior* 203; *Sixth Form* 182
Teacher:pupil ratio 1:10; **Average class size** 16
Fees per annum *(full boarding)* £15,975–£21,300; *(day)* £10,905–£14,520

Full range of subjects to GCSE, choice of A level or Scottish Highers in Sixth Form. Very strong music, art, theatre.

Splendid facilities for technology and there are excellent computing opportunities, including new internet access throughout the school. Golf course, salmon river, artificial ski-slope, indoor and outdoor shooting, skiing and water sports enhance a wide range of sports facilities. There is a new second AstroTurf pitch, a new science block and a new IT resource centre. Glenalmond is also strong on public speaking and debating. There are good European links.

Easy access to Glasgow and Edinburgh and to airports. Art, music and academic scholarships and all-rounder awards. Bursaries are available for service children and clergy children.

The college is a registered charity providing quality education for boys and girls.

Strathallan School

Forgandenny, Perth, Perth and Kinross PH2 9EG Tel: (01738) 812546 Fax: (01738) 812549
E-mail: admissions@strathallan.co.uk Website: www.strathallan.co.uk

Headmaster Mr B K Thompson MA
Founded 1913
School status Co-educational boarding and day
Religious denomination Non-denominational
Member of AGBIS, BSA, HAS, HMC, ISA, ISBA, SCIS, SHA
Accredited by British Council, HMC, ISA, ISC
Age range 10–18
No of pupils 451; *(full boarding)* 296; *Girls* 188; *Boys* 263
Teacher:pupil ratio 1:7
Average class size 10
Fees per annum *(full boarding)* £14,760–£20,685; *(day)* £9,210–£14,025

Strathallan is a boarding school (70 per cent of pupils are full boarders) that caters for pupils from all round the world. With pupils from the local area, and throughout Scotland, as well as from the UK, foreign nationals and Scots who live abroad, it is a Scottish school with an international outlook.

Academically, Strathallan is one of the strongest schools in the country, with excellent GCSE and A level results. Outside the classroom, Strathallan prides itself on providing opportunities for all pupils to excel in the widest range of areas. Its size makes it possible for everyone to feel very much part of the community and to take part in all its activities. Particular emphasis is placed on the pastoral care provided in the boarding houses, the positive relationship between teachers and pupils, and the small classes. Pupils also benefit from teaching, sport and extra-curricular activities of the highest standard.

3.3 Schools in Continental Europe and Overseas Schools Outside Europe

MAP OF SCHOOLS IN CONTINENTAL EUROPE AND OVERSEAS SCHOOLS OUTSIDE EUROPE

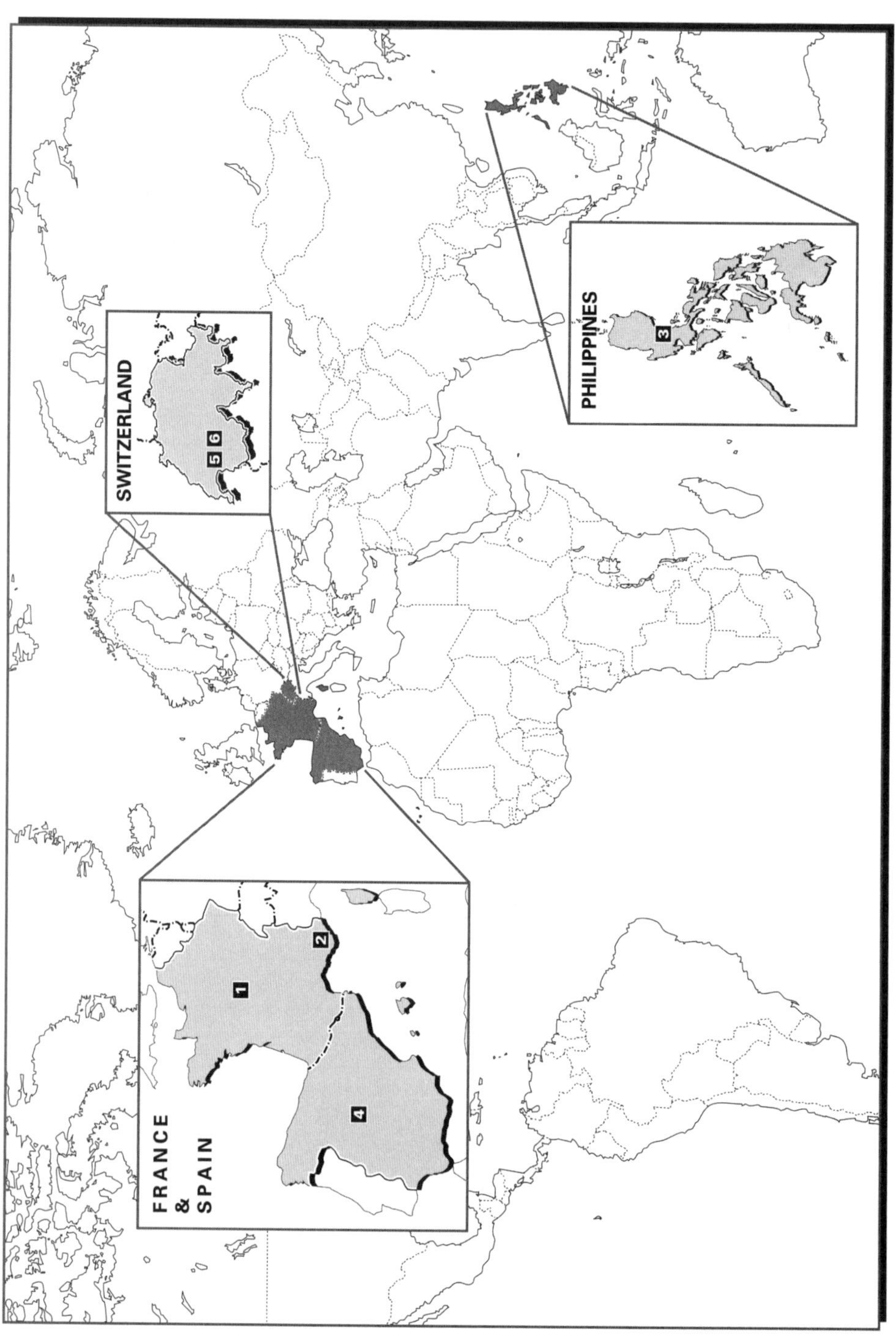

PROFILED SCHOOLS IN CONTINENTAL EUROPE AND OVERSEAS SCHOOLS OUTSIDE EUROPE

L'Ermitage – International School of France

46 Avenue Egle, Maisons Laffitte, France 78600 Tel: (+33) 1 39 62 0402 Fax: (+33) 1 39 62 5402
E-mail: ermitage@ermitage.fr Website: www.ermitage.fr

Head Mr C Hunter
Deputy Head Mrs V Wildman
International Section Co-ordinator Mrs T Thornewill
Founded 1941
School status Co-educational independent boarding and day
Religious denomination Non-denominational
Member of Round Square French Ministry of Education, Cambridge Exam Board. Member of Global Connections foundation.
Learning difficulties RA/DYS
Behavioural and emotional disorders RA/CB
Physical and medical conditions RA WA3/HEA
Age range 2–18; *boarders from* 8
No of pupils 904; *(full boarding)* 14; *(weekly boarding)* 101; *(day)* 789; *Nursery* 117; *Pre-prep* 258; *Prep* 279; *Senior* 69; *Sixth Form* 181; *Girls* 447; *Boys* 457
Teacher:pupil ratio 1:10; **Average class size** 20
Fees per annum *(full boarding)* €11,500–€19,000; *(weekly)* €6,500–€15,000; *(day)* €2,000–€9,000. Fees vary according to the choice of programme: French national, bilingual or IGCSE/A level

L'Ermitage, International School of France, is a co-educational day school also offering 5-day and 7-day boarding. The campus is located in the historic and highly residential park of Maisons-Laffitte, 10 miles west of Paris. Welcoming students from close to 40 nationalities, the school proposes a bilingual programme of instruction in French and English within the French national curriculum.

Pre-school and primary school pupils can participate in a bilingual class (English teacher in the morning; a French teacher in the afternoon), while francophone primary classes (year groups 1 to 6) receive 5 hours of English per week with special classes for native English speakers. In the Middle School (year groups 7 to 9), pupils can study history, science and civilization courses in English as well as a second foreign language (Chinese, German or Spanish). An intensive English course is also offered to new arrivals who may not have benefited from a bilingual primary education. The Brevet des Collèges diploma is taken by Francophone pupils at the end of 3ème (Year 10), whilst the International Brevet option is offered to bilingual pupils. Anglophone pupils or those of a sufficiently high level in English can study for the International GCSE.

The Upper School prepares students aged 16 to 18 for the French Baccalaureate (Economic, Literary and Scientific sections) and the International Option of the French Baccalaureate (American Section). L'Ermitage also offers the UK A level diploma, enabling pupils to take four subjects from a choice of eight entirely in English, as well as a variety of common core subjects (IT, French Civilization and European Studies).

Students can choose from a wide variety of outings and cultural activities and participate in different clubs and athletic teams. Numerous exchanges are also offered (USA, Europe and Asia). Non French-speaking students arriving from abroad can benefit from adaptation classes during their first year of stay in France.

The school makes every effort to integrate computer technology into the classroom (wireless, high-speed network, an intranet service, and an extensive range of computer facilities including interactive whiteboards and a 150-strong computer park) in order to enhance the creativity and innovation of its teachers and students alike.

In October 2005, L'Ermitage became the first French school to join the Round Square foundation.

Mougins School

615 Avenue Dr Maurice Donat, Font de l'Orme, BP 401, 06251 Mougins Cedex, France
Tel: (+33) 4 93 90 15 47 Fax: (+33) 4 93 75 3140 E-mail: information@mougins-school.com
Website: www.mougins-school.com www.gabbitas.net

Headmaster Mr B G Hickmore
Founded 1964
School status Co-educational independent day only
Religious denomination Non-denominational
Member of COBISEC
Learning difficulties CA SC/DOW MLD
Behavioural and emotional disorders RA
Physical and medical conditions TW WA1/W
Age range 3–18
No of pupils 422; *Prep* 169; *Senior* 211; *Sixth Form* 42; *Girls* 183; *Boys* 239
Teacher:pupil ratio 1:12; **Average class size** 22
Fees per annum *(day)* €4,370–€11,980

Mougins School is situated 10 km north of Cannes on a purpose-built campus. Facilities include a library, science laboratories, information technology centre, two art studios, music room, gymnasium, performing arts hall, dining room, outdoor games facility and an all-weather football pitch.

The school has a one-form entry system for students aged 3 to 18 from over 30 nationalities. Studies are based on the UK National Curriculum modified to meet the needs of an international market. Tests are taken at 7, 11 and 14, followed by IGCSE, GCSE, AS and A level examinations. ESOL is available.

The caring family atmosphere complements the high quality of the teaching and helps to enhance the academic, cultural and physical development of our students, producing excellent results, not only academically, but also in the sporting and artistic domains, all of which permit our students to go on to higher education in the best universities in Europe and the States. School buses allow us to organize field trips, sporting activities and competitions outside the school as well as residential educational visits.

The British School

36th Street University Park, Bonifacio, Global City, Taguig, Metro Manila, Philippines 1634
Tel: (+632) 840 15 70 Fax: (+632) 840 15 20 E-mail: admissions@britishschoolmanila.org
Website: www.britishschoolmanila.org www.gabbitas.net

Head of School Mr Chris Mantz Cert Ed, BA (Hons) MA (EdMan)
Head of Primary School Mr Glenn Hardy BSc (Hons) PGCE
Head of Senior School Mr Ian Clayton BA (Hons) PGCE
Founded 1976
School status Co-educational independent day only
Religious denomination Non-denominational
Member of CIS, COBISEC, FOBISSEA, IAPS, IBO
Age range 3–18
No of pupils 617; *Girls* 338; *Boys* 279
Average class size 17
Fees per annum Nursery £2,835; R–Y13 £6,666–£8,230

The British School Manila follows the UK National Curriculum with some modifications to reflect a multicultural student body. Children sit the National Curriculum tests at KS1, KS2 and KS3, as well as 11+, 12+ and 13+ if requested and GCSEs at the end of KS4.

The school is accredited to offer the IB diploma in KS5. We had our first class complete the Diploma in May 2005.

Teachers are all UK or Commonwealth trained and the maximum class size is 20 students. Each child is encouraged to develop at their own pace, benefiting from a high level of individual teacher attention and motivation. Emphasis is placed on self-discipline within a family atmosphere, providing an ideal environment for children of all nationalities.

King's College Madrid

Paseo de los Andes, 35, 28761 Soto de Vinuelas, Madrid, Spain
Tel: (+34) 918 034 800 Fax: (+34) 918 036 557 E-mail: info@kingscollege.es
Website: www.kingscollege.es www.gabbitas.net

Headmaster Mr D Johnson BEd Hons, MSc (Oxon) **Founded** 1969
College status Co-educational independent boarding and day
Religious denomination Non-denominational
Member of COBISEC, HMC, NABSS
Accredited by ISC ISC, Spanish Ministry of Education
Age range 1½–18; *boarders from* 11
No of pupils 1480; *(full boarding)* 20; *Prep* 902; *Senior* 427; *Sixth Form* 151; *Girls* 720; *Boys* 760
Fees per annum *(full boarding)* €14,313–€15,798; *(day)* €4,338–€8,853

Founded in 1969, King's College is the largest British school in Spain and the first to have had full UK accreditation through the Independent Schools Inspectorate.

It is a co-educational day and boarding school following the English National Curriculum which prepares pupils for IGCSE and GCE A levels and offers a wide range of subjects at both levels. There are optional Spanish studies and preparation for Spanish University entrance examinations.

With 1,480 pupils of more than 38 nationalities, the school has a complement of over 100 fully qualified teachers. All academic staff have British qualifications, except the Spanish teachers and some who teach modern languages. The average length of stay of the staff is over seven years.

Since it was founded over 35 years ago, the school has earned a reputation for high academic standards and excellent examination results with students going on to universities in Britain, USA and Spain amongst others. A very experienced Careers and University Entrance Advisory department is available to all students.

King's College is a modern purpose-built school set in a 12-acre site, surrounded by countryside but well connected to Madrid. A new purpose built Infant School for 200 children between the ages of 18 months and 6 years, is situated in the Chamartin area of northern Madrid. This school follows the same curriculum as the Infant Department at the main site in Soto de Vinuelas. Pupils transfer to the main school in Year 3.

The school has its own catering service and offers three-course midday meals. There is an optional bus service with a modern fleet of 18 vehicles covering Madrid and outlying areas.

Academic facilities King's College offers excellent academic facilities including seven science laboratories, three multimedia computer centres, a Sixth Form internet room, two libraries, two music rooms and an art studio. Recent additions include a purpose-built Early Learning Centre and an auditorium with seating capacity for 350 people.

Sports facilities On-site sports facilities include gymnasium, judo room, fitness centre, 25-metre heated indoor swimming pool, eleven-a-side and five-a-side football pitches, floodlit multi-sports area, tennis courts, stables and riding school.

Boarding facilities There are recently refurbished boarding facilities for boys and girls with rooms for one to three pupils over the age of 11. At present the residence is home to pupils from the UK, Russia, China, and Jamaica as well as students from expatriate families living in Spain. Resident pupils enjoy access to extensive sports facilities for afternoon/evening activities.

Extra-curricular activities The full range of extra-curricular activities offered by the school broadens students' general education, helping them to develop worthwhile leisure-time activities. Ballet, handicrafts, piano, judo, violin, riding, swimming and tennis are all offered as optional classes.

Admission The procedure for admission varies according to the age of the pupil. Importance is given to previous school records and from age 7 to 16 years candidates are required to sit entrance tests in mathematics and English.

Aiglon College

Rue Centrale, 1885 Chesières-Villars, Switzerland
Tel: (+41) 24 496 6126 Fax: (+41) 24 496 6162
E-mail: admissions@aiglon.ch
Website: www.aiglon.ch www.gabbitas.net

Headmaster The Revd Dr Jonathan Long BA(Hons) MA MTh DPhil DipRE DipTS
Founded 1949
College status Co-educational boarding and day
Religious denomination Non-denominational
Member of IAPS, ECIS, NEASC, Round Square, ADISR, COBISEC
Age range 9–18
No of pupils 350; *Girls* 165; *Boys* 185
Teacher:pupil ratio 1:6
Average class size 12
Fees per annum *(full boarding)* Sfr65,200; *(day)* Sfr45,600

Aiglon College offers a well-rounded education in a secure and friendly international community. The school is located on a 25-acre campus within an Alpine ski village. It is an independent, non-profit, co-educational, international boarding school with an enrolment of over 60 nationalities. The school is registered as a charitable trust in Switzerland, the UK, USA, the Netherlands and Canada. There are eight boarding houses, each with its own houseparents and tutors offering a high degree of pastoral care.

The academic programme is demanding and prepares students for GCSE and A level examinations as well as the American College Board. Courses are taught in English except in the first two years of the Junior School (ages 9 to 11) where the emphasis is based on French and English. The school offers an ESL (English as a Second Language) programme for all non-English speakers aged 10 to 12.

Facilities include a new computer centre, world languages centre, eight science laboratories, library and outstanding art and music departments. The school is also a centre for the College Board, TOEFL and some AICE exams at subsidiary levels. Aiglon's graduates are currently enrolled in leading international universities and colleges.

Sports and expeditions form an essential component of a well-rounded approach to the development of the students' personality and character. The wide range of sports include skiing, basketball, tennis, soccer, athletics, gymnastics, swimming and volleyball. Expeditions take place at weekends and activities include camping, climbing and skiing under expert and qualified supervision. Service and responsibility are fostered through social service and through the Round Square organization.

During vacations, Aiglon offers a Summer School and a Languages and Snowsports programme that combine expert language tuition with fun outdoor activities.

John F Kennedy International School

CH 3792 Saanen-Gstaad, Switzerland
Tel: (+41) 33 744 1372 Fax: (+41) 33 7448982
E-mail: lovell@jfk.ch
Website: www.jkf.ch

Founded 1950
School status Co-educational boarding and day
Accredited by the Department of Education Canton of Bern Switzerland
Learning difficulties SNU/DYS MLD
Behavioural and emotional disorders RA/ADD
Physical and medical conditions RA
Age range 4–14
No of pupils 60; *(full boarding)* 26; *(day)* 34; *Girls* 30; *Boys* 30
Teacher:pupil ratio 1:6
Average class size 10
Fees per annum *(full boarding)* Sfr45,300; *(day)* Sfr24,800

JFK was founded in 1950 in the village of Saanen, Switzerland, 3 kilometres from the world famous resort of Gstaad. Features include small classes, a family-like atmosphere and well-balanced programmes emphasizing strong academic skills and good study habits. The curriculum has been especially designed for international schools and is based on a clear philosophy of international education in a time of rapid global change and endeavours to foster a 'global viewpoint'. The programme also reflects recent developments in our understanding of how the brain works and how children learn. In addition, a conscious effort is made to take the learning process beyond the classroom through field trips, cultural activities and sports, including daily skiing in winter. Since 1973 the school has offered an outstanding summer camp for children aged 6 to 13 years.

Part 4

Reference Section

4.1
Scholarships

The following is based on information provided by schools. The entry age, where given, is the age at which scholarships are available to pupils. Please note that for each school, not every scholarship listed is offered at all the stated entry ages. Further details of scholarships available at individual schools may be found in Part Three: School Profiles. The abbreviations are as follows:

A Art
AA Academic ability
D Drama
G Games
I Instrumental music/Choral
O All round ability
S Science
6 VIth Form entry

ENGLAND

BEDFORDSHIRE

Bedford High School, Bedford AA I O
Bedford Modern School, Bedford
Entry age: 11+ A D G I
Bedford Preparatory School, Bedford AA
Bedford School, Bedford 6 A AA D G I O
Moorlands School, Luton Entry age: 7+ A AA I O

BERKSHIRE

The Abbey School, Reading Entry age: 11+, 16+ 6 AA I
The Ark School, Reading Entry age: 7 A AA I
Bearwood College, Wokingham
Entry age: 11/13 6 A AA D G I O S
Bradfield College, Reading
Entry age: 13+, 16+ 6 A AA I
Brigidine School Windsor, Windsor
Entry age: 11, 16 6 A AA D G I
Brockhurst and Marlston House Schools, Newbury AA
Cheam School, Newbury AA
Claires Court School, Maidenhead 6 A AA D G I O
Claires Court Schools, Ridgeway, Maidenhead A AA D G I O
Claires Court Schools, The College, Maidenhead 6 A AA D G I O
Dolphin School, Reading A AA D G I O
Downe House, Thatcham 6 A AA I
Eagle House, Sandhurst AA I
Elstree School, Reading Entry age: 7 AA
The Elvian School, Reading Entry age: 11+ 6 A AA G I
Eton College, Windsor 6 AA I
Heathfield School, Ascot A AA D G I
Hemdean House School, Reading AA I O
Highfield School, Maidenhead AA
Holme Grange School, Wokingham
Entry age: 11+ AA O
Horris Hill, Newbury AA O
Hurst Lodge School, Ascot
Entry age: various 6 A AA D I O
Langley Manor School, Slough AA G I O
Leighton Park School, Reading
Entry age: 12, 14, 17 A AA I O
Licensed Victuallers' School, Ascot 6 A AA G I
Luckley-Oakfield School, Wokingham
Entry age: 11 6 AA I
The Marist Senior School, Ascot
Entry age: 11 6 A AA D G I O
The Oratory Preparatory School, Reading AA G I
The Oratory School, Reading
Entry age: 11+, 13+ 6 A AA D G I O
Padworth College, Reading Entry age: 14, 16 6 A AA I

Pangbourne College, Pangbourne
Entry age: 11+, 13+, 16+ 6 A AA D G I O S
Papplewick School, Ascot Entry age: 7–11 A AA G I O
Queen Anne's School, Reading
Entry age: 11, 12, 13+, 16+ 6 A AA G I O
Reading Blue Coat School, Reading 6 A AA I
St Edward's School, Reading AA O
St Gabriel's , Newbury Entry age: 11, 16 6 A AA G I
St George's School, Ascot Entry age: 11+, 16+ AA I
St George's School, Windsor Entry age: 7+, 9+ AA I
St Joseph's Convent School, Reading 6 AA D G I
St Mary's School, Ascot 6 A AA I S
St Piran's Preparatory School, Maidenhead AA
Thorngrove School, Newbury AA G I O
Upton House School, Windsor A AA
Wellington College, Crowthorne 6 A AA D G I O

BRISTOL

Badminton School Entry age: 11+, 13+, 16+ 6 A AA I O
Bristol Cathedral School, Bristol
Entry age: 11+, 13+, 16+ 6 AA I
Bristol Grammar School, Bristol
Entry age: 7, 11, 13, 16 6 A AA D I O S
Clifton College, Bristol
Entry age: 13+, 16+ 6 A AA G I O
Clifton College Preparatory School
Entry age: 11+ AA I O
Clifton High School, Bristol
Entry age: 11+, 13+, 16+ 6 AA G I
Colston's Collegiate School, Bristol 6 A AA D G I O
Colston's Girls' School 6 A AA I O S
The Downs School, Wraxall Entry age: 8+ A AA G I O
Fairfield PNEU School, Bristol AA
Queen Elizabeth's Hospital
Entry age: 11, 13, 16 6 AA I S
The Red Maids' School
Entry age: 11+,13+, 16+ 6 AA G I O
Redland High School Entry age: 7, 11, 16 6 A AA I
Sacred Heart Preparatory School, Chew Magna Entry age: 3+, 11+ O
St Ursula's High School AA
Torwood House School O

BUCKINGHAMSHIRE

Bury Lawn School, Milton Keynes 6 AA
Davenies School, Beaconsfield A AA G I O
Gateway School, Great Missenden O
Godstowe Preparatory School, High Wycombe
Entry age: 8, 11 AA
High March School, Beaconsfield Entry age: 8 AA
Holy Cross Convent, Gerrards Cross
Entry age: 11+, 16+ 6 AA I O
Ladymede, Aylesbury Entry age: 7+ AA O
Milton Keynes Preparatory School, Milton Keynes A AA G I
Pipers Corner School, High Wycombe 6 I
St Mary's School, Gerrards Cross
Entry age: 11/16+ 6 AA I
Stowe School, Buckingham
Entry age: 13, 16 6 A AA G I O
Swanbourne House School, Milton Keynes
Entry age: 11+ AA G I
Thornton College Convent of Jesus and Mary, Milton Keynes Entry age: 11 AA
Thorpe House School, Gerrards Cross AA
Wycombe Abbey School, High Wycombe 6 AA I

CAMBRIDGESHIRE

Bellerbys College, Cambridge AA O
Cambridge Centre for Sixth-form Studies, Cambridge 6 AA O
Kimbolton School, Huntingdon 6 A AA G I O
The King's School Ely, Ely
Entry age: 11+ 6 A AA D G I O
The Leys School, Cambridge
Entry age: 11, 13, 16 6 A AA D G I O
MPW (Mander Portman Woodward), Cambridge 6 AA O
The Perse School, Cambridge 6 A AA I
The Perse School for Girls, Cambridge 6 I
Peterborough High School, Peterborough
Entry age: 11, 17 6 A AA I O
St Faith's, Cambridge Entry age: 7+ AA
St John's College School, Cambridge I
St Mary's School, Cambridge 6 AA I
Sancton Wood School, Cambridge D O
Wisbech Grammar School, Wisbech I

CHANNEL ISLANDS

Elizabeth College, Guernsey I O
Ormer House Preparatory School, Alderney AA
St George's Preparatory School, Jersey
Entry age: 7+ A AA G I O S
St Michael's Preparatory School, Jersey AA
Victoria College, Jersey AA I S

CHESHIRE

Abbey Gate College, Chester
Entry age: 11+, 16+ 6 AA I
Alderley Edge School for Girls, Alderley Edge 6 A AA G I
Brabyns School, Stockport AA
Cransley School, Northwich
Entry age: 11+ A AA G I O S
Culcheth Hall, Altrincham AA
The Grange School, Northwich 6 AA I
Hammond School, Chester AA D I
Hulme Hall Schools, Cheadle AA
The King's School, Macclesfield AA I
Macclesfield Preparatory School, Macclesfield AA G O
Mostyn House School, South Wirral
Entry age: 7, 11 AA G O
North Cestrian Grammar School, Altrincham AA
Oriel Bank, Stockport I
The Ryleys, Alderley Edge AA O

Stockport Grammar School, Stockport
Entry age: 11+ I
Terra Nova School, Holmes Chapel A AA D G I O S

CORNWALL

The Bolitho School, Penzance
Entry age: 10+, 13+ 6 A AA I O
Polwhele House School, Truro AA I
Roselyon, Par AA I O
St Joseph's School, Launceston
Entry age: 7+, 11+ AA G I O
St Petroc's School, Bude Entry age: 7+ A AA D G I O S
St Piran's School, Truro AA
Truro High School, Truro
Entry age: 11+, 16+ 6 A AA G I
Truro School, Truro 6 A AA I
Wheelgate House School, Newquay AA O

CUMBRIA

Austin Friars St Monica's School, Carlisle
Entry age: 11+ AA G I
Casterton School, Kirkby Lonsdale 6 A AA D G I O S
Chetwynde School, Barrow-in-Furness 6 AA G I O
Harecroft Hall School, Seascale AA
Holme Park School, Kendal Entry age: 7+ AA D G O S
Lime House School, Carlisle AA G O
St Bees School, St Bees 6 A AA G I
Sedbergh School, Sedbergh
Entry age: 13+, 16+, 17+ 6 A AA D G I O
Windermere St Anne's, Windermere
Entry age: 11+, 13+, 16+ 6 A AA D G I O

DERBYSHIRE

Derby Grammar School for Boys, Derby 6 6 AA I
Derby High School, Derby Entry age: 11/16 6 AA I O
Foremarke Hall School, Derby A AA D G I
Mount St Mary's College, Spinkhill
Entry age: 11+, 15+ 6 AA G I O
Ockbrook School, Derby A AA D G I
Repton School, Derby
Entry age: 13+, 16+ 6 A AA D G I O
St Wystan's School, Repton Entry age: 7+ AA G I O

DEVON

The Abbey School, Torquay AA O
Blundell's School, Tiverton
Entry age: 11, 13, 16 6 A AA G I O
Bramdean School, Exeter Entry age: 7/11 AA D G I
Edgehill College, Bideford 6 A AA D G I
Exeter Cathedral School, Exeter
Entry age: 7/12+ AA I O
Exeter Junior School, Exeter Entry age: 7+ AA
Exeter School, Exeter Entry age: 7, 11,
12, 13 6 A AA I S
Gramercy Hall School, Torbay AA G I
Grenville College, Bideford
Entry age: 11, 12, 13, 16+ 6 A AA D G I O S
Kelly College, Tavistock
Entry age: 11, 13, 16 6 A AA G I O
Lanherne Nursery and Junior School, Dawlish O
The Maynard School, Exeter 6 I
Mount House School, Tavistock AA
Plymouth College, Plymouth
Entry age: 11, 13, 16 6 A AA G I
St Christophers School, Totnes O
St John's School, Sidmouth
Entry age: 8, 11 A AA D G I O
St Margaret's School, Exeter 6 A AA D I
St Michael's, Barnstaple A AA D G I O
St Peter's School, Exmouth AA G I O
St Wilfrid's School, Exeter Entry age: 7 O
Shebbear College, Beaworthy
Entry age: 11+, 13+, 16+ 6 A AA D G I O
Stoodley Knowle School, Torquay O
Stover School, Newton Abbot 6 A AA G I O
Tower House School, Paignton
Entry age: 11 A AA D G I O S
Trinity School, Teignmouth 6 A AA D G I O S
West Buckland Preparatory School,
Barnstaple AA O
West Buckland School, Barnstaple 6 AA G I O

DORSET

Bryanston School, Blandford Forum
Entry age: 13, 16 6 A AA G I O
Canford School, Wimborne 6 A AA D G I
Castle Court Preparatory School, Wimborne AA I
Clayesmore Preparatory School,
Blandford Forum A AA G I O
Clayesmore School, Blandford Forum 6 A AA I O
Dorchester Preparatory School,
Dorchester 6 A AA D G I O S
Dumpton School, Wimborne Entry age: 7 A AA G I O
Hanford School, Blandford Forum I
Knighton House, Blandford Forum A AA D G I O
Milton Abbey School, Blandford Forum 6 A AA D G I
The Old Malthouse, Swanage
Entry age: 7+ A AA G I O
The Park School, Bournemouth AA I O
Port Regis School, Shaftesbury A AA G I O
St Antony's Leweston Schools, Sherborne
Entry age: 7–13,16 6 A AA D G I S
St Martin's School, Bournemouth AA
St Mary's School, Shaftesbury
Entry age: 11+, 13+, 16+ 6 A AA I
Sherborne Preparatory School, Sherborne AA I O
Sherborne School, Sherborne
Entry age: 13+, 16+ 6 A AA D G I O
Sherborne School for Girls, Sherborne 6 A AA I O
Talbot Heath, Bournemouth 6 A AA D G I O
Thornlow Preparatory School, Weymouth AA G
Uplands School, Poole Entry age: 11+, 12+, 13+ AA
Wentworth College, Bournemouth 6 A AA D G I
Yarrells School, Poole AA I O

COUNTY DURHAM

Barnard Castle School, Barnard Castle 6 A AA G I
Bow School, Durham Entry age: 7+, 8+ AA G I O
The Chorister School, Durham I
Durham High School For Girls, Durham
Entry age: 11, 16 6 A AA G I
Durham School, Durham
Entry age: 11–16 6 A AA G I O
Hurworth House School, Darlington AA G O
Polam Hall, Darlington
Entry age: 7, 11, 13, 16 6 AA G I O

ESSEX

Alleyn Court Preparatory School,
Southend-on-Sea Entry age: 7 AA I O
Bancroft's School, Woodford Green
Entry age: 11, 16 6 AA I
Brentwood School, Brentwood
Entry age: 11, 16 6 A AA I O
Chigwell School, Chigwell A AA D I O
Colchester High School, Colchester AA
College Saint-Pierre, Leigh-on-Sea O
Crowstone Preparatory School, Westcliff-on-Sea O
Felsted Preparatory School, Dunmow AA I
Felsted School, Dunmow 6 A AA D I O
Friends' School, Saffron Walden
Entry age: 11, 13, 16 6 A AA G I
Gosfield School, Halstead 6 AA D G I O
Herington House School, Brentwood D G I O
Holmwood House, Colchester A AA G I O
Loyola Preparatory School, Buckhurst Hill AA
New Hall School, Chelmsford
Entry age: 11, 13, 16 6 A AA D I O
Park School for Girls, Ilford AA
St Aubyn's School, Woodford Green AA
St Hilda's School, Westcliff-on-Sea O
St Margaret's School, Halstead Entry age: 8+ AA I
St Mary's School, Colchester Entry age: 11+ O
St Nicholas School, Harlow 6 A AA G I
Thorpe Hall School, Southend-on-Sea
Entry age: 7/11 AA

GLOUCESTERSHIRE

The Abbey School, Tewkesbury AA I
Berkhampstead School, Cheltenham AA G I
Bredon School, Tewkesbury A AA G O
Cheltenham College, Cheltenham
Entry age: 13, 16 6 A AA G I O S
Cheltenham College Junior School, Cheltenham
Entry age: 11+ A AA G I O
The Cheltenham Ladies' College,
Cheltenham 6 A AA G I
Dean Close Preparatory School, Cheltenham AA G I O
Dean Close School, Cheltenham
Entry age: 11+, 13+, 16+ 6 A AA G I O
Hatherop Castle School, Cirencester
Entry age: 7+ AA D G I O
The King's School, Gloucester 6 A AA G I O
Rendcomb College, Cirencester
Entry age: 11, 13, 16 6 A AA D G I
The Richard Pate School, Cheltenham Entry age: 7+ AA
Rose Hill School, Wotton-under-Edge AA
St Edward's School, Cheltenham 6 A AA D G I
Westonbirt School, Tetbury 6 A AA D G I O S
Wycliffe College & Preparatory School,
Stonehouse 6 A AA D G I O
Wycliffe Preparatory School, Stonehouse
Entry age: 11 A AA D G I O

SOUTH GLOUCESTERSHIRE

Silverhill School, Winterbourne O

HAMPSHIRE

Alton Convent School, Alton Entry age: 11/16 6 AA I
The Atherley School, Southampton 6 A AA D G I
Ballard School, New Milton Entry age: 7 A AA G I O
Bedales School, Petersfield 6 A AA I
Boundary Oak School, Fareham AA I
Brockwood Park School, Bramdean O
Churchers College, Petersfield 6 AA I
Ditcham Park School, Petersfield Entry age: 11 AA I
Dunhurst (Bedales Junior School), Petersfield I
Durlston Court, New Milton Entry age:
Over 7 in September of year of entry A AA G I
Hampshire Collegiate School, Embley Park,
Romsey 6 A AA D G I O S
Farleigh School, Andover AA O
Farnborough Hill, Farnborough 6 AA G I
The Gregg School, Southampton AA I
Highfield School, Liphook AA
Hordle Walhampton School, Lymington AA I O
King Edward VI School, Southampton
Entry age: 11+, 13+ AA I
Lord Wandsworth College, Hook
Entry age: 11+, 13+, 16+ 6 A AA D I O
Marycourt School, Gosport Entry age: 7 O
Mayville High School, Southsea A AA D G I
Meoncross School, Fareham Entry age: 11 AA
The Pilgrims' School, Winchester I
The Portsmouth Grammar School,
Portsmouth 6 A AA D G I O
Portsmouth High School GDST, Southsea
Entry age: 11+, 13+, 16+ 6 A AA D G I
Prince's Mead School, Winchester A AA G I
Rookesbury Park School, Portsmouth AA I
Rookwood School, Andover AA G I
St Mary's College, Southampton AA
St Neot's School, Hook O
St Nicholas' School, Fleet Entry age: 11, 13 AA I O
St Swithun's School, Winchester
Entry age: 11+, 13+, 16+ 6 AA I
Sherborne House School, Eastleigh A AA G I O
Stockton House School, Aldershot AA O
The Stroud School, Romsey A AA D G I O
Winchester College, Winchester
Entry age: 13, 16 6 AA I
Wykeham House School, Fareham AA
Yateley Manor Preparatory School, Yateley
Entry age: 7+ AA G I O

HEREFORDSHIRE

The Hereford Cathedral School, Hereford 6 A AA I
Lucton School, Leominster
  Entry age: 11, 13, 16 6 A AA D G I O S
St Richard's, Bromyard AA

HERTFORDSHIRE

Abbot's Hill School, Hemel Hempstead
  Entry age: 11 A AA G I
Aldenham School, Elstree 6 A AA G I O
Aldwickbury School, Harpenden AA
The Arts Educational School, Tring D I O
Berkhamsted Collegiate Preparatory School,
  Berkhamsted AA
Berkhamsted Collegiate School,
  Berkhamsted 6 A AA G I
Bishop's Stortford College, Bishop's Stortford
  Entry age: 11+, 13+, 16+ 6 A AA I O
Egerton-Rothesay School, Berkhamsted
  Entry age: 5+, 16+ A AA G I
Haberdashers' Aske's Boys' School, Elstree
  Entry age: 11, 13 AA I
Haberdashers' Aske's School for Girls, Elstree AA I
Haileybury, Hertford Entry age: 11, 13, 16 A AA I O
Haresfoot Preparatory School,
  Berkhamsted A AA D I O
Heath Mount School, Hertford
  Entry age: 7+, 11+ A AA
Immanuel College, Bushey Entry age: 11/16 6 A AA I
The Junior School, Bishop's Stortford College,
  Bishop's Stortford A AA I O
Lockers Park, Hemel Hempstead A AA G I O
The Princess Helena College, Hitchin
  Entry age: 11–18 6 A AA D G I
The Purcell School, Bushey I
Queenswood School, Hatfield 6 AA G I
The Royal Masonic School for Girls, Rickmansworth
  Entry age: 7, 11, 16 6 A AA D G I O
St Albans High School for Girls, St Albans
  Entry age: 11+, 13+, 16+ 6 I O
St Albans School, St Albans
  Entry age: 11+, 13+, 16+ 6 A AA I
St Andrew's Montessori School, Watford AA G I O
St Christopher School, Letchworth 6
St Columba's College, St Albans
  Entry age: 11+/13+ 6 AA I
St Edmund's College, Ware 6 A AA G I
St Francis' College, Letchworth 6 AA G I
St Margaret's School, Bushey 6 AA I O S
Sherrardswood School, Welwyn 6 AA O
Stanborough School, Watford AA G I
Stormont, Potters Bar Entry age: 7 AA
Westbrook Hay Preparatory School,
  Hemel Hempstead Entry age: 8+ AA G O
York House School, Rickmansworth AA G

ISLE OF MAN

King William's College, Castletown 6 A AA G I O

ISLE OF WIGHT

Ryde School, Ryde 6 AA I
Westmont School, Newport AA I O

KENT

Ashford School, Ashford 6 A AA D G I O
Babington House School, Chislehurst AA D G I O
Baston School, Bromley AA O
Bedgebury School, Cranbrook
  Entry age: 7, 11, 13, 16 6 A AA D G I S
Beechwood Sacred Heart School, Tunbridge Wells
  Entry age: 11+, 13+ 6 A AA D G I O S
Benenden School, Cranbrook
  Entry age: 11, 13, 16 6 A AA G I
Bethany School, Cranbrook
  Entry age: 11+, 13+, 16+ 6 A AA D G I
Bishop Challoner RC School, Bromley
  Entry age: 11+ AA I
Breaside Preparatory School, Bromley
  Entry age: 7+ AA
Bromley High School GDST, Bromley
  Entry age: 11/16+ 6 A AA G I
Cobham Hall, Gravesend 6 A AA D G I O S
Combe Bank School, Sevenoaks
  Entry age: 7+ AA D G I
Cranbrook School, Cranbrook I
Darul Uloom London, Chislehurst AA G O S
Derwent Lodge School for Girls, Tonbridge AA
Dover College, Dover
  Entry age: 11, 13, 16 6 A AA G I O
Duke of York's Royal Military School,
  Dover 6 A AA G I
Elliott Park School, Sheerness O
Farringtons School, Chislehurst 6 A AA G I
Gad's Hill School, Rochester
  Entry age: 11 A AA D G I O
Haddon Dene School, Broadstairs O
Hilden Grange School, Tonbridge AA I
Holmewood House, Tunbridge Wells AA
The Junior School, St Lawrence College, Ramsgate AA
Kent College, Canterbury
  Entry age: 11, 13, 16+ 6 A AA G I O
Kent College Pembury, Tunbridge Wells
  Entry age: 11, 13, 16 6 A AA D G I O
King's Preparatory School, Rochester AA I
The King's School, Canterbury 6 A AA I
King's School Rochester, Rochester 6 A AA G I
Marlborough House School, Hawkhurst AA
Merton Court Preparatory School, Sidcup AA D G I O
Northbourne Park School, Deal A AA G I O
Rochester Independent College,
  Rochester 6 A AA D O S
Rose Hill School, Tunbridge Wells
  Entry age: 11+ A AA D G I O
Sackville School, Tonbridge 6 A AA G I
St Christopher's School, Canterbury O
St Edmunds Junior School, Canterbury
  Entry age: 11 AA G I O
St Edmund's School, Canterbury
  Entry age: 11+, 13+, 16+ 6 A AA D G I O

St Lawrence College, Ramsgate
Entry age: 8, 11, 13, 16 — 6 AA G I O
St Mary's Westbrook, Folkestone — A AA G I O
St Michael's School, Sevenoaks Entry age: 7 — AA G I O
St Ronan's, Hawkhurst Entry age: 11 — AA
Sevenoaks School, Sevenoaks
Entry age: 11+, 13+, 16+ — 6 A AA G I O
Solefield School, Sevenoaks — I
Spring Grove School, Ashford
Entry age: 7+ — A AA D G I O S
Sutton Valence School, Maidstone
Entry age: 11+, 13+, 16+ — 6 A AA D G I O
Tonbridge School, Tonbridge
Entry age: 13+, 16+ — 6 A AA D G I
Walthamstow Hall, Sevenoaks
Entry age: 11+, 13+, 16+ — 6 A AA D I
Wellesley House School, Broadstairs — AA G I
Yardley Court, Tonbridge — AA O

LANCASHIRE

Arnold School, Blackpool
Entry age: 11+, 16+ — 6 A AA D G I
Bury Grammar School, Bury — 6 AA
Bury Grammar School Girls, Bury Entry age: 11 — AA
Clevelands Preparatory School, Bolton — AA O
Firwood Manor Prep School, Oldham — AA O
Heathland College, Accrington — AA I
The Hulme Grammar School for Girls, Oldham — AA
King Edward VII and Queen Mary School,
Lytham St Annes Entry age: 11, 16 — 6 AA G I
Kingswood College at Scarisbrick Hall,
Ormskirk — AA G I
Kirkham Grammar School, Preston — 6 AA I
Oakhill College, Clitheroe — AA O
Queen Elizabeth's Grammar School, Blackburn
Entry age: 11+ — AA S
Rossall Junior School, Fleetwood — 6 A AA G I O
Rossall School, Fleetwood
Entry age: 11, 13, 16 — 6 A AA G I O S
St Anne's College Grammar School,
Lytham St Annes — 6 AA
St Joseph's Convent School, Burnley — I
St Mary's Hall, Stonyhurst — A AA I
Sedbergh Junior School, Lancaster
Entry age: 11 — A AA D G I O
Stonyhurst College, Clitheroe
Entry age: 13, 16 — 6 A AA I O
Westholme School, Blackburn — 6 A AA I

LEICESTERSHIRE

Brooke House College, Market Harborough — 6 AA G O
The Dixie Grammar School, Market Bosworth
Entry age: 10, 11, 14, 16 — 6 A AA G I
Grace Dieu Manor School, Leicester — AA G
Irwin College, Leicester Entry age: 14, 16 — AA
Leicester Grammar School, Leicester — 6 A AA G I O
Leicester High School For Girls, Leicester — 6 AA I
Loughborough Grammar School, Loughborough
Entry age: 10+, 11+, 13+, 16+ — 6 AA I
Loughborough High School, Loughborough — AA I
Ratcliffe College, Leicester
Entry age: 11+, 13+, 16+ — 6 AA I
St Crispin's School (Leicester) Ltd., Leicester
Entry age: 7+, 11+, 13+ — AA G
Stoneygate School, Leicester — AA

LINCOLNSHIRE

Copthill School, Stamford Entry age: 11 — AA
Fen School, Sleaford Entry age: 7 — AA
Kirkstone House School, Bourne — A AA G I O
Lincoln Minster School, Lincoln — 6 AA G I
Maypole House School, Alford — AA O
Stamford High School, Stamford — 6 A AA I O
Stamford School, Stamford — 6 A AA I
Witham Hall, Bourne — AA O

NORTH EAST LINCOLNSHIRE

St James' School, Grimsby — 6 AA G I O

LONDON

Abercorn School, NW8 — O
Albemarle Independent College, W1K
Entry age: 14+, 19+ — AA
Alleyn's School, SE22 Entry age: 11+, 16+ — 6 A AA G I
Ashbourne Independent Sixth Form College,
W8 — 6 A AA D G I O S
Ashbourne Middle School, W8
Entry age: 13/16 — 6 A AA D O S
Bassett House School, W10 Entry age: 8 — AA
Belmont (Mill Hill Preparatory School), NW7
Entry age: 11 — AA D I S
Blackheath High School GDST, SE3
Entry age: 11+/16+ — 6 A AA I
Blackheath Preparatory School, SE3 — AA
Brampton College, NW4 — AA
Broomwood Hall School, SW12 — A AA O
Channing School, N6 — 6 AA I
City of London School, EC4V Entry age: 11+, 13+, 16+ 6
AA I
City of London School for Girls, EC2Y
Entry age: 11, 16 — 6 A AA I
Clifton Lodge Preparatory School, W5 — I
Colfe's School, SE12 — 6 A AA G I
Connaught House, W2 Entry age: 6, 8 — A AA I O
Davies Laing and Dick, W1U — 6 AA O
Devonshire House Preparatory School, NW3 — AA I
Dulwich College, SE21 — 6 A AA G I
Durston House, W5 — AA
Ealing College Upper School, W13 — 6 AA
Ealing Independent College, W5 — AA
Eaton House The Manor, SW4
Entry age: 8+ — A AA G I O
Eaton Square Schools, SW1V — O
Emanuel School, SW11 — 6 A AA D G I O
Forest School, E17 — 6 A AA D I S
Francis Holland School, SW1W
Entry age: 11+, 16+ — 6 AA I
Francis Holland School, NW1 — 6 I
Fulham Prep School (Prep Dept), W14 — A AA G I

Garden House School, SW3 AA I O
The Godolphin and Latymer School, W6 I
Hall School Wimbledon, SW20 A AA D G I O
The Hampshire Schools (Kensington Gardens), W2 AA G I O
The Hampshire Schools (Knightsbridge Under School), SW7 AA I O
The Hampshire Schools (Knightsbridge Upper School), SW7 AA I O
Hampstead Fine Arts Independent College, NW3 6 O
Hampstead Hill Pre-Preparatory & Nursery School, NW3 O
Harvington School, W5 D I
Heathside Preparatory School, NW3 AA
Hellenic College of London, SW1X AA
Hendon Preparatory School, NW4 AA G O
Highgate School, N6 AA I
Hill House International Junior School, SW1X Entry age: 11 A I
Hurlingham Private School, SW15 Entry age: 7+ O
Ibstock Place School, SW15 6 I
International Community School, NW1 6 AA O
The Italia Conti Academy of Theatre Arts, EC1M D
James Allen's Girls' School, SE22 Entry age: 11+, 16+ 6 A AA G I
Keble Preparatory School, N21 Entry age: 11 AA G O
King's College Junior School, SW19 AA I
King's College School, SW19 6 A AA I
Lansdowne College, W2 Entry age: 14+, 16+ 6 AA O
Latymer Upper School, W6 6 A D G I
Lycee Francais Charles de Gaulle, SW7 6 6 AA
The Lyceum, EC2A I
Mander Portman Woodward, SW7 6 AA
More House, SW1X 6 AA I
The Mount School, NW7 6 AA I
Newton Prep, SW8 AA
Normanhurst School, E4 Entry age: 11 AA
North Bridge House Lower Prep School, NW1 AA I
North Bridge House Senior School, NW1 I
Northcote Lodge School, SW11 AA
Notting Hill and Ealing High School GDST, W13 Entry age: 11+, 16+ 6 A AA D I O
Palmers Green High School, N21 Entry age: 11+ AA I
Parkgate House School, SW4 AA I
The Pointer School, SE3 AA D G O
Portland Place, W1B A AA I
Prospect House School, SW15 AA O
Putney High School GDST, SW15 Entry age: 11+, 16+ 6 AA I
Queen's College, W1G 6 A AA I
Queen's Gate School, SW7 6 O
Riverston School, SE12 AA G I O
The Roche School, SW18 Entry age: 7 AA
The Royal School, Hampstead, NW3 Entry age: 7, 16 AA
St Augustine's Priory, W5 6 I O
St Benedict's Junior School, W5 I
St Benedict's School, W5 Entry age: 11+ AA G I
St Margaret's School, NW3 AA
St Mary's School Hampstead, NW3 AA
St Paul's Cathedral School, EC4M I
St Paul's Girls' School, W6 6 A AA I
St Paul's Preparatory School, SW13 AA I
St Paul's School, SW13 6 AA I
Sinclair House School, SW6 O
South Hampstead High School, NW3 6 AA I
Southbank International School, Hampstead, NW3 6
Southbank International School, Westminster, W1B O
Streatham and Clapham High School, SW16 Entry age: 11, 16 6 AA I S
Sussex House School, SW1X I
Sydenham High School GDST, SE26 Entry age: 11/16+ 6 AA I
Sylvia Young Theatre School, NW1 Entry age: 10–14 D I
Thomas's Preparatory School, SW11 O
University College School, NW3 AA I
The Village School, NW3 AA
Virgo Fidelis, SE19 Entry age: 7–11 AA
Westminster Abbey Choir School, SW1P I
Westminster Cathedral Choir School, SW1P I
Westminster School, SW1P 6 AA I
Westminster Tutors, SW7 6 AA O
Westminster Under School, SW1P Entry age: 11+ I
The White House Prep & Woodentops Kindergarten, SW12 AA
Willington School, SW19 AA
Wimbledon High School GDST, SW19 6 AA I S
Woodside Park International School, N11 6 A AA D G I O

GREATER MANCHESTER

Abbey College, Manchester 6 AA
Branwood Preparatory School, Eccles O
Bridgewater School, Manchester Entry age: 11/16+ 6 AA
Chetham's School of Music, Manchester I
Manchester High School for Girls, Manchester Entry age: 11, 16 6 AA I
St Bede's College, Manchester I
William Hulme's Grammar School, Manchester Entry age: 11/16+ 6 AA I

MERSEYSIDE

Avalon Preparatory School, Wirral Entry age: 7 AA
The Belvedere School GDST, Liverpool 6 AA D I
Birkenhead High School GDST, Wirral 6 AA I
Birkenhead School, Wirral 6 AA I
Kingsmead School, Wirral Entry age: 7/11+ AA G I
Liverpool College, Liverpool 6 AA G I O
Merchant Taylors' School, Liverpool 6 AA
Merchant Taylors' School for Girls, Liverpool 6 AA O
Runnymede St Edward's School, Liverpool I
St Mary's College, Liverpool Entry age: 11/16+ 6 A AA G I
Streatham House School, Liverpool AA
Tower College, Prescot Entry age: 7, 11 AA I
Tower Dene Preparatory School, Southport Entry age: 5, 7 A AA G O

MIDDLESEX

Buckingham College Preparatory School, Pinner AA
Buckingham College School, Harrow 6 AA
Halliford School, Shepperton
Entry age: 11+ 6 A AA G I
Hampton School, Hampton
Entry age: 11+, 13 A AA G I O
Harrow School, Harrow on the Hill
Entry age: 13, 16 6 A AA G I
Heathfield School, Pinner 6 AA I
The John Lyon School, Harrow 6 A AA D G I
The Lady Eleanor Holles School, Hampton 6 AA I
Merchant Taylors' School, Northwood 6 AA I
North London Collegiate, Edgware AA I
Northwood College, Northwood
Entry age: 11+, 16+ 6 A AA G I
St Catherine's School, Twickenham
Entry age: 11 A AA G I O
St David's School, Ashford
Entry age: 11+, 16+ 6 A AA G I O
St Helen's School, Northwood 6 A AA D G I
St James Independent School for Boys (Senior), Twickenham O
Sunflower Montessori School, Twickenham I

NORFOLK

All Saints School, Norwich AA I
Glebe House School, Hunstanton A AA G I O
Gresham's Preparatory School, Holt AA
Gresham's School, Holt A AA D G I S
Hethersett Old Hall School, Norwich 6 AA O
Langley Preparatory School & Nursery, Norwich AA I
Langley School, Norwich
Entry age: 11, 13, 16 6 A AA D G I O
The New Eccles Hall School, Norwich
Entry age: 8 AA I O
Norwich High School for Girls GDST, Norwich 6 AA I
Norwich School, Norwich
Entry age: 9+, 11+, 16+ 6 AA I
Sacred Heart Convent School, Swaffham
Entry age: 11+ A AA D G I O
Taverham Hall, Norwich AA G I
Thetford Grammar School, Thetford
Entry age: 16+ 6 AA I
Town Close House Preparatory School, Norwich
Entry age: 7+ G I
Wood Dene School, Norwich A AA D

NORTHAMPTONSHIRE

Beachborough School, Brackley Entry age: 8–11 AA I O
Bosworth Independent College, Northampton 6 AA O S
Maidwell Hall, Northampton A I
Northampton High School, Northampton
Entry age: 11, 13, 16 6 A AA D G I
Great Houghton Preparatory School, Northampton A AA I
Northamptonshire Grammar School, Pitsford 6 AA I
Oundle School, Peterborough 6 A AA D I O
Quinton House School, Northampton 6 AA O
Winchester House School, Brackley A AA G I O

NORTHUMBERLAND

Longridge Towers School, Berwick-upon-Tweed
Entry age: 9, 11, 13, 16 6 AA G I
Mowden Hall School, Stocksfield AA
St Oswald's School, Alnwick AA O

NOTTINGHAMSHIRE

Bramcote Lorne School, Retford 6 AA G O S
Coteswood House School, Nottingham A AA D G I O
Dagfa House School, Nottingham Entry age: 11 I
Hollygirt School, Nottingham Entry age: 11+ AA I
Nottingham High School, Nottingham 6 AA
Nottingham High School for Girls GDST, Nottingham O
Ranby House, Retford Entry age: 11+ AA G I O
Rodney School, Newark AA D
Trent College, Nottingham 6 A AA D G I
Wellow House School, Newark A AA G I O
Worksop College, Worksop 6 A AA G I O

OXFORDSHIRE

Abacus College, Oxford O
Abingdon School, Abingdon 6 A AA I O
Bloxham School, Banbury Entry age: 11, 13, 16 6 A AA G I
Cherwell College, Oxford 6 AA
Christ Church Cathedral School, Oxford I
Cokethorpe, Witney 6 A AA D G I O
Cranford House School, Wallingford I O
d'Overbroeck's College, Oxford 6 A AA D I S
Ferndale Preparatory School, Faringdon AA
Headington School, Oxford Entry age: 11, 13, 16 6 A AA D G I
Josca's Preparatory School, Abingdon AA
Kingham Hill School, Chipping Norton
Entry age: 11+, 13+ 6 A AA D G I O
Magdalen College School, Oxford
Entry age: 7+, 13+, 16+ A AA G I
New College School, Oxford Entry age: 8 I
Our Lady's Convent Senior School, Abingdon 6 A AA I
Oxford High School GDST, Oxford 6 A AA G I
Oxford Tutorial College, Oxford AA
Radley College, Abingdon
Entry age: 13+ 6 A AA D I O
Rye St Antony School, Oxford 6 AA O
St Andrew's, Wantage AA
St Clare's, Oxford, Oxford Entry age: 16+ 6 AA O
St Edward's School, Oxford 6 A AA D G I O
St Mary's School, Wantage
Entry age: 11, 13, 16 6 A AA D G I O S
School of St Helen & St Katharine, Abingdon 6 AA I
Shiplake College, Henley-on-Thames
Entry age: 13+, 16+ 6 A AA G I
Sibford School, Banbury 6 AA I O
Summer Fields, Oxford AA I

Tudor Hall School, Banbury
Entry age: 11, 13, 16 A AA D G I
Wychwood School, Oxford 6 A AA I S

RUTLAND

Oakham School, Oakham 6 A AA D G I O S
Uppingham School, Uppingham 6 A AA I O

SHROPSHIRE

Adcote School for Girls, Shrewsbury 6 AA
Bedstone College, Bucknell 6 A AA G I O
Bellan House Preparatory School, Oswestry AA I O
Concord College, Shrewsbury 6 O
Dower House School, Bridgnorth
Entry age: 7, 8, 9 AA G O
Ellesmere College, Ellesmere 6 A AA D G I O S
Kingsland Grange, Shrewsbury Entry age: 7–11 AA G I
Moor Park School, Ludlow AA O
Moreton Hall, Oswestry Entry age: 11+, 13+, 16+ 6 A AA D G I O
The Old Hall School, Telford AA I
Oswestry School, Oswestry Entry age: 9+, 11+, 13+, 16+ 6 A AA G I O
Packwood Haugh School, Shrewsbury A AA G I
Prestfelde Preparatory School, Shrewsbury
Entry age: 7+, 11+ AA I O
Shrewsbury High School GDST, Shrewsbury 6 AA I
Shrewsbury School, Shrewsbury 6 A AA I O
Wrekin College, Telford Entry age: 11, 13, 16 6 A AA G I O

SOMERSET

All Hallows, Shepton Mallet Entry age: 11+ A AA G I O
Bruton School for Girls, Bruton Entry age: 11+, 13+, 16+ 6 A AA D G I O S
Buckland School, Watchet I
Chilton Cantelo School, Yeovil O
Downside School, Bath 6 A AA G I O
Hazlegrove (King's Bruton Preparatory School), Yeovil AA I
King's Bruton , Bruton 6 A AA D I O
King's College, Taunton 6 A AA D G I O S
King's Hall School, Taunton AA G I
Millfield Preparatory School, Street
Entry age: 7–13 A AA G I O
Millfield School, Street Entry age: 13, 14, 16 6 A AA G I O
The Park School, Yeovil Entry age: 8–18+ 6 A AA D I
Perrott Hill School, Crewkerne A AA D G I O
Queen's College Junior and Pre-Preparatory Schools, Taunton AA G I O
Queen's College, Taunton 6 A AA D G I
Taunton Preparatory School, Taunton
Entry age: 11+ AA G I
Taunton School, Taunton 6 AA G I O
Wellington School, Wellington
Entry age: 10+, 11+, 13+, 16+ 6 AA I
Wells Cathedral Junior School, Wells
Entry age: 8–11 AA I
Wells Cathedral School, Wells
Entry age: 11, 13, 16 6 AA I S

BATH & NORTH EAST SOMERSET

King Edward's School, Bath
Entry age: 11–18 6 A AA D G I
Kingswood School, Bath 6 A AA D G I O
Monkton Combe Junior School, Bath AA
Monkton Combe School, Bath 6 A AA D G I O
Paragon School, Prior Park College Junior, Bath AA G I O
Prior Park College, Bath 6 A AA D G I O
The Royal High School, Bath
Entry age: 11/16+ 6 AA I

NORTH SOMERSET

Sidcot School, Winscombe 6 A AA I O

STAFFORDSHIRE

Abbots Bromley School for Girls, Abbots Bromley Entry age: 11/16+ 6 A AA D G I
Abbotsholme School, Uttoxeter
Entry age: 11+, 13+, 16+ 6 A AA D G I
Brooklands School, Stafford AA O
Chase Academy, Cannock Entry age: 3+, 18+ AA G I O
Denstone College, Uttoxeter Entry age: 11, 13, 16 6 A AA D G I O
Edenhurst School, Newcastle-under-Lyme O
Lichfield Cathedral School, Lichfield
Entry age: 7, 9, 11 A AA D G I O
Newcastle-under-Lyme School, Newcastle-under-Lyme 6 AA G
St Dominic's Independent Junior School, Stoke-on-Trent Entry age: 8+ AA
St Dominic's Priory School, Stone AA
St Dominic's School, Stafford
Entry age: 11, 12 AA D G I
Stafford Grammar School, Stafford 6 A AA D G I O
Vernon Lodge Preparatory School, Brewood AA O
Yarlet School, Stafford Entry age: 11+ I

STOCKTON-ON-TEES

Teesside Preparatory and High School, Eaglescliffe 6 AA
Yarm School, Yarm Entry age: 7+, 11+, 16+ 6 AA I S

SUFFOLK

Amberfield School, Ipswich Entry age: 11/13+ A AA I
Cherry Trees School, Bury St Edmunds AA
Culford School, Bury St Edmunds 6 A AA D G I S
Fairstead House School, Newmarket AA
Felixstowe International College, Felixstowe AA O
Finborough School, Stowmarket 6 A AA G I O
Framlingham College, Woodbridge 6 A AA D I O S
Framlingham College Preparatory School, Brandeston Entry age: 11+/13+ A AA D I O
Hillcroft Preparatory School, Stowmarket AA G I
Ipswich High School GDST, Ipswich
Entry age: 11+ 6 AA I

Ipswich School, Ipswich Entry age: 11, 13, 16 6 A AA G I O
Moreton Hall Preparatory School, Bury St Edmunds A AA D G I
Orwell Park, Ipswich Entry age: 7+ A AA I O
Royal Hospital School, Ipswich Entry age: 11+ 6 A AA G I O
Saint Felix Schools, Southwold Entry age: 11, 13, 16 6 A AA D G I
St Joseph's College, Ipswich 6 AA G I O
South Lee Preparatory School, Bury St Edmunds Entry age: 8+, 11+ AA O
Stoke College, Sudbury AA I
Woodbridge School, Woodbridge 6 A AA I O

SURREY

Aberdour School, Tadworth AA
Amesbury, Hindhead AA G I
Barfield School, Farnham AA G I O
Belmont School, Dorking AA
Box Hill School, Dorking A AA D G I O
Bramley School, Tadworth Entry age: 7+ AA
Cambridge Tutors College, Croydon 6 AA
Canbury School, Kingston-upon-Thames AA O
Caterham School, Caterham 6 A AA D G I O S
Charterhouse, Godalming 6 A AA I O
City of London Freemen's School, Ashtead 6 A AA D G I
Claremont Fan Court School, Esher 6 A AA D G I
Cranleigh Preparatory School, Cranleigh AA I
Cranleigh School, Cranleigh Entry age: 13+, 16+ 6 A AA I O
Croham Hurst School, South Croydon Entry age: 11+, 16+ 6 AA G I
Croydon High School GDST, South Croydon 6 AA G I
Cumnor House School, South Croydon AA G I
Danes Hill School, Leatherhead AA
Downsend School, Leatherhead AA
Duke of Kent School, Ewhurst Entry age: 7+, 10+, 11+ AA O
Dunottar School, Reigate Entry age: 11, 14, 16 6 AA I
Edgeborough, Farnham O
Epsom College, Epsom Entry age: 13+, 16+ 6 A AA D G I O
Essendene Lodge School, Caterham AA O
Ewell Castle School, Epsom Entry age: 11+, 13+, 16+ 6 A AA G I O
Feltonfleet School, Cobham A AA I O
Frensham Heights School, Farnham A AA D I
Greenacre School for Girls, Banstead 6 A AA D G I O
Guildford High School, Guildford 6 AA I
Hampton Court House, East Molesey AA I
Haslemere Preparatory School, Haslemere A AA D G I O
Hawley Place School, Camberley Entry age: 7, 11 A AA D G I O
The Hawthorns School, Redhill AA I O
Hoe Bridge School, Woking Entry age: 7+ AA O
Homefield School, Sutton AA G O
Hurtwood House, Dorking Entry age: 16 6 D O S
King Edward's School Witley, Godalming 6 A AA I S
Kingston Grammar School, Kingston-upon-Thames 6 A AA G I
Kingswood House School, Epsom AA G
Lanesborough, Guildford Entry age: 8+ I
Lingfield Notre Dame School, Lingfield Entry age: 11+ 6 AA O
Lodge School, Purley AA I
Lyndhurst School, Camberley AA
Manor House School, Leatherhead Entry age: 7+, 11+ A AA D G I
Marymount International School, Kingston-upon-Thames Entry age: 11, 16 AA
Milbourne Lodge School, Esher AA
Notre Dame Preparatory School, Cobham O
Notre Dame Senior School, Cobham 6 AA
Oakfield School, Woking Entry age: 7+, 11+ AA I O
Old Palace School of John Whitgift, Croydon AA I
Parsons Mead, Ashtead 6 A AA I
Prior's Field School, Godalming Entry age: 11, 16 6 A AA D G I
Reed's School, Cobham 6 A AA G I O
Reigate Grammar School, Reigate 6 AA I O
Reigate St Mary's Preparatory and Choir School, Reigate Entry age: 8+ I
Ripley Court School, Woking A AA D G I O
Rokeby School, Kingston-upon-Thames A AA G I
Royal Grammar School, Guildford Entry age: 11+/13+ A AA I
Royal Russell School, Croydon Entry age: 11+/16 6 AA I
The Royal School, Haslemere Entry age: 11+, 13+, 16+ 6 A AA D G I O
St Andrew's (Woking) School Trust, Woking Entry age: 7+ A AA G I O
St Catherine's School, Guildford Entry age: 11/16+ 6 A AA G I O
St Edmund's School, Hindhead Entry age: 7/8 A AA G I O
St George's College, Weybridge 6 A AA I O
St Hilary's School, Godalming A AA D I
St Ives School, Haslemere A AA D G I O
St John's School, Leatherhead Entry age: 13+, 16+ 6 A AA G I O
St Teresa's School, Dorking 6 A AA D G I O
Sir William Perkins's School, Chertsey 6 AA I
Stowford College, Sutton Entry age: 11, 14 AA G O
Surbiton High School, Kingston-upon-Thames 6 A AA G I
Surrey College, Guildford Entry age: 15+ O
Sutton High School GDST, Sutton Entry age: 11+, 16+ 6 AA I
Tormead School, Guildford 6 A AA I
Trinity School, Croydon Entry age: 10+, 11+, 13+, 16+ 6 A AA G I O
West Dene School, Purley Entry age: 7 I
Whitgift School, South Croydon Entry age: 10–13, 16 6 A AA D G I O
Wispers School for Girls, Haslemere A D I
Woldingham School, Woldingham Entry age: 11+ 6 A AA D G I
Woodcote House School, Windlesham A AA G I O
Yehudi Menuhin School, Cobham I

EAST SUSSEX

Battle Abbey School, Battle
Entry age: 13/16+ 6 AA G O
Bellerbys College, Hove 6 AA
Brighton and Hove High School GDST, Brighton 6 AA
Brighton College, Brighton Entry age: 13+, 16+ 6 A AA D G I O
Brighton College Prep School, Brighton
Entry age: 11+ AA O
Buckswood School, Hastings AA G I
Claremont School, St Leonards-on-Sea A AA D G I O
Eastbourne College, Eastbourne
Entry age: 13, 16 6 A AA I O S
The Fold School, Hove Entry age: 3+ AA I
Lewes Old Grammar School, Lewes 6 AA I O
Moira House School, Eastbourne O
Moira House Girls School, Eastbourne AA D G I O
Lancing College Preparatory School at Mowden, Hove Entry age: 7+, 11+ AA
Newlands School, Seaford 6 A AA D G I O
Roedean School, Brighton
Entry age: 11+, 12+, 13+, 16+ 6 A AA D G I S
St Andrew's School, Eastbourne A AA D G I O
St Aubyns School, Brighton A AA G I O
St Bede's Prep School, Eastbourne A AA D G I
St Bede's School, Hailsham 6 A AA D G I
St Leonards-Mayfield School, Mayfield
Entry age: 11, 13, 16 6 A AA I
St Mary's Hall, Brighton 6 A AA D G I
Skippers Hill Manor Preparatory School, Mayfield AA D G O
Stonelands School of Ballet & Theatre Arts, Hove D O
Vinehall School, Robertsbridge AA I O

WEST SUSSEX

Ardingly College, Haywards Heath
Entry age: 7+, 11+, 13+ , 16+ 6 A AA D G I O S
Ardingly College Junior School, Haywards Heath
Entry age: 11+ A AA G I
Arundale Preparatory School, Pulborough
Entry age: 7–11 A AA G I O
Brambletye School, East Grinstead Entry age: 9+ I
Burgess Hill School for Girls, Burgess Hill 6 A AA D G I O
Conifers School, Midhurst AA I
Copthorne Prep School, Copthorne A AA G I
Dorset House School, Pulborough AA I
Farlington School, Horsham 6 A AA D G I O
Great Ballard School, Chichester
Entry age: 7 A AA D G I O
Great Walstead, Haywards Heath
Entry age: 7 – 11 AA D G I
Handcross Park School, Haywards Heath
Entry age: 7 – 11 AA G I
Hurstpierpoint College, Hurstpierpoint 6 A AA D G I O
Lancing College, Lancing 6 A AA G I O
Lavant House, Chichester Entry age: 11, 13 6 AA
Oakwood School, Chichester AA O
Our Lady of Sion School, Worthing 6 AA
The Prebendal School, Chichester Entry age: 7 I
Seaford College, Petworth
Entry age: 10+, 11+, 13+ 6 A AA G I
Shoreham College, Shoreham-by-Sea AA G I O
Slindon College, Arundel Entry age: 10 AA O
Stoke Brunswick, East Grinstead AA I O
Tavistock & Summerhill School, Haywards Heath AA
The Towers Convent School, Steyning AA
Westbourne House School, Chichester I
Windlesham House, Pulborough AA G I O
Worth School, Turners Hill Entry age: 11, 13, 16 6 A AA I

TYNE AND WEAR

Newcastle School for Boys, Newcastle upon Tyne AA
Central Newcastle High School GDST, Newcastle upon Tyne Entry age: 11+, 16+ 6 AA
Dame Allan's Boys School, Newcastle upon Tyne 6 AA
Dame Allan's Girls School, Newcastle upon Tyne
Entry age: 11 6 AA I
The King's School, Tynemouth
Entry age: 11+ 6 A AA I O S
La Sagesse School, Newcastle upon Tyne AA O
Newcastle Upon Tyne Church High School, Newcastle upon Tyne AA I
Sunderland High School, Sunderland 6 AA I
Westfield School, Newcastle upon Tyne 6 A AA G I O

WARWICKSHIRE

Abbotsford School, Kenilworth Entry age: 7 AA
Arnold Lodge School, Leamington Spa A AA I O
Bilton Grange, Rugby Entry age: 8+ AA G I O
The Croft Preparatory School, Stratford-upon-Avon
Entry age: 8 AA
The King's High School for Girls, Warwick 6 AA I
The Kingsley School, Leamington Spa 6 A AA D I
Princethorpe College, Rugby
Entry age: 11/18+ 6 A AA G I O
Rugby School, Rugby 6 A AA G I
Warwick School, Warwick 6 A AA I

WEST MIDLANDS

Abbey College, Birmingham 6 AA O
Al Hijrah School, Birmingham AA
Bablake School, Coventry 6 A AA I O
Birchfield School, Wolverhampton
Entry age: 11 A AA G I O
The Blue Coat School, Birmingham
Entry age: 7+ AA I O
Coventry Prep School, Coventry
Entry age: 7+ A AA I O
Edgbaston High School for Girls, Birmingham
Entry age: 11+ 6 AA G I
Elmhurst School for Dance, Birmingham 6
Eversfield Preparatory School, Solihull AA
Highclare School, Birmingham
Entry age: 11/16+ 6 A AA G I O
Hydesville Tower School, Walsall AA G I O

King Edward VI High School for Girls, Birmingham AA
King Edward's School, Birmingham Entry age: 11+, 13+, 16+ 6 AA I
King Henry VIII School, Coventry A AA I O
Mander Portman Woodward, Birmingham AA
Norfolk House School, Birmingham AA
Priory School, Birmingham Entry age: 11, 16 6 A AA D I
The Royal Wolverhampton Junior School, Wolverhampton AA I O
The Royal Wolverhampton School, Wolverhampton 6 AA G G I
St George's School, Edgbaston, Birmingham Entry age: 11+ 6 AA I O
Saint Martin's School, Solihull Entry age: 11+, 16+ 6 AA I
Solihull School, Solihull 6 A AA D I S
Tettenhall College, Wolverhampton Entry age: 11 6 A AA G I O
Wolverhampton Grammar School, Wolverhampton Entry age: 11+, 13+, 16+ 6 AA I O S

WILTSHIRE

Chafyn Grove School, Salisbury A AA G I O
Dauntsey's School, Devizes Entry age: 11+, 13+, 16+ 6 A AA D G I O S
Godolphin Preparatory School, Salisbury AA
The Godolphin School, Salisbury 6 A AA G I O
Grittleton House School, Chippenham A AA D G I S
La Retraite Swan, Salisbury Entry age: 7, 11, 14 A AA G I
Leaden Hall, Salisbury AA
Marlborough College, Marlborough Entry age: 13+, 16+ 6 A AA G I O
Norman Court Preparatory School, Salisbury Entry age: 7, 8, 11 A AA D G I O
Pinewood School, Shrivenham Entry age: 11+ AA O
Prior Park Preparatory School, Cricklade AA
St Francis School, Pewsey A AA G I O
St Mary's School, Calne Entry age: 11+, 13+, 16+ 6 A AA I O
Salisbury Cathedral School, Salisbury Entry age: 7, 10 A AA D G I
Sandroyd School, Salisbury AA I O
Stonar School, Melksham 6 A AA D G I O
Warminster School, Warminster Entry age: 7, 9, 11, 13, 16 6 A AA D G I O

WORCESTERSHIRE

Abberley Hall, Worcester Entry age: 8+ AA
The Abbey College, Malvern Wells 6 AA O S
The Alice Ottley School, Worcester 6 A AA G I
Bromsgrove Preparatory School, Bromsgrove Entry age: 11+ AA I O
Bromsgrove School, Bromsgrove 6 A AA D G I O
The Downs School, Malvern A AA D G I O
The Elms, Malvern AA G I O
Hartlebury School, Kidderminster A AA D G I S
Heathfield School, Kidderminster AA
Malvern College Preparatory and Pre-Prep School, Malvern A AA D G I O
Holy Trinity School, Kidderminster 6 AA I O S
King's Hawford, Worcester Entry age: 7+, 8+ AA
The King's School, Worcester AA I
Malvern College, Malvern 6 A AA D G I O
Malvern Girls' College, Malvern Entry age: 11+, 12+, 13+, 16+ 6 A AA G I
Moffats School, Bewdley A AA D G I O S
Royal Grammar School Worcester, Worcester A AA I
St James's School, Malvern Entry age: 11+, 13+, 16+ 6 A AA G I
St Mary's Convent School, Worcester Entry age: 11+, 16+ A AA G I
Saint Michael's College, Tenbury Wells 6 AA O S
Whitford Hall & Dodderhill School, Droitwich Entry age: 11+ AA I
Winterfold House, Kidderminster A AA G I O

EAST RIDING OF YORKSHIRE

Hull Grammar School, Kingston-Upon-Hull 6 AA O
Hull High School, Anlaby Entry age: 11 6 AA
Pocklington School, Pocklington 6 AA I O

NORTH YORKSHIRE

Ampleforth College, York Entry age: 13, 16 6 AA I O
Ashville College, Harrogate Entry age: 11–18 6 A AA D G I O
Aysgarth Preparatory School, Bedale I
Belmont Grosvenor School, Harrogate AA G I
Bootham School, York Entry age: 11+, 13+, 16+ 6 A AA I O
Bramcote School, Scarborough AA G I O
Catteral Hall School, Settle Entry age: 10, 11 AA I O
Cundall Manor School, York AA G I
Fyling Hall School, Whitby 6 AA G I O
Giggleswick School, Settle Entry age: 13, 16 6 A AA D G I O
Harrogate Ladies' College, Harrogate Entry age: 11+, 16+ 6 AA I O
Harrogate Tutorial College, Harrogate Entry age: 15+ 6 AA O
Howsham Hall, York AA G O
Lisvane, Scarborough College Junior School, Scarborough Entry age: 7–9 AA
Malsis School, Skipton AA I O
The Minster School, York I
The Mount School, York 6 A AA I
Queen Ethelburga's College, York Entry age: 11 6 A AA D G I O S
Queen Margaret's School, York 6 A AA I O
Queen Mary's School, Thirsk A AA G I
Read School, Selby Entry age: 11+, 13+, 16+ 6 A AA I
Ripon Cathedral Choir School, Ripon AA I
St Martin's Ampleforth, York Entry age: 7/12+ AA G I O
St Peter's School, York Entry age: 13/16+ 6 AA I O
Scarborough College & Lisvane School, Scarborough 6 A AA I

Terrington Hall, York A AA D G I O
Woodleigh School, Malton A AA D G I

SOUTH YORKSHIRE

Birkdale School, Sheffield Entry age: 11, 16 6 AA I S
Hill House St Mary's School, Doncaster A AA G I O
Sheffield High School GDST, Sheffield Entry age: 11, 16 6 AA I O
Westbourne School, Sheffield A AA G O

WEST YORKSHIRE

Ackworth School, Pontefract A AA I
Bradford Girls' Grammar School, Bradford I
Bradford Grammar School, Bradford Entry age: 11+ I
Bronte House School, Bradford Entry age: 9 AA
The Froebelian School, Leeds AA
Fulneck School, Pudsey 6 A AA G I O
Gateways School, Leeds Entry age: 11 6 A AA D G I
Ghyll Royd School, Ilkley Entry age: 7 AA
Hipperholme Grammar School, Halifax Entry age: 16+ 6 AA
Huddersfield Grammar School, Huddersfield AA I
The International Centre, Ackworth School, Pontefract 6 A AA D I
Leeds Girls' High School, Leeds 6 AA I
Leeds Grammar School, Leeds Entry age: 11+, 16+ 6 AA I
Moorlands School, Leeds A AA G I
Queen Elizabeth Grammar School, Wakefield 6 AA I
The Rastrick Independent School, Brighouse Entry age: 11+ O
Richmond House School, Leeds Entry age: 7/8 AA
Rishworth School, Rishworth Entry age: 11, 16 6 AA D G I O
Shaw House School, Bradford AA O
Silcoates School, Wakefield Entry age: 11 6 A AA D G I O S
Wakefield Girls' High School, Wakefield 6 AA
Wakefield Independent School, Wakefield AA
Wakefield Tutorial Preparatory School, Leeds O
Woodhouse Grove School, Apperley Bridge A AA G I O

NORTHERN IRELAND

COUNTY ANTRIM

Campbell College, Belfast A AA I
Methodist College, Belfast 6 I

COUNTY TYRONE

The Royal School Dungannon, Dungannon Entry age: 11–16 AA G I

SCOTLAND

ABERDEENSHIRE

Albyn School, Aberdeen A AA G I
Robert Gordons College, Aberdeen 6 AA G I O
St Margaret's School for Girls, Aberdeen AA I

ANGUS

The High School of Dundee, Dundee Entry age: 12 O
Lathallan School, Montrose A AA D G I O

ARGYLL AND BUTE

Lomond School, Helensburgh Entry age: 11, 16 6 AA I

CLACKMANNANSHIRE

Dollar Academy, Dollar A I

FIFE

St Leonards School & VIth Form College, St Andrews 6 A AA D G I

GLASGOW

Craigholme School, Glasgow Entry age: 12 AA
The Glasgow Academy, Glasgow Entry age: 11+ 6 AA
The High School of Glasgow, Glasgow AA
Hutchesons' Grammar School, Glasgow 6 AA
Kelvinside Academy, Glasgow 6 AA
St Aloysius' College, Glasgow AA

LANARKSHIRE

Hamilton College, Hamilton AA I

LOTHIAN

Cargilfield, Edinburgh AA I O
The Edinburgh Academy, Edinburgh 6 A AA I
Fettes College, Edinburgh 6 A AA G I O
George Heriot's School, Edinburgh Entry age: 11+ 6 A AA D G I
George Watson's College, Edinburgh 6 AA G I S
Loretto Junior School, Musselburgh Entry age: 10/11 A AA D G O
Loretto School, Musselburgh 6 A AA G I O
The Mary Erskine School, Edinburgh 6 AA I
Merchiston Castle School, Edinburgh 6 A AA I O

St Margaret's School, Edinburgh 6 A AA D G I
St Mary's Music School, Edinburgh Entry age: 9+ I
Stewart's Melville College, Edinburgh AA I

MORAYSHIRE

Gordonstoun School, Elgin
Entry age: 9 6 A AA D G I O

PERTH AND KINROSS

Ardvreck School, Crieff AA
Glenalmond College, Perth
Entry age: 12, 13, 16 6 A AA I O
Kilgraston (A Sacred Heart School), Perth A AA G I O
Morrison's Academy, Crieff 6 AA
Strathallan School, Perth
Entry age: 10+, 16+ 6 A AA I O

ROXBURGHSHIRE

St Mary's Preparatory School, Melrose O

STIRLING

Beaconhurst School, Stirling AA D O

WALES

BRIDGEND

St Clare's School, Porthcawl Entry age: 11+,
13+ ,16+ AA
St John's School, Porthcawl AA O

CARDIFF

The Cardiff Academy, Cardiff AA
The Cathedral School, Cardiff Entry age: 11 AA G I
Howell's School, Llandaff GDST, Cardiff
Entry age: 11, 16 6 AA I
Kings Monkton School, Cardiff 6 A AA G I

CARMARTHENSHIRE

Llandovery College, Llandovery Entry age: 11+,
17+ 6 A AA D G I O
St Michael's School, Llanelli 6 AA D G I O

CONWY

Lyndon Preparatory School,
Colwyn Bay 6 A AA D G I O S
Rydal Penrhos Senior School, Colwyn Bay 6 AA G I
St David's College, Llandudno Entry age: 11 A AA G I

DENBIGHSHIRE

Howell's School, Denbigh Entry age: 11 6 A AA D G I
Ruthin School, Ruthin Entry age: 11 6 A AA D G I O S

MONMOUTHSHIRE

Haberdashers' Monmouth School For Girls,
Monmouth 6 AA I
Monmouth School, Monmouth
Entry age: 11, 13, 16 6 AA G I
St John's-on-the-Hill, Chepstow A AA D G I O

NEWPORT

Rougemont School, Newport AA

PEMBROKESHIRE

Netherwood School, Saundersfoot
Entry age: 11, 12, 13 AA

POWYS

Christ College, Brecon Entry age: 11,
13, 16 6 A AA G I O S

SWANSEA

Ffynone House School, Swansea
Entry age: 11 6 A AA D G I O S
Oakleigh House, Swansea A AA D G I

4.2
Bursaries and Reserved Entrance Awards

The following is compiled from information provided by schools. For further information please contact the school direct. The abbreviations used are as follows:

E	Christian Missionary or full-time worker
F1	The Royal Navy
F2	The Royal Marines
F3	The Army
F4	The Royal Air Force
FO	Foreign Office
H	Financial or domestic hardship
M	Medical profession
T	Teaching profession
+	The Clergy

ENGLAND

BEDFORDSHIRE

Bedford High School, Bedford F1 F2 F3 F4 H
Bedford Modern School, Bedford H
Bedford Preparatory School, Bedford F1 F2 F3 F4 H
Bedford School, Bedford + F1 F2 F3 F4 H T
Dame Alice Harpur School, Bedford H
Moorlands School, Luton H T

BERKSHIRE

The Abbey School, Reading Entry age: 11+, 16+ H
The Ark School, Reading Entry age: 5+ H T
Bearwood College, Wokingham + E F1 F3 F4 H
Brigidine School Windsor, Windsor Entry age: 11 H
Dolphin School, Reading H T
Downe House, Thatcham H
Elstree School, Reading Entry age: 7 + E H T
Eton College, Windsor H
Heathfield School, Ascot
Entry age: 11+, 13+, 16+ + F1 F2 F3 F4 FO
Hemdean House School, Reading Entry age: 11+ H
Highfield School, Maidenhead Entry age: 7+, 12+ H
Horris Hill, Newbury F1 F2 F3 F4
Hurst Lodge School, Ascot F1 F2 F3 F4
Lambrook Haileybury, Bracknell T
Leighton Park School, Reading H
Luckley-Oakfield School, Wokingham F1 F2 F3 F4
The Oratory Preparatory School, Reading F1 F2 F3 F4 H
The Oratory School, Reading
Entry age: 11+, 13+ F1 F2 F3 F4 H T
Padworth College, Reading F1 F2 F3 F4 FO H
Pangbourne College, Pangbourne F1 F2 F3 F4 H
Queen Anne's School, Reading +
Reading Blue Coat School, Reading H T
St Andrew's School, Reading +
St George's School, Ascot Entry age: 11+, 16+ H
St Joseph's Convent School, Reading H

St Michaels School, Newbury H
St Piran's Preparatory School, Maidenhead E H T
Sunningdale School, Sunningdale T
Upton House School, Windsor H
Wellington College, Crowthorne F3 H
White House Preparatory School, Wokingham + H

BRISTOL

Badminton School H
Bristol Cathedral School, Bristol Entry age: 11+, 13+, 16+ H
Bristol Grammar School, Bristol H
Clifton College, Bristol + F1 F2 F3 F4 H T
Clifton College Preparatory School + F1 F2 F3 F4
Clifton High School, Bristol Entry age: 11+, 13+, 16+ H
Colston's Collegiate School, Bristol F1 F2 F3
Colston's Girls' School H
The Downs School, Wraxall Entry age: 8+ + F1 F2 F3 H
Fairfield PNEU School, Bristol H
Overndale School, Bristol H
Queen Elizabeth's Hospital Entry age: 11, 13, 16 H
The Red Maids' School H
Redland High School Entry age: 11, 16 H
Tockington Manor School, Bristol T

BUCKINGHAMSHIRE

Ashfold School, Aylesbury + E F1 F2 F3 F4
The Beacon School, Amersham H
Bury Lawn School, Milton Keynes H
Caldicott School, Farnham Royal H T
Davenies School, Beaconsfield H
Gayhurst School, Gerrards Cross + E H
Godstowe Preparatory School, High Wycombe Entry age: 8,11 T
High March School, Beaconsfield H T
Holy Cross Convent, Gerrards Cross + H
Ladymede, Aylesbury H
Milton Keynes Preparatory School, Milton Keynes H
Pipers Corner School, High Wycombe F1 F2 F3 F4
St Mary's School, Gerrards Cross + H
Stowe School, Buckingham E H
Swanbourne House School, Milton Keynes Entry age: 11+ + F1 F3 F4
Thornton College Convent of Jesus and Mary, Milton Keynes Entry age: 8, 11 F1 F2 F3 F4 H
Thorpe House School, Gerrards Cross H T

CAMBRIDGESHIRE

Bellerbys College, Cambridge H
Cambridge Arts & Sciences (CATS), Cambridge H
Cambridge Centre for Sixth-form Studies, Cambridge F1 F2 F3 H
Kimbolton School, Huntingdon H
The King's School Ely, Ely Entry age: 11+ + F1 F2 F3 F4 H
The Leys School, Cambridge Entry age: 11, 13, 16 F1 F2 F3 F4 H
Madingley Pre-Preparatory School, Cambridge H
MPW (Mander Portman Woodward), Cambridge H
The Perse School for Girls, Cambridge Entry age: 11 H
Peterborough High School, Peterborough F1 F2 F3 F4 H
St John's College School, Cambridge H
St Mary's School, Cambridge H
Sancton Wood School, Cambridge H T
Wisbech Grammar School, Wisbech H

CHANNEL ISLANDS

Ormer House Preparatory School, Alderney H
St George's Preparatory School, Jersey Entry age: 7 H T
St Michael's Preparatory School, Jersey + H
Victoria College, Jersey H

CHESHIRE

Abbey Gate College, Chester Entry age: 11+, 16+ H
Alderley Edge School for Girls, Alderley Edge H
Beech Hall School, Macclesfield + E H
Cheadle Hulme School, Cheadle Entry age: 11, 16 H
Culcheth Hall, Altrincham H
The Grange School, Northwich H
Hillcrest Grammar School, Stockport H
Hulme Hall Schools, Cheadle H T
The King's School, Chester Entry age: 11, 16 H
The King's School, Macclesfield H
Macclesfield Preparatory School, Macclesfield E
Mostyn House School, South Wirral Entry age: 4 H
North Cestrian Grammar School, Altrincham H
Oriel Bank, Stockport H
Pownall Hall School, Wilmslow + T
The Queen's School, Chester H
Ramillies Hall School, Cheadle F1 F2 F3 F4
Stockport Grammar School, Stockport Entry age: 11+ H
Terra Nova School, Holmes Chapel + E F1 F2 F3 F4 H
Wilmslow Preparatory School, Wilmslow H T
Yorston Lodge School, Knutsford +

CORNWALL

The Bolitho School, Penzance Entry age: 10+,13+ + F1 F2 F3 F4 H
Polwhele House School, Truro + H T
Roselyon, Par H
St Joseph's School, Launceston Entry age: 7+, 11+ H
St Petroc's School, Bude + F1 F2 F3 F4 H T
Truro High School, Truro Entry age: 11+, 16+ + E H
Truro School Preparatory School, Truro Entry age: 7+ H
Truro School, Truro H
Wheelgate House School, Newquay H

CUMBRIA

Austin Friars St Monica's School, Carlisle H
Casterton School, Kirkby Lonsdale E H T

Chetwynde School, Barrow-in-Furness H
Harecroft Hall School, Seascale + F1 F2 F3 F4 H
Hunter Hall School, Penrith H
Lime House School, Carlisle E F1 F2 F3 FO H T
St Bees School, St Bees + F1 F2 F3 F4 H
St Ursulas Convent School, Wigton H
Sedbergh School, Sedbergh
Entry age: 13+, 16+, 17+ + E F1 F2 F3 F4 H T
Wellspring Christian School, Carlisle E H
Windermere St Anne's, Windermere
Entry age: 11+, 13+, 16+ H

DERBYSHIRE

Derby Grammar School for Boys, Derby H
Derby High School, Derby H
Foremarke Hall School, Derby F1 F2 F3 F4 H
Michael House Steiner School, Heanor H
Mount St Mary's College, Spinkhill
Entry age: 11+ F2 F3 F4 FO H
Repton School, Derby Entry age: 13+,
16+ F1 F2 F3 F4 H
St Anselm's, Bakewell Entry age: 7 + F1 F2 F3 F4
St Wystan's School, Repton H

DEVON

Blundell's School, Tiverton Entry age: 11,
13, 16 F1 F2 F3 F4 FO H
Bramdean School, Exeter Entry age: 7 H
Edgehill College, Bideford + E F1 F2 F3 F4 H
Emmanuel School, Exeter H
Exeter Cathedral School, Exeter
Entry age: 7+ F1 F2 F3 F4 H
Exeter Junior School, Exeter H
Exeter School, Exeter Entry age: 7, 8, 11, 12, 13, 16 H
Exeter Tutorial College, Exeter H
Gramercy Hall School, Torbay H T
Grenville College, Bideford + F1 F2 F3 F4 H T
Kelly College, Tavistock Entry age: 11,
13, 16 E F1 F2 F3 F4 H T
The Maynard School, Exeter H
Mount House School, Tavistock T
Park School, Totnes H
Plymouth College, Plymouth H
St Christophers School, Totnes H
St John's School, Sidmouth Entry age: 8 F1 F2 F3 F4 H
St Margaret's School, Exeter E H
St Michael's, Barnstaple + F1 F2 F3 F4 H T
St Wilfrid's School, Exeter H
Sands School, Ashburton H
Shebbear College, Beaworthy + E F1 F2 F3 F4 H T
Stover School, Newton Abbot + F1 F2 F3 F4 FO H
Tower House School, Paignton
Entry age: 11 H
Trinity School, Teignmouth + F1 F2 F3 F4 H M T
West Buckland Preparatory School, Barnstaple H
West Buckland School, Barnstaple H

DORSET

Bryanston School, Blandford Forum H
Castle Court Preparatory School, Wimborne + E H
Clayesmore Preparatory School,
Blandford Forum + F1 F2 F3 F4 H
Clayesmore School, Blandford Forum F1 F2 F3 F4
Dorchester Preparatory School, Dorchester H
Dumpton School, Wimborne H T
Knighton House, Blandford Forum F1 F2 F3 F4 FO H T
Milton Abbey School,
Blandford Forum F1 F2 F3 F4 H T
The Park School, Bournemouth H
Port Regis School, Shaftesbury Entry age: 7+, 12+ T
St Antony's Leweston Schools, Sherborne H
Sherborne Preparatory School,
Sherborne F1 F2 F3 F4 H
Sherborne School, Sherborne F1 F2 F3 F4 H
Sherborne School for Girls, Sherborne H
Talbot Heath, Bournemouth H
Uplands School, Poole H
Wentworth College, Bournemouth F1 F2 F4
Yarrells School, Poole F1 F2 H

COUNTY DURHAM

Barnard Castle School, Barnard Castle F1 F2 F3 F4
The Chorister School, Durham + H
Durham High School For Girls, Durham + H
Durham School, Durham
Entry age: 11–18 F1 F2 F3 F4 H
Hurworth House School, Darlington H
Polam Hall, Darlington F1 F2 F3 F4 H

ESSEX

Alleyn Court Preparatory School,
Southend-on-Sea + H T
Bancroft's School, Woodford Green Entry age: 11 H
Brentwood School, Brentwood Entry age: 11–18 H T
Chigwell School, Chigwell H T
Cranbrook College, Ilford T
Dame Johane Bradbury's School, Saffron Walden H
Felsted School, Dunmow F1 F2 F3
Holmwood House, Colchester H
Littlegarth School, Colchester H
New Hall School, Chelmsford Entry age: 11 F1 F2 F4
St Hilda's School, Westcliff-on-Sea H
St Michael's School, Leigh-on-Sea E
St Nicholas School, Harlow H T
Thorpe Hall School, Southend-on-Sea H

GLOUCESTERSHIRE

The Abbey School, Tewkesbury + H
Beaudesert Park School, Stroud F1 F2 F3 F4
Bredon School, Tewkesbury F1 F2 F3 F4
Cheltenham College, Cheltenham F1 F2 F3 F4
Cheltenham College Junior School,
Cheltenham F1 F2 F3 F4
The Cheltenham Ladies' College, Cheltenham H

Dean Close Preparatory School, Cheltenham + E F1 F2 F3 F4 H
Dean Close School, Cheltenham + E F1 F2 F3 F4 H T
Hatherop Castle School, Cirencester H
Ingleside PNEU School, Cirencester H
The King's School, Gloucester + F1 F2 F3 F4 H T
Rendcomb College, Cirencester F1 F2 F3 F4
Rose Hill School, Wotton-under-Edge F1 F2 F3 F4 H T
St Edward's School, Cheltenham H
School of the Lion, Gloucester E H
Westonbirt School, Tetbury + F1 F2 F3 F4 FO H
Wycliffe College & Preparatory School, Stonehouse F1 F2 F3 F4 H T
Wycliffe Preparatory School, Stonehouse F1 F2 F3 F4 FO H T
Wynstones School, Gloucester H

HAMPSHIRE

The Atherley School, Southampton H
Ballard School, New Milton H T
Bedales School, Petersfield Entry age: 13+, 16+ H
Churchers College, Petersfield H
Daneshill School, Basingstoke T
Dunhurst (Bedales Junior School), Petersfield H
Durlston Court, New Milton H
Hampshire Collegiate School, Embley Park, Romsey + F1 F2 F3 F4 FO H T
Farnborough Hill, Farnborough H
Forres Sandle Manor, Fordingbridge F1 F2 F3 F4
The Gregg School, Southampton H
Highfield School, Liphook Entry age: 7+, 12+ E F1 F2 F3 F4 H
Hordle Walhampton School, Lymington H
King Edward VI School, Southampton Entry age: 11+, 13+ H
Mayville High School, Southsea H
The Pilgrims' School, Winchester H
The Portsmouth Grammar School, Portsmouth H T
Portsmouth High School GDST, Southsea H
Rookesbury Park School, Portsmouth F1 F2 F3 H
St Neot's School, Hook Entry age: 5+ H
St Nicholas' School, Fleet +
St Swithun's School, Winchester Entry age: 11–18 H
Salesian College, Farnborough H
Sherborne House School, Eastleigh Entry age: 5–11 H
Stanbridge Earls School, Romsey H
Stockton House School, Aldershot H
Winchester College, Winchester Entry age: 13, 16 H
Wykeham House School, Fareham H

HEREFORDSHIRE

The Hereford Cathedral School, Hereford + F1 F2 F3 F4 H T
Lucton School, Leominster E H
St Richard's, Bromyard F1 F2 F3 F4

HERTFORDSHIRE

Abbot's Hill School, Hemel Hempstead T
Aldenham School, Elstree H
Berkhamsted Collegiate Preparatory School, Berkhamsted H
Berkhamsted Collegiate School, Berkhamsted F3 H M T
Bishop's Stortford College, Bishop's Stortford F1 F3 F4 H T
Edge Grove, Aldenham Entry age: 7+ E F1 F2 F3 F4 FO H T
Egerton-Rothesay School, Berkhamsted H
Haberdashers' Aske's Boys' School, Elstree Entry age: 11, 13 H
Haberdashers' Aske's School for Girls, Elstree + H
Haileybury, Hertford H
Harpenden Preparatory School, Harpenden H
Immanuel College, Bushey H T
The Junior School, Bishop's Stortford College, Bishop's Stortford H
Lockers Park, Hemel Hempstead F1 F2 F3 T
Norfolk Lodge Nursery & Preparatory School, Barnet H
The Princess Helena College, Hitchin + E F1 F2 F3 F4 H
The Purcell School, Bushey H
Queenswood School, Hatfield H
The Royal Masonic School for Girls, Rickmansworth Entry age: 11+ F1 F2 F3 F4 H
St Albans High School for Girls, St Albans + H
St Albans School, St Albans Entry age: 11+, 13+, 16+ H
St Andrew's Montessori School, Watford H T
St Christopher School, Letchworth H
St Columba's College, St Albans H
St Edmund's College, Ware + F1 F2 F3 F4 H T
St Francis' College, Letchworth H
St Margaret's School, Bushey + H
Westbrook Hay Preparatory School, Hemel Hempstead H
York House School, Rickmansworth H T

ISLE OF MAN

King William's College, Castletown + F1 F2 F3 F4 H T

ISLE OF WIGHT

Ryde School, Ryde H
Westmont School, Newport + H

KENT

Ashford School, Ashford H
Baston School, Bromley H
Bedgebury School, Cranbrook + F1 F2 F3 F4 H
Beechwood Sacred Heart School, Tunbridge Wells Entry age: 11+, 13+ E F1 F2 F3 F4 FO H
Benenden School, Cranbrook Entry age: 11–18 H
Bethany School, Cranbrook + E F1 F2 F3 F4 H
Bickley Park School, Bromley H T
Bromley High School GDST, Bromley H
Cobham Hall, Gravesend H
Dover College, Dover F1 F2 F3 F4
Elliott Park School, Sheerness H

Farringtons School, Chislehurst E F1 F2 F3 F4
Gad's Hill School, Rochester H
The Granville School, Sevenoaks H
Hilden Grange School, Tonbridge H
Junior King's School, Canterbury +
The Junior School, St Lawrence College, Ramsgate + E F1 F2 F3 F4 T
Kent College, Canterbury Entry age: 11+, 13+, 16+ + H
Kent College Pembury, Tunbridge Wells F1 F2 F3 F4
King's Preparatory School, Rochester + E F1 F2 F3 F4 H
King's School Rochester, Rochester + F1 F2 F3 F4 H
Lorenden Preparatory School, Faversham Entry age: 7+ H
Marlborough House School, Hawkhurst T
Merton Court Preparatory School, Sidcup H T
Northbourne Park School, Deal + E F1 F2 F3 F4 H
Rochester Independent College, Rochester H
Rose Hill School, Tunbridge Wells H
Sackville School, Tonbridge H
St Christopher's School, Canterbury Entry age: 3–11 H
St Edmunds Junior School, Canterbury + F1 F2 F3 F4 FO
St Edmund's School, Canterbury Entry age: 11+, 13+, 16+ + F1 F2 F3 F4 FO H
St Lawrence College, Ramsgate + E F1 F2 F3 F4 FO H T
St Mary's Westbrook, Folkestone + F1 F2 F3 F4 H
St Michael's School, Sevenoaks H
Sevenoaks Preparatory School, Sevenoaks T
Sevenoaks School, Sevenoaks Entry age: 11+ H
Solefield School, Sevenoaks H T
Sutton Valence School, Maidstone Entry age: 11+, 13+, 16 H T
Tonbridge School, Tonbridge Entry age: 13+, 14+, 16+ H
Walthamstow Hall, Sevenoaks Entry age: 11+, 13+, 16+ + E H
Wellesley House School, Broadstairs + H T
Yardley Court, Tonbridge H

LANCASHIRE

Arnold School, Blackpool H
Beech House School, Rochdale H
Bolton School (Boys' Division), Bolton H
Bolton School (Girls' Division), Bolton Entry age: 11, 16 H
Bury Grammar School, Bury H
Bury Grammar School Girls, Bury H
Heathland College, Accrington H
The Hulme Grammar School for Girls, Oldham H
Kingswood College at Scarisbrick Hall, Ormskirk H T
Kirkham Grammar School, Preston H
Moorland School, Clitheroe F1 F2 F3 F4
The Oldham Hulme Grammar School, Oldham H
Queen Elizabeth's Grammar School, Blackburn Entry age: 11+ + H
Rossall Junior School, Fleetwood + F3
Rossall School, Fleetwood Entry age: 11 + F1 F2 F3
St Anne's College Grammar School, Lytham St Annes F1 F2 F3 F4 FO
Sedbergh Junior School, Lancaster F1 F2 F3 F4 H
Stonyhurst College, Clitheroe H

LEICESTERSHIRE

Leicester Grammar School, Leicester Entry age: 11,18 H
Leicester High School For Girls, Leicester H
Loughborough High School, Loughborough H
Manor House School, Ashby-de-la-Zouch + H
PNEU School, Loughborough +
Ratcliffe College, Leicester F1 F2 F3 F4
St Crispin's School (Leicester) Ltd., Leicester Entry age: 3+, 7+, 13+, 16+ H
Stoneygate School, Leicester + E H

LINCOLNSHIRE

Fen School, Sleaford Entry age: 4–5 E F1 F2 F3 F4
Kirkstone House School, Bourne H
Maypole House School, Alford H
St Hugh's School, Woodhall Spa F1 F2 F3 F4 T
Stamford High School, Stamford H
Stamford School, Stamford H
Witham Hall, Bourne H T

NORTH EAST LINCOLNSHIRE

St James' School, Grimsby + F1 F2 F4 FO H T

NORTH LINCOLNSHIRE

Brigg Preparatory School, Brigg +

LONDON

Albemarle Independent College, W1K Entry age: 14+, 19+ H
Alleyn's School, SE22 H
The American School in London, NW8 H
Arnold House School, NW8 H
The Arts Educational School, W4 H
Ashbourne Independent Sixth Form College, W8 + FO H M T
Ashbourne Middle School, W8 + F4 FO H M T
Bales College, W10 H
Belmont (Mill Hill Preparatory School), NW7 H
Blackheath High School GDST, SE3 H
Channing School, N6 H
City of London School, EC4V Entry age: 11+, 13+, 16+ H T
City of London School for Girls, EC2Y H
Colfe's School, SE12 H
Collingham College, SW5 FO H T
Dallington School, EC1V H
Davies Laing and Dick, W1U H
Dolphin School (Including Noah's Ark Nursery Schools), SW11 + E H
Dulwich College, SE21 Entry age: 11, 13 H
Dulwich College Preparatory School, SE21 Entry age: 7–8 H
Ealing College Upper School, W13 H
Emanuel School, SW11 H
Forest School, E17 +

Francis Holland School, SW1W
Entry age: 11+ + E FO H
Francis Holland School, NW1 + H
Garden House School, SW3 H
The Godolphin and Latymer School, W6 H
Hampstead Fine Arts Independent College, NW3 H
Hampstead Hill Pre-Preparatory & Nursery School, NW3 Entry age: 4+ H
Hellenic College of London, SW1X H
Hereward House School, NW3 +
Highgate School, N6 Entry age: 11+, 13+ H
Hurlingham Private School, SW15 H
International School of London, W3 H
James Allen's Girls' School, SE22 H
The Kerem School, N2 H
King Fahad Academy, W3 H
King's College Junior School, SW19 H
King's College School, SW19 H
Lansdowne College, W2 Entry age: 14+, 16+ H
Latymer Upper School, W6 H
Lyndhurst House Preparatory School, NW3 H
Mander Portman Woodward, SW7 FO T
More House, SW1X H
Naima Jewish Preparatory School, NW6 H
The Norwegian School, SW20 F1 F2 F3 F4 FO
Notting Hill and Ealing High School GDST, W13 H
Palmers Green High School, N21 Entry age: 11+ H
The Pointer School, SE3 + E F1 F2 F3 H
Putney High School GDST, SW15 H
Queen's College, W1G H
Riverston School, SE12 + H
The Roche School, SW18 H
Royal Ballet School, WC2E H
The Royal School, Hampstead, NW3
Entry age: 3–18 F1 F3 F4 H
St Benedict's School, W5 Entry age: 11+ H
St James Independent School for Boys, W14 H
St James Independent School for Senior Girls, W14 H
St James Independent School for Girls (Juniors), W14 H
St Johns Wood Pre-Preparatory School, NW8 H
St Margaret's School, NW3 H
St Paul's Cathedral School, EC4M H
St Paul's Girls' School, W6 H
St Paul's Preparatory School, SW13 H
St Paul's School, SW13 H
Sarum Hall, NW3 H
Sinclair House School, SW6 H
South Hampstead High School, NW3 H
Southbank International School, Kensington, W11 H
Southbank International School, Hampstead, NW3 H
Southbank International School, Westminster, W1B H T
Streatham and Clapham High School, SW16
Entry age: 11, 13, 16 H
Sydenham High School GDST, SE26 H
Sylvia Young Theatre School, NW1 Entry age: 10–14 H
University College School, NW3 H
The Village School, NW3 + H
Westminster Cathedral Choir School, SW1P H
Westminster School, SW1P H
Westminster Under School, SW1P H
The White House Prep & Woodentops Kindergarten, SW12 H
Willington School, SW19 H
Woodside Park International School, N11 H

GREATER MANCHESTER

Abbey College, Manchester M
Bridgewater School, Manchester Entry age: 11 H
The Manchester Grammar School, Manchester
Entry age: 11 H
Manchester High School for Girls, Manchester
Entry age: 11 H
Monton Prep School with Montessori Nurseries, Eccles H T
St Bede's College, Manchester H
William Hulme's Grammar School, Manchester H
Withington Girls' School, Manchester H

MERSEYSIDE

Avalon Preparatory School, Wirral H
The Belvedere School GDST, Liverpool H
Birkenhead High School GDST, Wirral H
Birkenhead School, Wirral H
Highfield School, Birkenhead H
Kingsmead School, Wirral + E F1 F2 F3 F4 H
Liverpool College, Liverpool + E F1 F2 F3 F4 H M
Merchant Taylors' School, Liverpool H
Merchant Taylors' School for Girls, Liverpool H
Streatham House School, Liverpool H
Sunnymede School, Southport H T
Tower Dene Preparatory School, Southport
Entry age: 5 F1 F2 F3 F4 FO H M T

MIDDLESEX

ACS Hillingdon International School, Hillingdon + H
Alpha Preparatory School, Harrow T
Halliford School, Shepperton H
Hampton School, Hampton Entry age: 11+, 13 H T
Harrow School, Harrow on the Hill + H
Heathfield School, Pinner H
The John Lyon School, Harrow H
The Lady Eleanor Holles School, Hampton H
The Mall School, Twickenham H
Merchant Taylors' School, Northwood H T
Newland House School, Twickenham H
North London Collegiate, Edgware H
Quainton Hall School, Harrow Entry age: 4+ H T
St David's School, Ashford F1 F2 F3 H
St Helen's School, Northwood F1 F2 F3 F4 H
St James Independent School for Boys (Senior), Twickenham H
Sunflower Montessori School, Twickenham E

NORFOLK

Beeston Hall School, Cromer H
Glebe House School, Hunstanton + T
Gresham's Preparatory School, Holt H
Gresham's School, Holt H
Hethersett Old Hall School, Norwich + F1 F2 F3 F4

Langley Preparatory School & Nursery, Norwich F1 F2 F3 F4 H
Langley School, Norwich Entry age: 10+, 11+, 13+, 16+ E F1 F2 F3 F4 FO H
The New Eccles Hall School, Norwich F1 F2 F3 F4 H
Norwich High School for Girls GDST, Norwich H
Norwich School, Norwich Entry age: 11+, 12+, 16+ H
Riddlesworth Hall, Diss F1 F2 F3 F4 H
Sacred Heart Convent School, Swaffham E H T
Taverham Hall, Norwich F1 F2 F3 F4
Thetford Grammar School, Thetford H
Wood Dene School, Norwich H

NORTHAMPTONSHIRE

Beachborough School, Brackley H
Bosworth Independent College, Northampton H
Maidwell Hall, Northampton F2 F4
Northampton High School, Northampton Entry age: 11+ H
Great Houghton Preparatory School, Northampton + H T
Northamptonshire Grammar School, Pitsford H
Oundle School, Peterborough H T
Quinton House School, Northampton H
St Peter's School, Kettering H

NORTHUMBERLAND

Longridge Towers School, Berwick-upon-Tweed + F1 F2 F3 F4 FO H
Mowden Hall School, Stocksfield F1 F2 F3 F4 H T
St Oswald's School, Alnwick E H T

NOTTINGHAMSHIRE

Bramcote Lorne School, Retford + F1 F2 F3 FO T
Greenholme School, Nottingham + E F1 F2 F3 F4 FO H T
Grosvenor School, Nottingham + F1 F2 F3 F4
Nottingham High School, Nottingham Entry age: 11 + 16 H
Nottingham High School for Girls GDST, Nottingham H
Nottingham High Junior School, Nottingham H
Ranby House, Retford Entry age: 11+ F1 F2 F3 F4
Rodney School, Newark H
Trent College, Nottingham F1 F2 F3 F4 H
Wellow House School, Newark H
Worksop College, Worksop + E F1 F2 H

OXFORDSHIRE

Abingdon School, Abingdon H
Bloxham School, Banbury + E F1 F2 F3 F4 H T
The Carrdus School, Banbury Entry age: 3–11 H T
Cherwell College, Oxford F1 F2 F3 H
Cokethorpe, Witney H
Cranford House School, Wallingford H
Dragon School, Oxford H
Emmanuel Christian School, Oxford Entry age: 5 H
Headington School, Oxford Entry age: 11+, 12+, 13+, 16+ +
Josca's Preparatory School, Abingdon H
Kingham Hill School, Chipping Norton + E F1 F2 F3 F4 FO H T
Magdalen College School, Oxford H
The Manor Preparatory School, Abingdon H
Our Lady's Convent Senior School, Abingdon H
Oxford High School GDST, Oxford H
Oxford Tutorial College, Oxford H
Radley College, Abingdon H
Rye St Antony School, Oxford F1 F2 F3 F4
St Andrew's, Wantage H
St Clare's, Oxford, Oxford H
St Edward's School, Oxford + F1 F2 F3 F4
St Mary's School, Wantage + F1 F2 F3 F4 H
School of St Helen & St Katharine, Abingdon H
Shiplake College, Henley-on-Thames F1 F2 F3 F4
Sibford School, Banbury F1 F2 F3 F4 H
Summer Fields, Oxford H
Windrush Valley School, Chipping Norton H
Wychwood School, Oxford H

RUTLAND

Oakham School, Oakham H
Uppingham School, Uppingham H

SHROPSHIRE

Adcote School for Girls, Shrewsbury + F1 F2 F3 F4 H
Bedstone College, Bucknell H
Bellan House Preparatory School, Oswestry + F1 F2 F3 F4 T
Concord College, Shrewsbury F1 F2 F3 F4
Dower House School, Bridgnorth H
Ellesmere College, Ellesmere H T
Kingsland Grange, Shrewsbury H T
Moor Park School, Ludlow H
Moreton Hall, Oswestry Entry age: 11+, 13+, 16+ E F1 F2 F3 F4 FO H T
Oswestry School, Oswestry F1 F2 F3 H T
Packwood Haugh School, Shrewsbury + F1 F2 F3 F4 H T
Prestfelde Preparatory School, Shrewsbury F1 F2 F3 F4 H T
Shrewsbury School, Shrewsbury H
Wrekin College, Telford F1 F2 F3 F4 H T

SOMERSET

All Hallows, Shepton Mallet Entry age: 11+ H
Bruton School for Girls, Bruton F1 F2 F3 F4 H
Buckland School, Watchet H
Chard School, Chard H
Chilton Cantelo School, Yeovil F1 F2 F3 F4 FO
Downside School, Bath Entry age: 11+, 13+, 16+ F3 H
Hazlegrove (King's Bruton Preparatory School), Yeovil F1 F2 F3 F4 H
King's Bruton , Bruton + F2 F4 H
King's College, Taunton + E F1 F2 F3 H

King's Hall School, Taunton + F1 F2 F3 F4
Millfield Preparatory School, Street
Entry age: 7–13 F1 F4 H
Millfield School, Street F1 F2 F3 F4 H
The Park School, Yeovil
Entry age: 8–18 + E F1 F2 F3 F4
Perrott Hill School, Crewkerne + F1 F2 F3 F4 H T
Queen's College Junior and Pre-Preparatory Schools, Taunton + F1 F2 F3 F4 H
Queen's College, Taunton F1 F2 F3 F4 H
Taunton Preparatory School, Taunton
Entry age: 11 + F1 F2 F3 F4 H
Taunton School, Taunton E F1 F2 F3 F4
Wellington School, Wellington
Entry age: 10+, 11+, 13+, 16+ F1 F2 F3 F4 H T
Wells Cathedral Junior School, Wells + H
Wells Cathedral School, Wells F1 F2 F3 F4 H

BATH & NORTH EAST SOMERSET

King Edward's School, Bath H
Kingswood Preparatory School, Bath + F1 F2 F3 F4
Kingswood School, Bath + F1 F2 F3 F4 H
Monkton Combe Junior School, Bath E
Monkton Combe School, Bath + E F1 F2 F3 F4 H T
Paragon School, Prior Park College Junior, Bath H
Prior Park College, Bath F1 F2 F3 F4 H
The Royal High School, Bath
Entry age: 11+,16+ F1 F2 F3 F4 H

NORTH SOMERSET

Sidcot School, Winscombe H

STAFFORDSHIRE

Abbots Bromley School for Girls, Abbots Bromley + F1 F3 F4 H
Abbotsholme School, Uttoxeter + E F1 F2 F3 F4 FO H T
Chase Academy, Cannock F1 F2 F3 F4 H
Denstone College, Uttoxeter + H T
Edenhurst School, Newcastle-under-Lyme + T
Hanbury Prep School, Hanbury +
Lichfield Cathedral School, Lichfield
Entry age: 3, 7 + F1 F2 F3 F4 H
Newcastle-under-Lyme School, Newcastle-under-Lyme H
St Dominic's School, Stafford H
Stafford Grammar School, Stafford H
Yarlet School, Stafford Entry age: 7 F1 F2 F3 F4 H T

STOCKTON-ON-TEES

Teesside Preparatory and High School, Eaglescliffe H
Yarm School, Yarm Entry age: 7+, 11+, 16+ H

SUFFOLK

Amberfield School, Ipswich H
Barnardiston Hall Preparatory School, Haverhill + F1 F2 F3 F4
Culford School, Bury St Edmunds F1 F2 F3 F4 H
Framlingham College, Woodbridge F1 F2 F3 F4 H
Framlingham College Preparatory School, Brandeston F1 F2 F3 F4 H
Hillcroft Preparatory School, Stowmarket H
Ipswich High School GDST, Ipswich
Entry age: 11–18 H
Ipswich School, Ipswich Entry age: 11, 13, 16 F1 F3 F4 H
Moreton Hall Preparatory School, Bury St Edmunds F1 F2 F3 F4 H T
Old Buckenham Hall School, Ipswich + E F1 F2 F3 F4
Orwell Park, Ipswich F1 F2 F3 F4 H T
Royal Hospital School, Ipswich
Entry age: 11–14, 16 F1 F2 H
Saint Felix Schools, Southwold F1 F3 F4 FO H T
St Joseph's College, Ipswich H
Stoke College, Sudbury H
Woodbridge School, Woodbridge H

SURREY

Aberdour School, Tadworth H
ACS Cobham International School, Cobham H T
ACS Egham International School, Egham H
Aldro School, Godalming H
Amesbury, Hindhead T
Box Hill School, Dorking F1 F2 F3 F4 H T
Bramley School, Tadworth Entry age: 7+ H
Cambridge Tutors College, Croydon H
Canbury School, Kingston-upon-Thames H
Caterham Preparatory School, Caterham
Entry age: 10+ + H
Caterham School, Caterham + E F1 F2 F3 F4 FO H
Charterhouse, Godalming H
Coworth-Flexlands School, Woking +
Cranleigh School, Cranleigh H T
Croham Hurst School, South Croydon
Entry age: 11+ 16+ H
Croydon High School GDST, South Croydon H
Drayton House School, Guildford H
Duke of Kent School, Ewhurst
Entry age: 7+, 10+, 11+ F1 F2 F3 F4
Dunottar School, Reigate H
Edgeborough, Farnham F1 F2 F3 F4 H
Epsom College, Epsom Entry age: 13+, 16+ M
Essendene Lodge School, Caterham H
Ewell Castle School, Epsom H
Feltonfleet School, Cobham H
Frensham Heights School, Farnham H
Glenesk School, Leatherhead H
Greenacre School for Girls, Banstead H
Guildford High School, Guildford
Entry age: 11+, 16+ + H
Halstead Preparatory School, Woking H
Haslemere Preparatory School, Haslemere T
Hawley Place School, Camberley H
The Hawthorns School, Redhill + FO H
Hazelwood School, Oxted Entry age: 7+, 11+ H
Holy Cross Preparatory School, Kingston-upon-Thames H T
King Edward's School Witley, Godalming
Entry age: 11–18 + E F1 F2 F3 F4 H T
King's House School, Richmond H

Kingston Grammar School, Kingston-upon-Thames H
Kingswood House School, Epsom + H T
Lingfield Notre Dame School, Lingfield
Entry age: 11+ H
Lyndhurst School, Camberley H
Marymount International School,
Kingston-upon-Thames H
Notre Dame Preparatory School, Cobham H
Oakfield School, Woking Entry age: 7 H T
Oakwood School & Nursery, Purley H
Parsons Mead, Ashtead + F1 F2 F3 F4
Prior's Field School, Godalming F1 F2 F3 F4 H
Reed's School, Cobham H
Reigate Grammar School, Reigate H
Ripley Court School, Woking Entry age: 7 H T
Royal Alexandra and Albert School, Reigate + H
Royal Grammar School, Guildford H
Royal Russell School, Croydon F1 F2 F3 F4 FO
The Royal School, Haslemere
Entry age: 11+, 13+, 16+ + F1 F2 F3 F4 H T
St Andrew's (Woking) School Trust, Woking H
St Edmund's School, Hindhead H T
St Ives School, Haslemere H
St John's School, Leatherhead Entry age: 13+, 16+ +
St Teresa's School, Dorking T
Sanderstead Junior School, South Croydon H
Shrewsbury House School, Surbiton T
Sir William Perkins's School, Chertsey H
Stowford College, Sutton E H
Surbiton High School, Kingston-upon-Thames + H
Sutton High School GDST, Sutton
Entry age: 11+, 16+ H
TASIS The American School in England, Thorpe H
Trinity School, Croydon Entry age: 10+, 11+, 13+ H
Warlingham Park School, Croydon H
Whitgift School, South Croydon
Entry age: 10–13,16 H
Wispers School for Girls, Haslemere F1 F2 F3 F4 H
Woodcote House School, Windlesham T
Yehudi Menuhin School, Cobham H

EAST SUSSEX

Ashdown House School, Forest Row + T
Battle Abbey School, Battle F2 F3 F4 M T
Bricklehurst Manor Preparatory, Wadhurst H
Brighton and Hove High School GDST,
Brighton H
Brighton College, Brighton + F3 H T
Brighton College Prep School, Brighton + F3
Eastbourne College, Eastbourne H
The Fold School, Hove H
Moira House School, Eastbourne H T
Moira House Girls School,
Eastbourne E F1 F2 F3 F4 H T
Lancing College Preparatory School at Mowden,
Hove + H
Newlands School, Seaford F1 F2 F3 F4
Roedean School, Brighton Entry age: 11+,
12+, 13+, 16+ H
Sacred Heart RC Primary School, Wadhurst H
St Andrew's School, Eastbourne F1 F2 F3 F4
St Aubyns School, Brighton + H T
St Christopher's School, Hove H
St Leonards-Mayfield School, Mayfield H
St Mary's Hall, Brighton + E F1 F2 F3 F4 H
Vinehall School, Robertsbridge F1 F2 F3 F4 H

WEST SUSSEX

Ardingly College, Haywards Heath + H
Ardingly College Junior School, Haywards Heath H T
Burgess Hill School for Girls, Burgess Hill H
Christ's Hospital, Horsham F1 F2 F4 H
Conifers School, Midhurst H
Copthorne Prep School, Copthorne H T
Cottesmore School, Pease Pottage H
Dorset House School, Pulborough FO H T
Farlington School, Horsham + F1 F2 F3 H
Fonthill Lodge, East Grinstead H
Great Ballard School, Chichester F1 F2 F3 F4
Great Walstead, Haywards Heath + E H T
Handcross Park School, Haywards Heath
Entry age: 7–11 H T
Lancing College, Lancing H T
Lavant House, Chichester H
Our Lady of Sion School, Worthing H
Pennthorpe School, Horsham H
The Prebendal School, Chichester Entry age: 7 H
St Peter's School, Burgess Hill H
Seaford College, Petworth Entry age: 10+,
11+, 13+ F1 F2 F3 F4 H
Shoreham College, Shoreham-by-Sea + H
Slindon College, Arundel Entry age: 10 F1 F2 F3 F4 H
Sompting Abbotts School, Sompting T
Stoke Brunswick, East Grinstead H
Tavistock & Summerhill School, Haywards Heath H
The Towers Convent School, Steyning H T
Windlesham House, Pulborough F1 F2 F3 FO H

TYNE AND WEAR

Central Newcastle High School GDST,
Newcastle upon Tyne Entry age: 11+, 16+ H
Dame Allan's Boys School, Newcastle upon Tyne H
Dame Allan's Girls School, Newcastle upon Tyne H
Grindon Hall Christian School, Sunderland + E T
The King's School, Tynemouth Entry age: 4, 11 + E H
La Sagesse School, Newcastle upon Tyne H
Newcastle Preparatory School,
Newcastle upon Tyne H
Newcastle Upon Tyne Church High School,
Newcastle upon Tyne +
Sunderland High School, Sunderland E H
Westfield School, Newcastle upon Tyne H

WARWICKSHIRE

Bilton Grange, Rugby Entry age: 8+ + F1 F2 F3 F4 H T
The King's High School for Girls, Warwick H
The Kingsley School, Leamington Spa H
Rugby School, Rugby H
Warwick School, Warwick H

WEST MIDLANDS

Abbey College, Birmingham H
Bablake School, Coventry H
Birchfield School, Wolverhampton F4 H
The Blue Coat School, Birmingham H
Edgbaston High School for Girls, Birmingham H
Elmhurst School for Dance, Birmingham F1 F3 F4 H
Eversfield Preparatory School, Solihull +
King Edward VI High School for Girls, Birmingham H
King Edward's School, Birmingham
Entry age: 11+, 16+ H
Newbridge Preparatory School, Wolverhampton +
Pattison College, Coventry H
Priory School, Birmingham H
The Royal Wolverhampton Junior School,
Wolverhampton F1 F3 H
The Royal Wolverhampton School,
Wolverhampton Entry age: 11+ F1 F2 F3 F4 H
St George's School, Edgbaston, Birmingham + H
Solihull School, Solihull +
Tettenhall College, Wolverhampton F1 F2 F3 F4
West House School, Birmingham + T
Wolverhampton Grammar School, Wolverhampton
Entry age: 11+, 13+, 16+ H

WILTSHIRE

Chafyn Grove School, Salisbury F1 F2 F3 F4 H T
The Godolphin School, Salisbury F1 F2 F3 F4
La Retraite Swan, Salisbury H
Leaden Hall, Salisbury +
Marlborough College, Marlborough
Entry age: 13+, 16+ +
Norman Court Preparatory School,
Salisbury F1 F2 F3 F4
Pinewood School, Shrivenham H
Prior Park Preparatory School, Cricklade F1 F2 F3 F4
St Francis School, Pewsey H
St Mary's School, Calne + H
South Hills School, Salisbury H
Stonar School, Melksham F1 F2 F3 F4
Warminster School, Warminster + H

WORCESTERSHIRE

Abberley Hall, Worcester Entry age: 8+ F1 F2 F3 F4 H
The Abbey College, Malvern Wells H
The Alice Ottley School, Worcester +
Bromsgrove Preparatory School,
Bromsgrove F1 F2 F3 F4 H
Bromsgrove School, Bromsgrove F1 F2 F3 F4 H T
The Downs School, Malvern F1 F2 F3 F4 H
The Elms, Malvern F1 F2 F3 F4 H T
Hartlebury School, Kidderminster H
Malvern College Preparatory and Pre-Prep School,
Malvern F1 F2 F3 FO
King's Hawford, Worcester +
The King's School, Worcester H
Malvern College, Malvern F1 F2 F3 F4 H T
Malvern Girls' College, Malvern
Entry age: 11+, 12+, 13+, 16+ F1 F2 F3 F4 H T
Moffats School, Bewdley + E F1 F2 F3 F4 FO H M T
River School, Worcester H
Royal Grammar School Worcester, Worcester H
St James's School, Malvern F1 F2 F3 F4
St Mary's Convent School, Worcester
Entry age: 11+, 16+ H
Winterfold House, Kidderminster H

EAST RIDING OF YORKSHIRE

Hull Grammar School, Kingston-Upon-Hull H
Hull High School, Anlaby Entry age: 11 H
Hymers College, Hull H
Pocklington School, Pocklington F1 F2 F3 F4 H

NORTH YORKSHIRE

Ampleforth College, York H
Ashville College, Harrogate
Entry age: 7 + E F1 F2 F3 F4 H T
Aysgarth Preparatory School, Bedale F1 F2 F3 F4 H T
Belmont Grosvenor School,
Harrogate + F1 F2 F3 F4 T
Bootham School, York
Entry age: 11+, 13+, 16+ H
Bramcote School, Scarborough E F1 F2 F3 F4 FO H T
Catteral Hall School, Settle F1 F2 F3 F4 T
Cundall Manor School, York F1 F2 F3 F4 FO
Giggleswick School, Settle
Entry age: 13, 16 F1 F2 F3 F4 H T
Harrogate Ladies' College, Harrogate + E F1 F3 F4 H
Harrogate Tutorial College, Harrogate H
Howsham Hall, York + H T
Malsis School, Skipton F1 F2 F3 F4 H T
Queen Ethelburga's College, York
Entry age: 11 + E F1 F2 F3 F4 FO M T
Queen Margaret's School, York + F1 F2 F3
Queen Mary's School, Thirsk F1 F2 F3 F4 H T
Read School, Selby Entry age: 11+, 13+, 16+ H
Ripon Cathedral Choir School, Ripon F1 F2 F3 F4
St Martin's Ampleforth, York F1 F2 F3 F4
St Peter's School, York Entry age: 13,
14, 16 + F1 F2 F3 F4 H
Scarborough College & Lisvane School,
Scarborough F2 F3 F4 H
Terrington Hall, York + F1 F2 F3 F4 T
Woodleigh School, Malton F1 F2 F3

SOUTH YORKSHIRE

Ashdell Preparatory School, Sheffield Entry age: 4 H
Birkdale School, Sheffield + H
Brantwood School for Girls, Sheffield H
Handsworth Christian School, Sheffield H
Rudston Preparatory School, Rotherham H T
Sheffield High School GDST, Sheffield
Entry age: 11–18 H
Westbourne School, Sheffield H

WEST YORKSHIRE

Ackworth School, Pontefract H
Alcuin School, Leeds H

Batley Grammar School, Batley H
Bradford Girls' Grammar School, Bradford H
Bradford Grammar School, Bradford
Entry age: 11+, 13+, 16+ H
Bronte House School, Bradford
Entry age: 7+, 8+ F1 F2 F3 H
The Froebelian School, Leeds H
Fulneck School, Pudsey + E F1 F2 F3 F4 H
Gateways School, Leeds H
Hipperholme Grammar School, Halifax H
Huddersfield Grammar School, Huddersfield H
Leeds Girls' High School, Leeds H
Leeds Grammar School, Leeds Entry age: 11+,16+ H
Queen Elizabeth Grammar School, Wakefield H
The Rastrick Independent School,
Brighouse + E F1 F2 F3 F4 FO H M T
Richmond House School, Leeds Entry age: 7/8 H T
Rishworth School, Rishworth H
Shaw House School, Bradford H T
Silcoates School, Wakefield
Entry age: 11 + E F1 F2 F3 F4 FO H M T
Wakefield Girls' High School, Wakefield
Entry age: 11+-16+ H

NORTHERN IRELAND

COUNTY ANTRIM

Cabin Hill School, Belfast F3
Methodist College, Belfast +
Royal Belfast Academical Institution, Belfast H

COUNTY ARMAGH

The Royal School, Armagh +

COUNTY DOWN

The Holywood Rudolf Steiner School, Holywood H

COUNTY LONDONDERRY

Coleraine Academical Institution, Coleraine + E

COUNTY TYRONE

The Royal School Dungannon, Dungannon Entry age:
11–16 + E F1 F2 F3 F4

SCOTLAND

ABERDEENSHIRE

Aberdeen Waldorf School, Aberdeen H
International School of Aberdeen, Aberdeen H
Robert Gordons College, Aberdeen H
St Margaret's School for Girls, Aberdeen H

ANGUS

The High School of Dundee, Dundee + H
Lathallan School, Montrose F1 F2 F3 F4 H

SOUTH AYRSHIRE

Wellington School, Ayr H

FIFE

St Leonards School & VIth Form College,
St Andrews + F1 F2 F3 F4 H T
Sea View Private School, Kirkcaldy H

GLASGOW

Craigholme School, Glasgow Entry age: 12 H
The Glasgow Academy, Glasgow Entry age: 11+ + H
The High School of Glasgow, Glasgow H
Hutchesons' Grammar School, Glasgow H
St Aloysius' College, Glasgow H

LOTHIAN

Belhaven Hill, Dunbar Entry age: 8+ H T
Cargilfield, Edinburgh F1 F2 F3 F4
Clifton Hall School, Edinburgh Entry age: 3 H
The Compass School, Haddington H
The Edinburgh Academy, Edinburgh H
Fettes College, Edinburgh F1 F2 F3 F4 H T
George Heriot's School, Edinburgh H
George Watson's College, Edinburgh H
Loretto School, Musselburgh F1 F2 F3 F4 H T
The Mary Erskine School, Edinburgh H
Merchiston Castle School, Edinburgh F1 F2 F3
St George's School for Girls, Edinburgh H
St Margaret's School, Edinburgh F1 F2 F3 F4 H
Stewart's Melville College, Edinburgh H

MORAYSHIRE

Gordonstoun School, Elgin Entry age: 9 F1 F2 H
Rosebrae School, Elgin H

PERTH AND KINROSS

Ardvreck School, Crieff F1 F2 F3
Craigclowan Preparatory School, Perth H T
Glenalmond College, Perth E F1 F2 F3 F4 H T
Kilgraston (A Sacred Heart School), Perth F1 F2 F3 F4 H T
Morrison's Academy, Crieff H
Queen Victoria School, Dunblane F1 F2 F3 F4
Strathallan School, Perth F1 F2 F3 F4 H T

STIRLING

Beaconhurst School, Stirling H

WALES

BRIDGEND

St John's School, Porthcawl H

CARDIFF

The Cathedral School, Cardiff H
Elm Tree House, Cardiff H
Howell's School, Llandaff GDST, Cardiff H

CARMARTHENSHIRE

Llandovery College, Llandovery Entry age: 11+, 17+ E F1 F2 F3 F4 H T
St Michael's School, Llanelli H

CONWY

Lyndon Preparatory School, Colwyn Bay E F1 F2 F3 F4 H
Rydal Penrhos Senior School, Colwyn Bay F3
St David's College, Llandudno F1 F2 F3 F4 H

DENBIGHSHIRE

Howell's School, Denbigh Entry age: 11 F1 F2 F3 F4 FO
Ruthin School, Ruthin Entry age: 5 F1 F2 F3 F4 H

GWYNEDD

Hillgrove School, Bangor E

MONMOUTHSHIRE

Haberdashers' Monmouth School For Girls, Monmouth H
Monmouth School, Monmouth Entry age: 11, 13, 16 F1 F2 F3 F4 H T
St John's-on-the-Hill, Chepstow F1 F2 F3 F4 H

NEWPORT

Rougemont School, Newport H

PEMBROKESHIRE

Netherwood School, Saundersfoot H

POWYS

Christ College, Brecon Entry age: 11+, 13+, 16 + F1 F3 F4 H T

SWANSEA

Ffynone House School, Swansea H
Oakleigh House, Swansea H

4.3
Specialist Schools

Schools in the directory which specialize in the theatre, dance or music are listed below. For full details about entrance requirements and the curriculum, parents are advised to contact schools direct.

Arts Schools

The Arts Educational School, Hertfordshire
The Arts Educational Schools, London W4
Barbara Speake Stage School, London W3
The Italia Conti Academy of Theatre Arts, London EC1
Pattison College, Coventry
Ravenscourt Theatre School, London W6
Sylvia Young Theatre School, London NW1

Dance Schools

Elmhurst School for Dance, Birmingham
Hammond School, Chester
Royal Ballet School, London WC2E
Stonelands School of Ballet & Theatre Arts, East Sussex
The Urdang Academy of Ballet, London WC2

Music Schools

Chetham's School of Music, Manchester
The Purcell School, Bushey
St Mary's Music School, Edinburgh
Yehudi Menuhin School, Cobham

4.4
Single-Sex Schools

Note: * denotes a co-educational school that educates boys and girls separately, either within a specific age range or throughout the school. For details consult the school listings in Part 2.

BOYS

ENGLAND

BEDFORDSHIRE

Bedford Preparatory School, Bedford	7–13
Bedford School, Bedford	7–18

BERKSHIRE

*Brockhurst and Marlston House Schools, Newbury	
Claires Court School, Maidenhead	11–16 (Co-ed VIth Form)
Claires Court Schools, Ridgeway, Maidenhead	4–11
Crosfields School, Reading	4–13
Elstree School, Reading	3–13 (Girls 3–7)
Eton College, Windsor	13–18
Horris Hill, Newbury	7–13
Ludgrove, Wokingham	8–13
The Oratory School, Reading	11–18
Papplewick School, Ascot	7–13
Reading Blue Coat School, Reading	11–18 (Co-ed VIth Form)
St Edward's School, Reading	4–13
St John's Beaumont, Windsor	4–13
*St Michaels School, Newbury	
Sunningdale School, Sunningdale	8–13

BRISTOL

Bristol Cathedral School, Bristol	10–18 (Co-ed VIth Form)
Queen Elizabeth's Hospital	11–18

BUCKINGHAMSHIRE

The Beacon School, Amersham	3–13
Caldicott School, Farnham Royal	7–13
Davenies School, Beaconsfield	4–13
Gayhurst School, Gerrards Cross	4–13
Kingscote Pre-Preparatory School, Gerrards Cross	3–7
Thorpe House School, Gerrards Cross	3–13

CAMBRIDGESHIRE

The Perse School, Cambridge	11–18

CHANNEL ISLANDS

Elizabeth College, Guernsey	2–18 (Co-ed VIth Form)
Victoria College, Jersey	11–19
Victoria College Preparatory School, Jersey	7–11

CHESHIRE

Altrincham Preparatory School, Altrincham	4–11
*The King's School, Macclesfield	
North Cestrian Grammar School, Altrincham	11–18
The Ryleys, Alderley Edge	3–13
St Ambrose Preparatory School, Altrincham	4–11

DERBYSHIRE

Derby Grammar School for Boys, Derby	7–18

DORSET

Sherborne School, Sherborne	13–18

COUNTY DURHAM

Bow School, Durham	3–13
Hurworth House School, Darlington	3–18

ESSEX

*Brentwood School, Brentwood	
Cranbrook College, Ilford	4–16
The Daiglen School, Buckhurst Hill	4–11
Loyola Preparatory School, Buckhurst Hill	3–11

HAMPSHIRE

The Pilgrims' School, Winchester 7–13
Salesian College, Farnborough 11–18
Winchester College, Winchester 13–18

HERTFORDSHIRE

Aldwickbury School, Harpenden 4–13
*Berkhamsted Collegiate School, Berkhamsted
Haberdashers' Aske's Boys' School, Elstree 5–18
Lochinver House School, Potters Bar 4–13
Lockers Park, Hemel Hempstead 7–13
Northwood Preparatory School, Rickmansworth 4–13 (Girls 3–4)
St Albans School, St Albans 11–18 (Co-ed VIth Form)
St Columba's College, St Albans 4–18
York House School, Rickmansworth 3–13 (Co-ed 2–5)

KENT

Bickley Park School, Bromley 2–13
Darul Uloom London, Chislehurst 11–0
Harenc School Trust, Sidcup 3–11
The New Beacon, Sevenoaks 4–13
Solefield School, Sevenoaks 4–13
Tonbridge School, Tonbridge 13–18
Yardley Court, Tonbridge 7–13

LANCASHIRE

Bolton School (Boys' Division), Bolton 7–18
Bury Grammar School, Bury 7–18
The Oldham Hulme Grammar School, Oldham 7–18

LEICESTERSHIRE

Loughborough Grammar School, Loughborough 10–18

LINCOLNSHIRE

Stamford School, Stamford 11–18

LONDON

*Al-Sadiq and Al-Zahra Schools, NW6
Arnold House School, NW8 5–13
Brondesbury College For Boys, NW6 11–16
City of London School, EC4V 10–18
Clifton Lodge Preparatory School, W5 4–13
Donhead Wimbledon College Prep School, SW19 7–11
Dulwich College, SE21 7–18
Dulwich College Preparatory School, SE21 3–13 (Girls 3–5)
Durston House, W5 4–13
Ealing College Upper School, W13 11–18 (Co-ed VIth Form)
Eaton House School Belgravia, SW1W 4–8
The Falcons School for Boys, W4 3–8
*Forest School, E17
The Hall School, NW3 4–13
Hawkesdown House School, W8 3–8
Hereward House School, NW3 4–13
Keble Preparatory School, N21 4–13
King's College Junior School, SW19 7–13
King's College School, SW19 13–18
Lyndhurst House Preparatory School, NW3 4–13
Mechinah Liyeshivah Zichron Moshe, N16 11–16
North Bridge House Upper Prep School, NW1 10–13
Northcote Lodge School, SW11 8–13
Pardes Grammar Boys' School, N3 11–17
St Anthony's Preparatory School, NW3 5–13
St Benedict's Junior School, W5 3–11
St Benedict's School, W5 11–18 (Co-ed VIth Form)
St James Independent School for Boys, W14 4–10
St Paul's Preparatory School, SW13 7–13
St Paul's School, SW13 13–18
St Philip's School, SW7 7–13
Sussex House School, SW1X 8–13
Tower House School, SW14 4–13
University College School, NW3 11–18
University College School, Junior Branch, NW3 7–11
Westminster Abbey Choir School, SW1P 8–13
Westminster Cathedral Choir School, SW1P 8–13
Westminster Under School, SW1P 7–13
Wetherby Preparatory School, W11 8–13
Wetherby School, W2 4–8
Willington School, SW19 4–13
Wimbledon Common Preparatory School, SW19 4–8
*Yesodey Hatorah Jewish School, N16
Yetev Lev Day School for Boys, N16 3–11

GREATER MANCHESTER

Kassim Darwish Grammar School for Boys, Manchester 11–16
The Manchester Grammar School, Manchester 11–18
Tashbar Primary School, Salford 3–11

MERSEYSIDE

Birkenhead School, Wirral 3–18
Merchant Taylors' School, Liverpool 7–18

MIDDLESEX

Buckingham College Preparatory School, Pinner 4–11
Buckingham College School, Harrow 11–18 (Co-ed VIth Form)
Denmead School, Hampton 2–11 (Girls 2–7)
Halliford School, Shepperton 11–19 (Co-ed VIth Form)
Hampton School, Hampton 11–18
Harrow School, Harrow on the Hill 13–18
The John Lyon School, Harrow 11–18
The Mall School, Twickenham 4–13
Menorah Grammar School, Edgware 11–18
Merchant Taylors' School, Northwood 11–18
Quainton Hall School, Harrow 4–13
St James Independent School for Boys (Senior), Twickenham 10–18
St John's Northwood, Northwood 3–13
St Martin's School, Northwood 3–13

NORFOLK

Norwich School, Norwich 7–18 (Co-ed VIth Form)

NORTHAMPTONSHIRE

Maidwell Hall, Northampton 7–13 (Girls day only)

NOTTINGHAMSHIRE

Al Karam Secondary School, Retford 11–16
Nottingham High School, Nottingham 11–18
Nottingham High Junior School, Nottingham 7–11

OXFORDSHIRE

Abingdon School, Abingdon 11–18
Christ Church Cathedral School, Oxford 2–13 (Girls 2–4)
Cothill House Preparatory School, Abingdon 8–13
Josca's Preparatory School, Abingdon 4–13 (Girls 4–7)
Magdalen College School, Oxford 7–18
Moulsford Preparatory School, Wallingford 5–13
New College School, Oxford 4–13
Radley College, Abingdon 13–18
Shiplake College, Henley-on-Thames 13–18 (Day girls 16–18)
Summer Fields, Oxford 7–13

SHROPSHIRE

Kingsland Grange, Shrewsbury 4–13
Shrewsbury School, Shrewsbury 13–18

SURREY

Aldro School, Godalming 7–13
Charterhouse, Godalming 13–18 (Co-ed VIth Form)
Chinthurst School, Tadworth 3–13
Cranmore School, Leatherhead 3–13
Cumnor House School, South Croydon 4–13
Elmhurst School, South Croydon 4–11
Ewell Castle School, Epsom 3–18 (Co-ed 3–11)
Haslemere Preparatory School, Haslemere 2–14
Homefield School, Sutton 2–13
King's House School, Richmond 4–13
Kingswood House School, Epsom 2–13
Lanesborough, Guildford 3–13
More House School, Farnham 9–18
Parkside School, Cobham 4–13 (Co-ed 2–4)
Priory School, Banstead 2–13
Reed's School, Cobham 11–18 (Co-ed VIth Form)
Rokeby School, Kingston-upon-Thames 4–13
Royal Grammar School, Guildford 11–18
St Edmund's School, Hindhead 2–13 (Co-ed day 2–7)
St John's School , Leatherhead 13–18 (Co-ed VIth Form)
Shrewsbury House School, Surbiton 7–13
Surbiton Preparatory School, Surbiton 4–11
Trinity School, Croydon 10–18
Whitgift School, South Croydon 10–18
Woodcote House School, Windlesham 7–14

WEST SUSSEX

Dorset House School, Pulborough 3–13
*Fonthill Lodge, East Grinstead
Slindon College, Arundel 9–16
Worth School, Turners Hill 11–18

TYNE AND WEAR

Newcastle School for Boys, Newcastle upon Tyne 3–13
Dame Allan's Boys School, Newcastle upon Tyne 8–18 (Co-ed VIth Form)
Royal Grammar School, Newcastle upon Tyne 8–18 (Co-ed VIth form)

WARWICKSHIRE

Warwick School, Warwick 7–18

WEST MIDLANDS

*Al Hijrah School, Birmingham
Birchfield School, Wolverhampton 4–13
*Darul Uloom Islamic High School and College, Birmingham
King Edward's School, Birmingham 11–18
West House School, Birmingham 1–11 (Girls 1–4)

NORTH YORKSHIRE

Aysgarth Preparatory School, Bedale 3–13 (Co-ed day 3–8)

SOUTH YORKSHIRE

Birkdale School, Sheffield 4–18 (Co-ed VIth Form)

WEST YORKSHIRE

Ghyll Royd School, Ilkley 2–11
Leeds Grammar School, Leeds 4–18
Queen Elizabeth Grammar School, Wakefield 7–18

NORTHERN IRELAND

COUNTY ANTRIM

Cabin Hill School, Belfast 3–13 (Co-ed kindergarten)
Campbell College, Belfast 11–18
Royal Belfast Academical Institution, Belfast 4–18

COUNTY DOWN

Bangor Grammar School, Bangor 11–18

COUNTY LONDONDERRY

Coleraine Academical Institution, Coleraine 11–19

SCOTLAND

LOTHIAN

The Edinburgh Academy, Edinburgh 5–18 (Co-ed VIth Form)
Merchiston Castle School, Edinburgh 8–18
Stewart's Melville College, Edinburgh 12–18 (Co-ed VIth Form)

WALES

CONWY

*Rydal Penrhos Senior School, Colwyn Bay

MONMOUTHSHIRE

Monmouth School, Monmouth 7–18 (Boarding 11–18)

GIRLS

ENGLAND

BEDFORDSHIRE

Bedford High School, Bedford 7–18
Dame Alice Harpur School, Bedford 7–18
St Andrew's School, Bedford 3–16 (Boys 3–7)

BERKSHIRE

The Abbey School, Reading 3–18
Brigidine School Windsor, Windsor 3–18 (Boys 3–7)
*Brockhurst and Marlston House Schools, Newbury
Claires Court Schools, The College, Maidenhead 3–16 (Boys 3–5, co-ed VIth Form)
Downe House, Thatcham 11–18
Heathfield School, Ascot 11–18
Highfield School, Maidenhead 3–11
Hurst Lodge School, Ascot 3–18 (Boys 3–7)
Luckley-Oakfield School, Wokingham 11–18
The Marist Senior School, Ascot 11–18
The Marist Preparatory School, Ascot 3–11
Queen Anne's School, Reading 11–18
St Gabriel's , Newbury 3–18 (Boys 3–7)
St George's School, Ascot 11–18
St Joseph's Convent School, Reading 3–18
St Mary's School, Ascot, Ascot 11–18
*St Michael's, Newbury
White House Preparatory School, Wokingham 2–11 (Boys 2–4)

BRISTOL

Badminton School 4–18
Colston's Girls' School 10–18
The Red Maids' School 11–18
Redland High School 3–18

BUCKINGHAMSHIRE

Godstowe Preparatory School, High Wycombe 3–13 (Boys 3–8)
Heatherton House School, Amersham 3–11 (Boys 2–5)
High March School, Beaconsfield 3–12 (Boys 3–5)
Holy Cross Convent, Gerrards Cross 3–18
Maltman's Green School, Gerrards Cross 3–11
Pipers Corner School, High Wycombe 4–18
St Mary's School, Gerrards Cross 3–18
Thornton College Convent of Jesus and Mary, Milton Keynes 2–16 (Boys 2–4)
Wycombe Abbey School, High Wycombe 11–18 (A few day places)

CAMBRIDGESHIRE

The Perse School for Girls, Cambridge 7–18
Peterborough High School, Peterborough 3–18 (Boys 3–11)
St Catherines Preparatory School, Cambridge 4–11
St Mary's School, Cambridge 11–18

CHANNEL ISLANDS

Beaulieu Convent School, Jersey 4–18
The Ladies' College, Guernsey 4–18

CHESHIRE

Alderley Edge School for Girls, Alderley Edge 3–18
Bowdon Preparatory School For Girls, Altrincham 2–12
Cransley School, Northwich 3–16 (Boys 3–11)
Culcheth Hall, Altrincham 2–16 (Boys 2–4)
*The King's School, Macclesfield
Loreto Preparatory School, Altrincham 3–11 (Boys 4–7)
Oriel Bank, Stockport 3–16
The Queen's School, Chester 4–18
Wilmslow Preparatory School, Wilmslow 2–11

CORNWALL

St Joseph's School, Launceston 3–16 (Boys 3–11)
Truro High School, Truro 3–18 (Boys 3–5)

CUMBRIA

Casterton School, Kirkby Lonsdale 3–18 (Day boys 3–11)

DERBYSHIRE

Ockbrook School, Derby 3–18

DEVON

The Maynard School, Exeter 7–18
St Margaret's School, Exeter 7–18
Stoodley Knowle School, Torquay 2–18

DORSET

Hanford School, Blandford Forum 7–13
Knighton House, Blandford Forum 3–13 (Day boys 4–7)
St Antony's Leweston Schools, Sherborne 2–18 (Boys 2–11)
St Mary's School, Shaftesbury 9–18
Sherborne School for Girls, Sherborne 11–18
Talbot Heath, Bournemouth 3–18 (Boys 3–7)
Wentworth College, Bournemouth 11–18

COUNTY DURHAM

Durham High School For Girls, Durham 3–18
Polam Hall, Darlington 4–18

ESSEX

Braeside School for Girls, Buckhurst Hill 3–16
*Brentwood School, Brentwood
Ilford Ursuline Preparatory School, Ilford 3–11
Park School for Girls, Ilford 7–18
St Hilda's School, Westcliff-on-Sea 2–16 (Boys 2–7)
St Mary's School, Colchester 4–16

GLOUCESTERSHIRE

The Cheltenham Ladies' College, Cheltenham 11–18
Gloucestershire Islamic Secondary School For Girls, Gloucester 11–16
Kitebrook House, Moreton-in-Marsh 4–13 (Boys 4–8)
Westonbirt School, Tetbury 11–18

HAMPSHIRE

Alton Convent School, Alton 2–18 (Co-ed 2–11)
The Atherley School, Southampton 3–18 (Boys 3–11)
Farnborough Hill, Farnborough 11–18
Portsmouth High School GDST, Southsea 3–18
St Nicholas' School, Fleet 3–16 (Boys 3–7)
St Swithun's School, Winchester 11–18
Wykeham House School, Fareham 2–16

HEREFORDSHIRE

Haberdashers' Redcap School, Hereford 2–11

HERTFORDSHIRE

Abbot's Hill School, Hemel Hempstead 3–16 (Boys 3–7)
*Berkhamsted Collegiate Preparatory School, Berkhamsted
Haberdashers' Aske's School for Girls, Elstree 4–18
The Princess Helena College, Hitchin 11–18
Queenswood School, Hatfield 11–18
Rickmansworth PNEU School, Rickmansworth 3–11
The Royal Masonic School for Girls, Rickmansworth 4–18
St Albans High School for Girls, St Albans 4–18
St Francis' College, Letchworth 3–18
St Hilda's School, Bushey 3–11 (Boys 3–5)
St Hilda's School, Harpenden 2–11
St Margaret's School, Bushey 4–18
St Martha's Senior School, Barnet 11–18
Stormont, Potters Bar 4–11

KENT

Babington House School, Chislehurst 3–16 (Boys 3–7)
Baston School, Bromley 2–16
Bedgebury School, Cranbrook 2–18 (Boys day 2–7)
Beechwood Sacred Heart School, Tunbridge Wells 3–18 (Boys 3–11)
Benenden School, Cranbrook 11–18
Bromley High School GDST, Bromley 4–18
Cobham Hall, Gravesend 11–18
Combe Bank School, Sevenoaks 3–18
Derwent Lodge School for Girls, Tonbridge 7–11
The Granville School, Sevenoaks 3–11 (Boys 3–5)
Kent College Pembury, Tunbridge Wells 3–18
Walthamstow Hall, Sevenoaks 3–18

LANCASHIRE

Bolton Muslim Girls School, Bolton 11–16
Bolton School (Girls' Division), Bolton 4–18 (Boys 4–7)
Bury Grammar School Girls, Bury 4–18 (Boys 4–7)
The Hulme Grammar School for Girls, Oldham 3–18
Tauheedul Islam Girls High School, Blackburn 11–16
Westholme School, Blackburn 3–18 (Boys 3–7)

LEICESTERSHIRE

Leicester High School For Girls, Leicester 3–18
Loughborough High School, Loughborough 11–18
Our Lady's Convent School, Loughborough 3–18 (Boys 3–5)

LINCOLNSHIRE

Stamford High School, Stamford 11–18

LONDON

School	Ages
*Al-Sadiq and Al-Zahra Schools, NW6	
Beis Soroh Schneirer, N3	3–9
Blackheath High School GDST, SE3	3–18
Bute House Preparatory School for Girls, W6	4–11
The Cavendish School, NW1	3–11
Channing Junior School, N6	4–11
Channing School, N6	4–18
City of London School for Girls, EC2Y	7–18
Eaton House The Manor, SW4	2–4
The Falcons School for Girls, W5	4–11
Falkner House, SW7	3–11 (Co-ed 3–4)
*Forest School, E17	
Francis Holland School, SW1W	4–18
Francis Holland School, NW1	11–18
Glendower Preparatory School, SW7	4–11
The Godolphin and Latymer School, W6	11–18
Grange Park Preparatory School, N21	4–11
Harvington School, W5	3–16 (Boys 3–5)
Islamia Girls' School, NW6	11–16
James Allen's Girls' School, SE22	11–18
Kensington Prep School, SW6	4–11
Lubavitch House Senior School for Girls, N16	11–18
Madni Girls School, E1	12–18
More House, SW1X	11–18
The Mount School, NW7	4–18
Notting Hill and Ealing High School GDST, W13	5–18
Palmers Green High School, N21	3–16
Pembridge Hall, W2	4–11
Putney High School GDST, SW15	4–18
Queen's College, W1G	11–18
Queen's College Prep School, W1B	4–11
Queen's Gate School, SW7	4–18
The Royal School, Hampstead, NW3	3–18
St Augustine's Priory, W5	4–18
St Christina's RC Preparatory School, NW8	3–11 (Boys 3–7)
St James Independent School for Senior Girls, W14	10–18
St James Independent School for Girls (Juniors), W14	4–10
St Joseph's Convent School, E11	3–11
St Margaret's School, NW3	4–16
St Mary's School Hampstead, NW3	2–11 (Boys 2–7)
St Paul's Girls' School, W6	11–18
Sarum Hall, NW3	3–11
South Hampstead High School, NW3	4–18
Streatham and Clapham High School, SW16	3–18 (Boys 3–5)
The Study Preparatory School, SW19	4–11
Sydenham High School GDST, SE26	4–18
Tayyibah Girls School, N16	5–18
Ursuline Preparatory School, SW20	3–11 (Boys 3–7)
The Village School, NW3	4–11
Wimbledon High School GDST, SW19	4–18
*Yesodey Hatorah Jewish School, N16	

GREATER MANCHESTER

School	Ages
Jewish High School for Girls, Salford	11–18
Manchester High School for Girls, Manchester	4–18
Manchester Islamic High School, Manchester	11–16
Withington Girls' School, Manchester	7–18

MERSEYSIDE

School	Ages
The Belvedere School GDST, Liverpool	3–18
Birkenhead High School GDST, Wirral	3–18
Merchant Taylors' School for Girls, Liverpool	4–18 (Boys 4–7)
Streatham House School, Liverpool	2–16 (Boys 2–11)

MIDDLESEX

School	Ages
Heathfield School, Pinner	3–18
Jack and Jill School, Hampton	3–7 (Boys 3–5)
The Lady Eleanor Holles School, Hampton	7–18
North London Collegiate, Edgware	4–18
Northwood College, Northwood	3–18
Peterborough & St Margaret's School, Stanmore	4–16
St Catherine's School, Twickenham	3–16 (Sixth form in 2006)
St David's School, Ashford	3–18
St Helen's School, Northwood	3–18

NORFOLK

School	Ages
Hethersett Old Hall School, Norwich	4–18 (Boys 4–7)
Norwich High School for Girls GDST, Norwich	4–18
Thorpe House School, Norwich	3–16

NORTHAMPTONSHIRE

School	Ages
Northampton High School, Northampton	3–18

NOTTINGHAMSHIRE

School	Ages
Hollygirt School, Nottingham	3–16
Nottingham High School for Girls GDST, Nottingham	4–18

OXFORDSHIRE

School	Ages
The Carrdus School, Banbury	3–11 (Boys 3–8)
Cranford House School, Wallingford	3–16 (Boys 3–7)
Headington School, Oxford	3–18 (Co-ed 3–4)
IQRA School, Oxford	10–16
Our Lady's Convent Senior School, Abingdon	11–18
Oxford High School GDST, Oxford	3–18 (Boys 3–6)
Rye St Antony School, Oxford	3–18 (Boys 3–8)
St Mary's School, Wantage	11–18
School of St Helen & St Katharine, Abingdon	9–18
Tudor Hall School, Banbury	11–18
Wychwood School, Oxford	11–18

SHROPSHIRE

School	Ages
Adcote School for Girls, Shrewsbury	4–18
Shrewsbury High School GDST, Shrewsbury	2–18

SOMERSET

Bruton School for Girls, Bruton 3–18

BATH & NORTH EAST SOMERSET

The Royal High School, Bath 3–18

STAFFORDSHIRE

Abbots Bromley School for Girls, Abbots Bromley 4–18
St Dominic's Priory School, Stone 3–18 (Boys 3–11)
St Dominic's School, Stafford 2–16 (Co-ed 2–7)

STOCKTON-ON-TEES

Teesside Preparatory and High School, Eaglescliffe 3–18

SUFFOLK

Amberfield School, Ipswich 3–16 (Boys 3–7)
Ipswich High School GDST, Ipswich 3–18

SURREY

Bramley School, Tadworth 3–11
Croham Hurst School, South Croydon 3–18
Croydon High School GDST, South Croydon 3–18
Dunottar School, Reigate 3–18
Greenacre School for Girls, Banstead 3–18
Guildford High School, Guildford 4–18
Halstead Preparatory School, Woking 3–11
Holy Cross Preparatory School, Kingston-upon-Thames 4–11
Laverock School, Oxted 3–11
Lodge School, Purley 3–18 (Boys 3–11)
Manor House School, Leatherhead 2–16
Marymount International School, Kingston-upon-Thames 11–18
Notre Dame Preparatory School, Cobham 2–11 (Boys 2–5)
Notre Dame Senior School, Cobham 11–18
Old Palace School of John Whitgift, Croydon 4–18
Old Vicarage School, Richmond 4–11
Parsons Mead, Ashtead 2–18
Prior's Field School, Godalming 11–18
Rowan Preparatory School, Esher 3–11
The Royal School, Haslemere 3–18 (Boys 2–4)
St Catherine's School, Guildford 4–18
St Ives School, Haslemere 3–11 (Boys 3–5)
St Teresa's Preparatory School, Effingham 2–11
St Teresa's School, Dorking 11–18
Sir William Perkins's School, Chertsey 11–18
Surbiton High School, Kingston-upon-Thames 4–18 (Boys 4–11)
Sutton High School GDST, Sutton 4–18
Tormead School, Guildford 4–18
Wispers School for Girls, Haslemere 11–18
Woldingham School, Woldingham 11–18

EAST SUSSEX

Brighton and Hove High School GDST, Brighton 3–18
Moira House School, Eastbourne 2–11
Moira House Girls School, Eastbourne 3–19
Roedean School, Brighton 11–18
St Leonards-Mayfield School, Mayfield 11–18
St Mary's Hall, Brighton 3–18 (Boys 3–8)

WEST SUSSEX

Burgess Hill School for Girls, Burgess Hill 3–18
Farlington School, Horsham 4–18
*Fonthill Lodge, East Grinstead
Lavant House, Chichester 3–18
The Towers Convent School, Steyning 4–16 (Boys 3–11)

TYNE AND WEAR

Central Newcastle High School GDST, Newcastle upon Tyne 3–18
Dame Allan's Girls School, Newcastle upon Tyne 8–18 (Co-ed VIth Form)
La Sagesse School, Newcastle upon Tyne 3–18
Newcastle Upon Tyne Church High School, Newcastle upon Tyne 2–18
Westfield School, Newcastle upon Tyne 3–18

WARWICKSHIRE

The King's High School for Girls, Warwick 10–18
The Kingsley School, Leamington Spa 3–18 (Boys 2–7)

WEST MIDLANDS

*Al Hijrah School, Birmingham
Birchfield Independent Girls School, Birmingham 11–16
Coventry Muslim School, Coventry 4–16
*Darul Uloom Islamic High School and College, Birmingham
Edgbaston High School for Girls, Birmingham 2–18
Highclare School, Birmingham 1–18 (Boys 1–11 & 16–18)
King Edward VI High School for Girls, Birmingham 11–18
Newbridge Preparatory School, Wolverhampton 3–11
Priory School, Birmingham 1–18 (Co-ed 1–11)
Saint Martin's School, Solihull 3–18
Woodstock Girls' School, Birmingham 11–15

WILTSHIRE

Godolphin Preparatory School, Salisbury 3–11
The Godolphin School, Salisbury 11–18
Leaden Hall, Salisbury 3–11 (Boys 3–4)
St Mary's School, Calne 11–18
Stonar School, Melksham 2–18

WORCESTERSHIRE

The Alice Ottley School, Worcester 3–19
Malvern Girls' College, Malvern 11–18
St James's School, Malvern 7–18
St Mary's Convent School, Worcester 2–18 (Boys 2–8)
Whitford Hall & Dodderhill School, Droitwich 3–16 (Boys 3–9)

EAST RIDING OF YORKSHIRE

Hull High School, Anlaby 3–18 (Boys 3–11)

NORTH YORKSHIRE

Harrogate Ladies' College, Harrogate 10–18
The Mount School, York 11–18
Queen Margaret's School, York 11–18
Queen Mary's School, Thirsk 3–16 (Boys 3–7)

SOUTH YORKSHIRE

Ashdell Preparatory School, Sheffield 4–11
Brantwood School for Girls, Sheffield 3–16
Sheffield High School GDST, Sheffield 4–18

WEST YORKSHIRE

Bradford Girls' Grammar School, Bradford 2–18
Gateways School, Leeds 3–18 (Boys 3–7)
Islamia Girls High School, Huddersfield 11–16
Leeds Girls' High School, Leeds 3–19
New Horizon Community School, Leeds 11–16
Moorfield School, Ilkley 2–11
Wakefield Girls' High School, Wakefield 11–18

NORTHERN IRELAND

COUNTY ANTRIM

Victoria College Belfast, Belfast 4–18

SCOTLAND

ABERDEENSHIRE

St Margaret's School for Girls, Aberdeen 3–18 (Boys 3–5)

GLASGOW

Craigholme School, Glasgow 3–18 (Boys 3–5)

SOUTH LANARKSHIRE

Fernhill School, Rutherglen 4–18 (Boys 4–11)

LOTHIAN

The Mary Erskine School, Edinburgh 12–18 (Co-ed VIth Form)
St George's School for Girls, Edinburgh 2–18 (Boys 2–5)
St Margaret's School, Edinburgh 1–18 (Boys 1–8)

PERTH AND KINROSS

Kilgraston (A Sacred Heart School), Perth 2–18 (Boys day 2–9)

WALES

CONWY

*Rydal Penrhos Senior School, Colwyn Bay

DENBIGHSHIRE

Howell's School, Denbigh 2–18

MONMOUTHSHIRE

Haberdashers' Monmouth School For Girls, Monmouth 7–18

4.5

Boarding Provision (Full, Weekly and Flexi-Boarding, Host Families)

The schools and colleges listed below offer boarding/residential accommodation. Full boarding is indicated by 'F', weekly boarding by 'W'. Many schools now offer Flexi-boarding (Fl), ie pupils may board for part of the week or on an occasional basis. Please note that in some cases independent Sixth Form colleges may offer accommodation with host families (H) or in hostels. For further details please contact schools direct.

ENGLAND

BEDFORDSHIRE

Bedford High School, Bedford F Fl
Bedford Preparatory School, Bedford F W Fl
Bedford School, Bedford F W Fl
Bedford School Study Centre, Bedford F

BERKSHIRE

Bearwood College, Wokingham F W Fl
Bradfield College, Reading F W
Brockhurst and Marlston House Schools, Newbury W Fl
Cheam School, Newbury F W Fl
Downe House, Thatcham F
Eagle House, Sandhurst F W Fl
Elstree School, Reading F Fl
Eton College, Windsor F
Heathfield School, Ascot F
Horris Hill, Newbury F
Hurst Lodge School, Ascot W Fl
Lambrook Haileybury, Bracknell F W Fl
Leighton Park School, Reading F W Fl
Licensed Victuallers' School, Ascot F W
Luckley-Oakfield School, Wokingham F W Fl
Ludgrove, Wokingham F
The Oratory Preparatory School, Reading F Fl
The Oratory School, Reading F Fl
Padworth College, Reading F W Fl
Pangbourne College, Pangbourne F W Fl
Papplewick School, Ascot F
Queen Anne's School, Reading F Fl
St Andrew's School, Reading Fl
St George's School, Ascot F Fl
St George's School, Windsor F W Fl
St John's Beaumont, Windsor F W
St Mary's School, Ascot F
St Michaels School, Newbury F W Fl
Sunningdale School, Sunningdale F
Wellington College, Crowthorne F W

BRISTOL

Badminton School F W Fl
Clifton College, Bristol F Fl
Clifton College Preparatory School F W Fl
Clifton High School, Bristol F W Fl
Colston's Collegiate School, Bristol F Fl
The Downs School, Wraxall F W Fl
Queen Elizabeth's Hospital F W Fl
Tockington Manor School, Bristol F Fl

BUCKINGHAMSHIRE

Ashfold School, Aylesbury W Fl
Caldicott School, Farnham Royal F
Godstowe Preparatory School, High Wycombe F W
Gyosei International School UK, Milton Keynes
Pipers Corner School, High Wycombe F W Fl

Stowe School, Buckingham F
Swanbourne House School, Milton Keynes F W Fl
Thornton College Convent of Jesus and Mary, Milton Keynes F W Fl
Wycombe Abbey School, High Wycombe F

CAMBRIDGESHIRE

Bellerbys College, Cambridge F
Cambridge Arts & Sciences (CATS), Cambridge F H
Cambridge Centre for Sixth-form Studies, Cambridge F W Fl
Kimbolton School, Huntingdon F Fl
The King's School Ely, Ely F W Fl
The Leys School, Cambridge F
MPW (Mander Portman Woodward), Cambridge Fl
Peterborough High School, Peterborough F W Fl
St Andrew's, Cambridge Fl
St John's College School, Cambridge F Fl
St Mary's School, Cambridge F W Fl

CHESHIRE

Hammond School, Chester F W
Ramillies Hall School, Cheadle W
Terra Nova School, Holmes Chapel F W Fl

CORNWALL

The Bolitho School, Penzance F W Fl
Polwhele House School, Truro W Fl
Truro High School, Truro F W Fl
Truro School, Truro F Fl

CUMBRIA

Casterton School, Kirkby Lonsdale F Fl
Harecroft Hall School, Seascale F W Fl
Holme Park School, Kendal Fl
Lime House School, Carlisle F W
St Bees School, St Bees F W Fl
Sedbergh School, Sedbergh F
Windermere St Anne's, Windermere F W

DERBYSHIRE

Foremarke Hall School, Derby F W Fl
Mount St Mary's College, Spinkhill F W Fl
Ockbrook School, Derby F W Fl
Repton School, Derby F
St Anselm's, Bakewell F Fl

DEVON

Blundell's School, Tiverton F W Fl
Bramdean School, Exeter W Fl
Edgehill College, Bideford F W Fl
Exeter Cathedral School, Exeter F W Fl
Grenville College, Bideford F W Fl
Kelly College, Tavistock F W Fl
Kelly College Preparatory School, Tavistock F W Fl
Mount House School, Tavistock F Fl
Plymouth College, Plymouth F W
St John's School, Sidmouth F W Fl
St Peter's School, Exmouth W Fl
Shebbear College, Beaworthy F W Fl
Stover School, Newton Abbot F W Fl
Trinity School, Teignmouth F W Fl
West Buckland Preparatory School, Barnstaple F Fl
West Buckland School, Barnstaple F Fl

DORSET

Bryanston School, Blandford Forum F
Canford School, Wimborne F
Clayesmore Preparatory School, Blandford Forum F W Fl
Clayesmore School, Blandford Forum F W
Hanford School, Blandford Forum F
International College, Sherborne School, Sherborne F
Knighton House, Blandford Forum F W Fl
Milton Abbey School, Blandford Forum F
The Old Malthouse, Swanage W Fl
Port Regis School, Shaftesbury F W Fl
St Antony's Leweston Schools, Sherborne F Fl
St Mary's School, Shaftesbury F
Sherborne Preparatory School, Sherborne F W Fl
Sherborne School, Sherborne F
Sherborne School for Girls, Sherborne F
Talbot Heath, Bournemouth F W Fl
Wentworth College, Bournemouth F W Fl

COUNTY DURHAM

Barnard Castle School, Barnard Castle F W Fl
The Chorister School, Durham F W
Durham School, Durham F W Fl
Polam Hall, Darlington F W Fl

ESSEX

Brentwood School, Brentwood F W
Chigwell School, Chigwell F W Fl
Felsted Preparatory School, Dunmow
Felsted School, Dunmow F Fl
Friends' School, Saffron Walden F W Fl
Gosfield School, Halstead F Fl
Holmwood House, Colchester W Fl
New Hall School, Chelmsford F Fl

GLOUCESTERSHIRE

The Abbey School, Tewkesbury W
Beaudesert Park School, Stroud F W Fl
Bredon School, Tewkesbury F W Fl
Cheltenham College, Cheltenham F
Cheltenham College Junior School, Cheltenham F Fl
The Cheltenham Ladies' College, Cheltenham F
Dean Close Preparatory School, Cheltenham F Fl
Dean Close School, Cheltenham F

Hatherop Castle School, Cirencester Fl
The King's School, Gloucester W Fl
Kitebrook House, Moreton-in-Marsh W
Rendcomb College, Cirencester F W Fl
Rose Hill School, Wotton-under-Edge F W Fl
Westonbirt School, Tetbury F W Fl
Wycliffe College & Preparatory School, Stonehouse F Fl H
Wycliffe Preparatory School, Stonehouse F W Fl
Wynstones School, Gloucester F W Fl H

HAMPSHIRE

Bedales School, Petersfield F
Boundary Oak School, Fareham W Fl
Brockwood Park School, Bramdean F
Dunhurst (Bedales Junior School), Petersfield F Fl
Hampshire Collegiate School, Embley Park, Romsey F W Fl
Farleigh School, Andover F W Fl
Forres Sandle Manor, Fordingbridge F W Fl
Highfield School, Liphook F
Hordle Walhampton School, Lymington F W Fl
Lord Wandsworth College, Hook F W Fl
Moyles Court School, Ringwood F
The Pilgrims' School, Winchester F W
Rookesbury Park School, Portsmouth F W Fl
Rookwood School, Andover F Fl
St John's College, Southsea F Fl
St Neot's School, Hook W Fl
St Swithun's School, Winchester F W
Stanbridge Earls School, Romsey F
Twyford School, Winchester W Fl H
Winchester College, Winchester F

HEREFORDSHIRE

Lucton School, Leominster F W Fl
St Richard's, Bromyard F W Fl

HERTFORDSHIRE

Aldenham School, Elstree F W Fl
Aldwickbury School, Harpenden W Fl
The Arts Educational School, Tring F
Beechwood Park School, St Albans W Fl
Berkhamsted Collegiate School, Berkhamsted F W Fl
Bishop's Stortford College, Bishop's Stortford F Fl
Edge Grove, Aldenham F Fl
Haileybury, Hertford F Fl
Heath Mount School, Hertford W Fl
The Junior School, Bishop's Stortford College, Bishop's Stortford F W
Lockers Park, Hemel Hempstead F Fl
The Princess Helena College, Hitchin F W Fl
The Purcell School, Bushey F
Queenswood School, Hatfield F Fl
The Royal Masonic School for Girls, Rickmansworth F W Fl
St Christopher School, Letchworth F W Fl
St Edmund's College, Ware F W Fl
St Francis' College, Letchworth F W Fl
St Margaret's School, Bushey F W Fl
Stanborough School, Watford F W Fl
Westbrook Hay Preparatory School, Hemel Hempstead Fl

ISLE OF MAN

King William's College, Castletown F W Fl

ISLE OF WIGHT

Ryde School, Ryde F W Fl

KENT

Ashford School, Ashford F W Fl
Bedgebury School, Cranbrook F W Fl
Beechwood Sacred Heart School, Tunbridge Wells F W Fl
Benenden School, Cranbrook F
Bethany School, Cranbrook F W
Cobham Hall, Gravesend F W Fl
Cranbrook School, Cranbrook F Fl
Darul Uloom London, Chislehurst F
Dover College, Dover F W Fl
Duke of York's Royal Military School, Dover F
Dulwich Preparatory School, Cranbrook, Cranbrook W Fl
Farringtons School, Chislehurst F W Fl
Holmewood House, Tunbridge Wells W Fl
Junior King's School, Canterbury F W Fl
The Junior School, St Lawrence College, Ramsgate F Fl
Kent College, Canterbury F W Fl
Kent College Infant & Junior School, Canterbury F W Fl
Kent College Pembury, Tunbridge Wells F W Fl
King's Preparatory School, Rochester F W Fl
The King's School, Canterbury F
King's School Rochester, Rochester F W
Marlborough House School, Hawkhurst Fl
Northbourne Park School, Deal F Fl
Rochester Independent College, Rochester F Fl
St Edmunds Junior School, Canterbury F Fl
St Edmund's School, Canterbury F Fl
St Lawrence College, Ramsgate F W Fl
St Mary's Westbrook, Folkestone F W Fl
St Ronan's, Hawkhurst Fl
Sevenoaks School, Sevenoaks F
Sutton Valence School, Maidstone F W Fl
Tonbridge School, Tonbridge F W
Wellesley House School, Broadstairs F W

LANCASHIRE

Kirkham Grammar School, Preston F W Fl
Moorland School, Clitheroe F W Fl
Rossall Junior School, Fleetwood F Fl
Rossall School, Fleetwood F Fl
Rossall School International Study Centre, Fleetwood F

St Anne's College Grammar School, Lytham St Annes F W Fl H
St Mary's Hall, Stonyhurst F W Fl
Sedbergh Junior School, Lancaster F W Fl
Stonyhurst College, Clitheroe F W Fl

LEICESTERSHIRE

Brooke House College, Market Harborough F
Irwin College, Leicester F
Loughborough Grammar School, Loughborough F W Fl
Ratcliffe College, Leicester F W Fl

LINCOLNSHIRE

Lincoln Minster School, Lincoln F W Fl
St Hugh's School, Woodhall Spa F W Fl
Stamford High School, Stamford F W Fl
Stamford Junior School, Stamford F W
Stamford School, Stamford F W Fl
Witham Hall, Bourne F W Fl

NORTH EAST LINCOLNSHIRE

St James' School, Grimsby F W Fl

LONDON

Ashbourne Independent Sixth Form College, W8 F
Bales College, W10
David Game College, W11
Dulwich College, SE21 F W
Dulwich College Preparatory School, SE21 W
Mill Hill School, NW7 F
Royal Ballet School, WC2E F
The Royal School, Hampstead, NW3 F W Fl
St Paul's Cathedral School, EC4M F
St Paul's School, SW13 F W Fl
Sylvia Young Theatre School, NW1 F W H
Westminster Abbey Choir School, SW1P F Fl
Westminster Cathedral Choir School, SW1P F
Westminster School, SW1P F W

GREATER MANCHESTER

Chetham's School of Music, Manchester F

MERSEYSIDE

Clarence High School, Formby
Kingsmead School, Wirral F W Fl

MIDDLESEX

Harrow School, Harrow on the Hill F
St David's School, Ashford F W Fl
St Helen's School, Northwood F W Fl
St James Independent School for Boys (Senior), Twickenham W

NORFOLK

Beeston Hall School, Cromer F Fl
Glebe House School, Hunstanton W Fl
Gresham's Preparatory School, Holt F W Fl
Gresham's School, Holt F W
Hethersett Old Hall School, Norwich F Fl
Langley School, Norwich F W Fl
The New Eccles Hall School, Norwich F W Fl
Riddlesworth Hall, Diss F W Fl
Sacred Heart Convent School, Swaffham F W
Taverham Hall, Norwich W Fl

NORTHAMPTONSHIRE

Beachborough School, Brackley Fl
Bosworth Independent College, Northampton F
Maidwell Hall, Northampton F
Oundle School, Peterborough F
Winchester House School, Brackley F W Fl

NORTHUMBERLAND

Longridge Towers School, Berwick-upon-Tweed F W Fl
Mowden Hall School, Stocksfield F W

NOTTINGHAMSHIRE

Al Karam Secondary School, Retford F Fl
Bramcote Lorne School, Retford Fl
Ranby House, Retford F W Fl
Rodney School, Newark Fl
Trent College, Nottingham W Fl
Wellow House School, Newark W Fl
Worksop College, Worksop F W Fl

OXFORDSHIRE

Abacus College, Oxford F
Abingdon School, Abingdon F W
Bloxham School, Banbury F W Fl
Cherwell College, Oxford F W
Christ Church Cathedral School, Oxford F
Cothill House Preparatory School, Abingdon F
d'Overbroeck's College, Oxford F H
Dragon School, Oxford F
Greene's Tutorial College, Oxford F W Fl H
Headington School, Oxford F W Fl
Kingham Hill School, Chipping Norton F W Fl
Moulsford Preparatory School, Wallingford W
Oxford Tutorial College, Oxford
Radley College, Abingdon F
Rye St Antony School, Oxford F W Fl
St Clare's, Oxford, Oxford F W Fl
St Edward's School, Oxford F
St Hugh's School, Faringdon W Fl
St Mary's School, Wantage F
Shiplake College, Henley-on-Thames F
Sibford School, Banbury F W Fl
Summer Fields, Oxford F
Tudor Hall School, Banbury F
Wychwood School, Oxford F W Fl

RUTLAND

Oakham School, Oakham F
Uppingham School, Uppingham F

SHROPSHIRE

Adcote School for Girls, Shrewsbury F W Fl H
Bedstone College, Bucknell F Fl
Concord College, Shrewsbury F
Ellesmere College, Ellesmere F W Fl
Moor Park School, Ludlow F W Fl
Moreton Hall, Oswestry F
Oswestry School, Oswestry F W Fl
Packwood Haugh School, Shrewsbury F
Prestfelde Preparatory School, Shrewsbury F Fl
Shrewsbury School, Shrewsbury F
Wrekin College, Telford F Fl

SOMERSET

All Hallows, Shepton Mallet F W Fl
Bruton School for Girls, Bruton F W Fl
Chilton Cantelo School, Yeovil F Fl
Downside School, Bath F W
Hazlegrove (King's Bruton Preparatory School), Yeovil F Fl
King's Bruton, Bruton F
King's College, Taunton F
King's Hall School, Taunton F W Fl
Millfield Preparatory School, Street F
Millfield School, Street F
The Park School, Yeovil F W Fl H
Perrott Hill School, Crewkerne F W Fl
Queen's College Junior and Pre-Preparatory Schools, Taunton F
Queen's College, Taunton F Fl
Taunton International Study Centre (TISC), Taunton F
Taunton Preparatory School, Taunton F Fl
Taunton School, Taunton F
Wellington School, Wellington F W Fl
Wells Cathedral Junior School, Wells F W Fl
Wells Cathedral School, Wells F Fl

BATH & NORTH EAST SOMERSET

Bath Academy, Bath F Fl H
Kingswood Preparatory School, Bath F W Fl
Kingswood School, Bath F W Fl
Monkton Combe Junior School, Bath F W Fl
Monkton Combe School, Bath F W Fl
Prior Park College, Bath F W Fl
The Royal High School, Bath F Fl

NORTH SOMERSET

Sidcot School, Winscombe F W Fl

STAFFORDSHIRE

Abbots Bromley School for Girls, Abbots Bromley F Fl
Abbotsholme School, Uttoxeter F W Fl
Chase Academy, Cannock F
Denstone College, Uttoxeter F W
Lichfield Cathedral School, Lichfield F W Fl
St Bede's School, Stafford F W Fl
Yarlet School, Stafford Fl

SUFFOLK

Barnardiston Hall Preparatory School, Haverhill F W Fl
Culford School, Bury St Edmunds F W Fl
Felixstowe International College, Felixstowe F
Finborough School, Stowmarket F W Fl
Framlingham College, Woodbridge F W Fl
Framlingham College Preparatory School, Brandeston F W Fl
Ipswich School, Ipswich F W Fl
Moreton Hall Preparatory School, Bury St Edmunds F W Fl
Old Buckenham Hall School, Ipswich F W
Orwell Park, Ipswich F W Fl
Royal Hospital School, Ipswich F
Saint Felix Schools, Southwold Fl
St Joseph's College, Ipswich F W Fl
Stoke College, Sudbury W Fl
Summerhill School, Leiston Fl
Woodbridge School, Woodbridge F W Fl

SURREY

ACS Cobham International School, Cobham F W
Aldro School, Godalming F
Belmont School, Dorking W Fl
Bishopsgate School, Egham W Fl
Box Hill School, Dorking F W
Cambridge Tutors College, Croydon H
Caterham School, Caterham F W Fl
Charterhouse, Godalming F
City of London Freemen's School, Ashtead F W Fl
Cranleigh Preparatory School, Cranleigh
Cranleigh School, Cranleigh F
Duke of Kent School, Ewhurst F W Fl
Edgeborough, Farnham Fl
Epsom College, Epsom F W
Feltonfleet School, Cobham W Fl
Frensham Heights School, Farnham F
Hall Grove School, Bagshot W Fl
Hampton Court House, East Molesey W Fl
Hurtwood House, Dorking F W Fl
King Edward's School Witley, Godalming F Fl
Marymount International School, Kingston-upon-Thames F W Fl H
More House School, Farnham
Prior's Field School, Godalming F W
Reed's School, Cobham F
Royal Alexandra and Albert School, Reigate F Fl
Royal Ballet School, Richmond
Royal Russell School, Croydon F W Fl
The Royal School, Haslemere F W Fl
St Catherine's School, Guildford F W Fl
St Edmund's School, Hindhead W Fl
St John's School, Leatherhead F Fl
St Teresa's Preparatory School, Effingham F W Fl

St Teresa's School, Dorking F W Fl
TASIS The American School in England, Thorpe F
Wispers School for Girls, Haslemere F W
Woldingham School, Woldingham F W Fl
Woodcote House School, Windlesham F
Yehudi Menuhin School, Cobham F Fl

EAST SUSSEX

Ashdown House School, Forest Row F
Battle Abbey School, Battle F W Fl
Bellerbys College, Hove F
Brighton College, Brighton F W Fl
Buckswood School, Hastings F W Fl
Eastbourne College, Eastbourne F
Greenfields School, Forest Row F W Fl
Michael Hall (Steiner Waldorf School), Forest Row F W Fl
Moira House School, Eastbourne F W Fl
Moira House Girls School, Eastbourne F W Fl
Newlands International College, Seaford F
Newlands School, Seaford F Fl
Roedean School, Brighton Fl
St Andrew's School, Eastbourne F W Fl
St Aubyns School, Brighton W Fl
St Bede's Prep School, Eastbourne F W Fl
St Bede's School, Hailsham F Fl
St Leonards-Mayfield School, Mayfield F W Fl
St Mary's Hall, Brighton F W Fl
Stonelands School of Ballet & Theatre Arts, Hove F Fl
Vinehall School, Robertsbridge F

WEST SUSSEX

Ardingly College, Haywards Heath F W Fl
Ardingly College Junior School, Haywards Heath F Fl
Brambletye School, East Grinstead F
Burgess Hill School for Girls, Burgess Hill F Fl
Christ's Hospital, Horsham F
Copthorne Prep School, Copthorne W Fl
Cottesmore School, Pease Pottage F
Cumnor House School, Haywards Heath F
Dorset House School, Pulborough W Fl
Farlington School, Horsham F W Fl
Great Ballard School, Chichester F W Fl
Great Walstead, Haywards Heath W Fl
Handcross Park School, Haywards Heath W Fl
Hurstpierpoint College, Hurstpierpoint F W Fl
Lancing College, Lancing F Fl
Lavant House, Chichester F W Fl
The Prebendal School, Chichester F W Fl
Seaford College, Petworth F W Fl
Slindon College, Arundel F W Fl
Sompting Abbotts School, Sompting W Fl
Stoke Brunswick, East Grinstead W Fl
The Towers Convent School, Steyning F W Fl
Westbourne House School, Chichester F Fl
Windlesham House, Pulborough F
Worth School, Turners Hill F W

WARWICKSHIRE

Bilton Grange, Rugby F W Fl
Rugby School, Rugby F
Warwick School, Warwick F W Fl

WEST MIDLANDS

Birchfield School, Wolverhampton W Fl
The Blue Coat School, Birmingham F W Fl
Darul Uloom Islamic High School & College, Birmingham
Elmhurst School for Dance, Birmingham F
The Royal Wolverhampton Junior School, Wolverhampton F
The Royal Wolverhampton School, Wolverhampton F W Fl
Tettenhall College, Wolverhampton F W Fl

WILTSHIRE

Appleford School, Salisbury
Chafyn Grove School, Salisbury F W Fl
Dauntsey's School, Devizes F
The Godolphin School, Salisbury F Fl
Leaden Hall, Salisbury F Fl
Marlborough College, Marlborough F
Norman Court Preparatory School, Salisbury F W Fl
Pinewood School, Shrivenham F W Fl
Prior Park Preparatory School, Cricklade F W Fl
St Mary's School, Calne F
Salisbury Cathedral School, Salisbury F Fl
Sandroyd School, Salisbury F Fl
Stonar School, Melksham F W Fl H
Warminster School, Warminster F W Fl

WORCESTERSHIRE

Abberley Hall, Worcester F Fl
The Abbey College, Malvern Wells Fl
Bromsgrove Preparatory School, Bromsgrove F W Fl
Bromsgrove School, Bromsgrove F
The Downs School, Malvern F W Fl
The Elms, Malvern F Fl
Malvern College Preparatory and Pre-Prep School, Malvern F Fl
Malvern College, Malvern F
Malvern Girls' College, Malvern F W
Moffats School, Bewdley F W Fl
St James's School, Malvern F W Fl
Saint Michael's College, Tenbury Wells F

EAST RIDING OF YORKSHIRE

Pocklington School, Pocklington F W Fl

NORTH YORKSHIRE

Ampleforth College, York F
Ashville College, Harrogate F W Fl
Aysgarth Preparatory School, Bedale F W Fl
Bootham School, York F W Fl

Bramcote School, Scarborough F W Fl
Catteral Hall School, Settle F Fl
Cundall Manor School, York F
Fyling Hall School, Whitby F W
Giggleswick School, Settle F
Harrogate Ladies' College, Harrogate F W Fl
Harrogate Tutorial College, Harrogate F W Fl H
Highfield Preparatory School, Harrogate F W Fl
Howsham Hall, York F Fl
Lisvane, Scarborough College Junior School, Scarborough F W Fl
Malsis School, Skipton F
The Mount School, York F W Fl
Queen Ethelburga's College, York F
Queen Margaret's School, York F W
Queen Mary's School, Thirsk F W Fl
Read School, Selby F W Fl
Ripon Cathedral Choir School, Ripon F W
St Martin's Ampleforth, York F Fl
St Peter's School, York F
Scarborough College & Lisvane School, Scarborough F W Fl
Terrington Hall, York F W Fl
Woodleigh School, Malton F W Fl

WEST YORKSHIRE

Ackworth School, Pontefract F W
Bronte House School, Bradford F W Fl
Fulneck School, Pudsey F W Fl
The International Centre, Ackworth School, Pontefract F W Fl
Rishworth School, Rishworth F W Fl
Woodhouse Grove School, Apperley Bridge F W Fl

NORTHERN IRELAND

COUNTY ANTRIM

Cabin Hill School, Belfast Fl
Campbell College, Belfast F W Fl
Methodist College, Belfast F
Victoria College Belfast, Belfast F W Fl

COUNTY ARMAGH

The Royal School, Armagh F W Fl

COUNTY DOWN

Rockport School, Holywood W Fl

COUNTY TYRONE

The Royal School Dungannon, Dungannon F W Fl

SCOTLAND

ANGUS

Lathallan School, Montrose W Fl

ARGYLL AND BUTE

Lomond School, Helensburgh F H

CLACKMANNANSHIRE

Dollar Academy, Dollar F W Fl

FIFE

St Leonards School & VIth Form College, St Andrews F Fl

LOTHIAN

Basil Paterson Tutorial College, Edinburgh H
Belhaven Hill, Dunbar F
Cargilfield, Edinburgh F W Fl
The Edinburgh Academy, Edinburgh Fl
Fettes College, Edinburgh F
Loretto Junior School, Musselburgh F W Fl
Loretto School, Musselburgh F W Fl
The Mary Erskine School, Edinburgh F W
Merchiston Castle School, Edinburgh F
St George's School for Girls, Edinburgh F Fl
St Mary's Music School, Edinburgh F
Stewart's Melville College, Edinburgh F W Fl

MORAYSHIRE

Gordonstoun School, Elgin F W

PERTH AND KINROSS

Ardvreck School, Crieff F
Glenalmond College, Perth F
Kilgraston (A Sacred Heart School), Perth F W Fl
Morrison's Academy, Crieff F W Fl
Queen Victoria School, Dunblane F
Strathallan School, Perth F

ROXBURGHSHIRE

St Mary's Preparatory School, Melrose W Fl

WALES

CARMARTHENSHIRE

Llandovery College, Llandovery F W Fl

CONWY

Lyndon Preparatory School, Colwyn Bay F Fl
Rydal Penrhos Senior School, Colwyn Bay F Fl
St David's College, Llandudno F W Fl

DENBIGHSHIRE

Howell's School, Denbigh F W Fl
Ruthin School, Ruthin F W Fl

MONMOUTHSHIRE

Haberdashers' Monmouth School For Girls, Monmouth F W Fl
Monmouth School, Monmouth F W Fl
St John's-on-the-Hill, Chepstow F W Fl

PEMBROKESHIRE

Netherwood School, Saundersfoot F W Fl

POWYS

Christ College, Brecon F W Fl

SWANSEA

Oakleigh House, Swansea

4.6 Religious Affiliation

The following index lists all schools specifying a particular denomination. However, it should be noted that this is intended as a guide only and that many of the schools listed also welcome children of other faiths. Schools which claim to be non- or inter-denominational are not listed. Parents should check precise details with individual schools. A full list of each school's entries elsewhere in the book is given in the main index at the back.

BUDDHIST

Dharma School, Brighton

CHRISTIAN

Abinger Hammer Village School, Dorking
Alderley Edge School for Girls, Alderley Edge
All Saints School, Norwich
Amberfield School, Ipswich
Ardvreck School, Crieff
The Ark School, Reading
Ashdell Preparatory School, Sheffield
Avon House, Woodford Green
Avondale School, Salisbury
Barnsley Christian School, Barnsley
Benedict House Preparatory School, Sidcup
Berkhamsted Collegiate Preparatory School, Berkhamsted
Berkhamsted Collegiate School, Berkhamsted
Bowbrook House School, Pershore
Bradford Christian School, Bradford
Bromley High School GDST, Bromley
Broomwood Hall School, SW12
Castle Court Preparatory School, Wimborne
Castle House School, Newport
Caterham Preparatory School, Caterham
Cedars School, Aldermaston
Chard School, Chard
Chase Academy, Cannock
Christ the King School, Sale
Clifton Lodge Preparatory School, W5
The Crescent School, Rugby
The Daiglen School, Buckhurst Hill
Dame Alice Harpur School, Bedford
Danes Hill School, Leatherhead
Darvell School, Robertsbridge
Dean Close School, Cheltenham
Derby Grammar School for Boys, Derby
Derwent Lodge School for Girls, Tonbridge
Ditcham Park School, Petersfield
Dolphin School (Including Noah's Ark Nursery Schools), SW11
The Dolphin School, Exmouth
Dower House School, Bridgnorth
Downham Prep School and Montessori Nursery, Kings Lynn
East London Christian Choir School, E8
Egerton-Rothesay School, Berkhamsted
Emmanuel Christian School, Oxford
Emmanuel School, Exeter
Emmanuel School, Derby
Eversfield Preparatory School, Solihull
Exeter School, Exeter
Filgrave School, Newport Pagnell
Fosse Bank Mountains School, Tonbridge
Francis House, Tring
The Froebelian School, Leeds
Gatehouse School, E2
Gateway Christian School, Ilkeston
Ghyll Royd School, Ilkley
Glenarm College, Ilford
Godolphin Preparatory School, Salisbury
Gracefield Preparatory School, Bristol
Grange Park Preparatory School, N21
Grangewood Independent School, E7
Great Walstead, Haywards Heath
Grey House Preparatory School, Basingstoke
Guildford High School, Guildford

Hamilton College, Hamilton
Handsworth Christian School, Sheffield
Haslemere Preparatory School, Haslemere
Heath House Preparatory School, SE3
Herne Hill School, SE24
Heswall Preparatory School, Wirral
Hillgrove School, Bangor
Holy Trinity School, Kidderminster
Honeybourne School, Birmingham
Howell's School, Denbigh
Hydesville Tower School, Walsall
Jack and Jill School, Hampton
Josca's Preparatory School, Abingdon
Joseph Rayner Independent School, Audenshaw
King of Kings School, Manchester
The King's School, Nottingham
King's School, Plymouth
The King's School Senior, Eastleigh
The King's School, Witney
The King's School, Primary, Witney
Kingham Hill School, Chipping Norton
Kings Primary School, Southampton
Kings School, Harpenden
Kingsmead School, Wirral
Kingston Grammar School, Kingston-upon-Thames
Kingsway School, Wigan
La Retraite Swan, Salisbury
La Sagesse School, Newcastle upon Tyne
Lady Barn House School, Cheadle
Langley Manor School, Slough
Laverock School, Oxted
Leicester Grammar School, Leicester
Lightcliffe Preparatory, Halifax
Lincoln Minster School, Lincoln
Lingfield Notre Dame School, Lingfield
Lisvane, Scarborough College Junior School, Scarborough
Lorenden Preparatory School, Faversham
Lucton School, Leominster
The Lyceum, EC2A
Mannafields Christian School, Edinburgh
Maranatha Christian School, Swindon
Maypole House School, Alford
The Mead School, Tunbridge Wells
Meadowpark Nursery & Pre-Prep School, Cricklade
Michael Hall (Steiner Waldorf School), Forest Row
Monton Prep School with Montessori Nurseries, Eccles
Mountjoy House School, Huddersfield
New Life Christian School, Croydon
Norfolk House Preparatory & Kids Corner Nursery, Sandbach
Norfolk House School, Birmingham
Norwich School, Norwich
Oakleigh House, Swansea
Paragon Christian Academy, E5
The Park School, Yeovil
Plymouth College, Plymouth
The Pointer School, SE3
The Portsmouth Grammar School, Portsmouth
Priory School, Shanklin
Putney Park School, SW15
The Rastrick Independent School, Brighouse
Red House School, Norton
Redcliffe School, SW10
Richmond House School, Leeds
Rickmansworth PNEU School, Rickmansworth
River School, Worcester
Roundstone Preparatory School, Trowbridge
Sacred Heart Preparatory School, Chew Magna
St Aubyn's School, Woodford Green
St Aubyn's School, Tiverton
St Christophers School, Totnes
St Dominic's School, Stafford
St Francis' College, Letchworth
St George's School, Edgbaston, Birmingham
St Helen's School, Northwood
St Hilda's School, Westcliff-on-Sea
St John's Senior School, Enfield
St Joseph's College, Ipswich
St Mary's Preparatory School, Lincoln
St Mary's Westbrook, Folkestone
St Matthews School, Northampton
St Michael's School, Leigh-on-Sea
St Oswald's School, Alnwick
School of the Lion, Gloucester
Sedbergh Junior School, Lancaster
Sherborne Preparatory School, Sherborne
Stoneygate College, Leicester
Stowford College, Sutton
Sunflower Montessori School, Twickenham
Sunninghill Preparatory School, Dorchester
Thomas's Kindergarten, SW1W
Thomas's Preparatory School, W8
Thorpe Hall School, Southend-on-Sea
Trent College, Nottingham
Trinity School, Croydon
Trinity School, Stalybridge
Twickenham Preparatory School, Hampton
Uplands School, Poole
Victoria College, Jersey
Vine School, Southampton
Wakefield Tutorial Preparatory School, Leeds
Warlingham Park School, Croydon
Warwick Preparatory School, Warwick
Wellspring Christian School, Carlisle
Westmont School, Newport
Weston Green School, Thames Ditton
Wetherby Preparatory School, W11
Wickham Court School, West Wickham
Willington School, SW19
Woodford Green Preparatory School, Woodford Green
Worksop College, Worksop
Yardley Court, Tonbridge
Yarm School, Yarm

CHRISTIAN SCIENCE

Claremont Fan Court School, Esher

CHURCH IN WALES

The Cathedral School, Cardiff
Christ College, Brecon
Ffynone House School, Swansea
Llandovery College, Llandovery
Monmouth School, Monmouth

CHURCH OF ENGLAND

Abberley Hall, Worcester
Abbey Gate College, Chester
Abbey Gate School, Chester
The Abbey School, Tewkesbury
The Abbey School, Reading
The Abbey, Woodbridge
Abbot's Hill School, Hemel Hempstead
Abbots Bromley School for Girls, Abbots Bromley
Abbotsbury School, Newton Abbot
Abingdon School, Abingdon
Acorn School, Nailsworth
Adcote School for Girls, Shrewsbury
Airthrie School, Cheltenham
Aldenham School, Elstree
Aldro School, Godalming
Aldwickbury School, Harpenden
The Alice Ottley School, Worcester
Alleyn Court Preparatory School, Southend-on-Sea
Alleyn's School, SE22
Amesbury, Hindhead
Ardingly College, Haywards Heath
Ardingly College Junior School, Haywards Heath
Arnold House School, NW8
Arnold Lodge School, Leamington Spa
Ashbourne PNEU School, Ashbourne
Ashdown House School, Forest Row
The Atherley School, Southampton
Aysgarth Preparatory School, Bedale
Ballard School, New Milton
Bancroft's School, Woodford Green
Barfield School, Farnham
Barnardiston Hall Preparatory School, Haverhill
Baston School, Bromley
Beachborough School, Brackley
The Beacon School, Amersham
Bearwood College, Wokingham
Beaudesert Park School, Stroud
Bedford Preparatory School, Bedford
Bedford School, Bedford
Bedgebury School, Cranbrook
Bedstone College, Bucknell
Beech Hall School, Macclesfield
Beechenhurst Preparatory School, Liverpool
Beechwood Park School, St Albans
Beeston Hall School, Cromer
Bellan House Preparatory School, Oswestry
Belmont School, Dorking
Benenden School, Cranbrook
Berkhampstead School, Cheltenham
Bethany School, Cranbrook
Bilton Grange, Rugby
Birchfield School, Wolverhampton
Bloxham School, Banbury
The Blue Coat School, Birmingham
Blundell's School, Tiverton
Bodiam Manor School, Robertsbridge
The Bolitho School, Penzance
Bow School, Durham
Bradfield College, Reading
Brambletye School, East Grinstead
Bramcote Lorne School, Retford
Bramcote School, Scarborough
Bramley School, Tadworth
Bredon School, Tewkesbury
Brentwood School, Brentwood
Brigg Preparatory School, Brigg
Brighton College, Brighton
Brighton College Pre-preparatory School, Brighton
Brighton College Prep School, Brighton
Bristol Cathedral School, Bristol
Broadwater Manor School, Worthing
Brockhurst & Marlston House Pre-Preparatory School, Thatcham
Brockhurst and Marlston House Schools, Newbury
Bromsgrove Pre-preparatory and Nursery School, Bromsgrove
Bromsgrove Preparatory School, Bromsgrove
Bromsgrove School, Bromsgrove
Bronte School, Gravesend
Broomfield House School, Richmond
Bryanston School, Blandford Forum
Buckingham College Preparatory School, Pinner
Burys Court School, Reigate
Caldicott School, Farnham Royal
Cameron House School, SW3
Canford School, Wimborne
Casterton School, Kirkby Lonsdale
Chafyn Grove School, Salisbury
Chandlings Manor School, Oxford
Charterhouse, Godalming
Cheam School, Newbury
Cheltenham College, Cheltenham
Cheltenham College Junior School, Cheltenham
Chigwell School, Chigwell
Chilton Cantelo School, Yeovil
The Chorister School, Durham
Christ Church Cathedral School, Oxford
Christ's Hospital, Horsham
Claremont School, St Leonards-on-Sea
Clayesmore Preparatory School, Blandford Forum
Clayesmore School, Blandford Forum
Clifton College, Bristol
Clifton College Preparatory School
Colfe's School, SE12
Colston's Collegiate School, Bristol
Conifers School, Midhurst
Conway Preparatory School, Boston
Coopersale Hall School, Epping
Copthorne Prep School, Copthorne
Cothill House Preparatory School, Abingdon
Cottesmore School, Pease Pottage
Coventry Prep School, Coventry
Cranford House School, Wallingford
Cranleigh Preparatory School, Cranleigh
Cranleigh School, Cranleigh
The Croft Preparatory School, Stratford-upon-Avon
Cumnor House School, South Croydon
Cumnor House School, Haywards Heath
Cundall Manor School, York
Dair House School Trust Ltd, Farnham Royal
Daneshill School, Basingstoke
Dean Close Preparatory School, Cheltenham
Deepdene School, Hove
Denmead School, Hampton
Denstone College, Uttoxeter

Derby High School, Derby
The Dormer House PNEU School, Moreton-in-Marsh
Dorset House School, Pulborough
Dover College, Dover
Downe House, Thatcham
The Downs School, Wraxall
Dragon School, Oxford
Duke of York's Royal Military School, Dover
Dulwich College, SE21
Dulwich College Preparatory School, SE21
Dulwich Preparatory School, Cranbrook, Cranbrook
Dumpton School, Wimborne
Duncombe School, Hertford
Durham High School For Girls, Durham
Durham School, Durham
Durlston Court, New Milton
Eagle House, Sandhurst
Eastbourne College, Eastbourne
Edenhurst School, Newcastle-under-Lyme
Edge Grove, Aldenham
Edgeborough, Farnham
Elizabeth College, Guernsey
Ellesmere College, Ellesmere
Elmhurst School for Dance, Birmingham
The Elms, Malvern
Elstree School, Reading
The Elvian School, Reading
Emanuel School, SW11
Hampshire Collegiate School, Embley Park, Romsey
Epsom College, Epsom
Eton College, Windsor
Eton End PNEU, Slough
Ewell Castle School, Epsom
Exeter Cathedral School, Exeter
Exeter Junior School, Exeter
Fairfield PNEU School, Bristol
Fairholme Preparatory School, St Asaph
Farlington School, Horsham
Felixstowe International College, Felixstowe
Felsted Preparatory School, Dunmow
Felsted School, Dunmow
Feltonfleet School, Cobham
Fen School, Sleaford
Fonthill Lodge, East Grinstead
Foremarke Hall School, Derby
Forest Preparatory School, E17
Forest School, E17
Forres Sandle Manor, Fordingbridge
Framlingham College, Woodbridge
Framlingham College Preparatory School, Brandeston
Francis Holland School, SW1W
Francis Holland School, NW1
Gayhurst School, Gerrards Cross
Giggleswick School, Settle
Glebe House School, Hunstanton
The Godolphin School, Salisbury
Godstowe Preparatory School, High Wycombe
Great Ballard School, Chichester
Grenville College, Bideford
Gresham's Preparatory School, Holt
Gresham's School, Holt
Haberdashers' Aske's Boys' School, Elstree
Haberdashers' Aske's School for Girls, Elstree
Haileybury, Hertford
The Hall School, NW3
Hallfield School, Birmingham
Halstead Preparatory School, Woking
Hammond School, Chester
Handcross Park School, Haywards Heath
Hanford School, Blandford Forum
Harrogate Ladies' College, Harrogate
Harrow School, Harrow on the Hill
Hatherop Castle School, Cirencester
Hazelwood School, Oxted
Hazlegrove (King's Bruton Preparatory School), Yeovil
Headington School, Oxford
Heath House Preparatory School, SE3
Heath Mount School, Hertford
Heathland College, Accrington
Hemdean House School, Reading
The Hereford Cathedral Junior School, Hereford
The Hereford Cathedral School, Hereford
Hethersett Old Hall School, Norwich
Highfield Preparatory School, Harrogate
Highfield School, Liphook
Highgate School, N6
Hilden Grange School, Tonbridge
Hilden Oaks School, Tonbridge
Hillcroft Preparatory School, Stowmarket
Malvern College Preparatory and Pre-Prep School, Malvern
Holme Grange School, Wokingham
Holme Park School, Kendal
Hordle Walhampton School, Lymington
Hull Grammar School, Kingston-Upon-Hull
Hull High School, Anlaby
Hurlingham Private School, SW15
Hurstpierpoint College, Hurstpierpoint
Innellan House School, Pinner
Ipswich School, Ipswich
James Allen's Girls' School, SE22
James Allen's Preparatory School, SE22
Junior King's School, Canterbury
The Junior School, St Lawrence College, Ramsgate
Kelly College, Tavistock
Kelly College Preparatory School, Tavistock
King Edward's School, Birmingham
King William's College, Castletown
King's Bruton , Bruton
King's College, Taunton
King's College Junior School, SW19
King's College School, SW19
King's Hall School, Taunton
King's Hawford, Worcester
King's Preparatory School, Rochester
The King's School, Chester
The King's School, Macclesfield
The King's School, Canterbury
The King's School Ely, Ely
The King's School, Gloucester
King's School Rochester, Rochester
The King's School, Worcester
Kingscote Pre-Preparatory School, Gerrards Cross
Kingshott School, Hitchin
Kingsland Grange, Shrewsbury
The Kingsley School, Leamington Spa

The Lady Eleanor Holles School, Hampton
Lambrook Haileybury, Bracknell
Lanesborough, Guildford
Lanherne Nursery and Junior School, Dawlish
Lavant House, Chichester
Laxton Junior School, Peterborough
Leicester Grammar Junior School, Leicester
Leicester Grammar School, Leicester
Leicester High School For Girls, Leicester
Lichfield Cathedral School, Lichfield
The Littlemead School, Chichester
Liverpool College, Liverpool
Lockers Park, Hemel Hempstead
Luckley-Oakfield School, Wokingham
Ludgrove, Wokingham
Magdalen College School, Oxford
Maidwell Hall, Northampton
Malvern College, Malvern
Malvern Girls' College, Malvern
The Manor Preparatory School, Abingdon
Marlborough College, Marlborough
Marlborough House School, Hawkhurst
Meadowbrook Montessori School, Bracknell
Merchant Taylors' School, Northwood
Merton Court Preparatory School, Sidcup
Merton House (Downswood), Chester
Micklefield School, Reigate
Milbourne Lodge School, Esher
Milton Abbey School, Blandford Forum
The Minster School, York
Monkton Combe Junior School, Bath
Monkton Combe School, Bath
Moorland School, Clitheroe
Moreton Hall, Oswestry
Morley Hall Preparatory School, Derby
Moulsford Preparatory School, Wallingford
Mount House School, Tavistock
Mowden Hall School, Stocksfield
Lancing College Preparatory School at Mowden, Hove
Netherwood School, Saundersfoot
The New Beacon, Sevenoaks
New College School, Oxford
New Lodge School, Dorking
New School, Exeter
Newcastle Upon Tyne Church High School, Newcastle upon Tyne
Norman Court Preparatory School, Salisbury
Northampton High School, Northampton
Northbourne Park School, Deal
Northcote Lodge School, SW11
Northwood Preparatory School, Rickmansworth
Oakham School, Oakham
Oakwood School, Chichester
Old Buckenham Hall School, Ipswich
The Old Hall School, Telford
The Old Malthouse, Swanage
Old Palace School of John Whitgift, Croydon
The Old School, Beccles
Old Vicarage School, Richmond
Oriel Bank, Stockport
Orley Farm School, Harrow
Oundle School, Peterborough
Packwood Haugh School, Shrewsbury
Pangbourne College, Pangbourne
Papplewick School, Ascot
Park Hill School, Kingston-upon-Thames
Parkside School, Northampton
Parsons Mead, Ashtead
Peaslake School, Guildford
Pennthorpe School, Horsham
Perrott Hill School, Crewkerne
The Perse School, Cambridge
Peterborough & St Margaret's School, Stanmore
Peterborough High School, Peterborough
Pilgrims Pre-Preparatory School, Bedford
The Pilgrims' School, Winchester
Pinewood School, Shrivenham
Pipers Corner School, High Wycombe
Plumtree School, Nottingham
Pocklington School, Pocklington
The Prebendal School, Chichester
Prebendal School (Northgate House), Chichester
Prestfelde Preparatory School, Shrewsbury
Prince's Mead School, Winchester
The Princess Helena College, Hitchin
Quainton Hall School, Harrow
Queen Anne's School, Reading
Queen Ethelburga's College, York
Queen Margaret's School, York
Queen Mary's School, Thirsk
Queen's College, W1G
Queen's College Prep School, W1B
Querns Westonbirt School, Tetbury
Radley College, Abingdon
Ranby House, Retford
Rathvilly School, Birmingham
Ravenscourt Theatre School, W6
Read School, Selby
Reading Blue Coat School, Reading
Reddiford, Pinner
Reed's School, Cobham
Reigate St Mary's Preparatory and Choir School, Reigate
Rendcomb College, Cirencester
Repton School, Derby
Riddlesworth Hall, Diss
Ripon Cathedral Choir School, Ripon
Rishworth School, Rishworth
Rock Hall School, Alnwick
Rodney School, Newark
Roedean School, Brighton
Rose Hill School, Wotton-under-Edge
Roselyon, Par
Rossall Junior School, Fleetwood
Rossall School, Fleetwood
Rosslyn School, Birmingham
Roxeth Mead School, Harrow
Royal Alexandra and Albert School, Reigate
Royal Russell School, Croydon
The Royal School, Haslemere
The Royal Wolverhampton Junior School, Wolverhampton
The Royal Wolverhampton School, Wolverhampton
Rugby School, Rugby
Rushmoor School, Bedford
Russell House School, Sevenoaks
Ryde School, Ryde

Saddleworth Preparatory School, Oldham
St Agnes PNEU School, Leeds
St Albans High School for Girls, St Albans
St Andrew's School, Eastbourne
St Andrew's School, Reading
St Andrew's (Woking) School Trust, Woking
St Anselm's, Bakewell
St Aubyns School, Brighton
St Bees School, St Bees
St Catherine's School, Guildford
St Christopher's School, Epsom
St Christopher's School, Hove
St David's School, Ashford
St David's School, Purley
St Edmunds Junior School, Canterbury
St Edmund's School, Canterbury
St Edmund's School, Hindhead
St Edward's School, Oxford
St Francis Preparatory School, Drifield
St Francis School, Pewsey
St Gabriel's School, Newbury
St George's School, Ascot
St George's School, Windsor
St Hilda's School, Harpenden
St Hilda's School, Wakefield
St Hugh's School, Woodhall Spa
St Hugh's School, Faringdon
St Ives School, Haslemere
St James' School, Grimsby
St James's School, Malvern
St John's College School, Cambridge
St John's Northwood, Northwood
St John's School, Leatherhead
St John's-on-the-Hill, Chepstow
St Lawrence College, Ramsgate
St Margaret's School, Halstead
St Margaret's School, NW3
St Margaret's School, Bushey
St Margaret's School, Exeter
St Martin's School, Bournemouth
St Martin's School, Northwood
St Mary's Hall, Brighton
St Mary's School, Gerrards Cross
St Mary's School, Calne
St Mary's School, Wantage
St Michael's, Barnstaple
St Michael's School, Sevenoaks
St Michael's School, Leigh-on-Sea
St Neot's School, Hook
St Nicholas' School, Fleet
St Olave's Preparatory School, SE9
St Paul's Cathedral School, EC4M
St Paul's Preparatory School, SW13
St Paul's School, SW13
St Peter's School, Kettering
St Peter's School, York
St Petroc's School, Bude
St Piran's Preparatory School, Maidenhead
St Ronan's, Hawkhurst
St Swithun's School, Winchester
St Wilfrid's School, Exeter
St Wystan's School, Repton
Salisbury Cathedral School, Salisbury
Sancton Wood School, Cambridge
Sanderstead Junior School, South Croydon
Sandroyd School, Salisbury
Sarum Hall, NW3
Saville House School, Mansfield
School of St Helen & St Katharine, Abingdon
Seaford College, Petworth
Sedbergh School, Sedbergh
Shaw House School, Bradford
Sherborne Preparatory School, Sherborne
Sherborne School, Sherborne
Sherborne School for Girls, Sherborne
Shernold School, Maidstone
Sherrardswood School, Welwyn
Shiplake College, Henley-on-Thames
Shoreham College, Shoreham-by-Sea
Shrewsbury House School, Surbiton
Shrewsbury School, Shrewsbury
Silchester House School, Maidenhead
Smallwood Manor Preparatory School, Uttoxeter
Snaresbrook College Preparatory School, E18
Solefield School, Sevenoaks
Solihull School, Solihull
Sompting Abbotts School, Sompting
Spratton Hall, Northampton
Stamford School, Stamford
Steephill Independent School, Longfield
Stepping Stones Nursery and Pre-Preparatory School, Marlborough
Stoke Brunswick, East Grinstead
Stoneygate School, Leicester
Stourbridge House School, Warminster
Stover School, Newton Abbot
Stowe School, Buckingham
The Stroud School, Romsey
The Study School, New Malden
Summer Fields, Oxford
Sunderland High School, Sunderland
Sunningdale School, Sunningdale
Sunnyside School, Worcester
Surbiton High School, Kingston-upon-Thames
Surbiton Preparatory School, Surbiton
Sussex House School, SW1X
Sutton Valence Preparatory School, Maidstone
Sutton Valence School, Maidstone
Swanbourne House School, Milton Keynes
Talbot Heath, Bournemouth
Taverham Hall, Norwich
Thomas's Kindergarten, Battersea, SW11
Thomas's Preparatory School, SW11
Thomas' Preparatory School Clapham, SW11
Thorpe House School, Gerrards Cross
Tockington Manor School, Bristol
Tonbridge School, Tonbridge
Town Close House Preparatory School, Norwich
Trevor Roberts', NW3
Trinity School, Teignmouth
Truro High School, Truro
Tudor Hall School, Banbury
Twyford School, Winchester
Uppingham School, Uppingham
Upton House School, Windsor
Vinehall School, Robertsbridge

Wakefield Independent School, Wakefield
Warminster School, Warminster
Warwick School, Warwick
Wellesley House School, Broadstairs
Wellington College, Crowthorne
Wellington School, Wellington
Wells Cathedral Junior School, Wells
Wells Cathedral School, Wells
West Buckland Preparatory School, Barnstaple
West Buckland School, Barnstaple
Westbourne House School, Chichester
Westbrook Hay Preparatory School, Hemel Hempstead
Westminster Abbey Choir School, SW1P
Westminster School, SW1P
Westminster Under School, SW1P
Westonbirt School, Tetbury
Widford Lodge, Chelmsford
The Willow School, SW8
Winchester College, Winchester
Winchester House School, Brackley
Windlesham House, Pulborough
Wisbech Grammar School, Wisbech
Witham Hall, Bourne
Wood Dene School, Norwich
Woodbridge School, Woodbridge
Woodleigh School, Malton
Worksop College, Worksop
Wrekin College, Telford
Wycombe Abbey School, High Wycombe
Wykeham House School, Fareham
Yateley Manor Preparatory School, Yateley
York House School, Rickmansworth
Yorston Lodge School, Knutsford

CHURCH OF SCOTLAND

The Glasgow Academy, Glasgow
Queen Victoria School, Dunblane

EPISCOPELIAN

Glenalmond College, Perth

GREEK ORTHODOX

Hellenic College of London, SW1X

JEWISH

Akiva School, N3
Davies Laing and Dick, W1U
Immanuel College, Bushey
Jewish High School for Girls, Salford
The Kerem School, N2
Lubavitch House Senior School for Girls, N16
Mechinah Liyeshivah Zichron Moshe, N16
Menorah Grammar School, Edgware
Naima Jewish Preparatory School, NW6
Pardes Grammar Boys' School, N3
Tashbar Primary School, Salford
Yesodey Hatorah Jewish School, N16
Yetev Lev Day School for Boys, N16

METHODIST

Ashville College, Harrogate
Bronte House School, Bradford
Culford School, Bury St Edmunds
Edgehill College, Bideford
Farringtons School, Chislehurst
Kent College, Canterbury
Kent College Infant & Junior School, Canterbury
Kent College Pembury, Tunbridge Wells
Kingswood Preparatory School, Bath
Kingswood School, Bath
The Leys School, Cambridge
Lyndon Preparatory School, Colwyn Bay
Queen's College Junior and Pre-Preparatory Schools, Taunton
Queen's College, Taunton
Rydal Penrhos Senior School, Colwyn Bay
St Crispin's School (Leicester) Ltd., Leicester
Shebbear College, Beaworthy
Truro School Preparatory School, Truro
Truro School, Truro
Woodhouse Grove School, Apperley Bridge

MORAVIAN

Fulneck School, Pudsey

MUSLIM

Al Hijrah School, Birmingham
Al Karam Secondary School, Retford
Al-Muntada Islamic School, SW6
Balham Preparatory School, SW12
Birchfield Independent Girls School, Birmingham
Bolton Muslim Girls School, Bolton
Brondesbury College For Boys, NW6
Coventry Muslim School, Coventry
Darul Uloom Islamic High School & College, Birmingham
Gloucestershire Islamic Secondary School For Girls, Gloucester
IQRA School, Oxford
Islamia Girls High School, Huddersfield
Islamia Girls' School, NW6
Jamahiriya School, SW3
King Fahad Academy, W3
New Horizon Community School, Leeds
Madni Girls School, E1
Manchester Islamic High School, Manchester
Noor Ul Islam Primary School, E10
Tayyibah Girls School, N16

QUAKER

Ackworth School, Pontefract
Bootham School, York
Friends' School, Saffron Walden
The International Centre, Ackworth School, Pontefract
Leighton Park School, Reading
Tregelles, York
The Mount School, York
Sibford School, Banbury
Sidcot School, Winscombe

ROMAN CATHOLIC

All Hallows, Shepton Mallet
Alton Convent School, Alton
Ampleforth College, York
Austin Friars St Monica's School, Carlisle
Barlborough Hall School, Chesterfield
Barrow Hills School, Godalming
Beechwood Sacred Heart School, Tunbridge Wells
Bishop Challoner RC School, Bromley
Brigidine School Windsor, Windsor
Bury Catholic Preparatory School, Bury
Carleton House Preparatory School, Liverpool
The Cavendish School, NW1
Claires Court Schools, The College, Maidenhead
Combe Bank School, Sevenoaks
Convent of Mercy, Guernsey
Cranmore School, Leatherhead
Donhead Wimbledon College Prep School, SW19
Downside School, Bath
Farleigh School, Andover
Farnborough Hill, Farnborough
FCJ Primary School, Jersey
Fernhill School, Rutherglen
Holy Cross Convent, Gerrards Cross
Holy Cross Preparatory School, Kingston-upon-Thames
Ilford Ursuline Preparatory School, Ilford
Kilgraston (A Sacred Heart School), Perth
Laleham Lea School, Purley
Loreto Preparatory School, Altrincham
Loyola Preparatory School, Buckhurst Hill
The Marist Senior School, Ascot
The Marist Preparatory School, Ascot
Marymount International School, Kingston-upon-Thames
Moor Park School, Ludlow
More House, SW1X
More House School, Farnham
Moreton Hall Preparatory School, Bury St Edmunds
Mount St Mary's College, Spinkhill
Mylnhurst RC School & Nursery, Sheffield
New Hall School, Chelmsford
Notre Dame Preparatory School, Cobham
Notre Dame Preparatory School, Norwich
Notre Dame Senior School, Cobham
Oakhill College, Clitheroe
Oakwood School & Nursery, Purley
The Oratory Preparatory School, Reading
The Oratory School, Reading
Our Lady of Sion School, Worthing
Our Lady's Convent Junior School, Abingdon
Our Lady's Convent School, Loughborough
Our Lady's Convent Senior School, Abingdon
Our Lady's Preparatory School, Crowthorne
Princethorpe College, Rugby
Prior Park College, Bath
Prior Park Preparatory School, Cricklade
Priory School, Birmingham
Ratcliffe College, Leicester
Runnymede St Edward's School, Liverpool
Rye St Antony School, Oxford
Sacred Heart Convent School, Swaffham
Sacred Heart RC Primary School, Wadhurst
St Aloysius' College, Glasgow
St Ambrose Preparatory School, Altrincham
St Anthony's Preparatory School, NW3
St Anthonys School, Cinderford
St Antony's Leweston Schools, Sherborne
St Augustine's Priory, W5
St Bede's College, Manchester
St Bede's School, Stafford
St Benedict's School, W5
St Bernard's Preparatory School, Slough
St Catherine's Preparatory School, Stockport
St Catherine's School, Twickenham
St Catherines Preparatory School, Cambridge
St Christina's RC Preparatory School, NW8
St Columba's College, St Albans
St Dominic's Priory School, Stone
St Edmund's College, Ware
St Edward's School, Cheltenham
St George's College, Weybridge
St George's College Junior School, Weybridge
St Gerard's School, Bangor
St John's Beaumont, Windsor
St John's College, Southsea
St Joseph's Convent, Chesterfield
St Joseph's Convent School, E11
St Joseph's Convent School, Reading
St Joseph's Convent School, Burnley
St Joseph's Preparatory School, Stoke-on-Trent
St Joseph's School, Nottingham
St Leonards-Mayfield School, Mayfield
St Margaret's School Convent of Mercy, Midhurst
St Martha's Senior School, Barnet
St Martin's Ampleforth, York
St Mary's College, Southampton
St Mary's College, Liverpool
St Mary's Convent School, Worcester
St Mary's Hall, Stonyhurst
St Mary's Hare Park School, Romford
St Mary's School, Shaftesbury
St Mary's School, Cambridge
St Mary's School, Ascot
St Mary's School Hampstead, NW3
St Michaels School, Newbury
St Philip's School, SW7
St Philomena's Preparatory School, Frinton-on-Sea
St Pius X Preparatory School, Preston
St Richard's, Bromyard
St Teresa's Catholic Independent & Nursery School, Princes Risborough
St Teresa's Preparatory School, Effingham
St Teresa's School, Dorking
St Thomas Garnet's School, Bournemouth
St Ursula's High School
St Winefride's Convent School, Shrewsbury
Salesian College, Farnborough
Sinclair House School, SW6
Stella Maris Junior School, Stockport
Stonyhurst College, Clitheroe
Thornton College Convent of Jesus and Mary, Milton Keynes
The Towers Convent School, Steyning
Ursuline Preparatory School, SW20
Ursuline Preparatory School, Brentwood
Virgo Fidelis, SE19
Vita Et Pax School, N14

Westminster Cathedral Choir School, SW1P
Winterfold House, Kidderminster
Woldingham School, Woldingham
Worth School, Turners Hill

SEVENTH DAY ADVENTIST

Dudley House School, Grantham
Fletewood School, Plymouth
Hyland House, E17
Newbold School, Bracknell
Stanborough School, Watford

UNITED REFORMED CHURCH

Caterham School, Caterham
The Firs School, Chester
Silcoates School, Wakefield
Sunny Hill House School, Wakefield

4.7

Schools Registered with CReSTeD (Council for the Registration of Schools Teaching Dyslexic Pupils)

Registered charity number 1052103
Information provided by CReSTeD

CReSTeD (the Council for the Registration of Schools Teaching Dyslexic Pupils) produces a twice yearly register of schools that provide for dyslexic children. The aim is to help parents and those who advise them to choose a school that has been approved to published criteria. CReSTeD was established in 1989 – its main supporters are the British Dyslexia Association and The Dyslexia Institute. Schools wishing to be included in the Register are visited by a CReSTeD consultant whose report is considered by the CReSTeD Council before registration can be finalised.

Consulting the Register should enable parents to decide which schools they wish to approach for further information. Dyslexic students have a variety of difficulties and so have a wide range of special needs. An equally wide range of teaching approaches is necessary. CReSTeD has therefore grouped schools together under four broad categories, which are designed to help parents match their child's needs to an appropriate philosophy and provision.

The four categories of the schools are described below:

SPECIALIST PROVISION SCHOOLS – SP

The school is established primarily to teach pupils with dyslexia. The curriculum and timetable are designed to meet specific needs in a holistic, co-ordinated manner with a significant number of staff qualified in teaching dyslexic pupils.

DYSLEXIA UNIT – DU

The school has a designated unit or centre that provides specialist tuition on a small group or individual basis, according to need. The unit or centre is an adequately resourced teaching area under the management of a senior specialist teacher, who co-ordinates the work of other specialist teachers and ensures on-going liaison with all mainstream teachers. This senior specialist teacher will probably have head of department status, and will certainly have significant input into the curriculum design and delivery.

SPECIALIST CLASSES – SC

Schools where dyslexic pupils are taught in separate classes within the school for some lessons, most probably English and mathematics. These are taught by teachers with qualifications in teaching dyslexic pupils. These teachers are deemed responsible for communicating with the pupils' other subject teachers.

WITHDRAWAL SYSTEMS – WS

Schools where dyslexic pupils are withdrawn from appropriately selected lessons for specialist tuition from a teacher qualified in teaching dyslexic pupils. There is on-going communication between mainstream and specialist teachers.

Note: **Qualified** means holding a BDA recognized qualification in the teaching of dyslexic pupils.

The list below includes those schools registered with CReSTeD which are listed elsewhere in this guide. For a full list of schools registered with CReSTeD, including specialist schools and maintained schools, contact CReSTeD on 01242 604852 or by email at admin@crested.org.uk, or by writing to The Administrator, CReSTeD, Greygarth, Littleworth, Winchcombe, Cheltenham, GL54 5BT. Alternatively, visit the website at www.crested.org.uk

DYSLEXIA UNIT

Avon House, Woodford Green
Bedgebury School, Cranbrook
Bloxham School, Banbury
Bredon School, Tewkesbury
Clayesmore Preparatory School, Blandford Forum
Clayesmore School, Blandford Forum
Clifton College Preparatory School
Cobham Hall, Gravesend
Danes Hill School, Leatherhead
Ellesmere College, Ellesmere
Finborough School, Stowmarket
Fulneck School, Pudsey
Grenville College, Bideford
Hazlegrove (King's Bruton Preparatory School), Yeovil
Hillcroft Preparatory School, Stowmarket
Holmwood House, Colchester
Hordle Walhampton School, Lymington
King's School Rochester, Rochester
Kingham Hill School, Chipping Norton
Kingswood College at Scarisbrick Hall, Ormskirk
Kingswood House School, Epsom
Lime House School, Carlisle
Mayville High School, Southsea
Merchiston Castle School, Edinburgh
Monkton Combe School, Bath
Mostyn House School, South Wirral
Moyles Court School, Ringwood
Newlands School, Seaford
Ramillies Hall School, Cheadle
Riddlesworth Hall, Diss
St Bede's Prep School, Eastbourne
St Bede's School, Hailsham
St Bees School, St Bees
St David's College, Llandudno
St James's School, Malvern
St John's School, Sidmouth
Sibford School, Banbury
Sidcot School, Winscombe
Slindon College, Arundel
Stanbridge Earls School, Romsey

Stowford College, Sutton
Tettenhall College, Wolverhampton
Wycliffe College & Preparatory School, Stonehouse
Wycliffe Preparatory School, Stonehouse

SPECIALIST CLASSES

Belmont School, Dorking
Bodiam Manor School, Robertsbridge
St Crispin's School (Leicester) Ltd., Leicester

WITHDRAWAL SYSTEM

Box Hill School, Dorking
Dover College, Dover
Malvern College Preparatory and Pre-Prep School, Malvern
Kilgraston (A Sacred Heart School), Perth
Milton Abbey School, Blandford Forum
Prior Park Preparatory School, Cricklade
Woodleigh School, Malton
Woodside Park International School, N11

4.8
Provision for English as a Foreign Language

This index is intended as a general guide only and is compiled upon the basis of information given to Gabbitas by schools. Parents should note that there are wide variations in provision and are advised to contact individual schools for further details.

Schools listed below with a 'U' have a dedicated English language unit or offer intensive initial tuition for students whose first language is not English. Schools with no 'U' displayed offer one-to-one English language tuition, or arrange this tuition, according to need, for students whose first language is not English.

Parents may also wish to refer to the list of International Study Centres on page 33.

ENGLAND

BEDFORDSHIRE

Acorn School, Bedford
Bedford School, Bedford

BERKSHIRE

The Ark School, Reading
Bearwood College, Wokingham U
Bradfield College, Reading U
Brockhurst and Marlston House Schools, Newbury
Cedars School, Aldermaston
Cheam School, Newbury
Claires Court School, Maidenhead
Claires Court Schools, Ridgeway, Maidenhead
Dolphin School, Reading
Eagle House, Sandhurst
Elstree School, Reading
The Elvian School, Reading
Holme Grange School, Wokingham
Horris Hill, Newbury
Hurst Lodge School, Ascot
Leighton Park School, Reading U
Licensed Victuallers' School, Ascot U
Luckley-Oakfield School, Wokingham
The Oratory Preparatory School, Reading
The Oratory School, Reading U
Padworth College, Reading U
Papplewick School, Ascot
Queen Anne's School, Reading
St George's School, Ascot
St John's Beaumont, Windsor U
St Joseph's Convent School, Reading
Upton House School, Windsor
Waverley School, Wokingham
White House Preparatory School, Wokingham

BRISTOL

Badminton School U
Clifton College, Bristol U
Clifton College Preparatory School U
The Downs School, Wraxall
Gracefield Preparatory School, Bristol
Queen Elizabeth's Hospital
Tockington Manor School, Bristol U
Torwood House School

BUCKINGHAMSHIRE

Akeley Wood School, Buckingham
Caldicott School, Farnham Royal
Godstowe Preparatory School, High Wycombe U

Grove Independent School, Milton Keynes
Holy Cross Convent, Gerrards Cross
Ladymede, Aylesbury
Maltman's Green School, Gerrards Cross
Milton Keynes Preparatory School, Milton Keynes
Pipers Corner School, High Wycombe
Stowe School, Buckingham
Thornton College Convent of Jesus and Mary, Milton Keynes
Thorpe House School, Gerrards Cross

CAMBRIDGESHIRE

Bellerbys College, Cambridge U
Cambridge Arts & Sciences (CATS), Cambridge U
Cambridge Centre for Sixth-form Studies, Cambridge
Kimbolton School, Huntingdon
The King's School Ely, Ely U
The Leys School, Cambridge U
MPW (Mander Portman Woodward), Cambridge U
Peterborough High School, Peterborough U
St Mary's School, Cambridge U

CHANNEL ISLANDS

St George's Preparatory School, Jersey

CHESHIRE

Culcheth Hall, Altrincham
The Firs School, Chester
Forest Park School, Sale
Hale Preparatory School, Altrincham U
Loreto Preparatory School, Altrincham
Mostyn House School, South Wirral
The Queen's School, Chester
The Ryleys, Alderley Edge
Terra Nova School, Holmes Chapel
Wilmslow Preparatory School, Wilmslow

CORNWALL

The Bolitho School, Penzance U
St Ia School, St Ives
Truro School, Truro

CUMBRIA

Harecroft Hall School, Seascale
Holme Park School, Kendal
St Bees School, St Bees U
Sedbergh School, Sedbergh U
Windermere St Anne's, Windermere U

DERBYSHIRE

Derby High School, Derby
Mount St Mary's College, Spinkhill U
Repton School, Derby U
St Anselm's, Bakewell

DEVON

Blundell's School, Tiverton
Bramdean School, Exeter
Trinity School U
Edgehill College, Bideford U
Exeter Cathedral School, Exeter
Exeter Tutorial College, Exeter U
Grenville College, Bideford U
Kelly College, Tavistock U
Plymouth College, Plymouth U
St Dunstan's Abbey-Plymouth College Junior School, Plymouth
St John's School, Sidmouth U
Shebbear College, Beaworthy U
Stover School, Newton Abbot U
Tower House School, Paignton
Trinity School, Teignmouth U
West Buckland School, Barnstaple U

DORSET

Bryanston School, Blandford Forum
Clayesmore Preparatory School, Blandford Forum
Clayesmore School, Blandford Forum
Dorchester Preparatory School, Dorchester
International College, Sherborne School, Sherborne U
Milton Abbey School, Blandford Forum
The Old Malthouse, Swanage
Port Regis School, Shaftesbury U
St Antony's Leweston Schools, Sherborne
St Mary's School, Shaftesbury
Sherborne School, Sherborne
Sherborne School for Girls, Sherborne U
Wentworth College, Bournemouth U

COUNTY DURHAM

Bow School, Durham
Durham School, Durham
Polam Hall, Darlington U

ESSEX

Brentwood School, Brentwood U
Chigwell School, Chigwell U
College Saint-Pierre, Leigh-on-Sea
Elm Green Preparatory School, Chelmsford U
Felsted School, Dunmow U
Friends' School, Saffron Walden U
New Hall School, Chelmsford U
Oaklands School, Loughton
St John's School, Billericay
St Margaret's School, Halstead U
St Mary's School, Colchester
St Philomena's Preparatory School, Frinton-on-Sea
Thorpe Hall School, Southend-on-Sea

GLOUCESTERSHIRE

The Abbey School, Tewkesbury
Bredon School, Tewkesbury U

Cheltenham College, Cheltenham
Cheltenham College Junior School, Cheltenham
The Cheltenham Ladies' College, Cheltenham
Dean Close Preparatory School, Cheltenham U
Dean Close School, Cheltenham U
Rendcomb College, Cirencester
Rose Hill School, Wotton-under-Edge
Westonbirt School, Tetbury U
Wycliffe College & Preparatory School, Stonehouse U
Wynstones School, Gloucester

HAMPSHIRE

Bedales School, Petersfield
Brockwood Park School, Bramdean U
Hampshire Collegiate School, Embley Park, Romsey
Glenhurst School, Havant
Hordle Walhampton School, Lymington
Lord Wandsworth College, Hook
Mayville High School, Southsea U
Rookesbury Park School, Portsmouth
St Mary's College, Southampton
St Nicholas' School, Fleet
Sherborne House School, Eastleigh
Stanbridge Earls School, Romsey
Twyford School, Winchester
Woodhill School, Chandler's Ford
Wykeham House School, Fareham

HEREFORDSHIRE

Lucton School, Leominster

HERTFORDSHIRE

Aldenham School, Elstree
The Arts Educational School, Tring
Bishop's Stortford College, Bishop's Stortford
Haileybury, Hertford
Lockers Park, Hemel Hempstead
The Princess Helena College, Hitchin
Queenswood School, Hatfield U
The Royal Masonic School for Girls, Rickmansworth
St Andrew's Montessori School, Watford
St Christopher School, Letchworth
St Edmund's College, Ware U
St Francis' College, Letchworth U
St Margaret's School, Bushey U
Stanborough School, Watford U

ISLE OF MAN

King William's College, Castletown

ISLE OF WIGHT

Ryde School, Ryde

KENT

Ashford School, Ashford
Bedgebury School, Cranbrook U
Beechwood Sacred Heart School, Tunbridge Wells U
Benenden School, Cranbrook
Bethany School, Cranbrook U
Bromley High School GDST, Bromley
Dover College, Dover U
Dulwich Preparatory School, Cranbrook, Cranbrook
Farringtons School, Chislehurst U
Harenc School Trust, Sidcup
Holmewood House, Tunbridge Wells
Junior King's School, Canterbury U
The Junior School, St Lawrence College, Ramsgate U
Kent College, Canterbury U
Kent College Infant & Junior School, Canterbury U
Kent College Pembury, Tunbridge Wells
Northbourne Park School, Deal U
Rochester Independent College, Rochester U
St Christopher's School, Canterbury U
St Edmunds Junior School, Canterbury
St Edmund's School, Canterbury
St Lawrence College, Ramsgate U
St Mary's Westbrook, Folkestone U
St Michael's School, Sevenoaks
Sevenoaks School, Sevenoaks
Sutton Valence School, Maidstone
Tonbridge School, Tonbridge
Walthamstow Hall, Sevenoaks
Wellesley House School, Broadstairs
West Lodge Preparatory School, Sidcup

LANCASHIRE

Bolton School (Girls' Division), Bolton
Clevelands Preparatory School, Bolton
Kingswood College at Scarisbrick Hall, Ormskirk
Kirkham Grammar School, Preston
Rossall School, Fleetwood U
Rossall School International Study Centre, Fleetwood U
St Anne's College Grammar School, Lytham St Annes U
Stonyhurst College, Clitheroe U

LEICESTERSHIRE

Brooke House College, Market Harborough U
Irwin College, Leicester U
Leicester Grammar School, Leicester U
Ratcliffe College, Leicester U
St Crispin's School (Leicester) Ltd., Leicester

LINCOLNSHIRE

Copthill School, Stamford
Kirkstone House School, Bourne
Stamford School, Stamford

NORTH EAST LINCOLNSHIRE

St James' School, Grimsby U

LONDON

Albany College, NW4
Albemarle Independent College, W1K U
The American School in London, NW8 U
Ashbourne Independent Sixth Form College, W8
Ashbourne Middle School, W8
Aston House School, W5
Bales College, W10
Barbara Speake Stage School, W3
Brampton College, NW4 U
Cameron House School, SW3
Collingham College, SW5
Connaught House, W2
Davies Laing and Dick, W1U U
Ealing Independent College, W5
Eaton House School Belgravia, SW1W
Eaton House The Manor, SW4
Eaton House The Vale, SW7
Eaton Square Schools, SW1V
Francis Holland School, SW1W
Gatehouse School, E2
Hall School Wimbledon, SW20
Heath House Preparatory School, SE3
Heathside Preparatory School, NW3
Hellenic College of London, SW1X
Hendon Preparatory School, NW4 U
International Community School, NW1 U
International School of London, W3 U
The Kerem School, N2
Lansdowne College, W2
Le Herisson, W6 U
Mander Portman Woodward, SW7 U
The Mount School, NW7 U
North Bridge House Senior School, NW1
North Bridge House Upper Prep School, NW1
Parkgate House School, SW4
Putney Park School, SW15
Riverston School, SE12
The Roche School, SW18
The Rowans School, SW20
The Royal School, Hampstead, NW3
St Augustine's Priory, W5
St Johns Wood Pre-Preparatory School, NW8
St Margaret's School, NW3
St Martin's, NW7
St Olave's Preparatory School, SE9
Southbank International School, Kensington, W11 U
Southbank International School, Hampstead, NW3 U
Southbank International School, Westminster, W1B U
Sylvia Young Theatre School, NW1
Westminster Tutors, SW7
Wetherby Preparatory School, W11
Willington School, SW19
Woodside Park International School, N11

GREATER MANCHESTER

Clarendon Cottage School, Eccles
St Bede's College, Manchester
Withington Girls' School, Manchester

MERSEYSIDE

Kingsmead School, Wirral
Liverpool College, Liverpool
Merchant Taylors' School for Girls, Liverpool
Newborough School, Liverpool

MIDDLESEX

ACS Hillingdon International School, Hillingdon U
Denmead School, Hampton
Halliford School, Shepperton
Little Eden SDA School & Eden High SDA School, Hanworth
The Mall School, Twickenham
St Christopher's School, Wembley
St Helen's School, Northwood U
Staines Preparatory School, Staines
Sunflower Montessori School, Twickenham

NORFOLK

Beeston Hall School, Cromer
Gresham's Preparatory School, Holt
Gresham's School, Holt U
Hethersett Old Hall School, Norwich
Langley School, Norwich U
The New Eccles Hall School, Norwich U
Norwich High School for Girls GDST, Norwich
Notre Dame Preparatory School, Norwich
Riddlesworth Hall, Diss U
St Nicholas House Kindergarten & Prep School, North Walsham U
Taverham Hall, Norwich U

NORTHAMPTONSHIRE

Bosworth Independent College, Northampton U
Maidwell Hall, Northampton
Northamptonshire Grammar School, Pitsford
Quinton House School, Northampton

NORTHUMBERLAND

Longridge Towers School, Berwick-upon-Tweed

NOTTINGHAMSHIRE

Dagfa House School, Nottingham
Hollygirt School, Nottingham U
Ranby House, Retford

OXFORDSHIRE

Abacus College, Oxford U
Abingdon School, Abingdon
Bloxham School, Banbury U
Cherwell College, Oxford
Christ Church Cathedral School, Oxford
Cokethorpe, Witney
Cothill House Preparatory School, Abingdon

d'Overbroeck's College, Oxford U
Greene's Tutorial College, Oxford
Headington School, Oxford
IQRA School, Oxford U
Josca's Preparatory School, Abingdon
Kingham Hill School, Chipping Norton
New College School, Oxford
Our Lady's Convent Senior School, Abingdon
Oxford Tutorial College, Oxford U
Rye St Antony School, Oxford
St Clare's, Oxford, Oxford U
St Mary's School, Wantage U
School of St Helen & St Katharine, Abingdon
Sibford School, Banbury U

RUTLAND

Oakham School, Oakham

SHROPSHIRE

Adcote School for Girls, Shrewsbury
Bedstone College, Bucknell U
Dower House School, Bridgnorth
Ellesmere College, Ellesmere U
Kingsland Grange, Shrewsbury
Moreton Hall, Oswestry U
Oswestry School, Oswestry U
Packwood Haugh School, Shrewsbury
St Winefride's Convent School, Shrewsbury
Shrewsbury School, Shrewsbury
Wrekin College, Telford

SOMERSET

All Hallows, Shepton Mallet
Bruton School for Girls, Bruton U
Chard School, Chard
Chilton Cantelo School, Yeovil
Downside School, Bath
Hazlegrove (King's Bruton Preparatory School), Yeovil
King's Bruton, Bruton
King's College, Taunton
King's Hall School, Taunton
Millfield Preparatory School, Street U
Millfield School, Street U
The Park School, Yeovil
Perrott Hill School, Crewkerne U
Queen's College, Taunton U
Taunton International Study Centre (TISC), Taunton U
Taunton Preparatory School, Taunton U
Taunton School, Taunton U
Wellington School, Wellington U
Wells Cathedral School, Wells U

BATH & NORTH EAST SOMERSET

Bath Academy, Bath U
Kingswood Preparatory School, Bath
Kingswood School, Bath U
Monkton Combe School, Bath U
Prior Park College, Bath
The Royal High School, Bath

NORTH SOMERSET

Sidcot School, Winscombe U

STAFFORDSHIRE

Abbots Bromley School for Girls, Abbots Bromley
Abbotsholme School, Uttoxeter U
Denstone College, Uttoxeter
Lichfield Cathedral School, Lichfield
St Bede's School, Stafford U
St Dominic's School, Stafford

SUFFOLK

Culford School, Bury St Edmunds
Felixstowe International College, Felixstowe U
Framlingham College, Woodbridge U
Framlingham College Preparatory School, Brandeston U
Ipswich School, Ipswich
Moreton Hall Preparatory School, Bury St Edmunds
Orwell Park, Ipswich
Royal Hospital School, Ipswich U
Saint Felix Schools, Southwold
Summerhill School, Leiston U
Woodbridge School, Woodbridge U

SURREY

Aberdour School, Tadworth
ACS Cobham International School, Cobham U
Aldro School, Godalming
Amesbury, Hindhead
Box Hill School, Dorking U
Cambridge Tutors College, Croydon U
Canbury School, Kingston-upon-Thames U
Caterham School, Caterham
Charterhouse, Godalming
City of London Freemen's School, Ashtead
Croydon High School GDST, South Croydon
Epsom College, Epsom
Ewell Castle School, Epsom
Grantchester House, Esher
Greenacre School for Girls, Banstead
Hampton Court House, East Molesey
Hawley Place School, Camberley
Hoe Bridge School, Woking
Hurtwood House, Dorking U
Kew Green Preparatory School, Richmond U
King Edward's School Witley, Godalming
King's House School, Richmond
Lodge School, Purley
Longacre School, Guildford
Marymount International School, Kingston-upon-Thames U
Notre Dame Preparatory School, Cobham
Old Palace School of John Whitgift, Croydon

Park Hill School, Kingston-upon-Thames U
Prior's Field School, Godalming U
Royal Ballet School, Richmond
Royal Russell School, Croydon U
The Royal School, Haslemere U
St Catherine's School, Guildford
St John's School, Leatherhead U
St Teresa's School, Dorking U
Stowford College, Sutton
Surbiton High School, Kingston-upon-Thames
Surbiton Preparatory School, Surbiton
Surrey College, Guildford U
Sutton High School GDST, Sutton
TASIS The American School in England, Thorpe U
Westbury House School, New Malden
Woldingham School, Woldingham U
Woodcote House School, Windlesham
Yehudi Menuhin School, Cobham U

EAST SUSSEX

Ashdown House School, Forest Row
Battle Abbey School, Battle U
Brighton College, Brighton U
Buckswood School, Hastings U
Eastbourne College, Eastbourne U
Greenfields School, Forest Row U
Moira House School, Eastbourne
Moira House Girls School, Eastbourne U
Lancing College Preparatory School at Mowden, Hove
Newlands School, Seaford U
Roedean School, Brighton U
St Andrew's School, Eastbourne U
St Aubyns School, Brighton
St Leonards-Mayfield School, Mayfield U
St Mary's Hall, Brighton U
Stonelands School of Ballet & Theatre Arts, Hove
Vinehall School, Robertsbridge

WEST SUSSEX

Ardingly College, Haywards Heath
Brambletye School, East Grinstead
Burgess Hill School for Girls, Burgess Hill
Cottesmore School, Pease Pottage
Dorset House School, Pulborough
Great Ballard School, Chichester
Hurstpierpoint College, Hurstpierpoint
Lavant House, Chichester
Seaford College, Petworth
Slindon College, Arundel
The Towers Convent School, Steyning
Windlesham House, Pulborough U

TYNE AND WEAR

Central Newcastle High School GDST, Newcastle upon Tyne
The King's School, Tynemouth
Sunderland High School, Sunderland
Westfield School, Newcastle upon Tyne

WARWICKSHIRE

Abbotsford School, Kenilworth U
Bilton Grange, Rugby
The Kingsley School, Leamington Spa
Princethorpe College, Rugby
Rugby School, Rugby

WEST MIDLANDS

Birchfield School, Wolverhampton
The Blue Coat School, Birmingham
Highclare School, Birmingham
Mander Portman Woodward, Birmingham
Priory School, Birmingham
The Royal Wolverhampton School, Wolverhampton U
Tettenhall College, Wolverhampton U

WILTSHIRE

Chafyn Grove School, Salisbury
Dauntsey's School, Devizes
Grittleton House School, Chippenham
Norman Court Preparatory School, Salisbury
Prior Park Preparatory School, Cricklade
St Margaret's Preparatory School, Calne
Sandroyd School, Salisbury
Stonar School, Melksham
Warminster School, Warminster U

WORCESTERSHIRE

Abberley Hall, Worcester U
Bowbrook House School, Pershore
Bromsgrove Preparatory School, Bromsgrove U
Bromsgrove School, Bromsgrove U
The Downs School, Malvern
Malvern College Preparatory and Pre-Prep School, Malvern
Malvern College, Malvern U
Moffats School, Bewdley
St James's School, Malvern U
Saint Michael's College, Tenbury Wells U
Sunnyside School, Worcester

EAST RIDING OF YORKSHIRE

Pocklington School, Pocklington

NORTH YORKSHIRE

Ashville College, Harrogate
Bootham School, York
Brackenfield School, Harrogate
Bramcote School, Scarborough
Catteral Hall School, Settle
Fyling Hall School, Whitby
Giggleswick School, Settle
Harrogate Ladies' College, Harrogate U
Harrogate Tutorial College, Harrogate U
Howsham Hall, York
Queen Ethelburga's College, York U

Queen Margaret's School, York
Read School, Selby
St Martin's Ampleforth, York
Scarborough College & Lisvane School, Scarborough
Terrington Hall, York

SOUTH YORKSHIRE

Ashdell Preparatory School, Sheffield
Brantwood School for Girls, Sheffield
Sheffield High School GDST, Sheffield

WEST YORKSHIRE

Ackworth School, Pontefract U
Batley Grammar School, Batley
Fulneck School, Pudsey U
Gateways School, Leeds
The International Centre, Ackworth School, Pontefract U
New Horizon Community School, Leeds
The Rastrick Independent School, Brighouse
Richmond House School, Leeds
Rishworth School, Rishworth U
Woodhouse Grove School, Apperley Bridge U

NORTHERN IRELAND

COUNTY ANTRIM

Victoria College Belfast, Belfast

COUNTY ARMAGH

The Royal School, Armagh U

COUNTY TYRONE

The Royal School Dungannon, Dungannon U

SCOTLAND

ABERDEENSHIRE

International School of Aberdeen, Aberdeen U
St Margaret's School for Girls, Aberdeen

GLASGOW

Hutchesons' Grammar School, Glasgow

LOTHIAN

Basil Paterson Tutorial College, Edinburgh U
Clifton Hall School, Edinburgh U
The Edinburgh Rudolf Steiner School, Edinburgh U
George Watson's College, Edinburgh
Loretto Junior School, Musselburgh U
Loretto School, Musselburgh
Merchiston Castle School, Edinburgh U
St George's School for Girls, Edinburgh U
St Serf's School, Edinburgh

MORAYSHIRE

Gordonstoun School, Elgin

PERTH AND KINROSS

Craigclowan Preparatory School, Perth
Glenalmond College, Perth
Kilgraston (A Sacred Heart School), Perth U
Morrison's Academy, Crieff
Strathallan School, Perth

WALES

BRIDGEND

St Clare's School, Porthcawl

CARDIFF

The Cardiff Academy, Cardiff
Kings Monkton School, Cardiff

CARMARTHENSHIRE

Llandovery College, Llandovery U

CONWY

Lyndon Preparatory School, Colwyn Bay
Rydal Penrhos Senior School, Colwyn Bay
St David's College, Llandudno U

DENBIGHSHIRE

Fairholme Preparatory School, St Asaph
Howell's School, Denbigh U
Ruthin School, Ruthin U

MONMOUTHSHIRE

Monmouth School, Monmouth
St John's-on-the-Hill, Chepstow

PEMBROKESHIRE

Netherwood School, Saundersfoot

POWYS

Christ College, Brecon U

SWANSEA

Ffynone House School, Swansea

4.9

Schools in Membership of the Constituent Associations of the Independent Schools Council

The schools listed below are all in membership of the Independent Schools Council in the UK. Please note that ISC-accredited special schools and overseas schools are not included. The constituent associations of the ISC include:

Association of Governing Bodies of Independent Schools (AGBIS)
The Girls' Schools Association (GSA)
The Headmasters' and Headmistresses' Conference (HMC)
The Incorporated Association of Preparatory Schools (IAPS)
The Independent Schools Association (ISA)
The Independent Schools' Bursars Association (ISBA)
The Society of Headmasters and Headmistresses of Independent Schools (SHMIS)

Further information about ISC can be found in Part 1.1.

ENGLAND

BEDFORDSHIRE

Bedford High School, Bedford
Bedford Modern School, Bedford
Bedford Preparatory School, Bedford
Bedford School, Bedford
Dame Alice Harpur School, Bedford
Moorlands School, Luton
Pilgrims Pre-Preparatory School, Bedford
Rushmoor School, Bedford
St Andrew's School, Bedford

BERKSHIRE

The Abbey School, Reading
Bearwood College, Wokingham
Bradfield College, Reading
Brigidine School Windsor, Windsor
Brockhurst and Marlston House Schools, Newbury
Cheam School, Newbury
Claires Court School, Maidenhead
Claires Court Schools - Ridgeway School, Maidenhead
Crosfields School, Reading
Dolphin School, Reading
Downe House, Thatcham
Eagle House, Sandhurst
Elstree School, Reading
The Elvian School, Reading
Eton College, Windsor
Eton End PNEU, Slough
Heathfield School, Ascot
Hemdean House School, Reading
Herries School, Maidenhead
Highfield School, Maidenhead
The Highlands School, Reading
Holme Grange School, Wokingham

Horris Hill, Newbury
Hurst Lodge School, Ascot
Lambrook Haileybury, Bracknell
Leighton Park School, Reading
Licensed Victuallers' School, Ascot
Long Close School, Upton
Luckley-Oakfield School, Wokingham
Ludgrove, Wokingham
The Marist Preparatory School, Ascot
The Marist Senior School, Ascot
The Oratory Preparatory School, Reading
The Oratory School, Reading
Pangbourne College, Pangbourne
Papplewick School, Ascot
Queen Anne's School, Reading
Reading Blue Coat School, Reading
St Andrew's School, Reading
St Bernard's Preparatory School, Slough
St Edward's School, Reading
St Gabriel's School, Newbury
St George's School, Ascot
St George's School, Windsor
St John's Beaumont, Windsor
St Joseph's Convent School, Reading
St Mary's School, Ascot
St Piran's Preparatory School, Maidenhead
Sunningdale School, Sunningdale
Upton House School, Windsor
Waverley School, Wokingham
Wellington College, Crowthorne
White House Preparatory School, Wokingham
Winbury School, Maidenhead

BRISTOL

Badminton School, Bristol
Bristol Cathedral School, Bristol
Bristol Grammar School, Bristol
Clifton College, Bristol
Clifton College Preparatory School, Bristol
Clifton College Pre-Prep, Bristol
Clifton High School, Bristol
Colston's Collegiate School, Bristol
Colston's Girls' School, Bristol
Colston's Lower School, Bristol
The Downs School, Bristol
Fairfield PNEU School, Bristol
Queen Elizabeth's Hospital, Bristol
The Red Maids' School, Bristol
Redland High School, Bristol
Sacred Heart Preparatory School, Chew Magna
St Ursula's High School, Bristol
Tockington Manor School, Bristol

BUCKINGHAMSHIRE

Ashfold School, Aylesbury
The Beacon School, Amersham
Bury Lawn School, Milton Keynes
Caldicott School, Farnham Royal
Chesham Preparatory School, Chesham
Crown House School, High Wycombe
Dair House School Trust Ltd, Farnham Royal
Davenies School, Beaconsfield
Gateway School, Great Missenden
Gayhurst School, Gerrards Cross
Godstowe Preparatory School, High Wycombe
Heatherton House School, Amersham
High March School, Beaconsfield
Kingscote Pre-Preparatory School, Gerrards Cross
Ladymede, Aylesbury
Maltman's Green School, Gerrards Cross
Milton Keynes Preparatory School, Milton Keynes
Pipers Corner School, High Wycombe
St Mary's School, Gerrards Cross
St Teresa's Catholic Independent & Nursery School, Princes Risborough
Stowe School, Buckingham
Swanbourne House School, Milton Keynes
Thornton College Convent of Jesus and Mary, Milton Keynes
Thorpe House School, Gerrards Cross
Wycombe Abbey School, High Wycombe

CAMBRIDGESHIRE

Cambridge Arts & Sciences (CATS), Cambridge
Cambridge Centre for Sixth Form Studies, Cambridge
Horlers Pre-Preparatory School, Cambridge
Kimbolton School, Huntingdon
The King's School Ely, Ely
The Leys School, Cambridge
The Perse School, Cambridge
The Perse School for Girls, Cambridge
Peterborough High School, Peterborough
St Catherines Preparatory School, Cambridge
St Colette's School, Cambridge
St Faith's, Cambridge
St John's College School, Cambridge
St Mary's School, Cambridge
Whitehall School, Huntingdon
Wisbech Grammar School, Wisbech

CHANNEL ISLANDS

Elizabeth College, Guernsey
The Ladies' College, Guernsey
St Michael's Preparatory School, Jersey
Victoria College, Jersey
Victoria College Preparatory School, Jersey

CHESHIRE

Abbey Gate College, Chester
Abbey Gate School, Chester
Alderley Edge School for Girls, Alderley Edge
Altrincham Preparatory School, Altrincham
Beech Hall School, Macclesfield
Brabyns School, Stockport
Cheadle Hulme School, Cheadle
Cransley School, Northwich
Culcheth Hall, Altrincham
The Firs School, Chester
Forest Park School, Sale

Forest School, Altrincham
The Grange School, Northwich
Greenbank, Cheadle
Hale Preparatory School, Altrincham
Hammond School, Chester
Hillcrest Grammar School, Stockport
Hulme Hall Schools, Cheadle
Hulme Hall Schools (Junior Division), Cheadle
The King's School, Chester
The King's School, Macclesfield
Lady Barn House School, Cheadle
Loreto Preparatory School, Altrincham
Mostyn House School, South Wirral
North Cestrian Grammar School, Altrincham
Oriel Bank, Stockport
Pownall Hall School, Wilmslow
The Queen's School, Chester
Ramillies Hall School, Cheadle
The Ryleys, Alderley Edge
St Catherine's Preparatory School, Stockport
Stockport Grammar School, Stockport
Terra Nova School, Holmes Chapel
Wilmslow Preparatory School, Wilmslow

CORNWALL

The Bolitho School, Penzance
Polwhele House School, Truro
Roselyon, Par
St Joseph's School, Launceston
Treliske, Truro
Truro High School, Truro
Truro School, Truro

COUNTY DURHAM

Barnard Castle School, Barnard Castle
Bow School, Durham
The Chorister School, Durham
Durham High School For Girls, Durham
Durham School, Durham
Polam Hall, Darlington

CUMBRIA

Austin Friars St Monica's School, Carlisle
Casterton School, Kirkby Lonsdale
Chetwynde School, Barrow-in-Furness
Harecroft Hall School, Seascale
Lime House School, Carlisle
St Bees School, St Bees
Sedbergh School, Sedbergh
Windermere St Anne's, Windermere

DERBYSHIRE

Ashbourne PNEU School, Ashbourne
Derby Grammar School for Boys, Derby
Derby High School, Derby
Foremarke Hall School, Derby
Mount St Mary's College, Spinkhill
Ockbrook School, Derby
Repton School, Derby
St Anselm's, Bakewell
St Wystan's School, Repton

DEVON

Blundell's School, Tiverton
Edgehill College, Bideford
Exeter Cathedral School, Exeter
Exeter School, Exeter
Grenville College, Bideford
Kelly College, Tavistock
Kelly College Preparatory School, Tavistock
Manor House School, Honiton
The Maynard School, Exeter
Mount House School, Tavistock
Plymouth College, Plymouth
St Aubyn's School, Tiverton
St John's School, Sidmouth
St Margaret's School, Exeter
St Michael's, Barnstaple
St Peter's School, Exmouth
Shebbear College, Beaworthy
St Dunstan's Abbey-Plymouth College Junior School, Plymouth
Stover School, Newton Abbot
Trinity School, Teignmouth
West Buckland School, Barnstaple

DORSET

Bryanston School, Blandford Forum
Canford School, Wimborne
Castle Court Preparatory School, Wimborne
Clayesmore Preparatory School, Blandford Forum
Clayesmore School, Blandford Forum
Dorchester Preparatory School, Dorchester
Dumpton School, Wimborne
Hanford School, Blandford Forum
International College, Sherborne School, Sherborne
Knighton House, Blandford Forum
Milton Abbey School, Blandford Forum
The Old Malthouse, Swanage
The Park School, Bournemouth
Port Regis School, Shaftesbury
St Antony's Leweston Schools, Sherborne
St Mary's School, Shaftesbury
Sherborne Preparatory School, Sherborne
Sherborne School, Sherborne
Sherborne School for Girls, Sherborne
Sunninghill Preparatory School, Dorchester
Talbot Heath, Bournemouth
Thornlow Preparatory School, Weymouth
Uplands School, Poole
Wentworth College, Bournemouth
Yarrells School, Poole

ESSEX

Alleyn Court Preparatory School, Southend-on-Sea
Bancroft's School, Woodford Green

Braeside School for Girls, Buckhurst Hill
Brentwood School, Brentwood
Chigwell School, Chigwell
Colchester High School, Colchester
Coopersale Hall School, Epping
Cranbrook College, Ilford
Crowstone Preparatory School, Westcliff-on-Sea
The Daiglen School, Buckhurst Hill
Dame Johane Bradbury's School, Saffron Walden
Elm Green Preparatory School, Chelmsford
Felsted Preparatory School, Dunmow
Felsted School, Dunmow
Friends' School, Saffron Walden
Glenarm College, Ilford
Gosfield School, Halstead
Heathcote School, Chelmsford
Holmwood House, Colchester
Ilford Ursuline Preparatory School, Ilford
Littlegarth School, Colchester
Loyola Preparatory School, Buckhurst Hill
Maldon Court Preparatory School, Maldon
New Hall School, Chelmsford
Oaklands School, Loughton
Oxford House School, Colchester
Park School for Girls, Ilford
Raphael Independent School, Romford
St Anne's Preparatory School, Chelmsford
St Aubyn's School, Woodford Green
St Cedd's School, Chelmsford
St Hilda's School, Westcliff-on-Sea
St John's School, Billericay
St Margaret's School, Halstead
St Mary's School, Colchester
St Michael's School, Leigh-on-Sea
St Nicholas School, Harlow
St Philomena's Preparatory School, Frinton-on-Sea
Thorpe Hall School, Southend-on-Sea
Ursuline Preparatory School, Brentwood
Widford Lodge, Chelmsford
Woodford Green Preparatory School, Woodford Green
Woodlands School, Brentwood

GLOUCESTERSHIRE

The Abbey School, Tewkesbury
Beaudesert Park School, Stroud
Berkhampstead School, Cheltenham
Bredon School, Tewkesbury
Cheltenham College, Cheltenham
Cheltenham College Junior School, Cheltenham
The Cheltenham Ladies' College, Cheltenham
Dean Close Preparatory School, Cheltenham
Dean Close School, Cheltenham
Hatherop Castle School, Cirencester
The King's School, Gloucester
Rendcomb College, Cirencester
The Richard Pate School, Cheltenham
Rose Hill School, Wotton-under-Edge
St Edward's School, Cheltenham
Westonbirt School, Tetbury
Wycliffe College, Stonehouse
Wycliffe Preparatory School, Stonehouse

HAMPSHIRE

Alton Convent School, Alton
The Atherley School, Southampton
Ballard School, New Milton
Bedales School, Petersfield
Boundary Oak School, Fareham
Churchers College, Petersfield
Daneshill School, Basingstoke
Ditcham Park School, Petersfield
Dunhurst (Bedales Junior School), Petersfield
Durlston Court, New Milton
Embley Park School, Romsey
Farleigh School, Andover
Farnborough Hill, Farnborough
Forres Sandle Manor, Fordingbridge
The Gregg School, Southampton
Highfield School, Liphook
Hordle Walhampton School, Lymington
King Edward VI School, Southampton
Lord Wandsworth College, Hook
Mayville High School, Southsea
Meoncross School, Fareham
Moyles Court School, Ringwood
Nethercliffe School, Winchester
The Pilgrims' School, Winchester
The Portsmouth Grammar School, Portsmouth
Portsmouth High School GDST, Southsea
Prince's Mead School, Winchester
Rookesbury Park School, Portsmouth
Rookwood School, Andover
St John's College, Southsea
St Neot's School, Hook
St Nicholas' School, Fleet
St Swithun's School, Winchester
St Winifred's School, Southampton
Salesian College, Farnborough
Sherborne House School, Eastleigh
Stanbridge Earls School, Romsey
The Stroud School, Romsey
Twyford School, Winchester
Winchester College, Winchester
Wykeham House School, Fareham
Yateley Manor Preparatory School, Yateley

HEREFORDSHIRE

Haberdashers' Redcap School, Hereford
The Hereford Cathedral Junior School, Hereford
The Hereford Cathedral School, Hereford
Lucton School, Leominster
St Richard's, Bromyard

HERTFORDSHIRE

Abbot's Hill School, Hemel Hempstead
Aldenham School, Elstree
Aldwickbury School, Harpenden
The Arts Educational School, Tring
Beechwood Park School, St Albans
Berkhamsted Collegiate Preparatory School, Berkhamsted
Berkhamsted Collegiate School, Berkhamsted
Bishop's Stortford College, Bishop's Stortford

CKHR Immanuel College, Bushey
Duncombe School, Hertford
Edge Grove, Aldenham
Egerton-Rothesay School, Berkhamsted
Francis House, Tring
Haberdashers' Aske's Boys' School, Elstree
Haberdashers' Aske's School for Girls, Elstree
Haileybury, Hertford
Haresfoot Preparatory School, Berkhamsted
Heath Mount School, Hertford
Homewood Pre-Preparatory School, St Albans
Howe Green House School, Bishop's Stortford
Immanuel College, Bushey
Kingshott School, Hitchin
Lochinver House School, Potters Bar
Lockers Park, Hemel Hempstead
Manor Lodge School, Radlett
Northwood Preparatory School, Rickmansworth
The Princess Helena College, Hitchin
The Purcell School, Bushey
Queenswood School, Hatfield
Rickmansworth PNEU School, Rickmansworth
The Royal Masonic School for Girls, Rickmansworth
St Albans High School for Girls, St Albans
St Albans School, St Albans
St Christopher School, Letchworth
St Columba's College, St Albans
St Edmund's College, Ware
St Francis' College, Letchworth
St Hilda's School, Bushey
St Hilda's School, Harpenden
St Margaret's School, Bushey
Sherrardswood School, Welwyn
Stanborough School, Watford
Stormont, Potters Bar
Westbrook Hay Preparatory School, Hemel Hempstead
York House School, Rickmansworth

ISLE OF MAN

The Buchan School, Castletown
King William's College, Castletown

ISLE OF WIGHT

Ryde School, Ryde

KENT

Ashford School, Ashford
Babington House School, Chislehurst
Baston School, Bromley
Bedgebury School, Cranbrook
Beechwood Sacred Heart School, Tunbridge Wells
Benenden School, Cranbrook
Bethany School, Cranbrook
Bickley Park School, Bromley
Bishop Challoner RC School, Bromley
Bromley High School GDST, Bromley
Bronte School, Gravesend
Cobham Hall, Gravesend
Combe Bank School, Sevenoaks
Derwent Lodge School for Girls, Tonbridge
Dover College, Dover
Duke of York's Royal Military School, Dover
Dulwich Preparatory School, Cranbrook, Cranbrook
Farringtons School, Chislehurst
Friars School, Ashford
Gad's Hill School, Rochester
The Granville School, Sevenoaks
Harenc School Trust, Sidcup
Hilden Grange School, Tonbridge
Hilden Oaks School, Tonbridge
Holmewood House, Tunbridge Wells
Junior King's School, Canterbury
The Junior School, St Lawrence College, Ramsgate
Kent College, Canterbury
Kent College Infant & Junior School, Canterbury
Kent College Pembury, Tunbridge Wells
King's Preparatory School, Rochester
The King's School, Canterbury
King's School Rochester, Rochester
Marlborough House School, Hawkhurst
The Mead School, Tunbridge Wells
The New Beacon, Sevenoaks
Northbourne Park School, Deal
Rose Hill School, Tunbridge Wells
Russell House School, Sevenoaks
Sackville School, Tonbridge
St David's College, West Wickham
St Edmunds Junior School, Canterbury
St Edmund's School, Canterbury
St Lawrence College, Ramsgate
St Mary's Westbrook, Folkestone
St Michael's School, Sevenoaks
St Ronan's, Hawkhurst
Sevenoaks Preparatory School, Sevenoaks
Sevenoaks School, Sevenoaks
Solefield School, Sevenoaks
Sutton Valence Preparatory School, Maidstone
Sutton Valence School, Maidstone
Tonbridge School, Tonbridge
Walthamstow Hall, Sevenoaks
Wellesley House School, Broadstairs
West Lodge Preparatory School, Sidcup
Yardley Court, Tonbridge

LANCASHIRE

Arnold School, Blackpool
Bolton School (Boys' Division), Bolton
Bolton School (Girls' Division), Bolton
Bury Grammar School, Bury
Bury Grammar School Girls, Bury
Clevelands Preparatory School, Bolton
Highfield Priory School, Preston
The Hulme Grammar School for Girls, Oldham
King Edward VII and Queen Mary School,
Lytham St Annes
Kingswood College at Scarisbrick Hall, Ormskirk
Kirkham Grammar School, Preston
The Oldham Hulme Grammar School, Oldham
Queen Elizabeth's Grammar School, Blackburn
Rossall Junior School, Fleetwood
Rossall School, Fleetwood

St Mary's Hall, Stonyhurst
St Pius X Preparatory School, Preston
Stonyhurst College, Clitheroe
Westholme School, Blackburn

LEICESTERSHIRE

The Dixie Grammar School, Market Bosworth
Fairfield Preparatory School, Loughborough
Grace Dieu Manor School, Leicester
Leicester Grammar School, Leicester
Leicester High School For Girls, Leicester
Loughborough Grammar School, Loughborough
Loughborough High School, Loughborough
Manor House School, Ashby-de-la-Zouch
Our Lady's Convent School, Loughborough
PNEU School, Loughborough
Ratcliffe College, Leicester
Stoneygate School, Great Glen

LINCOLNSHIRE

Copthill School, Stamford
Kirkstone House School, Bourne
Lincoln Minster School, Lincoln
St Hugh's School, Woodhall Spa
St Mary's Preparatory School, Lincoln
Stamford High School, Stamford
Stamford Junior School, Stamford
Stamford School, Stamford
Witham Hall, Bourne

NORTH EAST LINCOLNSHIRE

St James' School, Grimsby
St Martin's Preparatory School, Grimsby

NORTH LINCOLNSHIRE

Brigg Preparatory School, Brigg

LONDON

Abercorn School, NW8
Alleyn's School, SE22
Arnold House School, NW8
The Arts Educational School, W4
Avenue House School, London W13
Belmont (Mill Hill Preparatory School), NW7
Blackheath High School GDST, SE3
Broomwood Hall School, SW12
Bute House Preparatory School for Girls, W6
Cameron House School, SW3
The Cavendish School, NW1
Channing School, N6
City of London School, EC4V
City of London School for Girls, EC2Y
Colfe's School, SE12
Devonshire House Preparatory School, NW3
Dulwich College, SE21
Dulwich College Preparatory School, SE21
Durston House, W5
Ealing College Upper School, W13
Eltham College, SE9
Emanuel School, SW11
Falkner House, SW7
Finton House School, SW17
Forest School, E17
Francis Holland School, SW1W
Francis Holland School, NW1
Garden House School, SW3
Glendower Preparatory School, SW7
The Godolphin and Latymer School, W6
Grange Park Preparatory School, N21
Grangewood Independent School, E7
The Hall School, NW3
The Hampshire Schools (Kensington Gardens), W2
The Hampshire Schools (Knightsbridge Under School), SW7
The Hampshire Schools (Knightsbridge Upper School), SW7
Harvington School, W5
Hawkesdown House School, W8
Hellenic College of London, SW1X
Hendon Preparatory School, NW4
Hereward House School, NW3
Herne Hill School, SE24
Highfield School, SW18
Highgate School, N6
Hornsby House School, SW12
Ibstock Place School, SW15
The Italia Conti Academy of Theatre Arts, EC1M
James Allen's Girls' School, SE22
James Allen's Preparatory School, SE22
Keble Preparatory School, N21
Kensington Prep School, SW6
The King Alfred School, NW11
King's College Junior School, SW19
King's College School, SW19
Latymer Preparatory School, W6
Latymer Upper School, W6
Lyndhurst House Preparatory School, NW3
Mander Portman Woodward, SW7
Mill Hill School, NW7
More House, SW1X
The Mount School, NW7
Newton Prep, SW8
Norland Place School, W11
Normanhurst School, E4
Northcote Lodge School, SW11
Notting Hill and Ealing High School GDST, W13
Oakfield Preparatory School, SE21
Orchard House School, W4
Palmers Green High School, N21
Pembridge Hall, W2
Portland Place, W1B
Prospect House School, SW15
Putney High School GDST, SW15
Putney Park School, SW15
Queen's College, W1G
Queen's Gate School, SW7
Ravenscourt Park Preparatory School, W6
Redcliffe School, SW10
Riverston School, SE12
Rosemead Preparatory School, SE21

Royal Ballet School, WC2
The Royal School, Hampstead, NW3
St Anthony's Preparatory School, NW3
St Benedict's School, W5
St Christina's RC Preparatory School, NW8
St Christopher's School, NW3
St Dunstan's College, SE6
St James Independent School for Boys, W14
St James Independent School for Senior Girls, W14
St James Independent School for Girls (Juniors), W14
St Margaret's School, NW3
St Mary's School Hampstead, NW3
St Olave's Preparatory School, SE9
St Paul's Cathedral School, EC4M
St Paul's Girls' School, W6
St Paul's Preparatory School, SW13
St Paul's School, SW13
Salcombe Preparatory School, N14
Sarum Hall, NW3
Snaresbrook College Preparatory School, E18
South Hampstead High School, NW3
Southbank International School, Hampstead, NW3
Southbank International School, Kensington, W11
Streatham and Clapham High School, SW16
The Study Preparatory School, SW19
Sussex House School, SW1X
The Swaminarayan School, NW10
Sydenham High School GDST, SE26
Sylvia Young Theatre School, NW1
Tower House School, SW14
University College School, NW3
University College School, Junior Branch, NW3
Virgo Fidelis, SE19
Vita Et Pax School, N14
Westminster Abbey Choir School, SW1P
Westminster Cathedral Choir School, SW1P
Westminster School, SW1P
Westminster Under School, SW1P
Wimbledon High School GDST, SW19
Woodside Park International School, N11

GREATER MANCHESTER

Abbotsford Preparatory School, Manchester
Bridgewater School, Manchester
Chetham's School of Music, Manchester
The Manchester Grammar School, Manchester
Manchester High School for Girls, Manchester
Moor Allerton School, Manchester
St Bede's College, Manchester
William Hulme's Grammar School, Manchester
Withington Girls' School, Manchester

MERSEYSIDE

The Belvedere School GDST, Liverpool
Birkenhead High School GDST, Wirral
Birkenhead School, Wirral
Carleton House Preparatory School, Liverpool
Kingsmead School, Wirral
Liverpool College, Liverpool
Merchant Taylors' School, Liverpool
Merchant Taylors' School for Girls, Liverpool
Prenton Preparatory School, Wirral
Runnymede St Edward's School, Liverpool
St Mary's College, Liverpool
Sunnymede School, Southport
Tower College, Prescot

MIDDLESEX

ACS Hillingdon International School, Hillingdon
Alpha Preparatory School, Harrow
Ashton House School, Isleworth
Buckingham College School, Harrow
Denmead School, Hampton
Halliford School, Shepperton
Hampton School, Hampton
Harrow School, Harrow on the Hill
Heathfield School, Pinner
Innellan House School, Pinner
The John Lyon School, Harrow
The Lady Eleanor Holles School, Hampton
The Mall School, Twickenham
Merchant Taylors' School, Northwood
Newland House School, Twickenham
North London Collegiate, Edgware
Northwood College, Northwood
Orley Farm School, Harrow
Peterborough & St Margaret's School, Stanmore
Quainton Hall School, Harrow
Reddiford, Pinner
St Catherine's School, Twickenham
St Christopher's School, Wembley
St David's School, Ashford
St Helen's College, Hillingdon
St Helen's School, Northwood
St James Independent School for Boys (Senior), Twickenham
St John's Northwood, Northwood
St Martin's School, Northwood
Staines Preparatory School, Staines
Twickenham Preparatory School, Hampton

NORFOLK

Beeston Hall School, Cromer
Glebe House School, Hunstanton
Gresham's Preparatory School, Holt
Gresham's School, Holt
Hethersett Old Hall School, Norwich
Langley Preparatory School & Nursery, Norwich
Langley School, Norwich
The New Eccles Hall School, Norwich
Norwich High School for Girls GDST, Norwich
Norwich School, Norwich
Riddlesworth Hall, Diss
Sacred Heart Convent School, Swaffham
St Christopher's School, Norwich
Taverham Hall, Norwich
Thetford Grammar School, Thetford
Thorpe House School, Norwich
Town Close House Preparatory School, Norwich

NORTHAMPTONSHIRE

Beachborough School, Brackley
Laxton Junior School, Peterborough
Maidwell Hall, Northampton
Northamptonshire Grammar School, Pitsford
Northampton High School, Northampton
Northampton Preparatory School, Northampton
Oundle School, Peterborough
St Peter's School, Kettering
Spratton Hall, Northampton
Wellingborough School, Wellingborough
Winchester House School, Brackley

NORTHUMBERLAND

Longridge Towers School, Berwick-upon-Tweed
Mowden Hall School, Stocksfield

NOTTINGHAMSHIRE

Arley House PNEU School, East Leake
Bramcote Lorne School, Retford
Dagfa House School, Nottingham
Greenholme School, Nottingham
Grosvenor School, Nottingham
Highfields School, Newark
Hollygirt School, Nottingham
Mountford House School, Nottingham
Nottingham High School, Nottingham
Nottingham High School for Girls GDST, Nottingham
Nottingham High Junior School, Nottingham
Plumtree School, Nottingham
Ranby House, Retford
Rodney School, Newark
St Joseph's School, Nottingham
Salterford House School, Nottingham
Trent College, Nottingham
Waverley House PNEU School, Nottingham
Wellow House School, Newark
Worksop College, Worksop

OXFORDSHIRE

Abingdon School, Abingdon
Bloxham School, Banbury
The Carrdus School, Banbury
Chandlings Manor School, Oxford
Christ Church Cathedral School, Oxford
Cokethorpe, Witney
Cothill House Preparatory School, Abingdon
Cranford House School, Wallingford
d'Overbroeck's College, Oxford
Dragon School, Oxford
Ferndale Preparatory School, Faringdon
Headington School, Oxford
Josca's Preparatory School, Abingdon
Kingham Hill School, Chipping Norton
Magdalen College School, Oxford
The Manor Preparatory School, Abingdon
Moulsford Preparatory School, Wallingford
New College School, Oxford
Our Lady's Convent Senior School, Abingdon
Oxford High School GDST, Oxford
Radley College, Abingdon
Rupert House, Henley-on-Thames
Rye St Antony School, Oxford
St Edward's School, Oxford
St Hugh's School, Faringdon
St John's Priory School, Banbury
St Mary's School, Henley-on-Thames
St Mary's School, Wantage
School of St Helen & St Katharine, Abingdon
Shiplake College, Henley-on-Thames
Sibford School, Banbury
Summer Fields, Oxford
Tudor Hall School, Banbury
Wychwood School, Oxford

RUTLAND

Brooke Priory School, Oakham
Oakham School, Oakham
Uppingham School, Uppingham

SHROPSHIRE

Adcote School for Girls, Shrewsbury
Bedstone College, Bucknell
Castle House School, Newport
Concord College, Shrewsbury
Ellesmere College, Ellesmere
Kingsland Grange, Shrewsbury
Moor Park School, Ludlow
Moreton Hall, Oswestry
The Old Hall School, Telford
Oswestry School, Oswestry
Packwood Haugh School, Shrewsbury
Prestfelde Preparatory School, Shrewsbury
St Winefride's Convent School, Shrewsbury
Shrewsbury High School GDST, Shrewsbury
Shrewsbury School, Shrewsbury
Wrekin College, Telford

SOMERSET

All Hallows, Shepton Mallet
Bruton School for Girls, Bruton
Chilton Cantelo School, Yeovil
Downside School, Bath
Hazlegrove (King's Bruton Preparatory School), Yeovil
King's College, Taunton
King's Hall School, Taunton
King's School, Bruton
Millfield Preparatory School, Street
Millfield School, Street
The Park School, Yeovil
Perrott Hill School, Crewkerne
Queen's College Junior and Pre-Preparatory Schools, Taunton
Queen's College, Taunton
Taunton Preparatory School, Taunton
Taunton School, Taunton
Wellington School, Wellington

Wells Cathedral Junior School, Wells
Wells Cathedral School, Wells

BATH & NORTH EAST SOMERSET

King Edward's School, Bath
Kingswood School, Bath
Kingswood Preparatory School, Bath
Monkton Combe Junior School, Bath
Monkton Combe School, Bath
Paragon School, Bath
Prior Park College, Bath
The Royal High School, Bath

NORTH SOMERSET

Sidcot School, Winscombe

STAFFORDSHIRE

Abbots Bromley School for Girls, Abbots Bromley
Abbotsholme School, Uttoxeter
Brooklands School, Stafford
Chase Academy, Cannock
Denstone College, Uttoxeter
Edenhurst School, Newcastle-under-Lyme
Lichfield Cathedral School, Lichfield
Newcastle-under-Lyme School, Newcastle-under-Lyme
St Bede's School, Stafford
St Dominic's Priory School, Stone
St Dominic's School, Stafford
St Joseph's Preparatory School, Stoke-on-Trent
Smallwood Manor Preparatory School, Uttoxeter
Stafford Grammar School, Stafford
Vernon Lodge Preparatory School, Stafford
Yarlet School, Stafford

STOCKTON-ON-TEES

Red House School, Norton
Teesside Preparatory and High School, Eaglescliffe
Yarm School, Yarm

SUFFOLK

The Abbey, Woodbridge
Amberfield School, Ipswich
Barnardiston Hall Preparatory School, Haverhill
Cherry Trees School, Bury St Edmunds
Culford School, Bury St Edmunds
Fairstead House School, Newmarket
Finborough School, Stowmarket
Framlingham College, Woodbridge
Framlingham College Preparatory School, Brandeston
Hillcroft Preparatory School, Stowmarket
Ipswich High School GDST, Ipswich
Ipswich Preparatory School, Ipswich
Ipswich School, Ipswich
Moreton Hall Preparatory School, Bury St Edmunds
Old Buckenham Hall School, Ipswich
The Old School, Beccles
Orwell Park, Ipswich
Royal Hospital School, Ipswich
Saint Felix Schools, Southwold
St Joseph's College, Ipswich
South Lee Preparatory School, Bury St Edmunds
Stoke College, Sudbury
Woodbridge School, Woodbridge

SURREY

Aberdour School, Tadworth
ACS Egham International School, Egham
Aldro School, Godalming
Amesbury, Hindhead
Barfield School, Farnham
Barrow Hills School, Godalming
Belmont School, Dorking
Bishopsgate School, Egham
Box Hill School, Dorking
Bramley School, Tadworth
Canbury School, Kingston-upon-Thames
Caterham Preparatory School, Caterham
Caterham School, Caterham
Charterhouse, Godalming
Chinthurst School, Tadworth
City of London Freemen's School, Ashtead
Claremont Fan Court School, Esher
Clewborough House School, Frimley
Collingwood School, Wallington
Coworth-Flexlands School, Woking
Cranleigh Preparatory School, Cranleigh
Cranleigh School, Cranleigh
Cranmore School, Leatherhead
Croham Hurst School, South Croydon
Croydon High School GDST, South Croydon
Cumnor House School, South Croydon
Danes Hill Preparatory School, Leatherhead
Downsend School, Leatherhead
Duke of Kent School, Ewhurst
Dunottar School, Reigate
Edgeborough, Farnham
Elmhurst School, South Croydon
Epsom College, Epsom
Ewell Castle School, Epsom
Feltonfleet School, Cobham
Frensham Heights School, Farnham
Glaisdale School, Cheam
Glenesk School, Leatherhead
Greenacre School for Girls, Banstead
Greenfield School, Woking
Guildford High School, Guildford
Hall Grove School, Bagshot
Halstead Preparatory School, Woking
Haslemere Preparatory School, Haslemere
Hawley Place School, Camberley
The Hawthorns School, Redhill
Hazelwood School, Oxted
Hoe Bridge School, Woking
Holy Cross Preparatory School, Kingston-upon-Thames
Homefield School, Sutton
Hurtwood House, Dorking
King Edward's School Witley, Godalming
King's House School, Richmond

Kingston Grammar School, Kingston-upon-Thames
Kingswood House School, Epsom
Lanesborough, Guildford
Laverock School, Oxted
Lingfield Notre Dame School, Lingfield
Lodge School, Purley
Longacre School, Guildford
Lyndhurst School, Camberley
Manor House School, Leatherhead
Marymount International School, Kingston-upon-Thames
Micklefield School, Reigate
Milbourne Lodge School, Esher
Notre Dame Preparatory School, Cobham
Notre Dame Senior School, Cobham
Oakhyrst Grange School, Caterham
Old Palace School of John Whitgift, Croydon
Old Vicarage School, Richmond
Parkside School, Cobham
Parsons Mead, Ashtead
Prior's Field School, Godalming
Priory School, Banstead
Reed's School, Cobham
Reigate Grammar School, Reigate
Reigate St Mary's Preparatory and Choir School, Reigate
Ripley Court School, Woking
Rokeby School, Kingston-upon-Thames
Rowan Preparatory School, Esher
Royal Grammar School, Guildford
Royal Russell School, Croydon
The Royal School, Haslemere
Rydes Hill Preparatory School, Guildford
St Andrew's (Woking) School Trust, Woking
St Catherine's School, Guildford
St Christopher's School, Epsom
St David's School, Purley
St Edmund's School, Hindhead
St George's College, Weybridge
St George's College Junior School, Weybridge
St Hilary's School, Godalming
St Ives School, Haslemere
St John's School, Leatherhead
St Teresa's Preparatory School, Effingham
St Teresa's School, Dorking
Seaton House, Sutton
Shrewsbury House School, Surbiton
Sir William Perkins's School, Chertsey
Stowford College, Sutton
The Study School, New Malden
Surbiton High School, Kingston-upon-Thames
Surbiton Preparatory School, Surbiton
Sutton High School GDST, Sutton
Tormead School, Guildford
Trinity School, Croydon
Unicorn School, Richmond
West Dene School, Purley
Whitgift School, South Croydon
Wispers School for Girls, Haslemere
Woldingham School, Woldingham
Woodcote House School, Windlesham
Yehudi Menuhin School, Cobham

EAST SUSSEX

Ashdown House School, Forest Row
Battle Abbey School, Battle
Bodiam Manor School, Robertsbridge
Bricklehurst Manor Preparatory, Wadhurst
Brighton and Hove High School GDST, Brighton
Brighton College, Brighton
Brighton College Prep School, Brighton
Eastbourne College, Eastbourne
Greenfields School, Forest Row
Lewes Old Grammar School, Lewes
Moira House Girls School, Eastbourne
Mowden School, Hove
Newlands Manor School, Seaford
Newlands Preparatory School, Seaford
Roedean School, Brighton
St Andrew's School, Eastbourne
St Aubyns School, Brighton
St Bede's Prep School, Eastbourne
St Bede's School, Hailsham
St Leonards-Mayfield School, Mayfield
St Mary's Hall, Brighton
Skippers Hill Manor Preparatory School, Mayfield
Vinehall School, Robertsbridge

WEST SUSSEX

Ardingly College, Haywards Heath
Ardingly College Junior School, Haywards Heath
Arundale Preparatory School, Pulborough
Brambletye School, East Grinstead
Broadwater Manor School, Worthing
Burgess Hill School for Girls, Burgess Hill
Christ's Hospital, Horsham
Copthorne Prep School, Copthorne
Cottesmore School, Pease Pottage
Cumnor House School, Haywards Heath
Dorset House School, Pulborough
Farlington School, Horsham
Fonthill Lodge, East Grinstead
Great Ballard School, Chichester
Great Walstead, Haywards Heath
Handcross Park School, Haywards Heath
Hurstpierpoint College, Hurstpierpoint
Lancing College, Lancing
Lavant House, Chichester
Oakwood School, Chichester
Our Lady of Sion School, Worthing
Pennthorpe School, Horsham
The Prebendal School, Chichester
St Margaret's School Convent of Mercy, Midhurst
Seaford College, Petworth
Shoreham College, Shoreham-by-Sea
Slindon College, Arundel
Sompting Abbotts School, Sompting
Stoke Brunswick, East Grinstead
The Towers Convent School, Steyning
Westbourne House School, Chichester
Windlesham House, Pulborough
Worth School, Turners Hill

TYNE AND WEAR

Argyle House School, Sunderland
Ascham House School, Newcastle upon Tyne
Central Newcastle High School GDST, Newcastle upon Tyne
Dame Allan's Boys School, Newcastle upon Tyne
Dame Allan's Girls School, Newcastle upon Tyne
The King's School, Tynemouth
La Sagesse School, Newcastle upon Tyne
Newcastle Preparatory School, Newcastle upon Tyne
Newcastle Upon Tyne Church High School, Newcastle upon Tyne
Newlands School, Newcastle upon Tyne
Royal Grammar School, Newcastle upon Tyne
Sunderland High School, Sunderland
Westfield School, Newcastle upon Tyne

WARWICKSHIRE

Abbotsford School, Kenilworth
Arnold Lodge School, Leamington Spa
Bilton Grange, Rugby
The Crescent School, Rugby
The Croft Preparatory School, Stratford-upon-Avon
The King's High School for Girls, Warwick
The Kingsley School, Leamington Spa
Princethorpe College, Rugby
Rugby School, Rugby
Stratford Preparatory School, Stratford-upon-Avon
Twycross House School, Atherstone
Warwick Preparatory School, Warwick
Warwick School, Warwick

WEST MIDLANDS

Bablake School, Coventry
Birchfield School, Wolverhampton
The Blue Coat School, Birmingham
Coventry Prep School, Coventry
Davenport Lodge School, Coventry
Eastbourne House School, Birmingham
Edgbaston High School for Girls, Birmingham
Elmhurst School for Dance, Birmingham
Eversfield Preparatory School, Solihull
Hallfield School, Birmingham
Highclare School, Birmingham
Hydesville Tower School, Walsall
King Edward VI High School for Girls, Birmingham
King Edward's School, Birmingham
King Henry VIII School, Coventry
Mayfield Preparatory School, Walsall
Newbridge Preparatory School, Wolverhampton
Norfolk House School, Birmingham
Priory School, Birmingham
The Royal Wolverhampton Junior School, Wolverhampton
The Royal Wolverhampton School, Wolverhampton
Ruckleigh School, Solihull
St George's School, Edgbaston, Birmingham
St Martin's School, Solihull
Solihull School, Solihull
Tettenhall College, Wolverhampton
West House School, Birmingham
Wolverhampton Grammar School, Wolverhampton

WILTSHIRE

Chafyn Grove School, Salisbury
Dauntsey's School, Devizes
The Godolphin School, Salisbury
Heywood Preparatory School, Corsham
La Retraite Swan, Salisbury
Leaden Hall, Salisbury
Marlborough College, Marlborough
Norman Court Preparatory School, Salisbury
Pinewood School, Swindon
Prior Park Preparatory School, Cricklade
St Francis School, Pewsey
St Margaret's Preparatory School, Calne
St Mary's School, Calne
Salisbury Cathedral School, Salisbury
Sandroyd School, Salisbury
Stonar School, Melksham
Warminster School, Warminster

WORCESTERSHIRE

Abberley Hall, Worcester
The Alice Ottley School, Worcester
Bowbrook House School, Pershore
Bromsgrove Preparatory School, Bromsgrove
Bromsgrove School, Bromsgrove
The Downs School, Malvern
The Elms, Malvern
Green Hill School, Evesham
Hartlebury School, Kidderminster
Heathfield School, Kidderminster
Hillstone School (Malvern College), Malvern
Holy Trinity School, Kidderminster
King's Hawford, Worcester
The King's School, Worcester
The Knoll School, Kidderminster
Malvern College, Malvern
Malvern Girls' College, Malvern
Moffats School, Bewdley
Royal Grammar School Worcester, Worcester
St James's School, Malvern
St Mary's Convent School, Worcester
Whitford Hall & Dodderhill School, Droitwich
Winterfold House, Kidderminster

EAST RIDING OF YORKSHIRE

Hull Grammar School, Kingston-Upon-Hull
Hull High School, Anlaby
Hymers College, Hull
Pocklington School, Pocklington

NORTH YORKSHIRE

Ampleforth College, York
Ashville College, Harrogate
Aysgarth Preparatory School, Bedale

Bootham School, York
Bramcote School, Scarborough
Catteral Hall School, Settle
Clifton Preparatory School, York
Fyling Hall School, Whitby
Giggleswick School, Settle
Harrogate Ladies' College, Harrogate
Howsham Hall, York
Lisvane, Scarborough College Junior School, Scarborough
Malsis School, Skipton
The Minster School, York
The Mount School, York
Queen Ethelburga's College, York
Queen Margaret's School, York
Queen Mary's School, Thirsk
Read School, Selby
Ripon Cathedral Choir School, Ripon
St Martin's Ampleforth, York
St Olave's School (Junior of St Peter's), York
St Peter's School, York
Scarborough College & Lisvane School, Scarborough
Terrington Hall, York
Woodleigh School, Malton

SOUTH YORKSHIRE

Ashdell Preparatory School, Sheffield
Birkdale School, Sheffield
Brantwood School for Girls, Sheffield
Hill House St Mary's School, Doncaster
Mylnhurst RC School & Nursery, Sheffield
Rudston Preparatory School, Rotherham
Sheffield High School GDST, Sheffield
Westbourne School, Sheffield

WEST YORKSHIRE

Ackworth School, Pontefract
Batley Grammar School, Batley
Bradford Girls' Grammar School, Bradford
Bradford Grammar School, Bradford
Bronte House School, Bradford
Cliff School, Wakefield
The Froebelian School, Leeds
Fulneck School, Pudsey
Gateways School, Leeds
The Gleddings School, Halifax
Hipperholme Grammar School, Halifax
Lady Lane Park School, Bingley
Leeds Girls' High School, Leeds
Leeds Grammar School, Leeds
Moorfield School, Ilkley
Moorlands School, Leeds
Queen Elizabeth Grammar School, Wakefield
The Rastrick Independent School, Brighouse
Richmond House School, Leeds
Rishworth School, Rishworth
Silcoates School, Wakefield
Sunny Hill House School, Wakefield
Wakefield Girls' High School, Wakefield
Westville House Preparatory School, Ilkley
Woodhouse Grove School, Apperley Bridge

NORTHERN IRELAND

COUNTY ANTRIM

Belfast Royal Academy, Belfast
Campbell College, Belfast
Methodist College, Belfast
Royal Belfast Academical Institution, Belfast

COUNTY DOWN

Bangor Grammar School, Bangor
Rockport School, Holywood

COUNTY FERMANAGH

Portora Royal School, Enniskillen

COUNTY LONDONDERRY

Coleraine Academical Institution, Coleraine

COUNTY TYRONE

The Royal School Dungannon, Dungannon

SCOTLAND

ABERDEENSHIRE

Robert Gordons College, Aberdeen
St Margaret's School for Girls, Aberdeen

ANGUS

The High School of Dundee, Dundee
Lathallan School, Montrose

ARGYLL AND BUTE

Lomond School, Helensburgh

CLACKMANNANSHIRE

Dollar Academy, Dollar

FIFE

St Leonard's School & VIth Form College, St Andrews

GLASGOW

Craigholme School, Glasgow
The Glasgow Academy, Glasgow
The High School of Glasgow, Glasgow
Hutchesons' Grammar School, Glasgow
Kelvinside Academy, Glasgow
St Aloysius Junior School, Glasgow

LOTHIAN

Belhaven Hill, Dunbar
Cargilfield, Edinburgh
Clifton Hall School, Edinburgh
The Edinburgh Academy, Edinburgh
Fettes College, Edinburgh
George Heriot's School, Edinburgh
George Watson's College, Edinburgh
Loretto School, Musselburgh
The Mary Erskine School, Edinburgh
Merchiston Castle School, Edinburgh
St George's School for Girls, Edinburgh
St Margaret's School, Edinburgh
Stewart's Melville College, Edinburgh

MORAYSHIRE

Gordonstoun School, Elgin

PERTH AND KINROSS

Ardvreck School, Crieff
Craigclowan Preparatory School, Perth
Glenalmond College, Perth
Kilgraston (A Sacred Heart School), Perth
Morrison's Academy, Crieff
Strathallan School, Perth

RENFREWSHIRE

St Columba's School, Kilmacolm

ROXBURGHSHIRE

St Mary's Preparatory School, Melrose

WALES

CARDIFF

The Cathedral School, Cardiff
Howell's School, Llandaff GDST, Cardiff
Kings Monkton School, Cardiff
Westbourne School, Cardiff

CARMARTHENSHIRE

Llandovery College, Llandovery
St Michael's School, Llanelli

CONWY

Lyndon Preparatory School, Colwyn Bay
Rydal Penrhos Senior School, Colwyn Bay
St David's College, Llandudno

DENBIGHSHIRE

Howell's School, Denbigh
Ruthin School, Ruthin

GWYNEDD

St Gerard's School, Bangor

MONMOUTHSHIRE

Haberdashers' Monmouth School For Girls, Monmouth
Monmouth School, Monmouth
St John's-on-the-Hill, Chepstow

NEWPORT

Rougemont School, Newport

POWYS

Christ College, Brecon

4.10
Educational Associations and Useful Addresses

The Allied Schools
Cross House
38 High Street
Banbury
Oxon OX16 5ET
Tel: (01295) 256441
Fax: (01295) 275350
E-mail: n.coulson@alliedschools.org.uk
Website: www.alliedschools.org.uk
General Manager: Nevil Coulson MA, MBA

The organization provides management, financial, helpline and other support services to member schools, as well as operating a communications network between school governors, heads, bursars and other staff for the exchange of information and ideas. The Allied Schools include:

Stowe School
Wrekin College
Canford School
Harrogate Ladies' College
Westonbirt School
Riddlesworth Hall Preparatory School (associate)

The Association for the Education and Guardianship of International Students (AEGIS)
Tel/Fax: (01453) 755160
E-mail: secretary@aegisuk.net
Website: www.aegisuk.net
Secretary: Janet Bowman

The Association promotes best and legal practice in all areas of guardianship and the care of international students, under 18 years of age, at school or college in the United Kingdom. All members, including school members, are required to adhere to the AEGIS Code of Practice and undertake to follow guidelines on caring for international students. Guardianship organizations are admitted to membership after a successful accreditation inspection.

Association of Governing Bodies of Independent Schools (AGBIS)
Field House
Newton Tony
Salisbury
Wiltshire SP4 0HF
Tel: (01980) 629831
Fax: (01980) 629774
E-mail: sec@agbis.org.uk
Website: www.agbis.org.uk
Secretary: Brigadier S Rutter-Jerome

The aim of the association is to advance education in independent schools, to promote good governance and administration in independent schools and to encourage co-operation between their governing bodies. For details please contact the Secretary.

Association of Heads of Independent Schools
St Nicholas School
Redfields House, Redfields Lane
Church Crookham
Fleet
Hampshire GU52 0RF
Honorary Secretary: Mrs A V Whatmough

Membership of AHIS is open to the Heads of girls' independent secondary schools and girls' co-educational junior independent schools which are accredited by the Independent Schools Council (see below).

Association of Nursery Training Colleges
The Chiltern College
16 Peppard Road
Caversham
Reading RG4 8JZ
Tel: (0118) 9471847

Provides information and advice on careers in child care, as nannies and nursery workers. Also gives information on Diplomas, National Vocational Qualifications (NVQs) and Montessori training in child care and education offered at Chiltern College in Reading (www.chilterncollege.com), the Norland College in Bath (www.norland.co.uk), and the Montessori Centre International, whose headquarters are in London (www.montessori.ac.uk).

Association of Tutors
Sunnycroft
63 King Edward Road
Northampton NN1 5LY
Tel: (01604) 624171

Fax: (01604) 624718
Website: www.tutor.co.uk
Secretary: Dr D J Cornelius

The professional body for independent private tutors. Members provide advice and individual tuition to students at all levels of education. The tutoring may be supplementary to full course provision or may be on a full course basis.

Boarding Schools' Association (BSA)
Grosvenor Gardens House
35–37 Grosvenor Gardens
London SW1W 0BS
Tel: (020) 7798 1580
Fax: (020) 7798 1581
E-mail: bsa@boarding.org.uk
Website: www.boarding.org.uk
National Director: Adrian Underwood BA (Hons), MA, FRSA

The BSA has the twin objectives of promoting boarding education and developing quality boarding through high standards of pastoral care and boarding facilities.

A school can join the BSA only if it is a member of one of the constituent associations of the Independent Schools Council or, for state-maintained boarding schools, a member of SBSA (the State Boarding Schools Association). These two bodies require member schools to be regularly inspected by the Independent Schools Inspectorate (ISA) or OFSTED. Parents and prospective pupils choosing a boarding school can therefore be assured that BSA member schools are committed to providing the best possible boarding environment for their pupils.

For further information about the BSA Professional Development Programme please contact:

Tim Holgate BSc (Hons), MSc
BSA Director of Training
4, Manor Farm Cottages
Etchilhampton
Devizes
Wilts SN10 3JR
Tel/Fax: (01380) 860953
E-mail: training@boarding.org.uk

British Accreditation Council
The Chief Executive
42 Manchester Street
London WIU 7LW
Tel: (020) 7224 5474
Fax: (020) 7224 5475

E-mail: info@the-bac.org
Website: www.the-bac.org

British Association for Early Childhood Education (Early Education)
111 City View House
463 Bethnal Green Road
London E2 9QY
Tel: (020) 7739 7594
Fax: (020) 7613 5330

A charitable association which advises on the care and education of young children from birth to eight years. The association also publishes booklets and organizes conferences for those interested in early childhood education.

British Dyslexia Association
98 London Road
Reading, Berkshire RG1 5AU
Tel: (0118) 966 2871
Fax: (0118) 935 1927
E-mail: helpline@bdadyslexia.org.uk
Website: www.bdadyslexia.org.uk
(Helpline/Information Service 10am–12.45pm and 2pm–4.45pm Mondays, Wednesdays and Fridays)

Children's Education Advisory Service
Trenchard Lines
Upavon
Pewsey
Wilts SN9 6BE
Tel: (01980) 618244
E-mail: enquiries.ceas@gtnet.gov.uk

To support Service families and entitled civilians in obtaining appropriate educational facilities for their children and to provide high quality, impartial advice on all aspects of education worldwide.

Choir Schools Association
The Minster School
Deangate, York YO1 7JA
Tel: (01904) 624900
Fax: (01904) 557232
E-mail: info@choirschools.org.uk
Administrator: Wendy Jackson

An association of schools educating cathedral and collegiate boy and girl choristers. Membership comprises the following schools:

The Abbey School, Tewkesbury
Bristol Cathedral School, Bristol
The Cathedral School, Llandaff
Chetham's School of Music, Manchester
The Chorister School, Durham
Christ Church Cathedral School, Oxford
Exeter Cathedral School, Exeter
Hereford Cathedral Junior School, Hereford
The King's School, Gloucester
The King's School, Worcester
King's College School, Cambridge
The King's School, Ely
King's Preparatory School, Rochester
Lanesborough, Guildford
Lichfield Cathedral School, Lichfield
Lincoln Minster School, Lincoln
Magdalen College School, Oxford
The Minster School, Southwell
The Minster School, York
New College School, Oxford
Norwich School, Norwich
The Pilgrim's School, Winchester
Polwhele House, Truro
The Prebendal School, Chichester
Ripon Cathedral Choir School, Ripon
St Edmunds Junior School, Canterbury
St George's School, Windsor
St James's School, Grimsby
St John's College, Cardiff
St John's College School, Cambridge
St Mary's Music School, Edinburgh
St Paul's Cathedral Choir School, London EC4
Salisbury Cathedral School, Salisbury
Wells Cathedral School, Wells
Westminster Abbey Choir School, London SW1
Westminster Cathedral Choir School, London SW1

Associate Members
Ampleforth College, Ampleforth, North Yorkshire
Portsmouth Grammar School, Portsmouth
Queen Elizabeth Grammar School, Wakefield
Reigate St Mary's Preparatory and Choir School, Reigate
The Cathedral School, Chelmsford
St Edward's College, Liverpool
The King's School, Peterborough
Warwick School, Warwick

Council for Independent Further Education (CIFE)
Dr Norma R Ball
Executive Secretary
75 Foxbourne Road
London SW17 8EN
Tel: (020) 8767 8666
Fax: (020) 8767 9444

CIFE, founded in 1973, is a professional association for independent colleges of further education which specialize in preparing students (mainly over statutory school leaving age) for GCSEs, A and AS levels and university entrance. In addition, some colleges offer English language tuition for students from abroad and degree-level tuition. The aim of the association is to promote good practice and safeguard adherence to strict standards of professional conduct and ethical propriety. Full membership is open to colleges which have been accredited either by the British Accreditation Council for Independent Further and Higher Education (BAC) or by the Independent Schools Council. Candidate membership is available to colleges seeking accreditation by either body within three years which otherwise satisfy CIFE's own stringent criteria for membership. All CIFE colleges, of which there are currently 24 spread throughout England, with concentrations in London, Oxford and Cambridge, have to abide by exacting codes of conduct and practice; and the character and presentation of their published exam results are subject to regulation, the accuracy of the information presented requiring in addition to be validated by BAC as academic auditor to CIFE. Colleges in full membership are subject to re-inspection from time to time by their accrediting bodies. Further information and a list of colleges are available from the Secretary.

CReSTeD (Council for the Registration of Schools Teaching Dyslexic Pupils)
Registered Charity No: 1052103
Greygarth, Littleworth
Winchcombe
Cheltenham GL54 5BT
Tel/Fax: (01242) 604 852
E-mail: admin@crested.org.uk
Website: www.crested.org.uk
Chairman: Dr M C V Cane

The CReSTeD Register is to help parents and those who advise them to choose schools for dyslexic children. Its main supporters are the British Dyslexia Association and the Dyslexia Institute who, with others, established CReSTeD to produce an authoritative list of schools, both maintained and independent, which have been through an established registration procedure, including a visit by the CReSTeD selected consultant.

Department for Education and Skills
Sanctuary Buildings
Great Smith Street
London SW1P 3BT
Tel: (08700) 012345
Website: www.dfes.gov.uk

The Dyslexia Institute: National Training and Resources Centre
Park House, Wick Road
Egham
Surrey TW20 0HH
Tel: (01784) 222300
Fax: (01784) 222333
E-mail: info@dyslexia-inst.org.uk
Website: www.dyslexia-inst.org.uk

The Dyslexia Institute (DI), the UK's leading provider of services for dyslexic people, has 27 main centres and over 140 smaller teaching units throughout the country. It carries out assessments for children and adults who may be dyslexic, provides tuition and trains specialist teachers, as well as developing teaching materials and conducting research. Registered Charity No: 268502.

Gabbitas Educational Consultants
Carrington House
126–130 Regent Street
London W1B 5EE
Tel: (020) 7734 0161
Fax: (020) 7437 1764
E-mail: market@gabbitas.co.uk
Website: www.gabbitas.co.uk

Gabbitas offers friendly, independent, expert advice on all stages of education and careers:

- choice of independent schools and colleges;
- educational assessment services for parents concerned about their child's progress at school;
- Sixth Form options – A and AS level, International Baccalaureate and vocational courses;
- university and degree choices and UCAS applications;
- careers assessment and guidance;
- extensive guidance for overseas students transferring into the British system;
- specialist services including guardianship for overseas students attending UK boarding schools and testing services in English, Maths and Science.

Gabbitas also provides a full range of services for schools, including the appointment of Heads and staff as well as consultancy on any aspect of school management and development.

The Girls' Day School Trust (GDST)
100 Rochester Row
London SW1P 1JP
Tel: (020) 7393 6666
Fax: (020) 7393 6789
E-mail: info@wes.gdst.net
Website: www.gdst.net

The GDST has been making a distinctive contribution to education for girls since it was founded in 1872. Today the GDST owns and runs 25 schools throughout England and Wales with a concentration of 12 schools in London, making it the largest group of independent schools in the UK, currently educating 20,000 students each year – some 9 per cent of girls in the fee paying sector. GDST schools encourage creativity, articulate self-expression and enterprise in girls who are prepared to participate fully in the challenges of 21st century life.

The GDST is a Registered Charity (No 306983).

The Belvedere School, Liverpool
Birkenhead High School, Birkenhead
Blackheath High School, London SW3
Brighton and Hove High School, Brighton
Bromley High School, Bromley
Central Newcastle High School, Newcastle-upon-Tyne
Croydon High School, Croydon
Heathfield School, Pinner
Howell's School, Cardiff
Ipswich High School, Ipswich
Kensington Preparatory School, London SW6
Norwich High School for Girls, Norwich
Notting Hill & Ealing High School, London W13
Nottingham High School for Girls, Nottingham
Oxford High School, Oxford
Portsmouth High School, Portsmouth
Putney High School, London SW15
Royal High School, Bath
Sheffield High School, Sheffield
Shrewsbury High School, Shrewsbury
South Hampstead High School, London NW3
Streatham & Clapham High School, London SE26
Sydenham High School, Sydenham
Wimbledon High School, London SW19

GDST schools are non-denominational. Entry is by interview and test appropriate to the pupil's age. All schools have a junior department. Kensington is a preparatory school only. The Royal High School, Bath, also takes boarders. Howell's School in Cardiff has a co-educational Sixth Form Centre. For further details contact the schools direct, the GDST office for a general prospectus or the GDST website (www.gdst.net) which has links to all the schools.

The Girls' Schools Association (GSA)
130 Regent Road
Leicester LE1 7PG
Tel: (0116) 254 1619 Fax: (0116) 255 3792
E-mail: office@gsa.uk.com
President: Dr Brenda Despontin
General Secretary: Ms Sheila Cooper

The GSA exists to represent the 208 schools whose Heads are in membership. Its direct aim is to promote excellence in the education of girls. This is achieved through a clear understanding of the individual potential of girls and young women. Over 110,000 pupils are educated in schools which cover day and boarding, large and small, city and country, academically elite and broad based education. Scholarships and bursaries are available in most schools.

The Headmasters' and Headmistresses' Conference (HMC)
130 Regent Road
Leicester LE1 7PG
Tel: (0116) 285 4810
Fax: (0116) 247 1167

Membership Secretary: R V Peel
Secretary: G H Lucas

Membership of the HMC consists of 245 Heads of major boys' and co-educational independent schools. The object of the annual meeting is to discuss matters of common interest to members.

The Incorporated Association of Preparatory Schools (IAPS)
11 Waterloo Place
Leamington Spa
Warwickshire CV32 5LA
Tel: (01926) 887833
Fax: (01926) 888014
E-mail: hq@iaps.org.uk
General Secretary: John Morris

IAPS is the main professional association for Heads of independent preparatory and junior Schools in the UK and overseas. There are some 570 schools whose Heads are in membership, accommodating over 130,000 children.

The Independent Schools Association (ISA)
Boys' British School
East Street
Saffron Walden
Essex CB10 1LS
Tel: (01799) 523619
Secretary: Timothy Ham

There are approximately 300 schools in membership of ISA. These are all schools which have been accredited by the Independent Schools Council Inspection Service. This and the requirement that the school should be good of its kind are the criteria for membership. ISA represents schools with pupils throughout the age range. The majority of schools are day schools, but a significant number also have boarders. Membership of the Association enables Heads to receive support from the Association in a number of ways and enables pupils to take part in many events organized by ISA.

The Independent Schools' Bursars Association (ISBA)
Unit 11–12, Manor Farm
Cliddesden, Basingstoke
Hants RG25 2JB
Tel: (01256) 330369
Fax: (01256) 330376
E-mail: office@theisba.org.uk
Website: www.theisba.org.uk
General Secretary: Mr Jonathan Cook

Membership of ISBA includes over 800 independent schools. Objectives include the promotion of administrative efficiency and exchange of information between schools.

The Independent Schools Careers Organisation (ISCO)
12A Princess Way
Camberley, Surrey GU15 3SP
Tel: (01276) 211888
Fax: (01276) 691833
E-mail: admin@isco.org.uk
Website: www.isco.org.uk

ISCO exists to help young people, from age 15 upwards, to make informed choices about further and higher education and start out on the right career path. It has membership schemes for parents and schools and a network of Regional Directors who work to promote and support careers education and guidance of the highest quality. It provides a range of publications and software, as well as training and conferences for teachers, work experience for sixth formers, information for parents and guidance in individual cases. The magazine Careerscope is published three times a year and is available on subscription.

Independent Schools Examinations Board
Jordan House, Christchurch Road
New Milton
Hants BH25 6QJ
Tel: (01425) 621111
E-mail: ce@iseb.co.uk

Details of the Common Entrance examinations (see the section on Examinations and Qualifications) and copies of past papers are available from the General Secretary at the address above.

Independent Schools Council (ISC)
St Vincent House
30 Orange Street
London WC2H 7HH
Tel: (020) 7766 7070
Fax: (020) 7766 7071
General Secretary: Jonathan Shephard
ISC is a federation of the following associations:

The Association of Governing Bodies of Independent Schools (AGBIS)
The Girls' Schools Association (GSA)
The Headmasters' and Headmistresses' Conference (HMC)
The Incorporated Association of Preparatory Schools (IAPS)
The Independent Schools' Association (ISA)
The Independent Schools' Bursars Association (ISBA)
The Society of Headmasters and Headmistresses of Independent Schools (SHMIS)

The total membership of ISC comprises about 1,300 schools which are accredited by ISC and inspected on a six-year cycle by the Independent Schools Inspectorate (ISI) under arrangements agreed by the DfES and OFSTED. ISC deals with matters of policy and other issues common to its members and when required speaks collectively on their behalf. It represents its members in discussions with the Department for Education and Skills and with other organizations and represents the collective view of members on independent education.

The Round Square Schools
3 Cronks Hill Close
Meadvale, Redhill
Surrey RH1 6LX
Tel: (01737) 217134
Fax: (01737) 217133
E-mail: Hollandkay@msn.com
Secretary: Kay Holland

An international group of schools which follow the principles of Kurt Hahn, founder of the Salem School in Germany and Gordonstoun in Scotland. There are now 50 member schools in 12 countries: Australia, Canada, England, Germany, India, Kenya, Oman, Scotland, South Africa, Switzerland, Thailand and the United States. Member schools arrange regular exchange visits for pupils and undertake aid projects in India, Kenya, Eastern Europe and Thailand. All member schools uphold the five principles of outdoor adventure, community service, education for democracy, international understanding and environmental conservation. UK member schools are as follows:

Abbotsholme, Uttoxeter (Co-ed)
Box Hill, Dorking (Co-ed)
Cobham Hall, Gravesend (Girls')
Gordonstoun, Elgin (Co-ed)
Hellenic College, London (Co-ed, Day)
Wellington College, Crowthorne (Boys', Girls in Sixth Form)
Westfield, Newcastle upon Tyne (Girls')
Windermere St Anne's (Co-ed)

SATIPS
Professional Support for Staff in Independent Schools
Cherry Trees, Stebbing
Great Dunmow
Essex CM6 3ST
Tel/Fax: (01371) 856823
E-mail: admin@satips.com
Website: www.satips.com
General Secretary: Andrew Davis
Administrator: Mrs P M Harrison

SATIPS – founded in 1952 – is a source of professional support and encouragement for staff in preparatory, and other schools. We are now one of the foremost providers of subject-based and cross-curricular INSET courses for prep school and other staff. SATIPS is a registered charity. In 1993 the Society widened its appeal by changing its emphasis from purely preparatory school teachers to any school staff, especially those in independent schools. In particular, teachers who have pupils in Key Stages 1, 2 and 3 will find the membership of SATIPS useful: we are particularly interested in making contact with colleagues in the maintained sector. The Society publishes 19 Broadsheets each term in all subject areas and runs conferences (mostly one-day) at various venues during the year. We offer school and individual membership.

The Secondary Heads Association (SHA)
130 Regent Road
Leicester LEI 7PG
Tel: (0116) 299 1122
Fax: (0116) 299 1123
E-mail: info@sha.org.uk
Website: www.sha.org.uk
General Secretary: J E Dunford

SHA represents Heads, Deputy Heads, Assistant Heads and Bursars in all types of secondary schools and colleges.

The Society of Headmasters and Headmistresses of Independent Schools (SHMIS)
5 Tolethorpe Road
Oakham
Rutland
LE15 6GF
Tel: (01572) 755426
Fax: (01572) 756234
E-mail: gensec@shmis.org.uk
Website: www.shmis.org.uk
General Secretary: David Richardson

A society of some 95 schools, most of which are co-educational, day and boarding, and all of which educate children up to the age of 18.

Steiner Waldorf Schools Fellowship
Kidbrooke Park
Forest Row
East Sussex RH18 5JA
Tel: (01342) 822115 Fax: (01342) 826004
E-mail: info@swsf.org.uk
Website: www.steinerwaldorf.org.uk
Chairman: Christopher Clouder

The Steiner Waldorf Schools Fellowship represents the 32 autonomous Steiner Waldorf Schools and 45 Early Years Centres in the UK and Eire. There are now over 890 schools worldwide. Key characteristics of the education include: careful balance in the artistic, practical and intellectual content of the international Steiner Waldorf curriculum; co-educational from 3 to 19 years. Shared Steiner Waldorf curriculum for all pupils. GCSE and A Level examinations. A broad education based on Steiner's approach to the holistic nature of the human being. Co-operative school management – usually a variable parent payment scheme. Steiner Waldorf education is rapidly gaining in popularity all over the world.

Woodard Schools (The Woodard Corporation)
High Street
Abbots Bromley
Rugeley
Staffordshire WS15 3BW
Tel: (01283) 840893

The Woodard Corporation has 37 schools throughout the country, including 14 Affiliated schools. All have an Anglican foundation and together they form the largest independent group of Church Schools in England and Wales.

Member Schools

Southern Area

Ardingly College, Haywards Heath
Ardingly College Junior School, Haywards Heath
Bloxham School, Banbury
Hurstpierpoint College, Hassocks
Hurstpierpoint Junior School, Hassocks
Lancing College, Lancing
Mowden School, Hove

Midland Area

Abbots Bromley School for Girls, Rugeley
Denstone College, Uttoxeter
Ellesmere College, Ellesmere
Prestfelde, Shrewsbury
Ranby House, Retford
Smallwood Manor Preparatory, Uttoxeter
Worksop College, Worksop

Eastern Area

Peterborough High School, Peterborough
St James's School, Grimsby

Western Area

The Cathedral School, Llandaff
Grenville College, Bideford
King's College, Taunton
King's Hall School, Taunton
St Margaret's School, Exeter

Northern Area

The King's School, Tynemouth
Queen Mary's School, Thirsk

Affiliated Schools

Alderley Edge School for Girls, Alderley Edge
Archbishop Michael Ramsey Technology College, London (Voluntary Aided)
Bishop of Hereford's Bluecoat School, Tupsley (Voluntary Aided)
Bolitho School, Penzance
Crompton House Church of England School
Derby High School, Derby
Grammar School for Boys, Derby

St Aidan's Church of England Technology College
St Peter's Collegiate School, Wolverhampton (Voluntary Aided)
St Wilfred's Church of England High School and Technology College
St Olaves Grammar School, Orpington
St George's Church of England School, Gravesend
St Peter's Church of England High School, Stoke on Trent
The King's School, Wolverhampton

4.11
Glossary of Abbreviations

ABRSM	Associated Board of the Royal Schools of Music
ADD	Attention Deficit Disorder
ADISR	Association des Directeurs d'Instituts de la Suisse Romande
AEB	Associated Examining Board
AGBIS	Association of Governing Bodies of Independent Schools
AHIS	Association of Heads of Independent Schools
AICE	Advanced International Certificate of Education
ANTC	Association of Nursery Training Colleges
ARCS	Accreditation, Review and Consultancy Service
ARELS	Association of Recognised English Language Services
AVDEP	Association Vaudoise des Ecoles Privees
BACIFHE	British Accreditation Council for Independent Further and Higher Education
BAGA	British Amateur Gymnastics Association
BAYS	British Association for the Advancement of Science
BHS	British Horse Society
BSA	Boarding Schools Association
CAE	Cambridge Certificate in Advanced English
CASE	Council for Advancement and Support of Education
CEE	Common Entrance Examination
CIFE	Council for Independent Further Education
COBISEC	Council of British International Schools in the European Community
CReSTeD	Council for the Registration of Schools Teaching Dyslexic Pupils
CSA	Choir Schools Association
DfES	Department for Education and Skills
ECIS	European Council for International Schools
EFL	English as a Foreign Language
ESL	English as a Second Language
ESOL	English for Speakers of Other Languages
FCE	Cambridge First Certificate in English
FOBISSEA	Federation of British International Schools in South-East Asia

FSEP	Federation Suisse des Ecoles Privees
GBA	Governing Bodies Association
GBGSA	Governing Bodies of Girls' Schools Association
GDST	Girls' Day School Trust
GSA	Girls' Schools Association
HAS	Head Teachers' Association of Scotland
HMC	Headmasters' and Headmistresses' Conference
IAPS	Incorporated Association of Preparatory Schools
IB	International Baccalaureate
IBO	International Baccalaureate Organisation
IBSCA	International Baccalaureate Schools and Colleges Association
IBTA	Independent Business Training Organisation
ICG	Independent Colleges Group
IGCSE	International General Certificate of Secondary Education
ISA	Independent Schools Association
ISBA	Independent Schools Bursars' Association
ISC	Independent Schools Council (formerly Independent Schools Joint Council or ISJC)
ISCIS	Independent Schools Council Information Service (formerly ISIS)
ISCO	Independent Schools Careers Organisation
ISI	Independent Schools Inspectorate
ISIS	Independent Schools Information Service
LAMDA	London Academy of Music and Dramatic Art
LISA	London International Schools Association
MSA	Middle States Association of Colleges and Schools (USA)
NABSS	National Association of British Schools in Spain
NAHT	National Association of Head Teachers
NAIS	National Association of Independent Schools
NE/SA	Near East/South Asia
NEAB	Northern Examinations and Assessment Board
NEASC	New England Association of Schools and Colleges
OFSTED	Office for Standards in Education
OUDLE	University of Oxford Delegacy of Local Examinations
PET	Cambridge Preliminary English Test
PSE	Personal and Social Education
RSA CLAIT	Computer Literacy and Information Technology
SATIPS	Society of Assistants Teaching in Preparatory Schools
SCIS	Scottish Council of Independent Schools
SGS	Scottish Girls' Schools
SHA	Secondary Heads Association
SHMIS	Society of Headmasters and Headmistresses of Independent Schools
SpLD	Specific Learning Difficulties
STABIS	State Boarding Schools Information Service
WJEC	Welsh Joint Education Committee

Abbreviations used to denote Special Needs provision in the profiles section are as follows:

Special needs support provided (independent mainstream schools)

Learning difficulties

CA Some children with special needs receive help from classroom assistants

RA There are currently very limited facilities for pupils with learning difficulties but reasonable adjustments can be made if necessary

SC Some children with special needs are taught in separate classes for specific subjects

SNU School has a dedicated Special Needs Unit, which provides specialist tuition on a one-to-one or small group basis by appropriately qualified teachers

WI There is no dedicated Special Needs Unit but some children with special needs are withdrawn individually from certain lessons for one-to-one tuition

Behavioural disorders/emotional and behavioural difficulties/challenging behaviour

CA Some children with behavioural problems receive help from classroom assistants

CO Trained counsellors available for pupils

RA There are currently very limited facilities for pupils with behavioural disorders but reasonable adjustments can be made if necessary

ST Behaviour management strategies identified in school's behaviour management policy

TS Staff trained in behaviour management available

Physical impairments/medical conditions

AT Adapted timetable for children with health problems

BL Materials can be provided in Braille

CA Some children receive help from classroom assistants

DS Signing by staff and pupils

HL Hearing loops available

IT Specialist IT provision available

RA There are currently very limited facilities for pupils with physical impairments or medical conditions but reasonable adjustments can be made if necessary

SL Stairlifts

SM Staff with medical training available

TW Accessible toilet and washing facilities

W School has wheelchair access (unspecified)
WA1 School is fully wheelchair accessible
WA2 Main teaching areas are wheelchair accessible
WA3 No permanent access for wheelchairs; temporary ramps available

Special needs

ADD Attention Deficit Disorder
ADHD Attention Deficit/Hyperactivity Disorder
ASD Autistic Spectrum Disorder
ASP Asperger's Syndrome
BESD Behavioural, Emotional and Social Disorders
CB Challenging Behaviour
CP Cerebral Palsy
DOW Down's Syndrome
DYC Dyscalculia
DYP Dyspraxia
DYS Dyslexia
EPI Epilepsy
HEA Health Problems (eg heart defect, asthma)
HI Hearing Impairment
IM Impaired Mobility
MLD Moderate Learning Difficulties
PMLD Profound and Multiple Learning Difficulties
SLD Severe Learning Difficulties
SP&LD Speech and Language Difficulties
TOU Tourette's Syndrome
VI Visual Impairment
WU Wheelchair User

4.12
Further Reading

Schools and Further Education

Schools for Special Needs: A complete guide
11th Edition: Gabbitas Educational Consultants
*The definitive guide to special needs education in the UK
£19.99 Paperback ISBN 0 7494 4409 6 600 pages 2005

How to Pass Secondary School Selection Tests
Contains over 600 Practice Questions
Mike Bryon
*Ideal for 11+ common entrance & SATS
£8.99 Paperback ISBN 0 7494 4217 4 224 pages 2004

Everything You Need to Know about Going to University
3rd Edition: Sally Longson
"comprehensive resource to help you make the right choices." —Mandy Telford, former National President, National Union of Students,
£9.99 Paperback ISBN 0 7494 3985 8 192 pages 2003

Educational Reference

British Qualifications
A complete guide to professional, vocational & academic qualifications in the United Kingdom
36th Edition
"The single best one-volume reference on British educational awards in print." —*World Education News & Reviews*
£45.00 Paperback ISBN 0 7494 4484 3 1072 pages 2006
£70.00 Hardback ISBN 0 7494 4483 5 1072 pages 2006

British Vocational Qualifications
A directory of vocational qualifications available in the United Kingdom
8th Edition
"Splendid. . . Every imaginable accessible procedure is packed into its pages." —*New Statesman*
£40.00 Paperback ISBN 0 7494 4485 1 472 pages 2006

Careers

The A–Z of Careers & Jobs
13th Edition: published in association with *The Times*
"The perfect starting point for students and school leavers" —*Education & Training*
£14.99 Paperback ISBN 0 7494 4627 7 416 pages 2006

also available:

Careers & Jobs in Hospitality & Catering £7.99 Paperback ISBN 0 7494 42246 8 128 pages 2005
Careers & Jobs in IT £7.99 Paperback ISBN 0 7494 4245 X 144 pages 2004
Careers & Jobs in Nursing £7.99 Paperback ISBN 0 7494 4249 2 136 pages 2004
Careers & Jobs in Sport £7.99 Paperback ISBN 0 7494 4248 4 128 pages 2005
Careers & Jobs in the Media £7.99 Paperback ISBN 0 7494 4247 6 128 pages 2005
Careers & Jobs in the Police Service £7.99 Paperback ISBN 0 7494 4204 2 112 pages 2004
Careers & Jobs in Travel & Tourism £7.99 Paperback ISBN 0 7494 4205 0 112 pages 2004

What Next after School?
All you need to know about work, travel & study
4th Edition: Elizabeth Holmes, published in association with *The Times*
"A wealth of practical information about the world of work, training and higher-education" —*Evening Standard*
£7.99 Paperback ISBN 0 7494 4504 1 224 pages 2006

What Next after University?
Work, travel, education & life with a degree
2nd Edition: Simon Kent, published in association with *The Times*
"Covers everything from basic work, travel and education options and graduate recruitment tests to finding a home and personal finance." —*Girl About Town*
£8.99 Paperback ISBN 0 7494 4251 4 224 pages 2004

Job Applications

Great Answers to Tough Interview Questions
6th Edition: Martin Yate
"The best book on job-hunting." —*Financial Times*
£8.99 Paperback ISBN 0 7494 4356 1 240 pages 2005

The Ultimate CV Book
Write the perfect CV and get that job
Martin Yate
*Over 100 samples of job-winning CVs
£9.99 Paperback ISBN 0 7494 3875 4 256 pages 2002

The Ultimate Job Search Letters Book
Write the perfect letter and get that job
Martin Yate
£9.99 Paperback ISBN 0 7494 4069 4 256 pages 2003

Readymade Job Search Letters
Every type of letter for getting the job you want
3rd Edition: Lynn Williams, published in association with *The Times*
"The first book I've seen which specifically deals with letters. . . . A really useful resource."—*Phoenix Journal*, Keele University
£8.99 Paperback ISBN 0 7494 4277 8 208 pages 2004

Readymade CVs
Sample CVs for every type of job
3rd Edition: Lynn Williams, published in association with *The Times*
"A resource book offering several ways to design your CV for a multitude of needs." —*All About Money Making*
£8.99 Paperback ISBN 0 7494 4274 3 176 pages 2004

Property

The Complete Guide to Buying & Selling Property
How to get the best deal on your home
2nd Edition: Sarah O'Grady
Published in association with the *Daily Express*
"Valuable, no-nonsense information." —*Ideal Home*
£8.99 Paperback ISBN 0 7494 4194 1 256 pages 2004

The Complete Guide to Renovating & Improving Your Property
Liz Hodgkinson
"Focuses on major renovation work, from obtaining planning permission to employing and managing contractors."
—*What Mortgage*
£9.99 Paperback ISBN 0 7494 4199 2 224 pages 2004

Also available:

The Complete Guide to Letting Property
5th Edition: Liz Hodgkinson
£10.99 Paperback ISBN 0 7494 4355 3 264 pages 2005

The Complete Guide to Buying Property Abroad
4th Edition: Liz Hodgkinson
£12.99 Paperback ISBN 0 7494 4418 5 304 pages 2005

The Complete Guide to Buying Property in France
3rd Edition: Charles Davey
£10.99 Paperback ISBN 0 7494 4419 3 304 pages 2005

The Complete Guide to Buying Property in Italy
Barbara McMahon
£9.99 Paperback ISBN 0 7494 4151 8 224 pages 2004

The Complete Guide to Buying Property in Portugal
Colin Barrow
£9.99 Paperback ISBN 0 7494 4303 0 240 pages 2005

The Complete Guide to Buying Property in Spain
Charles Davey
£9.99 Paperback ISBN 0 7494 4056 2 208 pages 2004

Personal Finance

A Complete Guide to Family Finance
Essential advice on everything from student loans to inheritance tax
Roderick Millar: published in association with the *Daily Express*
*Comprehensive and practical advice on everything you need to know about saving, investing and insuring for the future.
£12.99 Paperback ISBN 0 7494 4203 4 368 pages 2004

How the Stock Market Works
A beginner's guide to investment
2nd Edition: Michael Beckett
"Not just for investors, but for anyone who wishes to understand our financial system."
—Neil Collins, City Editor, *Daily Telegraph*
£8.99 Paperback ISBN 0 7494 4190 9 208 pages 2004

How to Write Your Will
15th Edition: Marlene Garsia
"A practical and easy-to-read guide." —*Pensions World*
£8.99 Paperback ISBN 0 7494 4471 1 200 pages 2005

Relocation

Working Abroad
The complete guide to overseas employment
26th Edition: Jonathan Reuvid
"Anyone involved in working abroad will quickly come to look upon this as their bible."
—*Personnel Today*
£12.99 Paperback ISBN 0 7494 4427 4 464 pages 2005

Kogan Page publishes books on Business, Management, Marketing, HR, Training, Careers and Testing, Personal Finance, Property and more.

Visit our website for our full online catalogue:
www.kogan-page.co.uk

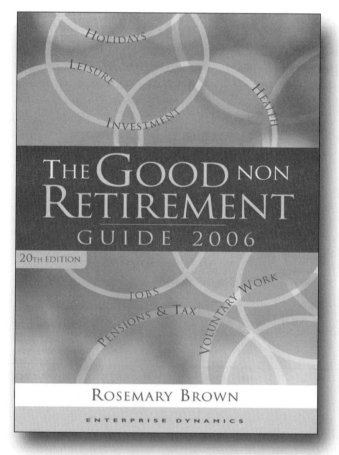

4.13
Main Index

A

B

C

D

E

F

G

H

I

J

K

L

M

N

O

P

Q

R

S

T

U

Y

READER ENQUIRY CARD

If you would like further information about our Advisory, Guardianship or other services, please complete and return this card. No stamp necessary if posted within the United Kingdom.

Name: ____________________

Address: ____________________

____________________ Tel: ____________________

Please indicate which area of our services might interest you:

____

Please tell us where you obtained a copy of this Guide:

Bookshop/Library (name and town): ____________________

School/advisory service etc (please give details): ____________________

____

Other (please give details): ____________________

READER ENQUIRY CARD

If you would like further information about our Advisory, Guardianship or other services, please complete and return this card. No stamp necessary if posted within the United Kingdom.

Name: ____________________

Address: ____________________

____________________ Tel: ____________________

Please indicate which area of our services might interest you:

____

Please tell us where you obtained a copy of this Guide:

Bookshop/Library (name and town): ____________________

School/advisory service etc (please give details): ____________________

____

Other (please give details): ____________________

BUSINESS REPLY SERVICE
Licence No WD 598

GGIS 12

GABBITAS EDUCATIONAL CONSULTANTS Ltd
CARRINGTON HOUSE
126–130 REGENT STREET
LONDON
W1B 5EE

BUSINESS REPLY SERVICE
Licence No WD 598

GGIS 12

GABBITAS EDUCATIONAL CONSULTANTS Ltd
CARRINGTON HOUSE
126–130 REGENT STREET
LONDON
W1B 5EE